To Ted,

   Who continues to show the
way — in respect and gratitude,
always —

   Howard

NATIVE AMERICAN RESOURCES SERIES

General Editors

Jack W. Marken, South Dakota State University

Michael Tate, University of Nebraska at Omaha

Advisory Board

Brenda Child, University of Minnesota; R. David Edmunds, Indiana University; Arlene B. Hirschfelder, Teaneck, NJ; Karl Kroeber, Columbia University; A. LaVonne Ruoff, University of Illinois, Chicago; Emory Sekaquaptewa, University of Arizona; Virginia Driving Hawk Sneve, Rapid City, SD; Clifford E. Trafzer, University of California, Riverside

1. *Handbook of the American Frontier: Four Centuries of Indian–White Relationships*, by J. Norman Heard
   Volume I: *Southeastern Woodlands*. 1987.
   Volume II: *Northeastern Woodlands*. 1990.
   Volume III: *The Great Plains*. 1993.
   Volume IV: *The Far West*. 1997.
   Volume V: *Chronology, Bibliography, Index*. 1998.

2. *Oliver La Farge and the American Indian*, by Robert A. Hecht. 1991.

3. *Native American Resurgence and Renewal: A Reader and a Bibliography*, by Robert N. Wells Jr. 1994.

4. *The Navajo as Seen by the Franciscans, 1898–1921: A Sourcebook*, edited by Howard M. Bahr. 2004.

The Navajo as Seen by the Franciscans, 1898–1921

A Sourcebook

Edited by
Howard M. Bahr

Native American Resources Series, No. 4

The Scarecrow Press, Inc.
Lanham, Maryland • Toronto • Oxford
2004

SCARECROW PRESS, INC.

Published in the United States of America
by Scarecrow Press, Inc.
A wholly owned subsidiary of
The Rowman & Littlefield Publishing Group, Inc.
4501 Forbes Boulevard, Suite 200, Lanham, Maryland 20706
www.scarecrowpress.com

PO Box 317
Oxford
OX2 9RU, UK

British Library Cataloguing in Publication Information Available

Library of Congress Cataloging-in-Publication Data

The Navajo as seen by the Franciscans, 1898–1921 : a sourcebook / edited by Howard
M. Bahr.
    p. cm. — (Native American resources series ; no. 4)
  Includes bibliographical references and index.
  ISBN 0-8108-4962-3 (hardcover : alk. paper)
  1. Navajo Indians—History. 2. Navajo Indians—Missions. 3. Navajo Indians—
Religion. 4. Franciscans—Missions—Southwest, New—History. 5. Christianity and
culture—Southwest, New—History. I. Bahr, Howard M. II. Series.
E99.N3N385 2004
979.1004'9726—dc22

                                                                    2004002489

In the life of St. Patrick we read that he one day saw in a vision the infants and children of distant Erin, stretching out their hands toward him, begging and entreating him to come to their land to bring them the light and the grace of faith. Thus, too, the red man and his children are stretching out their hands today toward you, dear reader, and all the Catholics of the land, imploring you to help them in receiving and preserving the light and the grace of faith. Shall we, and can we in defiance of the claims of Christian charity, nay common humanity, allow these our brethren in the household of the faith, to be perverted, or to be forced back into savagery and heathenism, without extending the hand of Catholic fellowship and Christian benevolence? Shall and can we suffer their children to be deprived of the faith born and nourished in their hearts through the untiring efforts and labors of our missionaries and their mission schools?

Leopold Ostermann, O.F.M.

Contents

Abbreviations

BCIM Bureau of Catholic Indian Missions Papers. Marquette University Special Collections and University Archives, Milwaukee, Wisconsin.

BHP Berard Haile Papers. AZ132. University of Arizona Library Special Collections, Tucson.

FAC Franciscan Archives Cincinnati. 5000 Colerain Avenue, Cincinnati, Ohio.

FFP Franciscans, St. Michaels, Arizona: Papers. AZ500. University of Arizona Library Special Collections, Tucson.

FMN "Die Indianer-Mission unter den Navajos" (after September 1902, "Die Franziskaner-Mission unter den Navajo-Indianern"). Series published in *Sendbote des göttlichen herzens Jesu* or *Der Sendbote*, German-language periodical published by Franciscan Fathers' Province of St. John the Baptist.

FMSW *Franciscan Missions of the Southwest*. Annual published by Franciscan Fathers, St. Michaels, Arizona. 1913–1922.

FWW "Franciscans in the Wilds and Wastes of the Navajo Country." Series published 1901–1909 in *St. Anthony's Messenger*.

Series Editor's Foreword

The establishing by the Franciscans of a mission at Cienega (later called St. Michaels) on the Navajo reservation in 1898 began a relationship that proved beneficial to both the Indians and the Franciscans. Upon arrival, Father Superior Juvenal Schnorbus, Father Anselm Weber, and Brother Placidus Buerger set about learning the language and the culture of the Navajo before trying to convert them to Catholicism, actions unique among missionaries who invariably tried to impose their religion, language, and culture on the Indians. In 1900 Father Anselm, now elevated to superior, was joined by Fathers Leopold Ostermann and Berard Haile. This trio of gifted, committed missionaries would devote the rest of their lives to working among and learning from the Navajo. Many other friars would join these pioneers as the mission grew, but these three, in that critical first decade, would set the pattern.

The enlightened philosophy followed by these Franciscans was stated by Father Berard at his Golden Jubilee in 1948:

> It seemed to me one had to study [the Dineh's] customs, their outlook on life, on the universe, natural phenomena, their concepts of the origin of man, vegetation and animals, before one could approach them on religious matters. Here were human beings, intelligent, ingenious, industrious, religious, enormously so; why then approach them on a 'you're all wrong, listen to me' basis? Traditions of such long standing cannot be uprooted by such matter-of-fact statements as we are accustomed to, owing to our training.[1]

Applying this philosophy, the Franciscans spent their early years at St. Michaels immersing themselves in the language, culture, and reservation life of the Diné. Each of them appears to have focused on different aspects of Navajo life. As Peter Iverson says in his *Diné: A History of the Navajos*,

> Father Anselm Weber . . . emerged as a key figure in this struggle [to consolidate and extend the Navajo land base]. Weber worked indefatigably for Diné land interests from soon after he arrived in Diné Bikéyah in 1898 until his death in 1921. He helped obtain the vitally important addition to the southern portion of the Navajo reservation in 1907. . . . Weber also took on railroad and livestock interests as he battled for individual Diné on the checkerboard lands. He wrote thousands of letters to the Office of Indian Affairs, [to] individual superintendents . . . , the Land Office, the Board of Indian Commissioners, members of the U.S.

House of Representatives and the U.S. Senate, the Santa Fe Railway, and the
Bureau of Catholic Indian Missions. His insistent voice made a difference.[2]

Father Berard became an authority on the Navajo language and is responsible
for helping to record and preserve the great religious ceremonies performed in the
Diné "sings." Father Leopold, a "thoroughgoing and scientific student" of both
Navajo language and culture,[3] collaborated in the preparation of the influential
Ethnologic Dictionary and later wrote important early anthropological articles on
Navajo customs and lifestyles.

So successful were these Franciscans in becoming trusted friends and helpers
of the Navajo that when Protestant missionaries wanted to set up a dormitory school
they were rebuffed by Charley Mitchell, a Navajo leader, who spoke for most of his
people when he said in council in 1916:

> You ministers seem to make trouble for us wherever you are. You report the
> Indian for the smallest of offenses, some of you even tried to take away or help
> take away lands that belong to the Indians; in fact, the districts in which you have
> located report dissension and a world of trouble. On the other hand, we know the
> priests. They do not meddle with every little trouble that arises; they don't gossip
> like you do; they do not oppose our singings as you do; they help us along in our
> land and other ways and we know them for years to be the same good people they
> were when they first came to us.[4]

The Navajo as Seen by the Franciscans, 1898-1921 is a collection of articles
and other writings by Franciscan priests telling about their experiences on the
Navajo reservation from 1898 to 1921, the years of Father Anselm's life among the
Navajo (from 1900 on he was Father Superior of the mission). Some articles focus
on the customs and domestic life of the Navajo, others on the experiences of the
missionaries as they worked among the People. Many of the articles, originally
written to help eastern readers understand the Diné, are located in nearly inaccessible journals. Some, particularly those by Father Anselm, appeared in German
language journals and have been translated by Father Emanuel Trockur and Marie
Bradford Durrant.

Professor Bahr's headnote to each selection sets it in context and adds
information useful to the scholar and the general reader. The book is a fascinating
account of the sensitivity of the Franciscans to the Navajo, with whom they became
friends. It is a tribute to these priests that their efforts in the early decades of the last
century both contributed to the welfare of the People of that era and continue to
benefit the Navajo of today.

Jack W. Marken
Professor Emeritus
South Dakota State University

Notes

1. Quoted in Murray Bodo, ed. *Tales of an Endishodi: Father Berard Haile and the Navajos, 1900–1961*. Albuquerque: University of New Mexico Press, 1998, xxii.

2. Peter Iverson, *Diné: A History of the Navajos*. Albuquerque: University of New Mexico Press, 2002, 104.

3. Robert L. Wilken, *Anselm Weber, O.F.M.: Missionary to the Navaho, 1898–1921*. Milwaukee, Wisc.: Bruce, 1955, 117.

4. Berard Haile, "The Sequel," *St. Anthony Messenger* 24 (July 1916), 71.

Foreword

Anselm Weber, Juvenal Schnorbus, and Placidus Buerger hardly viewed themselves as heroes; but they certainly knew they were pioneering new territory as midwestern, German-rooted Franciscan friars moving among the Navajo people in 1898.

Since joining the Franciscans some 35 years ago, I have heard the stories of these men and other early missionaries to the Southwest. The tales are the stuff of legend in our Franciscan community. Prompted by the vision and fortune of Mother Katharine Drexel, they boarded trains to move west—to touch and change the lives of their new "flock." But in the process their own lives were deeply touched and profoundly changed.

Of course, I have seen these early missionaries through the eyes of a proud younger brother. Working with Howard Bahr during his frequent visits to our archives has given me the wonderful opportunity to see them through eyes that are neither Franciscan nor Catholic. His search for information and his probing questions have challenged me to revisit events and reread letters from a fresh perspective.

The more I learned about the receptive stance and positive impact of these men on the Navajo people (and, just as important, the impact the Navajo people had on these men), the prouder I was to be part of the community that fostered and celebrated more than 100 years of mutual ministry with the Navajo.

Bahr's thorough search for relevant texts and his reverence for the materials at his disposal are the dream of every archivist, and I look forward to additional volumes and additional research visits. I am delighted that through his scholarly and engaging work, others will come to know these men, my brothers, who were in so many ways ahead of their time.

Dan Anderson, O.F.M.
Archivist
Franciscan Province of St. John Baptist

Acknowledgments

My greatest debts are to the Franciscans, beginning with those who, in the early 1990s when I was working on a bibliography of Navajo materials, answered my questions, allowed me access to their archives, and thus set the stage for my discovery of and growing fascination with the records of their work among the Navajo. Early on, I enjoyed the hospitality and encouragement of Father Martan Rademaker at St. Michaels, Father Peter Ricke, archivist of the Province of Our Lady of Guadalupe in Albuquerque, and especially Father Leonard Foley, then archivist at the St. Francis Center of the Province of St. John Baptist in Cincinnati. Father Leonard hosted my visits to the center and seemed to share my delight in retrieving long-lost glimpses of Navajo life from his files.

The archive at the St. Francis Center is no more; it has been expanded and replaced by Franciscan Archives Cincinnati, one of the best environments anywhere for serious scholarly work. I owe a huge debt to its director, Father Dan Anderson, who has been unfailingly helpful, from providing desk space and copy facilities to personally facilitating my search of the materials under his stewardship, and when I failed, continuing that search himself. He has done a little of everything, whatever was needed, providing essential bibliographies and biographies of the friars, advising on matters of style and presentation, translating Latin phrases and quotations, and correcting my spelling. I am also indebted to Father Marcan Hetteberg, who himself spent many years as a Franciscan missionary to the Navajo, partly for his direct assistance at the archive in helping to answer particular questions or locate fugitive materials, but especially for the fruit of his own experience in Navajoland, his memory, and his personal network of friends, associates, and people who know the territory. If he didn't know an answer, he knew names, places, times, where to look, and whom to call. Father Don Rewers of the Franciscan Archives, less directly involved in Navajo matters, was also consistently supportive. I value the friendship and intellectual example of these good men.

I have also drawn materials and insights from the Franciscan Fathers collections at the University of Arizona Libraries, Special Collections, in Tucson, and from the records of the Bureau of Catholic Indian Missions at Marquette University Libraries in the Department of Special Collections and University Archives. I acknowledge the helpful efforts of librarians and staff members at both institutions, and especially the encouragement and assistance of Mark G. Thiel, archivist at Marquette University Libraries. The facilities and collections at the Harold B. Lee Library at Brigham Young University have been a continuing source of relevant material and essential services, and their interlibrary loan division was especially helpful in solving problems of access to scarce periodicals.

Part of the travel associated with this project was funded by faculty research grants from Brigham Young University's College of Family, Home, and Social Sciences, and additional institutional support was provided by the BYU's Department of Sociology. The administrative support of Deans Clayne L. Pope and David B. Magleby, and of Department Chair Vaughn R. A. Call, is acknowledged with thanks.

Valerie Nye at the New Mexico Archives and Record Center went far beyond the required standard of helpfulness in finding, finally, an official record of a 1907 governor's pardon for New Mexico Territorial Penitentiary inmate Des Chee Nee, thus providing a happy ending to the story left unresolved in his letters preserved in the Franciscan Archives.

In addition, I am indebted to the translators who have made many of Father Anselm Weber's German-language articles published in *Der Sendbote* accessible to an English-language readership. Some of the pieces I have used were translated decades ago by Father Emanuel Trockur in the course of his historical research and writing. Many others have been translated expressly for this volume by Marie Bradshaw Durrant. Her cheerful willingness to interrupt her own busy research and family schedule to unlock these "hidden" resources is acknowledged with many thanks.

Finally, I owe a continuing debt to my wife and intellectual partner, Kathleen S. Bahr, who tolerated my absences, read chapters, critiqued my logic, shared and augmented my enthusiasm for the topic, and provided a continuing environment of support and love that made it possible for me to lose myself, sometimes for many days at a stretch, in the worlds of the Navajo and the Franciscans.

Permissions

Grateful acknowledgment is made to the following libraries and copyright holders for permission to reprint the selections specified:

Materials owned or controlled by the Archives of the Franciscan Province of St. John Baptist of Cincinnati: From *Der Sendbote*: Anselm Weber, "Eine Weihnachtsfeier unter den Navajo–Indianern im fernen Westen," 26 (March 1899): 199–203 (translated by Father Emanuel Trockur); Anselm Weber, "Die Indianer-Mission unter den Navajos," 27 (March, April 1900): 201–4; 284–89; 26 (June, July, August 1899): 469–74, 551–57, 635–39; 28 (December 1901); 995–99; 29 (January 1902): 24–28; 46 (April 1919): 323–28 (translated by Father Emanuel Trockur); Anselm Weber, Die Indianer-Mission unter den Navajos," 28 (April, May, June, July 1901): 292–97, 376–80, 467–71, 554–60; 30 (March 1903): 214–20; 31 (August, September, December 1904): 681–84, 765–66, 1030–34; 32 (December 1905): 1083–88; 33 (January, February, March, and May–September 1906): 28–33, 120–26, 222–26, 411–15, 510–14, 596–601, 704–9, 804–8; 34 (June 1907): 513–18; 35

(November 1908): 979–82 (translated by Marie Bradshaw Durrant). Egbert Fischer, "Die Franziskaner-Mission unter den Navajo-Indianern," *Sendbote* 42 (December 1915): 1118–23 (translated by Marie Bradshaw Durrant).

From *Provincial Chronicle*: Emanuel Trockur, "Background of the Indian Missions," 11 (Fall 1938): 3–16; "Franciscan Missions among the Navajo Indians: IV," 13 (Winter 1940–41): 73–76, 80–90; "Franciscan Missions among the Navajo Indians: VI," 14 (Fall 1941): 37–42, 47–53, 56–57.

From *Franciscan Missions of the Southwest*: Leopold Ostermann, "The Last Warrior of the Navajo Tribe," 3 (1915): 45–48; "Navajo Names," 6 (1918): 11–15; Marcellus Troester, "Our Mission at Lukachukai, Arizona," 3 (1915): 30–38; Anselm Weber, "On Navajo Myths and Superstitions," 4 (1916): 38–45; "Navajos on the Warpath," 7 (1919): 1–17; Gertrude Honaghani, "The Navajo Woman and Her Home," 9 (1921): 35–36.

From unpublished or privately published materials owned or controlled by the Archives of the Franciscan Province of St. John Baptist of Cincinnati: Manuscripts: Anselm Weber, *The Navajo Indians: A Statement of Facts*. St. Michaels, Arizona. Franciscan Fathers, 1914; and "The Navajo Indians: A Statement of Facts," Box DEC.241. Correspondence: Egbert Fischer to Provincial Rudolph Bonner, 11 January 1916 and 30 June 1916, Box DEC.062. Berard Haile to Anselm Weber, 3 August 1904, Box DEC.077. Berard Haile to Provincial Rudolph Bonner, 2 December 1918, Box PLA.323. Fidelis Koper to Provincial Rudolph Bonner, 7 December 1917, Box PLA.376. Leopold Ostermann to Provincial Rudolph Bonner, 23 February 1918, Box PLA.071. Leopold Ostermann to Anselm Weber, 2 June 1918, Box DEC.248. Anselm Weber to Provincial Rudolph Bonner, 2 August 1916, Box DEC.062. Anselm Weber to Provincial Rudolph Bonner, 23 May 1918 and 26 May 1918, Box DEC.247. Anselm Weber to Provincial Rudolph Bonner, 2 November 1918, Box DEC.245. Anselm Weber to Provincial Eugene Buttermann, 12 February 1912, Box DEC.247; 29 May 1912, Box DEC.246. Anselm Weber to E. P. Davis, 21 April 1919, Box DEC.250. Anselm Weber to Deschini, 15 December 1905, and to the writer of Des Chee Nee's letters 27 January 1906; Des Chee Nee to Anselm Weber 19 December 1905, 9 January 1906, 17 January 1906, 4 February 1906, circa 1 August 1906, 9 September 1906, 29 November 1906, 9 December 1906, 10 February 1907; Des Chee Nee to Chee Gema Gay 12 November 1905; Des Chee Nee to Charles Day 10 December 1905; A. M. Bergere to Anselm Weber 12 January 1906; Alexander Read to Anselm Weber 26 January 1906; Des Chee Nee to Henry Dodge 8 July 1906, all from Box DEC.245. Anselm Weber to Berard Haile, 17 May 1911 and 16 October 1911, Box DEC.245. Anselm Weber to Berard Haile, 23 January 1916 and 13 February 1916, Box DEC.241. Anselm Weber to Howel Jones, 16 November 1920, Box DEC.242. Anselm Weber, "The Navajo Indian Trouble of 1905," memo to William Ketcham, 15 March 1907, Box DEC.332. Anselm Weber to William H. Ketcham, 14 November 1910, Box DEC.250. Anselm Weber to Charles S. Lusk, 8 August 1918 and 28 February 1919, Box PLA.071. Anselm Weber to Hugh L. Scott, 13 January 1921, Box DEC.242. Anselm Weber to S. A. M. Young, 13 March 1919, Box PLA.071. Photographs: Navajo gathering for a chicken pull; Navajo family at Oak Springs; Armed Navajo at Chin Lee; Home of Tsiischbischi; Tsiischbischi and our students at Santa Fe; and Father Anselm and first communicants at breakfast.

Materials originally published in St. Anthony Messenger, *reprinted by permission of St. Anthony Messenger Press, Cincinnati, Ohio*: Berard Haile, "A Council at St. Isabel Mission," *St. Anthony Messenger* 23 (May 1916): 553–54; "The Sequel," *St. Anthony Messenger* 24 (July 1916): 67–72; and "Do the Navahos Pray?" *St. Anthony Messenger* 29 (January 1922): 353–54.

Leopold Ostermann, from the series "Franciscans in the Wilds and Wastes of the Navajo Country," *St. Anthony Messenger* 8 (February, March, April, May 1901): 298–301, 327–30, 366–69, 401–4; 9 (June, August, September 1901, April, May 1902): 10–12, 80–83, 118–21, 366–71, 402–5; 10 (October, November, December 1902 and January, February, March, April, May 1903):152–56, 188–94, 222–27, 260–65, 295–99, 332–34, 369–72, 404–7; 11 (June, July, August 1903): 10–14, 44–48, 82–86; 12 (December 1904, January 1905): 225–27, 258–61; and 17 (September 1909): 118–21.

Leopold Ostermann, from the series "Little Mission Stories from Our Own Southwest," *St. Anthony Messenger* 34 (February, March, April, May 1927): 466–67, 524–25, 578, 634–36; 35 (June, July, November 1927): 22–23, 75–77, 301; 36 (November 1928): 309–11.

Manuscripts in the collection of, and reprinted here by permission of the University of Arizona Library, Special Collections, Tucson: Berard Haile, "Random Notes," "Do the Navahos Pray?" "Navaho Ethics," "Pawn, Games, Homelife," and untitled manuscripts beginning "The subject of Navaho sacrifices," "The Navaho is, of course, a heathen," and other untitled notes and drafts, Berard Haile Papers (AZ132), Box 5; "Mission of Im. Conc. B.M.V. . . . Notes—1904," "St. Isabel's," and untitled manuscripts beginning "Letters which reach us from time to time," and "It is not customary among the Navahos," Berard Haile Papers (AZ132), Box 1.

Leopold Ostermann, "The Navahos and Christianity," typescript, Franciscan Fathers Papers (AZ500), Box 45.

Correspondence, all from Franciscan Fathers Papers (AZ500): Celestine Matz to Anselm Weber, 10 January 1919; Leopold Ostermann to Henry C. Dodge, 18 December 1918; and Anselm Weber to Leopold Ostermann, 15 February 1921, Box 1. Anselm Weber to Provincial Chrysostom Theobald, 13 July 1904, Box 33.

Materials from the Bureau of Catholic Indian Missions Records collection, reprinted here by permission of Marquette University Libraries, Raynor Memorial Libraries, Department of Special Collections and University Archives, Milwaukee, Wisconsin: Correspondence: William H. Ketcham to Isadore B. Dockweiler, 16 July 1921; to Ludger Oldegeering, 5 April 1921; to Leopold Ostermann, 6 October 1921; to Marcellus Troester, 29 June 1921; to Anselm Weber, 22 February 1921. Charles S. Lusk to Leopold Ostermann, 8 February 1992. Leopold Ostermann to William H. Ketcham, 28 October 1921; to Charles S. Lusk, 22 January 1922; to Anselm Weber, 18 June 1918. Marcellus Troester to Leopold Ostermann, 25 January 1922. Anselm Weber to William H. Ketcham, 8 December 1915, 4 July 1918, 18 June 1919, 6 October 1919, 16 February 1921; to Charles S. Lusk, 14 October 1916, 1

October 1917, 16 December 1918, 1 February 1919. Photograph: Students at St. Michael's School, early 1900s.

Photographs in the collection of, and reprinted here by permission of, the Franciscan Friars, St. Michael's Mission, Province of Our Lady of Guadalupe of the Order of Friars Minor, Albuquerque, New Mexico: Father Anselm visits Dine Tsosi (cover photograph); St. Michael's Mission, circa 1900; Father Leopold and friends at a summer gathering; At the hogan of the Silversmith; Navajo "desperadoes" of the Beautiful Mountain disturbance; and Father Anselm, Chee Dodge, and medicine man Bizhoshi.

Introduction

Howard M. Bahr

I first came to know the Franciscan literature on the Navajo more than a decade ago, while working on *Diné Bibliography to the 1990s*.[1] It was a literature from "the road less traveled," a view of the Navajo grounded in an alternative standpoint. Familiarity soon led to awe at its scope and great respect for much of its content. Marginal to mainstream scholarship on the Navajo, it incorporated a history largely neglected outside of Roman Catholic publications. Yet that history continues to impact Navajo life, and some of the unsung contributions of the early Franciscan friars continue to benefit the Navajo people. Perhaps, given the seemly modesty of friars committed to sacrifice of self in service to others, the general unfamiliarity with their lives and achievements is to be expected. By Franciscan standards it may be appropriate. Even so, it seemed to me that many of their early accounts of life among the Navajo deserved a wider audience.

Also instructive, and still relevant, is the friars' work as middlemen and sometimes advocates, helping to bridge the cultural divide between the Navajo people and the intrusive bureaucracies of institutional America that have changed and sometimes threatened their lives and lands. The texts, published and unpublished, created by the Franciscans and their associates in the course of their labors, constitute a seldom-quoted, little-read, generally difficult-to-access literature of enormous importance to the history of Navajo-white relations.[2] It mirrors the Navajo of the late 19th and early 20th centuries, reflected in the writings of men and women who were committed enough to live among the Navajo for very long periods, and who served them as teachers, advocates, counselors, and medical missionaries, while worrying about their souls and administering the holy sacraments.

The Navajo as Seen by the Franciscans, 1898-1921 is the first of a projected two-volume collection of portrayals of life among the Navajo by the Franciscan missionaries. It spans the first grand phase of the Navajo missions, the era directed and dominated by Father Anselm Weber, who arrived with the first contingent of friars in 1898, and from 1900 until his passing in 1921 was the mission's Father Superior. No subsequent Superior would serve as long, nor make such historic contributions to the future welfare of the Navajo people.

This first quarter-century of the Navajo missions was a time of extraordinary service and innovation. In retrospect, and especially in view of the problems the Navajo missions would face in future decades in finding and keeping suitable missionaries, one wonders how it came to be that of the first four missionaries sent, three devoted the remainder of their lives to the Navajo. Perhaps more important, one marvels that those three—Anselm Weber, Leopold Ostermann, and Berard Haile—were missionaries of such surpassing commitment and diversity of talent.

Other men of stature and talent would arrive, who would later make historic contributions to the mission and the tribe: Marcellus Troester in 1906, Emanuel Trockur in 1917, and they are represented in this book. However, in those critical first decades, it was the trio of Fathers Anselm, Leopold, and Berard who were the key figures in building rapport with the People by living an ethic of meaningful service to them, mastering Navajo language and culture, establishing the physical and institutional bases of mission educational and pastoral care, and, not least, in their literary contributions.

The interplay of the Franciscan missionaries and the Navajo is one of the great cultural confluences in American history. It is the coming together of two starkly different ways of life, each millennia old, each evolving in a different direction from the other prior to contact. The encounter is also an interchange between two language streams, the English of the conquering invaders and the Navajo of the subdued natives. The confluence of these cultural streams occurs within a wider matrix of differing culture and power relations, a context in which both the Navajo and the Catholic worldviews are alien, minority, suspect, and devalued.

The Franciscans embodied the culture of European Christendom, as represented in the Roman Catholic Church, an important, sometimes dominant influence in the colonization of the New World since Columbus. Yet in its American context and in its missions to the Indians of the United States, the Church itself was marginal. It was a minority religion, an object of prejudice and ethnic discrimination, a target of nativist agitation and political action from the "Know Nothing" party of the 1850s to the immigration restriction acts of the 1920s and beyond.

The Franciscans came to teach, to "civilize" the Navajo, but they were themselves a culture at risk, beset by opposition and competition. In addition to the Navajo medicine men they sought to supplant, they faced competition from Protestant missionaries, regulation from the government, and opposition from elements of white society whose interests were at odds with those of the friars. Often it was this last group that proved most difficult. In 1902 Father Anselm wrote that "life out here in the 'Wild West' is a battle indeed—not with the redskins, as many might imagine; they are an innocent and peaceable class of people—but with shrewd and irresponsible, though fairly well-educated white men, who seem to find their greatest and only pleasure in taking advantage of others, whether they be red or white."[3]

The work of the missionaries was complicated by the prior need to know the Indians and their problems, and then to take their part, when it seemed right to do so, against forces that threatened them. Initially the friars' greatest challenge was to master the Navajo language. When the Navajo learned that the friars could be trusted, the missions became a tribal resource. They functioned as private aid and social service centers where the needy were not turned away and the friars were willing to assist the Navajo as dispensers of charity and agents of acculturation, sometimes interceding for them in bureaucratic or legal matters, or helping in other ways to ease their accommodation to the dominant culture.

President Ulysses Grant's "peace policy" toward the Indians had parceled out to various Christian denominations the task of civilizing the Indians. The Navajo had been assigned to the Presbyterians, whose preliminary efforts at schooling Navajo children had been ineffectual at best. By the time the Franciscan missionaries arrived in 1898, federal policy on Indian education had changed and religious schools for Indian children were no longer subsidized by the government. Officially the government was neutral to religion; in practice, the inertia of the previous decades of Protestant administration continued to marginalize Catholics.

The Franciscan missionaries were marginal in other ways. Members of a mendicant order based in a midwestern city, they were the products of German-American culture, American citizens for whom English was a second language and whose first public reports of their mission work were published in German-language periodicals. If their ultimate object was to save Indian souls, their pragmatic tool for doing so was the school where Indian children would learn the ways of civilization and the English language, albeit sometimes in German accent. Celebrating their first Christmases on the reservation, the friars would teach the Navajo to sing German-language Christmas carols.

There was also the matter of poverty. The early years of the mission were subsidized by grants from the fortune of Mother Katharine Drexel, and there were sufficient resources to build some essential mission buildings, but neither the financial support nor the available personnel were ever equal to the challenge at hand. From the outset the friars' writings contain appeals to readers for support in the form of cash, used clothing, and necessary mission supplies. Occasionally, a missionary had to make a tour of parishes elsewhere in the country seeking funds from the laity, or to appeal to Catholic charitable organizations. There was always an element of self-support involved in the Navajo missions, and sometimes it conflicted with the spiritual work. Over the years the friars served as postmasters, gardened, raised chickens, sold hay and honey, and worked in scores of other fund-raising or cash-saving enterprises. After the first years there were always more places on the reservation where the friars had been invited to establish churches, schools, or medical facilities than there were funds to build with and people to send. Later, the simple maintenance of existing facilities would become problematic.

The other parties to this historic confluence, the Navajo people, were reeling from a series of shocks to their physical well-being and the integrity of their culture that might have destroyed a less resilient people. In 1868 they had returned home from Fort Sumner, the remnant of a proud people who had suffered profound physical and psychological dislocation. A decade before that, they had been the masters of their vast homeland, farmers and herders and raiders, a people who "raided as harvesting machines reap grain from its golden stalks, for pure caloric gain."[4]

That way of life ended in the Navajo War of 1863–1864, when the U.S. military temporarily solved the "Navajo problem" by tearing out Navajo orchards, destroying their crops and herds, rounding up the starving Navajo in midwinter, and marching them 300 miles from Fort Defiance to Fort Sumner in eastern New Mexico. There the government tried to force them to become farmers in a land not their own. The crops failed, the Navajo sickened and died, and after four years the costly experiment ended. The Navajo were permitted to return home to a greatly reduced land base.

They were a changed people. In the words of Clyde Kluckhohn and Dorothea Leighton,

> Probably no folk has ever had a greater shock. Proud, they saw their properties destroyed and knew what it was to be dependent upon the largess of strangers. Not understanding group activity and accustomed to move freely over great spaces, they knew the misery of confinement within a limited area. . . .
>
> Fort Sumner was a major calamity to The People; its full effects upon their imagination can hardly be conveyed to white readers. . . . One can no more understand Navaho attitudes—particularly toward white people—without knowing of Fort Sumner than he can comprehend Southern attitudes without knowing of the Civil War.[5]

By 1898, the Navajo had had 30 years to rebuild, to practice coexistence with the long arm of the federal government, 30 years to struggle with the ever more numerous whites over use of lands that for centuries had been Navajo lands. "From 1868 to the present," Kluckhohn and Leighton wrote in 1946, "the persistent theme in Navajo history has been the struggle with the whites for land."[6]

The Navajo had increased in number from perhaps 9,000 in 1868 to about 19,000, but they had not become acculturated. Only a few of their children had attended government schools, only a handful of adults spoke English, and government efforts to recruit students to boarding schools, viewed by Navajo parents as kidnapping, had provoked clashes with officials that had escalated to the intervention of federal troops. Economically there had been some recovery, but there were good years and bad years, and the decade of the 1890s was mostly bad. The period 1893–1900 was a time of "economic collapse," in which drought, hard winters, and a down cycle of the national economy combined to push as many as one-fourth of the Navajo into destitution.[7]

By winter of 1894–1895 "the poorer of the Indians had eaten up their flocks, so at the beginning of the winter they had nothing to eat except their horses and burros, which they began to kill for food."[8] Things improved somewhat the following years, but then came the winter of 1898–1899, when one-fifth of the sheep on the reservation either froze to death or starved. Over the decade as a whole, "the intensified herding economy collapsed, and with it, prosperity vanished."[9]

The time seems hardly propitious for the introduction of another white man's religion and the establishment of another white man's school. Yet from the conjuncture of the Franciscan missionary and the impoverished and suspicious

Navajo would come extraordinary outcomes of great benefit to the Navajo people. One is tempted to call them gifts to the Navajo from the Franciscans, but in truth they are interaction effects, the products of a combination of Franciscan and Navajo thought and personality in a particular historical setting, and both sides are essential to the remarkable synergy set into motion by the arrival of three Franciscan missionaries on October 7, 1898.

The missionaries faced a subdued but wary people impoverished by economic cycles beyond their understanding or control, a people who resented the efforts of the white man to steal their land, of the white government to steal their children, of the white establishment generally to demean and destroy their culture. Father Anselm Weber reported that "suspicion is a way of life here," and Father Leopold Ostermann was not imagining things when, in 1906, he discerned "a strong feeling against the whites prevalent among the Indians . . . some even going so far as to say that all the Americans living on the reservation ought to be killed."[10]

The Franciscans, themselves multipli-marginal in American society, would become unlikely advocates for Navajo rights, Navajo land, and Navajo culture, such that their efforts, in addition to establishing a network of mission schools and churches and a small core of faithful believers among the "pagan" Navajo, would yield: 1) over 1.5 million additional acres to the Navajo reservation, 2) a written Navajo language where before there had been none, 3) an unparalleled record of traditional Navajo chants and rituals, 4) a treasure trove of priceless historical photographs of Navajo people and Navajo life in the early decades of the 20th century, and 5) a systematic.census of the Navajo people that would come to be the most complete record of Navajo kinship ties anywhere.

The Franciscans realized that to gain access to the people's souls, they would have to minister to their physical needs, especially in times of hunger and cold, sickness and death, and to serve as advocates or middlemen who could help the Navajo deal with the Anglo establishment: the law, the government, the railroads, the cattlemen, and the settlers.

Franciscans as Observers of Navajo Life

One reason to credit the standpoint and experience of the Franciscans as students of the Navajo is the sheer extent of their personal immersion in the daily life of the people. Without minimizing the importance of the theoretical sophistication, scientific training, and scholarly detachment that professional researchers bring to the field, it is worth noting that in terms of years spent living among the Navajo—or, for that matter, among any of the "native" peoples whose cultures are the subject of scholarly study—the professional anthropologist or sociologist is something of a carpetbagger. Typically, he or she arrives, establishes contacts and rapport, and "does fieldwork" among the people for anywhere from a few months to, in rarer cases, a few years. Often episodes of intensive fieldwork are separated by intervals of several years away from the field, so that the total duration "on site" in an anthropological career may amount to only a few years, scattered over several decades.

For instance, Bronislaw Malinowski's classic studies of the Trobriand Islanders were based on two years of residence among them; he had earlier spent six months elsewhere in New Guinea.[11] Franz Boas's famed ethnographies of the Northwest Coast Indians derive from a total of only 30 months fieldwork, and in his entire life, counting both his year in Baffinland and a year in Mexico when he did little fieldwork, Boas's personal total of fieldwork amounted to not more than five years.[12]

In contrast, the Franciscan missionaries whose writings are collected in this volume came to stay, often for life. Of course there were other friars who, after a few months or years among the Navajo, moved on, and there were also some who lived among them for long periods but had neither the interest nor the skills to describe Navajo life and the interplay of Navajo and Anglo culture.

Data collection by the professional scholar is far more efficient than that of the priest. The latter is less concerned in documenting particulars of the people's culture than in serving the members of that culture, both individually and collectively. Thus the friar who teaches, visits, and ministers among the people, as compared to the professional researcher, may be both less attuned to systematic observation and less motivated to inquire into a situation's nonobvious aspects. On the other hand, both as a result of long familiarity with his charges and his necessary participation in many of their more intimate moments—instructions before marriage, birth and baptism, marriage and divorce, sickness and death—the priest is likely to observe aspects of Navajo life less open to the "disinterested" scholar. Presumably the latter is less concerned to know the Navajo for themselves, and for their benefit, than to know them in the interest of a professional agenda.

Stated differently, many Franciscans who served the Navajo invested their lives in that service. They committed their time and energy to providing the Navajo with material assistance and access to the sacraments. Ideally, their primary motivation was genuine concern for the individual Navajo and not advancement of a professional career, as may be seen in Father Anselm's appeal to the motive of altruistic self-sacrifice in an effort to recruit Sisters to come help teach Navajo children: "Is there anything greater than to merge one's entire being into the lives and needs of a race other than our own? Can you imagine a vocation more pleasant, more appealing to the best and noblest instincts of a womanly heart, than to become the mother of the lonely, poor, and most forsaken?"[13]

Even in the secular literature there is occasionally the suggestion that the "eye of love" is capable of seeing some things better, more clearly, than the coldly analytic eye of science. It has been said that "reason reveals the way the world is; emotion and desire move us to respond to that world with action and feeling."[14] Presumably everyone responds with both reason and emotion, but the scientific observer is taught to minimize, insofar as possible, personal emotional involvement, desire, or caring, and to emphasize reason, observation, and accurate recording of data, with only as much commitment, concern, or emotion in evidence as is necessary to maintain rapport with the subject population, for whom observation and recording are far less important than emotion and action.

Among those who affirm that caring and moral commitment may *increase* one's capacity for accurate observation is the philosopher Margaret Olivia Little, who writes that in much scientific work "there is a tendency to view emotion and desire with deep suspicion . . . as something that infects, renders impure, and constantly threatens to disrupt" the functions of distanced reason. Affect tends to be seen as "a source of contamination, which we must control and, in the end, transcend." Yet, Little continues, "what one is attentive to is largely a function of . . . one's affect," that is "what one is attentive to reflects one's interests, desires, in brief, what one *cares* about."[15] Especially relevant to Franciscan missionaries responsible for the spiritual welfare of their Navajo brothers and sisters is the judgment that "it is extremely unlikely that one will be reliably sensitive to moral saliences unless one cares about recognizably moral ends." Moreover, "the attentiveness necessary to good moral judgment is best ensured . . . when we care, not simply about impersonal moral ideals such as justice, but about *people themselves*."[16]

There are serious ethical questions inherent in observing others for the sake of goals beyond the welfare of the persons in question. The external, professional objective changes the very nature of "observation." In the role of "investigator," one observes from a stance in which "we objectify the person in a certain way: we see her as a means to aiding our agenda, including agendas as laudable as furthering justice or diminishing suffering," and observing in the interest of our agenda means that we may miss or distort essential elements of the situation, aspects of the experience that might be more accessible if we observed "from a stance of caring for the person herself." Therefore, "to see clearly what is before us, we need to cultivate certain desires, such as the desire to see justice done, and the desire to see humans flourish, but we must also, more particularly, work at developing our capacities for loving and caring about people."[17]

These very capacities are enhanced by the long-term, personal commitment of the Franciscan friar to the welfare of his flock. To the degree that caring and loving increase one's ability to see and understand, the Franciscans will have access to a different, if not deeper, understanding of the Navajo than will the professional observers. (True, the well-trained observer combines both caring and dispassionate observation, but in academic contexts it is the observer/recorder role that is the more highly valued, for it produces the ultimate "product" that justifies fieldwork in the first place.) To put it bluntly, in terms that anyone who has ever done ethnographic fieldwork will recognize, sometimes you have to choose between what's good for the career (get the data and don't worry too much about problems that will still be here after you're gone) and what's good for the people you are studying.

The issue boils down to the primary justification for the encounter. Why is the observer or change agent "there" at all? Even allowing for the fact that everyone has mixed motives, it is useful to ask the *cui bono?*—"who benefits?"—question that has proved so fruitful in the sociological analysis of organizations.[18] Is the observer there primarily for her own benefit, or for that of the people? For some roles (anthropologists, traders, government agents) the answer seems fairly obvious; for others (priests, medical personnel, some secular teachers) there is a higher probability of motives that are seriously mixed, and sometimes there is a primary commitment to the welfare of the people. If we allow, as we must, that persons in all these positions arrive with biases attached, then from the standpoint of our quest for a greater understanding of the Navajo people, the relevant question is either 1) Whose vision is least clouded?, or better, 2) As everyone's vision is clouded, whose distinctive vision of things are we missing? There being no all-inclusive view, no impartial and unlimited standpoint, there is strength in the cumulative vision. That vision necessarily includes perspectives based in long acquaintance, despite their sometime characterization as "marginal" in the sense of being beyond or partially outside the accredited "expert" view.

Perhaps in an era when much scientific objectivity is demonstrably mythical, we can still muster two cheers for disinterestedness, or perhaps for disinterestedness other than that associated with the field-worker's career prospects. If so, then we must also applaud commitment not to knowledge, method, or career, but to *people*, which is one way of casting the difference between a Franciscan's assignment to a tribal people and the field experience of a visiting social scientist.

Another important difference between the penurious priest and the professional researcher is that of audience. To shift metaphors, both the hopeful graduate student and the established scholar are oriented to audiences outside of, beyond, the "quarry" where are mined the texts upon which academic progress is constructed. Social scientists write first of all for their peers, perhaps also for a wider general public, but typically not for their subjects, the anonymous and pseudonymous ones whose stories provide the raw material for their texts (although in these days of tribal literacy, researchers know that some of their native subjects will also be reading their reports).[19]

The essential issue for the visiting field-worker generally is some variation on "how can I use this?" or "how can these observations be turned into a meaningful contribution to my discipline?" In contrast, the missionary is committed to the "quarry" itself, that is, to the communities of people whose stories, texts as texts, are only of secondary interest, far less important than the people themselves and the welfare of their souls.

Usually when the Franciscan missionary produced a text, he wrote in service of the People—to beg for resources to enable him to serve his flock better, to generate interest in the mission work and perhaps recruit supporters and potential coworkers, to influence the opinion of lawmakers and other influentials, to seek advice and assistance from his superiors—and not for the sake of personal promotion grounded in the writing itself.

Recently anthropology, and to a lesser degree some of the other social sciences, have taken a reflexive turn that asks, among other things, whether their methods and findings have any utility for the "subject" populations. Increasingly, there are questions about the ethics of "taking" from tribal communities more than is "given back" to them. Professional standards now include the recommendation that some attention be paid to the needs of the community one studies. Still, disciplinary goals and professional achievement remain the primary justifications for academic fieldwork.

In contrast, the Franciscan's primary, explicit commitment is to the welfare, both here and hereafter, of those among whom he serves. If theological priorities ascribe more importance to spiritual salvation than temporal welfare, still the temporal and the spiritual are known to be interrelated, and the friar must keep a pragmatic eye on both. The audience for his work includes his peers, the people he serves, and his God, and acts of self-interest that interfere with the interests of those he serves are seen as sinful. His relationship to those he serves is to mirror, insofar as circumstances allow, the love of Christ.

A central question for the reader is whether the writings of observers who are formally, personally committed to serving and loving the Navajo people merit attention alongside, and not in an inferior position to, the writings of professionals committed more to academic disciplines and sound scholarly practice than to the long-term benefit of the People.

Consider also the difference between *studying* a people as a distinct and purposeful activity and learning to know them as a by-product of living and working among them. Presumably either avenue to knowledge will yield a recognizable core of information, an area of common understanding, but it also seems likely that each will contribute insights of its own. Surely both ways are legitimate and useful, but the priorities of academia and the realities of modern professionalism have elevated the knowledge of the disinterested expert while tending to underrate and neglect the knowledge grounded in commitment, sacrifice, and love.

Each of the four Franciscan fathers whose writings comprise most of this book lived among the Navajo, except for brief assignments or medical treatment and convalescence elsewhere, from their initial assignment to the Navajo missions to the end of their lives. Father Berard and Father Emanuel each lived among the Navajo for more than half a century, Father Leopold, for almost 30 years, Father Anselm, for over 20 years. Each of these men, and most of the other writers represented in this collection, demonstrates the commitment of caring and the deeper awareness of the other that accompanies such commitment. Each personifies the "first lesson about affect's role in moral epistemology," namely that "to see clearly what is before us, we need to . . . work at developing our capacities for loving and caring about people."[20]

Editorial Practice

My primary objective is to make more readily available to today's readers the views of the Navajo produced by the Franciscans when they were writing for themselves and their own, both in their personal writings—correspondence, journal entries, internal memoranda, administrative reports—and when they addressed the Catholic laity and potential donors in national publications like *St. Anthony Messenger* and *Indian Sentinel*, or narrower, more regional audiences in mission magazines such as *Catholic Pioneer* and the *Padres' Trail*, or, more selective and sophisticated, their own confreres, Franciscans and members of other orders, in the *Provincial Chronicle* or the German-language *Der Sendbote*.

Selection of items has been governed by criteria of accessibility, relevance, and interest or appeal. According to the criterion of accessibility, the more difficult to access a piece is, for instance, because it was never published, never published in English, or appeared in a truly obscure journal, the higher its rating for possible inclusion here. The criterion of relevance refers to historical importance, my sense that essays or other materials reflect events that "made a difference" either generally or in the lives of individual Navajo. Thus it seemed important to include the friars' accounts of such decisive events as the confrontations between Navajo people and the U.S. military in 1905 and 1913, and of Father Anselm's role in lobbying successfully for extensions to the reservation and helping individual Navajo to obtain secure title to their land when many of their white neighbors were doing everything they could to wrest it from them.

The criterion of interest or appeal is more personal. I assume that most people like to pass on a good story or to share the atypical and the well-expressed experience. My immersion in the Franciscan archives has yielded much that, in my judgment, is worthwhile: much that illuminates Navajo history, that offers alternative perspective on events and trends, or that is surprising, amusing, occasionally compelling, and often inspiring. I take pleasure in offering these "gems" for more general appreciation.

The Franciscan writings on the Navajo include both the "primary" source, the firsthand account of families visited, events observed, actions taken in which the writer participated directly, and also the "secondary" source, the historical record based to some extent on the writings of others. Emanuel Trockur is well represented in the latter genre, for in addition to his half-century of personal experience among the Navajo, he was the great historian of the Franciscan missionaries, drawing upon the writings of his confreres and a variety of external sources to describe the beginnings of the Franciscan missions to the Navajo, the history of government involvement in Indian education, and the antecedents of the "Navajo crisis" at mid-century. In selecting items for this book, I have favored the primary source, but both personal experience and the well-documented historical account are necessary to tell the story coherently.

Some of the chapters in this book are more than a century old. Many were published in little mission magazines or Franciscan journals that today are not readily available in most libraries. Others are internal reports or position papers not intended for publication. There are also selections from diaries and personal correspondence, and from notes and rough drafts that seem never to have gone beyond the draft stage. In trying to recast these materials in a standard, contemporary format, I have made minor editorial changes, removing unnecessary punctuation (current usage is less free with commas and semicolons), changing archaic spellings, deleting unnecessary references to previous or forthcoming articles, and correcting a few typographical errors. Sometimes I have deleted parts of a selection that did not pertain directly to Franciscan-Navajo relations, or that seemed tangential to the main themes a chapter was intended to convey. In other instances, short pieces or segments have been combined. I have added and deleted headings, divided lengthy paragraphs, and as may be seen by reference to the title note of each selection, freely changed or created titles. In no case, as far as I can tell, has the editing altered the meaning of a statement or a passage of text.

Throughout the book the standard spelling for the name of these people to whom the Franciscans were sent is "Navajo." In accordance with contemporary usage, it is spelled with a *j* even in selections by Father Berard Haile, who made a compelling argument for the correctness of "Navaho" and spelled it that way in his work.[21]

The extent and freedom of editing have varied by type of selection. Correspondence I have defined to be largely "set" as written and sent, and so have tried to minimize editorial changes. Still, I have corrected spelling, capitalization, punctuation, and obvious typographical oversights, for the objective here is to tell a story, not to critique the friars' spelling.

Most freely edited were pieces translated from the German and chapters based on previously unpublished drafts and documents, some of which had not been finally edited and polished by their authors. In all cases, my intent has been to edit as I would want my own manuscripts and publications edited a century hence to improve their consistency and flow for a future audience.

Two categories of text that have not been changed in the interest of uniformity are Navajo language words and place names. Both categories are "moving targets," in that they were in the processes of creation and evolution during the period the Franciscan fathers wrote the materials collected here. The Franciscans were themselves producing a written Navajo language and experimenting with alternate orthographies, and even in their own writings the presentation of a Navajo word varies over time. Similarly, place names evolve, such that, for example, Chin Lee and Chinlee become the present-day Chinle. Leaving things as they were, with respect to place names and Navajo words, seemed preferable to imposing an artificial and anachronistic uniformity. Where two or more usages seem to have overlapped, I have chosen one for the sake of consistency. Thus, references to Chinlee have been changed to Chin Lee. Otherwise, the spelling of Navajo terms and the names of places have been left as they appear in the source documents.

A related problem is the contemporaneous use of different names for the same places and people. The issue of multiple Navajo names is dealt with in some detail in chapter 35, "Navajo Names." As for alternative names for the same place, or different spellings of the same name, perhaps the most frequent is St. Michaels, Arizona, where the school and mission the fathers founded is properly designated St. Michael's Mission, while the post office and village at the same place is St. Michaels, without apostrophe. The friars themselves, more often than not, leave out the apostrophe even when referring to the mission, and the most appropriate and simplest rule is to follow their lead and use "St. Michaels" in all instances except when stating the formal, proper name of the mission or school.

It is customary to render words and phrases from languages other than English in italics. Here there are two exceptions to this rule, place names and proper names. Thus, the Navajo word for "Mr.," *hastin*, is italicized when used in contexts other than proper names, but when incorporated as a name, for example, Hastin Naez, it appears in standard text. A similar usage applies to place names. Despite their derivation from Navajo terms, when used to name particular places, neither Chin Lee nor Tse-heli are italicized.

Editorial comments or additions, both introductory to and within the texts, are bracketed. So are editorial endnotes to selections, to distinguish them from the author's notes. However, notes to bracketed introductory or other editorial comment, obviously mine, are unbracketed. A few frequently cited sources and archives are identified in the notes by abbreviations.[22]

Notes

1. Howard M. Bahr, *Diné Bibliography to the 1990s: A Companion to the Navajo Bibliography of 1969* (Lanham, Md.: Scarecrow Press, 1999).

2. There is one major exception to the generalization that Franciscan contributions to Navajo studies have been underrated or neglected, and that is the writings of Father Berard Haile. He is widely admired for his work on the Navajo language and his writings on Navajo ceremonials, including many posthumous works coauthored by others based on his manuscripts. Father Murray Bodo's recent *Tales of an Endishodi: Father Berard Haile and the Navajos, 1900–1961*, makes Father Berard's reminiscences of his early years among the Navajo available for the first time, and also reprints two essays by Father Anselm Weber, "Opening of St. Michael's School—Indians' Attack at Round Rock," and "The Snake Dance of the Hopi or Moqui Indians."

3. Anselm Weber, FMN 29 (August 1902): 641. Translated by Emanuel Trockur.

4. John Major Hurdy, *American Indian Religions* (Los Angeles: Sherbourne Press, 1970), 150.

5. Clyde Kluckhohn and Dorothea Leighton, *The Navaho*, rev. ed. (Cambridge, Mass.: Harvard University Press, 1974), 41.

6. Kluckhohn and Leighton, 43.

7. Garrick Bailey and Robert Glenn Bailey, *A History of the Navajos: The Reservation Years* (Santa Fe, N.Mex.: School of American Research Press, 1986), 100–102.

8. Bailey and Bailey, 102. They are quoting Mary Eldridge, government field matron.

9. Bailey and Bailey, 104.

10. Leopold Ostermann, "Navajo Indian Mission at Chin Lee, Arizona," FMSW 2 (1914): 27.

11. Bronislaw Malinowski, *A Diary in the Strict Sense of the Term* (Stanford, Calif.: Stanford University Press, 1989), xiii.; Phyllis Kaberry, "Malinowski"s Contribution to Field-work Methods and the Writing of Ethnography," in *Man and Culture: An Evaluation of the Work of Bronislaw Malinowski*, ed. Raymond Firth (London: Routledge & Kegan Paul, 1957), 77.

12. Leslie A. White, "The Ethnography and Ethnology of Franz Boas," *Bulletin of the Texas Memorial Museum* 6 (April 1963):10–11.

13. Anselm Weber, "The Sisters of Blessed Sacrament for Indians and Colored People," *St. Anthony Messenger* 9 (January 1901): 267–68.

14. Margaret Olivia Little, "Seeing and Caring: The Role of Affect in Feminist Moral Epistemology," *Hypatia* 10 (Summer 1995): 120.

15. Little, 120, 122.

16. Little, 123.

17. Little, 124.

18. Peter M. Blau and W. Richard Scott, *Formal Organizations: A Comparative Approach* (San Francisco: Chandler, 1962).

19. See, for example, Caroline B. Brettell, ed., *When They Read What We Write: The Politics of Ethnography* (Westport, Conn.: Bergin & Garvey, 1993).

20. Little, 124.

21. Berard Haile, "Navaho or Navajo?" *The Americas* 6 (1949): 85–90. Reprinted in Murray Bodo, ed., *Tales of an Endishodi: Father Berard Haile and the Navajos, 1900–1961* (Albuquerque: University of New Mexico Press, 1998), 145–50.

22. Origin of the abbreviations is identified by the italicized letters below: *B*ureau of *C*atholic *I*ndian *M*issions Papers, or BCIM; *B*erard *H*aile *P*apers, or BHP; *F*ranciscan *A*rchives *C*incinnati, or FAC; Franciscans, St. Michaels, Arizona: Papers, shortened to *F*ranciscan *F*athers' *P*apers, or FFP; the series, "Die *F*ranziskaner-*M*ission unter den *N*avajo-Indianern," or FMN; the journal *F*ranciscan *M*issions of the *S*outh*w*est, or FMSW; and the series, "*F*ranciscans in the *W*ilds and *W*astes of the Navajo Country," or FWW.

Part 1

BEGINNINGS

1

The Birth of the Navajo Missions[1]

Emanuel Trockur, O.F.M.

[Originally entitled "Fifty Years among the Navajo," this historical sketch by Father Emanuel Trockur is almost entirely devoted to the challenges and accomplishments of the earliest years of the Navajo missions. Only the final paragraph of the piece, not reprinted here, shifts focus from the early 1900s to the years following Father Anselm Weber's passing in 1921. At the time of its writing Father Emanuel had been a missionary to the Navajo for over three decades and had established himself as the unofficial historian of the mission. Reading this carefully crafted overview of early mission history, intended for the sympathetic Catholic lay readership of the *Indian Sentinel*, I was impressed that neither stylistically nor in judicious selection of material could I produce a better opening to the story of the Franciscan ministry to the Navajo. Accordingly, although its publication date is midcentury rather than the early 1900s, we begin with Father Emanuel's tribute to the founders.]

The romance which attaches to the beginnings of important historical undertakings hovers over the birth of the Navajo missions. On October 7, 1898, three Franciscan friars, Fathers Anselm Weber, Juvenal Schnorbus, and Brother Placidus Buerger, arrived at Cienega, a day's trip from the railroad, and took possession of a small, scantily furnished building that awaited them there. This they blessed and placed under the protection of St. Michael the Archangel. A large wooden cross, which they set up prominently in front of their dwelling, proclaimed that the building, originally designed as a trading post, was to serve a far different purpose. They were ready to begin at last the long, persevering work of Christianizing America's largest Indian tribe, then supposed to count 20,000 souls, who were scattered over thousands of square miles in northeastern Arizona and northwestern New Mexico.

Various attempts had been made, back in Spanish colonial days, to evangelize the Navajo. These Indians had attracted the notice of the pioneer Franciscan missionaries among the Pueblo Indians along the Rio Grande River. As early as 1629, Fray Alonso de Benevides reported in his famous "Memorial" the baptism of a Navajo chief. But they were a nomadic and widely roaming people, and repeated failures to gather an appreciable number of them for instruction and services frustrated the friars in their attempts to establish even a single successful mission.

The project of a new, if belated, attempt to bring the Gospel to the Navajo finally shaped up 50 years ago. Upon the representations of Monsignor Joseph A. Stephan, then director of the Bureau of Catholic Indian Missions, the provincial and councillors of St. John's Province of the Franciscans accepted this task. Little time was lost in selecting the first missionary band. They, in turn, set forth from Cincinnati on their mission as soon as they were assured that a humble shelter awaited them. Unheralded and practically unnoticed was their entry into the land of magnificent distances, lofty mountains, desert wastes, and rugged canyons that is the Navajo reservation.

There they met surprises such as they might scarcely have expected even in far-off China or Africa. Reports about the Navajo and their new field of labor which they had received before coming had been encouraging. But the real situation, they soon discovered, was quite different. If they had the impression that all of Arizona is a land of perpetual sunshine and mild climate, they were promptly disillusioned. On February 7, 1899, exactly four months after their arrival, the thermometer indicated a shivering temperature of 30 degrees below zero.

Though the new mission was not located upon the Indian reservation proper, where the friars might have had reason to fear government interference, they later found plenty of opposition and unpleasant experiences where they were. Even official Washington contributed its share of difficulties and embarrassments.

Then the actual prospects for conversions were not as hopeful as the missionaries might have assumed. In fact, during their first four years, the total results of their spiritual ministrations added up to a mere dozen baptisms. It is true that they did not find the Navajo savage barbarians, but a peaceable, industrious people. However, with the rarest exceptions, none of them understood a word of English.

The study of the Navajo language naturally became the new missionaries' first occupation. With the aid of Indians who knew no more English than the missionaries knew Navajo, they set about gathering a collection of words. This was done by holding up an article or pointing to it and asking the word for it. These words were then written down as carefully as possible. In this way they composed a small dictionary after about three months and trained their vocal cords to pronounce 3,000 of the strange words so that an Indian would understand them.

They soon discovered that only a few Indians lived in the neighborhood of the new mission. As for the reservation, it is difficult to believe how far apart one cabin usually is from the next. Nor is the Navajo family always at one home, for they follow their sheep from one seasonal grazing place to another. Roads were few in the early days, and these were mere wagon trails which were bad enough at their best. The surest and safest means of travel was by horseback. Many were the times that Father Anselm made trips of several hundred miles that required days of riding.

At Fort Defiance, Arizona, long before abandoned as a military post, was a large government boarding school. Only eight miles from St. Michaels, it offered a splendid opportunity for religious work among the pupils. Later, a Catholic chapel was built there.

The desired expansion of religious work to other points was necessarily very, very slow. On the reservation, the secretary of the interior could set aside plots of land as mission sites. But to obtain these concessions required much correspondence and the unraveling of endless red tape. It was not until 1907 that a mission with two resident priests was established at Chinle, although this promising locality had been visited regularly for more than five years. Next followed the mission at Lukachukai, and in 1920 Tohatchi, long an outmission from St. Michaels, was provided with a beautiful chapel and became the residence of a priest.

On his many long trips over the mountains and barren wastes, what struck Father Anselm particularly was the fact that thousands of children on the reservation lacked the opportunity of an education. The establishment of a large boarding school was, therefore, eventually decided upon. Mother Katharine Drexel, who was deeply interested in the Navajo cause, offered to pay for the building and to send Sisters of her community to the mission as teachers. Her generous intervention solved one problem.

To solve the next one, namely, the recruitment of pupils for the new school, Father Anselm spent weeks in the saddle traveling thousands of miles. In conferences with headmen and in speeches before large groups of Indians gathered at trading posts or for some ceremonial observance, he clearly and persuasively explained the purpose of an education, with particular emphasis on the benefits and need of moral training. He frankly admitted that it was not in his power to force parents to send their children to school, nor his desire.

Never before had the Navajo heard such "straight talk." When the school was opened on December 3, 1902, 57 pupils were on hand. Among them were 27 children from a remote district where 10 years before the Indians had almost murdered the government agent and threatened to go on the warpath unless he would recede from his policy of compulsory education. The attendance at St. Michaels increased from year to year until it reached 250 pupils, when the capacity of the school was reached.

When Father Anselm passed to his eternal reward in 1921, four other mission centers had been established on the reservation, besides the headquarters, St. Michaels, and its mission school. He had proved to be an able guiding spirit of the missions during their formative years. His missionary initiative and enterprise and his manifest interest in the welfare of the Navajo had won for him regard in government circles and the respect and trust of the Indians of the reservation.

Note

1. From Emanuel Trockur, "Fifty Years among the Navajo," *Indian Sentinel* 28 (November 1948): 131–33.

2

Beginnings of St. Michael's Mission and School[1]

Anselm Weber, O.F.M.

[The *Indian Sentinel*, official organ of the Catholic Indian Missions, was published by the Bureau of Catholic Indian Missions, headquartered in Washington, D.C. In the mid-1890s its director, Monsignor Joseph A. Stephan, had collaborated with Mother Katharine Drexel in securing a location for the Navajo mission and arranging for the Franciscan friars of the Province of St. John Baptist to serve there. When the bureau created the *Indian Sentinel*[2] in 1902, it was natural that the Navajo missions should be highly visible there, both in feature stories and in appeals for assistance. The *Sentinel* was distributed "in the interest of the Society for the Preservation of the Faith among Indian children," and its readers were an important source of funding for missionary work. In 1908, the tenth anniversary of the arrival of the first missionaries in Navajo country, the *Sentinel* published a decade overview by Father Anselm. Although in later chapters we return to these first years of the mission, drawing upon the friars' correspondence and regular reports to Catholic periodicals to provide a more intimate, day-to-day view of things, Father Anselm's overview belongs here at the beginning. This article, an effort by the mission Superior to highlight the decade's most significant events and accomplishments, sensitizes us to key events treated more fully later, and also provides background or pattern against which the more focused later segments may be interpreted.]

In northwestern New Mexico and northeastern Arizona a tract of land equaling about twice the size of the state of Massachusetts has been set aside for the 20,000 Navajo Indians who from time immemorial have been living in this locality. They certainly were here when the Spaniards under Coronado arrived in this part of the country in 1540. They must have been here long before that, since all their myths and legends and traditions are localized in and between their "sacred" mountains which bound their territory—*Debentsa,* that is, Big Sheep, the San Juan Mountains of Colorado, in the north; *Sizna-jini,* that is, Dark-streaked Belt, Pelado Peak of New Mexico, in the east; *Tsodzil,* that is, Tongue Mountain, Mt. Taylor of New Mexico in the south; and *Dook'ooslid,* that is, Snow-capped Mountain, the San Francisco Mountains of Arizona, in the west—though the numerous prehistoric ruins and cliff dwellings which dot their country show that they were preceded by a different people.

Were we to believe their myths we would say that they emerged from four different worlds into this, the fifth one. A small lake in the San Juan Mountains in southwestern Colorado is given by them as the place whence they came into this world. This small lake is surrounded, the Indians say, by precipitous cliffs and has a small island near its center, from the top of which rises something that looks like the top of a ladder. Beyond the bounding cliffs there are four mountain peaks which are frequently referred to in the songs and myths of the Navajo. They fear to visit the shores of this lake, but they climb the surrounding mountains and view its waters from a distance. Space does not permit me to relate the amusing incidents of their emergence into this world.

There is no doubt in my mind that they originally came from the steppes of Tartary, in Asia, across Bering Strait, since the various dialects of their language can easily be traced from Arizona to the very shores of the strait. They belong to the Athapascan or Diné stock, a race whose diffusion is only equaled by that of the Aryan or Semitic nations of the Old World. Stretching from the northern interior of Alaska down into southern Arizona and New Mexico, it is a linguistic line of more than 4,000 miles in length, extending diagonally over 42 degrees of latitude, like a great tree whose trunk is the Rocky Mountain Range, whose roots encompass the deserts of Arizona and New Mexico, and whose branches touch the borders of Hudson Bay and of the Arctic and Pacific Oceans. West of the Rocky Mountains they are to be found to the borders of the Eskimo tribes. From west to east they roam, undisputed masters of the soil, over almost the entire breadth of the American continent. South of the Canadian boundary, Diné tribes, or remnants thereof, are found all through Oregon, northern California, Arizona, and New Mexico, the Navajo, Apache and Lipanes being the most southern. The Navajo, therefore, seem to have been the vanguard, as it were, of some great national migration, started from some cause or causes on the steppes of Asia over Bering Strait southward, a supposition borne out not only by the traditions of the northern Diné tribes, but also by those of the Navajo concerning the *Diné Nahodloni,* that is, "other Navajo."

Prior to 1863 the Navajo were the highway robbers of the plains, the terror of the country, and, like the Ishmaelites of old, their hands were raised against all, and the hands of all against them. They fought the Utes, the warlike Apaches, the fierce Comanches, but especially the Pueblo Indians and the Mexicans. Quick, alert, and experienced, the Navajo frequently appeared in numbers as suddenly as a flash of light, took what they wanted, killed those who resisted, or took them along as slaves, and as suddenly disappeared again. But General Carson, or, as he is familiarly known in the Southwest, Kit Carson, in 1863, with a regiment of soldiers from New Mexico, and 100 Ute Indians, killed their stock and destroyed their crops, thus forcing them through starvation to surrender. They were transferred to Fort Sumner, in southeastern New Mexico, whence when they returned to their old homes in 1869, they were completely subdued. Ever since, they are a peaceful, pastoral people, living by, with, and off their flocks of sheep and goats.

The present commissioner of Indian Affairs, the Hon. Francis E. Leupp, very aptly describes the present Navajo as follows:

To the great Northern tribes the Navajo present a characteristic contrast. Their remoteness from any of the denser white settlements and the slow and uneven development of the country around them have kept them from much, if any contact with civilization, so that they are today about as primitive as any tribe in the United States.

They are Indians through and through, clinging as far as practicable to their old style of dress and their old manner of living. Lithe of figure, handsome of face, magnificent horsemen, bright, responsive, cheerful fellows, they win their way to the hearts of all who know them.

They object, for the most part, to experimenting with our methods in their crude agriculture, and I am by no means sure that they cannot teach us a thing or two about wresting a scanty living out of their alkali clay and sand.

They are also clever silversmiths. With two or three simple instruments for beating and engraving metal into ornamental forms, they produce results of rare beauty.

The Navajo have learned that thrice blessed is he who has nothing, for from him can nothing be taken away. Denizens of a desert too forbidding to tempt white cupidity, they have escaped pillage because nobody believes the booty would be worth the trouble of robbing them. The government has done little or nothing for them beyond maintaining an agency and a few schools, and they have enjoyed no income from invested funds. Yet the years come and go with rarely a complaint from the Navajo. With neither present wealth nor future prospects to distract their thoughts from the simple life and the duty of making a living, they are getting along pretty well, all things considered. At any rate they seem happy and contented. Their wants are few, and what they can raise on their little patches of tilled land or earn by selling their blankets and silverware is supplemented, among those who need more, by an occasional turn at manual labor off the Reservation.

The white farmers within reach would rather have them for help in the fields than anybody else. The young men are in great demand as pliers of the pick and shovel wherever there is any railroad building in the neighborhood. The contractors of the Santa Fe line tell me that they have no better employees for industry, honesty, cheerfulness, and a disposition to render a full day's work for a full day's pay.

They have not yet learned the meaning of a strike. As long as they are decently treated they are perfectly willing to keep at their tasks, and they are peaceful among themselves and never interfere with their fellow laborers of other races. In more than one respect they could be imitated with advantage by people who have enjoyed the benefits of a higher civilization.

Though the Navajo may not be counted among the 'progressive' members of their race according to our artificial standards, they have proved their right to be considered good Americans.

One day the descendants of such fine fellows will be heard from—unless by mistaken kindness, or the opposite extreme, we ruin them in the meantime.

This promising field for missionary endeavor attracted the attention of the late lamented Very Reverend Monsignor Stephan, director of the Bureau of Catholic Indian Missions at Washington, D.C., and Mother Katharine Drexel, foundress of the Sisterhood of the Blessed Sacrament.

In 1896 Monsignor Stephan purchased for missionary and school purposes a ranch of 200 acres, situated in a fertile valley just south of the Navajo reservation line, three miles west of the New Mexico and Arizona line, and 27 miles northwest of the town of Gallup, the nearest railway station. The Navajo call this valley *Tsohotso*, Large Meadow, while the early Spanish explorers had called it *Cienega Amarilla*, Yellow Swamp. There are several good, perennial springs in this valley which indicate an abundance of underground water, and in wet seasons portions of it are quite marshy and swampy. Toward the end of summer all places in the valley, not cultivated, are covered with a dense growth of *Gymnolomia multiflora*, the bright golden yellow blossoms of which are very profuse and probably suggested to the Spaniards the name of Yellow Swamp.

The funds for this purchase, $3,000, were generously supplied by Mother Katharine Drexel. After securing a site for a mission, the next difficulty was to get missionaries to take charge of it. After some fruitless negotiations with several provinces of different orders, several secular priests were taken into consideration, one of whom was Reverend Antonio Jouvenceau, who had spent many years among the Indian and Mexican missions of New Mexico and Arizona.

Finally, on September 3, 1897, Monsignor Stephan, through the courtesy of Reverend Godfrey Schilling, O.F.M., applied by letter to the Very Reverend Raphael Hesse, O.F.M., provincial of the Franciscan Province of St. John the Baptist of Cincinnati, Ohio, asking him to appoint some Fathers to take charge of the Navajo Indian Mission. On October 12 he personally paid a visit to the Very Reverend provincial, and on the very next day, October 13, 1897, a conference of the provincial councillors was held and the mission definitely accepted.

During the month of March 1898, Mother Katharine Drexel came to Cincinnati to see the Very Reverend provincial and to arrange with him some details regarding the acceptance of the mission. On the following July 26, the Chapter Conference, held at Mount Airy, Ohio, appointed the Reverend Juvenal Schnorbus, O.F.M., Superior of St. Michael's Mission, with the Reverend Anselm Weber, O.F.M., as assistant, and Venerable Brother Placidus Buerger, O.F.M., as lay-brother.

But as the buildings on the place had to be remodeled and needed repairs, the missionaries could not leave Cincinnati till October 3. They arrived at the mission on the 7th and said Mass for the first time at St. Michael's on the 11th.

Living in a house originally intended as an Indian trading store, in an Indian country more than twice the size of the state of Massachusetts, in the midst of a nomadic tribe of more than 20,000 pagan Indians who knew no other than their own barbaric Indian language, our task was certainly not an easy one.

Proceeding from the Catholic principle that the missionary, to do effective and lasting work, must speak the language of his flock, we began by studying their exceedingly difficult language and by reducing it to writing. By patient and persistent effort and the use of good interpreters, we fairly succeeded in constructing the language, in composing a catechism, a part of the Bible history, and some prayers. Besides, we gathered a copious vocabulary, a long list of verbs with their various conjugations, and fixed a number of grammatical rules. We gave instruction to a small number of Indian boys, sent five of them to St. Catharine's Industrial School at Santa Fe, baptized a number of sick children, and visited the Navajo in the neighborhood, trying to awaken their interest in our Holy Faith.

On July 14, 1900, the Very Reverend Dennis Schuler, O.F.M., visitator general, who subsequently was elected minister general of our whole order, paid St. Michael's a visit for a few days. He was very much interested in our work and personally visited some Indian families of the vicinity.

In the Provincial Chapter, which was held on the following September 27, at which the Very Reverend Dennis Schuler presided, the Reverend Juvenal Schnorbus, O.F.M., was transferred to Cincinnati, the Reverend Anselm Weber, O.F.M., who was, at the time, in California for his health, was appointed Superior, and the Reverend Fathers Leopold Ostermann and Berard Haile his assistants.

On October 31 of the same year, 1900, Mother Katharine, accompanied by her cousin, Miss Josephine Drexel, of New York, and by Mother M. Evangelist, Superioress of St. Catharine's, Santa Fe, paid her first visit to St. Michael's Mission. At our invitation, about 20 chiefs or headmen of the Navajo tribe met at the mission on November 2 to hold a council with the Reverend Mother concerning a school to be built for the instruction and education of their children. After a series of speeches in which some displayed no mean rhetorical talents, and after a long list of questions relating to the nature of the school, the methods of instruction, and the advantages of education, most of them consented to send their children and promised to try and induce others to do the same. Mother Katharine regretted very much that the limited number of her Sisters made it necessary to postpone the building for some time, but promised to begin the building in the fall of the following year, so that the school could be opened in 1902.

In 1902, Mother Katharine Drexel, having bought two more ranches, so that we now have 440 acres in all, of which, however, barely one-half is arable land, let the contract for a large boarding school with a capacity for 130 pupils. Much of the work, such as excavating, quarrying and hauling rock, and freighting lumber, was done by the Indians. The school is built of native stone, quarried near the building site, and consists of a main front building, to which are added three wings to the rear. It is a spacious, well-equipped, well-ventilated building. It was completed in December of the same year, except the water system, which was finished the following spring.

The mission property and school building has cost Mother Katharine about $70,000. Space does not permit me to relate all the troubles I had in securing title to our land. A Mormon and an American even placed mining claims on it to prevent us from obtaining title.

Until recently, the Navajo have been very averse to sending their children to school. Being a sturdy and independent race, their whole nature revolts against anything and everything that savors of compulsion. Only 15 years ago they were on the point of entering upon the warpath because a more zealous than prudent Indian agent attempted to take their children to school by force. In fact, they did attack the agent with the intention of killing him, knocked him down, broke his nose, and bruised him badly before his police succeeded in rescuing him; even then he was beleaguered until an army officer with a troop of soldiers came to the rescue.

When the government with its police force, farm implements to be issued to such as would send their children to school, and a number of other inducements did not succeed in filling its schools, it seemed a desperate undertaking for me to try and succeed where the government had, at least partially, failed. But, previous to the opening of our school I spent months in the saddle, visited the Navajo as far as a hundred miles away from us, gathered them especially at the homes of their chiefs, held councils with them, gave them a chance to express their opinions and objections, refuting them as best I could, enlarging especially upon the moral and industrial education to be imparted at our school.

I also laid special stress upon the fact that we had come to stay; that, after their children had left our school, we would consider them our special friends, would remain in touch with them, and would assist them in making practical use of what they had learned at school—a point in which the government had been singularly deficient. I also dwelled upon the fact that I could not use any force or drastic means to induce them to send their children; if they did not see the advantage of a good education and did not care to send their children voluntarily, why, we did not want them.

Even such as had been at the point of going upon the warpath 10 years previous not to be forced to send their children to school, promised to send them to us, stating that, until now, they simply had been told they must send their children to school, but, I having explained to them why they should send them, they saw the advantages and would send them with pleasure.

Mother Katharine Drexel, Mother Evangelist, and 11 Sisters of the Blessed Sacrament arrived on October 19, 1902, and prepared for the opening of the school.

On December 3, 1902, the feast of St. Francis Xavier, the school was opened with solemn High Mass celebrated by Reverend Berard Haile, O.F.M., captain of the school, with 57 pupils in attendance.

The midnight Mass on Christmas was the first one celebrated in the beautiful school chapel, which was finished only a few days previous.

The following year it was no small task to induce the parents to return the pupils to school and to add 30 more. Unfortunately, six pupils of the 87 enrolled that year died in rapid succession. It was very difficult to dissuade the parents from taking the sick children out of the school and delivering them up to their medicine men.

The Navajo have a great fear and dread of a corpse and everything connected with it. They will never enter a hut in which an Indian has died; hence, when so many died at our school, they imagined the infirmary full of ghosts and were loath to permit their children to remain there. Only a few of the nearest relatives are allowed to attend to the burial of a Navajo. When we had the first funeral at our school, I gathered all the children and explained to them our belief in the resurrection of the body and tried to show them the unreasonableness of their dread of a corpse. I added, however, I did not wish to compel anyone to be present at the funeral, though I would be much pleased if they would overcome their fear. All attended.

We impart religious instruction to the children in their Indian mother tongue, and the quick and ready answers given by the pupils show that they are by no means inferior to the whites so far as memory, intelligence, and understanding are concerned.

In the beginning of June, the older pupils were instructed well enough to receive the holy sacrament of baptism. Some had made the request to be baptized some time before; and when I baptized two orphan girls, of the age of five, on the first Sunday of June, some of the older ones felt chagrined, saying they thought they had the right to be baptized first.

Twenty-three of the higher class asked to be baptized. Having spent a week in special preparation, I baptized them on June 12. This was a great feast of joy, not only for those baptized, but also for us and the good Sisters, since these were the first pupils baptized, as a class, publicly in the chapel.

The following year (1905–1906) 96 children were enrolled. On June 3, 1906, during a levitical High Mass, some of our Navajo pupils received their First Holy Communion. Altar and chapel were beautifully decorated. The Indian first-communicants, between the ages of 12 and 18, the boys in black and the girls in white, sincere and devout, presented a most touching spectacle, and there were few dry eyes in our chapel that morning. Among the 32 first-communicants, 18 boys and 14 girls, were seven who had received baptism the day before.

Until the present writing, 105 of our pupils have been baptized. It certainly augurs well for the school and the Navajo that all the pupils without a single exception, some of them 18 years old, who had arrived at the proper age and were sufficiently instructed, have asked to receive baptism. Of these 105, 15 have died either at school or at home.

Forty-eight of our pupils have made their First Holy Communion, and they receive the sacraments every month, except during vacation, though one of the older pupils, who lives eight miles from here, never fails to come to Mass on Sundays, and one Saturday evening he rode up in a perfect hurricane of wind and rain to go to confession. The parents of very few of our pupils live in our immediate neighborhood; some live even a hundred miles from here. Last year (1906–1907) we had 118 pupils, and this year (1907–1908) it seems our school will be attended to its full capacity by 130 pupils.

The community of 13 Sisters of the Blessed Sacrament, in charge of the school, are doing most excellent work as teachers and educators.

The school is well graded, and this year, the sixth year of its existence, there are six classes, that is, five grades and a class for beginners—new children. The course of study includes catechism; arithmetic or number; English, which comprises reading, spelling, memory lessons, composition work, penmanship, and elementary grammar; U.S. history; geography and map drawing; a little music; and natural science.

The children are, as a rule, very intelligent. Were it not for the drawback of their nonknowledge of the English language (and the Navajo is not a linguist by any means), their class work would be excellent, equaling that of white children. Of course, English is the stumbling block; though they learn to understand it much more readily than to speak it. Their ready minds perceive this, and it renders them timid in expressing themselves in English through fear of making mistakes. Number is their strong point. Some of the children have made a grade each year.

In the way of industrial work the girls are taught plain sewing, dressmaking, cutting and fitting, blanket weaving, laundry work, domestic science, that is, cooking. how to set table, care of dining room, silver, serving at table, and so on. The older girls take turns in the kitchen monthly to prepare the meals and were very proud when the Sister allowed them once to prepare supper for a guest. Some of the older ones have also been taught a little nursing. Last year Mary Halede, one of the oldest girls, was able to teach blanket weaving to a class of smaller girls. Some of them are very dexterous in the use of the needle.

The boys are taught farming and gardening; at times they also take a turn at mason work and carpentering; they assist in laundry and bakery. As in all Indian schools, half of the time is devoted to class work, the other half to industrial work.

For the last five years we have been giving religious instruction once every week in the government school of Fort Defiance, eight miles north of this place.

After we had resided for almost five years in an old stone building which originally had been intended for a trading store, we were at last enabled to erect a more roomy and commodious residence, and a chapel, thanks to the kind liberality of our Very Reverend provincial, Father Louis Haverbeck, O.F.M., successor to the Very Reverend Raphael Hesse, under whom the mission had been accepted, seconded by a liberal contribution from Mother Katharine. The residence and chapel were begun on April 22, 1903, and finished about the middle of September.

To civilize and Christianize a nomadic people is naturally a difficult task. The nature and condition of the Navajo country is such as to force them to live very scattered, so that, excepting a few favored localities, one seldom sees two Navajo huts within hailing distance, or even within sight of each other. For the same reason they are almost constantly driving their herds and flocks from place to place. It is impossible for us to reach all the Navajo from our present mission. To do justice to them and to our work we should have at least four centers with resident missionaries, chapels and schools, and mission stations in localities where there are or will be larger agricultural settlements. I projected such a second center in the Chin Lee Valley, about two miles from the mouth of Cañon de Chelly and 60 miles from St. Michaels. I selected the place on account of its agricultural possibilities and its central location. There are plans and estimates for irrigation at the Indian Office at Washington, which are to enable the government to settle about 400 families in that valley.

Having secured the consent of the Indians, the government has granted us 160 acres for missionary and educational purposes. Thereupon we had an old dilapidated Indian trading store in the neighborhood of our grant repaired to serve as a temporary dwelling house and chapel. Through a few generous donations ($500 by Mother Katharine, and $300 by Mrs. Nurre of St. Bernard, Ohio, not to mention others) and the proceeds of some lectures in the East, we were able to build a mission house at Chin Lee in 1905, and at the last Provincial Chapter the Reverend Leopold Ostermann, O.F.M., was appointed Superior at that place, with Reverend Marcellus Troester, O.F.M., as his assistant, and Venerable Brother Gervase Thuemmel, O.F.M., as lay-brother. A large room serves as temporary chapel, which, we hope, will soon be replaced by an adequate chapel building, especially since the government has decided to build a boarding school with a capacity for 100 pupils at that place, only a quarter of a mile from our mission house.

Although our work has been largely preparatory, learning and constructing the language, gaining the confidence and goodwill of the Indians—in ways too numerous to mention—we have, till now, baptized in all 148 children and adults, among them Dine Ts'ossi, the last war chief of the Navajo.

The results of our nine years' work may not be as apparent as we might wish, but we must not forget that we are sowing the seed, hoping, with the help of God, to reap an abundant harvest in the end.

Enthusiasts and so-called reformers who think they can change the face of the earth in a day or a year at most, who can brook no delay, who crave for recognition and immediate results, would certainly leave the field in disappointment. I think, not enthusiasm, but a reasonable interest, patient and persistent effort, with confidence in divine providence and the all-powerful grace of God, are required above all. Under what difficulties and trials and persecutions has not our Holy Faith been spread in Europe, and what glorious results have followed in the end! If the meritoriousness of a work is to be judged by its difficulties and the opposition it arouses among the enemies of our Holy Faith, then, no doubt, the work among the Indians is the most meritorious work in our country.

The Catholic Indian schools are the groundwork of Indian Christianization; but if the work begun at the school is to bear lasting fruit, it must be supplemented by hard and persistent missionary work in the field. I am quite certain that the government policy in civilizing the Indian very often failed because it would not or did not care to see beyond the walls of the school. If the great work in the Catholic Indian schools is not to be in vain, we must see to it that the children, after leaving school, obtain good homes, that they practice what they have learned; that they have ample opportunity to live up to their holy religion; that they cooperate with the missionaries in the civilization and Christianization of their relatives and friends and neighboring members of the tribe. That, however, requires men and means; it requires chapels and catechists for widely separated localities, and arduous and continuous missionary labors in the field.

Though we have to wrestle with almost insurmountable difficulties in this land of a strange tongue, in the land of magnificent distances, in the land of the Bedouins of America, yet with the grace of God and the help of good and generous friends we hope to succeed.

Notes

1. From Anselm Weber, "St. Michael's Mission and School for the Navajo Indians," *Indian Sentinel* 5 (1908):14–27.

2. The *Indian Sentinel* began as an annual, shifted to quarterly publication in July 1916, and then to monthly issues from January 1936 until it ceased publication in 1962. From 1903 to 1918 there was a German-language edition, *Indian Wache.*

3

First Christmases[1]

Anselm Weber, O.F.M.

[Soon after arriving in the mission field, Father Anselm began writing monthly reports for *Sendbote des göttlichen herzens Jesu*, the German-language periodical published by the Franciscan Fathers' Province of St. John the Baptist in Cincinnati. Its subscribers were primarily German-speaking Americans, although apparently it had a substantial audience in Germany as well. It is reported that its widest readership came when copies were sent to all Franciscan monasteries in Germany.

In the official chronicle of the mission, Father Superior Juvenal Schnorbus wrote, "After having been repeatedly asked by our Very Reverend Provincial to write some articles about this mission for the *Sendbote*, a German monthly, Father Anselm kindly volunteered to do so, and in the beginning of February he wrote the first article and sent it with one of the photos of our mission house to Cincinnati, Ohio."According to Father Juvenal, that first article "appeared in the March number of the *Sendbote* and was given a cordial reception as letters from various sources show."[2]

The resulting series, "*Die Indianer-Mission unter den Navajos*" (renamed after September 1902 "*Die Franziskaner-Mission unter den Navajo-Indianern*") began with that March 1899 article on the missionaries' first Christmas among the Navajo. On that day, the Franciscans were surprised by the number of visitors they received, all expecting presents in honor of the white man's holiday. The friars shared newly baked bread and distributed some medals and rosaries, but did not have gifts for everyone. Father Anselm concluded his report with the promise that "next Christmas things will be different in this regard, at least if those kindhearted readers who learn of our mission for the first time from this article show themselves as charitable as the comparatively few who have known of the mission," and added an explicit statement of his intent in writing this and future articles, namely "to awaken and stir up an interest for this mission, and to insure the cooperation of the readers in this good work, especially by their fervent prayers." In the official history, Father Juvenal was even more candid: "The reasons for the writing of these articles . . . are to interest the numerous readers of said monthly in behalf of this mission, so as to obtain their devout prayers for its success as also to give them an opportunity of sharing in the good works and merits of all, laboring for the conversion of the Navajo, by financial aid donated for this noble cause."[3]

The volunteer had shouldered a perpetual assignment. For the rest of his life, when not prevented by travel or ill health, he faithfully submitted monthly reports on happenings among the Franciscans in the Navajo country. Occasionally, he assigned the task to others; and after his passing, others assumed the burden and the series continued, but while he lived and worked, he carried the *Sendbote* responsibility. Father Anselm wrote for many other outlets—pamphlets and books for the Franciscan Fathers' own St. Michaels Press, newspaper and encyclopedia articles, pieces for Catholic magazines such as *St. Anthony Messenger* and *Indian Sentinel*—and he both edited and contributed items to the mission's short-lived (1913–1921) annual, *Franciscan Missions of the Southwest*. But in sheer volume and number of items, only his massive correspondence overshadows the 200 plus articles he wrote for *Sendbote*. They amount to an ongoing public journal of his missionary activities that continues, with few interruptions, over the entire period of his ministry, from March 1899 until December 1920. In 1915, discussing a recently published article in the series, one he had delegated to another friar because "I had written nothing the month before, and could not have written anything that month," he offered a rare comment on his personal feelings about the ongoing *Sendbote* assignment: "Well, many people like to read such writings, and it is no fun to write an article every month—for me."[4]

Father Anselm's final *Sendbote* contribution appeared posthumously in 1922. His articles remain an irreplaceable primary source on the mission's early history. In the opinion of Father Emanuel, "were it not for these literary contributions, which Father Anselm made to the *Sendbote* until the time of his death in 1921, the material for a compilation of the early history of the Navajo missions would be very meagre indeed."[5]

In order that the reader may judge whether, in fact, things were different the following year, as the friars hoped, the selection below combines the report on Christmas 1898 from that first article of the *Sendbote* series with Father Anselm's thirteenth contribution, the tale of Christmas 1899.]

Lest I get ahead of my story it will be necessary for me to preface this article with a few explanations. The kind readers of the *Sendbote* no doubt know that on October 3 of last year two fathers of the Cincinnati Province of Franciscans, Friar Juvenal Schnorbus, as Superior, and Friar Anselm Weber together with Brother Placidus Buerger departed from Cincinnati for the Indian Mission among the Navajo in Arizona. This mission had just a short time before been accepted by the Cincinnati Province. Here permit me to state briefly that the reservation of these Indians embraces the northwest portion of the state of New Mexico and the northeast part of Arizona which lies about 30 miles north of the Santa Fe Railroad. The tribe numbers about 17,000 souls, all heathens. Our mission is located near the southern boundary line of the reservation, 30 miles northwest of Gallup, New Mexico, the nearest railway station.

Christmas 1898

Accustomed as we had been to the splendor which accompanied the celebration of Christmas day in Cincinnati, we now felt that we would have a more quiet and perhaps by contrast even a sad Christmas this year. In some measure it was so, too. The beautiful altar, the personal gift of Mr. Firnstein of Pustet and Co., who graciously undertook to furnish our chapel with all necessary articles, had been most beautifully decorated. In the absence of a choir of jubilant youthful voices and feeling that we could not permit the day to pass without musical expression of our Christmas joy, I sang some of the old familiar hymns during the first Holy Mass which Father Superior began at 5:00, while Father Superior acted as choir during my Holy Masses which began at 7:30. By next Christmas, so thought Father Superior, we might have a well-trained choir of Indian children who can then sing their hymns to the Christ child.

At the breakfast table five or six Indians made their appearance and entertained me, not by words, but—well, that goes without saying. Within half an hour there were 17 in our spacious kitchen (by the way, kitchen and dining room), men and women with their children. Gradually it dawned upon us that on this day the Indians were taking a particular interest in us. An old squaw walked up to the brother and said "*Kishmus, Kishmus*, money, peso" (Christmas, Christmas, money, or a dollar). Although the Indians know but very few English words, it must be said this one word, *Kishmus* seems to be known by all. Brother's answer was, "No money, no peso" (dollars, unfortunately, continue to be rather *rarae aves*), but he did give each one something to eat. A little fellow of about seven years came up to me and shaking my hand, said: "*Bueno, bueno*" (good, good). As a rule Indian children are rather shy; but when shortly thereafter Father Superior entered the room he did the same toward him. The latter placed a medal in his little hand, and the boy's face beamed with joy. Soon we hope to have this boy in school so that we might make a Christian of him. It seemed this visiting would never end, and when we felt that it would soon be over with, in comes our employee, Thomas Osborne, after a short visit with our Negro neighbor, followed by 16 Indians of the wilderness. Mr. Osborne had locked up his shack and gone over to the Negro's place where he hoped he would be free from visitors. Only the day before this Negro [George Overton] in self-defense had knocked an Indian down several times and had warded off several others in a not exactly gentle manner, and so Osborne thought he would have no visitors on this day. (From this it may be seen that the Navajo are not red angels; why, if they were there would be no reason for our being here to convert and civilize them.) But Mr. Osborne was wrong; after he had distributed the last of his belongings, he finally decided to come with the entire following to us. Between 70 and 80 Indians visited us that day.

Here was an unusual opportunity to make some interesting observations, and particularly did we notice the number of children on hand. Some sat at the table while others stood while taking their meal. Still others, especially the women, made themselves comfortable on the floor with the children while the rest stood by the stove to warm themselves. Some of the women had very young babes wrapped tightly in a certain something composed of two boards and a wicker work of yucca leaves (botanically known as Adams' needles). I have never heard the name of this affair, which the Indians find so convenient to carry their babes on their backs. The tress work served the purpose of a roof. Should I recommend this cradle to my kind readers? No doubt it would be less expensive than a baby buggy; and besides they could place their children nicely against the wall or in a corner, where they would have to remain in a peculiar state of noisy immobility.

The conversation of the men varied from serious to jovial; the women talked and laughed, and the youngsters gave expression to their emotions by crying. There was a small fat-cheeked boy with red painted face who was particularly adept in this art.

A frail-looking woman had with her a small baby boy who wore nothing but a thin shirt and very thin breeches; another wore only a thin shirt, and this in the midst of winter when the thermometer stood below zero; I fail to remember how many degrees.

Too bad that we cannot favor our reader with a picture of this interesting group, but it is impossible, for we have not even a Kodak. Every phase of Indian morphology and Indian facial features were here represented, from giant forms with aquiline noses and sharply defined features to the very opposite; forms, so small that even we had to look down upon, and whoever knows us, will know that at least we two, not including the brother, are not so very tall. One of the men might very easily have been mistaken for a little sunburnt Italian.

The features of our Navajo are for the most part, in spite of their differences, quite intelligent and expressive. Some appear solemn, almost angry; others, meek and kind; others are quiet and reserved; others, lively, and even mischievous. This goes to prove that there is not a distinct Navajo type; it further confirms their traditions that, although the Navajo are a united nation with a language of their own, they nevertheless have assimilated in past centuries with the Pueblos, Yumas, and many other tribes. But I have digressed.

An Indian who as pathfinder at Fort Wingate had considerable association with the whites, and mastered the English language to some extent, attempted to explain to the others a picture which hung in our kitchen and portrayed the transfigured Christ, standing upon the universe bearing the cross and surrounded with pictures of the 14 Stations of the Cross. To assist him in his efforts I produced our illustrated Holy Bible, and endeavored in my rather faulty Navajo to explain, among other things, the meaning of "*Kishmus*." If we had had a crib, it would have been a much easier task, and the crib would have undoubtedly given no little joy both to young and old. In the afternoon, Charles Day, the son of one of our two neighbors, called with a few Indians who wanted to see how we celebrated Christmas, particularly whether we danced (every one of their religious ceremonies is accompanied by a dance). One of these, a silversmith of some prominence, asked us whether, if he would place his eight-year-old son in our school, we would appoint him later on as teacher. Who knows, but that, since the young fellow seems to be a wide-awake chap, we might, God willing, have him trained and become an *ednishodi* (a man with a long gown, as we are called). We escorted them into the chapel, where Mr. Day, who has literally grown up with the Navajo and knows the language perfectly, explained everything, especially the statues and pictures, which latter showed the Crucifixion and the mysteries of the Rosary and the Way of the Cross. Naturally, since Mr. Day was a Protestant, Father Superior had to explain many things to him beforehand. When he had finished with his clever interpreting, Mr. Day expressed his opinion that the silversmith would spend the following week in explaining to other Indians what he had seen and heard here. We then gave both of them copies of these pictures, which as former premiums of the *Sendbote* are all well known to the readers.

As already mentioned, these visits took us all by surprise. We little expected that the Indians with their children would come to visit the whites on this day in order to receive presents. Luckily, the brother had baked the day before and we were able at least to give everyone something to eat, but all available dishes had to be put into service. When the number was not so great Father Superior distributed medals and rosaries, articles which the Indians prize very highly. Men and women, as well as the children, placed the rosaries about their necks; they told us that they frequently used them in place of earrings. If we had given of these articles to everyone, there would have been nothing left in this line either. If our neighbors had put us wise to this custom of the Navajo, we would undoubtedly have provided at least a small present for each child, as the Indians expected from their *ednishodi*, even though it might have occasioned an appreciable shortage of funds.

Next Christmas things will be different in this regard, at least if those kindhearted readers who learn of our mission for the first time from this article show themselves as charitable as the comparatively few who have known of the mission, and to whom we now take occasion to express our sincere thanks and in the name of the Navajo wish heartily God's blessing. Furthermore, the poorer Indians continually lay claim upon our charitableness, disregarding the fact that we clothe and board free of charge the Indian pupils in our school. For since the government school, only nine miles away, does this same thing, it would be impossible for us to hope for any results unless we did likewise. The *Sendbote* office will be glad to promptly direct whatever gifts are offered to the proper address. . . . By the way, I should like to make another very earnest request of the good readers of the *Sendbote*, and that is that they offer their fervent prayers to the Sacred Heart of Jesus for the conversion of our deeply heathen and superstitious Navajo. . . .

The purpose of this and following articles is nothing else than to awaken and stir up an interest for this mission, and to ensure the cooperation of the readers in this good work, especially by their fervent prayers; for if our labors and efforts are not supported by the ardent prayers of many, we cannot hope for any marvelous results. This will more easily be realized when you will have learned of the powerful influence which the heathenish and superstitious ideas of these Navajo have upon their mode of living. And yet we do hope with the help of many . . . that all our efforts will bring such wonderful results, that ere long we will have developed our retail business into a wholesale pursuit that will in the near future demand the presence of an actual standing army of friars in this extensive reservation.

Christmas 1899

Our second celebration among the Navajo has become a matter of history. If the readers of *Sendbote* were to ask how we celebrated it, I should say practically in the same manner as the first one, with the exception that, due to the kind gift of a crib by a person whose generosity toward this mission I have had occasion to mention before, we were enabled to impress the significance of the feast upon our Navajo, not only orally but visually as well.

In contrast to last year's deep snow and bitter cold, we had a typically spring day, and the number of Indian visitors was correspondingly greater this year. Fifty-six redskins were on hand for the last Holy Mass at 9:00. It was impossible to admit all of these into our home at one time, so we appointed our young pupil, Albert Chee, to be doorkeeper, a duty he fulfilled with great pride and no less tact and ability. Admitting about 10 at a time, he closed the door and assisted us in serving them. As on the previous Christmas, so on this day every Indian type, every age, and a great variety of dress styles were represented: little children with dirty hands ranging on through all stages of Indian civilization to men in fully acceptable American costume. The last is rarely met with, except at Fort Defiance and Gallup.

Apparently finding it more convenient than to sit on chairs, the women squatted down on the floor with their children; large and small accepted their gifts, insignificant though they were, with a broad smile and then all joyfully left the kitchen to make way for the next group. By 11:00 approximately 200 Indians had passed in and out of our kitchen on their "*Kishmus*" visit. For the most part they carried their presents in the folds of their blankets, which they carry about their shoulders in a manner similar to that of the old Romans carrying their togas. The children, however, lost no time in tasting their candy while the grownups, among them not a few women, rolled cigarettes and began to smoke them before leaving. Pipes are not used by the Navajo, neither do they smoke cigars, for they have not yet acquired a heavy smoker's taste; but they do enjoy a small, thin cigarette and love to expel the smoke through their noses.

A few months ago Charley Day and I stopped at a trading post about 80 miles distant from here where we met a rather sophisticated young lady from the East, who apparently was disgusted with the manner of living of these savages. As soon as she learned that Charley Day spoke the Navajo language fluently—the eighth wonder of the world, which she must behold with her own eyes—she hurried into the trading post to find him unconcernedly conversing with the Indians in their own tongue. Remarking that if she could only speak thus with the Indians, she would feel more at home among them and might be able to make herself useful by calling their attention to so many things which would be to their benefit, as for instance the serious evil of cigarette smoking, she asked Charley to tell the Indians this in her name. With a significant blink of the eye, he complied. The Indians, strong and living pictures of health, without putting their cigarettes aside, stared wide-eyed at the pale, withered lady and finally broke into a cynical laughter, whereupon one of them asked her what evil might befall them. They were smoking at the moment and they felt no ill effects; after all, smoking can't be so bad. Shaking her head as if in pity for the blindness of these poor people, she went away. She must have thought it merely necessary to tell the Indians something and then they would with eager willingness do just "this or that." Really, the Navajo use tobacco very little; they smoke as a rule only when they visit the trading posts, where they obtain the tobacco for nothing, and only the "civilized" Navajo indulge in chewing tobacco.

If the Navajo never smoke a pipe, how could they ever be said to smoke the pipe of peace? A peace pipe among the Navajo has so far not been found by any of us, nor have we even heard of one. In fact, if we should speak to our Navajo of the ceremonies of the pipe of peace, they would hardly know what we were speaking about. I myself believe this warlike tribe has never made use of the pipe of peace; neither have they wielded a tomahawk. Those, of course, who are versed in Indian literature generally will find it difficult to imagine an Indian without these two reminders of war, but in Navajo land there is no such Indian.

To return again to the religious celebration of Christmas, I would remind my readers that I wrote a year ago that our Father Superior hoped that our Indian pupils would be able to sing hymns to the infant Savior in their own language by the next Christmas. Due to difficulties of the language and other circumstances which we could not foresee at the time, we have not made the progress we desired. We did succeed, however, with the aid of Blind Luke, in translating a few Christmas hymns and adapting them to the German melodies. Among these is the beautiful German hymn, "*Ihr Kindelein kommet.*" In Navajo it begins thus: "*Dine baalchinni hako daahlzo,*" "Navajo children come ye all." I will not venture to proceed either with the Navajo nor the German transliteration, and that for two reasons. My readers would not understand the Navajo, and the German would present a mere jumble without poetry or rhythm. Our Indian pupils, Blind Luke, and two of his relatives, youngsters of about 15 years, who frequently are our guests at the noonday meal, were the only ones to sing to the Christ Child in the Navajo language. May the newborn Savior bless our pupils and the mission, so that by Christmas 1900 a large number of Navajo children will assemble about the crib.

The above-mentioned hymn is frequently being sung by our pupils and Blind Luke is even trying to sing it in the German language, though the German pronunciation provides innumerable difficulties. He tells us that the German words—rather, the words of Ednishodi Naes, that is, of the Tall Priest (Father Frederic) [Frederic Hartung, who following his ordination in 1899 spent a few months in the Navajo mission] are horrible and sound just like the Moqui Indian language. There it is; now we know how the German language sounds to a Navajo Indian.

Notes

1. From Anselm Weber, "Eine Weihnachtsfeier unter den Navajo-Indianern im fernen Westen," *Sendbote* 26 (March 1899): 199–203; and FMN 27 (March 1900): 201–4. Translated by Father Emanuel Trockur.

2. Juvenal Schnorbus et al., "History of the Ranch, About Seven Miles South of Fort Defiance (Cienega) Arizona, Now St. Michaels Missions," FAC Box PLA.376 St. Michael's, env. St. Michael's Earliest History 1898–1907, 7.

3. Schnorbus et al., 7.

4. Anselm Weber to Berard Haile, 19 December 1915, FAC Box DEC.241 Anselm Weber, Writings, fd. Missiology—Anselm and Emanuel II (AV7).

5. Emanuel Trockur, "Franciscan Missions among the Navajo Indians: III," *Provincial Chronicle* 12 (Spring 1940): 150.

4

"Suspicion Is almost a Virtue Here"[1]

Anselm Weber, O.F.M.

[Learning the Navajo language was basic to all other missionary aims, and once settled in Navajo territory it became the friars' first priority. A related challenge was obtaining students, for the friars intended to reach adult Navajo through their children. Not only would a few children under instruction serve as an exemplary beginning for the projected boarding school, but their continued availability and assistance would hasten the friars' mastery of the Navajo language. Father Anselm's *Sendbote* articles of summer 1899 cover the initial recruitment of students and the friars' efforts to compile a Navajo dictionary and to set down principles of Navajo grammar and usage during the previous winter and spring. In this selection, in charming and intimate detail, are recounted initial encounters with Navajo parents over teaching their children, along with the various "exchanges" whereby the missionaries traded their time, hospitality, and other resources for help with the language. Father Anselm highlights the innovative techniques whereby over a remarkably short period the friars created the best English-Navajo dictionary in existence, and he names significant contributors to the effort: Whitehair, the elderly survivor of Fort Sumner; the Navajo-Ute Percy Hayden; Peshlakai the silversmith; the "Day boys," sons of trader Samuel Day; Blind Luke; and the first Navajo students, Carl Yazhe and Albert Tschi. Along the way, there are revealing glimpses of individual Navajo and Navajo families, their attitudes, and problems, as recorded in those first months when the friars' definitions of things were still open and fluid. Here, too, are intimations of the continuing challenge the missionaries would face in relations with government programs and personnel that often were competitive with if not downright obstructive to the efforts of the Franciscan missionaries.]

❖

Our chief occupation up to this time has been the learning and reducing to writing of the Navajo language. We have, of course, made repeated attempts at having some boys remain with us here with the view of instructing them and thus inaugurating at least a moderate beginning of actual missionary work. At the same time we hoped they would be of invaluable assistance to us insofar as their Navajo conversation would more readily accustom our ears and tongues to the peculiar Navajo sounds. But right here we met with considerable opposition.

Seeking Students

At the very beginning, rumors were afloat that we would demand payment for giving instructions; then, too, it was objected that the children would have to return home every evening despite the great distances and weather conditions. Fortunately, however, these false rumors and excuses, whether put forth by red or white rascals, are constantly being brought to our knowledge by the Indians themselves, and thus we are in position to disillusion them without much delay.

And yet excuses of every nature were always forthcoming: "If the uncle or aunt send their children, then of course we will send ours," "after the snow has melted," or "when we shall no longer need our son in the capacity of sheepherder," "if he himself wants to go," "if my wife has no objection," "if my husband is satisfied," and so on. The kind readers of the *Sendbote* may be inclined to sneer at such actions of our uncivilized Indians; but is it not true that similar tactics are resorted to even in highly civilized communities? Take the case of sending Catholic children to public schools. How often does not the mother offer the excuse that the husband has so decided and there is nothing else left for her to do? In the matter of buying a new hat or other wearing apparel, all deference to her husband disappears; as long as she gets what she desires, she cares not for how long he might insist to the contrary. There is no desire on my part to refer here to my readers, for I feel certain that they have always succeeded not only in getting new hats whenever necessary, but also in arranging to send their children to Catholic schools.

The past winter was here, as it has been everywhere, of rather long duration; much snow fell and it was quite cold. For three months the ground was covered with snow, and at one time the thermometer registered as low as 32 below zero. This was indeed disastrous to the Navajo, who live, so to say, from hand to mouth, and fail to make proper provision either for themselves or their stock—an impossibility for the most of them after all, considering the poor quality of the soil. Many head of sheep, goats, burros, and horses were lost by hunger and the cold. What little feed we were able to part with, we gave to those who were in greatest need. Whenever they came to us for their many wants, we seized the opportunity to request them to send their children to our school, but without success.

An Indian named Shorthair once pestered us for a full hour with questions about the school which we were contemplating. He had a son whom he might send, but he was not exactly sure that his wife would agree to it, or perhaps the boy himself would not care to go. The latter might be afraid to remain with us and so it might be necessary even that he himself remain here with his son for a few days. It would require a few days before he could inform us as to his decision, but just now he would like to have some feed for a starving mule. A worthy conclusion, but just what we expected after such a diplomatic introduction. A few days later, while I was visiting at the home of our colored neighbor [George Overton] with a certain Mr. [George] Thacker, a Catholic who owns a trading post 40 miles west of here, in comes Shorthair. Since Mr. Thacker has been associated with the Navajo from his boyhood and thus mastered their language, I told him of the quasi-agreement made by Shorthair. Thacker then asked him as to his final decision. Shorthair expressed his opinion that the superintendent at Fort Defiance would not be satisfied to have him send his son to us; besides, the Indians would receive wagons and other gifts if they sent their children to the government school. Then the Negro asked him whether he intended to barter his children away to the government school. After much useless talking, Mr. Thacker's driver, a young Indian, also entered the conversation. He declared that he had attended the government school at Fort Defiance, had made strenuous efforts to learn something but failed, and now, if he desired to have his son educated, he would send him to us, and so on.

That same evening Shorthair told our helper [Thomas Osborne] that the Indians would hold a meeting in which they would decide whether they would send their children to us or not. Thus far we have no word regarding this proposed meeting.

A gentleman of Fort Defiance has told me of the arrangement by which wagons, farm implements, and other things on are given out to the Indians. The reservation is divided into eight districts, in each of which a reliable Indian acts as headman. The agent confers with these men and may suggest, for instance, that since he has a given number of wagons, axes, or shovels, he will distribute these among the Indians of the various districts, provided they will send a certain number of children to the government school. Then, of course, a council is held in which it is decided just which children are to attend school and who is entitled to the gratuities. The agent himself has told me that it is his intention not to give anything to the Indians of this vicinity who will not send their children to school. He did not state whether he was referring also to such as would send their children to our school. Of course, that would be very unjust, and yet —.

Our readers may judge from all this how difficult it will be for us to persuade parents to send their children to our school. In the very first place we have no wagons to give them, for our purse is not as large as that of Uncle Sam. It is not at all surprising that as a result of such precedents on the part of the government the Indians will expect to be rewarded in some way in every instance where they send their children to school.

The family of a certain Slinky took particular advantage of our charity last winter. He repeatedly came to us to tell of his great distress: his wife was always sick; he had no money, no sheep, and nothing to eat. He had promised to send his son to school in the spring, irrespective of what others might do. To tell the truth, we did not place much stock in his promises, but of course that did not influence us to such an extent that we refused to assist him in his needs.

We came by our first pupil in a rather whimsical way. One day a youngster of perhaps eight years came over the hills to our place only to leave again very shortly. Two days later he was here again. Father Superior [Father Juvenal] gave the timid little fellow an apple, but he dared not enter the house. On the following day he summoned up enough courage to enter. The Brother [Placidus] gave of the best we had to eat and placed a rosary around his neck. During the next three days he paid us nine visits, sometimes accompanied by his sisters. Father Superior had learned in the meantime that the youngster's mother was a poor widow in bad health and living in a little hut away from the road. He accordingly gave him some eatables to take home with him. On the last of these three days during which he paid us regular visits, I rode over to the mother's home and requested her to entrust the boy to our care. She replied that he liked it so well at our place that he himself would be glad to stay with us. She was not opposed to this plan, but she did not want us to send him to the East to school, as seemed to be the policy of the government schools. This naturally was an easy condition, for whither could we send our pupils anyway? Possibly later we might send one or the other to our college at Cincinnati. The following day, Sunday, the mother came with the entire family to leave her boy with us, and we treated them to what they no doubt considered a royal dinner. At any rate, that was the first meal at which they had had enough to eat for some time.

Lest we might lose our first pupil, it was naturally a matter of great concern to us to get another pupil as soon as possible. That same afternoon, therefore, I made inquiries at the neighboring Navajo huts, but alas, with results equal to those of Uncle Sam in the Philippines. In one of the huts I found a half dozen half-nude children squatted around a fire on the ground; the mother was not at home, and the father had been gone several days. At another place the mother appeared quite startled on learning the purpose of my visit. She called her little son to her side, apparently fearing that I might take him away by force. Embracing and caressing him, she pleaded that he was her only child and she did not want to part with him. I wonder what impression she has formed of us that she does not want to entrust her darling to us. She offered one excuse which was not at all noble: the little fellow must start the fire for her every morning. As though she herself, a young and able-bodied woman, or her tall and strong husband were unable to do it! I did not find our old friend Slinky at home, but asked his son to tell him that we now had a pupil and that he ought now fulfill his promise of long ago and send his son the next day so that both might have companionship.

That same evening at half past nine there was a violent knock at the door. Due to a superstitious fear of the spirits, Indians will rarely venture out at night; what was our surprise to find one outside the house at this late hour. It was the brother of our new pupil, who came to tell us that his mother was very sick, possibly even dead by that time, and he wanted to take his little brother home with him, and so on. Thinking this was merely a pretext to take the boy away from us—suspicion is almost a virtue here—I did not disturb the little boy and went to the home myself. Arriving at the [adjacent] Negro's home, the Indian told me he must summon a medicine man for his mother and disappeared in the darkness.

The Negro was kind enough to accompany me. When we entered the Navajo hogan we found the woman lying on a blanket which was spread on the ground in the farthest end of the hut. Around the roaring fire which sent out terrific heat and unbearable smoke were squatted the children, relatives, and neighbors. The woman was quite sick and her condition seemed to be growing worse; with a feeble voice she called her children to her side and told them that now she must leave for "*tschindi tcha*," the world of spirits. Her children approached in tears, and the eldest daughter raised her up and taking water, which contained the reputed holy roots, began to wash her mother's brow and chest. The Negro explained to me that this was a sort of baptism that is, according to Navajo custom, always conferred upon those in danger of death. Soon thereafter the patient became unconscious. In spite of my assurance that she was still alive, the children and relatives appeared convinced that she was dead and set to mourning.

We had been there but a short time when the son breathlessly rushed into the hogan to tell me the welcome bit of news that he had not called on the medicine man. Just as he was reaching the latter's home, he had seen a ghost which was coming directly toward him, so he took to his heels. Oh, thought I, if not only one, but a legion of spirits would appear to all who call upon the medicine men, so that this inhumane practice of blood sucking might be forever discontinued!

At the Negro's suggestion, I then sent the son with a note to our helper at the mission, Mr. Osborn, asking for a particular medicine. His fear of ghosts had disappeared, and he quickly obeyed.

I had already removed quite a bit of the burning wood from the fire, and yet I could no longer endure the heat within the hut. As I was walking to and fro outside, I was fairly frightened at the sight of two Indians hurrying toward me with giant strides; they must have thought a *tschindi* (spirit) was on their trail. I soon recognized the Indian whom I had sent for the medicine. The Negro administered several doses of the medicine, and the patient rallied and fell into a quiet sleep. This brought about a great change in the mourners, whose weeping gave place to rather lively discussion.

A very old squaw, a relative of the sick woman, thereupon called me her grandson. If a Navajo would flatter you, particularly if he is seeking a favor, it may happen that you will receive every title of relationship, beginning with grandson and all the way up to grandfather. My grandmother then told me the priests are good; they are not like certain other white people who—; but I do not want to discredit my white brothers. However, if what my grandmother then told me about white people is true, I can readily understand that the Navajo will fare much better, the less they come in contact with the whites.

We left the place after midnight. Our patient has since recovered under the care of the physician of Fort Defiance, Dr. C. J. Finnegan. . . .

On the following day our old friend Slinky brought his son to the mission. His first question was whether we would provide his son with a new suit of clothes; that was just like an Indian. A few days later we dressed the boys in the clothes in which they came to us and had them pose for a photograph before the hut of our helper, which was their home, school, and dormitory. They themselves brought out their blankets and covered their heads according to Navajo fashion. For the reason which I have already explained, it was found necessary nevertheless to employ all our powers of persuasion before they were willing to submit to this procedure. Just as we were prepared to take the picture, the sister of our first pupil appeared on the scene and began to talk to her brother. As soon as she realized what was going on she hurriedly sought the far corner of the hut, in order to avoid the evil *naltsos*, but as the picture will show, she did not succeed.

Our two pupils, Carl Yazhe, that is, "small," age eight, and Albert (Slinky) Tschi, that is, "red," age 14, are very fine and wide-awake chaps, and they seem to like it here. They are applying themselves diligently to reading and writing and are a great help to us in the matter of learning Navajo, especially in the enunciation of words. If we ask them what this or that is called in Navajo, they invariably come back with the question: "What do you call it in *belakana* (American)?"

I shall conclude this rather lengthy article by expressing the hope that we shall in the very near future be enabled to erect the necessary buildings to house a large number of children from all parts of the reservation, whom we might instruct not only in the ideals of civilization but also and above all in the truths of our holy religion. When the time arrives that we shall have erected the required buildings and we shall have surveyed the entire reservation for the purpose of bringing the older people into the fold of Jesus Christ and the younger generation into our school, there will no doubt be plenty of material on hand wherewith to interest the kind readers of *Sendbote*. It is within the power of my esteemed readers to hasten this time; the manner in which it is to be done I leave to their own resourcefulness.

Learning the Language

Before we came to the Navajo, misinformed individuals gave us the assurance that a large number of this tribe understood and spoke either the English or the Spanish language, and although it had been our intention from the very beginning to acquire the Navajo tongue, this bit of information was indeed very encouraging for it indicated that we would be able to associate with the natives from the very outset. Actual conditions, however, disclosed quite the contrary. Only a very few understand any English, namely those who have attended school at Fort Defiance or elsewhere. As for the rest, their vocabulary includes only the words "Kishmus," "Washington," and "money," while they are unable to give the English appellations of any of the neighboring localities, such as Fort Defiance, Gallup, and so on. However, there are not a few who are possessed of a copious vocabulary of English curse words—not exactly a compliment for the whites who live among them. Of words derived from the Spanish and incorporated into the Navajo language with some variation, there are at most one dozen. Very few Navajo understand Spanish, with the exception of these words, which naturally are known to all, and if they may be said to understand Spanish at all, it is only to the extent that they are able to negotiate a sale or trade of a sheep, horse, or blanket in Spanish, or rather Mexican, as we say here.

But when they desire to ask a favor, or, to speak plainly, to beg, you may be sure they will exhaust the entire supply of English and Spanish words at their command. Under these circumstances it was an absolute necessity that we apply ourselves at once to the study of the language, a task which loomed even more difficult before us when, after very extensive inquiries, we learned that there was not a single publication which treated this subject. Dr. Gustav Brühl of Cincinnati, Ohio, . . . called our attention to a certain doctor of the U.S. Army, Dr. Washington Matthews, who had spent 15 years in the vicinity of our mission, at Fort Wingate, and who utilized all his spare time in the study of the language, traditions, morals, customs, and religious ceremonies of the Navajo. In order to gain the confidence of the Indians, he had never permitted a belittling expression regarding their heathenish customs to escape his lips in the presence of an Indian. In fact, his earnest research work and his participation in their heathen ceremonies only increased their conviction that he actually shared and cherished their peculiar views, with the result that he was enabled more than anyone else to search into their profoundest mysteries. We have purchased a copy of his chief work, *Navajo Legends*, while he himself either presented or loaned to us his other works, which number about 20 treatises of various lengths.

In one of his letters he wrote that we would not have an exactly clean field in which to sow the seed of the Gospel, but that we would meet with a highly developed cult which it would be necessary to destroy; that the construction of the language is more complicated than that of any of the Aryan or Semitic languages; and that we might be prepared for many very great surprises. These surprises which he prophesied, by the way, have not failed to make their appearance. Since these works contain the translations of many heathen songs, we soon after our arrival were in possession of a very large number of Navajo words. However, not content with these alone, we made use of every opportunity to get words from the Indians who visited us and whom we gave to eat, and added them to our list.

It is evident, therefore, that Brother Placidus is playing no insignificant role in our study of the Navajo language. The Indians call him *Tschiia ilinni,* which means food maker, as little Carl Yazhe confidingly whispered into my ear a short time ago. They find it very easy to put up with such a food maker.

The Navajo furthermore appear astonished at seeing us putting their language down in writing. They knew well enough that English could be written, but it was unheard of that anyone could express their sounds on paper. They seemed to distrust us, therefore, and asked us repeatedly to recite to them what we had written, which always elicited a hearty laugh, so highly amusing did it seem to them to hear a *belakana* (American) reproduce their sounds from the written page. Last winter, several men and women came to the mission to find shelter against the severe cold of their miserable huts, and one of them went so far as to dictate a long list of Navajo words which I was to write down and then read to him. I never shall, I believe, again have to stand a more difficult examination nor be put to a severer test. Of the many Navajo who were of great assistance to us in collecting words, I wish to mention only a few.

A short time after our arrival we became acquainted with an old, quite well-to-do and prominent Indian, and the only surviving headman of the sad days of the tribe's captivity at Fort Sumner. Of this Babylonian captivity and their return to the promised land (?) I hope to write later, God willing. This Indian, Whitehair, had spent the night with us. While he was taking breakfast, I sat down beside him, armed with pencil and a pad, and began pointing to various objects, all the while pronouncing the word "Navajo" with interrogatory inflection—the expression *disch daolje*, "what is that called?" was at that time unknown to us. The old man quickly caught my meaning and very accommodatingly set to answering my questions. After breakfast, on his own initiative he went from one object to the other, mentioning the Navajo name, hardly allowing me time to write them. After he enumerated all the objects about him that he could name, he began with himself, giving first the word "hair" and then the parts of the body and articles of clothing. I thought now he must be at the end of his knowledge, but no. He began to give me faithful imitations of the sounds produced by the animals, as the sheep, goat, cow, and so forth, and after each one to add the Navajo name in a very serious tone of voice. Thus, he certainly paid well for his lodging and breakfast. But this was not the only time that he visited us and helped in enlarging our treasury of words. On one occasion, apparently trusting us more than his own tribesmen, he purposely left his hat hanging on the wall. The Navajo as a rule wear no head covering, only a headband. After a few months, Whitehair came back. Instead of taking his hat, he entered upon the procedure of hanging his stockings beside it on the wall. Father Superior, however, advised him that it would be better to take both home with him, to which he then agreed.

Shortly after making our acquaintance with Whitehair, a young Indian called on us. To our surprise, he asked us in English to help him out. His English was very poor and broken and fairly interlarded with scraps of Navajo, but it was English just the same. He had attended the government school at Fort Defiance for five years and, since he was at the time engaged as helper of the physician there, was generally known by the people as doctor. In school he had received the name of Percy Hayden. Father Superior once asked him his Indian name but he curtly replied that he did not know. A Navajo will hardly ever divulge his own name to white people; the only way to learn it is to ask others. Percy, however, did eventually yield to the urgings of Father Superior and gave him his Navajo name, but it was only after he had consulted with his mother in the matter. The English meaning of the name in like manner appeared to be unknown to him until his mother gave him permission to tell it. It means "An Indian murdered by a white man and buried in the sand." When he was asked when this took place, he replied: "Oh, about 100 years ago." His mother, moreover, is not a Navajo, but a Ute Indian, who had been captured by the Navajo and brought here as a slave. Her hut and all her belongings were only a short time ago destroyed by fire. The cold and hunger of the past winter had greatly diminished the numbers of her flock, and besides, she was not in good health.

Percy was, therefore, a very frequent visitor at the mission. Our help and apparent preference shown to this despised son of a former slave aroused the envy and jealousy of other Indians to such an extent that Percy himself deemed it advisable to discontinue his visits for a time and asked his mother to come in his stead. With his assistance we enlarged our word treasury to the extent of only about 300 words, for in spite of his many years of attendance at school, his English, as has already been remarked, was very faulty. This will be evident from the following conversation, which, I am sorry to say, will hardly permit the proper German translation.

Percy and his mother had just taken a meal, and Father Superior was busying himself with collecting the charges in Navajo words. Several questions were answered satisfactorily, but for the most part, Percy's reply was just one word: "*holla*," which means "I do not know." Finally, Father Superior told him that that one word *holla* seemed to be the one he knew best of all, to which he made the unabashed reply, "*Ou*," yes. When Father Superior asked him what the Navajo word for *son* was, he answered, "*Tschoochanaai*." Father Superior then explained that he did not mean the sun in the sky. He pointed to Percy's mother and said, "That is your mother; you are her son—." Percy did not permit him to continue, but interrupted with his pet expression: "*holla*." Father Superior thereupon told him that he must certainly know that word, that he surely knew the Navajo expression for the son of a mother, but Percy yelled out at the top of his voice, "*Holla! holla! holla*!!!" and then broke out in boisterous laughter. From then on, all further efforts for that day were futile.

The silversmith Peshlakai, "White Iron,"gave us the names of tools used in carpentry and other professions, names which for the most part are practically unknown to the other Indians. This singular individual (he may not be a singular Navajo after all) shrewdly married three sisters in order that he might have three wives, but only one mother-in-law, and then, lest he should ever see the latter again, bribed a third person to prevail upon her to move to the other end of the reservation. He took this precaution in view of the deeply rooted Navajo conviction that if a man ever beheld his mother-in-law, he would instantly be struck dumb and blind. Dumb? Well, that is not unlikely. But blind? Hardly. Yet, it must be remembered that the Navajo never trim their fingernails.

Illustrated books, especially the catalog of Montgomery Ward & Company of Chicago, proved to be another aid in the gathering of still more words from those who visited us as well as our two pupils. Our mission is naturally in poor circumstances and lacks many objects which we would like to point out to the Indians who know not a word of English, in order that they might give us the Navajo names thereof.

Mr. Thacker visited us for the first time on January 24 and was kind enough to enrich our collection with about 80 Navajo words and short colloquialisms. At our previous meeting I had endeavored with his aid to translate the Lord's Prayer into Navajo, but our efforts resulted in complete failure. At the third word, "who" (art in heaven), we were brought to a halt, for the Navajo do not employ pronouns in their language. At my suggestion that we might say at least, "Thou art in heaven," Mr. Thacker replied that was impossible, and turning to the young Indian who accompanied him, asked him to explain the Navajo conception of heaven to me. His explanation was as follows: After death, the Navajo spirit hovers near the body for about four days, during which time the relatives and neighbors must remain within the immediate vicinity of the home of the deceased. They are forbidden to work or to wash themselves (due to lack of water, this latter operation takes place seldom enough). On the evening of the fourth day, a spirit comes and conducts the soul of the deceased to *tschindi tcha*, that is, into the communion of the spirits. The gist of the explanation was that the Navajo language does not contain a noun or expression for "heaven," and that the nearest approach we could make would be by saying, "Thou livest among the spirits." For, strange to say, the language even lacks a mode of expressing "Thou art," at least in this particular sense. At the first petition, "Hallowed be Thy Name," Mr. Thacker gave up in despair and declared that the Navajo have no word either for hallowed or for name. In fact, all such general terms as bless, praise, blame, honor, obey, and so forth, lack a counterpart in the Navajo tongue.

And yet only a short time ago Father Superior received a letter from a gentleman living in Paris, France, asking whether he or his fellow missionaries had learned the language sufficiently to enable them to translate the prayers of the church, the catechism, and so on, into Navajo. This gentleman was a member of the Geographic Society and had spent about six years on the Indian reservations of Arizona and New Mexico; he had applied himself for years to the study of Indian languages, or, as he states more correctly, of American languages, and was now engaged in preparing to publish the results of his travels and studies. He would gladly include our translations in his publication and offered to send our mission as many copies as we might desire.

A generous offer, free of cost indeed! We certainly wish this kind friend no ill, but in the interest of our mission we are seized by a secret hope that his work will not be ready for publication very soon, for it is simply out of the question for us to comply with his request at this early date. Later on, after we shall have better familiarized ourselves with the language, we hope to transliterate the prayers and truths of our holy religion into such modes of expression as the lack of general and spiritual terms of Navajo demand.

Although we have from the very beginning been taking great pains to learn the Navajo language, still I must admit that the results have thus far not measured up to the efforts put forth. Very often it was found that words received from Indians were incorrect, due partly to the fact that they failed to understand us correctly in our English or in the sign language to which we had to resort in many instances, and partly because on our part we did not grasp the Indian sounds accurately.

Even the material gathered from books proved frequently to be unreliable, as the following incident will show. I had read that *achalani sikkes* means "hello, my friend," and on one occasion used this salutation on meeting old Whitehair. He began to laugh, repeated the greeting, and placing his arms around my shoulder conducted himself very strangely, I should say endearingly. His actions remained inexplicable to me until I learned later on that this salutation is applicable almost exclusively to squaws, and then only when they meet their relatives and close friends after a long absence. Under these circumstances, this greeting is uttered accompanied with tears and tender embraces. Thus without any fault of my own I had fallen into what could have been an even more serious mistake.

Dr. Washington Matthews made use of three phonetic systems in his various works. After making a comparative study of these we selected the alphabet employed by the Bureau of Ethnology of Washington [D.C.], copying from other works and rewriting all our words accordingly. We soon discovered that even Washington is not infallible, for his alphabet included letters for sounds that do not occur in Navajo, sounds which the Navajo themselves are unable to produce, while on the other hand it lacked characters for sounds which actually occur in the language, and very frequently at that.

Thus we could not consider as absolutely accurate what we had recorded according to this system. By the beginning of February [1899], however, we had sufficiently familiarized ourselves with the sounds of the language that we could devise an alphabet of our own, which as much as possible agreed with the English, although it included elements of the German, French, and Arabic languages, as well as such as, at least to our knowledge, are not met with in any other tongue.

Very few people will realize the difficulty we experience in the proper conception and reproduction of sounds in a language which differs so widely from all others with which we are conversant. The sounds of the mother tongue are mastered by long and continuous practice, which renders our vocal organs highly proficient in the art of accurate enunciation. Certain sound combinations, the character of which depends upon the position of the vocal organs and on the force with which the breath is expelled through the mouth or nose, are even acquired automatically without any conscious effort on our part. And so we may often observe that children, after their earlier years of childhood, will reproduce strange and unknown sounds of other languages in a manner closely resembling those of their mother tongue—a fact which close observers and attentive teachers and professors no doubt will have noticed especially in their spelling classes. Dictate to a student such words as he has never heard before and you will be convinced.

The experience of those who set to reducing a strange language to writing is the same. To mention only one example, the alphabet of the Bureau of Ethnology contains a *k* to designate two sounds, which at first thought would appear to demand the sound of *k*; but one of these sounds is actually a hard explosive *tl*, the other approximately the English *thl*.

A beginner, asking for a piece of string, would very likely make his request with the word *klo*. The Navajo hearing him would appear confused, for he would not know whether hay or a fish or a rope or perhaps even a prairie dog was wanted. The word *klo* does not occur in the Navajo language and is found only in the writings of the Bureau of Ethnology; yet, this word has much in common with the names of the four objects just mentioned.

The distinguished linguistic scholar, Franz Boas, tells us that in writing a certain word in the Eskimo tongue on three different occasions, he wrote it differently each time. He further states that it is an easy matter to detect the nationality of anyone who for the first time writes words of a foreign tongue, for he will reproduce the sounds by a peculiar imitation of the sounds of his mother tongue. This will, no doubt, be the case with those who know only one language; but I believe this statement will hardly apply to those who are thoroughly familiar with several languages.

No one will therefore be surprised to know that our original annotations had to be repeatedly corrected and rewritten, and that the Indians enjoyed more than one hearty laugh on hearing our attempts at producing their sounds. A squaw went so far in her quips as to suggest that we grease our lips a little.

On December 18 the sons of our neighbor, Mr. Samuel Day, visited us and gave us an idea of the appallingly irregular Navajo verbs. Since these boys had, so to say, grown up with the Navajo and spoke the language fluently, we planned to enter into an agreement with them, whereby they would give us instructions in Navajo in exchange for our instructing them in other branches [of knowledge], which agreement was finally made on December 28. The Days were quite busy at the time, so we could not begin our classes until January 23. Mr. and Mrs. Day had both completed a high school course in their youth and appreciated the value of a higher education. It had therefore grieved them very much to know that in this isolated district their three sons would be deprived of the opportunity of receiving an education. Of course, Mrs. Day, who had been a teacher at one time, did all in her power to supply an education. They, therefore, rejoice at our arrangement as much as we ourselves, in the hope that it will continue for a long time to come. So much the better for us; the peculiar Navajo language offers so many difficulties that we shall be very glad to employ the aid of the Day boys for a considerable length of time.

In this connection, permit me to say that the white people in Gallup and Fort Defiance, and those who conduct Indian trading posts, among these latter, one who has been married to a Navajo squaw for 30 years, seem to hold little encouragement for us in the matter of acquiring the Navajo language. They say it is impossible for anyone who has not grown up with the Navajo to learn their difficult language. During the many years of their association with the Navajo they have acquired the Navajo language merely to the extent that they are able, although with considerable difficulty, to conduct ordinary business with the Indians. But after all, they are even now willing to take advantage later on of the results of our studies.

The two Protestant preachers at Fort Defiance have likewise made an attempt at learning the language. An attempt was all, however, for they have long ago thrown up the game and are now contenting themselves with an English-language talk to the children at the government school on Sundays. One of them told me that they had abandoned their efforts for the reason that the Navajo had no general or abstract ideas and that it was consequently impossible to instruct them in religion in their own language. True enough, the Navajo do possess but a few spiritual and general concepts; but I believe that if they knew all that might possibly be conveyed to them about religion in their own tongue, their religious knowledge would surpass that of the average American who is constantly boasting of his high culture. I admit we cannot say, in Navajo, for instance, "You shall not commit sin," since a general term for "sin" is lacking. But why can we not say, "You shall not lie, or steal, or commit adultery, or kill, and so on?" That would be even more precise and more forcible than the dull expression, "You shall not commit sin." There will be no danger that a preacher will ever lose himself in a maze of abstractions in his conversation with the Navajo. And here we find no little advantage.

The Day boys have been coming to the mission daily except Saturday and Sunday for the purpose of mutual instruction. In order that we might obtain all the words known to our teachers, we resolved upon a certain system according to which on February 7 we began the translation of a small Webster's dictionary. Father Superior and Charley Day began with *A* and Samuel Day, Jr., and I, with *Z*. Writing various forms of verbs and adjectives and jotting down every peculiarity of grammar that occurred to our minds, we slowly but surely pushed onward from both ends of the book until we met at the letter *L* on April 26.

Father Superior at once undertook a thorough revision of the work in company with Charley Day, who is a far better Navajo scholar than his younger brothers. Not only had we but Charley himself had learned a great deal during the course of this procedure, and it was found that there was little material on hand that did not stand in need of improvement. This revision was completed on June 16, and the number of Navajo words has attained the stately figure of 2,850. This number will be increased from time to time, and at this very moment—I am writing this on June 16—Father Superior is beginning to enlarge it by an addition of the names of various plants. While it is quite an easy matter to obtain the Navajo names of plants, the flora of this western country is a closed book as far as our knowledge goes, and consequently the botanical and English names are unknown to us. But what are professors for, who have attained to prominence in a particular science to which they have dedicated their lives? This thought prompted us to gather plants and flowers, to carefully write down their Navajo names, and then send them to our experienced professor of sciences and expert botanist, Father Markus Kreke, O.F.M., of Cincinnati, who promptly supplied us with the botanical appellations. In this way we are enlarging our vocabulary and he his collection of specimens.

Dr. Washington Matthews has also published an article on the Navajo names of plants. . . .

I just remarked that in compiling our vocabulary we wrote down various forms of verbs and adjectives. Thus far we have 700 such forms of verbs and 77 of adjectives, and I doubt very much, whether there are two alike or which are subject to identical variations. Confronted with such unheard-of irregularities, it is not at all surprising that the Day boys frequently were unable to give complete information in these matters in which the Navajo themselves often experience difficulty.

We, therefore, on May 24 engaged a poor blind Indian named Luke, who had attended the government school for five years, and began with his help to revise, correct, and complete our vocabulary—a task which we hope to finish in a few weeks, so that we might begin the writing of a catechism, and at the same time make a final copy of all the material thus far collected.

The photograph accompanying this article introduces to our readers our teachers and pupils, to whom we are so deeply indebted. In the foreground are our two Indian pupils in Sunday attire: little dark-skinned Carl Yazhe, and the lighter-complexioned Albert Tschi. In the center is Blind Luke, who in spite of his blindness is always jovial and in leisure hours may be heard singing Navajo songs of which he has committed a large number to memory. Behind these and leaning against a wall of stone are the Day boys: Charles Day in the center, Samuel at his right, and William at his left.

Our Indian pupils, particularly the smaller one, present rather unpleasant faces, but I am sure that my readers will understand that it frequently happens that, at the moment critical when our countenance is to be impressed forever upon the film, we are all apt to present a face that is far worse than the actuality.

I have introduced these people as our teachers as well as pupils. Pupils they are all, indeed, and even blind Luke is beginning to brush up on his badly tarnished English. I have told you in how far our two Indian boys are our teachers in a previous article. Even William Day is giving us lessons in Navajo, although not as regularly as his two elder brothers. But these, as you will no doubt know, do not make up the total of our extraordinary teachers, for we are learning from each and every one who is able and willing to give us any information.

Just recently I read of a Catholic Indian missionary who, left to his own devices, spent 14 years in acquiring the Skalzi Indian tongue before he was able to publish a catechism in that language. No doubt it would require that long a time for us here, were it not for the fact that we are favored with the aid of such as fully understand the Navajo language, and we are living in hopes that in a comparatively short time we will be able to announce the chief truths of our holy religion to these Indians in their own tongue. May I request the readers of *Sendbote* to earnestly pray with us to God, the Giver of all things, that we may successfully and soon attain this end.

Note

1. From Anselm Weber, FMN 26 (June–August 1899): 469–74, 551–57, 635–39. Translated by Father Emanuel Trockur.

5

Father Anselm's 1899 San Juan Exploration[1]

Emanuel Trockur, O.F.M.

[No one was better suited to tell the story of the Navajo missions than Father Emanuel Trockur. Most of his 68 years as a friar were spent as a Navajo missionary, beginning at St. Michaels in 1917. Thus, "he knew Anselm Weber, Leopold Ostermann, Marcellus Troester and all the friars since. He was acquainted personally with many of the tribal headmen and leaders in this long developing period . . . [and] knew so many of the government officials on a name to name basis."[2] He was personally involved in the growth of the Church on the reservation, the evolution of tribal government, and the increasing interpenetration of Navajo life by federal agencies.

According to Father Emanuel's own account, among his first tasks were "deciphering Father Anselm's *Sendbote* articles and also typing letters for him."[3] Typescripts of many of his "decipherings" remained in his papers, and some are reprinted in this volume.

His reputation as the greatest historian of the Navajo missions is grounded both in his writings and in his long-term effort to accumulate and preserve the "valuable effects" of mission history, many of which now comprise the Franciscan Fathers collection at the University of Arizona Library Special Collections.

Beginning in 1938 with "Background of the Indian Missions,"[4] Father Emanuel published a serious history of the Navajo missions in the Franciscan's *Provincial Chronicle*. Counting that "background" piece there were nine installments, the last eight being numbered chapters in the series, "Franciscan Missions among the Navajo Indians," concluding in the Fall 1943 issue of the *Chronicle*. Our present chapter reprints most of installment IV, which drew upon Father Anselm's *Sendbote* articles in recounting the friars' initial indecision about whether Cienega (St. Michaels) was the best location for mission headquarters, and Father Anselm's first journey to the San Juan river valley near Farmington, New Mexico, to scout out the possibilities there.

Of course, the style of Father Emanuel's history is very different from Father Anselm's folksy reports to *Sendbote* readers. As we lack the space to tell the entire story in Father Anselm's words, Father Emanuel's summary serves both to cover that important San Juan reconnaissance and to introduce the master historian of the Franciscan missions at his scholarly best.]

❖

When Monsignor Stephan in 1895 purchased the Meadows Ranch as the site for a mission and school, doubts were expressed in many quarters[5] as to the good judgment of the director of the Bureau of Catholic Indian Missions in making this selection. Some there were who held that Cienega was too near the government establishment at Fort Defiance; others seemed to feel that it was too far removed from the railroad; still others, viewing the project from quite another angle, raised objections on the score that the colonization of a worthwhile group of Navajo at this point would be out of the question.

Among those who favored another locality was Father Antonio Jouvenceau[6] of Park View, New Mexico, whose parish extended into the San Juan region and embraced the northeastern part of the Navajo country. There can hardly be any doubt that the proposal to establish the central Navajo mission in this area was originally conceived by Father Jouvenceau and that he strongly advocated his plan before his archbishop, who had only recently been transferred from Arizona and who, as bishop of Tucson, had accepted the friars for the Navajo missions in the year 1897. Bishop Bourgade was promoted to the archdiocesan see of Santa Fe on January 7, 1899, exactly three months after the arrival of the friars at Cienega.[7]

On October 2 of that year[8] Father Juvenal met Father Provincial Raphael Hesse at the train at Lamy, New Mexico, and accompanied him and Father Charles Schoeppner to the ancient city, where they attended the ceremonies in which the newly appointed archbishop was invested with the pallium two days later. Incidentally, the chronicler notes[9] that the appearance of the friars in the City of the Holy Faith[10] created no little sensation among the older Mexican people who shed tears at the remembrance of the brown-robed Franciscans who had labored so faithfully among them in years gone by.

On the day after the festivities, October 5, 1899, the friars had a highly interesting and very important interview with their archbishop, during which His Grace broached the question of the advisability of locating the chief Navajo mission base in his diocese instead of that of Tucson; in the first place, he said that because of a scarcity of priests, he was particularly desirous of having Franciscans in his diocese to give missions and retreats for the Mexicans; in the second place, it appeared to him that the San Juan country to the north offered a much more favorable field for successful work among the Navajo than Cienega. He regretted very much that Father Jouvenceau had already left the city to return to his large parish and he, therefore, urged the friars to enter into correspondence with him and arrange for a meeting at an early date somewhere in the San Juan area.

Cienega or San Juan Country?

It could not be gainsaid that the close proximity of Cienega to the agency and government school at Fort Defiance, where every inducement was offered Indian parents to send their children to school—inducements which the mission could not possibly duplicate—loomed up as more than an imaginary obstacle and impediment to overcome; the distance from the railroad appeared to be another real drawback, as was the impossibility of getting the Indians to settle in the vicinity in appreciable numbers. And this latter was perhaps the most serious of all the objections in view of the fact that the dominating thought in the archbishop's Navajo mission plan was to establish a mission center among the Navajo along the lines of the gloriously successful missions of the Franciscans in California.

On the other hand, there were numerous worthy circumstances that argued strongly enough for Cienega as a suitable base of missionary activities among the Navajo. While the nearness of a government school might be considered derogatory to the success of a Catholic school, it would tend to bring the contrast between the two into bolder relief, while at the same time it would provide convenience and opportunity in giving religious instructions to the pupils in attendance at Fort Defiance, only eight miles away. There was an abundance of water in the north, but there was not a shortage of water at Cienega, which actually was an oasis in the desert, with an abundant water supply from nearby springs and artesian wells. And as to a source of water for irrigation purposes, there was Black Creek which carried the run-off from Defiance Plateau and the Chuska mountain ranges through the promising valley just to the east. It was true, the distance from the railroad was 29 miles and freight charges from Gallup were 35 cents per hundredweight, but railroad facilities in the San Juan region were practically non-existent.[11]

From Cienega one could travel 60 miles south, or 90 miles north, 150 miles east or west and still remain in the Navajo country, and thus, as far as accessibility to important points was concerned, Cienega was undoubtedly more favorably and strategically located than any spot in the San Juan area which comprised only the far northeastern portion of the Navajo domain. True, it was just another dot on the vast reservation which was twice the size of the state of Massachusetts, and living here was only a handful, comparatively speaking, of the 18,000 Indians that made up the tribe. But for that matter, there was not then, nor is there to this day, a place in the entire reservation where Indians lived in such numbers that it might deserve the name of a village. Scattered beyond the mountains to the four points of the compass throughout this great expanse of barren wastes, rock-walled canyons, wooded plateaus, and charming valleys lived the Indians to whose benighted souls the friars had resolved to bring the light of the Catholic Faith. And what a laborious task, they must have realized, stood before them! Not one church or chapel, not even parishioners, as was at least the case with the early pioneer priests of our land, who followed the Catholic settlers into the wilderness in order to provide opportunity for them to practice their religion and to invite backsliders to return to the Faith of their fathers. Here again, as in the learning of the language, they found themselves face to face with the absolute necessity of laying the very foundations, for their field was an entirely new one; indeed, a pagan enclosure in which the seed of the Gospel had been only sparsely and superficially sown and which had seen or heard little of education or civilizing influences, for in all that country there were only two schools: the government boarding school at Fort Defiance, Arizona, and the government day school at Tohatchi, New Mexico.[12]

Exploring San Juan

It may be said that the friars were evidently quite satisfied that the valley of Cienega afforded a natural location for a mission. Still, they were willing and ready to give the proposition of their archbishop earnest and careful consideration. Immediately, therefore, after his return from Santa Fe on October 6, 1899,[13] Father Juvenal wrote a letter to Father Jouvenceau at Park View, and in accordance with arrangements made in their correspondence, Father Anselm set out on horseback on November 2,[14] bound for the San Juan basin, to the northeast and beyond the Chuska Mountains. As guide and companion he took with him Charley Day, who had made the trip before and was familiar with the mountain passes, arroyos, and stopover points en route. The reconnaissance journey of more than 530 miles had its full measure of experiences, surprises, near-accidents, reverses, joys, and disappointments. Going by way of Crystal, New Mexico, where they stopped at the Moore trading post to enjoy a hearty meal about 2:00 in the afternoon, they crossed the rugged Chuska range via Cottonwood Pass, and with 55 miles behind them for the first day, spent the night at a Protestant mission at Two Grey Hills. One of the lady missionaries was a distant relative of the Days, and the party was received very cordially. Father Anselm writes that he was in no condition to entertain and retired shortly after supper; his hearing had been affected, and when he learned that the mountains they had just crossed were 9,500 feet above sea level, he became convinced that the high altitude was to blame. At any rate, he remarks, it is customary here to attribute almost every bodily indisposition to this cause.

A Mr. Thompson had joined Father Anselm and Charley Day at Crystal; at about 10:00 the next morning the three resumed their journey, [stopping] to have a noon lunch, consisting of crackers and canned peaches, at Bennett Peak, 12 miles farther on. By 4:00 they had traversed the dreary waste and reached the Hog Back; passing through the "Bad Lands" of Chaco Canyon by daylight, they reached the San Juan River after dark. Leaving Father Anselm at the bank of the river, the two companions drove to a neighboring Indian camp to make inquiry regarding the ford at that place; they soon returned with the information that there was no danger. All drew their saddle cinches a few notches tighter and then plunged into swift current, Mr. Thompson, who was accustomed to this crossing, taking the lead. It was Father Anselm's first experience fording a "real" river, and he happily remarks that, though his heart missed several beats, he gained the other side of the raging stream without mishap. A ride of only about a half mile, which gave them a total of 100 miles for the two days, brought them to another Protestant mission at Jewett, New Mexico. "And once again," Father Anselm humorously comments, "I found myself, like many a politician, in the hands of my enemies."

This mission at Jewett, as also the one at Two Grey Hills, was founded and maintained by "The Women's National Indian Association" for the purpose of discovering suitable mission sites on the Navajo reservation, of "clearing the way" for missionary activities and later selling out to any sect that might have a desire to carry on the work. In addition to their allowances from the association, the women in charge of both projects held positions as government field matrons, which netted each an annual salary of $720. The missionary at Jewett[15] was a native of Massachusetts, strong of body, very energetic, and zealous, and, according to Father Anselm, had done more good than anyone else in the way of instructing the Navajo in agriculture and irrigation, as well as inducing them to settle down and better their living conditions. The Indian settlements west of the Hog Back and north of the river were not only living testimony of her full-hearted and practical endeavors, but also definite proof of the possibility of persuading the Navajo to abandon their nomadic mode of life and to establish themselves permanently.[16]

At Farmington

The next morning the party continued toward Farmington—Father Anselm says 25 miles away—and as they followed the river eastward, the startling contrast of the day before, which saw them through the barren and forbidding desert, impressed the friar explorer very deeply and brought to his mind the words of the Old Testament: "And Lot, lifting up his eyes, saw all the country about the Jordan, which was watered throughout before the Lord destroyed Sodom and Gomorrah, as the paradise of the Lord" (Gen. 13:10). After a ride of five miles through this picturesque garden in a New Mexican desert, they arrived at the home of Mr. Thompson, whose father at one time had been government farmer for the Indians there. From the elder Thompson Father Anselm received much valuable information during his brief visit. After dinner he and Charley were again on their way, and riding via Fruitland and Olio,[17] they entered Farmington, the largest and most beautiful village in the San Juan country, situated west of the confluence of the Las Animas and San Juan Rivers. Here it was learned that the only Catholics were one Irish and two Mexican families living outside the town.

This third day's journey was, indeed, a revelation to Father Anselm. The north side of the river for many miles was an unbroken series of rich farms and fruit orchards, made fertile and productive by the waters that were led in a maze of winding irrigation ditches from the Las Animas and San Juan Rivers. The view across the river revealed another picture: vast stretches of sloping desert lands that seemed to be rolling from the pretentious cliffs northward into the river, with a scattering of small Indian fields and squat hogans, but little of vegetation except a few groves of cottonwood trees here and there on the banks of the river. This picture of outstanding contrasts stirred up a host of surmises, misgivings, and hopes in Father Anselm's mind. Certainly, he thought, there was, and that not so long ago, a time when this northern side of the river presented a view equally as disconsolate and cheerless as that to the south. And if the hands of poor and seemingly helpless men have been able to erect a paradise here, why can not our wealthy and powerful Uncle Sam do likewise for the red-skinned wards that he has so graciously taken under his protective mantle?

At Farmington, Father Anselm engaged an Indian guide to direct him and Charley on a visit to the Indian families living on the south side of the San Juan. After visiting a Mexican family the following morning, they forded the Las Animas River and proceeded to ford the San Juan. The Indian guide led the way, and as he approached the middle of the stream, his horse began to flounder in the quicksand. The rider promptly dismounted and waded to the opposite shore where he hurriedly removed his clothing and returned to drag his struggling animal to safety. Father Anselm and Charley had both struck the treacherous quicksand, but they wisely turned back at the first sign of danger. The guide beckoned them in all seriousness to come on, but they were not to be convinced. Rather than take any chances they rode back to Farmington, where they learned that they would find a safe crossing less than three miles to the west and only a short distance from the eastern reservation boundary. This was the so-called Kings Crossing, where the stream was indeed deep and wide, but where a rock bottom assured the horses of a firm footing; they forded the river here without any trouble or danger whatsoever.

The Indian, with his half-drowned steed, soon caught up with them and led them to the east reservation line only about one-fourth mile to the west. Here they met a few Indians who were just preparing to move south for the winter. Questioning revealed that very few Indians made their homes here, and the scouting party, realizing that it would be useless to go farther into the reservation, retraced their steps, and on their return they halted at the home of a Mexican named Eleutherio Vigil. This man had a good farm which he would have been glad to sell at $40 per acre.

Back at Farmington, Father Anselm was informed that there were two broad valleys east of the town and south of the river, each about 20 miles long, with irrigation projects, which, however, were no longer in operation. Some years before, so the reports went, a large number of Navajo, under their chief, Mattheo, settled here and became very successful farmers, but when the ditches and irrigation works later failed in their purpose, everyone moved away. A Mr. Allen[18] kindly offered to escort Father Anselm to this locality, and on the following day they crossed the San Juan River to drive to the home of Antonio Medina, eight miles away. Father Anselm left Charley at the latter place to rest and feed the horses[19] and to make arrangements for dinner. On the ride up the valley with Mr. Allen, everything was found just as reported, but commenting upon the prospects and recalling the failure of the government at Kings Crossing, where four years previously an irrigation superintendent had squandered thousands of dollars to produce nothing more than a project on paper, Father Anselm gave utterance to the following gem of bitter sarcasm:

Indeed, if we had plenty of money or if we only had the backing of the government, this would most certainly be an ideal place to found a large and flourishing Indian settlement, modeled after the old Franciscan missions in California; but those missions, be it remembered, were founded under the "cruel" and retrogressive rule of Spain; in this glorious land of ours, in this marvelous age of enlightenment and under our humane governmental rule, we do things of this nature in another way and, of course, more efficiently; simple, too, for all we have to do is: compel the young savages to go to school a few years and then let them on their own; in no time at all our incomparable system infallibly leads the wild aborigines to true civilization and contentment.[20]

Meantime, Charley Day was having the time of his life trying to converse with Senor Medina; the latter knew no English, and Charley, no Spanish. Finally, after exhausting every thinkable means of making himself intelligible, Charley in utter despair asked his host in Indian whether he understood the Navajo language. The reply:"And how!" brought on a spirited conversation in the language which was common to both. Medina later produced his rosary, several religious medals, and pictures and began to instruct his Protestant visitor in Catholic Faith and practice. When Father Anselm and Mr. Allen returned, they found the two seated on a bench, the Mexican with a Spanish New Testament in hand, translating into Navajo for Charley's benefit. Medina then, with Charley interpreting, told Father Anselm how happy he was to be visited by a Catholic priest; he had not seen one for many years, and now, only a few days after he had dreamed that a padre would visit him, his dream had unexpectedly come true.

Taking dinner at Medina's home, Mr. Allen departed for Farmington. Father Anselm and Charley rode up Gallegos Canyon—Father Anselm prefers to call it a valley—for a distance of nine miles to a trading post conducted by Dick Simpson, an Englishman, who welcomed them in true "unEnglish" style and lodged them for the night. Disappointed at not finding any Indians or even the trace of a settlement here, they left the next morning; bearing in a northeasterly direction, they crossed the San Juan River at Bloomfield and continued on to Aztec, where they hoped to meet Father Jouvenceau. There seems to have been some confusion in the arrangements, however, for when they inquired about the town they were informed that the padre would not be in Aztec until the following week.

With plenty of time on their hands, they decided to do some more reconnoitering, and the next day they set out for Largo, a Mexican village 15 miles to the southeast. Father Anselm planned to say Mass the following morning for the kind people he met here, but he needed more than an adobe church for that purpose, and since, according to the sacristan, the vestments, and so on, had been taken to the mission station at Alcatraz, this was impossible. With information that Kutz Canyon, which was one of the three localities recommended as a favorable mission site by Father Jouvenceau, was only a few miles to the west, hiring a Navajo horseman as guide, they went there after a good rest at Largo; but they found only six Navajo families, who, for the most part, were employed in Mexican ranches. They crossed the San Juan River once more, intending to visit the trading post of Romulo Martinez. Apparently changing their plans however, they bore westward with Angels Peak, or Los Gigantes and El Huerfano and El Huerfanito, massive stone formations that rose to great heights from the level plains, as their direction finders. Near these peaks lived more Navajo than they had found at any place thus far visited. The Chico, about 30 miles south of the river, with its abundant growth of grass, plentiful piñon and cedar trees, and fine perennial springs, appeared still more inviting and promising, but there were only a few Indians living there; furthermore, it was about 40 miles from Farmington and nearly 100 miles from the nearest railroad station, Durango, Colorado. Our scouts halted here just long enough to speak with an Indian family and take a light lunch, after which they pushed on to the "Bad Lands," where they spent the night at the trading post conducted by J. Walling.

After releasing their Indian guide, they took a southern course to enter into the very heart of the Indian country where, east of the reservation, upwards of 700 Indians were reported to be living in the vicinity.[21] This was Pueblo Bonito, situated about three miles east of the point where Chaco Canyon and Escavada Wash unite; it has been so named after the vast ruins of a large prehistoric community dwelling which has since been excavated and explored and become a national monument. Situated about 60 miles south of the San Juan, 40 miles north of the Santa Fe Railway, about 50 miles west of Nacimiento (Cuba), and probably 75 miles east of Cienega as the crow flies, but more than 100 miles by road, the encouraging features of Pueblo Bonito as a mission site quickly faded. Father Anselm and Charley arrived here shortly after noon and spent almost an entire day.

Horse Trading

Two days later they were again at Farmington. Father Anselm spent the greater part of a day negotiating a trade of his lame saddle horse for an Indian pony. The exchange was not a very fortunate one, for the only point in favor of the pony was that it was not lame. Father Anselm kept him one day and traded again at Aztec. It happened that Charley had just bought a horse there at public auction and was about to give his newly acquired steed a trial ride; the hotel proprietor, with an eye for business, offered Father Anselm his own horse for a short ride to accompany Charley. "Meek as a lamb," was the assuring comment of the shrewd horse trader, who had undoubtedly made many a horse deal before. Father Anselm began to realize very quickly that the westerner uses his figures of speech rather loosely, for he almost that same minute was having the ride of his life; it seemed to him the horse never intended to stop, and on his return, he took a side street and raced at breakneck speed through the town where, at the outskirts, the rider finally brought him under control. This was a real horse, thought Father Anselm, and no further sales talk was required to complete the deal. With the surrendering of his Indian pony and ten dollars in cash he came into possession of his faithful mount, whom he named "Swallow" and whom he used on many a later expedition on the reservation. To play safe, though, he also purchased a new bit. The "meek" lamb, however, seemed always to have been the master, and eventually after repeated outbreaks of unruliness, uncontrollable speed, and viciousness, Father Anselm in sheer self-defense gave him to Charley Day in exchange for the work of repairing an old trading post at Chin Lee and converting it into a chapel and residence.[22]

Father Jouvenceau arrived by stagecoach from Durango in the afternoon of November 14.[23] After an exchange of happy greetings and having partaken of a Mexican meal, they both set out for Largo in a rickety conveyance, which after the seats had several times collapsed, literally "went on the rocks" with a broken wheel. Charley Day had been leading Father Anselm's horse—he did not take Swallow for this short ride—and thus he had a way of going on, while the others[24] had to cover the last few miles to Largo on foot.

Father Antonio, as he was commonly known, made a very deep impression upon Father Anselm, who enthusiastically speaks of him as one of the most brilliant priests in the Southwest. As superintendent of Indian contract schools in New Mexico in the days of Indian commissioner [Thomas J.] Morgan, he had gained a broad knowledge and experience in Indian matters and had particularly become interested in the spiritual needs of the Navajo Indians to whose cause he frequently endeavored to recruit missionaries from among his priestly acquaintances. His house at Largo was soon filled with visitors who seemed to fully appreciate his visits, which came at such long intervals; a number of Indian pupils had come all the way from the government school at Fort Lewis, Colorado, 60 miles distant, in order to attend Holy Mass and receive the sacraments. Conversation, during which views and plans were thoroughly discussed, lasted far into the night, and the next morning Father Anselm and Charley returned to Aztec, where the former mounted his Swallow for the trip back to Cienega. Of their return voyage nothing is further recorded except that they passed through Farmington and arrived at Cienega on November 18.[25]

The information gathered on their visit is summed up as follows by the chronicler:

The Indians east of the mountain ranges (the region around Little Water, 30 miles east of Fort Defiance, where there is a Government school, excepted), more especially those east of the reservation, are very little influenced by the Agency and Government school. Those at Jewett and north of this place a little distance along the river seem to be influenced by the "Mission" at Jewett, where there is also a "mission school" attended by thirteen children—an increased attendance not being desired. The children sent to school are sent to the Fort Lewis Government school in southern Colorado. Since quite a number of them had and still have some contact with Mexicans, they might, even on this account, be more disposed to send their children to a Catholic school and receive the teachings of our Holy Religion. Between Jewett and Farmington (25 miles) about 20 families farm in summer; a farmer appointed by the Government and residing opposite Fruitland, a Mormon village, instructing them; in fall they move farther south. Near Largo about six families are living. These two are the only Navajo settlements on the San Juan River east of Jewett. Many Navajo had been farming eight miles east of Farmington on the San Juan River, but since the irrigation ditch became out of repairs, they moved away. The next settlement is thirty miles south of Largo at the Chico.

The center of all the Navajo settlements east of the mountain ranges and south of the San Juan (east of Jewett) is unquestionably around Pueblo Bonito (where Chaco Canyon and Escavada Wash meet) sixty miles south of the San Juan River, thirty miles east of the reservation line, forty miles directly north from Santa Fe railroad line, one hundred and ten miles north of west from Albuquerque, sixty miles east of La Posta and about fifty miles east of Nacimiento, both Mexican villages, attended to from the parish of Jemez (about 110–120 miles from Cienega). Taking all this into consideration a school and mission on the San Juan might be successful, if a large tract of land could be bought and irrigated on the south side of the San Juan River between Farmington and Largo, and if the Navajo could be induced to settle on this land permanently. At that time land could have been bought there for 7–10 dollars per acre, but now the Mormons are settling there and gold has been discovered about eight miles east of Farmington.

One more possibility remains of having a successful school and mission just east of the reservation line, three miles west of Farmington, if Mr. McHenry succeeds in obtaining the office of Superintendent of Irrigation on the Navajo reservation and an appropriation of about $40,000. In that case he would irrigate thousands of acres of fertile land between Farmington and Jewett. Although this cause has been endorsed by many influential persons, also through the Rev. Mother Katharine by the Indian Commissioner at Washington, he has until August, 1900, not succeeded in obtaining this office.[26]

Cienega Preferred

For the reasons implied in the above statement and since only about 1,000 Navajo were found to be living east of the reservation,[27] it was decided that the San Juan sector, so much farther away from "civilization" than Cienega and not even on the reservation, could no longer be considered *the* strategic location for the central Navajo mission; but since it was not without genuine merits for a mission and day school project, the matter was not definitely abandoned.

Here, indeed, was an opportunity for the friars to follow in the footsteps of their pioneer confreres in California[28] by gathering the Indians together into villages or settlements and instructing them in agriculture and possibly also developing other profitable industries; that would, of course, have demanded enormous expenditures of money in the construction of irrigation ditches, and so forth, which only the government could have afforded. But what could be expected of the government whose policy regarding the Indians, as Father Anselm sarcastically writes, "often failed because it would not or did not care to see beyond the walls of the school."[29] Yes, the school seemed to be everything and yet, sad to say, going through school without acquiring any sense of morality, the children returned to their parents and relatives like the helpless children they had been when they left home. No opportunity was given them to make use of the education they had received, and, lacking all incentive and initiative, as well as all sense of responsibility, they soon returned to their primitive Indian life to take up the blanket; and many, no doubt overcome by a feeling of disappointment and dissatisfaction over it all, plunged lower in the scale of human existence than if they had never attended school.

Father Anselm reported his findings to Archbishop Bourgade, who subsequently requested our province to take over the parish of Pena Blanca, which consisted of Pena Blanca itself, four Mexican settlements, La Bajada, La Canada de Cochiti (now abandoned), Sile and Thornton (the present-day Domingo), the mining camps of Bland and Colle, and the three Indian villages, Cochiti, Santo Domingo, and San Felipe.[30] In the latter part of March 1900, Father Anselm, in company with Father Juillard, made an inspection tour of the newly proffered parish. On April 4 he sent his report to Father Provincial, who forthwith accepted the parish, and on June 10 Father Francis de Sales Stuerenberg took charge and replaced the diocesan priest, Father Noel Dumarest.[31] This was the first mission accepted by the St. John Baptist Province in New Mexico.

The archbishop was not losing sight of the Navajo that lived in his diocese, and his determination to have mission work inaugurated among them at all events was far from declining, for immediately after recording the acceptance of the Pena Blanca parish, the chronicler writes:

> Since the Most Reverend Archbishop of Santa Fe has also offered us the parish of Jemez,[32] west of Pena Blanca, covering the territory between Pena Blanca and the Navajo Indians, the Navajo south of the San Juan River and east of the reservation could much easier be attended to from the outskirts of this parish (La Posta or Nacimiento, where it might be feasible to build a school for the Navajos later on) than either from the San Juan River or St. Michael's Mission. But there are only about 1,000 Navajos (persons, not families) living east of the reservation, certainly a small fraction of the 20,000. Cienega, with its almost central location for all the Navajos, has on the whole, advantages which could not easily be equaled at any other place.[33]

Nevertheless, as already stated, the rejection of a San Juan project was by no means a closed question; in fact, a few years later the founding of a mission with plans to establish a day school in that area was attempted. Numerous circumstances conspired against its success, and the attempt proved to be a trial in more ways than one.[34]

Notes

1. From Emanuel Trockur, "Franciscan Missions among the Navajo Indians: IV," *Provincial Chronicle* 13 (Winter 1940–1941): 73–76, 80–90.

2. John Lanzrath, "Emanuel Trockur's Bequest,"*Provincial Chronicle*, n.s. 1 (Fall 1978): 78.

3. Emanuel Trockur, "Incidents in Navajoland." FFP Box 47, fd. 1.

4. Emanuel Trockur, "Background of the Indian Missions," *Provincial Chronicle* 11 (Fall 1938): 3–16.

5. Anselm Weber, FMN 30 (November 1903): 964, 966.

6. Weber, FMN 31 (January 1904): 34. Father Jouvenceau had designated Kutz Canyon, Gallegos Canyon, or the Chico, all in New Mexico, as his choice for the location of Navajo mission headquarters—a fact that argues for his belief that the entire Navajo tribe was originally assigned to the charge of our province. Father Anselm Weber, in a letter written to Father Provincial Eugene Buttermann on February 13, 1910, stresses this point when he writes: "I wish to mention that, when we accepted this mission, we accepted the whole Navajo tribe, not only those in Arizona but those also in New Mexico." (Letter in St. Michaels Archives.) With the establishment of the diocese of Gallup, New Mexico, on August 25, 1940, announcement of which was released by the Apostolic Delegation on December 26, 1939, the entire Navajo reservation has been brought under the jurisdiction of the new diocesan head, the Most Reverend Bernard T. Espelage.

7. Father Bourgade was appointed vicar apostolic of Arizona on May 1, 1885, and became the first bishop of Tucson on May 8, 1897.

8. [Father Emanuel here refers to the "Chronicle of St. Michael's," recorded first by Father Juvenal Schnorbus, with later entries by Father Anselm Weber, Father Frederick Hartung, and, after October 15, 1900, by Father Leopold Ostermann. The typescript version of this document on file at Franciscan Archives Cincinnati (Box PLA.376 St. Michael's, env. St. Michael's Earliest History 1898–1907), entitled "History of the Ranch, about Seven Miles South of Fort Defiance (Cienega) Arizona, Now St. Michael's Missions," is paginated differently from the copy cited by Father Emanuel. I have added an author entry and changed title and page references to match the typescript copy in the Cincinnati archives.] Juvenal Schnorbus et al., "History of the Ranch," 11. Father Provincial was enroute to California, and Father Charles Schoeppner, then pastor at Wichita, Kansas, accompanied him as far as Cienega. Cf. *Provincial Chronicle* 12 (1939–1940): 69.

9. Schnorbus et al., "History," 11.

10. The original name was "*La Ciudad Real de la Santa Fe de San Francisco*," or "The Royal City of the Holy Faith of St. Francis." The city was founded in 1605 when the Spanish government was transferred thither from San Gabriel. Cf. Jerome Hesse, "Glimpses into the History of the Catholic Church in New Mexico," FMSW 6 (1918): 27.

11. The nearest railroad station at that time was at Durango, Colorado, which is about 80 miles from the present-day Shiprock Government School and about 50 miles from Farmington. A narrow gauge road, the Denver and Rio Grande, brought its first train to Farmington on September 19, 1905. Today, Farmington is still at the end of this line. According to the letter of Father Anselm, plans were under way in 1910 to construct "a new railroad from Farmington to Gallup, or rather from Durango, Colorado, through the Navajo Reservation to Clifton, Arizona, either passing through Farmington and Gallup, or a few miles to the west of these towns." The survey for this route was completed as early as the year 1903. Weber, FMN 30 (December 1903):1078.

12. Fort Defiance school was begun in September 1881. Cf. Richard Van Valkenburg, *A Short History of the Navajo People* (Window Rock, Ariz.: Navajo Service, U.S. Department of Interior, 1938): 49. Tohatchi was opened in 1895, and was known by the whites as "Little Water."

13. Schnorbus et al., "History," 12.

14. Weber, FMN 27 (May 1900): 373; 30 (November 1903): 966 ff.; 31 (January 1904): 34 ff.; (February 1904): 125 ff.; also "Notices of the Order," *St. Anthony Messenger* 7 (1899–1900): 283.

15. Her name was Mary L. Eldridge. Several letters relating to Navajo matters, which she wrote to Father Anselm, are preserved in St. Michael's archives.

16. This part of the memorable San Juan trip is described in Weber, FMN 30 (November 1903): 964–69. Father Anselm relates that by that time both missions, Jewett and

Two Grey Hills, had been taken over by the Presbyterians, and it was already apparent that they would have fared much better had the Association retained its hold of them.

17. According to Father Anselm, from Jewett to Thompson's was five miles, and from here to Fruitland, seven miles; the writer checked these distances in the summer of 1940 and found that from Jewett to Fruitland is only eight miles; three miles from Fruitland is Kirtland (Olio), which in the early 1890s was known as Olio Mesa. From here to Farmington the highway measures about nine and one-half miles. As a rule, Father Anselm's distance calculations will be found remarkably exact, but when he says it was 12 miles from Jewett to Fruitland, he either made a poor guess or a detour to Thompson's must account for the extra four miles.

18. This was probably Frank B. Allen, proprietor of the Grand Livery Feed and Sale Stable, whose advertisement appears in the *San Juan Times* in this year.

19. From Father Anselm's narrative it may be presumed that he loaned [borrowed] a horse from Senor Medina for this short trip.

20. Weber, FMN 30 (December 1904): 1080.

21. Vicinity, Father Anselm notes parenthetically, is to be construed according to the western acceptation of the term, and in that sense it could be understood to comprise a radius of as much as or more than 25 miles.

22. Weber, FMN 31 (January 1904): 38.

23. Schnorbus et al., "History," 12.

24. Father Anselm does not state who else was with them, but it is not unlikely that a Mexican helper of Father Jouvenceau, or the owner of the conveyance, was driving.

25. The *San Juan Times,* a weekly newspaper published at Farmington, New Mexico, 9 (no. 24), Friday, November 10, 1899, records this visit as follows: "Father Anselm Weber, who is now located at Seneca as a missionary to the Navajo, arrived in Farmington Saturday accompanied by Charles Day of Fort Defiance, as a guide. Father Weber came here to look up a location somewhere on the south side of the San Juan River for an industrial school and mission for the Navajo and Mexicans, which is to be built by Miss Drexel of Philadelphia.." The following week's issue had this to say: "Rev. Anselm Weber, who has been here for the past two weeks looking over this section with a view of determining the feasibility of establishing an industrial school for the Navajo Indians, mention of which was made in last week's *Times,* departed for his home at Seneca yesterday. Father Weber is well pleased with this section, and his report will be in favor of establishing the school. Father Weber is a friar of the Franciscan Order of Minors, and the work, if taken up, will be by this order, probably assisted by the sisterhood of the Blessed Sacrament, an order established and presided over by Mother Katharine (Miss Drexel of Philadelphia) for the education of the Indians and Negroes. We were in error last week in stating that the school would be for the education of the Mexicans. It will be only for the benefit of the Navajo Indians." [*San Juan Times*, 9] (no. 25), Friday, November 17, 1899.

26. Schnorbus et al., "History," 12–14.

27. Schnorbus et al., "History," 16.

28. Weber, FMN 31 (February 1904):126.

29. Anselm Weber, "St. Michael's Mission and School for the Navajo Indians,"*Indian Sentinel* 5 (1908):27; Weber, FMN 29 (February 1902): 111, 115.

30. Both Bland and Colle are no longer in operation. In the year 1918 La Madera, Golden, Ortiz, San Pedro, Madrid, and Cerrillos were added to the parish. The latter place has a resident priest since 1928.

31. Cf. . . . FMSW 8 (1920): 29; Weber, FMN 27 (July 1900): 554. The Reverend Noel Dumarest, a member of the Third Order of St. Francis, died of tuberculosis at St. Joseph Hospital, Albuquerque, New Mexico, on January 13, 1905; he was buried in the cemetery

beside the church in Pena Blanca on January 17. A brother, the Reverend Michael Dumarest, former assistant to Father Juillard at Gallup, is still active in the capacity of pastor in the pueblo of Isleta, New Mexico. Cf. FMN 32 (1905): 284; "Chronicle of the Order: Pena Blanca, New Mex.," *St. Anthony Messenger* 12 (1904–1905): 322. It appears that Father Francis Stuerenberg had been temporarily assigned to the cathedral at Sante Fe, where he arrived about the end of April 1900. Cf. Weber, FMN 27 (July 1900): 552.

32. In 1744 the friars Delgado and Irigoyen entered the Navajo domain by way of Jemes. Cf. Zephyrin Engelhardt, *Franciscans in Arizona* (Harbor Springs, Mich.: Holy Childhood Indian School, 1899): 208. From 1828, with the expulsion of the friars by the Mexican government, Jemes was administered by diocesan priests. In 1902 it was taken over by the Cincinnati Province of St. John the Baptist, with Fathers Barnabas Meyer, pastor, and Florentine Meyers as assistant. Cf. Fridolin Schuster, "The Mission at Jemes," FMSW 1 (1913): 24.

33. Schnorbus et al., "History," 16.

34. Anselm Weber, *Indian Sentinel* (April 1918): 27.

6

First Impressions and Councils with Headmen, 1900[1]

Leopold Ostermann, O.F.M.

[At the Provincial Chapter (meeting of the order's elected body of governing officials) of September 27, 1900, Father Juvenal Schnorbus was transferred to Cincinnati, Father Anselm was appointed Superior at St. Michaels, and two volunteers to the Navajo missions, Father Leopold Ostermann and Father Berard Haile, were appointed as his assistants. Father Leopold, a seminary classmate of Father Anselm's, had spent the decade following his ordination teaching languages (Latin, German, Greek, and French) and history at the St. Francis Seminary in Cincinnati, then serving in parishes in Ontario, Illinois, and Kentucky. Father Anselm's biographer suggests that Anselm had requested the appointment of his old classmate, and that Father Leopold was more than willing to join the Navajo missions. In the months preceding his new appointment he is described as "all aflutter over the prospect of going southwest."[2]

The new assistants arrived at St. Michaels on October 12. Three days later Father Anselm returned from his California convalescence, "took charge of the mission," and began delegating responsibilities. Father Leopold's literary talents were immediately called into play: on October 16 he was assigned the responsibility of keeping the mission chronicle.[3]

Within a few days he had accepted a much heavier assignment: to write a monthly article for the English-language Franciscan journal, *St. Anthony's Messenger*. Father Anselm, already burdened by the monthly *Sendbote* obligation, was happy to offer the open-ended *St. Anthony's Messenger* opportunity to his trusted associate. The new series, "Franciscans in the Wilds and Wastes of the Navajo Country," and its author were introduced by Father Anselm in the January 1901 issue,[4] and Father Leopold's initial installment, the story of his first days in Navajo land, appeared the following month. Father Leopold faithfully fulfilled this assignment through nine years and 102 episodes, finally concluding in the October 1909 *Messenger*.

The Cincinnati Franciscans had been publishing *Der Sendbote* since 1876 and in 1892 had added another German-language journal, *St. Franciscus Bote*. *St. Anthony's Messenger*, founded in 1893, was intended to offer English-speaking Catholic workers "the light of faith" as an alternative to socialistic, communistic, or anarchistic responses to the problems of the working class in modern industrial society. Its editors assumed that "most readers subscribed to no other magazine," and by the time Father Leopold began reporting on missionaries among the Navajo, the *Messenger* included "departments to address a whole range of everyday family concerns" and served "as an all-purpose magazine for the Catholic community."[5]

Father Leopold's early Navajo essays have a distinctive style. He can hardly contain his enthusiasm and wonder at the beauty of the land, the adventure of the work, each new natural vista, cultural variety, or human opportunity. It is as if the language does not contain enough adjectives, or that no single word or phrase can possibly convey what he sees and feels, and so he is compelled to multiply phrase on phrase, to pile image upon image. Later, when he had been isolated and over-worked at Chin Lee for many years, the palpable effervescence would disappear, there would be bouts of depression, and his prose style would come to more closely resemble the sober realism of Father Anselm and Father Berard. But in 1900, everything was new and magical, and the reader cannot help but share in the wonder of it all. Besides, Father Leopold seems to have been a faithful reader of Charles F. Lummis's *Land of Sunshine: The Magazine of California and the West*, and so, augmenting his own interests and enthusiasms, here and there in his early work are discernible stylistic and topical echoes of Lummis.]

"St. Michael's Mission, among the Navajo Indians, Apache County, Arizona," such was to be my address in the future; so I read it on the Chapter paper last September, and as it was written, so it came to pass. On October 2, I received orders from my Very Reverend Father Provincial to get ready for sunny Arizona, and a week later I bade farewell to all the comforts and refinements of civilization and exchanged them for the society of the semibarbarous Navajo. I arrived in company with Reverend Berard Haile, O.F.M., whose destination was the same as mine, at Gallup, N.M., on October 12, 1900. On the same day, we drove with Reverend Juvenal Schnorbus, O.F.M., to the place of our future labors: St. Michael's Mission, about 30 miles northeast of Gallup. (Gallup on the Santa Fe route is our nearest railway station.)

The country between here and Gallup is not very attractive as far as vegetation is concerned; nothing but dusty sagebrush and greasewood, a few bristling cacti, and sharp-leaved yucca plants, and some sporadic piñons, crippled, dwarfed, and twisted. However, one will readily overlook the absence of a rich and diversified flora, when viewing the strange grandeur of the surrounding scenery, endlessly shifting and changing. The dry and dreary wastes; the sandy valleys and water-courses; the arroyos with their perpendicular banks of adobe; the sage-covered plains, with here and there a coyote skulking about in the brush, or a colony of prairie dogs poking up their heads out of their burrows and watching with curiosity the strange passers-by; the wild and weird rocks; the bald and bold cliffs in their grotesque shapes and fantastic forms; everything spanned over by a clear, deep blue sky, with here and there filmy streaks of fleecy clouds; all bathed and dazzling in golden sunshine; all these make the scenery extremely interesting, beautiful, and fascinating, particularly for one who, just coming from the East, views it for the first time.

St. Michaels is situated about one mile south of the Navajo Indian Reservation, in a valley which may be called fertile in comparison to the surrounding country. To the north, south, and northeast are large fine meadows, which yield annually a good crop of hay and alfalfa, and on account of which the Indians have named this section *Tsoho-tso*, that is, Large Meadow. On the east and west are hills rising up gradually, until they, about four or five miles from the mission, meet the mountains. The mission house itself is built on a small eminence, in the form of an oblong square, containing three rooms, or apartments, of which the front room is utilized as a chapel, the rear as kitchen, dining room, parlor, and general utility room, and the middle is partitioned off into four small rooms for three Fathers and one Brother. Besides this house there is on the ranch another small house of two rooms, which serves as a dwelling for our interpreter, a medicine man, and a few Indian boys; also a barn, stable, hennery, and carpenter's shop, that is what we call it anyway. All these buildings are built in primitive western style. . . .

Neither are we missionaries the only palefaces that live in this valley. About one-fourth of a mile southwest of us lives Mr. John Wyant and wife, who owns a trading post; southeast, about the same distance, is the homestead of Mr. Samuel E. Day and family. Mr. Day is at present the clerk at the agency, for which reason the Indians call him Naa'ltsos, the Tall, or Long Book. Northeast of us about one mile is another trading post owned and operated by Mr. Thomas Osborne, who is known among the Indians as Atsiddi, Blacksmith, in reference to his former occupation. North about one-fourth of a mile is the cabin of a Negro, George Overton, whom the Indians have named Naakai 'lizhin, The Black Mexican. Mr. Wyant is simply called John, nothing but only John. I may here also add the names which the Indians have given the missionaries: Father Anselm, Superior, is Tsish chilli, Curly Hair; my own name is Ednishodi Tso, Big Priest; Father Berard is Ednishodi Yazhe, Little Priest; and Brother Placidus is Chi-iya'ilini, Food Preparer, or Cook. . . .

A Visit to Tsehili

My first experience with the Indians I had on a visit to Tsehili, five days after I arrived at the mission. The object of this visit was to get some Navajo boys, who had been promised us for the Indian school at Santa Fe. When our Fathers took charge of St. Michael's, two years and some months ago, they were soon visited by numbers of Indians, who inquired of them who they were, what they wanted, what were their intentions, and so on. Among these, one of the most conspicuous was a certain Charlie Mitchell, or Charlie Tso, that is, Big Charlie, a very influential chief, living about 58 miles north of us, at a place called Tsehili. All the Indians of that region look up to Charlie, and whatever he says or does is well considered and generally followed. It is his sincerest wish to see the Navajo educated and civilized.

When, therefore, all his questions were satisfactorily answered, and after he himself had accompanied Father Juvenal to Santa Fe and visited the Indian school there, which is taught by Mother Katharine Drexel's Sisters, he, upon his return home, visited every Indian family in the neighborhood and even undertook long journeys over hills and mountains and did his best to induce the Indian parents to send their children to school. Many promised to send them as soon as we would have a school at the mission (the foundation of which will be laid next summer). Some few consented to sending them to distant Santa Fe.

In consequence of this, an agreement was made between Charlie Tso and Father Juvenal Schnorbus, O.F.M., to the effect that on a certain day of October (last year) Charlie was to assemble the parents, and the children for Santa Fe at his house, and Father Juvenal was to drive up and get them.

In the meantime, the annual Chapter of our Province took place at Mt. Airy, Ohio. Father Juvenal was transferred to Cincinnati, Ohio; Father Frederick Hartung, who had been staying here for his health, was assigned to Pekin, Illinois; Father Anselm Weber, who was sent here two years ago, and who had been spending the last five or six months in California by orders of the physician, was appointed Superior of the mission, with Father Berard Haile and myself as his assistants.

Last October 15, Father Anselm arrived and took charge of the mission, Father Juvenal having left the day previous, and on October17 he and I set out on our northern trip. We had sent our interpreter, Mr. Frank Walker, a Navajo half-breed, ahead on horseback the day before, to keep the men there in case they were waiting for us, and he promised us that at the third creek which we would cross—Whisky Creek—we would meet an Indian guide, who would lead and direct us safely to Charlie's house. Up to there we were to keep just on the "main road."

We started off about 5:45 a.m. Fifty-eight miles on a heavy, lumbering farm wagon, over stick and stone, may not seem to be exactly a pleasure trip, but I must confess there are very few trips which I enjoyed more. Everything was new to me, so strange, so much different from the East. The wild wooded mountain range to our left, the bare sun-scorched and weather-beaten peaks, points, and buttes of the Chusca range to our right, the peeping prairie dogs, the prowling coyotes, the large flap-winged ravens, a soaring eagle, arid valleys and plains, acres and acres of sage and greaseweed, stunted piñons and stately pines, the majestic King and Queen [rock formations], solemn Black Rock, frowning Black Mountain, the placid surface of Red Lake, and so on, never permitted my interest to flag a moment. It seemed like a drive on some other planet, or into some ghoulish fairy land. One almost expected to see the coyote turn into a werewolf, the ravens into Stymphalides, the eagle into a roc, and some of the lone-standing rocks into giants.

At noon, arriving on the crest of a hill, we rested an hour in a small piñon copse. First we saw that the horses had their dinner, then we took some provisions from the wagon, straddled a log in good western style, regaled ourselves with cold meat, bread, canned tomatoes, and water, and at 1:00 p.m. we were again on the road. We were then about 30 miles from home. We had crossed two creeks already and now we came to the third. "This must be old Whisky," we said, and looked about for our promised guide, but never the shadow of a guide was to be seen far and near. Without hesitating long we drove briskly forward, for we were still on the so-called main road. About 5:00 p.m. we came to a large rock where the road forked off in two different directions. What now? One knew as much as the other. After a few moments thought, Father Superior threw a few handfuls of hay upon the road, where it divided, in order to attract the attention of the Indian guide, when he would come there, and direct him which trail to follow. Then we drove on to the left.

We had not driven but about four or five miles farther, when we heard the trample of horses in the rear, and looking around we saw three Indians on horseback. Two of them turned off from the road and galloped over the plain. The third one rode up to us, told Father Superior that he had been sent by our interpreter to show us the way, that we could get to Charlie's place on this road, although a little later than on the other one; that he had brought his two boys with him from [for] Santa Fe. He then shook hands with both of us and rode on ahead.

By this time it was beginning to get dark. We tried to keep pace with the guide as well as we could, but our two horses were well nigh pegged out, and as we entered a pine forest, the guide, with his horse, disappeared from view in the darkness. It was now so dark that we could hardly distinguish the wagon ruts, and were afraid every moment of driving against a tree or upsetting the wagon. Father Superior finally got off and led the way on foot, in order to avoid any mishap. After going thus forward slowly for some time we suddenly heard someone cry out: "*Kójego! kójego!*," that is, "This way! this way!" It was our guide, who had waited for us there at a place where we had to turn off from the road and drive right into the dense forest. He told us we had but a short distance yet to go to Charlie's house, and stayed with us. But in that short distance our poor horses refused twice to go forward, being totally fagged out by the 58-mile drive.

The Home of Charlie Tso

However, we soon came to Charlie's house, before which a cheerful fire was blazing, and were heartily welcomed by him. It was then about 7:45 p.m. Of the chiefs who were to meet us there, three had arrived. These were Naakai Diná-e, which name in its literal translation would signify: The Mexican Navajo; but as the Naakai Diná-e are a particular clan of the Navajo tribe, the name means one belonging to that clan. The second was Tsish Chilli, Father Superior's namesake, a good-looking, finely built young man, who derived his name from an immense bush of curly, kinky, jet-black hair; he is a brother-in-law of Naakai Diná-e. The third one was our guide. His name is Naakai Diná-e bi-daghan' das-gelligi, that is, The Mexican Navajo with a Black Moustache. He had brought his wife and his two boys with him. His home is over the mountains, near the so-called Ship Rock. This is a large rock, standing alone in a desertlike region, in the extreme northwestern part of New Mexico. Viewed from a distance it presents very closely the shape and form of a large ocean steamer, and is visible more than a hundred miles.

When we arrived at Charlie's house we took the flour, coffee, sugar, canned fruits, tobacco, and so on, which we had brought along for ourselves as well as for our red visitors, into the house, and Mrs. Charlie prepared us a supper at the fire outside. After supper we sat around the blazing stove with the Indians, smoking, and Charlie Tso, the three above-named Navajo, and Father Superior began to talk, at length, over educational matters and about the school which was to be erected at the mission. Frank Walker did the interpreting. Tsish Chilli and Naakai Diná-e were so much pleased with what they heard that they promised to cross the mountains next morning and try to get a few more boys for the school.

After this, the first council dispersed, and we were glad to subside for the night, being pretty tired from the day's drive. . . .

The next morning we had more leisure to look about the place and neighborhood. Charlie Tso's, or Charlie Mitchell's home is in a beautiful valley, through which there flows a creek, called the Tsehili Creek. The word *Tsehili* means "Flowing through the Rock." This creek is so called because it flows into the Canyon del Muerto, Canyon of the Dead, at the entrance of which there is a huge perforated rock, through which the water of the creek flows. Canyon del Muerto has a very tragic history, from which it derives its name, and which I shall relate at some later date, when I have a chance to visit the place and get more particulars.

Charlie has several houses, of which the main one is a large, square, solidly built stone house, about 35 feet long and 15 feet wide, erected at the foot of a hill. This house Charlie has offered to Father Juvenal as a mission station, or gathering place for the Indians, when once we go about to different parts of the reservation. It contains one large room, which may conveniently be used for a chapel. The floor is covered with good flooring boards, and there are two windows, one toward the north, the other toward the southwest. In the middle of the western wall is a door which leads out upon a porch, or veranda, with a floor of stamped clay. As we enter the door, the first thing we see, and are surprised to see, is a real, sure-enough stove with a half-dozen civilized high-backed chairs standing solemnly around it. Over against the eastern wall stands a bench, some six or seven feet long, with a wash basin on it. Over it, on nails, are hanging a coal oil lamp with a small tin reflector, two mirrors, and a few photographs. Along the southern wall is a rack loaded with saddles, harness, saddlebags, blankets, pelts, and so forth. In the northwestern cor-corner stands a real table, and beside it a chair with water bucket and dipper. The windows are glazed with real glass and furnished with calico curtains on the inside. All around the wall, hats, diverse pieces of men's clothing, headbands, rifles, revolvers, cartridge belts, saddle blankets, beads, pictures, and so on, are hanging on pegs or nails.

Among the pictures the two most conspicuous are one representing our Lord crucified, with the Apostles and Evangelists at the four ends of the cross, and one representing St. Dominic receiving the rosary from the Blessed Virgin, surrounded by the 15 mysteries of the Rosary. Both have been premium pictures of past volumes of *Der Sendbote* and have been given to Charlie by Reverend Father Juvenal. When visitors come in and look at these pictures, Charlie tries to explain to them what they represent. Above the table, the fourth part of a newspaper is tacked against the wall, showing the portrait of Colonel Theodore Roosevelt in his roughrider uniform. In the northeast corner of the room leaning against the wall is an old spring mattress, the condition of which seems plainly to say that it had seen its best days before the present generation knew how to form syllogisms. At the side of it were stacked six or seven Navajo blankets, upon which we deposited our own blankets and mantles. Every evening when we manifested our intention of retiring, Charlie would go to that northeast corner of the room, unfold the spring mattress on the floor, and cover it nicely with the blankets, but despite the blankets I could easily count the springs on my side of the mattress, even if I lay perfectly quiet. However, we slept well every night.

Besides this stone house, Charlie has two or three other Indian huts, or *goghán*s, in which his family lives. We and our interpreter were lodged in the stone house, where we spent three and one-half days and slept four nights. During the day, as also the two following days, the most influential chiefs of the neighborhood put in their appearance, in all about 12 or 13, and fine men they were, too. Besides those already named I shall make more particular mention of Tsish Bizhi, Naat'ani Tsossi, Billy, and Chi, or Henry Dodge, a half-breed Mexican, in the course of my description.

The Navajo and Tobacco

First, something about their mode of smoking; for smoking seems to most of us so intimately connected with Indian life, that we think nothing more natural than the following sentence: the Indian is to smoking, as smoke is to fire. Strange as it may seem, I haven't seen a single one of them smoke a pipe. In the East, I know, an Indian without a pipe would be looked upon like a clock without hands, or a duck without feathers. Pipes are really not to be found among the Navajo, and if you spoke to them of the calumet or pipe of peace, they would understand you about just as much as if you undertook to explain to them the perihelion or aphelion of the planets; but I was told some time ago by Mr. Lorenzo Hubbell, an Indian trader whose trading post is about 35 miles from the mission, and who is our *next* neighborhood in the west (this is a land of magnificent distances), that in times past the Navajo did make use of pipes. This seems probable, too, for in the first place Mr. Hubbell assured me of having a few specimens of old Navajo pipes in his possession, and second, their language has a word for pipe which does not seem to be of recent origin: *nat'os-tse*, tobacco stone.

However, they all, even the women, are inveterate cigarette smokers, which they have learned from the Spaniards and Mexicans. The smoking tobacco mostly used in these parts is Durham's Bull Mixture, which may likely be well known to many readers. . . . They call it *Bégashi nat'o*, Cow or Bull tobacco, from its seal, which is on every package. Cigar in their language is *Nat'o n'l-cho-nigi*, ill-smelling tobacco, and cigarette, *Nat'o bi'l-das-dissigi*, wrapped tobacco. They are very handy in rolling their cigarettes, and it is quite interesting to watch them. It is a very solemn and deliberate proceeding.

First, they pull out their cigarette paper, or take one if there are any near at hand, make a crease in it, and hold it in position with the thumb and the two first fingers of the left hand. Then they take the package of Durham's in the right hand and pour the quantity of tobacco they wish to smoke into the crease, shove the package into their pocket again, or drop it on the table or floor, and begin to roll the cigarette with the thumbs and two first fingers of each hand, talking or listening to others the while. (That is just like civilized cigarette smokers do it; or do the civilized palefaces do it like the red rovers of the plains and forests?) Now they light it with an air of great satisfaction; if they have no match, they simply hold it into the fire, or into the stove, if there be any. In smoking they inhale the smoke and emit it from the nostrils and mouth at the same time, just like civilized dudes, enjoying it immensely and watching the curling smoke floating in the air, with a mien of perfect self-contentedness.

Councils with Headmen

Now let us return to Charlie's stone house again. That morning two influential headmen arrived, Tsiish Bizhi and Naat'ani Ts'ossi, and a council was held that same forenoon. All sat around the stove in a large circle, in the center of which, just in front of the stove, lay a package of Durham's with matches and cigarette wrappers on the floor. Whoever wished, helped himself, dropped the things where he had picked them up, and went through the proceedings described above. The question of sending children to the Santa Fe school was thoroughly ventilated. They had hundreds of doubts to be solved and hundreds of questions to be answered. They love very much to have real long talks over a thing before deciding, and the longer the talk, the better pleased they are. In these talks they often display no mean rhetorical talents and accompany their words with easy, natural, graceful and very appropriate gestures. In fact, I think they indulge in gestures even more than Frenchmen, which is saying a great deal, and tying down their hands in the middle of a speech would have the same effect upon them as taking the wind out of the sails would have upon a ship.

One cannot blame them for being slow and extremely careful, and for proposing almost numberless doubts and questions when dealing with palefaces, when one remembers how often they have been cheated, deceived, and defrauded by governmental promises. They must necessarily be suspicious and distrustful. However, I think we have their goodwill and confidence now. They are very much attached to their children, seemingly even more so than white parents, and would surely never consent to sending them any place if they were not convinced beforehand that their children will be kept and treated well.

The chief speaker at the council in question was Tsiish Bizhi, Braided Hair. He has his name from the fact of wearing his hair in two large braids, which passing over his shoulders hang down in front, the ends touching his belt. He is a pretty well-to-do Navajo living in the Lukaichukai Mountains, about 25 miles farther north, and had hitherto strenuously opposed every school for Navajo children. A straight, erect, well-built and well-proportioned figure, with noble and regular features and muscular form, is Tsiish Bizhi. He has thoughtful, intelligent, keen-looking eyes, energetic and firmly set jaws, a fearless demeanor and the gait of a chief, is a fine horseman and an excellent shot.

More than an hour he spoke and proposed questions, his last questions concerning the moral education of children in our schools. Father Superior then told him that herein precisely lay the difference between our schools and the schools of the government, that we do not only instruct the children in reading and writing, in ciphering and speaking English, and so on, but also try especially to impress upon their minds and instill into their hearts the principles of true Christian morality; that we teach them what to do, and what to avoid in order to become better men and women; teach them how to be useful members of the community in which they live; and that even after they leave the school we would remain in touch with them, visiting and advising them. In a word, our aim is to teach their children how to be happy in this world and also in the next.

After listening attentively to these words, which Mr. Frank Walker interpreted faithfully to him, the air of suspense and mistrust which was upon the face of Tsiish Bizhi during the council vanished, and walking resolutely across the circle to where we were sitting, he shook hands with us and said to Father Superior: "My father, and my chief, what I have heard from you pleases me very much. I now go to bring you my son and my nephew." Without further words he left the room, mounted his horse, and rode off. Two days later he returned with his son, a bright and intelligent looking lad of about ten years, and his nephew. We are convinced that in Tsiish Bizhi, or Braided Hair, we have gained a true faithful friend who may be trusted in every way and who will do us every favor in his power.

Some Navajo Customs

In describing the Indian, his ways, habits, mode of life, and so on, many writers profusely make use of such attributes as solemn, reticent, somber, morose, sullen, and others more. This may be true of some Indians, but of our Navajo it certainly is not true, at least not of those whom we met at Tsehili. On the contrary, I have found them very sunny and social. Evenings after supper when they were gathered around the stove in the stone house, and had their cigarettes lighted, they talked very freely, joked and jested, told stories, laughed heartily, and enjoyed themselves very much.

Most of the Navajo whom I have hitherto seen wear American clothes or some part of American clothing, if it only be a necktie. Such of them as have no coats make use of blankets, *beelt-laddi*, of diverse colors to wrap about the upper part of the body. It makes a very picturesque appearance to see about a dozen of them on their tough, hardy little ponies, galloping along the ridge of a hill, or along the bottom of a valley, with their multicolored blankets wrapped about them. Some wear the broad-rimmed western slouch hat, others the traditional headband, called *ch'a*, which consists of a piece of cloth, black, white, red, or many-colored, sometimes nothing else but a large handkerchief, *ch'a s'tlinnigi*, rolled up and tied about the head over the forehead, leaving the top bare.

They carry their hair, as a rule, long, tied up in a knot in the back, something after the fashion which years ago was known among the ladies of the civilized world as waterfall style. Some, however, have their hair shorn after the old Westphalian straight cut pattern. Every few days they wash their hair and head, using as soap the root of the yucca plant, *talawush*, commonly called Adam's Needle. This root, when put into water and worked and kneaded with the hands, makes a fine lather, and has, I think, even stronger cleansing qualities than ordinary soap, and it keeps the scalp free from dandruff. Otherwise they are not very intimate with soap.

On their feet they wear self-made moccasins called *k'e*. Naat'ani Ts'ossi has U.S. 25-cent pieces as buttons on his moccasins. I also saw an Indian boy, the son of a wealthy Navajo, who had a whole row of such buttons down along the front of his coat. Like all other Indians, the Navajo are exceedingly fond of silver ornaments and other personal adornments and therefore take pride in displaying upon their person very beautiful silver necklaces, rings, ear-pendants, bracelets, belts, hatbands, and beads. Of beads, however, the most valued are cut turquoise, which are found in mines near Santa Fe. Santa Fe in their language is called *Yo-tgo*, that is, Bead Water. I was told they call it thus because a dry river flows through the city in which the Indians probably used to hunt for beads. Charlie Mitchell has a necklace of ground shells, turquoise, and other stones, which once belonged to the celebrated Navajo war chief Manuelito, and which is said to be worth about $150. Bows and arrows are no longer in use; boys sometimes use them yet to shoot prairie dogs. They have been displaced by six-shooters and winchesters. The once dreaded and deadly tomahawk has disappeared entirely, or rather has been buried long ago and never dug up again. But I am digressing too far, I see, so let us return to Charlie's stone house in Tsehili valley.

Navajo Cooking

It was the second morning of our stay at Tsehili; Friday, October 19, 1900, a bright, beautiful morning. The crimson, golden, and purple hues which had been playing about the pine tops and mountain peaks began to flit and to fade, and the sun's rays, like golden arrows, began to penetrate into our valley. Before the house—about 10 or 15 steps west—a crackling fire was already blazing up brightly. What time it was I don't know. Having forgotten to wind up my watch, it was not running, and Father Superior was not near enough at hand to be asked. Anyhow, Charlie's squaw and two or three squaws of visiting chiefs were sitting, or rather were squatted around the fire, busy with preparing breakfast. This is a good chance, I thought, to go and see them cook. So I went out and slowly approached the fire.

The chief cook was D'a-ha-ba, Charlie's squaw and lady of the house. She is a somewhat heavyset lady with very good-natured features; talks, jokes, and laughs very much, is very devoted to Charlie, and is extremely affectionate toward her baby, which she always keeps within reach. It was even there at the fire near her, wrapped and strapped up in its *ave-ts'al*, its Indian cradle.

These Indian cradles are quite different from the civilized pieces of furniture of that name. They have no rockers and consist of nothing else but a board or a frame interwoven with ropes or willows, just large enough for an infant to lie on. At the lower end is a small footboard and at the upper end a tiny round roof or canopy of bent laths. The child, wrapped in its little blanket, is placed on the board, or plaited bed, with its feet resting on the footboard and its head under the canopy, and strapped down so that it can move neither hand nor foot. On the upper end of this contrivance a band is attached, by which the whole concern may conveniently be hung up on a nail or limb, and which the mother places over her forehead when carrying the child so that it rests on her back and has plenty of chance and leisure to take in the surrounding sceneries and landscapes. Several times during the councils Mrs. Charlie came into the stone house, carrying this *ave-ts'al* and its little ruddy occupant in her arms. She never sat on a chair, however, but simply squatted right down on the floor at Charlie's side and listened with interest to the speeches until the little one got restive and gave unmistakable proofs of life, when she noiselessly left the room again. She also seems to be very cleanly and orderly in her habits and diligent at her work.

Beside her, at the fire, were sitting two more squaws. The name of one I haven't heard; the other was Yoa-qa'ta'l-'lin-bi-tsi, The Late Bead Chanter's Daughter, the wife of Naakai-Dinae-bidagha-nda's-tqelligi, The Mexican Navajo with the Black Mustache, one of the visiting chiefs whom I have mentioned already several times. Nearby, a few small boys were amusing themselves. One of them, a little lad of four or five years, whose entire suit consisted of nothing more than a little calico shirt imprinted with green flowers, was just flinging a piece of wood at a coyote-looking dog who when struck let off a series of penetrating war yells, pulled in his tail, lowered his head, and slunk limping from the scene, keeping a side glance on Little-shirt, till he disappeared behind the house.

In the fire on one side stood a steaming coffee pot, all black from smoke; on the other a frying pan, in which small pieces of mutton, *debé-bitsi*, were sizzling. The squaws were busy with the dough, which they were just rolling out into a long roll about three inches thick and perhaps two feet long. Of this roll they would squeeze off a chunk about as large as a good-sized fist. Then they would begin to knead and squeeze, to press and pat this chunk till it had the form of a cake about six inches in diameter and a little more than one-fourth-inch thick. This was then placed on a large, flat heated stone. While they were preparing the next cake, *na-nes-kad-de*, they watched the one on the hot stone and turned it over occasionally till it was sufficiently baked and showed brown spots. These *na-nes-kad-de* didn't taste bad either.

When the *esdsan*, the ladies, had finished their culinary preparations, and the meal being ready, Charlie came in, spread a piece of canvas over the table, placed three coffee cups and a shaving mug with teaspoons on it, brought in the coffee and cakes, and lastly the mutton in a large round dish, which he, with a large butcher knife, placed in the center of the table, and then invited us to breakfast, dinner, or supper, as the case may have been, excusing himself for the lack of dishes. Knives and forks were dispensed with. Each one took out his pocket knife, dug into the center dish, fished out his mutton, and did the rest with teeth and fingers. We enjoyed it so much, and had such good appetite, that with several cups of *coqye* many a *na-nes-kad-de* vanished, and of the *debé-bitsi* nothing remained but the bones, and they were ready to bleach.

As I have already mentioned, we had brought with us some flour, sugar, salt, crackers, and canned vegetables. Father Superior also bought a sheep at the place, for ourselves as well as especially for a treat to the visiting Indians. An Indian can eat any time of the day or night. In season or out of season, hungry or not hungry, he is ever blessed with a good, never-failing, insatiable appetite. Fill his stomach and his friendship, love, and confidence are yours. Hence the old saying: "The way to the Indian's heart goes through his stomach." He will eat almost anything, but there are some things upon which he draws his line, as the following anecdote will show.

Some time ago two young Navajo had been at Gallup, where they had a more or less glorious time. Toward evening, when they started for home, both had three sheets in the wind. Among other things they had bought some bread, butter, and other groceries, which were stowed away under the seat of their wagon. Indians are exceedingly fond of butter and will eat it by the spoonful. When they were well on their way, one of them felt as if he wanted to eat a good piece of butter bread. It was quite dark already then. He succeeded in finding the bread, and asked his brother to hand him the butter. Butter is not churned in these parts, but it is imported from other places and is put up and sold in round wooden boxes. His brother handed him the box; he put a good thick layer of butter on his bread and began to eat with a hearty appetite. After the first bite he asked: "What is the matter with the butter? It tastes awfully bitter and has a very queer smell!" The horses were stopped, a match was lighted, and then they found that instead of the box of butter, they had opened the box of—axle grease. This settled all eating for the balance of the way.

On that same morning, Friday, October 19, 1900, we had our third council with the headmen. The chief speaker on this occasion was Naat'ani Ts'ossi, Slender Chief. He is, indeed, very slender, but not tall, and like all—at least like most little men—of a pretty sanguine disposition. His features are regular, his movements quick, yet not hasty or abrupt, the expression of his face earnest when speaking. In all he makes the impression of a thoroughly sunburnt, mercurial little Switzer, who is bound to have his say. Outside of the council he is very social, likes to tell or hear a good joke or story, and laughs heartily and enjoys it. He had about the same to ask and to say as did Tsiish Bizhi the day before.

When his last question was answered to his satisfaction, he expressed himself much pleased with what he had heard, promised to do for our school whatever he could, and wound up with a hearty handshake. He had brought with him two boys—not his own—and, we are sure, will assist us in getting more when once we have a school.

On the same day another Indian arrived, who goes by the name of Old Billy. He is a brother of Tsiish Bizhi, or Braided Hair, and is of medium height but walks very stooped, although he is not very old. There was once a time when his figure was straight as an arrow, but severe attacks of rheumatism have contracted his muscles and bent his frame. There is a continual smile on Billy's face, and as he walked into the room with a somewhat drawn gait and stooped shoulders, a pair of leather gauntlet gloves and a quirt in his hand, a very slouchy slouch hat on his head held fast by a string, large silver rings dangling from his ears, a sunny smile for everyone present, one was inclined to think that he was not capable of harming a child, and yet our interpreter told us that he, some time ago, had shot and killed a medicine man, which, however, was done in pure self-defense, as the medicine man fired on him first.

I will relate the story of the shooting and killing according to the details given me by Frank Walker, our interpreter.

The Death of a Medicine Man

Billy's home is about six miles farther north from Charlie Tso's place. Besides Tsiish Bizhi, he has another brother. There was in the family also a sister, who, however, had died some years before, leaving a little girl in their care. The three brothers, who loved their sister very much, thought a great deal of their niece, and cared well for her. About three years ago the girl took sick, and a medicine man—the head medicine man of that region—was called in to perform his ceremonies over her and to banish the evil spirits.

The Navajo, like other Indians, do not believe that sicknesses are caused by organic disorders, but they believe them to be real entities, evil spirits. When a person takes sick, an evil spirit takes possession of him, and the indisposition, the pains, and other consequences of the sickness are to them nothing else but the manifestations of the evil spirit. Hence their strong belief and their great confidence in their medicine men. The medicine men, who are well paid for their services in sheep, horses, beads, and so on, and who are feasted at the expense of the sick person as long as their ceremonies last, foster this belief by every means in their power. For this reason they accompany their ceremonies with much show and noise: they dance around the sick man, sometimes wearing hideous masks, chant weird songs with peculiar melodies and isotonous cadences, shake rattles at him, administer potions of certain herbs, and so forth, so that if any evil spirits really had taken possession of the sick person, they surely would flee, and that quickly and far.

Others pretend to suck disease out of the patient and then draw from their own mouths pebbles, pieces of charcoal, tiny arrows, or bodies of insects, claiming that these are the diseases which they have extracted. There are, however, some who make use of various plants and herbs in the treatment of sicknesses, and these, in simple, acute cases, they administer without prayer, sacrifice, or incantation. But the greater part of the medicine men are cheats and charlatans who are making a good and easy living off the superstitious fears and beliefs of their fellow tribesmen.

The ceremonies of the medicine man whom Billy had engaged for his sick niece had no effect upon her condition; she seemed rather to become worse. When Billy noticed this he told the medicine man so, adding that he and his medicine were no good and he had better leave and stay away. Tsiish Bizhi, knowing his brother Billy's temper, and wishing to avoid trouble, warned the medicine man and also told him to leave. The medicine man then went, but having left his medicine bags and other paraphernalia at the house, he returned toward evening, armed with a winchester. Leaving the winchester outside, he entered the *goghan*. Billy and Tsiish Bizhi, having spent a few sleepless nights at the bedside of their sick niece, were very tired and worn out, and as the patient had begun to feel much better that day, they lay down to rest and sleep.

Meanwhile, the medicine man took some herbs, prepared a potion for the sick girl, and gave it to her. She immediately became worse, complained of pain and dryness in the throat and all over the body, and told her uncles that the medicine man had given her something. The medicine man then protested that that which he had given her was good medicine. However, toward morning the poor girl died. Billy then demanded of him directly to tell him what he had given her. The medicine man now became very insolent and left the *goghan*, followed by Billy. Outside they exchanged angry words and finally got into a scrap.

The medicine man drew his revolver and fired twice. Billy seized hold of the weapon; the first shot went into the air and the second shot burned Billy's hand. Now Tsi'ish Bizhi came rushing out to help his brother, but Billy told him to keep away; he would settle the rascal himself. The two grappled with each other, but the medicine man being the stronger soon threw Billy to the ground and fell on him. In the shuffle Billy got the revolver into his hand, shot twice, and crawled out from under his antagonist. The wounded man made some movements, when Billy gave him a third bullet, which put an end to all motion and life.

But let us return to Tsehili and take a look at the surrounding country. The country about Charlie's place is very picturesque, hills and valleys, mountains and forests form a panorama of fascinating interest. Going east from his house and ascending the hill, one is struck with surprise. A large plain, the end of which is lost in the depth of the forest, lies spread out before your wondering gaze. This plain is covered with large trees, mostly pines, some from 2½ to 3 feet in diameter, hundreds of feet high, and straight as a torch. The trees do not stand densely crowded, and as there is no underbrush, the forest assumes the aspect of a clean, well-kept deer park. Further east about three miles a beautiful mountain raises its rock-peak heavenward. The sides of this mountain ascend sloping upward several hundred feet; then there suddenly rises up a vast, solid, perpendicular rock, about one-third of the mountain's height. To look at it one cannot help but to admire it as it stands there in bold relief against the eastern sky, towering in silent, majestic grandeur over the surrounding country. When I first saw it, I thought and said to myself: "Surely there stands nature's altar, ready for a sacrifice to its Creator."

Navajo Theology and Father Anselm's Discourse

At the house I met that evening Mr. Henry Dodge, a Mexican half-breed, whom the Indians commonly call Chi, that is, Red. He belongs to the Jemez clan of the Navajo tribe and owns, in partnership with a Mr. Aldrich, of Gallup, a trading post about 30 miles from Charlie's place, near the center of the reservation. Chi is a special friend of Charlie and is by far the most intelligent and influential man in these parts, and perhaps throughout the whole Navajo tribe. He speaks Navajo perfectly and English well; his word has great weight with every Navajo, so that one might almost call him the uncrowned king of the Navajo. He has aided the missionaries greatly by his words and his influence in gaining the confidence of the Indians. He is a little above the middle height, of dark complexion, has jet black, bushy hair, an intelligent forehead, chin and jaws indicative of energy, and peculiarly bright and twinkling eyes.

The next morning Chi rode over to his trading store, and he returned to Tsehili toward evening. Tsish Chilli and Naakai Dinae, who had ridden over the mountains two days before in order to try and get us a few more boys for Santa Fe, had also returned; however, without result, as Charlie had been everywhere already for the same purpose. That evening, Saturday, October 20, 1900, after supper, when all were, as usual, assembled around the stove smoking, some sitting on chairs, others lying on sheep skins, the conversation turned upon the religious beliefs, traditions, and legends of the Navajo. On this field Charlie showed considerable knowledge.

Their Genesis begins with an emergence up through four successive worlds, until the surface of this, the fifth world, is reached. They have really no history of the Creation or of a Creator, but begin their legend with an already created world, filled with intelligent and speaking animals and beasts. When Charlie was asked how the first things came into existence he was ready with various explanations, but when the story of the chicken and the egg was sprung on him, when he was forced back to the very first chicken and asked who made it and how it came to be, he was at first a little at loss, but determined not to be balked he, with a desperate dash, such as his forefathers were wont to make when closed in by Apaches or Utes, or by Uncle Sam's Bluecoats, found a way out, saying it had been made by the morning's twilight.

However, they have a legend which tells of a First Man and a First Woman who came into existence in the fourth world by a special act of creation. They did not die like our first parents; they are still living in some form; they are immortal and divine and possess great power. And not only man has such an immortal, divine original prototype, but every animal in the world has the same, and most of these prototypes, if not all, are objects of veneration and worship. Sometimes this worship is even extended to their mortal descendants, as is the case with the bear and to a certain extent with the coyote. For this reason the bear and the coyote, and also other animals, play very important parts in their religious myths and legends, and to this day the bear, the coyote, and the rattlesnake are perfectly safe and secure in the Navajo country, as far as the Indian is concerned.

They have a great number of gods, for example, a sun god, a water god, *yei* or genii, war gods, alien gods, and many other individual gods. Besides these there are local gods by the score; mountains, rocks, lakes, rivers, creeks, springs, and cañons have their gods or genii, with prayers and sacrifices, legends and myths. They see the power of their gods in the wind and rain, in the storm and snow, in the clouds and sunshine, in the thunder and lightning. The number of local gods is so large that Dr. Washington Matthews says a complete list of them will probably never be obtained. One peculiarity of their mythology is that they have no supreme god, none who is at the head of their legion and who has any authority over the others. Their gods stand much on a level of equality, just like their men, who acknowledge no highest or head chief. The chiefs that are, possess but a temporary and ill-defined power and influence, which depends largely upon their personal merit, oratory, or reputation for wisdom.

Among the gods, the alien or stranger gods are inimical to man. They are, one may say, the counterpart of the giants and ogres in ancient European mythologies: Besides these there are a host of evil spirits haunting the earth, which men must fear and dread. These they call *chi'ndi*, which word may be rendered in English by "devils."

Such and other things, interspersed with myths and legends, were spoken of by the Indians, Chi doing the interpreting. When Charlie and his colleague were finished with their Navajo wisdom, Chi went to one corner of the room and, lying down on a few sheep skins, he said to us: "You have now heard what they say; they would like to hear what you have to say." Then Father Superior began and told them in plain, simple, and clear language the history of Creation, of the fall of our first parents, and of the necessity of a Divine Redeemer; of the birth, life, miracles, suffering, and death of Christ the Redeemer; of His resurrection, the founding of His church, and His ascension into heaven; of His coming again at the end of the world, the resurrection of the dead; of judgment, the reward of the good and punishment of the wicked; of the descent of the Holy Ghost, and the beginning of our Holy Church, with a short extract of the history of the Church and of heresies; of the civilizing influence of Christianity upon the once barbarous nations of Europe, and upon the savage Indian tribes of California and Paraguay, and so on.

At first Mr. Frank Walker did the interpreting, but soon Chi got interested, and when Frank asked him to take his place he was at once more than willing. The further the narrative progressed the more interested was Chi; he warmed up more and more as one sacred truth was evolved from the other, until his whole mind seemed to be thinking of nothing else and living in that which he heard. Finally, when the talk was running about the resurrection and ascension of Christ; about the resurrection of the dead and judgment, he leaped to his feet and, standing out on midfloor, his face beaming and eyes sparkling, accompanying his glowing words with at once energetic, yet exceedingly graceful gestures, he rendered those parts in flowing Navajo in a manner which would have done credit to any born orator of many years' training and practice.

Of his audience some were smoking their cigarettes, and listening attentively; others were resting their chins on the palms of their hands with their eyes riveted on Chi's lips; others were sitting with their elbows on their knees and their eyes bent thoughtfully upon the floor. Frequently the flow of Chi's speech was interrupted by exclamations of "*ou*," that is, "yes," or by an assenting grunt. After the talk was over they expressed their satisfaction, adding that they liked very much to hear such things. As it had become very late by this time, the assembly soon disbanded and retired, they to their blankets and sheepskins, and we to our old spring mattress, praying to God to bless the seed which had been cast into their pagan hearts with His grace, so that the wilds and wastes of the Navajo country may become white harvest fields for His earthly kingdom, the Church, as well as for His eternal kingdom of heaven.

The next morning, Sunday, October 21, 1900, the names of the boys who were to go to Santa Fe, with those of their parents, were taken down on paper to be handed over to the agent at Fort Defiance, for such are the instructions of our government at Washington. Following are the names in Navajo, with the Christian names of the boys in parentheses: 1) Hashke yitadasghut (Stephan); 2) Azhun (James); These two are sons of Qastqin Baibi-tsilli and were brought to us by Naat'ani Ts'ossi; 3) Nein'l-inni (Paul), son of Tsiish Bizhi and Dsi'l k'iji qa'ta'lin-ni bitsi; 4) Choi (Joseph), son of Sa'li and Sanni, and nephew of Tsiish Bizhi; 5) Tgolli (Willie); 6) Dine Ts'ossi (Charlev), son of Naakai Dinae bidagha ndastgeligi and Yoa-qa'ta'l-'lin bi-tsi; and 7) Foley Yazhe (John), son of John Foley.

About noon we left Tsehili and set out upon our return trip homeward. But before leaving Tsehili I must tell the readers how Charlie Tso came to the name of Charlie Mitchell.

How Charlie Tso Became Charlie Mitchell

Back in the early 1880s, when Charlie Mitchell, the English champion of the prize ring, was at his best and highest, a certain Mr. N. [probably Father Leopold here refers to trader Frank Noel] opened up a trading post among the Navajo Indians. In those days a *belagana*, or an American, was an abomination in the eyes of a Navajo, and it was not the safest thing to meet him in his own country. Consequently the said Mr. N. had many annoyances to suffer at the hands of his intended red customers. Charlie Tso was for peace, and he did all he could in the way of talking and persuading to induce his fellow tribesmen to preserve the peace. He tried to make them believe that the white man was their friend, that he had not come to harm or defraud them or to take their land from them; that it was a great advantage to them to have a store near at hand, where they could purchase many things which they had not, and which they needed.

But he spoke to deaf ears; they would not listen to him, nor believe him. One day a crowd of Navajo was in the store, and they proceeded to inaugurate a wild-woolly-west scene. After having intimidated the storekeeper, they began to play pandemonium, upsetting things and knocking them into splinters and smithereens. At this juncture Charlie Tso entered. Taking in at a glance what was going on, seeing how all his words and advice were disregarded, his ire rose up to the boiling point. Seizing an ax handle, he was with one leap in the midst of his fellow vandals, laying about right and left in right good Navajo style, and in less time than it takes to tell it, the store was cleared and as quiet as along the Potomac at midnight. Later on when the rescued trader used to tell this story, he invariably wound up by saying: "That fellow is a regular Charlie Mitchell." Ever since, the name of the English champion of pugilism has clung to him, and to the end of his days he will remain Charlie Mitchell, and his children will bear the family name of Mitchell.

Return to St. Michaels

So much for that. It is now time to leave beautiful Tsehili and its hospitable denizens. Our team is hitched up and the broncos of the Indians are saddled. The hard bed of the wagon has been made somewhat comfortable—as far as that word goes in these parts—by the canvas cover of a tent and a few Navajo blankets. The seven little redskins are lifted into the wagon, and we consult as to the best road home. We agree to stop at the trading post of Mr. J. B. Moore, about 25 miles from Tsehili. Having agreed upon this, Father Superior thought it advisable to ride ahead on horseback to notify Mr. Moore of our coming, as it probably would be well toward evening when the large wagon would arrive there. Naat'ani Ts'ossi offered him his horse and volunteered to drive the team, as my own geography, topography, and points of compass were all in a Gordian knot. Father Superior accepted this offer, and with him all the visiting Indians, squaws and all, mounted their broncos or their donkeys and were off. I climbed up on the seat with Slender Chief, and off moved our Studebaker, too, with seven bright, smiling faces in its boxy bed.

Naat'ani Ts'ossi, knowing every foot of the country as well as I knew my own pockets, did not follow the road but made many a shortcut over rough fields and plains grown over sparsely with sage bushes. At one place where the road was exceptionally bumpy, the iron pins which held our seat in position were lifted out of their sockets, and I went sprawling in the most undignified manner back into the wagon bed among the little reddies, who enjoyed this involuntary maneuver very much, with the exception of one, who was rubbing the top of his scalp and making a face like a jug of vinegar. As Naat'ani Ts'ossi could speak no English, and I no Navajo, I tried at least to improve the time with learning a few Navajo words from him and in telling him their signification in English. At one place he pointed out to me a prairie dog, pronouncing the word "*dlo*." I pronounced it after him several times, and when he was satisfied, he asked: "*Qaat'ish oliyé belagana bi-zad?*" "What is it called in the American (English) language?" He tried very hard to say prairie dog, but the nearest he got was pway-wee-dog. The Navajo language has no r (f, p, th, v, and x are also wanting).

We arrived at Moore's between 4:00 and 5:00 p.m. Mr. Moore was not at home but visiting his cattle ranch in Colorado. We were, however, very kindly and hospitably received by Mrs. Moore and Mr. John Foley, who was employed at the store. If we had any misgivings as to being welcome with our train of about 20 Indians, such misgivings were soon dispelled. Mr. Moore has built near his store a roomy *goghan*; this and another room Mrs. Moore cheerfully left to the Indians, gave them a sack of flour, some coffee and sugar, leaving the cooking and baking to the Navajo squaws, which they are but too glad to do so long as they have anything to cook or to bake. After supper Father Superior bought new pants, shirts, and hats for the boys; for although their Navajo attire was by no means *reductio ad absurdum*, yet the boys were not exactly fit to be taken into civilized society bedizened with it.

After having spent almost five days with the Navajo in Navajo style, we were glad to enjoy once again civilized company, table, and bed. We had all reason to feel most grateful to Mrs. Moore, who treated us, indeed, very nobly. She not only let us have the boys' clothing at cost price, but also refused absolutely to accept of any recompense for our own board and lodging or for that of the Indians. In point of hospitality the wild, woolly West can serve as an example for the selfish, enlightened East.

The next morning about 8:00 Father Superior started off on horseback for Fort Defiance in order to present the names of the boys to the agent. He was accompanied by Charlie Tso, Tsiish Bizhi, and two other Indians. The rest of the Indians left again for their homes after they had taken leave of the children. This done, our lumbering ambulance was once more moving, about a half hour later, on the road toward St. Michael's Mission, about 35 miles. The road from Moore's to the mission is a very good road, mostly a little downgrade with no hills of any size to climb. The greatest part leads through the same valley through which we went up six days ago. We again pass Bosco Redondo, a huge round forest-crowned rock, Black Mountain, Red Lake, Black Rock, and so forth, already mentioned. About seven miles north of the mission it passes about one mile east of Fort Defiance. Mr. Frank Walker, our interpreter, acted as driver on the home stretch. The boys were beaming with joy at the good long ride, and teeming with life and mirth. They were having "lots of fun" all along the road. The little fellow with the calico shirt, of whom I have already made mention, was the clown of the crowd. He kept his companions in the best and merriest humor all the way. But pants was too much civilization for him at one time; the transition was too sudden, so he simply pulled them off until we got near the mission.

The next day Father Superior took them to Gallup, New Mexico. When they were about halfway between St. Michaels and Gallup, while they were stopping to take a lunch and to rest the horses, a messenger drew up and told them that two of the boys had been enrolled as government scholars in the Defiance school; consequently, we could not take them away. Of this fact we had been totally ignorant. The zealous, quick-witted superintendent of the government school had made this momentous and most important discovery at 10:00 a.m., October 22, 1900; and as the agent is supposed to be responsible before God and his country for such children, he (the superintendent) sent a messenger posthaste after them to rescue them from the clutches of Romanism and, perhaps, of several other Rs.

Father Superior had to turn the two boys over to him, although they had not visited the school at the Fort during the last year, and although the boys and the other Indians who were present protested emphatically against such proceedings. For such is the import of the infamous Browning Ruling of September 30, 1896, the pith of which is that "Indian parents have no right to determine which schools their children shall visit." This abortive excrescence of some narrow-minded head, with a brain overheated with bigotry, has been made a law in this "land of the free and home of the brave"; made a law by men who on a Fourth of July will mount a dry goods box, or a plank scaffold, and tell their audience, with much squirming, writhing, and wriggling, that this country has fought and bled for a constitution that grants to every human being, born or unborn, political and religious freedom and liberty; that this country is chosen by Providence to spread this political and religious liberty over the saddened face of this enthralled planet of ours, even as soothing butter is spread over the hot toast. Happily this inky blotch upon the Constitution of the United States has been removed a few months ago by a repeal of the said rank, rotten, rancid ruling.

The older one of the two boys soon left the school without leave, and returned to the wilds and wastes of his country. The smaller one is, perhaps, still there, and the other five have been taken to Santa Fe, where they will remain until a school is erected at the mission.

Notes

1. From Leopold Ostermann, FWW 8 (February–May 1901): 298–301, 327–30, 366–69, 401–4; 9 (June, August–September 1901): 10–12, 80–83, 118–21.

2. Robert L. Wilken, *Anselm Weber, O.F.M.: Missionary to the Navaho, 1989–1921* (Milwaukee, Wisc.: Bruce, 1955), 57–58.

3. Juvenal Schnorbus et al., "History of the Ranch, about Seven Miles South of Fort Defiance (Cienega) Arizona, Now St. Michael's Missions," FAC Box PLA.376 St. Michael's, env. St. Michael's Earliest History 1898–1907, 19.

4. Anselm Weber, "The Sisters of Blessed Sacrament for Indians and Colored People," *St. Anthony's Messenger* 8 (January 1901): 262–68.

5. Daniel Hurley, "*St. Anthony Messenger*: 100 Years of Good News," *St. Anthony Messenger* 100 (June 1992): 12–13.

7

Fall 1900: Students to Santa Fe, Headmen to Cienega[1]

Anselm Weber, O.F.M.

[Father Leopold closed the previous chapter with the statement that five Navajo boys had been taken to Santa Fe to attend school. Father Anselm, accompanied by three Navajo headmen, personally delivered the boys to the Sisters at St. Catherine's School. There they were pleasantly surprised to find Mother Katharine Drexel and her cousin Josephine Whorton who, traveling incognito, were visiting the Southwest. Father Anselm had learned that the Mountain Chant, one of the most important Navajo ceremonies, was soon to be performed in the vicinity of St. Michael's Mission. Knowing that headmen from all over the reservation would be in attendance, and wishing to take advantage of this opportunity for Mother Katharine to meet and address them, he invited the visiting Sisters to come to mission on the day of the dance. They came, and when the Navajo dances were over, the headmen and many others gathered at the mission for a historic exchange with "Reverend Sister Mary," who spoke on behalf of Mother Katharine.

Father Anselm's report of these events to his *Sendbote* readers is richly detailed, from his account of the Navajo inspecting the Santa Fe school—"three real Navajo headmen in the different classrooms"—to his reaction to Mother Katharine's effort to teach Indian boys to throw rocks at a tin can: "Women can't throw at all, and especially such a millionaire child!" An incident at the dance reveals that even at this early date he has great personal authority with the Navajo. He is one of a handful of whites amid hundreds of Navajo, a mere observer. Yet when the "excessive enjoyment" of "dark water" leads to a fight and one of the protagonists draws a revolver, it is Father Anselm who steps into "a whole throng of wrestling, fighting Indians" and confiscates the firearm. His description of the dance itself is a historical treasure, and his careful management of the subsequent meeting of headmen with Mother Katharine at St. Michaels is a case study in strategic information control. Here are exhibited some of the skills that would serve Father Anselm, and the Navajo, so well in his future efforts as mediator and advocate.]

❖

In Santa Fe a very pleasing surprise was waiting for me. The Reverend Sister Mary [Mother Katharine Drexel, traveling incognito to avoid publicity], who by the way is much better known by her two other names, had arrived in Santa Fe just before with her wealthy, generous niece from New York, who is traveling under the name Ms. Warden [Josephine Whorton]. They intended to visit our mission with the headmistress of the school in Santa Fe, the Reverend Mother Evangelist, to inspect it, to designate the building site for the school to be established, and so on. When I heard this, I soon developed a plan for a campaign to recruit Navajo for the future school. In about one week the biggest Indian dance that the Navajo know was supposed to take place 25 miles from our mission. I knew that influential headmen from all corners of the reservation would gather there. Therefore, I made the recommendation that the Reverend Sisters and Ms. Warden should arrange it so that they arrived on the day of this dance at our mission. I would then attend this dance and try, with the help of Big Charlie [Mitchell], Henry Dodge, and Frank Walker, to arrange for the assemblage of headmen to visit our mission on the following day to discuss questions about the school with us and the Reverend Sisters and to reach a mutual agreement. Good meals and food for their horses would be adequately provided for. The Reverend Sisters directly agreed with this recommendation. Big Charlie and Henry Dodge also declared themselves ready to use their entire influence with their fellow Navajo in this matter.

We stayed for two days in Santa Fe, mostly to give Henry Dodge and Tsiischbischi [Braided Hair] the opportunity to become familiar through their own observations with the successful activities of the Sisters and the whole setup of this outstanding school, down to the smallest details. It was most likely an unusual sight for the Sisters as well as the Indian children—three real Navajo headmen in the different classrooms, following the proceedings with interest. Actually, Henry Dodge was the only one who could really evaluate the children's accomplishments. Their tests in reading and writing, in music and song, especially in mathematics, far surpassed his expectations. We also got the chance to admire their accomplishments in mechanics.

While we observed the lessons, the head Mother brought a man with his son to us and said she was afraid she was being deceived by this man. He spoke Spanish, was probably a Mexican, but claimed to be a Navajo Indian and wanted to enroll his son in the school under this pretext. Such cases are not really rare. In fact, the man didn't even look like an Indian. However, when Henry Dodge spoke to him in Navajo, he answered him in fluent Navajo. As a young boy, he was taken from the Ute Indians and sold to a Mexican. He stayed with him and later married a Mexican.

The young, wild, Navajo boys had not yet come to the realization that they should remain calm in the school. Little six-year-old John Foley, a half-blood Indian, was humming a loud Navajo song, and when the sister reprimanded him he threw his slate pencil at her face. He had good aim—a talent which he probably inherited from his father, who is recognized as the best shot in Arizona and New Mexico. The seed doesn't fall far from the tree!

The son of Tsiischbischi, whom I mentioned in my last letter—I gave the boy the name Paul—showed such high spirits during our trip but in the enclosed school got very homesick for the open air of the Lukachukai mountains and wouldn't stop crying. To help him think of other things, the Reverend Sister Mary took the Navajo boys out of the school, brought them to an open, sandy place, set up an old metal can as a goal, and began to throw toward it. But oh my goodness, what a throw! Women can't throw at all, and especially such a millionaire child! But the young Indians joined in the sport with excitement, and the poor can was bombarded from all sides. Even little Paul forgot his homesickness and turned out to be *facile princeps* of the arena.

The next day I took the young bunch out, and with much effort I succeeded in driving the melancholy out of the little one. He asked me in which direction Gallup lay, how far it was to there, when he could go home again, and so forth. The questions allowed me to glimpse his sly intentions, as a result of which I warned the Sisters to keep a watchful eye on him so that he didn't take a French leave. When we were ready to depart, the little one began to cry bitterly. His father, however, contained himself and had him led away before we took off. Probably very few would have had enough courage to separate from their children under such circumstances. After we were under way, the little one threw himself on the ground and cried out with the pain of being separated from his father. But what did he want to do? Then the doors were closed and the Reverend Sister Mary stood at the window, seeking to soothe him in her gentle manner. The fit actually only lasted about 15 minutes. Since then he has shown no trace of homesickness. The Reverend Mother wrote me shortly that he is handling himself very well, is a very lively boy, and is making good progress in his learning.

It was easy to see that the separation had likewise affected his father. Clouded and somber, he sat on the train with a sinister countenance, brooding, and couldn't be induced to talk or to eat. I tried to comfort him—in vain! Then Henry Dodge came to my aid. He said he couldn't watch this anymore. He told me to go sit with Big Charlie and send Tsiischbischi back to him. No sooner had Tsiischbischi sat down beside him when all the conversation on the train went quiet, and all eyes turned to the last bench in the train where the unique Navajo lute was playing with such power that someone at the other end of the train could differentiate each note. Even four politicians, Republicans and Democrats, who had been arguing contentedly with the greatest enthusiasm over gold and silver, the Philippines and sheep herding, boodle and election fraud forgot for a few moments their earth-shattering issues. But all of this didn't bother our Henry Dodge in the least. With true Indian imperturbability, he spoke to the poor Tsiischbischi with great power, as if he had a whole regiment of recruits before him.

What did he say to him? He asked what had actually caused him to be so overcome with grief. Who was he actually angry with? Me? The Sisters? Himself? Hadn't he made this decision himself after much reflection? Tsischbischi couldn't hold out against such big guns for long and soon regained his earlier open, cheerful self again.

No less than Henry Dodge, the imposing figure of Charlie Mitchell aroused the attention and curiosity of all the passengers. One asked me what kind of an Indian that was; whether he was a chief; whether he was perhaps returning from a trip to Washington, and so forth. In complete American clothing, with a long overcoat and studious glasses, one could have thought he was a paleface, if his dark skin color and especially his long, black hair and his expensive shell and turquoise necklaces had not clearly exposed him as an Indian.

As we arrived in Albuquerque that evening, where the train remained for over an hour, I led Big Charlie and Tsiischbischi through the marketplace of the city. Right at the beginning we passed a branch of the Salvation Army in full activity. The Indians were more than a little surprised about this "army" and could hardly believe that these were American men and women. They thought they were Mormons or something similar. After that I took them into several shops, where I had to make a few small purchases. In the last one, two young men were very interested in my two companions. They especially admired Charlie's necklaces, mentioned before, and were quite amazed when in answer to my question he told them they had cost him $160. The young men then gave each of the Indians a cigar. When Tsiischbischi, who had never before smoked a real stogie, tried to light his, he had no success. He didn't realize that you had to bite off the tip first, for which he was laughed at heartily by the young men. When I remarked that these Indians only smoked cigarettes, the young men gave them each a pouch of tobacco and cigarette papers.

Returning home, my first worry was to find out when the big Indian dance would take place. Since this was going to be very soon, I had to return immediately to Gallup and telegraph the Reverend Sisters. They arrived in Gallup on the last of October. Around noon we left Gallup and reached the mission around 5:00 p.m. Even though we were all a bit tired from the long journey of 30 miles, we made plans right away to go to Red Lake, 25 miles from here, where the great Indian dance was to take place that very evening at 9:00. The Reverend Sisters, however, didn't come to the dance.

If some of my esteemed readers have found this letter somewhat less than interesting, I promise to more than make up for it in the following articles about the Indian dance.

In closing, I must mention that many of our poor Navajo have very little to get them through the winter even until the next harvest. All of last winter we had the most beautiful fall weather—without snow and without rain. The result of this unusual drought is that their harvest failed completely. Already—I'm writing this on February 17—they have pawned off all of their few belongings and jewelry to get food. How many of them, especially those who don't have sheep or goat herds, will manage to survive until the next harvest is a mystery to us. Because of this we will be having many more demands than usual for support in the form of food and clothing, and I must confess that we, with trust in God and the generosity of our valued readers, have already gone further in this than our limited means allow. It is very hard to turn away the truly needy, especially children, whose hunger you can read in their faces, as long as there is still anything edible in the house.

To those who, in their noble generosity, have supported our mission thus far, we express our heartfelt thanks in our name and in the name of our thankful Navajo. May God bless you a hundredfold.

An Evening at the Dance

In keeping with my promise, I must try to describe an Indian dance this time, even if it is only an attempt and the description naturally falls short of the reality. "Indian dance?" Of course one should use discretion with regard to the way the whites see things, where all similar performances are labeled dances. For them, the dance is most likely the essential part—not so for the Navajo, who call such performances *chatcha'l*, or songs. If I were free to create a name, I would choose the words "evening entertainment." The "dance" which shall be the topic of this article, by far the most interesting the Navajo have, has the name *dsi'l k'idschi chatcha'l*, or song on a mountain [Mountain Chant or Mountainway]. This dance may only be performed in the winter, when the thunder is silent and the rattlesnakes are hibernating. If the Navajo were to talk about their chief gods at any other time or speak of their sayings from olden times and worship the gods with song, they would, in their opinion, be prematurely struck down by lightning or killed by the bite of a rattlesnake.

This dance is performed to heal a sickness, to call on the gods for a good harvest and abundant rain, as a graphic representation of their religious sayings, and to pass on their religious symbolism. All of this applies even more to the nine-day secret ceremonies in the so-called medicine lodge, which take place regularly before the open "evening entertainment." The main goal of the latter, which is open to all, is most certainly conversation and entertainment. Even the person who organizes the ceremonies and dances and argues over the expenses usually has the purpose of distinguishing himself with his clan and making a name for himself, because his (or her) sickness which needs healing is mostly only imagination.

I will spare my readers from a description of the nine-day ceremonies, which are not unfamiliar to me, with their truly beautiful sand mosaics, their extensive symbolism, and the myths and sayings founded upon it, because for most of you this would be extremely boring. Let us rather begin by visiting the actual entertainment. At 6:00 in the evening, Father Leopold, our interpreter, our neighbor Mrs. Wyant, and Miss Warden, our associate, mounted their horses and departed. Father Berard and our dreaded medicine man, "the little bean shooter," who found himself in open custody of us, completed the party on horseback. A half-hour later, I mounted my good Swallow, who honored his name on this evening by carrying me the 25 miles, partly against my will, in two and one-half hours.

When I was still about 10 miles from my destination, I could already glimpse the mighty fire where the dance would take place. Coming nearer, I saw a large ring of piñon wood by which the flaming bonfire was enclosed. The enclosure was about eight feet high. The ring, meant to encircle the observers, measured 40 feet in diameter, with an opening, an entrance, in the east. Just after sunset, a medicine man sat himself east of the huge woodpile where the entrance was and began to sing and to rattle. Everyone seized this opportunity and built the ring with the nearby piñon wood. It was finished in about an hour, and the exhausted medicine man stopped his singing and rattling.

Within the ring, small fires were lit all around, and the Indians—men, women, and children—were camped around them in utter confusion. Woe to the dog who strays into the ring! Horses and other animals are likewise denied entrance. Also, no one is allowed to watch the dance over the enclosure from outside or through the holes; this part of the auditorium is appointed for the ghosts of the bears and other animal gods. At the west end of the ring the song choir and the "orchestra" are stationed.

What is the orchestra made up of? To begin with, [it is made up] of eight musicians, who sat around a holy basket, holding a serrated piece of wood, with one end resting on the basket, and going rhythmically back and forth over the notches with another piece of wood in their right hand. Next to a second inside-out basket sat a Navajo who used this basket like a drum. The others swung their rattles, which were made from a gourd covered with buffalo skin and sewed together with deer sinew. The handles were formed like the end of a buffalo tail. The sound is caused by the valuable turquoise stone found in the rattles. Almost without interruption, song and music continue until daybreak.

As I arrived and entered the enclosure, the first dance, called *Naigahi*, was in full swing. Thirteen figures, slender, supple, and flexible, wearing only white loincloths and moccasins, their whole bodies covered with white clay so that they looked like a group of marble statues, circled the mighty, flaming woodpile, first stepping, then hopping and jumping, now imitating the cry of a jackal, then again letting out other unnatural sounds. Now turning here, now there, small, graceful, swinging rods with tufts of eagle down at the farthest ends, they assumed first a graceful pose, then a forced and unnatural one, then a threatening demeanor. After they had thus crossed the fire several times, they began to thrust their rods against it, and we soon remarked that they were trying to light on fire the tufts of down fastened to the ends of their rods. But because of the intense heat, it was almost impossible for them to get close enough to the fire. One rushed wildly toward the fire but pulled back just as quickly from the fearful glow. Another laid himself on the ground like a scared lizard and tried to wriggle to the fire. Others tried to catch the showering sparks to set the feathers on fire. One moved close to the glowing mass, threw himself suddenly onto his back and thrust his rod in the flames. After many unsuccessful attempts, one of them finally succeeded in sticking the down into the fire and lighting it.

As soon as one succeeded in lighting the tuft, he swung it up and down, at a full run, and the tuft returned to its original state. Triumphantly, he raised his rod, brandished it in the air, and gave an exultant cry. Then he rushed in wild leaps to the exit and immediately disappeared into the medicine lodge outside of the enclosure.

But how was it possible that the feather tuft reappeared after it had been burned? Well, the rod of sumac, approximately three feet long, was all sewn together so that it was only one-half inch thick, except at the upper end where the tuft was attached. This end, this knob, was about an inch thick. On the other end of the rod was a ring which was hollowed so that it could easily be slipped up to the knob on the other end. Another tuft of down was fastened onto this ring that couldn't be seen because the dancer held this end, including the ring with the down, in his hand. As soon as the tuft on the other end was burned, he swung the rod downward, let the ring with the second tuft slip upward to the knob at the other end, swung the rod up high again, and held it there brandishing it in circles to keep the ring with the feathers from sliding back down to his hand. All of this took place with such skill and with such speed that one couldn't detect the actual course of events.

After a long pause, a loud whistle rang out from the medicine lodge, from a pipe made out of eagle leg. At the same time, two large, muscular figures appeared. Their bodies were covered with white clay, their forearms and legs painted black with white zigzag stripes representing lightning, and around their loins each wore a silver belt and a wide, red loincloth. They had three eagle feathers on their heads, and on each arm a tuft of eagle feathers fastened together with deer sinew. Each dancer held an arrow in his hand. While they marched several times around the flaming fire, a buffalo skin was spread out on the west side in front of the orchestra, and the sick person who had organized the dance was brought there. After he took his place sitting on the skin, both dancers planted themselves in front of him. Each gripped his arrow about eight inches from the tip, between the pointer finger and the thumb, held it high and gave a coyote-like cry, as if to say: "I will swallow the arrow this far." Then each appeared to force the arrow slowly and painfully eight inches down into his throat. With the arrows apparently in their throats, the dancers, each holding his arrow with both hands, executed a dance to the left and right in short, extremely rapid steps, so well done as to create the impression that they were suffering unspeakable pain. Then they pulled the arrows out of their throats and held them high as before with a triumphant cry, as if to say: "We swallowed them this far!"

After this, each after the other went to the patient on the buffalo skin, and held the arrow to his feet, knees, hands, shoulders, back, head, and mouth, each time imitating the cry of a coyote. Each danced one more time around the fire and left the enclosure.

Swallowing the arrows was very easy, by the way. The arrow was made out of two parts: one with the stony point made of hard wood, the other, completely covered with eagle feathers, was made of the hollow stalk of a sunflower. To swallow, the Indian took the stony arrow head firmly between his teeth and pulled the hollow stalk covered with feathers toward him, so that the actual arrow shaft disappeared up to the arrow head in the hollow stalk instead of into his throat. The deception, by the way, was perfect.

There followed a long pause. We had spread out our blankets on the north side of the circle next to a campfire and had made ourselves very comfortable there, as the Indians do. As we busied ourselves heating our coffee on the campfire and consuming our modest lunch, as were most of the Indians, some could not resist the temptation for something "stronger." The liquor was horribly expensive—from 75 cents per sip, and from $2.50 up to $5.00 per bottle. Where was the agent, with his white assistants, whose presence at such events was especially desired? Probably between the sheets. Although he had some of his Indian police there, I think the *tchodi'lchi'l*, or dark water, tasted just as good or in some cases even better to them than to the less civilized Indians. In any case it was not the Indian police but the "wild" Indian headmen who gave practical admonitions against drinking during the pause. As a result of excessive enjoyment of the liquor, a fight finally broke out between a powerful full-blood and a slight, but contentious and sly, half-blood Indian. I saw that as the Navajo drew his revolver, the brother of the one threatened grabbed his arm and held it tight, as a whole throng of wrestling, fighting Indians formed around the three. In order, if possible, to avoid an accident, I went quickly into the middle of them and in the blink of an eye the dangerous gun disappeared into my coat pocket.

It was now not quite midnight. The different dances and entertainments would continue until dawn. From the medicine lodge a shrill whistle announced the beginning of the third dance. Immediately a line of about 20 dancers came through the opening in the enclosure and danced around the burning logs. At the head of this dance procession was a Navajo in traditional clothing, who swung the so-called *tsin di'ni*, or lamentation stick, to drive away or keep away the devil. This is a thin, flat board sewed together on one end, painted black, and sprinkled with hematite. The lamentation stick can only be made out of spruce that has been struck by lightening. The stick was about ten inches long and two inches wide, with a two-foot-long tail fastened to it, by which it was swung about in circles. Three small turquoise stones were set in the wood to represent eyes and a mouth.

The leader was followed by *Chaaskiddi*, or the hunchback, dressed in traditional clothing with silver necklaces and a silver belt, completely masked, having a sheep skin on his back with several eagle feathers forming a half circle attached to it. Next came the two head dancers, *alil fahi*, called "slender performers," sparsely clothed and heavily painted; following were the rest of the dancers in traditional clothing with piñon branches in their hands. Singing a somewhat monotone but very powerful melody, they danced energetically around the bonfire. Now in a circle, now stopping and turning to the fire, they danced back and forth, swinging the branches into the fire, and by the glow of the flame making their bows. After they had danced around the fire several times like this, they joined the orchestra on the west end of the enclosure, where they sat down to help the choir with their songs for the next dance.

Only the two head dancers, "slender performers," stayed between the fire and the orchestra, standing about ten steps apart. Their thin, muscular bodies were colorfully painted; their heads and arms were adorned with eagle feathers, their necks with real coral. They wore scarves of red silk and silver belts around their loins, lovely moccasins on their feet, and held in their hands thin pipes decorated with feathers. Their profiles reminded one of the frame of a paper kite. They stood across from each other, ready to start the dance.

At the given sign the orchestra started to play, the choir to sing, the rattlers to rattle, the leader to swing his lamentation stick, and the two dancers to dance. In complete harmony with the music and song, the dancers performed an extraordinarily elegant dance, a series of wonderful dance forms and evolutions. First forward, then backward, now across from each other, then next to each other again, they danced in short, powerful, shuffling steps, often changing places, the decorated pipes swinging rhythmically until finally, side by side, with powerful, elegant hops, the dancers stomped out of the enclosure. Soon they came hopping in again in the same manner and performed the same dance in a somewhat altered fashion for the second and third times. This dance is so peculiar, demanding such flexibility and elasticity of the muscles, that it is likely that only the strongest, most muscular, as well as most limber, Indians could perform it to such perfection.

Later, three other Indians were the main dancers. Adorned much like the two "slender performers" but fully masked, their bodies covered with white clay, their dances were no less diverse and beautiful than those of their predecessors. Three times they appeared in the enclosure and, with the music and song, put their accomplished art to the test. The dance around the huge fire, described above, in which a large number of Navajo in traditional clothing take part, also was repeated often.

Between the different dances a few illusion tricks were performed. The first consisted of a feather in a basket performing a lively dance, apparently without any assistance from the surrounding Navajo. Later I saw how several medicine men tried to make a number of eagle feathers float into the air with the magic words, "*Dohi, dohi!*" ("Up, up!"). The medicine men had built an enclosure around themselves to hide their doings from observers. I and a few others, however, didn't pay any attention to this circle and entered it. So I saw how the medicine men were trying to fasten the feathers to a tightly stretched string held by two Navajo. Despite their "*Dohi, dohi!*" the feathers fell from the string to the ground again and again. The Navajo from whom, with the help of big Charlie, I had wrested a dangerous six-shooter shortly before, and who seemed to be in quite high spirits, proposed openly that I might be more of a sorcerer than the medicine men, and he called to me, "*Ednishodi bifischtschilligi: Dohi, dohi, dohi!*" which caused more than a little amusement among the bystanders. However, even without my assistance the medicine men finally succeeded in fastening all the feathers to the string, whereby the two Navajo with the "floating" feathers between them solemnly exited the enclosure.

At the end the most interesting dance, the actual fire dance, was supposed to follow; but sadly it was omitted this time. I have, however, spoken with many who have observed the fire dance and can, therefore, give the assurance that the following description of the dance from the honorable Washington Matthews (who served as army doctor for 15 years at Fort Wingate) is absolutely not exaggerated. He writes:

The fire dance or fire play was the most picturesque, striking, and interesting of all the dances. At times, before the dancers entered, you could hear peculiar tones mixed with the ringing of the buffalo horns, similar to the cry of a sand crane. These tones grew louder and came nearer and nearer until they were heard at the eastern entrance. Just then ten men, with no more clothing than the dancers in the first dance, came into the circle. All of them, with the exception of the leaders, carried in each hand a torch made of the fibers of cedar bark, and one carried two extra torches for the later use of the leaders. The last also carried four small bunches of the same material in his hands. Four times they all danced around the fire and swung the cedar bark into it. After they had danced four times around the fire this way, they stopped on the east side of it. The leaders approached the fire, caught one of the small cedar-bark bunches on fire, let out the above-mentioned heron or crane cry, and threw the burning bunch towards the east over the hedge of the enclosure. The same ceremony was repeated on the southern, western, and northern sides. However, before he threw the bunch towards the north, he first ignited the torches of the dancers. As often as a bunch was thrown over the hedge, some in the audience would blow in their hands and make a movement as if they were throwing something at the bunch. After all the torches were lit, all the dancers leaped and sprang in a wild dance around the fire. First they stayed close together and spit at each other with a certain juice which was supposed to contain medical power. However, as the space between them became greater, they sprang and ran after each other, seemingly without order, while the air currents that were created from the fast running and racing seemed to wind the fire around their hands and arms in long, glowing stripes. Then they touched their own bodies and the bodies of those in front of them with the burning torches. No one ever turned around or looked behind himself. Then one of them dealt the dancer in front of him a powerful blow with his burning torch; another grabbed the flame with his hands as if it were a sponge, and since he remained close to the dancer in front of him, he rubbed that dancer's back with the fiery sponge as if he wanted to wash him; then another who couldn't catch the dancer in front of him rubbed his own back with the burning cedar torch and bore this while he ran two or three times around the fire or until he had caught up with the dancer in front. As often as the burning torches were used, the above-mentioned crane's cry could be heard, so that it seemed at times as if a whole train of these birds were hovering in the darkness over the dance area. If a torch went out, it was relit in the great fire at the center and the furious dance continued. If a torch became so short that it could not be held comfortably any more, the dancer let it fall and with a crane's cry, raced from the enclosure. One after the other disappeared like this until all had left the enclosure. Now several from the audience stood up, picked up the scattered remains of the torches, lit them at the fire, and washed their hands with the flames. This was supposed to be a protection against the evil effects of the fire.

How was it that these fire dancers came away with no real burn wounds? It is likely that the flaming cedar bark doesn't give off that much heat and more than likely that the white clay with which the dancers covered their skin is a very poor conductor of heat. However, the thought that the dancers may have protected themselves like that against the effects of the fire hardly lessens the impression that this dance must have on the audience.

Washington Matthews closed his description of this dance with the observation that he had seen many fire scenes on stage, several fire-eating performers in civilized lands, and the fire dances of other Indian tribes, but that none of these could compare, none even come close, to the fire dance of the Navajo.

On Caring for Navajo Children

As the dawn began to break and the different dances neared their end, we set off from the "Song on the Mountain" to celebrate the beautiful All Saints Day [November 1] in the valley of Cienega. About 10:00 a.m., little by little, the Indians began to arrive at our mission. As I went with the two Reverend Sisters to our log cabin, the Indians were all lying in front stretched out in a line on the ground, using their blankets as beds and their saddles as pillows. One way or another, they simply had to catch up on the sleep lost during the dances. Sister Mary wisely remarked that it would likely be impossible to undertake anything today with these sleep-deprived Navajo. Thus we decided to postpone conversation with them until the next day.

They began to come to life that evening. We had bought them a few sheep and gave them flour, sugar, coffee, potatoes, and other foodstuffs as well, and made coffee-can pots and so forth available for their use. Several squaws from the neighborhood were ready nearby to take care of the baking, cooking, and roasting just to be able to take part in the meal. While the Navajo enjoyed their meal, their ponies stood in a long line and gave our good hay its proper honor—a rare treat for these small, tough, tenacious horses.

The next afternoon our conversation with the headmen and other Navajo took place. On the veranda of our log cabin, the Reverend Sisters and Ms. Whorton took their places in chairs. In front of them, forming a half circle, the Indians took their places, some in chairs, some on wood blocks. At the outer end between them sat our translator, so that he could turn to the Indians as well as the Sisters. Fathers Leopold, Berard, and my humble self regretted that there were no more chairs and stood on the veranda, thus securing "freedom of movement."

The conversation was opened with a long speech by Pesh'lakai J'lini A'lts'osigi, Slim Silversmith. . . . In his thoughtful, calm way he sketched a somber picture of the situation of those young people who had been away to school. After attending school for years in Fort Defiance or in the East and returning home again, after a few months you could hardly tell they had ever seen the inside of a school. They were just more malicious, more shifty, and more dishonest than the others. No one was taking care of them, no one took them on as their own. The government has them taught to read and write so that they can rely on themselves, but as a result of this they are much poorer than children who never attend school. These have worked, earned something for themselves, learned sheep or goat herding, and established a home for themselves, while the returning students are poor as beggars. With what they learn in school they have no opportunities to earn a living, and at school they don't learn how to provide for themselves on the reservation. Growing accustomed to a better lifestyle during the years at school only makes them dissatisfied and unhappy when they have to do without these comforts on the reservation. In closing, he thought this was not just his personal opinion but that of a majority of the Navajo.

Our friend Pesh'lakai had a point. I had heard similar observations repeatedly from other Indians and had enough opportunities during our presence here to become convinced that much of what he brought up was absolutely right. Therefore his speech didn't surprise me at all. However, others, like the Reverend Sisters, took it that the speech was given just to make them unhappy and discourage them.

Right after this, Charlie Mitchell began to speak, and it was soon obvious that he was trying to convince the Indians, after all that he had seen and heard from us in the school at Santa Fe, that our school would achieve completely different, much more positive results. The Navajo were waiting for the Reverend Sister Mary, who had answered some of their questions, to stand and give them a speech. However, she remarked that she had heard such good and positive things about the eloquence of the Navajo headmen that she would be very happy to take the opportunity now just to listen to their persuasive words. She would prefer it if the headmen would explain their opinions, needs, and wishes to her. So they did this.

In addition to those already mentioned, seven other headmen from every part of the reservation, living anywhere from 18 to 100 miles from here, gave long, brilliant speeches. I won't go any further into their many complaints about the past or try to cover their confidence and hopes for our mission and the school established here. When the opportunity arose, the Reverend Sister Mary answered their questions and cleverly met their objections that a school education for their children was useless by reminding them of the respect and success of Henry Dodge (who was not present). He owed all of this in large part to his education. She also inserted clever remarks and let them know of the good intentions of the Reverend Mother Katharine and her associates.

More than 10 years ago the Reverend Mother had already taken into consideration how so many other Indian tribes were enjoying the advantages of a good education through religious associations, while the great and famous tribe of the Navajo—which had so much over the other tribes, whose members were so intelligent and industrious, whose women were so skillful at weaving blankets that their name was known throughout the land—was still lacking the advantages of such education. So Mother Katharine decided that she would take special responsibility for this tribe, more than any other, and let their children receive the blessings of a good education.

One headman remarked that when they came to "specific places" to visit their children they were treated "condescendingly," and further both they themselves and their ponies had to go hungry. Reverend Sister Mary responded that mission supplies were not unlimited—we didn't receive any support from Washington; everything had to be covered by our private resources. If, for example, one of us decided to help his brethren with his private belongings, he could not give as much as he would really like to because then his property would soon be depleted and the source of his good deeds would soon run dry. It costs a lot to build a school and to keep it in good condition. But even if we couldn't give them wagons, farm equipment, and so forth, as did the government, the Indians were still welcome at any time. Their horses and they themselves would not lack for good food. However, one chief, Sandoval, from San Juan River, couldn't keep himself from remarking that a hungry dog would be given something to eat at one time or another, but if he repeated his visits too often, people would get sick of him and just give him a kick. He feared that in the end the Indians would become such a bother to us through their visits and would receive similar treatment—a comparison which caused much general amusement. But the Reverend Sister assured them that her red brothers would be welcomed anytime they visited the mission or the school.

By the way, no one seemed to doubt this assurance, because every headman brought up in his speech the friendly reception which they had found here. Not only they themselves but also their horses were taken care of, and they praised us about how with us they felt good and at home and with their friends. All of them promised to share with their neighbors what they had said and heard here. Not just to send their own children but also to try to convince all others who were under their authority to do so. In return, the Reverend Sister promised that the foundation of the new school would be laid in the year 1901, and the school should be finished and opened in the following year. Both of them, the Reverend Sister and the Indians, regretted that the Reverend Mother didn't have enough Sisters to open the school one year earlier.

Actually, the conversation could have ended then, but one very critical question remained unanswered. One of the oldest speakers had complained that the parents weren't notified when their children were sick. Naturally, he was assured that we would be very conscientious in such matters, and the parents could stay here when their children were dangerously ill. Not satisfied with that, he demanded that parents should be allowed to take their sick children home so that the medicine men could perform their hocus-pocus over them, complaining bitterly that the government school would never allow them to do this.

I knew that those from the government schools gave them the runaround with nonanswers to this request, which only made our stand that much harder. After we have instructed the children in the Catholic faith and baptized them, it is impossible for us to allow them to die as heathen. Because I know my flock and knew what a hold the medicine men have on these superstitious people, I advised the Reverend Sister to completely ignore the challenge, for I had reason to fear that if we just quickly brushed this challenge aside the whole purpose of this meeting would be frustrated. However, when the next two speakers stressed this point very forcefully as well, the Reverend Sister decided it was not advisable to strengthen the impression that we were letting them bask in this concession through our silence. I had to agree with her, but asked her to allow me to answer this critical question.

As the four remaining speakers also emphatically insisted on this point, and I persevered in silence about it, they became, as I believe, almost bewildered with me, because they demanded several times that I not forget the answer to this question. No danger of that! For I was thinking of nothing else during the time than how I could best resolve this question. My plan was, incidentally, soon set: First, everything else should be resolved, then I wanted to go into a long explanation to try to convince more of them of our way, introduce the situation well, then bring in the big guns against their demand, finally divert their attention back away from this question, and then end the meeting without further ado, without giving them the opportunity to start speaking about it again.

So I told them we had not come here for ourselves. If we had had our own benefit in mind, had looked to our own comfort, we would have stayed in the East where we could have had a comfortable location, a beautiful house, and everything that we could wish for as our own. We didn't come to make money—who was giving us anything here? Our friends knew that we used all the money that is sent to us that we don't use in our own upkeep for the needs of our red brothers. Only the love of our red brothers has moved us to leave our beautiful home to do what we have become accustomed to through years of study, to help them. The same goes for the Reverend Sisters. No one has forced the Reverend Mother Katharine to give her fortune for the benefit of the Navajo. Like the other rich Americans, she could have used her money in the East for herself. But she has a good heart; she loves the Indians. That is why she bought this land; that is why she is now building a beautiful, big school for their children and sending her Sisters here to teach them everything so that there is no difference between the children of the white men and the red men.

When we came here, the Navajo often asked us when our wives would be coming; why didn't we marry? But neither we nor the Reverend Sisters marry, so that we can dedicate our whole attention, our whole time, all of our abilities and power undivided to them. We didn't have families so that we can be like fathers to their children, and the Sisters can be like mothers. In our school they should have pleasant living quarters protected against the harsh weather, warm clothing, and good beds. Most Navajo died from consumption. Why? Not just because of the climate but because they didn't know how to prevent it. The Americans came from near and far to this region to be healed of consumption, while the Navajo here perished from it. Would we then allow Navajo parents to take their sick children from the warm rooms and good beds and to go home to their poor huts where they would be exposed to wind and weather, where the wind presses through every crack and crevice? Would we not then be committing murder to their children? We know how much the Navajo love their children, but we don't want to love the little ones any less and couldn't take it to be guilty of their deaths.

Now with regard to their medicine men, aren't we medicine men also? Didn't they believe that our prayer to the great God whom we came to preach to them about, who created the heavens and the earth, would be more effective than the prayer of their medicine men? Also, we didn't demand their horses and goats and sheep for our blessings and prayers. By the way, we didn't just have in mind to educate their children in reading, writing, and mathematics but also in agriculture and business, in everything which would be useful for their future progress. Also, they should, when possible, learn to read and write in their mother tongue. Schooling and education are not the end results but only preparation for their future lives. If the school evolved we would be in constant contact with them and regard them as belonging to a family and support them with word and deed.

I closed my remarks with that, stepped immediately from the veranda toward them, gave the Reverend Sisters a sign to follow me, and let them know that the conversation was finished. Our bond was strengthened and sealed with friendly handshakes. The conversation had gone well for everyone. Not one syllable about the earlier demand was uttered. After a few friendly words with each headman and the women, who were nearby preparing lunch, we took our leave from our red brothers and sisters.

Note

1. From Anselm Weber, FMN 28 (April–July 1901): 292–97, 376–80, 467–71, 554–60. Translated by Marie Bradshaw Durrant.

8

Mission to the San Juan, 1904

Berard Haile, O.F.M., and Anselm Weber, O.F.M.

[From the time of his first visit to the San Juan River area in northwestern New Mexico, Father Anselm planned to establish a mission there, amid the "vast possibilities for irrigation and permanent settlements." There the federal government was helping to construct irrigation works for the Navajo, and the cooperative agent stationed there had identified possible sites where a mission might be located. Father Anselm had promises of support from Mother Katharine Drexel and her aunt, Mrs. Joseph Whorton Drexel, for a Navajo day school where pupils could attend and yet "still be with the parents whom God has given them."[1] So in the spring of 1903 Father Anselm, Father Berard, and several others traveled to the San Juan, met with Navajo headman Sandoval and agent Samuel Shoemaker, and scouted possible mission sites. In August Father Anselm returned again to the San Juan, and on August 21 he, Mr. Shoemaker, and a council of local Navajo met to finalize agreement on a mission site to be located on a "semi-island" in the San Juan River near Kirtland, New Mexico, a few miles downstream from Farmington.

Unfortunately, the most influential headmen in the region were unable to attend this council, and Father Anselm was not accompanied by his usual Navajo interpreter, Frank Walker, but rather by Tom Morgan, thought to be somewhat less accomplished. Even so, things at the council seemed to go well, and after some discussion the Navajo enthusiastically approved granting the desired site to the friars. Mr. Shoemaker endorsed the selection and forwarded official requests, and by year's end the island was officially designated for the future San Juan mission.

Father Anselm appointed Father Berard to head the new mission. On April 7, 1904, Father Berard departed St. Michaels for his new field of labor, accompanied by the interpreter Frank Walker. Arriving at the San Juan, they encountered newly appointed Indian agent William T. Shelton, who challenged the Franciscan's right to the island. After three weeks of waiting for official clarifications, including the necessity for Berard to return to St. Michaels for documents and numerous communications to Washington, Mr. Shelton's concerns were overridden and Father Berard was authorized to begin work. In the meantime, he had become concerned about the suitability of the location, noting is his journal, "My present impression is one of doubt as to the durability of damming this arm of the river and I am in favor of throwing a bridge across and run chances on high-water tide." Despite his reservations, now that the location had been officially approved for a second time, he proceeded, with Navajo assistance, to build a breakwater to protect the island when the river ran high.

Father Berard had not been present the previous August when Mr. Shoemaker and Father Anselm had obtained the Navajo's approval for the site, and now, working with some of the men who had been there, he learned of promises supposedly made to the Indians that contradicted Father Anselm's report of the event. As time went by, and as his familiarity with and confidence in the local Navajo increased, Berard found himself torn between loyalty to Father Anselm's view of things and that held by the natives, who were certain that, among other things, Father Anselm had promised them a boarding school, not a day school. Eventually, the question would prove moot, for it would develop that other parties had prior legal claim to the mission site. In the meantime, Father Berard's belief that the San Juan Navajo were telling the truth as they understood it seemed to suggest that his Superior's perceptions were incorrect or that he had not told Father Berard the whole truth. As Berard explored the contradictions, he learned that much of the trouble lay in faulty translation during the fateful council of August 21. Father Anselm had said one thing, the Navajo had heard another, and the translator had either been unaware of the misunderstanding or had not bothered to correct it.

While finally it was established that translation problems might explain the discrepant positions, Father Berard's apparent acceptance of the recollections of the San Juan Navajo over Father Anselm's account of things seriously damaged the relationship between the two friars, especially from Father Anselm's viewpoint. To Father Anselm, Berard's position, even if temporary, manifested intolerable disloyalty and lack of confidence in his Superior, and perhaps inappropriate ambition as well. Later that summer, while Father Berard was on leave visiting relatives in the East, Father Anselm wrote to Father Provincial Chrysostom Theobald, indicating his displeasure with Berard and suggesting that he would not object to having Berard transferred elsewhere. To Anselm, Father Berard's commitment to the Navajo missions did not seem very deep, he was independent and ambitious, and his prickly disposition, often sarcastic and angry-appearing, was not a positive attribute in work among the Navajo.

The record is not clear as to why the recommended transfer did not take place. One reason may be Berard's subsequent apology to Anselm and his plea that their relationship be allowed to return to its former level of familiarity, confidence, and respect. In retrospect, it was a very near thing, one of those hinges upon which history turns. Over the next half century no single Franciscan, nor, for that matter, no other white man, would contribute more than Father Berard to the creation of a written Navajo language and the documentation of traditional Navajo culture. For Berard Haile in the late summer of 1904, most of the "scholarship [which] laid the foundation of twentieth-century study of the Navajo language"[2] lay ahead, along with decades of unselfish pastoral service to the Navajo people. It was a very near thing.

Father Berard kept a journal of his San Juan experience for the period April 7 through June 5, 1904. It chronicles his growing awareness of the discrepancy between the San Juan Navajo's perception of things and the definition of the situation implicit in his instructions from Father Anselm. The journal concludes with the apparent resolution of that discrepancy when, back at St. Michaels, Father Berard confronts Father Anselm and, later, the interpreter Tom Morgan. The first segment below contains those portions of Father Berard's journal for the period May 9 through June 5 relevant to the misunderstanding about what the Navajo had been promised versus what the Franciscans were now prepared to deliver. Next is presented Father Anselm's assessment of the situation as communicated to Provincial Chrysostom Theobald. Finally, there is the full text—seven handwritten pages—of Father Berard's plea to Father Anselm that their estrangement be resolved, that somehow relations between them be allowed to return to their former pleasant and productive state.]

❖

"I Could Not Doubt the Truth of Their Statements"[3]

On Monday, May 9, I took a walk through the various fields in the vicinity. Found the Indians busy at work with plow, and so forth. Mr. "Adobe" conversed with us for a while and remarked that during winter he and I would be the only inhabitants of the vicinity. Previous to this conversation I have obtained views on various subjects concerning this locality, a day school, and so forth. First of all, the Indians, that is, such as look upon us as friends, did not wish us to select the "island" because they themselves wished us to locate just opposite on the table land. In studying the matter over, my personal view is in their favor. I have no fear for the dam. This at its worst will allow water to flow over its bank. But it will throw the current against the banks of the island, and the river will always remain a menace to the occupants. This holds good, it is true, only in high tide. But one exceptional high tide is also sufficient to endanger a building and cause any amount of damage to fields and ditches. I should be in favor of another and safer site.[4] For this reason a school is under reconsideration. A day school is also a puzzle. I am opposed to it as something impracticable among the Navajo.

We had discussed this question at home [St. Michaels] and had come to the conclusion that the San Juan country only would offer a practical solution to the question. This was owing, in our opinion, to the stationary disposition of these Indians. I learn, however, that, first, even these regions are vacated after harvest and that the Indians repair to the mountains for the winter. This is on account of their flocks and for fuel. Second, even in the summer they are often gone for other work, after finishing their work on their fields, so that they are continually shifting and roaming about. Third and finally, it appears that if an Indian resolves to send his child to school, it should replace his home and he [the parent] does not wish to

bother with his child while at school. I had the pleasure of receiving Sandoval Tlo
tsai as guest today. Among other things we discussed these questions also. I learned
from him that the soil on the island is loose or washed in by continual floods. . . .
At the bottom it is "river rock-bed." As to school, he has no use for day schools. He
contends that it limits the pupils to the neighborhood, which is only too true. Also,
that we cannot expect the children living on the upper flat to attend school every
day, which again I cannot gainsay. Finally, that we should find ourselves in the
position of "herding" the children to school every morning. Besides, he made
mention of the many objections to schools raised by the Indians and which are
unavoidable, [and] that this may eventually empty the schools especially among a
low class of Indians as those in the neighborhood. He therefore considers a
boarding school the only successful venture and pleads that if we build a school it
might be none other than a boarding school.

I admit that I am forced to this same conclusion by personal experience at St.
Michael's. The Navajo is critical beyond measure when the education of his child
is concerned. He compares one school with another, its furniture, cleanliness,
dishes, food, and so on, and I fear that with our moderate allowance and annuity we
would scarcely find ourselves in a position to compete with better equipped modern
government schools. However, I have now fully resolved to conduct a day school
personally for a time and see whether or not a temporary "summer school" can be
conducted on the day-school plan. Sandoval advised me to make the acquaintance
of two chiefs southeast of here (at *Tgeł sakad* standing-reeds) at Dick Simpson's
place. These are Chałbaí nibiyé' (Roan Hat's . . . Son) and Gastginłtso'itso (Big
Yellow Man). I shall follow his advice at a later date.

Remarks were dropped also about Tom Morgan the interpreter. It was said by
both Sandovals [father and son] that his interpreting may have been correct but that
he showed little regard for the Indians' interest. By this I understand they meant to
say that he did not call Father Superior's attention to their way of looking at things.
They even suspected that he suppressed many things for fear of causing trouble
between them and Shoemaker. This they concluded from the fact that Mr.
Shoemaker never became angry at what they said, many things having been said for
this very purpose. Again the elder Sandoval had had in mind to call the above-
mentioned chiefs into council in our favor, which he did not do on hearing that a
"scrub" interpreter was with us. They ask Frank [Walker, Father Anselm's usual
interpreter] to stay here and do so repeatedly.

On Tuesday, May 10, gave Indians powder and so on for blasting at a point
seven miles from here. Indians were very grateful for the assistance. The chief from
this district also paid me a visit. Impressed me as a very sensible man. Expresses
his opinions in a modest and quiet manner. Discussed the selection of land and also
school question. Stated that he had objected to granting us the island as a place ill-
suited for our purposes; had hinted at the constant danger of the locality, especially
in regard to children; but that all his and his followers' warnings had remained
unheeded. That both Mr. Shoemaker and Father Anselm had insisted on the island;
that Mr. Shoemaker even had stated, that he had appointed him as chief, and in so
doing, had relied on his assistance; that he expected him to "go behind" and not to

lead, that he wanted that island and nothing else. Whereupon they all had given up further discussion as useless and given up the island and told them: "The dirt is yours, but the trees and brush is ours." To which assent had been given. This struck me as rather strange. My instructions had been: "Don't chop all the trees down, but let some stand; it'll look better." And as to the above-mentioned agreement it was explained to me that the Indians had asked only to use this brush and timber for their ditches and houses, fences, and so on, and that this had been most pleasantly agreed to. However, a clash seems unavoidable inasmuch as the Indians would come and claim any tree suitable to their fancy. Let it serve our purpose ever so much, how could we refuse? And what about clearing the place? Could not such trees as we allowed to stand "to look better" be claimed by our neighbors? Complications of this nature may cause friction at some time or another.

It strikes me, too, that the Indians had been willing to further our interests in selecting a good place for us. In fact, everyone assured me that they could not grasp why we were so persistent in demanding as poor a site as that island. And that they finally acquiesced in the "bull-headedness" of their visitors. It does really appear that they frequently find a happy way of qualifying a person's actions.

This chief, called Nakai dinaé, also spoke of the school. As it was always understood by me this school was to be a day school and nothing else, at least for the beginning. This locality was selected as offering the best, or at least good, opportunities for a venture at the solution of the problem. Thus far all the Indians are surprised at the turn which matters are taking with my arrival. This chief informed me that they understood this was to be a "real school." He stated that they had mentioned they were glad to have a school in their neighborhood; and hoped to see beds, tables, their children well clad, well fed, and they themselves relieved of the trouble of going very far (to Fort Lewis) [Colorado] to see them; that this was often impossible and that, as soon as our school was opened, they would put their children here instead of at the other schools. Upon this no mention was made of a day school. For if at that time mention had been made of "sending their children to school in the morning and sleeping in the hogans at night," they would have resented the idea and told Tsishchilli [Father Anselm] they didn't wish to send their children to school in this manner. If their children were at school they should remain there altogether. That was the only kind of school they liked. Thus the impression was left in their minds that a boarding school was to be erected here in their "immediate" neighborhood. And, the chief assured me, this news spread rapidly and created quite an excitement. All were glad and rejoiced and planned out how many children they would send to us. And "as Indians are," he continued, they exaggerated things. Some [Navajo] even said they [Franciscans] would build immediately, though he [Nakai dinaé] kept his peace, owing to "his way of doing" in believing and acting upon information he received personally.

I explained the whole situation to him and begged him to inform his people that I was here, and was studying the situation. I referred to our beginnings at St. Michaels, our steady growth in influence, our school and present good progress. As to this new mission, since a day school was not to be considered, I could not give any certainty and definite information further, than that the mission as established would not be relinquished. Yet all this convinces me of the complicated state of affairs here. Shall recommend this mission to our Blessed Patroness at Mass. . . .

Thursday, May 12. This is Ascension Day and a holy day. After celebrating Mass and taking breakfast, saddled horses and rode to the camp of Indians to whom I had given the powder. Found their ditch in fair shape. Its head is along and below a high rock bank. It can be used only in high tide, its purpose being to flood the soil once or twice a year. It meets a curve in the river bed and at rapids, which cause this point to be a very dangerous one. The Indians' purpose is to create a solid bank by means of log-and-rock houses in the present river bed. The quicksand of the river would gradually cement the joints. The cottonwoods along the river furnish the logs, which are spliced and jointed, and fastened with baling wire. The rock is thrown into these cabins from the top of the bank, a height of about 30–50 feet. They had put in six of these cabins, two of them, however, having been washed out by the current. The space between these cabins and the river bank they intended to fill out with gravel and such. This can be done only from the precipitous bank above. By blasting they hoped to throw enough down, or at least create a terraced descent, in order to facilitate access to the ditch.

I found the Indians gathered in a spacious hogan over a *biji* ceremony. They thanked me for the assistance I had given them and told me they would not give up, since the ditch was their only support and hope. They spoke of the agent's arrival there and that he desired them to come to his office and sign a petition to Washington for the purpose of assistance; that it would take a large sum of money to do any efficient work on their ditch and he would recommend their petition to the government. They thanked him for this and assured him they did not look for payment for any work done on the ditch, in order to remain in possession of it, that they wished to claim this ditch and nothing more. They then went on to tell me their opinion of Mr. Shelton; that they had very little confidence in his promises and cited instances in which he had promised them plows and farm implements and then either told them it was not so, or that he would first inspect their fields, or divided the ownership of these implements in such a way, that wrangling and quarreling over them had to ensue.

After they had finished their tales I took advantage of the occasion and explained who we were and our objects in settling among them: That we were a body of men; and sent here by our Superiors; were unmarried, in order to devote ourselves better to our work. This caused merriment, as also about Sisters; that we were independent of government, and not in connection with Protestant preachers; that on account of the record these had, we expected to be treated with suspicion until we were better known. I referred to our mission at St. Michaels, our connection with their headmen, our school, and the beginning of this mission. I found these Indians attentive listeners. Their chief is a man of about 45 years of age and very sensible ideas. They were about 22 all told in that neighborhood. They impressed me as a better class of Indians than these in my immediate vicinity.

In the evening Frank mentioned in the course of his conversation a remark that Sandoval had made to him. They had talked over the school matter and our work. Young Sandoval remarked that we might begin with religious instruction and

Sunday School with the "*atchín biyāzh*," or coming generation, but leave them, the older ones alone. They had their religion and ceremonies and were used to them. They might attend a sermon and "say yes" to what they heard; but when "it came to changing their views and accepting ours, it was quite a different thing."

In thinking over this matter I could not but help see the difficulty of our position, and of instructing this people in a new religion especially. At the same time the opinion of some of my confreres in the East, that [the efforts of] this mission were of no use "since you can't do anything" with them, seemed to find nourishment and confirmation. We contend for supplanting our religion for theirs; we ask them to put aside their religious practices for ours. A difficult task, I admit, my Blessed Mother, but this is your work and not mine! Let them look to you for arguments! My own are weak, but I shall append them for reference.

It seems we have full sway as far as the "rising generation" goes. The elders' generation contend that the "American" religion is good enough for the Americans, therefore let us alone! But I hope that their love for their children is deep and I know it is, for a child has "preference even to its mother" and "many a Navajo has perished in the effort to save his child." But if this be so, we possibly may reach them through their children in two ways: By educating them and appealing to their love for their children. Both, in my opinion, should go together. Do we not appeal to whites through their children? Call their attention to the futility of education in school if not combined with education at home? Perhaps an appeal to their desire for the welfare of their children may introduce a better education in their homes. Let's try it, at least. Appeal to their toil, their daily hardships, accumulation of wealth, all for their children!

Another one is their married life. "Try! Try to find a woman that is true among the Navajo and vice versa." Happy marriages—an exception. And in this connection if American methods are better in regard to farming, and so on, perhaps the Catholic marriage is a better institution, and so forth. Let us not indulge in despondency before we have made a test. I admit of the difficulty in appealing to many "American" models and asking us to convert them [the Navajo]. But these need other arguments, and after all we are trying persuasion and not force, grace and not only human efforts.

Friday, May 13. Asked heads of the families in the neighborhood to come for consultation on school. I had four of them in council: Adobe, Barba's Wero, Sandoval, and Shorty. Dick Simpson's brother-in-law alone did not appear. These five constitute the heads of the families in the neighborhood. Adobe has, as far as I can learn, four sons-in-law; Barba's, one; Shorty, two; Dick, one or two; and Sandy, none.

Opened council by explaining the meaning of day school, that for this I had been sent here to try the experiment; that $600 was all we could figure on, that this annuity was granted by a charitable lady in the East, that she wished their children to remain with their parents and not be penned up in a boarding school, that she imagined the Indians would like this better since they lived, in her imagination, in colonies, where such a scheme could be realized; and that I wished their opinion in the matter before either venturing at its materialization, or its final settlement in discarding the plan as impracticable.

Barba's opened with a remark that they had expected the chief [Father Anselm] for the discussion, which I settled by stating that I had his opinion a few days before this and now looked for their opinions, as representing the families here.

He then began with "the beginning," namely, granting the island. He stated that council had been called in presence of Mr. Shoemaker and Father Weber; stated that they [the Navajo] had been willing to give them or us a place up "above" belonging to "Julian"; that this was their own choice and they thought would be the best place in the neighborhood, but that Mr. Shoemaker—who did all the talking and Tsishchilli none at all—simply insisted on the island. This they could not understand. They raised objections to this selection on account of the river; but Shoemaker said they would fix that part by damming; that the river formed a natural barrier (fence) which they desired, and so on. [Barba's said that] after long discussion they finally stated that this particular island was in the possession of Julian's family to whom decision belonged. After the second summons he [Julian] appeared and opposed the selection, telling Tsishchilli, whom alone he addressed, that they [the Navajo] did not think the island would suit their [the friars'] purposes. However, talk was no use. So he [Julian] asked what they wished to do with it. Then both, Tsishchilli and Shoemaker, said they wished to put a big school there much like at St. Michaels. Adobe then spoke up and said: "He [Father Anselm] even said to me: 'You saw it, Adobe, didn't you?'" "Yes, I saw it!" "Well, we want to put one here too."

The Indians also asked whether they could put their children from Fort Lewis here. To which Shoemaker said: "Yes, all your children now at Fort Lewis shall go to school here," which statement Tsishchilli repeated. The Indians then told them that this was fine; that Fort Lewis was far; that they could not get to see their children very often on this account; and that they certainly would gladly prefer to put their children here. It was then stated that these children would form the basis, the foundation of the school, that later on others would follow, and so on; that these children should be put to school here as soon as it were finished. The children at Fort Lewis and the old women even know this and expect it and discuss it.

Objections were raised on account of visitors. How would they be treated, and if they intended to stay three or four days, would they be provided for? This was assured and they would certainly be provided for! Mention was made of goats and sheep coming in there on the island; that they used this place for greasewood and sagebrush and shade! That if Americans were there and their [the Navajo's] sheep straggled over there, they should be stoned and trouble arise with occupants on this account. That Tsishchilli might say no; and that if they did have trouble on this account he would say that he had not been there and it was not his fault. Such conclusions as these, though astute I must say, were not allowed to enter their minds, and they were promised that this should not be allowed to cause the least trouble!

Again, mention was made of conditions in winter. Most of these objections [in the earlier council] originated with Sandoval, in the presence of the chief and the neighboring Indians. Since I had them repeated very often and asked repeatedly concerning them, and even carried these statements on paper, I know that I am correct as to these. Now Sandoval asked how it would be in winter. Since Indians vacated this vicinity, and occasionally they would come to see their children from a distance, whether or not this would be objectionable. [He was answered] certainly not, since we would always be provided with hay and plenty to eat!

These promises were such, as seemed so enormously assertive and bold, that I questioned them repeatedly so as not to be mistaken concerning them. The references made to the school, to clothes, beds, visits of their children, provision for visiting Indians, transfer of pupils from Fort Lewis to this school, but especially to the vacancy of this locality in winter, almost upset me. Why had I been sent here at all? Why had these promises not been made mention of to me? Why was I sent here to experiment with a day school, when promises of a boarding school had been made to these Indians and trumpeted through the country? Why was a boarding school completely lost sight of, and why had I been left under the impression that these Indians were prepared for a day school and that, if anywhere, this plan would work here? Why was the annuity for a day school assigned to this place at all? Is it stating too much when I say that this whole transaction savors of gross double-dealing and misjudgment of the Indians' extreme sensibility of honor?

Let me add here that Sandoval was pleased with the outlook [offered by Mr. Shoemaker and Father Anselm], together with the other Indians; that he and they gave their account and told Shoemaker and company to start tomorrow; that there was plenty of work and they should like to see it go on, especially how they would manage the river. Remarks as these were pompously trumped off by stating that what seemed enormous to the Indians was merely a slip of the finger for the American; that these priests would make an ideal spot of it; raise alfalfa, corn, wheat, melons, beans and fruit, and so on. Anything else?

In reference to above statements as to provision for visitors, Sandoval stated in presence of the groups that Tsishchilli had said he would personally look after that, because he would be here himself. Sandoval doubted this and said "*do-noshdlã'da*," "You will send another man here and things will change!" "No, no, I will be here myself. I return home now and [will be] here after three months since it takes so long to fix these papers. But after that I will be here myself to look after things and appoint somebody to superintend the work." This portion of the conversation I had repeated to me. Sandoval added that though he did not believe this with certainty, he thought all things had panned out well, when he was appointed as foreman of that dam. He thought that something similar had been intended at the time of the above council.

I can write in truth that all this had an overwhelming effect on me. I went as far as to question them whether they understood enough English collectively to know whether these things had been truly interpreted to our party. But they said they could not say this, because they understood very little English. However, from the interpretation of the promises made by our party to them, I could not doubt the truth of their statements. As to the question of a day school, they all stated that the school to be erected here was never explained to them in such a manner, as if their children "were to go to school in the morning and eat a sheep with them in the evening"; that they always thought it would be a "good and real" school, not half-work, but everything that goes to make a school: clothes, beds, and that their children would stay in school; references were made to transfer from Fort Lewis to [the] school at St. Michaels; to the winter months; to the permission granted at the time that the children of the neighborhood might occasionally spend a night with their parents if so desired; statements, which in my opinion, would hardly be interpreted in favor of a day school. What could be done?

I explained to them that we personally did not believe in the day-school plan for the Navajo; that it would be feasible only after the Navajo lived together, could tell time, and were disciplined like white children to go to school at the appointed hour. At the same time, since $600 was allowed for this purpose, we thought it best to try the plan; that I was here for that purpose and would now work against the plan as impracticable. As to the boarding school, nothing could, in my opinion, be done but to work on the plan of St. Michaels, which was built up in five years. [I explained] that this mission would not be given up, but maintained. They were glad to hear that I agreed with them on this point and asked me to work for a boarding school as had been promised them.

My impression of this whole council may easier be imagined than described. In a conversation with Sandoval—whom I trust and found a faithful friend—I explained my whole view of the present status of affairs. Among other things I confided to him that I would work for two points upon my return, namely, a change of our selection [for the mission site] and the school plan.

I am more than ever confirmed in my view that in matters concerning the Indians, these and not Americans are to be consulted and trusted if possible. In this instance I come to the conclusion that less trouble would have arisen, and a more satisfactory solution arrived at, and a better location been selected, if Mr. Shoemaker had been left with his ditches and dirt. A selection had already been made for us by the Indians themselves, a site had been chosen, which easily could have been brought under irrigation. The Indians themselves, under old Sandoval's direction, had selected this place as most suitable for a school and our purposes, so that I say Mr. Shoemaker has made this selection and we have permitted ourselves to be drawn into selecting a worse spot than even an Indian's meanness could have chosen. Yet I hope, if properly managed, we can yet repair this blunder. Once before I have learned that there are many blunders made in the Indian service. They usually cost a neat little sum of money. This blunder has cost us in the neighborhood of $350, and if not repaired I venture at the prediction that it may cost us a hundred times as much in repairing damages caused by floods! Again, if a man breaking a promise is stamped a liar, ought we not be very careful in making promises to Indians? Or, is an Indian less sensitive on the point of honor than we are? Perhaps not so much among themselves as in their dealings with whites! And I have experienced it often enough how readily they call a person a liar. Yet we boast of being their friends! Refer to frequent frauds, double-dealing, cheating, lies, breach of promise by whites; on which account we wish to be their counselors, advisers, and friends! And yet what promises we make! How careless we are in proposing our plans, leaving them often under the impression as if these plans were to be realized in the nearest future, even appointing a certain period for their materializing. Such impressions were undoubtedly created at the point when this selection of a site was made; and though we might favor the interpretation that an allowance must be made [by the Navajo] for [the unpredictability of] gathering of funds, [unanticipated] delay in the work, yet no such apprehensions were hinted at [in the previous meeting], while this could easily have been done. Prudence required this, and our experience at our "Mother-house" might have inspired greater caution!

And what prospects for funds did we have at the time of selection? Were we not continually in debt at the other mission, let alone expenses for traveling to and fro until this mission had been permanently established!

And yet speak of a boarding school, fine fields, any amount of work for the Indians! And in such a manner, as left no doubts in their minds as to its accomplishment in the near future! Four or five years of intercourse with this tribe has apparently not taught us a lesson in the ABCs of prudence and discretion. And our influence with them? Yes, there is some show of and for it. But even at best, when it comes to a test I believe that even in our opinion it would amount to very little. At least, our influence does not prompt them to give us their entire confidence in their own private and family affairs. If such a thing as trusting a white man *entirely* is possible for a Navajo or rather on his part, we can undoubtedly claim that they do not give us their entire confidence. And as long as this condition is true, we might use a little caution, at least, and especially in our promises to them!

Hash, I believe, is considered to be a stew of finely cut-up (or chewed) meat, potatoes, and spices. Metaphorically it may signify a medley in a state of affairs. I like hash but not very much of it and despise anybody else's. I therefore hate to face a mixed-up state of affairs caused by others. And in this instance I must face promises made by others, whose fulfillment requires enormous sums of money. Here's hoping that our Immaculate Patroness will clear the situation!

Saturday, May 14. I receive copy of [a] letter of Father Superior to Mrs. Drexel. Mention is made of a day school to be erected by her munificence, so that a day school and not a boarding school had been intended. It removed all doubts from my mind, as I had feared I may have been mistaken in my orders. . . .

Saturday, May 21. Owing to condition of affairs here and news of my sister's ill-health, am feeling pretty gloomy. Nevertheless, entertain my friend Sandoval Jr. and give him charge of house [which Berard had rented]. Receive further intelligence from him about school to the effect that the "real" school is to be finished and in running order by September 1, which if not done would make hard feelings with Indians. He stated again that he had asked Tsishchilli when work would begin, whether immediately, whether children could be taken from Fort Lewis for this school term, and to this he received answer that he did not think children could go to "our" school during this school year, that papers had to be sent to Washington, but that in the spring and during summer work would be pushed so that their children would not need to go to Fort Lewis in September. "This," he said "is in me, just as if it had been said yesterday. And if Tisishchilli comes here and does not want to believe you, I'll tell him what he said." There is then nothing to be gained by my lengthened sojourn here. . . .

Wednesday, May 25. Reach St. Michaels and find that Father Superior denies all that Indians said and that he had intended a day school from the very start. The interpreter had understood a boarding school and his attention had not been called to the difference. This leaves the blunder on our side, though I await further developments. Father Superior stated that he did not think it necessary to call their attention to the day school any more than by mentioning a day school.

When I told him that one of the Indians stated that he had promised to take charge of the mission personally, he denied this, also that any mention was made of the fact that the Indians move to different localities in winter. He stated that Indians had at first objected to schools in general, and had objected to the island, also that Mr. Shoemaker had been in a very angry mood, so that he had begged him to drop the matter of selecting a place until later. Shoemaker, however, insisted upon getting the island.

May 26–June 5. During this period, am thinking over the matter and imagine, to express it mildly, that this situation is a very peculiar one. Discuss matters freely with Father Superior, suggest a change of site, which is rejected and only agreed to, providing "he deems the island unsafe." As to feasibility of a day school my reasons against it have no weight, and it appears as if I am to believe I did not venture at its realization at all. I receive compliments in this mild shape on various occasions and, of course, must accept them as gracefully as they are given. At times I am disgusted, then again hopeful of a fortunate settlement of affairs. Father Superior also consented to accompany me or follow me to the river "to set those fellows straight." This may prove to be the best course to follow, though I anticipate some interesting arguments. Hope to leave second week of June.

Sunday, June 5. Mr. Morgan returned, and I have an understanding with him and discuss the situation. I inset his statement: "That he interpreted or tried to, as best he could, whatever was said by Superintendent Shoemaker and the Indians; that he interpreted the meaning of a day school, by explaining to Indians that their children were to come to school in the morning and return in the evening, which would take place the next day again, and thus five times a week. The Indians objected that they had no children, since their children were at Fort Lewis and such children as were at home with them were needed to assist them or to carry water, herd sheep, and catch horses. But it was explained to them that their children could still help them; that they should be at school during the day and return home after it got cooler toward evening, when the best time to work set in. This satisfied the Indians, who now asked whether they could put children from Fort Lewis and other schools into this one. This found a favorable reply and assurance that the children from Fort Lewis could be transferred to this school. The Indians then gave their consent to this understanding, but made no promises to put certain children into the school. They only consented to the plan of putting such children into our school.

[Morgan said he told them] that this school was to be a day school in the beginning and later on, "perhaps" a boarding school. The reason for this was lack of funds, which might later on be received, so that a boarding school would be erected, perhaps in five years or so. Reference was made to the beginnings at St. Michaels, to erection of the school there, and the statement made that it would be similarly here on the river. The interpreter also stated that it seemed to him as if Father Weber spoke about this "prospective" boarding school in this manner, because he was afraid he would not get a piece of land. [Morgan stated] that Mr. Shoemaker told them they ought to rejoice at the prospects of getting a fine school in such close proximity; that they always complained of the great distance of the government schools; that this would be a fine school, just like at the *Cienega*, which he knew; that "these people" would put up such a fine building here also; that they had plenty of money and could afford to put up a fine building; that it was for their own [the Navajo's] interest to have a building and school of this description in their own neighborhood.

Thoughts like these disposed them favorably toward the school and all objections vanished. Too much stress, in my opinion, was laid on this prospective boarding school, so that the Indians seemed to have forgotten all about the day school. However, when I mentioned to Mr. Morgan that the Indians had made statements to the effect that nothing whatever had been mentioned of a day school, that they always understood that this was to be a "real good" school, and that had a day school been intended they would never have been satisfied with such a plan, [he said] he thought that this was a made-up scheme on their part. And when I disputed this he went on to say that I did not know the Navajo; that they might have made up what each one was to say, and that he thought they had done so. To this I answered that I thought it highly improbable that Indians such as Tlotsai, Nakai dinaé and that council—Indians living at different points and interviewed separately—would agree even as far as repeating the very words of that first council; and that Frank, the interpreter, admittedly knew his people and believed that they told the truth. [To this, Morgan] kept his peace with a smile and said that it was a made-up story, and that he knew he had not made up his own.

As to the selection of land, the interpreter stated that Father Weber had asked for a tract just opposite the "island" but that the Indians objected to this as belonging to Julian Badani; but advised to build at "*Tgasotse*" just opposite two buttes. Mr. Shoemaker objected to this, however, as being rocky and valueless and "sterile" soil. [Morgan also stated] that after Father Weber had spoken in an easy manner to the Indians, had told them of our intentions, plans, and successes, to which all Indians apparently listened with pleasure, but which apparently irritated Mr. Shoemaker, the latter asked to be allowed to talk; "he'd fix it."

He then went on to state to them what he had done for them in the years he had been with them; how he had helped them, had given them a chief who should assist him whenever he wanted to benefit them, and that he now asked for a piece of land, the island, and wanted the chief to give it to them.

Objections were raised on the grounds that they used that island for timber and brush and grazing [and] that if a school was to be erected there, it would be danger-ous for their children on account of high water in spring. As to the first, they [the Navajo] finally obtained permission to use some of the timber; and as to brush they [were told they] would not need any more of it since the government would take out a ditch to cover the whole flat; and as to the danger of drowning, this also would be averted by cutting off the river. The Americans knew how to do such things, that while they never could succeed in putting a ditch across to the island, the Americans would change that whole island: that "these people" had more money than the Navajo; that they could afford to spend lots of money and would do it, to make this a fine place, raise anything, have fields and—. Incidentally, the interpreter remarked that Father Weber took a stroll with him through the island and remarked that with "those groves" and fine soil, the place would be changed into a paradise before long. Yes, in paradise—lost.

After such hopeful discussions the Indians consented, leaving the decision with Sandoval's brother. He appeared after having been summoned three times. On his arrival, he made no objections, but advised his neighbors to consent, since he knew by experience that if the Americans wanted a piece of land they would get it in spite of their objections. As to Father Superior's having said that he would return there personally, the interpreter emphatically denied this and said that he had said he did not know whether he could come personally since he had to be at St. Michaels also. But in that event he would send another, perhaps two and even three, since one was coming from East in fall.

As to the time of building he interpreted that perhaps they should commence in fall providing papers of approval would arrive in time and funds could be secured; if not, then they would wait until spring. The majority consented to have building on the island after objections had been refuted. Morgan also remembered that Mr. Shoemaker had remarked at the table that a day school would be just the thing for these people! When asked of his opinion as to the feasibility of a day school, he [Morgan] stated that he did not think it would be successful.

I come to the belief now that, owing to the frequent references made to "these people" and "their lots of money" and "the fine school at Cienega," and raising funds and beginning in fall, if possible, and if not, in spring, the Indians easily could be misled, and to lose sight of the day school entirely. And since even this interpreter gained the impression that the Indians were forced into the grant [of the island], I am only confirmed in my previous view of the transaction.

"I Should Not Regret His Loss"[5]

[Probably Father Anselm never read Father Berard's "view of the transaction" as recorded in his journal, but if Berard did, as he reported, discuss these matters "freely" with Father Anselm, it is unlikely that he was able to hide his sense, so plain in the journal entries, that Father Anselm was at least partly to blame for the misunderstanding, for the "hash" that had developed. In June, Father Anselm accompanied Father Berard back to the San Juan to straighten things out, held another council with the Navajo, this time with Frank Walker as interpreter, "denied" the prevailing understanding of statements he had made at the earlier council, and reiterated the position that the friars had funding only for a day school.

As may be seen in Anselm's report to the Provincial, some of Father Berard's comments at the time further alienated his Superior.

Due to his sister's illness, Father Berard received permission to leave the mission field for a family visit. While he was away, Father Anselm reconsidered the situation and on July 13 filed the following report to his Provincial on how matters stood at the San Juan and on Father Berard's problematic future in the Navajo missions.]

I regret the necessity of writing to you about the San Juan River. You know, and our Fathers know through the *"Sendbote,"* what pains I have taken to secure a location on that river, because there is no doubt in my mind that, eventually, it will be *"the"* Navajo country. The flat in which I made the selection is the largest and best located on the river, and, if irrigated, it would give homes to a large number of families. There is no doubt in my mind but that it will be irrigated, even though the Navajo would have to take out the ditch themselves.

I did not wish any Protestant minister to locate in that neighborhood before us, and did not deem it advisable to postpone the matter.

Though I thought and had been assured there were Indians enough in the immediate neighborhood to justify a small day school before the irrigation ditch was taken out, still, I made the selection more on account of the good prospects of having a much larger settlement in the future. This as a preamble.

You know how anxious P. Berard was to go to the river. At first he asked me to let him go to do missionary work (without an interpreter, which I knew was preposterous), urging me to "do something," calling this place "Bluff City," and so on. But before he left, not missionary work, but the day school seemed to have become the main thing, he offering himself to teach in person until the buildings were up and Sisters secured. You know I had $600 from Mrs. Drexel for the San Juan, which, together with the money for his intentions, I turned over to him.

The first thing he did was to build a dam across the then dry channel to throw all the water to one side of the "island"; this was necessary, since during high water, which was anticipated, it would have been impossible to reach the "island" on foot. I had allowed him to build the dam, to buy the most necessary furniture, and so forth. Though he did not succeed in doing any missionary work, he succeeded in building the dam and kept in good humor, still intending, at least during the first 17 days of his stay, to open up a small day school. He was clamoring for funds to do "work" on the "island" and to build, though he knew I had no assurance of getting any more money this year. As you know I was "in hopes" that Mrs. Drexel would furnish the money to erect the building. When I obtained her refusal and notified him, it was "all off"; he would not believe that her refusal was final, asked for her letter and permission to write her himself (his letter was certainly "a peach"); but a copy of her letter finally convinced him. Shortly afterward he wrote: as matters were standing, he thought it useless to remain any longer, and hardly possible to arrive at an understanding by mail—he soon arrived.

While these last letters were passing, the Indians began to "talk objections," and he was seemingly only too eager to listen; instead of denying their statements (which he knew were untrue, unless he took me for a liar and a hypocrite) and trying to placate them, he attached great importance to their statements, even wrote them down in their presence.

I cannot fully explain the reasons for their soreness without becoming too prolix. I will only state that I had been handicapped in making the selection by not having Frank Walker (who was in jail), but Tom Morgan, with me as interpreter, by being unable to have the chief Sandoval with me, who had left a few days before for Colorado, and by having Mr. Schoemaker, who was agent at the time, who had invited himself to accompany me to the council, and who, as I learned later, is very much disliked by the Indians on the river.

As to the Indians' statements, they maintained I had promised them a large boarding school like the one here, that I myself in person would come to the San Juan, that I would start the building in three months from the time I made the selection, and so on. They also maintained there were not enough children in the immediate neighborhood for a day school; they would move away in winter; they had no clocks and could not tell the time when the children were to be at school, and so forth.

I will state here, though I thought and had been assured there were more Indians in that settlement than there really are, I never dreamt of having a large day school until the irrigation ditch was taken out and the flat settled more; but since P. Berard was so eager to start with a few children, I was not averse to it.

When P. Berard came home he told me he believed the Indians' statements, and he would not credit my denial until it was corroborated by Tom Morgan, the interpreter. He told me he was utterly opposed to a day school; he had described the day school to the Indians as though the pupils would not receive any clothing whatever, or any meals at school, while we could have begged the clothing easily, and while in all Indian day schools the noon meals are furnished to them.

I decided to go with him to the San Juan and straighten out matters if possible. In the meantime he made his suggestions. Considering the "island" unsafe (though that occurred to him first after a stay of about three weeks when the Indians began objecting, and after he had spent on the dam $175), he asked for three weeks to look around for another location; then he wished to use the $500 Mother Katharine had promised and what was left of the $600 to erect dwelling rooms, asking me to give him a third of our income to live on. A few days afterward, however, he suggested to go over to the San Juan, bring everything back, and take charge again of our school here. He did not persist in this, however, after Father Norbert (who wished to accompany him and stay a while at the San Juan) told him he was making a fool of himself by beginning a thing and then giving it up on account of such small difficulties. His pride was aroused by that and the publicity the affair had obtained through our publications, and he decided to return.

I would not decide anything, of course, until I had been at the San Juan myself. At the San Juan I had a council with the Indians, heard their assertions, denied them, explained, and so on. When the Indian "Sandy" brought his objections against a day school, P. Berard laughed immoderately, then said to Frank Walker: "Yes, and Frank you tell them that I promised Sandy to do all I could to assist him in opposing a day school." I knew now what I had suspected: that he himself had encouraged the Indians in their opposition.

I told the Indians that the $600 yearly was promised by a lady who was utterly opposed to boarding schools, who thought it wrong to separate the children from their parents, and, consequently, if they would not have a day school, we could not have the money for any other purpose; the $500 had also been promised under the suppositions that they would have a day school; whether I could have that money under the present circumstances was also doubtful. When at last I saw that things had gone too far, I gave up the idea of a day school, anyway for the near future, and told them if I could get the money for that purpose we would erect a mission house on the "island."

Seeing the attitude of the Indians, more especially expressed in the significant question, whether, since we would not now build a school, we would have to get another "paper" from Washington to hold the "island," I decided to write to Mother Katharine for the $500, ask your permission, and let P. Berard put up a few rooms on the "island"; when, on the following day, I was informed that one Mormon had a deed to [a] portion of "island," while another had filed on the rest of it. Then also your letter came, giving P. Berard permission to go to Pittsburg. I have inquired at Land Office, band, if plats are correct, the Mormons have no title to "island" or portion of it. I shall make further inquiries in the matter.

When I told P. Berard about the Mormons claiming the "island," he said: "So the San Juan farce is over; it did not last very long, did it?"

Now as to P. Berard, I knew he was very peculiar, but I did not think he was as changeable and unreliable, not to use any stronger expression, as I found him since the San Juan affair began.

I mentioned to you when you were here that he wanted a chance, and if he were no success as an Indian missionary on the San Juan, he would apply to return East; subsequently, he made the same statement to Frank Walker.

The fact is, the Indians not only in our immediate neighborhood, but on this side of the mountains, do not care for him, dislike him, on account of his treating them in an abrupt and harsh way. I knew perfectly well he could not do any efficient missionary work among these Indians; but I *did* hope, if he came to the San Juan, where he was practically unknown, and where he would be practically independent, he would not only try to make a success of it, but would actually do so.

I have lost all hopes that he will ever be able to do any missionary work among the Indians, and I could not recommend that he should return to the San Juan. Of course, I could let him have charge of our school as heretofore, but he said he would not be chaplain unless he had complete charge of the school, unless he could "run" it; he did not wish that anybody should "stick his nose in it." But I cannot permit him to do so. *I* must induce the parents to send their children to school, and to return them each year, and God knows it is not an easy task, and I cannot permit him to snub them when they come to see their children, especially when they are sick, to determine how long they may remain, and how the Sisters are to treat them, and what and how much they are to give them, and so on. I have permitted too much of that, not exactly to the benefit of our school, and some of the Sisters, especially the Reverend Mother, are not disinclined to listen to such suggestions and restrictions. Besides, if I am to look after the spiritual welfare of the children after they leave school, I ought to know them and be allowed to "stick my nose into the school" whenever I please.

P. Berard has become restive, cannot bear to be dependent, and will, in my opinion, not last longer than another year, no matter what occupation he may have. When he returned from his visit to Jemez last year he was all eagerness to go to Nacimiento, attend to the Mexicans in that mission and the Navajo in that part of the country, began to study Spanish, and so forth—it would have made him independent.

In my mind it is time lost for him to return, but time gained for his successor if the change is made now. I am inclined to think he would be glad to remain "East" if he were not too proud to ask for a change. I am writing to him today and enclose copy of my letter to him. I desire him to know where he is at before the conference takes place. You may rest assured I am not writing this letter "on the spur of the moment," but after due consideration.

Since I can rely on no one, and the bulk of work rests with me, and I do not know how long my physical strength will endure, I would be very thankful if you could send a younger, an energetic, but at the same time friendly, patient and persistent Father out here; I am inclined to think that P. Herculan, whom you mentioned, would "fill the bill."

I certainly would appreciate it very much if you could send a second one of similar "caliber" (to take the place of E'nishodi Hashke'e, that is, the angry priest, as the Indians call him—though I should not regret his loss even though you could not send any one to take his place). . . .

[Father Anselm enclosed a copy of his letter to Father Berard, written the same day. It tersely announced the end of the San Juan mission for the present, and held out little hope of other compatible mission work for Berard:

At any rate, building on the San Juan this year is out of the question, especially since it is not worth while beginning with the $500, which, moreover, may not be granted when Mother Katharine hears about the day-school affair.

Neither do I see my way clear for next year, since my intention [is] to induce Mrs. Drexel to give the $600 per year for Jemez day school, and the lady of Detroit to give her $6,000 for the San Juan—failed. . . .

Besides, if a new "farce" is to be inaugurated on the San Juan, there may be different actors in the play. Nothing shall be done until I have the money to build and our support in that locality is secured.

Upon your return I see nothing awaiting you, when next school-year begins, except the chaplaincy of the school, though not its complete management, and not the management of the visiting Indians at school.[6]

Father Berard did not receive his Superior's letter and its chilling message until he returned to the San Juan from his sojourn in the East. In the meantime, he sent Father Anselm several chatty reports on his travels, possible fund-raising opportunities, and plans for the future, each assuming the continuance of the San Juan mission. On July 29, from Denver, he wrote, "As to my stay at the river, I await your orders and settlement of the land question. Can we give up the 'Belle Isle'? If not, all right. I ought to know, however. In any case, I shall probably make arrangements to hold the cabin through the winter and pay rent in advance."[7] Two days later, writing from Durango, Father Berard concluded his letter with reference to a recent interview with Father Provincial:

> I am confident, that he is convinced you have taken the best course. I have done all in my power to support your actions and to increase our confratrum'[s] great estimate of you and your diplomacy. I am assured you expected this of me, though at times, I admit, I am, somewhat, nay very cranky and ugly toward you. Pardon these slips, especially since our purposes and work are unanimous and inseparable. Well I hope to find a letter from you when I arrive at Kirtland.[8]

The anticipated letter was indeed waiting at Kirtland. As we have seen, it effectively canceled the San Juan mission for the present, suggested there would be "different actors in the play" if and when it was resumed, and offered "nothing awaiting you" at St. Michaels. Father Berard's immediate response, so starkly, painfully at variance with the enthusiasm and presumed camaraderie of his letters of just days before, is perhaps the most important letter of Father Berard's entire career. To the contemporary reader, and possibly to Father Anselm at the time, it suggests that Father Anselm had underestimated Berard's commitment to him, and to the Navajo mission. Other factors, such as Father Berard's recent interview with the Provincial and the quality of his personal relations with Father Anselm following this correspondence and his return to St. Michaels, must have played a part in the decision to "keep" him. Still, one cannot read Berard's plea to his Superior without sympathy, nor doubt that Anselm's heart was softened. Father Berard stayed.]

"The Mistake Is Mine, Not Yours"[9]

My Father Superior,

It hurts me to address you in this very distant manner after the cordiality and intimacy I have enjoyed with you for the last four years. I sincerely hope, however, that it may be in my power to restore that same relation by this explanation. I refer to your letter of 13 ult., which reached me only today. And from the fact that I hasten here at Kennedy's to answer, what I consider charges, ought to show my own anxiety in this matter. It is useless, I presume, to signify my sorrow at the failure of your proposed transfer of moneys in regard to this mission. Or to take any further steps here, or show any interest in the San Juan as long as these, imaginary I hope, charges remain. Thence to the referred passages. "Besides, if a new 'farce' (it. yours) is to be inaugurated at the S.J. there may be different *actors* (it. mine) in the 'play' (it. mine). Nothing shall be done until I have the money, etc. Upon your return I see nothing awaiting you, when next school year begins, except the chaplaincy of the school, *though not its complete management and not the management of the visiting Indians at school.*" (It. mine.) These charges underlying these passages accuse me, as I understand them, of an ambition, the goal of which is nothing short of simply ousting you from the position you now hold! Let me acknowledge right here, that, as I know you and Father Leopold, such a charge could never have originated with you. I consider nobody else the author, but that impudent lanky convalescent, for whom, I regret, I have shown too much consideration and intimacy perhaps.[10] I could refer you to the treatment I received at his hands upon his arrival at St. Michaels, or, too, to the more recent things at San Juan, of which you are fully aware, and upon which occasion I received your fullest approval. Your own admission at the time of our ride to Farmington gave ample occasion to the view that he created universal dissatisfaction. How, in the face of such circumstances, you could form such an opinion of me, merely on his report, and without offering any proves [proofs?] to me for such odious statements and orders, I fail to grasp. Perhaps he has falsely reported me. Let me state what I actually did say. He at one time confidentially (which among confratres would be considered impudence) asked me what I intended to do in the future. I then stated that I had a choice between three things; either to work on the San Juan; or, in the event of my unsuitableness for that position, to have the entire chaplaincy (by which I only meant devoting myself to the instruction of the children, that is, take all instructions, private, public, and individual, and Sundays. This is nothing new to you, since I repeatedly offered my services to you to this effect. From which it is plain, I hope, that I wished to do this only with your consent). Perhaps I was unfortunate in my use of words, and said management instead of chaplaincy. But under no circumstance can he or anyone accuse me of having aspired to the entire management of the school. I protest against such charges and wish to be faced with the accuser. On the contrary, several of suggestions to that effect have been spurned by me and referred to you. And, again, though I have listened to complaints, these have been referred to you, whenever it proved to be serious. I believe you are forced to acknowledge this. As to visiting Indians, I can claim that if ever in your presence at St. Michaels, I have made dispositions in regard to visiting Indians, I have either referred them to you or Father Leopold, or made mention of my own dispositions afterward. Whether this always met with your pleasure or not I scarcely can say. But whether this could reasonably give occasion to such foul aspersions, I never found necessary to inquire or consider until now. If so, the mistake is mine, not yours. I apologize for the same and shall certainly strive to be more scrupulous than before. As to the third alternative, only a perseverance in upholding such charges against me shall induce me to ask for my removal.

After having proposed to you to either take charge of San Juan personally, or ask P. Provincial to send another man to San Juan whom I might assist with what little knowledge I have of the language, I was confident that no sinister motive would be ascribed to my application for the post; as also to my applying to you for independence of this mission from St. Michaels. On the contrary, I had all reasons to expect that, after thoroughly considering what I had to expect here and nevertheless exchanging this lonesome life for the comfort of Arizona, and so on, someone, most of all my confratres at St. Michaels, would believe in my devotedness to the cause. It is hard, to say the least. And still more hurtful since a mere report has brought it on. In the face of all of this I yet believe that, owing to the distances, this place ought to be independent, whether I consent to direct it, or others, in your own words "act the play." The choice is not mine, but my consent to take an active part here hardly will be denied to me. But I hope it never comes to that. On the contrary, I hope our old affectionate relations will be restored again.

To be complete, I ought to touch on the "farce." I must premise, however, that some people have called me a barefaced liar, because apparently I coincide with their opinions and, to their own chagrin, they eventually find that I hold just the opposite view. I do this simply out of devilment, and partially also to encourage the other party, to "give me his whole soul." I admit that upon one occasion I have in your and Father N's. [Father Norbert's] presence (perhaps imprudently) acquiesced in a view, which, I am convinced, is his own only. Can't four years of my best efforts convince you that I took and still take at least some interest in this matter? The choice to remain or go has at every visitation been left to me; have I ever signified my displeasure at your treatment, our methods, the work, and so on, to any of them? To say naught of a farce! Ridiculous! At the last visitation you signified to Father Provincial my intention of opening this mission. Both of you gave your heartiest approval. To both of you I stated that in my opinion this mission would afford me easier methods of acquiring the language than the dry study of grammar. Both agreed, only that you added, "This would be nothing for me." I hope, for heavens' sake, you have not come to designate this mission a farce, or ever imagined that *I* looked upon it as such. Thanks! I for one do *not* wish to "play the part of an actor," nor do I, without resenting it, wish to be looked upon as a fool.

True, when I returned from my second visit to St. Michaels again, I was impressed, as if you thought I was making trouble where there was none, in other words only imagining a status, which, in reality, was far from existence; consequently, that you made a mistake in sending me here. This letter seems to confirm this view (though not expressly stated and even perhaps not intended). It would surprise me very much, especially since our last interview after the council. Then you admitted every one of my contentions, save the safety of the island. While you were thoroughly convinced, as your succeeding actions warrant, of the futility of an Indian day school here, it, at the same time, showed you some of the difficulties I had to contend with. Yet I should be glad, in the interests of the Navajo, if another could succeed where we vainly looked for success. And, if there has been anything farcical in the whole work, I rest assured, you will not hold me responsible for it. On the contrary, I am of opinion that the difficulties here were such, as few could and would have surmised. My conversations and correspondence with you also bear me witness that on *all* occasions I sought your council. Yet after all I may not have been free of faults, though these have not been intentional. And since I am considered to be "too full of prunes and ambition" a change ought to take place at the San Juan.

In the intervening period of my leave and return I have forgotten which things you desired to remain at the lodgings here. I await your speedy answer as also orders in regard to the renting of the house. Do you wish rent to be paid or not?

Yours,

Father Berard, O.F.M

Kirtland, N.M.

P.S. I expect, at least, that the differences under consideration be strictly confined to ourselves.

Notes

1. Robert L. Wilken, *Anselm Weber, O.F.M.: Missionary to the Navaho*. Milwaukee: Bruce, 1955, 130, 137.

2. Murray Bodo, ed., *Tales of an Endishodi: Father Berard Haile and the Navajo*, 1900–1961. Albuquerque: University of New Mexico Press, 1998, xxi.

3. Berard Haile, handwritten journal, BHP Box 1, fd. 3.

4. As it turned out, Father Berard's doubts about the safety of the "island" were well founded. It was totally washed away in the San Juan flood of October 6, 1911. Wilken, 138.

5. Anselm Weber to Provincial Chrysostom Theobald, 13 July 1904. FFP Box 33, fd.

6. Anselm Weber to Berard Haile, 13 July 1904. FFP Box 1, fd. 6.

7. Berard Haile to Anselm Weber, 29 July 1904. FAC Box DEC.077. Haile, Berard. fd. Haile, Berard: Letters to Anselm Weber and Katharine Drexel.

8. Berard Haile to Anselm Weber, 31 July 1904. FAC Box DEC.077. Haile, Berard. fd. Haile, Berard: Letters to Anselm Weber and Katharine Drexel.

9. Berard Haile to Anselm Weber, 3 August 1904. FAC Box DEC.077. Haile, Berard. fd. Haile, Berard: Letters to Anselm Weber and Katharine Drexel.

10. Here Berard refers to Father Norbert Gottbrath, "the tubercular theological student," who according to the mission chronicle was sent to St. Michaels in August 1903 "in the interest of his health." He remained there for 18 months, departing February 1, 1905, for Cincinnati to continue his studies. Later Father Norbert attended medical school, and in 1913 Father Anselm tried unsuccessfully to arrange for the priest-physician to serve on the Navajo reservation. Wilken, 149, 211; Juvenal Schnorbus et al., "History of the Ranch, about Seven Miles South of Fort Defiance (Cienega) Arizona, Now St. Michaels Missions," FAC Box PLA.376 St. Michaels, env. St. Michaels Earliest History 1898–1907, 25, 27.

Part 2

INDIAN POLICY

9

Federal Policy and Indian Missions, 1869–1916[1]

Emanuel Trockur, O.F.M.

[We have already encountered, in Father Emanuel's narrative of the 1899 expedition to the San Juan (chapter 5) an installment of his nine-part series, "Franciscan Missions among the Navajo Indians," published sporadically in the *Franciscan Chronicle*, 1938–1943. Here we present portions of the inaugural article of the series. Father Emanuel explicitly labeled this first article as "background," a review of "modern missionary activities in general among the Indians" that was essential to understanding the particular situation of the Franciscans among the Navajo. Writing in an era of more firmly established federal neutrality and secularism, Father Emanuel apologized for the need "to delve into past unpleasantries with the morbidity of a scandal-monger," yet he insisted that unless readers understood the spirit of anti-Catholic bigotry that had influenced the legislation and sometimes the administration of federal Indian policy in earlier decades, they could not appreciate the struggles and achievements of the early missionaries. Indian policy, however well intentioned, in practice often worked to the detriment of its wards and their advocates. Federal administration and regulation, whether even-handed or, as the Franciscans sometimes complained, deliberately biased against Catholics, seemed as often to impede as to facilitate the friars' efforts to "civilize" the Indians.

When assessing the history of federal Indian policy as it affected the Indian missions, it is important to distinguish formal "Indian policy" from the day-to-day working relationships between the friars and various agents of the government. A formal policy might seem unfair, even patently anti-Catholic; yet friars, working within the unfortunate policy, would still establish positive and productive relationships with government officials at various levels. Typically, the Franciscans were on excellent terms with key federal administrators, and these relationships worked both ways. Indeed, many times it was the government agent who came to the friars with requests for assistance and information.

Competition with the Protestants for Indian souls, Indian support, Indian children, and Indian land for mission sites was conducted in light of, and with reference to, federal oversight and authority. Each side of the competition might appeal to highly placed officials or committees, and each might define the official stance of government neutrality as in fact favoring the opposition. Furthermore, within the broad arena of "government relations," the Catholic fathers were forced to "play politics," not only to confront Protestant missionaries in the field, but to identify potential problems and to resist Protestant attempts to have enacted, either in Congress or the courts, policies unfavorable to Catholics. Father Emanuel writes of the necessity for constant overview of Indian legislation in Congress by the Bureau of Catholic Indian Missions, "to prevent the Protestant sects from using the strong arm of the Government to aid them to Protestantize the Indians of our country." Also, it is noteworthy that it is in present tense, not past, that Emanuel refers to the high cost of the struggle with Protestantism: "Thus, whilst we are striving to sow the good seed of Catholic doctrine into the Navajo mind, we must at the same time be ever rooting up the bad seed of Protestantism which presents a more formidable obstacle to our efforts than paganism itself."[2]]

By way of introduction to the work of the Franciscan Fathers of the Province of St. John the Baptist among the Navajo Indians since the year 1898, it should be both interesting and enlightening to review beforehand the development of modern missionary activities in general among the Indians of our land. Thus, we shall obtain a fair and clear picture of the difficult field into which our Province ventured and be enabled to adjudge properly and appreciate more fully the varied and unsuspected hardships amid obstacles that were involved in the work of these brave and zealous pioneers.

Government Policy

Prior to the year 1869 the policy of our government in its dealings with Indians was practically devoid of every element of a helpful and constructive character. Educational facilities among the Indians were supplied for the most part by various religious organizations, which were encouraged by the government to establish schools and in many instances received financial aid for their maintenance. The result was often hostility between the government and the Indians and friction and controversy between the numerous religious interests in the field.

In his message to Congress in December 1869, President Grant, agreeing with the first Board of Indian Commissioners,[3] which he himself had appointed, that the government Indian policy must be changed from one of "spoliation, outrage and murder, unjust and iniquitous beyond the power of words to express," declared the advisability of enlisting the aid of religion in the cause of Indian education and civilization. He inaugurated a new policy which became known as the *Peace Policy*, in contradistinction to the one of extermination and strife which had prevailed theretofore, and asked the various denominations to cooperate with the government toward that end. Accordingly, he invited representatives of all the churches to come to Washington to deliberate with him as how to formulate and carry out his designs. The Methodists, Presbyterians, Congregationalists, and Episcopalians were among those who responded; the Catholic Church was represented by the illustrious Jesuit missionary of the Northwest, Father De Smet.[4]

At this meeting the president pledged the solemn word of the administration that the government would provide clothing, food, and tuition for all Indian pupils attending mission schools of whatsoever denomination. This policy was most favorably received, and, acting on the well-meant invitation and promise of the president, the denominations began to erect schools on the various reservations throughout the country, the Catholic Church alone expending the sum of $1.5 million in the new project.

Unfortunately, however, the Indian Office later decided to assign only one denomination to each tribe, to the exclusion of all others—plainly against the spirit of the Constitution inasmuch as it militated against freedom of conscience—and with little regard to the previous affiliations of the Indians. At that time there were 72 Indian agencies, and in 38 of these, Catholics had been the first to establish themselves. Yet only eight agencies were assigned to the Catholic Church, and 80,000 Catholic Indians were given over to Protestant missionaries.[5] The Catholic pueblo of Jemes[6] in New Mexico was, for example, given over to the Presbyterians, and Pine Ridge and Rosebud in South Dakota to the Episcopalians.[7] Thus, Catholic tribes were entrusted to Protestant sects and Protestants to Catholic missionaries with the most confusing and detrimental results, as might well be imagined.

Anti-Catholic Bigotry

It was not long after this that the same forces that had jumbled and perverted the original peace policy began to invade the halls of Congress and the Senate, even the Executive Mansion, and clamored that no more appropriations should be given to sectarian and denominational schools. This agitation to have government allowances withdrawn was begun when it was realized that 3,500 Indian pupils were attending Catholic schools under this plan, and it "appeared" that the Catholic Church was monopolizing government aid. It is, therefore, quite apparent that anti-Catholic bigotry was at work from the beginning, seeking to secure passage of legislation in Congress that would cripple the efforts of the Church on the one hand, or to promote those of the Protestants among our Indians on the other.[8]

With every form of opposition and complaint brought to bear against the Catholic "monopoly" which actually educated its pupils at about one-half the per-capita allowance that the government required in its own schools, the victory went to the objectors who, it is safe to say, were chiefly instrumental in having this very policy adopted in the first place. Beginning, then, with the fiscal year of 1896, all government appropriations for such purposes were annually decreased by 20 percent, until in 1901, under the pretext that such action was in perfect accord with the Constitution, these government funds were discontinued entirely.

This drastic legislation, wholly unprepared for and unforeseen by the Catholics, naturally left all their mission schools without any funds; whereupon Commissioner of Indian Affairs Browning, apparently moved by a desire to relieve the situation as much as possible, offered to purchase all mission school plants and to incorporate the teachers into the Civil Service and allow them to remain until they should be replaced through the operation of Civil Service regulations—an offer that was later repeated by Commissioner W. A. Jones, but which was declined by Catholic missions in the main. Protestants, however, welcomed the new arrangement and sold their buildings to the government, retaining most of their regular personnel as government employees, while their ministers continued to conduct their "nonsectarian" services every Sunday as before.

Why did the Catholics refuse to sell their buildings as the Protestants had done? Could they not have retained their teachers and employees in the same manner? Yes; but for how long? Past experience had taught them to be suspicious and fear for the future, and they quickly detected the trap that was being set for them. That their suspicions were well grounded developed from the numerous instances which occurred later. An example: in 1874 the government school at Tualip, Washington, was given to the Sisters of Divine Providence. In 1902 a Protestant superintendent was placed over them, and they resigned and left.[10]

Next came the "Browning Ruling" issued by Commissioner Browning on November 30, 1896, which declared that "parents have no right to designate which school their children shall attend." Only after six years, on January 18, 1902, was this ruling recalled at the instigation of Archbishop Ireland.[11] On November 29 of that year the succeeding commissioner, W.A. Jones, issued a circular which, though it seemed to annul the Browning Ruling's intent, nevertheless required parents who wished to enroll their children in other than government schools to appear personally before their superintendents and declare such intention in writing. There can be no doubt but that every effort was being put forth to put the Catholics to rout. This was clearly indicated when parents who sent their children to other than government schools—these were only Catholic schools, of course—were deprived of rations.

Is it then a rash statement when I say that at the bottom of all these monstrous rulings and all this agitation against the use of government funds was anti-Catholic bigotry? In no instance was it claimed that the mission schools were inefficient, that their teachers were incapable or unsuccessful, or that the Indians were in any way dissatisfied with them. Such claims could not have been made, much less established in the face of published reports of Indian commissioners, agents, and superintendents, and the testimony of senators and congressmen which bore eloquent tribute to the unprecedented work accomplished by the Catholic Indian schools, whose only crime was that they were Catholic *and* successful. It was at this crucial time that Mother Katharine Drexel, foundress and Superior of the Sisters of the Blessed Sacrament, came to the rescue and saved the Catholic schools from disaster, when she promised to support them until such time that the Catholic people themselves would be enabled to do so. For many years she did this practically alone.

Still, as it became more difficult from year to year to collect sufficient funds to supplement those furnished by Mother Katharine for the support of 60 Indian schools in the charge of the Bureau of Catholic Indian Missions,[12] Father William H. Ketcham, director of the bureau, found himself forced to surrender partly, at least, some of the buildings to the government. However, he did not sell them as the Protestants had done from 1895 to 1908, but decided to lease them for the term of one year—a clever arrangement which left a way open to correct any unjust dealings or treatment that might occur.[13] At the end of the term, the teaching Sisters, who were employees of the government, remained free to resign from the Indian Service and the schools could retain their status as purely Catholic institutions.

Tribal Funds

From the very beginning Father Ketcham had always firmly maintained that such Indians as possessed "tribal funds," though they were held by the government in the U.S. Treasury for the Indians, could legally request the appropriation of such funds for the education of their children in the schools of their own choice. Approaching President McKinley on the subject, he had already received the assurance that the president sincerely hoped that the law could be interpreted as liberally as possible in favor of the Church. The president referred the matter to the secretary of the interior who, to all appearances, "pigeonholed" it. As soon as President Roosevelt took office, Father Ketcham again took up his pet argument and, in spite of the fact that Archbishop Ireland had expressed himself as being very dubious of the outcome, he called upon the president in person. Mr. Roosevelt agreed that the proposition was perfectly just and reasonable, and promised to order such a disposition of tribal funds if he found it legally permissible to do so.

The Hon. Charles J. Bonaparte, general counsel for the Catholic Indian Bureau, at Father Ketcham's suggestion, then prepared a comprehensive memorandum of the entire question which was presented to the attorney general for his consideration. The attorney general subsequently affirmed the Catholic contention. On January 22, 1904, President Roosevelt called a meeting of his cabinet for a thorough review of the matter. The resulting decision of the attorney general affirmed Father Ketcham's contention and permitted monies that belonged strictly to the Indians to be used for the education of the Indian children in confessional schools.[14]

It is certain that President Roosevelt did not order the appropriation of Indian money for the support of the mission schools from political motives, because this order was not made known generally. The decision of the attorney general was not published. But no sooner did it leak out than a flood of protests and complaints stormed Washington. Congress reached such a state of agitation as though the very foundations of the republic were tottering.[15]

The alarm was spread by the Episcopal bishop Hare of South Dakota, who had two Indian schools under his supervision. On January 5, 1905, he wrote a stinging letter in which he attacked the Catholic Church and the administration. The Indian Rights Association came out in a strong pamphlet against the measure, and on January 21, 1905, the *Outlook* of New York[16] registered a vigorous protest in an article under the caption: "A Mischievous Appropriation." Representative Stephens of Texas and Senator Bard of California came to the rescue by airing their views in the House and Senate. In a letter addressed to him by the minister of a Baptist church in Kentucky—complaints came from all over the country—the president was informed that he was making a most serious mistake in permitting such a disreputable thing that would bring ruin to all parties concerned. As a citizen of this land of liberty, purchased with blood, the writer begged the chief executive in the name of the Lord of heaven and earth to be true to God and poor, suffering humanity, and refrain from such acts as would bury his good name in shame and disgrace.[17]

President Roosevelt refused to yield, and declared in a letter to the secretary of the interior that the Indians had a moral right to use their own money for the education of their children in any school or institution of their choice, and that the Indian Department would continue to respect the wishes of the Indians as long as Congress would not decree the contrary or the courts would rule that the decision of the attorney general had been erroneous.[18]

It is no wonder that the Bureau of Catholic Indian Missions was now contemptuously labeled a "Catholic Lobby" and accused of meddling in politics. These charges were, of course, unfounded and were made because the bureau, with its eye constantly on Indian legislation in Congress, was ever on the alert to prevent the Protestant sects from using the strong arm of the government to aid them to Protestantize the Indians of our country. A Catholic "lobby" of this nature was absolutely necessary to protect Catholic missions and the religious rights of the Indians against Protestant hostility which attempted to manipulate the government into crushing Catholic Indian mission work. An explanation of all this jealous frenzy is to be found in the fact that the Catholic Church had many Indian schools attended by several thousand children, while the Protestants had few Indian schools and few pupils. Had the tables been turned, the situation would undoubtedly have been viewed differently.

But since the bigots could make no effect on the administration nor succeed in putting through hostile legislation in Congress, they now attempted to achieve their ends through the courts. The question was brought before the Equity Court of the District of Columbia in the form of a test case in which the Indian Rights Association, under cover of three Protestant Sioux Indians of the Rosebud Agency of South Dakota, Reuben Quick Bear, Ralph Eagle Feather, and Charles Tackett, sought to bring an injunction against the secretary of the interior and the treasurer, forbidding the contracting with any mission school whatsoever for support and education of Indian pupils with the aid of trust or treaty funds. Judge Ashley C. Gould, on April 4, 1907, decided that the trust funds were available for that purpose, but that the use of treaty funds in such case was unlawful. The result of this decision was that five of the eight mission schools lost their support coming from Indian monies. To the Catholic schools it meant an annual loss of $62,600.

But, as was to be expected, neither party to the suit was satisfied with this decision, and the case was referred to the Court of Appeals, which on November 29, 1907, affirmed that not only trust funds but treaty funds as well could be used for the support of the pupils in the so-called contract schools.[19]

The main contention of the Indian Rights Association was that Congress, in an appropriation act passed on June 7, 1897, had declared it to be "the settled policy of the government to hereafter make no appropriation whatever for education in any sectarian schools." In the course of the opinion, Judge Wright, after reviewing the law creating both the trust and treaty funds and the authorities, stated that the declaration of the above-mentioned act applied only to money appropriated in *that* act, and that it could not establish "the settled policy of the government." To have such a settled policy it would be necessary for each succeeding Congress to so state. The opinion further declared that "it seems inconceivable that Congress should have intended to prohibit them (the Indians) from receiving religious education at their own cost, if they desired it; that such an intent would be only to prohibit the free exercise of religion among the Indians and such would be the effect of the construction for which the complainants contend."

As a result of this decision, President Roosevelt ordered the renewal of the contracts of all eight schools.

The Indian Rights Association then appealed to the Supreme Court, which, in 1908, upheld the decision of the Court of Appeals.[20]

Religious Garb in Government Schools

But bigotry kept marching on to raise its battered head in a new strategy when Congressman Stephens, who now was chairman of the Indian Committee of the House,[21] introduced a resolution on June 21, 1911, which directed the secretary of the interior to make a comprehensive report to Congress regarding religious schools which had been taken over by the government during the preceding six years: whether religious emblems or symbols of any kind were being displayed in the classrooms or whether employees were wearing any religious garbs. It is significant that the only schools taken over in that time were Catholic schools, and thus we find the old axiom applied: "*Duo, quum faciunt idem, non est idem,*" or "*Quod licet Jovi, non licet bovi.*" When Protestant schools were purchased by the government and their teachers were "blanketed into" the Civil Service, there was no protest or complaint from either side, but when Catholics preferred to lease their buildings to selling them, it was a different story.[22]

On January 27, 1912,[23] Indian Commissioner Robert G. Valentine, without consulting with the president or the secretary of the interior, issued his famous ukase, which would have banned all teachers wearing religions garbs—Catholic

Sisters—from government schools. "In the public schoolrooms, or on the grounds when on duty, insignia or garb has no justification," said the edict, which further required that "where such an employee cannot conscientiously do that (leave off such garb while engaged at lay duties as government employees) he will be given a reasonable time, not to extend, however, before the opening of the next school year after the date of this order, to make arrangements for employment elsewhere than in Federal Indian Schools."

Two weeks later, President Taft received the following telegram from Charles L. Thompson, president of the Home Mission Council of the National Protestant Mission Boards and Societies:[24]

> New York, February 1, 1912.
> The President, the White House,
>   Washington, D.C.
>   The action of the Honorable Commissioner of Indian Affairs, issued January 27, relative to sectarian insignia and garb in Federal Indian Schools, is to our minds so manifestly American in spirit, so judicial and righteous that we heartily approve and commend it. We did not know such an order was in preparation. But we now express our commendation, and ask that nothing be permitted to weaken its force. We desire representatives to have a conference with you if you find opportunity and occasion for this.
>   Charles Thompson

Mr. Taft apparently paid no heed to this "follow-up" of the scheme, and without waiting for the desired conference promptly suspended the order a few days later, with the declaration that the matter should first be thoroughly investigated and all interested parties be permitted to present their views of the question. The Jesuit weekly *America*[25] commented upon this action of the president as follows: "If the whole proceeding from Commissioner down to Mission Boards was a trap laid for the President by foes in the Republican Party and even in his own entourage to embarrass the candidate for reelection on the eve of a National Convention, Mr. Taft took the bull by the horns and showed himself equal to the occasion."

Father Anselm Weber, O.F.M., however, considered this one of Mr. Taft's many political blunders: had he sternly declared himself and denounced the commissioner as an unloyal official who had overstepped his authority and was now stirring up a political broil just before the elections, had he staunchly insisted that if any changes in this matter were to be made, Congress or the courts would make them, the unpleasant affair would have been set down by a single stroke.[26]

At the direction of the president, Commissioner Valentine revoked the order in the following curt instruction addressed to superintendents in charge of Indian schools, under date of February 6, 1912:

> By direction of the President, the order issued in Circular No. 601, supplementing the existing religious regulations in Indian schools, has been revoked and action

thereunder suspended pending a hearing to be given the parties in interest before the Secretary of the Interior. You will be governed accordingly.
(Signed) Robert G. Valentine. Commissioner.

The investigation which was undertaken at the president's suggestion revealed that, out of 2,000 teachers in Indian schools under government supervision, there were 51 who wore religious garbs and who were regularly classified members of the Civil Service.[27] In his report to the commissioner, Secretary of the Interior Fisher pointed out that no sectarian religious instruction was being given in any of these schools at the time, and he was of the opinion that there was no legal prohibition against the employment of government teachers who wore religious dress. However, he also held that such a regulation was within his authority and therefore "in order to secure more apparent equality of treatment between denominations interested" he now decided that henceforth no teachers wearing a religious garb should be incorporated into the service.

After eight months of wrangling and bitter animosity, President Taft finally announced his decision which coincided with that of the secretary of the interior. He held to the revocation of the order as originally framed, but the policy involved became effective as far as new teachers in the service were concerned. In other words, no new Sisters could be admitted to positions in government schools, but those that had been "blanketed in" up to that time were allowed to remain.

Proselyting

From the foregoing it should not be too difficult to judge who were playing politics and to what extreme they were willing to go in order to embarrass and intimidate the administration. It must also be clear that, while they appeared honest and sincere in their sanctimoniously vehement protests against government aid which they had originally secured through their own efforts, against sectarianism and our nuns in government schools, their demands for nonsectarianism were nothing else than a camouflaged insistence upon the fullest freedom for Protestantism. This was quite evident as far back as the year 1902 when Commissioner Jones[28] issued rules and regulations concerning religious worship and instructions in Indian schools. These regulations placed all government schools upon the same plane as the Protestant establishments which had previously been bought by the government, inasmuch as all pupils, irrespective of creed, were required to attend a strictly "undenominational service." Pupils were urged to "affiliate with some denomination—preference being left to the pupil," but no way was left for the pagan pupils to acquaint themselves with Catholic doctrine. Priests were permitted to give nonsectarian instructions only for fear that "unseemly discussion of sectarian matters, proselyting, or other conduct would tend to create strife among religious denominations." Thus it was permissible to try to make Protestants out of pagans—the Catholic priests were perfectly welcome to contribute their aid to this end—but to attempt to make

Catholics out of these pagans, such a thing was strictly prohibited, because it might have constituted an "unseemly discussion of sectarian matters."

At about this time a special appropriation was made in the Indian Appropriation Act for the education of 120 pupils at the Hampton, Virginia, Normal and Agricultural College, an institution conducted under Protestant auspices and which had a department for the education of Protestant ministers. Despite these facts, Congress had declared Hampton a nonsectarian institution. Never was an objection raised on the part of Catholics against government aid to Hampton, but why did not the Indian Rights Association or the *Outlook* and other champions of nonsectarianism do so?

To return to the rules issued by Commissioner Jones: Father Anselm Weber, O.F.M., "the apostle of the Navajo," presented his views on the question to the succeeding Commissioner Leupp. Mr. Leupp graciously promised to give the matter his serious consideration, but when Father Weber read the amendments which the commissioner had drawn up, he wrote: "I recalled the old Latin quotation: *"Parturiunt montes, et nascitur ridiculus mus.""*[29] Commissioner Leupp's amendments to the rules for religious instruction to government schools had not touched upon the question in its bearing on pagan children, and since the Indian Department declined to commit itself to any plan beforehand, the situation remained practically the same as before.

It was not until Mr. Valentine came to office that a fair and just plan was devised. Under the new rules promulgated by him, it was provided that pagan children could be instructed in the religion of their parents' choice. Attendance was made obligatory, the government was assumed to be taking the place of the parents of children while at school, and school officials were held responsible for the fulfillment of the parents' wishes, which were to be expressed in writing.

Mr. Valentine came into office when, on April 15, 1909, he was appointed to succeed Commissioner Leupp, who resigned his position because of ill health. Father Anselm went to Washington the following September,[30] and after several conferences with Mr. Charles S. Lusk, secretary of the Catholic Indian Bureau,[31] Mr. J. H. Dortch, chief of the Division of Indian Education, and Commissioner Valentine, a new set of fair and just regulations was drawn up and submitted to the Executive Committee of the Indian Department. Their acceptance and publication were immediately greeted by vigorous protests from 17 Protestant denominations, who proceeded to attempt their revocation. Mr. Gates, a member of the Board of Indian Commissioners, was their chief spokesman at a meeting called by the department. With the accustomed "logic and consistency" of his predecessors he opposed practically everything. He insisted that preachers be permitted to conduct the so-called undenominational services, that the hymns rejected by the Catholics be not forbidden, and that Protestant and Catholic children remain free to attend or not attend their respective churches, while Catholic, Protestant, and pagan pupils should be forced to attend the nonsectarian services. Father Ketcham, who was present at the urgent request of the commissioner, once more proved himself equal to the occasion. He countered in such clear and unmistakable language that the delegation left the conference room dumbfounded.

The new rules were finally issued on March 12, 1910. The nonsectarian service was retained, it is true, but with the understanding that it was to be conducted by "the superintendent of the school or some employee designated by him, but not by a minister or priest."

During the summer of 1910 Father Weber visited the Navajo in their homes, attending meetings, feasts, and dances for the purpose of obtaining written requests from parents for the instruction of their pagan children in Catholic doctrine at the government school at Fort Defiance, Arizona. His trip of about a thousand miles on horseback and by buggy yielded signatures for a total of 198 pupils, and on February 7, 1911, he had the happiness of giving Catholic instructions to pagan children for the first time at Fort Defiance, more than 12 years after the friars had entered the Navajo mission field.[32]

Inconsistency

The ultimate demands of the objectors invariably betrayed the spirit of their opposition and the hidden reasons for their capricious contentions, and, naturally, contradiction and inconsistency seemed to meet them on every side. Had they pursued their arguments in the religious garb dispute to their logical conclusions, they might have obtained legislation forbidding anyone wearing any sort of religious badge or insignia from entering an Indian classroom. Teachers in such schools might have been required to deny positively affiliation with any religion, or it might have become necessary to entrust the education of Indian children to men and women who were destitute of any religious belief whatsoever. It might also have been enacted that all teachers in government Indian schools wear a particular style of dress, such as our city police, railroad trainmen, or soldiers and sailors wear. But no; they cannot afford to be too consistent and must prefer to allow their bigotry to lead them so far away from the path of logic that they can see no violation of constitutional rights or principles, unless these "violations" prove disadvantageous to them or favorable to Catholics.

Thus, while teaching secular branches by those who wear a religious garb must constitute an infraction of the Constitution, it must by all means be provided that no legislation be enacted that would prohibit the teaching of religion or engaging in religious activities among Indian children by such as wore no distinctive religious garb. Even before the religious garb question was disposed of, YMCA secretaries had established themselves in government school buildings or at least on the school grounds. Notable instances were: Haskell Institute at Lawrence, Kansas; Sherman Institute at Riverside, California; and the Carlisle Indian School at Carlisle, Pennsylvania. It was the ancient Trojan horse clothed in the mantle of nonsectarianism—Protestantism in its simplest form—but housed in quarters that were furnished free of charge by the government which further supplied light, heat, and other privileges equally gratis.

Although not employees of the government and without any actual official status, these secretaries came to be looked upon as government aides at least, and it was quite natural that they should experience no difficulty in imposing their plans upon the superintendent in charge and in having whatever regulations they cared to suggest put into effect. As a result, Catholic pupils at Haskell[33] were discriminated against and insulted because of their faith so that in some instances they gave up their religion in order to escape oppression. They were permitted to absent themselves from Catholic services so that they might attend a "Y" meeting; but, on the other hand, non-Catholics were strictly forbidden to attend a Catholic gathering at any time. Although attendance at Mass was compulsory according to the rules, from 10 to 25 percent of the Catholic pupils were regularly absent. When Catholic children received Holy Communion, they were deprived of breakfast and had to fast until noon. On one occasion when four Catholic girls requested a late breakfast after receiving Holy Communion, they were told that they could find their breakfast in the "slop barrel."

These shocking conditions were repeatedly brought to the attention of the Indian Office, and time and again a fair deal for Catholics was requested, but action was always deferred, and for months the shameful state of affairs continued until Father Philip Gordon, a Chippewa Indian priest and newly appointed chaplain for the Catholics there,[34] preferred charges against the authorities and demanded an investigation. In the meanwhile Cardinal Gibbons, Cardinal Farley, and Archbishop Prendergast, members of the Catholic Indian Mission Board, wrote a joint letter to Secretary Lane, requesting that a home be provided for a priest-chaplain, the same as was being provided for the YMCA secretary. Of course, the secretary of the interior even was unable under the laws to do this and instead he wired the superintendent at Haskell to see that the "Y" secretary be ordered immediately to move off the government premises. The charge that said secretary had been housed at government expense was not investigated, as the said gentlemen had already moved from the grounds when the inspectors arrived.

On February 18, 1916, a set of rules was drafted and an understanding entered into between Superintendent John R. Wise of Haskell and Father Gordon, which later became standard in all other government Indian schools.

Back to Our Navajo Indians

It will appear that I have gotten ahead of my story which was supposed to be an introduction to our labors among the Navajo. Besides, many of my readers may have begun to feel that it is out of place and quite useless to review these or any other similarly unpleasant incidents of the past. Why, they may have thought, reopen old wounds and revive ancient bitterness, ill-feelings, and suspicions that should long ago have been put aside? The purpose of this article is not to highlight these unfortunate outbursts of bigotry and hatred of the Catholic religion, nor to denounce all Protestants in general. The writer was reared in the midst of Protestants in the Middle West and attended a public school, except for one year, before entering college to prepare for the priesthood. In all his school days he had not heard or witnessed such evidences of intolerance and bigotry as he found later in the Navajo missions. Protestants as a rule mind their own affairs, but it seems there is never a want of bigoted and narrow-minded ministers of the various sects who, in their misguided zeal and blind fanaticism, are constantly occupied in leading the people astray. Many instances could be enumerated where Protestant ministers have employed malicious, lying, and most uncharitable tactics in their attempts at poisoning the minds of our Navajo at Fort Defiance,[35] Chin Lee,[36] Tohatchi,[37] Keams Canyon,[38] Shiprock, and elsewhere on the reservation, and we have the word of one of the ministers himself that he undertook his work among the Navajo with instructions to "fight the Catholics."

What we set out to do by this article was not primarily to delve into past unpleasantries with the morbidity of a scandal-monger, but rather to furnish a general and fairly adequate review of conditions with which our pioneer missionaries had to contend in their new field. The statements are of facts that have become history, disagreeable and disgusting, it is true, but facts just the same, and even though not everything that is true ought be served up for general consumption, it has been deemed necessary in the present instance to dwell upon these facts inasmuch as they present our work from an angle which is only too rarely taken into account and without which a proper perspective and background of the Navajo mission activities cannot be obtained.

It may be truthfully said that Protestantism in its various forms and with its conflicting doctrines of the Presbyterian, Baptist, Episcopalian, Dutch Reformed Churches, and so on, all of whom do not hesitate to malign Catholic doctrines, priests, and nuns, has gotten the Indian confused. "If the Christians so fight among themselves," they will argue, "why should we join any of them?" Thus, while we are striving to sow the good seed of Catholic doctrine into the Navajo mind, we must at the same time be ever rooting up the bad seed of Protestantism which presents a more formidable obstacle to our efforts than paganism itself. We believe that the slow rate of progress accompanying our efforts at Christianizing and civilizing the Navajo may be attributed in great measure to this one factor alone. In practically every instance where we have met opposition, the Catholic contention has been the correct one; and when this contention was not upheld, it was not because it was wrong, but because the government, which felt itself bound to neutrality in such matters, always found its way out by resorting to compromise in order that the conflicting parties would remain at peace.

Much criticism has been aimed at the efforts and "meager results" produced by the Navajo missionaries, but what has been said here should serve to point out that these men were and still are confronted by circumstances and conditions quite different from those found in established parishes in the East, conditions which furthermore are not similar to those met by the earlier missionaries in these parts, who converted entire tribes or baptized thousands on a single visit.

For the first six years, the friars occupied themselves almost exclusively in making friends of the Navajo and learning their difficult language and strange customs. It was not until the year 1904 that the first Catholic school was opened on the Navajo reservation, and with this one exception, their contacts were, for the most part, with pupils at government schools where nonsectarian instructions only were permitted. First rules for religious instructions in government schools, as already stated, were issued in 1902, but it was not until 1910, with the appearance of the Valentine regulations, that provision was made for the Catholic instruction of pagan pupils.

These regulations brought brighter prospects and tended to dispel the false impression that the Catholic religion was an intruder in this pagan field and also to discredit the oft-repeated claim that our government was Protestant and desired that its wards should be Protestant likewise. Immediately, large classes of catechumens were organized, and during the year 1912 a total of 126 pupils of the Fort Defiance school received holy baptism. Up to that time there had been only 275 baptisms recorded at St. Michael's Mission; as of August 1, 1938, this number has grown to 2,279, while the Fort Defiance records count 1,856 baptisms.

From St. Michaels and Fort Defiance the work was extended to Chin Lee and Lukachukai, later to Tohatchi, Keams Canyon, Shiprock, and Fort Wingate. More recently, chapels have been erected at other vantage points on the reservation, and in 1932 a Catholic day school was opened at Houck. St. Michael's School, wholly supported by Mother Katharine Drexel, remains the only Catholic boarding school in the vast Navajo country. Besides the 293 pupils in attendance there during the past year, approximately 1,700 more Navajo children received Catholic instruction at other widely separated government day and boarding schools.

Notes

1. From Emanuel Trockur, "Background of the Indian Missions," *Provincial Chronicle* 11 (Fall 1938): 3–16.

2. Trockur, 7, 15.

3. Instituted by Act of Congress, April 10, 1869.

4. Cf. speech delivered by the Reverend Dr. Henry G. Ganns, Financial Agent of Catholic Indian Schools, at Dayton, Ohio, June 21, 1903.

5. This glaring injustice induced the Catholic bishops of the United States to organize the Catholic Commission for Indian Missions on January 2, 1874. Anselm Weber, FMN 41 (December 1914): 1092.

6. *Sendbote* 39 (January 1912): 11.

7. In 1878; but in 1905, under President Theodore Roosevelt, choice of religion was granted.

8. In 1892 Indian Commissioner Morgan attempted to "freeze out" a Catholic Indian school in Montana. Lawrence Benedict Palladino, *Indian and White in the Northwest: A History of Catholicity in Montana, 1831–1891* (Lancaster, Pa.: Wickersham, 1922), 267.

9. June 30, 1900. *Indian Sentinel* (1902–1903): 10, 29; Weber, FMN 29 (March 1902): 204; 30 (May 1903): 399; 30 (October 1903): 878.

10. Weber, FMN 40 (January, February 1913): 17, 108.

11. Weber, FMN 30 (July 1903): 579.

12. This new title of the Catholic Commission for Indian Missions was assumed in 1881. *Indian Sentinel* 1 (1916): 26.

13. Weber, FMN 40 (February 1913): 109.

14. Weber, FMN 32 (June 1905): 502.

15. Weber, FMN 2 (July 1905): 598.

16. *Outlook* (January 21, 1905): 149.

17. A German translation of this curious letter can be found in Weber, FMN 32 (July 1905): 600 ff.

18. Weber, FMN 32 (August 1905): 702.

19. The distinction between trust funds and treaty funds may be briefly explained as follows: Some Indian tribes had acquired funds by the sale of lands and timber, the proceeds of which were deposited in the U.S. Treasury. Monies of this character were known as Indian trust funds. Other tribes received compensation by appropriations which were made annually by Congress in payment of debts or in pursuance of treaty stipulations. These were known as treaty funds. Collectively these funds, which could in no way be considered public funds, were called "Tribal Funds." Weber, FMN 35 (October 1908): 886 ff.; 42 (June 1915): 546.

20. Weber, FMN 35 (October 1908): 891 ff.

21. Weber, FMN 39 (February 1912): 112 ff.; 40 (February 1913): 109; *Catholic Telegraph*, Oct. 10, 1912.

22. Weber, FMN 40 (February 1913): 109 ff.

23. Weber, FMN 40 (February 1913): 109 ff.

24. *America* (February 17, 1912): 446.

25. *America* (February 17, 1912): 446.

26. Weber, FMN 40 (February 1913): 110.

27. *Catholic Standard and Times* (September 26, 1912).

28. Weber, FMN 40 (January 1913): 20.

29. Weber, FMN 40 (January 1913): 20.

30. Weber, FMN 37 (February 1910): 108 ff.

31. Mr. Lusk had been associated with the bureau from its inception in 1874.

32. *Indian Sentinel* (April 1918): 18.

33. *True Voice*, Omaha, Nebraska (March 3, 1916).

34. *Indian Sentinel* (July 1916): 15; Weber, FMN 43 (May 1916): 445.

35. Weber, FMN 38 (April 1911): 319; 40 (October 1913): 885; 41 (February 1914): 118; 43 (April, June, November 1916): 353, 548, 1032. See also letter of Father Anselm Weber, O.F.M., to Indian Commissioner Cato Wells, 12 April 1916.

36. Weber, FMN 43 (December 1916): 1122.

37. *St. Anthony Messenger* 36 (1928–1929): 590 ff.

38. *St. Anthony Messenger* 36 (1928–1929): 365 ff.

10

What Are We Doing for the Indians?[1]

Leopold Ostermann, O.F.M.

[Father Leopold's "What Are We Doing for the Indians?" is in sharp contrast to the polite scholarship of Father Emanuel's history of U.S. Indian policy, with its apologies to readers for seeming "to delve into past unpleasantries" or for highlighting "these unfortunate outbursts of bigotry and hatred of the Catholic religion." Some of the difference is attributable to audience: the *Provincial Chronicle* served fellow Franciscans, while *St. Anthony's Messenger* addressed the Catholic laity. Some may be due to the contrasting career positions of the authors: Emanuel, writing in the late 1930s, had already served among the Navajo for two decades, and might be considered established and settled. Leopold, beginning this series of articles late in 1902, had not yet completed his second year in Navajo country. Perhaps the greatest difference is one of scope: Father Emanuel's topic is Indian education in the United States after 1869; Father Leopold's is the failure of Anglo-American Indian policy across the centuries, and probably into the future, in contrast to the often misunderstood and misrepresented achievements of the Spanish and French colonialists and the contemporary Canadians. Finally, there is the difference of intent: Father Emanuel, as historian, writes to inform and to record, to tell a story and at the same time to preserve it for posterity. Father Leopold also tells a story, but his rhetoric impacts the here and now; it is intended to generate popular support for the Catholic Indian missions, to touch hearts and open pocketbooks.

Here again the writing reflects the energy and enthusiasm of Leopold's first years in the Southwest. Also, these early pieces show little evidence that either Father Leopold or his editors felt the need of editorial constraint, either in the interest of political civility or for fear of further alienating the political/sectarian opposition. Here Father Leopold is permitted to say it as he sees it, and so the reader comes upon "narrow-brained writers, whose minds' eyes are hazed and blazed by prejudice and bigotry," a Protestant "pulpit-clown dishing out humbug," expensive federal pro-grams which "make useless parasites of the next generation of our Indian wards," opposition to Catholic Indian schools "from certain Mephistophelean quarters," and a former Indian commissioner whose programs are "the action of either a weak-minded jingo or a hysterical crank."

"What Are We Doing for the Indians?" is a series within a series. It consists of 11 consecutive installments of "Franciscans in the Wilds and Wastes of the Navajo Country," running from October 1902 through August 1903. It is fascinating, powerful stuff, arguably some of the best writing Father Leopold ever did.]

A school for the education of Navajo children is at present being erected at St. Michaels, Arizona. We are in hopes that this mustard seed, planted through the generosity of Mother Katharine Drexel, may, by the grace of God, grow and become a tree large enough to shelter with its branches the whole Navajo tribe. Until now little has been done for these red rovers, ever since they have been conquered and forced to give up their roving life and confined within the limits of a reservation. The Navajo—exclusive of the Apaches, who were originally nothing else but outlying bands of Navajo—number about 20,000 souls. Almost all of these are even now as much pagans as were their early forefathers in the wilds and on the steppes of Tartary, although they have been more or less in contact with the white man about 300 years or longer. And more than this: If we except Canada under French, and the Southwest under Spanish rule, we will find among the tribes who still exist about the same condition. How is this possible? Let us see.

The Indians When First Discovered

What were the Indians when first discovered by the fair-skinned Europeans? They were a brave, haughty, fearless people; every tribe a sovereign, independent branch. They were the lords and masters of a whole continent, and as fond of rushing headlong after their chieftains into the thick of the fight as were the flaxen-haired, skin-clad hordes of Angles and Saxons, who followed the call of Hengist and Horsa. Their winter dress of well-tanned buffalo robes and buckskin was more healthful and more protective against wind and weather than the blankets and the shirts and the trousers of gay prints and flashing calicos they now wear. Their venison, buffalo meat, fish, corn, beans, squashes, pumpkins, and wild fruits and berries were more wholesome and gave them more strength and nourishment than the occasional rations of beef, salt pork, bacon, potatoes, heavy wheat flour, and dyspeptic baking powder. Their free outdoor life fitted their bodies for the hardships of every season, sharpened the quickness of their senses, and diminished the dangers and causes of sicknesses. Their sense of right, justice, honor, and truthfulness was keener than now; their standard of temperance and sobriety infinitely higher than since they have become acquainted with the white man's firewater.

War was with the Indian—as it was with our own ancestors—a manly and honorable occupation, but the Indian never was the human tiger he is generally described to have been, whose every thought and energy were bent upon shedding the blood of his fellow beings. In his home life he was—as now—peaceful, tolerant, social, good-natured, humorous. However, he was an inveterate devotee of the *"dolce far niente"* [sweet idleness], deeming every muscular exertion, outside of fishing, hunting, and fighting, as beneath the dignity of man, and when his passions were aroused he was as fierce, vindictive, and relentless as an ancient Teuton, as cunning and treacherous as a Greek, in his modes of torture as ingenious as a refined Roman, and in need or want he had the principles of the modern communists and helped himself to the superfluities of his enemies. Like an old Persian, he never forgot a favor nor an insult. He was more spiritual-minded than a Celt; he peopled the forests and valleys and hills and springs and rivers and air and earth with spirits good and evil, whom he was constantly invoking, or trying to reconcile.

Indians Today

What are the Indians today? What have we done for them? We have broken their proud, independent spirit; we have made war on them, or have given them provocations until we had the desired pretext for war, then hundreds fell before the disciplined, well-drilled lines of the white soldiers, and whole tribes became a memory. We have taken their lands without giving them any recompense, and have kept on shoving them onward with the setting sun, and have silenced their protests with the crack of the rifle and the boom of the cannon. We have killed their buffaloes for mere sport, leaving their carcasses to rot on the plains; have destroyed their forests, slaughtered their game, desecrated the resting places of their ancestors, ruined their hunting grounds, broken up their homes, and have penned them within the fixed limits of a reservation, of which perhaps the greater part is such where, as Mr. Charles F. Lummis says, "a horned toad may scratch out a living when single, but would inevitably starve if led into matrimony."

What are the Indians of today? What have we done for them? Thousands and millions of emigrants from all lands and nations have come to our shores. They have been welcomed, have not only become our friends, but our very brethren. And the Indians—the Native Americans par excellence—are still set aside, are strangers and foreigners in the land owned and lorded over by their ancestors long before the hyphened Anglo-Saxon was ever dreamed of. They are shunned and spurned by "the superior race," are cut off from all intercourse with those whose civilization they are expected to accept; are cried out as lazy because they do not become civilized fast enough; as indolent, because they do not turn into experienced farmers or expert mechanics without being properly taught and shown; as stupid, because they cannot learn to read, write, and cipher overnight; as half-witted because they cannot acquire the heaven-born English tongue—the only worthy channel of instruction and education—in a half-dozen hours.

What are the Indians of today? Excepting the Osages and Pueblos, the majority of them are poor people, clad in thin, cheap calico, sometimes grotesquely botanical in aspect and intensely howling in colors, but insufficiently warm or protective. Most of their homes are poor, cheerless, unlovely places: tepees of hide, wickings [wickiups] of branches, or hogans of trunks covered with ground, with nothing in them but a few sheepskins or blankets and a fire. What has the white man done for the Indian? He has brought him rum, smallpox, tuberculosis, and syphilis, has taught him to lie, cheat, and defraud, to swear, curse, and get drunk. He has made a rascal, morally and physically, of the savage with whom he has come in contact, and whom he has not sent to the happy hunting grounds. The best Indians, therefore, are those who live far away from the railroads and who have not come in contact with the whites, or but very little. There one yet finds frank hospitality, natural grace and cheerfulness, happy humor and sociability.

What have we done for the Indians? In Canada, men like Fathers Jogues and Brebeuf; in the Northwest, men like Fathers Ravalli and De Smet; in the Southwest, men like Fathers Junipero Serra and Juan Ramirez; in the East, men like Lord Calvert and William Penn have done a world of good for the Indian, but where is their work now? The insatiable Anglo-Saxon shark (who is undoubtedly the biggest thing on earth) has swallowed and digested it long since, save a few ruined remnants. Indeed, our race has scarcely done a single thing it should have done. There is hardly a single fact to which we may point with pride, but our ten fingers are not sufficient to point to facts of which we must be ashamed.

It cannot be denied that the Indian suffered many wrongs, great and small, at the hands of the early settlers and later. He resented and resisted these wrongs; fought hard and bitterly against what he deemed an unjust, unscrupulous nation of invaders. His warfare partook of the character of his rugged mountains, his wild valleys, his turbulent streams, and his intricate forests. When the Indian, decked out in feathers and war paint, filled his quiver with arrows, grasped tightly the handle of his tomahawk, and went out upon the war trail, his intention was to kill and not to be killed. Who would, therefore, blame him if instead of rushing with foolhardy bravery into an open, exposed position before the muzzle of his enemy's rifles, he preferred those tactics which have lately been adopted by the Americans in the Philippines, and by the British in South Africa? What these two giant twin-intelligences do ought surely not to be considered skulking treachery or cowardly assassination in the savage.

The ancient Britons defended their home and country against the Romans, against the Angles and the Saxons; the English against the Normans; the Irish, the Boers, and the Poles fought valorously against the invaders of their country—all these we consider brave people fighting for their home and hearth. But did the Indian not fight for the same purpose? Why should we admire and praise the one and brand the other a "red devil"? His religion demanded that a captive should die for every tribesman slain, unless the dead warrior's family, as frequently happened, chose to adopt the prisoner, and then his fate was worse than death: a life of slavery. But we are told they tortured prisoners inhumanly at the stake. In the British Museum is a collection of instruments of torture, used in England a few hundred years ago, which would give an Iroquois chief an epileptic fit, or drive a Mohawk warrior crazy with envy. Then why should the Indian be so continually held up as a treacherous, bloodthirsty savage and his descendants held under the ban of that belief for all time?

Students of history, and of the Indian question in particular, know that the early Indians were not "human tigers and red devils," and that the Indians of today are not a lot of low, lazy, dirty, shiftless ragamuffins (except where they have been made such by good-for-nothing whites), but how many others share this knowledge? How many really care about sharing it? How many who "know it all" will tell you, with a precision that could decide the fate of empires, that absolutely too much is said, done, and written about the Indians, who are fast dying out? But my dear, oracular wiseacres, let me tell you that we shall have Indians with us (at least the Navajo) until the boom of doom is sounded, and it will take generations to say, to do, and to write enough in order to undo what has been done, or to supplant the utterly false and untrue ideas and theories of the past.

To mention but one point. How many, even among educated Catholics, know the real truth of the glorious past of our Southwest, which has no parallel in history? How many know of the first discoverers and explorers little more than that they were a band of red-handed cutthroats, their soldiers a pack of merciless bloodhounds, and their missionaries a gang of superstitious religious fanatics and ignoramuses? How many, even such who are supposed to be well-versed in history, declare the whole exploration and conquest of the Southwest by the Catholic Spaniards nothing else but a large-scaled marauding and buccaneering expedition of a crowd of robbers, murderers, and incendiaries? How many, who still have no other idea of the Indian but that he is a howling savage, dancing and hopping around a big fire, with bloodshot eyes and streaked with war paint, brandishing his tomahawk and yelling worse than a graduate of some Eastern university? Or that he is a stolid, stupid brute, a low, lazy beast, whose extinction is a blessing for the rest of decent mankind?

It is, therefore, very gratifying to see that of late the cause of the Indian has been championed by Catholic papers and magazines; that his past and present wrongs and his future needs have been clearly and repeatedly set before the people; that current errors and lies, which for more than 300 years have passed as genuine history, have been exposed and as far as possible corrected; that earnest and glowing appeals to aid the Indians, to save their schools, of which a bigoted government had tried to rob them, have gone through almost all Catholic papers; that not only Catholics, but also fair-minded Protestants have stigmatized the sectarian maneuvers of bigoted employees in our government Indian schools and have acknowledged the "permanent good" wrought among the different tribes by the Catholic schools.

French and Spanish Pioneers

What have we done for the Indian? Our consideration of this question is not a very cheerful or consoling meditation, nor does it include a single fact that would reflect credit, praise, or honor upon our race and nation. And yet this dark, gloomy question has a very bright and cheerful side, but in order to see it, one must forget New England and look to those regions which were explored and colonized by the French and Spanish. These two nations, formed by a union of the Celtic, Roman, and Teuton blood, were the only real and successful pioneers of true civilization in the New World. Just as the hard, crude iron is thrust into the fire and tempered while it cools down, in order to make a good, reliable blade that will not bend or twist when used, so, too, the impetuosity of the Celt united to the burning ambition of the Roman, and tempered by the sound, solid philosophy of the Teuton have fitted the French and Spanish to succeed where other nationalities would have failed or destroyed, and an everlasting pity it is that they could not continue their work.

Well, what have they done for the Indians? They did not burn down the homes of the Indian and place him before the alternative of either moving uncomplainingly farther westward or of being shot down like a "red dog." They did not condemn or despise him, but taught, educated, and instructed him. They did not consider him a howling heathen or a brutish savage, who was best after being killed, but a human fellow being, for whom Christ has shed His blood, who had an immortal soul worth as much as their own, and who was capable of being educated and civilized. They made a Christian and a citizen of him; they did not exterminate, but they civilized and preserved his race. There is not a single extinct tribe of Indians whose extermination is due to French or Spanish cruelty and barbarism. How does that compare with the early history of the colonization along the Atlantic coast by the Pilgrims and Puritans, whose present-day descendants know so much about French cruelties and Spanish atrocities, while they extol their Indian-exterminating forefathers as the only good thing that ever struck the shores of the western continent?

What have the French and Spanish done for the Indian? The brilliantly successful missionary work of the French Jesuits in Canada and in the Northwest is pretty well known, at least among Catholics in general. Names like those of Fathers Jogues, Brébeuf, Marquette, De Smet, and the like, have become household words. They are names expressive of the highest type of heroism and self-sacrifice; names which represent not only hundreds, but thousands of converted, instructed, and civilized Christian Indians; not only one, but many decades of years spent in patient, zealous work, not *against* but *for* and *with* the Indians, years of toil and travel, of dangers and hardships, of want and exposure, of love and labor, of success and suffering.

The work of the Spanish Franciscans and Dominicans in the Southwest is not so well known. The Southwest has been, until late years, a comparatively little-known, and grossly misrepresented region, so much that "Spanish conquest" has almost become a synonym of bestial brutality, and the padres stereotyped figures of incarnate bigots and fanatics.

John Gilmary Shea, in his *History of the Catholic Missions among the Indian Tribes of the United States, 1529–1854*,[2] begins the part treating of the old Spanish missions with these words: "The Spanish conquests in the Western world have long been chronicled by national hatred as scenes unsurpassed cruelty and tyranny, and to most it seems certain that Spanish America must be as completely cleared of its aboriginal inhabitants as the parts in which we live. Cruelties, indeed, were practiced, but they did not form the general rule." That is to say, cruelties were seldom and far between, and against the express laws of the Spanish rulers, whereas in New England men like Eliot and Penn are isolated figures and form the exceptions to the general rule. "The part taken by the missionaries," Mr. Shea goes on to say, "ever the steadfast friends of the Indian, has been singularly misrepresented, and they seldom figure in English accounts unless as persecutors. Yet never did men more nobly deserve a niche in the temple of benevolence than the early and later Spanish missionaries."[3] Why? What have they done for the Indian? "To give even a skeleton of Spanish missionary work in the two Americas," says Mr. Lummis, "would fill several volumes." "In 1617—three years before Plymouth Rock—there were already *eleven* churches in use in New Mexico." Speaking of Pecos, he says: "Above their grey mounds [the ruins of 'many-storied Indian houses'] still tower the walls of the old church, which was built before there was a Saxon in New England." "A century before our nation was born, the Spanish had built in one of our Territories half a hundred permanent churches, nearly all of stone, and nearly all for the express benefit of the Indians. That is a missionary record which has never been equaled elsewhere in the United States even to this day."[4]

What, then, have the Spaniards done for the Indians, civilly and socially? After they had brought them to the understanding that they must obey the new government, they treated them with humane kindness and generous mercy; they let their existing laws and governments continue, and added such laws as would promote their welfare; they protected them in the undisturbed possession of their lands and homes; reduced them into orderly, law-abiding communities; placed them at par with the Spaniards; made them crown vassals of the king of Spain, consequently Spanish citizens, who enjoyed all the rights and privileges of native Spaniards, and this, too, to such an extent that time and again Spaniards complained that the Indians were much better treated than they themselves.

The so-called "blood baths and butcheries," which the Spaniards are said to have perpetrated, when studied up and sifted down according to the latest discoveries and researches, generally lose much of their crimson dye, like red bunting on a rainy Fourth of July. They are, as a rule, overdrawn by about two-thirds, and liberally fringed with extras, and even when reduced to their actuality, are now acknowledged to have been necessary military actions. Let us try to imagine what would have been the result if our own "Howling-Wilderness" Smith, or "Water-and-Bottle-Cure" Waller had been in the boots of Coronado or Cortez, or if the Spaniards had been of the type of the "pig-sticking" lancers employed by England in the late Boer war, or if the Spanish padres had been of the same stamp as grim old Increase Mather, the New England Puritan preacher, who after the sickening massacre of the Pequods, in which men, women, and children were indiscriminately killed (most of them burned), cried out: "This day we brought 600 Indian souls to hell!" I think I am not mistaken if I say that, in that case the Southwest would now be a country of "prehistoric races," and that the Pueblos along the Rio Grande would be as mysterious as the cliff dwellings in the canyons of Arizona, or the mounds in the Miami and Mississippi valleys.

What have the Spaniards done for the Indians religiously and morally? They uprooted and overthrew pagan religions, which had been existing probably thousands of years, and whoever knows anything of the tenacity with which the Indian clings to the legends, beliefs, and ceremonies of his forefathers will realize what a tremendous task it was. They threw down and broke their hideous idols, crusted with the blood of human victims, and burned many of their picture-written books of magic, superstition, and ceremonies. A great cry of condemnation against the Spanish missionaries has been raised on this account, and it still rings from "Dan to Bersabee." They have been accused of burning piles and heaps of valuable historical documents and records, and of destroying fine and irreplaceable works of art, and so forth.

This is what one Reau Campbell has to say:

What might have served to enlighten upon the history of the earlier races that inhabited the land (Mexico), was destroyed by the fanatics, who saw in the temples they found evidences of civilization almost superior to their own, and of a religion so nearly identical, that it seemed only a creed of the one they professed; the jealous bigotry that threw down the graven stones, and tore the pictured parchments to fragments, wiped out volumes of history and placed bloody chapters in their stead.[5]

And again: "Whatever of chronological data there may have been in the picture writings of the Aztecs was destroyed in the fanatical fires that destroyed the temples of Tenochtitlan."[6] And the following passage, which is, indeed, a gem of petrified ignorance:

As we read the little of Aztec history that the Spanish fanatic left unburned we may well wonder at the similarity of their religion to that of the Christians, and we are apt to conclude that the ancient Mexicans were not the pagans they have been painted; true, they practiced human sacrifice, but was it less in cruelty than in the sacrifice of human life by the Inquisition?[7]

The notorious burning of the great library at Alexandria (700,000 rolls of manuscript) seems to have been but the flamelet of a match compared to the historical-record bonfire kindled by the Spanish missionaries in Mexico, where every man, woman, and child seems to have been occupied with writing history and running daybooks or diaries. Such narrow-brained writers, whose minds' eyes are hazed and blazed by prejudice and bigotry, remind one of an astronomer looking at the sun through a telescope, on the lens of which are a few atoms of dust. He tells the world, with the accuracy and metaphysical certainty of a mathematician, that he has discovered large spots and blotches on the sun; they must be immense lakes or oceans, and he can tell you, almost to the gallon, how much water they contain. Let them clean their lenses; let them forget all else, but that they are men who are expected to have nerve and character enough to tell the truth impartially, manfully, and in a straightforward manner. In order that they may do this, let them study their subject before writing on it, and let them use the proper, truthful, and authentic sources, and not be like an idiot, who leads his horse into a millinery store to have it shod. Let them think that they do not know it all, that there is still something for them to learn, and that their yellow intellectual X-rays are not the only things which are enlightening the race of Adam. Let them lock up their fenced-in sanctums of science and wisdom in the knowledge-puffed East, and if they are writing on Western subjects, let them come "Out West," or at least consult the papers and pamphlets, the records and reports, and so forth, of men who have been there, and who have spent years there, not like butterflies hovering from blossom to blossom, but who, like bees, have gone into things, have investigated, studied, and made researches among the old documents and memorials; men who were real scientists, and who lived and labored for truth and science. Volumes of New Mexican history have been blotted out, it is true; but by whom? By the Franciscan and Dominican fanatics? No, by the *American soldiers,* who sold bundles of rare old valuable documents at Santa Fe for the price of waste paper or old rags, and burned armfuls of them on the plaza of Santa Fe.

But men who are capable of delivering themselves of such rank rot would not hesitate to accuse the Almighty Himself of vandalism for throwing down and breaking Dagon, the idol of the Philistines; or to brand Daniel a bigot for destroying Baal of the Babylonians; or to stigmatize St. Paul a fanatic, for burning the books of magic at Ephesus. Yet this is just exactly what the Spanish padres did in Old and New Mexico. By such means they proved to the pagans that their gods were false, were mere puppets, their religious ideas gross hallucinations, and their ceremonies empty humbug.

The Spanish padres were, indeed, apostles, imitators of the great Apostle of the Gentiles, who "in journeying often, in perils of waters, in perils of robbers, in perils from the Gentiles, in perils in the city, in perils in the wilderness, in perils in the sea, in perils from false brethren, in labor and painfulness, in many watchings, in hunger and thirst, in many fastings, in cold and nakedness," led on the Indian, step by step, until they had finally achieved the conversion of a continent and a half of savages to Christianity. "Never did any other people anywhere," says Mr. Lummis, "complete such a stupendous missionary work."[8] And the life and morals of the neophytes were such that even to this day, those times are referred to as the "golden age of the missions."

What have the Spaniards done for the Indians with regard to science and art? They educated the Indians, not according to the principle: "Let the brutes learn English," but while they taught them the Spanish language, they learned and studied the language of the Indians; they taught them to read and write not only Spanish, but also their own tongue, printed books and paper for them, improved their methods of farming and stock raising, brought them implements of iron and steel, and taught them their use. "Each priest that came to this country," says E. T. Mills in the *Scientific American,*

> was a master mechanic; he knew something of all trades and much of many. He taught the Indians, and as soon as one became proficient, he in turn communicated his knowledge to the others. By so doing there was spread among the people the greatest amount of learning in the shortest space of time. The work accomplished by these pioneers of Western civilization, as shown by the relics from their workshops now in existence, is of superior quality to that which may be found in many factories of the present day.

There are collections existing of articles manufactured by Indians who were pupils of the padres. In these collections are found chains, bear traps, hammers, pulleys, flatirons, scissors, plowshares, scales for measuring gold, scales for measuring rations, nails, cowbells, hub bands, bits of almost all tools, and although they did not work with the tools and machines, nor with the facilities and improvements of modern times, yet their work has been pronounced by competent judges just "as good as any workman can turn out now."

Bits and bridles of iron, inlaid with silver; saddles with fancy leatherwork, and clever hand carvings; large copper bowls, handsomely finished and exquisitely decorated; beautiful hand-carved chairs, benches, balustrades, confessionals, altars, and so on, the remains of oil presses, flour mills, wine presses, blacksmith shops, sawmills, and workshops by the old mission buildings show that almost every trade has been taught and practiced.

Many of the old ruins of churches, convents, aqueducts, built by the Indians under the supervision of the padres, show a taste for architecture and a skill in engineering which excites wonder and admiration even in our days. Charles A. Keeler says of the old mission ruins: "They form today, ruined as they are, some of the most noteworthy examples of architecture in America," and of the mission church of San Xavier del Bac, in Arizona, Mr. Lummis says that it "is beyond cavil, the finest Mission edifice in the United States."

Speaking of their success as teachers, the last-named author says: "Not only did their intellectual activity breed among themselves a galaxy of eminent writers, but in a very few years there was a school of important *Indian authors.* It would be an irreparable loss to knowledge of the true history of America if we were to lose the chronicles of such Indian writers as Tezozomoc, Camargo, and Pomar in Mexico; Juan de Santa Cruz, Pachacuti Yamqui Salcamahuay in Peru, and many others. And what a gain to science if *we* had taken pains to raise up our own aborigines to such helpfulness to themselves and to human knowledge!"

I would like very much to dwell longer upon the work of the Spaniards in the Southwest and Mexico. Nothing can be more interesting to American readers than detailed descriptions of the hero soldiers and hero priests who first lighted the lamp of Christianity in the New World; of the benefits, civil and social, religious and moral, which they brought to the Indian; of the knowledge and art, the trades and crafts, which once flourished in "the new Kingdom of St. Francis," but this would fill many volumes. However, this short sketch will, I think, give the reader some idea of what the Spaniards have done for the Indian.

And now, one more glance at the Spanish pioneers. Not only have they been described as human fiends, devoid of every nobler sentiment or motive; not only have their missionaries been set down as fanatics who made immense bonfires of historical records which never existed and wiped out imaginary volumes of history; but they have also been represented as lazy and ignorant numbskulls, who not even kept any records of their own times and doings. Reverend J. D. Baldwin, a New England preacher who also had other occupations which did not require the reverend prefix to his name, generally refers to them as "The Franciscan and Dominican fanatics, whose learning and religion consisted of ignorance and bigotry," and of the Spanish pioneers in general, he says they "could be robbers and destroyers, but they were not qualified in any respects to become intelligent students of American antiquity." This certainly is the quintessence of ignorance and bigotry in a distilled form.

Reverend J. T. Roche writes in *Donahoe's Magazine*, July 1902: "The records of those early Spanish pioneers are well-kept; wherever the Spaniard has set his foot he has left behind him excellent material for the future historian. The reports of the governors and missionaries are still accessible and the labors of men like Hodge, Lummis, Bandelier, Morgan, and Winship have made the path of present day students moderately easy." And Mr. Lummis writes:

> One very important feature must not be lost sight of. Not only did these Spanish teachers achieve a missionary work unparalleled elsewhere by others, but they made a wonderful mark on the world's knowledge. Among them were some of the most important historians America has had; and they were among the foremost scholars in every intellectual line, particularly in the study of languages. They were not merely chroniclers, but students of native antiquities, arts, and customs—such historians, in fact, as are paralleled only by those great classic writers, Herodotus and Strabo. In the long and eminent list of Spanish missionary authors were such men as Torquemada, Sahagun, Motolinia, Mendieta, and many others; and their huge volumes are among the greatest and most indispensable helps we have to a study of the real history of America.[9]

However, the power and influence of the missions are now gone, their work destroyed by politicians, land grabbers, cattle kings, and other sharks; their people are dead or scattered; their ruins slowly crumbling to dust. And should this consideration not stir up in the heart of every Catholic the firm purpose of doing what can be done, and of saving what can be saved of our present Indian missions, especially our Indian schools? Therefore, dear reader, do not forget that there is a society for the preservation of these schools. . . .

Farce and Failure in Government Schools

After having considered the question, "What have we done for the Indian?"let us now change its grammatical form a little by placing it in the present tense: "What are we doing for the Indian?" A good introduction of this question will be found in the following extract from the letter of the superintendent of one of the largest government Indian schools in the Southwest:

> For years I have held to the conviction, that Indian education should be along religious (sectarian) lines. Our system of so-called religious training is farcical and would be laughable, if it did not concern such a dreadfully serious thing as the moral welfare of children committed to our care. The best we dare do here is to prevent proselytizing. There are eleven Catholic employees, and while they do not dare do anything *sectarian,* they have had catechism classes for Catholic children, and recited the rosaries during Lent.

The religious training of Indian children in our government schools certainly is, to say the least, a very peculiar affair. The rule of the Indian Department, bearing on this subject, reads as follows: "The pupils shall be encouraged to attend the churches and Sunday-schools of their respective denominations, and shall be accompanied by employees, detailed by the superintendent, for that purpose. Pupils who cannot thus be accommodated, shall be assembled during some suitable hour for religious and ethical exercises of a strictly undenominational character."

Yes, that sounds well enough, but pause a moment, and reflect, how often will it really happen, that the almost exclusively Protestant teachers will *encourage* the Catholic pupils to visit their own churches on Sundays? And if the children of the whites, as a matter of fact, stand in need of such encouragement, how much more necessary will it be for Catholic Indian children, whose religious education at home must of necessity be somewhat scant and deficient? Add to this that the children must move the whole week either in an anti-Catholic Protestant, or, at least, in a religiously indifferent atmosphere, and the negative, or rather, the positively pernicious results of these schools will not be surprising. Moreover, these schools are, as a rule, built several miles away from the city, for instance at Phoenix, Arizona, and at Santa Fe and Albuquerque, New Mexico. At these three just-mentioned schools, at least, a wagon is at the disposal of the Catholic as well as the Protestant pupils to convey them to their respective churches on Sundays. This seems a most generous privilege, indeed; but how often in a year will it thus happen, that each Catholic pupil will see the inside of a Catholic church, especially in such schools in which the great majority of pupils are [not] Catholics? How many Catholic pupils will be too bashful or too backward to ask for this privilege? How many will never disclose their religion under the supposition that thus they will be in better standing with their Protestant teachers, or that the Protestant religion is more fashionable, more American, and easier?

To remedy this disadvantage to some extent, Mother Katharine Drexel had a hall built near the government's Carlisle Indian school, in which Catholic services are held for the Catholic pupils of said school. It has been suggested of late by a prominent clergyman of Santa Fe, that a similar hall or chapel be erected near the government school at Santa Fe for the same purpose, but why should not the government schools be compelled to place a classroom or their "chapel" at the disposal of Catholic priests to conduct Catholic services for the Catholic pupils on Sundays, as is done in many of our public institutions, and even in one or two Indian schools? It seems, however, that some persons in authority are apprehensive, lest the Protestant ministers might ask for the same privilege, which would open every avenue to their pernicious activity. Well, I do not think there is a single case on record in which such privileges have ever been denied *them*.

If the Protestant ministers restricted their activity in the government Indian schools to keeping services for the really Protestant Indian pupils only, no one could reasonably object, I think. But as things actually are, Protestant Sunday schools and Bible classes are regularly kept; Y.M.C.A. and Y.W.C.A. and Christian Endeavors and Epworth Leagues and a half dozen other "what-nots" are introduced; Protestant ministers keep their services and sermons—and all this under the specious pretense of "nonsectarianism." Does this need proofs? Hardly, at least not for one who is in any way conversant with the actual conditions. Is not the "nonsectarian" Sunday school obligatory in each and every government Indian school? And is the word *nonsectarian* not practically accepted as a synonym of Protestant? And how many such schools are there in which the Protestant minister does not put in his regular appearance at regular intervals?

From the *Native American*, the official paper of the government Indian school at Phoenix, Arizona, the largest in the Southwest, with attendance of more than 600 pupils, a large number of whom are Catholic, I cull the following very interesting items:

> The exercises of the second Commencement week in the life of the Phoenix industrial school were ushered in on Sunday evening, May 18, when the sermon to the class was preached by the Rev. Louis Halsey, D.D., of Phoenix. The quartet choir of Dr. Halsey's church accompanied him, and their beautiful singing led the devotional spirit of the congregation, as was evidenced by their hushed attention. Our children, too, sang the hymns with fervor.

> The Indian oratorical medal contest was held at the Presbyterian church last Monday evening, under the auspices of the Y.C.T.U. The church was crowded. The devotional exercises consisted in a short scripture lesson and a prayer by Rev. Lapsley McAfee. The medal was won by William Peters, and Rev. McAfee presented it to him. The benediction was pronounced by Rev. Lewis Halsey. Prayer by Rev. C. V. Cowan.

> The new quarterlies for the Boy's Bible-class came this week. The boys should appreciate the gift of these from the Presbyterian church in town, and make good use of them. Mr. McAfee conducted the Boy's Bible-class Sunday afternoon.

Now and then ministers passing through Phoenix honor the Indian pupils with their sermons; for instance, the Rev. Dr. McIntyre, a Methodist minister of Chicago, Rev. Schneider, of Los Angeles, et al.

Every Sunday morning, Sunday-school; in the afternoon, Bible-class; in the evening, meeting of Y.M.C.A. and Y.W.C.A.

But all this is evidently not enough for the intensely religious Protestant, that is, nonsectarian fervor of the government officials at the Phoenix Indian school, the superintendent of which is a Protestant ex-minister. I quote again from the *Native American*:

A new and very pleasant feature of the Sunday afternoon program is the short out-of-door service, held at the close of the band concert. As the last melodious notes die away, the bugle sounds, and our boys and girls come trooping in from all parts of the grounds to mass themselves about the band stand, or, as on last Sunday, on the east side of the office building, where they join in singing a few of their favorite hymns and enjoy a simple, interesting talk from one of the Phoenix pastors. On the first Sunday Dr. McAfee called their attention to . . . (etc.)

The second meeting was held by Dr. Roland. Last Sunday's service was taken in charge by Dr. Halsey. Rev. Mr. Cowan conducted the open-air service on Sunday afternoon. Next Sunday Rev. Mr. Rowland comes. On other Sundays, the Rev. Black, Zumwalk, . . . (etc.)

One more quotation:

The open-air meetings, a pleasant feature of our Sunday afternoons, closed for the summer with a very clear and helpful address by Dr. McAfee, in which he illustrated by a series of interesting chemical experiments the truth that "the blood of Jesus Christ his son cleanseth us from all sin." He held the attention of the boys and girls from beginning to end as he explained to them the uselessness of depending upon education, repentance, individual effort, baptism or church membership to wash away the stain of sin from the heart. It was a straightforward talk that will not soon be forgotten. To Dr. McAfee and the ministers from other churches who have given their time and thought to thus helping the school we say a hearty 'thank you,' and wish them a pleasant vacation.

Now pause a moment, dear reader, and imagine, if possible, this religious pulpit-clown dishing out such humbug, which contains so much idiocy as might well have been hatched out behind the bars of an insane asylum, to Indian children, a large percentage of whom are Catholic. Think of "those ministers of other churches, who have given their *time* and *thought* to helping the school," that is, the Indian youth, to such budding ignorance, to such blooming nonsense, to such ripe blasphemy! But, by the way, where were those honey-tongued ministers, who are now swarming over the Southwest, and who are bubbling and boiling over with fervent zeal for the salvation of the Indian, where were they when the fathers and grandfathers of these very pupils were on the warpath; when the Apache and the Navajo were making red history with the blood of such whom they considered unjust invaders of their lawful country? Where was their burning zeal then? Then they were *rarae aves*, scarcer than dodoes; then the Catholic missionary had an undisputed field, he was welcome to toil and labor alone, and to risk his scalp. But now, since it has become safer among the Apache and Navajo—and among Indians in general—even at midnight, than it is in New York or Chicago at high noon, it is such an Apostolic work to play the role of the cuckoo.

But goodness me! Is there anything wrong, anything sectarian in all this? Is there any attempt made at proselytizing, at robbing the children of their Christian faith, and at paving the way to rank and blank infidelity? Are the children not well housed, fed, and cared for? Are they not well instructed and civilized? What more do we want? How intolerant and fanatical we Catholics are! Can we not shut up and let the lights shine? Must we always be enemies of true enlightenment and civilization? Must we continually be waving the dark lantern of ignorance, inherited from the Dark Ages?

What are we doing for the Indian? In a letter to the *Church Progress* of St. Louis, the Mother Superior of St. John's Mission school, in Arizona, below Phoenix, some time ago wrote:

> When St. John's school was filling with pupils and everything going on prosperously, they were disturbed by the Agent, who took away some of the pupils to transfer them to the government school. This is the really sorrowful side of the picture. After all possible and devoted painstaking on the part of the missionaries and teachers, laboring among the poor, wronged Indians, for whose want of religious freedom you can not but feel great pity, these officials come to destroy the fruit of their labors in its bud. The Indians all through this valley are very good. The great majority of them are pagans. There are also some Protestants among them. All, however, show themselves well disposed towards accepting Christianity, and would directly become Catholics, did not the fear of the Agent prevent. Those poor parents, who send their children to us, are deprived by this official of all government support. Freedom of conscience is thus denied them, and their miserable lot is worse than slavery. Regardless of their own wants, they are willing, however, to make any sacrifice for their good Padre and Sisters.

This smacks of the boots and knouts of Russia, and coming, as it does, from this "sweet land of liberty," it certainly is a slap in the face of our much vaunted and flaunted liberty and freedom. Happily, however, this strutting little autocrat has since been brought to the understanding that the Pima Agency is not a Russian province, and that he is not a Turkish grand-vizier.

About the Umatilla school, near Pendleton, Oregon, the *Native American* writes:

> From a private letter we take the following: 'The Presbyterian minister in Pendleton has a service for children once a month, and has invited us to let our children attend. Last month Miss McDowell took a number of them to the service

and they took part; sang their pretty hymns, besides reciting portions of Holy Scripture. The rector and the Presbyterian minister hold services for us every two weeks at the school, and they take great interest in our work. The Pendleton people are so lovely to our school, and especially the ministers.'

Are not all these things eminently nonsectarian, that is, according to the rule of the department, "religious and ethical exercises of a strictly undenominational character"? Would not the Catholics be justified under these conditions and circumstances, not only to insist upon the right of giving Catholic instruction, and of keeping Catholic services for the Catholic Indian pupils in the government schools themselves—which could hardly be refused—but also to demand that, wherever Protestant ministers have access to the pagan Indian pupils, the same privilege should be granted to the Catholic priest? And should this be refused, a persistent agitation ought to be kept up until the doors of the government schools are closed against the Protestant ministers as well.

However averse the officials at Washington may be to Catholics, it is pretty certain that if a well certified case is brought, in the proper way, to the notice of the Indian Department, it would not venture to commit an act of open, flagrant injustice. Neither is the honorable commissioner of Indian Affairs, W. A. Jones, the bigot as whom he has often been represented; he is, on the contrary, a man of broad and liberal views. His odious order to withhold the rations from children attending Catholic schools is not his order, but the order of a higher authority.

By writing thus I do not wish to create the impression that government Indian schools, even with Catholic instruction and Catholic services, could in any way be a substitute for Catholic Indian schools. At best such an arrangement is but a miserable makeshift, a means to neutralize, to some extent, Protestant influence, and to assert our equal rights with them. But as long as the Catholics of this country do not even raise the means for the maintenance of existing Catholic Indian schools—not to mention the erection of new ones—the only thing to be done is to save what can be saved, especially by insisting upon the right of giving Catholic instruction, and of keeping Catholic services for the Catholic Indian pupils in the different government schools, and also of making use of all means available to thwart the intention of Protestant ministerial bigots, as it appeared in the abolition of our contract schools.

This intention was none other than, by discontinuing government appropriations, to make Catholic Indian schools impossible, to force all Indian children into government schools, and then to gather them into the ample fold of the so-called Pure Gospel through Protestant teachers, Protestant influence, nonsectarian Protestant Sunday schools, and undenominational Protestant ministers. This intention can only be thwarted successfully if we do not shirk any labor, sacrifice, or expense supporting our Catholic Indian schools, and if we do it *now*.

What are we doing for the Indians? Making a farce of our endeavor to civilize and educate them. . . . Our governmental method of educating Indians has been declared a failure by President Roosevelt, Commissioner W. A. Jones, Senator Vest [George Graham Vest, of Missouri], and others who are in a position to know what they are saying. At the National Education convention, held at Minneapolis some months ago, several speakers asserted openly that the present system of government school education among the Indians is most detrimental to their welfare. This conclusion is shared by Colonel R. H. Pratt, head of the Carlisle, Pennsylvania, institution. Writing to the *New York Tribune* some time ago, he says of the late Reverend and General T. J. Morgan, formerly commissioner of Indian Affairs:

> Morgan succeeded in foisting upon, and in committing the government to his scheme of race and tribe-building schools, and this is the real weakness of the present Indian school system. As a result the present Indian Commissioner, Mr. Jones, is denouncing the schools and claiming that they are not doing what the government has a right to expect. The present Indian system, including schools, applied to any nationality of foreigners emigrating to America, would not only sap their manhood, but would continue them foreigners indefinitely, though living in this country.

These very Morgan schools, so sweepingly scored by Colonel Pratt, are the schools which were supported by all the Protestant denominations, and by all the bigoted, *patriotic* (?) organizations. They were held up for the admiration of heaven and earth as the only real thing in civilizing the Indians, while the Catholic contract schools, which, according to Senator Vest's testimony, alone brought lasting good to the red man, were cried down as hotbeds of ignorance and superstition, and were denied repayment for the expenditures made to educate Indian children, payments which had solemnly been promised them.

What are we doing for the Indians? Trying to civilize them in a hop, step, and jump. We have the crazy notion that the aborigines of this continent can and should be suddenly turned away from the customs of their forefathers; we have the grand plan of making the Indian in one generation the equal, competing neighbors of the white man, who has reached his present civilization after centuries of careful, uninterrupted race training; we entertain the wild idea of turning out Indian teachers, lawyers, capitalists, manufacturers, journalists, doctors, artists, and so on, equal in skill, learning, and workmanship, to any paleface in the world; we think ethnologists who insist that the savages need development along the lines of their traditions as herders, farmers, rovers, and so forth, are blooming idiots; we have Anglo-Saxon intelligence enough to expect that the Indian should and ought to be civilized at a bound, and be flung into the fierce struggle for existence just as a pup is thrown into the water with "swim or die." Have the "lights of the universe" forgotten how their own ancestors in Britannia's forests were civilized; how long it took to make them decent Christians, and that hardly 150 years ago they were yet burning innocent persons as witches at the stake in New England? Why, then, expect the savage to drop all the ideas, customs, and traditions of a thousand and more years by a simple, almighty "presto, change?"

What are we doing for the Indians? Making their lot worse than it was. During the months of September and October last, Dr. Henry M. Baum, of Washington, D.C., the noted archaeologist, made a ten-week trip through the southwestern country. Dr. Baum was at the head of an exploring party which had been making investigations of the prehistoric ruins of Arizona, New Mexico, and Colorado. He also devoted much of his time to a study of the conditions among the Indians. "Ever since 1873," says Dr. Baum,

> when I had a council with Red Cloud, I have been interested in the Indian question, and have followed up the work among the tribes. This summer I made it a special object to study the conditions on the various reservations and what progress had been made in the government schools. The schools I visited particularly were those at Fort Defiance, Little Water, and Keam's Cañon, Arizona, and some of the Pueblo Indian schools in New Mexico.
>
> It was the almost unanimous opinion of the men and women engaged in educational work among the Indians that under present conditions nothing is being accomplished, and the Indian is left in worse condition than before.
>
> The present system of Indian schools maintained by the government is a curse to the Indian race. The whole scheme of dealing with our Indian wards is wrong, and is a disgrace to the United States.

Dr. Baum said that he had seen, over and over again among the Moquis and Navajo, children that had been to school for from three to seven years, who were living in the hogans and pueblos exactly as before they had begun their education. Those who have been to school are despised by their people. Instead of being looked up to, they are looked down upon. With all the efforts of the government to educate the Indian, I do not believe there are any notable cases where he has been improved.

What are we doing for the Indians? Sacrificing millions to make them unhappy. From the last annual report of Indian commissioner Jones to Congress we have learned that in the last 20 years fully $45 million has been expended by the government in turning out specimens of spoiled, demoralized Indians, whose number is estimated at 20,000. And according to further testimony of the honorable commissioner, if the present rate of expenditure continues for another 20 years, it will take $70 million to make useless parasites of the next generation of our Indian wards. And, indeed, what else can we expect of such young red-skinned graduates? When their so-called education is finished, they are sent back to where they came from, and there they find everything the reverse of that to which they have become accustomed. The one may read, write, and cipher ever so well, the other may be an expert typesetter, another a skillful watchmaker, or a crack football player, yet that is not what he needs then and there. He is neither a good Indian in the sense that he knows how to gain a livelihood as his fathers did before him, nor does he, thanks to his education, know anything of farming, stock breeding, sheep herding, gardening, irrigating, or anything which his circumstances require. He begins to feel like a grasshopper in a chicken coop; he is unhappy, and either becomes a careless, work-shy loafer, or begins to follow on the trail of his companions who have never seen a school. It will be a piece of unimaginable idiocy on the part of our government if in the next 20 years it spends the enormous sum of $70 million in thus demoralizing and handicapping the Indian in his youth.

What are we doing for the Indians? Making a lottery, or a huge bunco game of the schools in which they are supposed to be instructed and educated. Senator Vest says he found Indian schools with 1,500 children on their rolls, and not ten in attendance, except on the days when the Indian agent distributed free meat, when every one of the 1,500 put in an appearance. He also found schools conducted by unsuccessful Protestant ministers and broken-down politicians, receiving $1,200 a year with a free house for work which was shamefully neglected. To what extent this work was neglected may be judged from the following extract from Senator Vest's speech: "When I cross-examined them (the broken-down ex-ministers and politicians), I found their actual attendance was about three to five in the hundred in the enrollment." The whole Indian system was simply a lottery, a cuckoo's nest, a huge bunco game practiced on the government, which had to foot the bills in full while its Indian wards received not only no equivalent, but nothing at all.

What are we doing for the Indians? Educating them in nonsectarian government schools, many of which are simply seminaries of sectarianism. Reverend Aloysius Bosch, S. J., writing a few months ago from Holy Rosary Mission in South Dakota to the *Ohio Waisenfreund*, says that in the Indian government schools no religious denomination is allowed to conduct services for the members of its own profession, for that would be sectarian. However, as they cannot get along without exterior services of some kind, all the children are assembled to a so-called general and nonsectarian prayer meeting. And whereas, furthermore, a general, colorless Christianity neither exists nor can exist, one of the teachers, or a Presbyterian or an Episcopalian minister, takes charge of the meeting, and such men will seldom fail in putting more or less sectarian coloring on the affair.

The very fact, too, that the pupils of such schools see the ministers of different denominations conducting those amphibious prayer meetings will naturally impress them with the opinion that one religion is as good as the other, will make them indifferent as to which is the true form of Christianity; they will finally give their name to some sect or other not knowing why or wherefore. At the beginning of this school year a young Catholic Navajo girl (both parents were Catholics) was transferred from the Santa Fe government school to the Indian school at Hampden, Virginia—another strictly nonsectarian institution—and in a few months she was an Episcopalian.

But more than this, in the official paper of the Haskell Institute, Lawrence, Kansas, one of the Indian pupils described how they are taught to *understand* the Holy Scripture. Several volumes of the Bible are placed on tables, certain texts are selected to be studied by heart, and the following Sunday these are recited and explained. The paper goes on to inform us that this pupil came to Haskell with the express intention of learning English in order to fit himself for missionary work among his people, and, adds Father Bosch, Haskell is training him to become a Protestant preacher.

Of the Catholic Mission Indians in southern California, Reverend B. F. Hahn writes in *St. Michael's Almanac*:

The government of the United States has established fourteen day-schools and two boarding schools for them. In these schools the children are taught Protestant prayers, Protestant Bible, and Protestant religion. Preachers visit these schools or the teachers who are all Protestant with the exception of a few employees at the boarding schools, teach them. Thus the Catholic Indian families, still true to their religion, will see their children return home Protestants.

What are we doing for the Indians? Making infidels of them and corrupting their morals. Last July, while over in New Mexico, I met a gentleman, who, by the way, is of Israelitic descent. He is and has been for many years a trader among the Pueblo Indians and has lived much of his life in the different pueblos. Speaking of the religious and moral progress of the Pueblos in late years, he said, among other things, that according to his experience, which was based upon the observations of many years, there were two factors which were working very detrimentally upon the Pueblos, one in a religious and the other in a moral direction, namely, Protestant preachers and government schools. Concerning the first, he said all the Pueblos are Catholics—at least as much of Christianity as they yet possess is Catholic—and they retain much of the teachings of the old Spanish missionaries. Now, Protestant missionaries of various shades and colors come in among them and teach them things different from those which the old padres taught. The Indian is puzzled; he does not know what to think or believe, and the consequence is that he loses what he has of the Catholic faith. He does not become a Protestant, or only so long as money and provisions are served him, and turns with more tenacity to his old pagan rites and ceremonies. He becomes a total infidel, or rather an intensified heathen.

Concerning the government schools, he said that of all the girls whom the Indians send to the government schools, nine-tenths are seduced and ruined. This statement seemed to me so monstrous, that I asked him if he was not "putting it on a little strong," but he said, by no means, he was not talking simply to say something; he was speaking from experience founded on facts, which had come under his own observation; he would not hesitate to say the same thing even if I were not a Catholic priest. He also gave this as a reason why the Indians of the pueblo of Cochiti refused point blank to send any girls to the white man's schools. If they *must* send children to school, they said, they were willing to send some boys, but no girls.

Shortly after, this was confirmed to me by a priest who for some months had been chaplain of the hospital at Santa Fe, where he had occasion of seeing many of these pitiful victims, who had been held good enough for nothing else but to "carry the white man's burden." When they leave the hospital, they are forced by some means or other to marry some Indian.

Since learning the above, I have been assured that in a certain large Indian government school somewhere in the Southwest (name was mentioned) at least seven out of every ten Indian girls are ruined, and this not by Indians, but by whites, and frequently, too, with the connivance of the school officials. I was told that often buggies or carriages are driven up to this school in the afternoon, and men ask for grown-up Indian girls to take home *to assist in housework*. The girls are taken away and returned later, no questions asked and nothing said, although there can hardly be a misunderstanding as to the meaning of *assisting in housework.* Is this not horrible? No wonder that the objection to our Catholic Indian schools is so vigorous and bitter from certain Mephistophelean quarters.

Therefore, dear reader, do not fail to join the Society for the Preservation of the Faith among Indian children; help save our Indian schools, and with them the little ones themselves. It ought not be difficult for you to sacrifice 25 cents a year for this cause if you remember those sweet words of Christ, which will count at the last great reckoning: "As long as you did it to one of these my least brethren, you did it to me" (Matt. 25, 40).

Federal Policy and "Civilization"

What are we doing for the Indians—making useless parasites of them? Bitter, indeed, and sweepingly condemning are the complaints about the Indians of the Ponca, Otoe, and Oakland Reservation in Oklahoma, which the Indian agent, Mr. Erwin, made in his annual report to the Indian commissioner last year. He says that of all the Indians who had not been educated in reservation schools (schools on reservations), or who had visited such schools but a few years, hardy a single one will do a stroke of work; that, as a general rule, the graduates of the government schools are the laziest and most useless members of the tribe; that among the different tribes almost all the work is done by middle-aged persons, who are strong and healthy and know neither how to read nor to write English; that the educated Indians, returning from school, try to excuse their slothfulness by saying they have nothing wherewith to work, no money, no implements, no stock. This is true enough. However, Mr. Erwin has noticed that they manage to live, to buy horses and buggies from their annuities and rents and to loan [borrow] money from the banks without any prospects of ever paying it back again. Furthermore, he says that every able-bodied Indian, man or woman, could get work at reasonable wages, but the majority of them are addicted to drinking and gambling, spend their time in doing nothing, and immorality and vices of every kind are multiplying. And this depravation will continue and will increase until they are forced to work.

Sad, very sad, conditions, indeed, and who is to blame for them? Chiefly and in first place, the government. Our Indian policy has all these years been systematically training up the Indians to become dependent wards and confirmed sluggards; our Indian school system, by taking the children off the reservations and sending them to distant Carlisle, Haskell, Hampden, and so on, and putting a veneer of knowledge on them there, has succeeded in turning out a lot of fops and dudes, who are as shy of work and as useless as their ornamental Caucasian sidepieces. Seldom has our Indian policy and our Indian school system been more openly and more sweepingly scored than by Mr. Erwin, and Catholic Indian missionaries, who have so often raised their warning voice against that system, could feel a certain degree of satisfaction at this acknowledgment of so signal a fiasco, if it were not for the irreparable damage done to thousands of souls.

What are we doing for the Indians? Trying to make farmers of them, but how and with what success? On some of the reservations not only wagons are issued to the Indians, but also shovels, picks, hoes, mattocks, rakes, and so on. All these implements are certainly very useful for working and tilling the soil, for planting, farming, and harvesting, and they are undoubtedly issued to the Indians for that purpose. But not the least thing is done to show and to teach them the use of these tools; neither is a single grain of corn or wheat or a single seed of grass or of vegetables given with these implements. How can anyone expect that, under such circumstances, Indians, whose forefathers were rovers for many generations, should settle right down to work, become self-supporting, and raise crops like old experienced farmers of Indiana? Of what advantage will it be to them to dig up and work the soil if they have naught to plant therein? It is like giving into the hands of a child pen and paper and expecting it to learn how to write well and correctly without patient showing and teaching, and without furnishing the ink. And this is about the way the Indian seems to look at it, for most of such implements are allowed to go to ruin after having been used very little or not at all. The Indian, not getting what he expected, gets disgusted, lays or throws his useless farming tools aside, and returns to the old life, that is, has a good time when there is plenty and starves when there is nothing—quite homeopathic! Of course, I am speaking now of nomad or roving tribes, not of Pueblos, for these latter were probably the great-grandnephews of farmers when the Spaniards first met them.

The latest view of the whole and sole solution of the Indian question may be summed up in three words: "Make them work." Why not, then, give them irrigation where it is needed, supply them with seeds, and appoint industrial teachers to go about and show them what and how? This could be done with half, and, perhaps, less than half the present expenses. But instead of this, good old Uncle Sam keeps on throwing shovels, pitchforks, and so forth, at them; keeps on building large, costly school houses hundreds of miles away from their homes for them; forces the only schools which are doing them lasting good to close down; employs an army of teachers and officials to look after *their interests;* throws out millions with both hands and imagines himself "a spectacle for God, angels and men."

What are we doing for the Indians—making enthusiastic patriots of them? It was ex-commissioner Morgan who, during his term of office, conceived the brilliant, infallible scheme of civilizing the Indians by introducing among them the celebration of the glorious Fourth of July. And, indeed, how could the red savages fail to be uplifted; how could they fail to turn away from the dark, narrow trails of their forefathers and march with firm step and double-quick time, à la Yankee Doodle, on the bright, asphalted boulevard of modern progress and enlightenment when they saw the Star-Spangled Banner, the emblem of liberty and civilization, unfurled and flung to the breeze; when they saw and participated in the grand processions and turnouts; when they heard the boom of cannon and the smatter of smaller arms; when they listened to the glowing eulogies on the origin and significance of that day; when their pockets were filled with fire crackers, pinwheels and sky rockets, while the band played on? Why, failure was simply out of the question. The Indian would be borne up in spite of himself; he would not be able to hinder it; he would be like a feather in a chimney; nilly-willy, he would float up into the higher regions of light and progress, where he, the *red* man, would mount up to the halcyon heights of the *white* man. However, the scheme turned out rather *blue*.

Reverend F. Digmann, S.J., wrote from Rosebud Agency, South Dakota, that at these celebrations the pagan element, with its pagan customs, ceremonies, and dances, took the lead, and the whole affair turned out to be a revival of the old pagan traditions and proved a serious stumbling block on the road to civilization.

Now our flag, with its stars and stripes, is as dear to me as it is to our own president, and I think just as much as any inhabitant of Philadelphia or Boston that we ought to celebrate the Fourth of July in a fitting and appropriate manner, with grateful hearts and exterior manifestations of joy and patriotism; but to use our national standard and our national birthday for such purposes and in such a manner as to make them ridiculous, or as if one could work miracles with them, seems to me to be the action of either a weak-minded jingo or a hysterical crank.

What are we doing for the Indians—helping them to make giant strides toward civilization? The following extracts from an order issued by the Indian Bureau a year ago, which at the time of its appearance furnished the newspapers of the country rich material for merriment, indicate a few of these giant strides:

The wearing of long hair by the male population of your agency is not in keeping with the advancement they are making, or will soon be expected to make, in civilization. The wearing of short hair by the males will greatly hasten their progress toward civilization. . . .

On many of the reservations the Indians of both sexes paint . . . this paint melts when the Indian perspires, and runs down into the eyes . . . causes many cases of blindness.

You are therefore directed to induce your male Indians to cut their hair, and both sexes to stop painting. . . . Non-compliance with this order may be made a reason for discharge (of employees) or for withholding rations and supplies. . . . [I]f they become obstreperous, a short confinement in the guardhouse at hard labor, with shorn locks, should furnish a cure.

The wearing of citizen's clothing instead of the Indian costume and blanket, should be encouraged.

Indian dances and so-called Indian feasts should be prohibited. In many cases these dances and feasts are simply subterfuges to cover degrading acts and disguise immoral purposes. You are directed to use your best efforts to the suppression of these evils.[10]

With regard to grandeur and sublimity of conception this scheme eclipses that of Mr. Morgan almost totally. Mr. C. F. Lummis comments at length upon these civilizing prescriptions, concerning the hair cutting and change of clothing. He asks, "What would you think of a law compelling every voter to shave his face smooth every day? Or to have his hair clipped once a month? Or to wear cutaway coats and creased trousers?"[11]

And should that which a legislative body would not dare to force upon the voters of this country be foisted upon the Indian? Has he no rights at all? Is he not a human being with a nature just as sensitive as that of the white man? And is his personality less strong and less to be considered than that of the overbearing paleface? "Equal rights to all!" is one of our favorite cries, and if we mean it why not, then, put detectives, armed with clippers, on the trail of Buffalo Bill and divine healers? Why not have a watchful eye on poets and painters? Why not appoint a barber for Castle Garden [once a concert hall, later an immigrant station in New York City] to look out for Paderewski and other piano and violin artists who come to this country and exhibit, besides their art, such savage customs on their persons? What the Indians think of this haircut order is best illustrated in the words of one of the Moquis: "The government did not give us our hair, therefore the government has no right to take it away from us." A Navajo asked a certain agent why he did not cut off the long hair from his chin. The agent said it was his style to have long hair on his chin, to which the Indian replied that it was his style to have long hair on the top of his head. And in the *Native American* of October 25, 1902, I read the following notice: "Aguahis, a Yuma Indian, has brought suit in the Superior Court of San Diego, California, to recover damages in the sum of $5,000 from Supt. J. S. Spear, of the Fort Yuma Indian School, for depriving him of his long, flowing hair."

"As for painting the face," says Mr. Lummis,

> is there any law yet to forbid an American woman to put on face powder—or even rouge—if she wishes? It is neither sanitary nor pretty, but who has authority to put a lady in the guardhouse for it? As to the paint "causing blindness by running down into the eyes," it may do so when the Indian stands on his head long enough to perspire.
>   'Rations and supplies,' where they are given, are not the alms of the Indian office, but a sacred obligation of the government. Should these pledges be broken and an Indian starved to death because he does not rub his nose in the dirt?[12]

With regard to dancing, if laws are to be made for its prohibition, why not make them where they will do the most good? Why not prohibit our sensuous, voluptuous waltzes and round dances? Our lascivious, obscene ballet dances? Our crazy, idiotic jigs and hops? What is used more to "disguise immoral purposes," an Indian dance or a modern masquerade ball? What causes more "degrading acts," the dance plaza of the Indian or the ballroom of the white man? And where will one meet more objectionable features, in an Indian dance corral or at one of our fashionable street fairs? The Indian never dances for amusement or sensual pleasures; all his dances are religious ceremonies. It is true, some very few of them have objectionable features, but even those have a religious significance for the Indian and are considered as such by him. Moreover, the dances being religious ceremonies, they are almost exclusively conducted and performed by medicine men. And just this fact contains a point for our legislators which they seem never to consider.

The medicine men exert about the same influence over the Indians as the Ewarts exerted over the old Germans, or the Druids over the ancient Celtic tribes. We know from history that once their influence was broken, these people were speedily converted and civilized. If those in authority would instruct all the agents to try, by wise and prudent means, to destroy the influence of the medicine men, these pagan dances and feasts would disappear ipso facto, and they would do more toward civilizing the Indians than by prohibiting long hair, face painting, blanket wearing, and dancing.

Our Indian System a Curse?

What are we doing for the Indians? The *Literary Digest*, under the caption: "Is Our Indian System a Curse?" informs its readers that D. A. Sanford of Bridgeport, Oklahoma, who has been for eight years a missionary among the Cheyenne and Arapahoe Indians, finds that one of the greatest obstacles to his work is the U.S. Indian Service. This service, Mr. Sanford declares, "is degrading and debauching the Indian," is making him a "vagabond," is destroying his home, and is killing the younger Indians who go to the government boarding schools, where they are carried off by scrofula and consumption.[13]

Following are a few sentences from Mr. Sanford's letter to *The Red Man and Helper*, a weekly published at the Carlisle, Pennsylvania, Indian Industrial School:

> The present methods are the most vicious possible. . . . If it were the purpose of the government to degrade and debauch the Indian to prevent him from becoming self-supporting, it would be hard to conceive any more effective method. . . . People generally suppose that education is a good thing, and that an excellent work is carried on at Indian schools, while they are blinded to the fact that these schools in many cases are made the tools for maintaining a vicious agency system. The "Home" should be the center around which all civilizing influences should cluster. The present government methods tend to destroy the home. Settled homes are what these Indians need. But it is very difficult for these Indians to maintain settled homes under present government methods. Rightly treated, many of them would be glad to establish settled homes. . . . The great mortality among these Indians is due, in my opinion, very largely to the vicious government methods in practice. . . . I regard the United States government methods as largely responsible for the deaths of large numbers of these Indians. Many people think and say that the Indian cannot stand civilization. That is not so. It is *not* civilization that kills the Indian, but the vicious methods in practice. . . . Again, it does not take a hundred years to civilize an Indian. Go about it rightly and it is quicker done than most people suppose. But the vicious methods in practice tend to keep the Indian uncivilized and to degrade him, to make the rising generation worse than their fathers.

Colonel R. H. Pratt, head of the Carlisle school says, in the same issue of the same paper, that Mr. Sanford does not overstate the conditions, and then proceeds to make the following rather strong and startling statement:

'I look upon *slavery* for the Negro as exemplifying a *higher quality of Christianity* than any scheme that either *church or state* has originated and carried out in *massing, controlling* and *supervising the Indians.*' After describing how much the Negro has gained in civilization during slavery by having been taken into the homes of the white man, he concludes with saying that 'the Indians *are still largely incapable, useless, dependent paupers, most dreadfully expensive because denied all privilege of proper association and contact. It is just about the most disheartening outlook any people could possibly have.*'[14]

The italics in the above quoted remarks of Colonel Pratt are mine. As far as *sectarian* churches and government methods are concerned, Colonel Pratt is perfectly right. But if his knowledge of American history goes beyond the *all-important* landing of the Mayflower, then he certainly should have said *sects* instead of *church*, and of the schemes *originated and carried out,* he should have excepted the *reductions* of the early French Jesuit and Spanish Franciscan missionaries, who did not *deny the Indians the privilege of proper association and contact.* No sincere and truthful student of history will any longer deny the great benefits and the marvelous progress in civilized life, learning, and arts brought to the Indians by "massing, controlling, and supervising" them on the Jesuit and Franciscan reductions.

But these missionaries had two faults, which seem to make their work unworthy of notice: First, they were members of the Catholic Church, which alone, as Senator Vest says, "is a crime with some people," probably because the Catholic Church is the only church that is *not* a sect; second, they had the misfortune of having been of French or Spanish descent. Yet, in spite of this, so long as they were "massing, controlling, and supervising" the Indians, there was no "disheartening outlook" for them; neither were the Indians "incapable, useless, dependent paupers." Take southern California, for instance. At the time of the secularization of the missions, they contained 30,650 Indians, 424,000 head of cattle, 62,500 horses, 321,500 sheep, and raised annually 122,500 bushels of wheat and maize. When this property was turned over to the governmental authorities for distribution (?) then the "disheartening outlook" began. Eight years later, 1842, many of the missions were closed, the Indians had dwindled down from 30,000 to 4,450, their cattle from 424,000 to 28,000, and their other stock in proportion. And ever since, conditions have continued to go from bad to worse, like a cancerous ulcer, until now "it is just about the most disheartening outlook any people could possibly have."

What are we doing for the Indians? I am very much afraid I am tiring the readers with the frequent repetition of this question. And yet, there is much more to say about it. However, from what has been said so far, we have learned that that which the government is doing for them had better not be done, that the government efforts are partly mad, blind, fitful experiments, resulting in ridiculous popgun effects, partly one-sided endeavors, by which the Indian is educated for this world alone, and left in ignorance as to the next life; that many of the employees in government Indian schools, especially broken down ministers and politicians, neglect their work shamefully, have no other motive for their work but the salary, or misuse their position for "unsectarian" proselyting; that many of our government Indian schools are veritable hotbeds of bigotry, infidelity, and immorality; that our government methods of civilizing the Indian are a dead weight, a drawback, a handicap, a curse to the rising generation of red men; that our government system of Indian education has become an unravelably muddled mess.

What the *New Orleans Picayune* said of our much-lauded and idolized public schools applies equally well to the government Indian schools: "It is time that the philanthropists and statesmen of this great Republic should arouse themselves to the realization of the fact that man has a spiritual nature as well as an intellectual, and that education must be addressed to the former as well as to the latter." Applied to the Indian schools, this simply means: it is high time to return to the methods of the Jesuits and Franciscans of 300 years ago; for this is the point never lost sight of by the Catholic Indian missionaries and instructors. In fact, just this point has called the Catholic Indian schools into existence; this point has made the Catholic Church the greatest civilizing power the world has ever seen.

This lesson she impressed upon the mind of the fiery Celt of Erin, and with it she sent him to his neighbors, the Angles and Saxons—then as barbarous and ignorant as Patagonians—to teach them Christian decency and civilization. The heaven-extolled Anglo-Saxon civilization is really nothing more nor less than an heirloom of the Catholic Irish monks and missionaries, vitiated, however, and jingoized in the days of Old Hal, the wife killer, and later. The same lesson the Catholic Church taught the fierce Teuton, and with it made him the carrier of Christian civilization throughout Europe. And what she has done for the Gael and the Goth, or, on our own continent, for the Canadian and Californian tribes, she can do again if given any chance, for the wild Sioux and the fierce Apache. In fact, she is yet doing it among the Nez Percés and Couer d'Alêne Indians of the Northwest, where her missionaries have stayed without interruption since the missions were founded.

What Shall We Do for the Indians?

Many a reader may think that my writings have no connection with the Navajo and their country. This is partly true, and partly not. The Navajo being a tribe of Indians, the Indian question must necessarily also affect them, and, moreover, as we have established a mission among this tribe and erected a school for their children—which is at present being maintained by the generosity of Mother M. Katharine Drexel—the Indian school question touches the Navajo also.

The reader will remember into what a precarious condition our Indian mission schools were thrown, when in June 1900, according to an act of Congress, all government aid was withdrawn from them. It was a blow that threatened their very existence, together with all the fruits of the patient labors, the untold privations, the sacrifice of health, even life, during many decades, nay centuries, of Catholic teachers and missionaries. In late years, when there are no longer any reeking tomahawks, dripping scalping knives, blood-curdling war whoops, hissing arrows, and twanging bowstrings to give nervous prostration to fathers of a family; when "digging up the hatchet" and "going on the warpath" have gone out of business, missionaries of every dye seem to have received a special vocation of Christianizing the Indian, particularly when a good salary and a little side issue in the shape of a trading store or a government position hangs thereby. In the latter case the spiritual part of the vocation often takes a backseat; for are not some of the superintendents of government Indian schools Protestant ex-ministers? Even the Presbyterians, who with their rigid doctrine of predestination can scarcely have logically any serious object or motive as missionaries among pagans, have followed the example of Saul, and gone where they are certainly out of place, but unlike Saul, they fail to see it.

These multicolored missionaries—each one of whom is by far more infallible than we Catholics believe the Pope to be—have conceived the idea that the Catholic missionaries, missions, and schools among the Indians ought to be ousted, because they were doing the Indians more good than they themselves, and legislators of the same light intellectual caliber have lent them their aid. Every sect, however new its brand, has carte blanche among the wards of the nation, for the education of the Indian is to be "nonsectarian," and the signification of this word is so well established now that it cannot well be misunderstood anymore. The prefix *non* has become as double-headed as the prefix *in* in the word *investigable,* and retains its negative signification only in reference to that church, which planted the standard of Christianity on the western continent when there was not yet a single Protestant on the face of the earth.

Being myself a missionary among the Indians, I deemed it my duty to contribute my share toward instructing and enlightening our Catholic people as to the real status of the Indian question, and as to the danger into which our missions and schools have been placed by that famous act of Congress; an act made in an edifice crowned with the statue of "Justice," blindfolded and holding the scales in her hand; an act made by men who are in honor bound to support a constitution that grants religious liberty to every human being within the confines of "Hail Columbia, Happy Land." I have tried to point out these dangers by answering the questions: "What have we done for the Indians?" and "What are we doing for the Indians?" It was not my object to run down our government as such, but to show what certain jingoes, who seem to be of the opinion that they are the whole government, were capable of! Neither have I suffered myself to be carried away by bias or bigotry; therefore, all my quotations, with very few exceptions, were taken from books, papers, or articles written by non-Catholics (Protestants, infidels, and Jews), the names of whom I have always given.

On the contrary, my object was to bring home to the readers the fact that the dangers which menace our Indian schools and missions are not imaginary, and that the appeal for help, made by the archbishops and the introduction of "The Society for the Preservation of the Faith among Indian Children," with a fee of 25 cents a year, is not a money-making scheme to help the missionaries to big salaries and a comfortable life (we shall hear of some of these comforts later), but *dire necessity*. I will, therefore, proceed with the Indian question, placing it now in the future tense. "What shall we do for the Indians?" Help them, of course! But how? . . .

To encourage you, and to interest you still more for our Indian schools, I am going to submit to your consideration a few motives why the Catholics of this country should unite in maintaining and upholding our Indian schools.

1) First motive: Christian Justice. We have seen what flagrant injustice has been done the red men of this country, since the landing of the Pilgrims, in the way of robbing them of their lands and homes. It is true, now and then, in very rare and exceptional cases, the Indian was paid for his land, but he was forced to be satisfied with the white man's price. As a rule he was driven off by brute force. With sword and musket he was told to follow the course of the big day star, until he had crossed the Father of Waters, where finally certain arid and barren strips of land were set aside for him and called reservations. Neither does this cruel and barbarous eviction of Indians belong to a bygone time. In our own days we must witness the shameful sight of how a company of very wealthy gentlemen evicted 300 mission Indians from the so-called Warner's Ranch in southern California, where they and their fathers before them had been living since times immemorial. Only for Mr. Charles F. Lummis, of Los Angeles, California, through whose manly efforts new homes were procured for them, they would have simply been cast out like a litter of superfluous kittens to shift or die, and had they dared to offer resistance, the old powder and bullet argument would have brought them to time.

Thus the Indian was robbed of his hunting grounds, his fisheries, and his planting fields; neither has he learned or been taught to make his living by farming or industry. After all this it will not be difficult to see that now Christian justice requires that the inhabitants of the country who robbed him of all he had must see that he has the necessities of life or that he be placed in a condition to acquire them himself.

And what applies to his corporal welfare applies in a higher degree to his spiritual progress. Having by their greed and cruelty placed the Indian in different circumstances, the whites now have the obligation of supplying the Indian with the means of raising himself to their own plane. This means is education. He should be educated to become a self-supporting, self-respecting man, a good citizen, and above all a practical Christian, and should, at the same time, be instructed in those sciences, arts, professions, and industries by which he can, like his white brother, successfully take up the struggle for existence.

Our government has acknowledged this obligation of justice, and has *tried* to give the Indian an appropriate education. But we have seen what a miserable failure the government—or rather the jingoes and the bigots who were acting in the name of the government—has made of its attempt to make good and useful citizens of the

Indians; have seen how a score of prominent men—all non-Catholics—have declared themselves against the methods of educating Indians as practiced heretofore in government schools.

After all these years of experimenting upon the Indians with their nonsectarian government school system, they are at last beginning to see the wisdom of one of Ruskin's remarks on modern education: "The three facts which it is most advisable that a man entering life should accurately know are: first, where he is; secondly, where he is going; and, thirdly, what he had best do under the circumstances." Yet it will evidently take many another year until this truth penetrates certain ironclad intellects and armor-plated skulls. For such, the following word of Senator Vest ought to be of interest: "I would give this question of the education of Indian children the same sort of consideration that I would if I were building a house or having any other mechanical expert business carried on. I had infinitely rather see these Indians Catholics than to see them blanket Indians on the plains, ready to go on the warpath against civilization and Christianity."

The man who spoke thus was a member of the Senate Committee on Indian Affairs, and as such had visited and examined Indian schools in Montana and Wyoming, government as well as mission schools. He tells us that the Jesuits, who have charge of the Catholic Indian schools of those territories, had grasped the true meaning of education so far as the red man is concerned. And, in fact, Catholic missionaries alone have succeeded in planting into the hearts of the red race the principles of a truly practical, civil, and religious life. That is the sort of education the Indian receives in our Catholic schools.

Therefore, dear reader, consider it an act of Christian justice to help maintain our Indian schools.

2) Second motive: Christian Sympathy. The Indian is poor and helpless. And even if he had sufficient means and money to send his children to the school of his choice and preference, he could hardly do so. If he thinks and acts as if he possessed the natural rights and the natural authority of a father over his own children, his course causes surprise; he is considered as overbearing and impudent, and as overreaching the boundaries of his rights; is, in fact, looked upon as a bucking bronco, who must be brought to time. Rations are, therefore, refused him and his children, and anything else is done that may make such an unwarranted course difficult, irksome, or impossible, with the sanction of bigoted government officials, tyrannical agents, or high-stilted superintendents.

The Indian is less a free man in this "Land of the Free" than any immigrant who landed at Castle Garden just yesterday. Being a part of the corrupted and corrupting political spoils system, our Indian policy changes with every change of government. One party declares him a citizen, the other denies him all citizen's rights; one party pronounces him a free man and his own master, the other an irresponsible ward of the nation, incapable even of choosing a school for his children, particularly if he be so idiotically foolish as to wish his children to visit a Catholic school. And thus he is a plaything in the hands of ignorant bigots and unscrupulous political jugglers for whom his existence and his conditions must serve to pave the way to gain influence and wealth.

The Catholic Indian school, on the contrary, is not an El Dorado for political heelers or enterprising missionaries; neither do those who are working in and for it consider it in the light of a stock exchange, from which they expect to derive liberal and paying dividends. The Catholic Indian school never changes its program; has always the same end and aim in view, namely, to educate the Indian for this life as well as for the next; to develop the intellectual and the moral side of his nature simultaneously; to teach the Indian the true principles of religion and morality, and to show him how to become self-respecting and self-supporting; in short, to make him a practical Christian and a useful citizen. A generation or two of this sort of education, and the red man will be a totally different being.

Therefore, if we are inclined to have pity and sympathy even with the dumb brute in its helplessness and misery, how much more, then, with the Indian, our brother in Christ? And how can we give expression to this pity and sympathy in a better and a more Christian manner than by sacrificing a mite of our superfluity toward helping those schools which alone are doing, and have been doing, lasting good to the Indian?

3) Third motive: Christian Gratitude. If, on the account of the lack of means, the Catholic Indian schools would be forced to discontinue, all their pupils would be placed before the alternative of either returning to the wilderness or of going to the government schools. What the government schools are—managed as they are now—we have seen; and what going back into the wilderness means, we can easily imagine.

It is true, there are a few government Indian schools in which Catholic instruction for Catholic pupils is allowed from once to three times a week; but they are white ravens, and besides, how is this permission complied with? In the government Indian school at Santa Fe, New Mexico, the Sisters of the Blessed Sacrament had been giving religious instruction to the Catholic pupils every Sunday afternoon, until the Hon. Commissioner W. A. Jones allowed religious instructions three times a week. Then the superintendent—who seems to belong to that category of officials whom Sir Walter Scott describes in the person of Master Robert Laneham, when he says, "There has been seldom a better portrait of the pragmatic conceit and self-importance of a small man in office"—got up on his highest stilts and solemnly announced to the sisters that such instructions were forbidden entirely for the future. The case was carried to Washington from whence, after several months' delay, the "small man in office" received a hint to lower his all-important personality a few pegs and to let the sisters give the Catholic instruction to Catholic pupils on Sundays, as before.

And thus it is in almost all government Indian schools: a Turkish pasha of six horsetails, or the kaiser of Germany, or even the czar of holy Russia would not cast a consumptive shadow—even if they turned around twice—beside some of our Olympic Indian-school despots, who seem to imagine themselves the very main and marrow of the government of the United States of America. In fact, the whole Catholic Church owes them an abjectly humble apology for her very existence. Heaped and steeped as they are in unconstitutional sectarianism, every sect or sectlet has preference to the one Church from which it has desected itself, or been desected, and who herself is not a sect.

To give religious instructions under such circumstances has been designated by Reverend Mother M. Katharine Drexel, foundress and superioress of the Sisters of the Blessed Sacrament, "a miserable makeshift," and I am sure every true Catholic will agree with her. For are not the Catholics of this country convinced that their children would lose their faith, or at least become very indifferent, if sent to the undenominational public schools? And have they not, for this very reason, for years brought great sacrifices to maintain their parochial schools, in order to afford their children a good religious education? And this, by the way, is one of the reasons why Catholics need never complain of empty churches, nor their priests drum up sensational topics for their sermons, nor make religious clowns of themselves in the pulpit to "draw a crowd," nor need they hire whistling soloists, nor turn their churches into lunchrooms to fill the benches.

Now, if Catholic or parochial schools are considered a necessity for the preservation of the faith among the children of the whites, who have other opportunities and advantages besides, for example, well-instructed parents, Sunday school, and so on, then our mission schools must be considered doubly so with regard to the Catholic Indian children, who if sent to a government school are forced to attend Protestant services and Sunday school and listen to the discourses of Protestant preachers, and who only too often have such teachers that will not miss an opportunity of casting slurs and reflections upon their religion, its ceremonies, customs, feasts, services, ministers, teachings, and so forth.

However, I feel it to be but a debt to justice to caution the reader against casting *all* Protestant teachers in the government Indian schools into the same mold. It certainly is not my intention to create the idea that *all* non-Catholic teachers in our government Indian schools are razor-edged bigots, nor to cause them to imagine that *all* of them are gaunt, lank individuals with dark hair, frowning brows, glistening eyes, sharp noses, thin compressed lips, square-set jaws, and twitching muscles. Even the superintendents are not *all* of the "small-man-in-office" type. There are exceptions to this, as to every other rule, which should gladly and cheerfully be acknowledged; some even deserve credit for their sensibleness, frankness, and candidness. Such a one is a certain teacher among the San Diego Indians in southern California. He writes in the *Los Angeles Times* as follows:

> When I first went to Mesa Grande I went with the good Protestant determination to fight Catholicism among the people to the bitter end, and convert them to my own religious views. But after being among them a short while, seeing the old people kneeling for hours on their pain-racked knees saying their devoted prayers, and seeing their intense desire finally brought to fruition—of replacing the old brush chapel, of which they were ashamed, with the neat adobe worshiping place which stands there now—I saw the folly of proselyting; and now what I try earnestly is not to confound their minds with new doctrines, but to make them better Catholics.

You, too, dear reader, can help to make better Catholics of the Indians by helping to support and maintain our mission schools among them. Reflect for a moment that you were born, baptized, and raised a Catholic; that your faith is the most precious gift you possess, more precious than all the gem-studded crowns and all the glittering gold and all the flashing jewels of this world; that the good God has given you this gift gratuitously and has denied it to thousands of others who are as deserving of it as you. Have you ever thought of this? Have you ever felt grateful for it? . . . Let, then, your heart expand in gratitude toward God, and show your gratitude in a really and genuinely Christian manner by lending your aid in preserving that faith in the hearts and souls of others, especially in the souls of, I may say, the most neglected of God's children, our own Indians.

4) Fourth motive: Christian Generosity. The enormous sums contributed annually by the sects toward foreign and home missions are astonishing, almost incredible. Protestants of every sect seem to find no difficulty whatever in raising funds for missionary purposes, and their contributions in the aggregate assume proportions almost fabulous. Consider, for instance, the following startling figures: One sectarian denomination, in 1901, devoted $1,477,306 to home and foreign missions; in addition to this, it appropriated $178,486 specifically for the perversion of those who are virtually our coreligionists (*Methodist Year Book*, 1902); another denomination contributed $1,220,603 for home and foreign missions (*American Baptist Year Book*, 1901); still another sect collected for the same end $2,304,593 (*Minutes of the General Assembly of the Presbyterian Church*, 1901).

In 1901 more than $18 million was collected for Protestant missions. Of this sum the Protestants of the United States contributed $5.5 million. In New Mexico alone the Presbyterians paid in one year $60,000 for missionary work, and in Arizona and New Mexico the Protestants spend annually the sum of $200,000. And to what purpose? Last July, while traveling through a part of New Mexico, I visited the villages of San Rafael, Cubero, Cebolleta, and a few others. The inhabitants of these villages are all Mexicans and exclusively Catholic. Yet in almost every one of them was either a Protestant preacher or a schoolmaster, sometimes both united in the same individual, sometimes the latter was the wife of the former, fishing for the children. The same thing is carried on in the different pueblos along the Rio Grande, for example, at the pueblo of Jemez the Catholic school was forced to discontinue on account of the lack of funds; now there is a Protestant school there, with the misfit name of government school. There are zealous missionaries trying hard to establish Catholic day schools at Santo Domingo, San Felipe, and other pueblos, but see no way of maintaining them in the future. Thus large sums of money are annually thrown out for the perversion of the Catholic Pueblo Indians and the Catholic Mexicans.

Neither is this astounding liberality of the sects toward their respective missions of recent date. Within 20 years after the Civil War, $22 million was contributed by northern Protestants for endowments of educational institutions in behalf of the Negroes of the South, all these institutions being strictly religious. In 1895 the Presbyterians spent $927,000 for American home missions, besides vast sums for foreign missions. According to a statement apparently authorized, the five leading denominations in the United States contribute annually $88 million for the support of their respective churches and missions. And these contributions are not exacted as a compulsory tax, but are bestowed as voluntary offerings.

Protestants ask for millions and obtain them. We are greater in numbers, and although we are poorer in worldly wealth, should not our zeal and love for the true faith be as great as theirs for their erroneous creeds? Shall they be more generous toward the dissemination of error than we are toward the spread of truth? Oh, what could not, and should not, the mighty membership of the Catholic Church do in this direction? Shall 10 million of the faithful shirk the sacred responsibility of saving to the faith 2,000 Indian children? Shall they allow their endangered red brethren to grope about in darkness without any effort of helping their missionaries to show them the light? Shall and will the Catholic clergy and laity of this country allow our Indian missions to be destroyed at the nod of bigots?

Let the Catholics of this country not forget how much they owe to the generosity of the Catholics of Europe, who, since 1822, through various societies, have contributed to the Church of this country the sum of more than $7 million. Shall we be less generous to our dependent Indians than Europe was to us? Let our Catholics also bear in mind the words of Mr. Charles F. Lummis, a non-Catholic: "It seems to me that any American, not to say any Catholic American, could not better employ part of his money than in aiding the support of the Indian schools conducted by these noble and unselfish women (Catholic sisters), now frowned upon and even actively antagonized by the partisan spirit of our politicians."

To these words of Mr. Lummis, the *Ave Maria* very appropriately remarks: "There is no one in this country who knows the needs of the Indian better than this Protestant man of letters. Let us hope that his earnest words will inspire Catholics to deal generously, and non-Catholics to deal justly, with the disinherited wards of the nation."

5) Fifth motive: Christian Ambition. Squarely and unequivocally the question put to us now is: Are the Indian schools and missions to be abandoned, and are the red men and their children to be turned over to the sects?

When we abandon the Indian schools we virtually abandon the Indian missions. And when we abandon the Indian missions we take from the Indian people not only the presence of the numerous sisterhoods who teach in the schools, but in many instances the priest also, who ordinarily could not live among them but for the shelter of the schools, from which he, like the Indian child, receives food and clothing, and often nothing more. Hence we take from the Indian the Holy Mass, the Blessed Sacrament, and all the sacraments. In many places, even with the schools, the Indians have Mass only once or twice a month, and in some places not more than two or three times a year; but were the schools abandoned, the consolations of Holy Mass and the sacraments would be denied the most unfortunate of all peoples.

One of the latest schemes of giving our Indian schools the coup de grace is the refusal of rations to children and parents unless the children go to government schools. In one of his latest speeches in the Senate, Senator Vest, who throughout his long, honorable, and brilliant public career has always been a faithful friend and a zealous advocate of the Indian's cause, characterizes this scheme as follows:

> We are confronted with the fact that the Commissioner of Indian Affairs, in direct violation, as I believe, of the Constitution of the United States, undertakes to starve the Indians, the father, the mother, and the children of school age. Yes, and in plain violation of solemn treaties by which we obtained their land, they do not get their rations unless these children are sent to government schools. . . . I should be obliged to any lawyer or Senator to tell me how the order of the Commissioner of Indian Affairs agrees with the Constitution of the United States, which says that there shall be no discrimination on account of religious opinion or membership in any religious sect. . . . I deny that that order of the Commissioner of Indian Affairs is the law or should be called the law—but I affirm that the status of the question now is that unless an Indian father and mother send their children to a govern-ment school, no matter what they think in regard to the education of these children, not only the father and mother, but the children are refused rations, so that the whole family may starve, unless they change their religious opinion and come within that order. . . . The Constitution of the United States means, and every commentator has said so, the Supreme Court has said so, that there shall be no discrimination on account of religious opinion or the exercise of any religious opinion, and here we have this outrageous and infamous order, which says that poor, innocent children shall be refused the rations to which they are entitled under treaty unless they are sent to the government schools. . . . It is astonishing how little attention is paid to any right, constitutional or otherwise, of the Indians. . . . Now if an Indian is a Catholic and his wife is a Catholic, as many of them are, and wants to send his children at his own expense to a Catholic school, to a private school, the children are to be starved; notwithstanding the treaty provides for furnishing rations to them. The Indian and his wife or squaw are to be starved in defiance to the Constitution and the treaty, unless his children are sent to a day school. If there is any way in a committee of conference to put any provision in the bill (Indian Appropriation Bill, last February) to remedy this great outrage, I hope it may be done.

This matter was brought up before the Board of Indian Commissioners, 10 in number, two of whom are Catholics, Archbishop Ryan, of Philadelphia, and Mr. Bonaparte, of Baltimore, the other eight being members of other religious denominations. This board unanimously decided that the ruling of the Indian commissioner against the children who attended the Catholic Indian schools was unjust, and when the bill came before Congress, an amendment, prepared by the Indian Commission to cover the defect caused by the Indian commissioner's decision, was presented. The amendment read as follows: "That no rations shall be withheld from any Indian entitled thereto under any treaty with the United States by reason of the fact that the child or children of such Indian may be in attendance upon any school other than a government school."

The adoption of this amendment would have made it possible to do justice to the Indian children attending Catholic schools. But there was a man in the U.S. Senate, a thread-brained, little-souled man, who was unwilling to grant the unanimous consent necessary to the passage of the bill. That man was Henry Cabot

Lodge, junior senator from Massachusetts; by his cast-iron bigotry he killed the amendment, and the starving-out experiment continues. It is, consequently, left to the religious fervor and ambition of our Catholic people to defeat, or to render ineffective, the malicious and unconstitutional designs and plans of the *Brownies* in office.

In 1889 T. J. Morgan was commissioner of Indian Affairs, and Daniel Dorchester was superintendent of Indian schools. Both were Protestant preachers. Both misused their positions for sectarian purposes; it was this pair *of a feather* who, in open violation of the constitution of their country, inaugurated the uncharitable and unAmerican campaign against the good work of the Catholic schools and missions among the Indians, only because their success was an eyesore to them. It was they who started the ball of bigotry rolling down the mountain of their ignorance and prejudice, and from that day to this there have been agents to keep the ball moving in its course, that is, to work against the Catholic missions. Along with Morgan and Dorchester we have the unpleasant memory of Hoke Smith, Browning, and other understrappers who by their words and deeds added weight and speed to the Morgan-Dorchester ball, which was to become an avalanche that would squelch the Catholic Indian schools out of existence.

Well, the ball struck, it rolled into Congress, and seems to have hit a great part of the members of that august body on a spot where they must have had a dent instead of a bump on their phrenological contour. The appropriations allotted to mission or contract schools by solemn treaty of the government were withdrawn, and since they have totally ceased in 1900, our Indian schools have been placed in a position in which they must struggle hard for their existence. As has been said above, the question which confronts us now is simply this: Are the Indian missions to be abandoned, and is the red man to be turned over to the sects? We hope that the religious fervor of our Catholics will answer: No! and that their Christian ambition will willingly furnish the means of saving and maintaining them; for "if we cannot look after the religious and educational needs of the Indian," says the *Ave Maria,* "the Protestant societies are extremely willing to try."

6) Sixth motive: Christian Charity. Our Indian schools were erected by the Church at the invitation of the U.S. government, at an expense of $1.5 million, with the promised support of the administration. The refusal to continue this support left the Church in a dire dilemma. The following passage taken from an "Appeal of the American Federation of Catholic Societies" to all the affiliated branches of the federation ought to touch a sympathetic chord in the heart of every Catholic:

> Had it not been for the timely and providential help of a most heroic type of Catholic womanhood, who gave her wealth and consecrated her life to the uplifting of the downtrodden races, the Church would have been confronted with a condition that we shrink from contemplating. Honor, justice, duty, impel us to come to the aid of our Holy Church in her hour of sore need, to lighten the weight of this holy woman, who alone carries the Red Man's burden, to save the jeopardized souls of our Indians. Shall we allow the repeated appeals of our Archbishops to go unheeded? Shall we let this devoted woman stand alone between a just God and His avenging wrath to atone for a 'Century of Dishonor'?

Shall she alone offer her life as a vicarious reparation for the national crime, which makes the Indian an alien, an exile, a pauper in the land which God gave him by the most sacred of titles? Shall we contribute to this catalogue of iniquities by our own sinful indifference, which allows Catholic brethren among the Indians to be forced into apostasy, and screen ourselves under the cowardly plea, 'Am I my brother's keeper?'

In the life of St. Patrick we read that he one day saw in a vision the infants and children of distant Erin, stretching out their hands toward him, begging and entreating him to come to their land to bring them the light and the grace of faith. Thus, too, the red man and his children are stretching out their hands today toward you, dear reader, and all the Catholics of the land, imploring you to help them in receiving and preserving the light and the grace of faith. Shall we, and can we in defiance of the claims of Christian charity, nay common humanity, allow these our brethren in the household of the faith to be perverted, or to be forced back into savagery and heathenism, without extending the hand of Catholic fellowship and Christian benevolence? Shall and can we suffer their children to be deprived of the faith born and nourished in their hearts through the untiring efforts and labors of our missionaries and their mission schools?

And does this involve any great or extraordinary sacrifice on the part of the individual Catholic? No. There are about 12 million Catholics in this country. Of these 12 million there are surely two million who could easily afford to give five cents a year, and would never miss nor feel it; this would make a sum of $100,000; or if only 400,000 would join the Preservation Society, at 25 cents a year, it would realize the same sum, and keep our Indian schools and missions in a condition to continue their work among the Indian tribes. Is there any reason why this could and ought not to be done?

Reverend Father Ketcham, director of the Catholic Indian Bureau, closes his report for 1901–1902 with the following words:

There appears to be only one legitimate conclusion, namely: the Catholic Indian Mission School is an absolute necessity, and the day (God grant it may never come) the Church of America discontinues the Mission schools, that day she turns her Indian children over to the sects, and practically withdraws from Indian mission work. *Shall* the schools be supported? The outlook is not bright. But in spite of two years of the gloomiest prospects, they are still in operation. *Can* they be supported? There is certainly enough surplus money among the Catholics of the country to support them; there *must* be found *some way* of inducing the people to minister unto Jesus Christ in the person of his suffering Indian brethren.

Some may, perhaps, say that every diocese has its orphanage, its seminary, or other charitable institutions to support, besides there are charitable societies and extra collections for missionary and benevolent purposes, so that the strain and the drain is too much. But before speaking or thinking thus, consider the five following little points: First, there is a great difference between the eastern and western part of our country; out here most dioceses are poor. A plain, simple country church in the East would be a fine cathedral in many parts of the West. Catholics live scattered and far between, the Catholic Indians are poor and needy, and most of our western dioceses must struggle hard to hold what they have. It would, therefore, be impossible for them to maintain the Indian schools. Second, the support of the Indian schools and missions is an affair that does not touch any diocese or dioceses in particular, but touches us all; it is general. Third, we contribute toward foreign missions in Africa and China; we have the Infant Jesus Society to save Chinese children. This is certainly very praiseworthy, but who is nearer to us, the Mongol or the Indian? Fourth, in their "Appeal" our archbishops speak as follows:

> Parish and diocesan needs cannot justly be pleaded as a reason for lack of generosity to the missions anymore than a man who owes two debts could be relieved of the duty of paying one because he had paid the other. If the people give liberally to the missions, they will be more generous to their parish churches, because turning a deaf ear to worthy appeals dries up the fountains of the heart and renders it callous even to urgent calls of domestic charity, while frequent and generous almsgiving begets the *habit* of contributing to all good works, and brings down upon the giver the lavish benedictions of God.

Fifth, the words of Holy Scripture: "He that hath mercy on the poor lendeth to the Lord: and He will repay him" (Prov. 19, 17). "And with what measure you mete, it shall be measured to you again" (Matt. 7, 2). "The pot of meal shall not waste, nor the cruse of oil be diminished" (3 Kings 17, 14). "Amen I say to you; as long as you did it to one of these my least brethren, you did it to me" (Matt. 25, 40).

7) Seventh motive: The Future Glory and Welfare of Our Country. Before closing the Indian question, I must warn the readers against a very popular illusion. We are frequently told that the Indians are fast dying out. With pathetic accuracy the time has been set, when the last red man, the last scion of a once noble, interesting, mighty, and numerous race, shall behold for the last time the sun setting upon the land of his forefathers. He sits in the twilight's gloaming at the entrance of his lodge, a buffalo skull at his feet, chanting his melancholy death song and wishing to lay his weary limbs to rest in the last long sleep with his fathers, and then the curtain noiselessly drops upon the history of the First Americans. Humorists, with no regard whatever for the feelings and the misery of others, who would not hesitate to crack a supposed joke on a widow surrounded by crying and starving children, tell us with cynical pleasantry that the Indian cannot survive soap and civilization. All this is blooming nonsense and rampant ignorance, based probably on the past history of New England.

The question of whether the Indians are dying out or not is one that must not be answered according to the past history of New England, but according to present actualities. In the first place, we need not expect the landing of any more Pilgrim fathers, who, as Mr. C. F. Lummis puts it, after landing "first fell upon their knees, then upon the Indians." Then, the rising generation of Americans are far more broad-minded and tolerant than their Puritanical sires and recognize in the Indian a human being who has a right to live on God's earth. The days of the Jacks, Bobs,

Bills, and the like, the Indian killers, and other dime-novel-hero-brutes are past; the Indians themselves are again in their normal state, namely, peaceful, and have no desire of making war upon the whites, if left alone, or if treated with justice—when treated at all.

Mr. L. A. Maynard writes of the Indians in *Leslie's Weekly*:

> These people are increasing in number, despite all the untoward conditions under which they live. The census of 1890 gave the number of the Indians in the United States, exclusive of Alaska, as 249,000; the census of 1900 gives them as 270,000. Careful ethnologists see no reason to suppose that since America was discovered there has ever been a time when the Indians on our territory were materially more in number than they are now.

The last part of this remark applies especially to our Southwest, where the Pueblo Indians, as Mr. Lummis says, are now practically as numerous as they were when first discovered by the Spaniards.[15]

The oft-repeated assertion that the Indian is incapable of enduring the strain of a higher civilization, hence our efforts at his betterment are vain, Mr. Maynard emphatically denies:

> The difficulties that lie in the peculiar status of the Indians themselves are the least among the difficulties which have always embarrassed and often nullified every sincere, honest, and unselfish effort toward the uplift, and the betterment of the red man. These obstacles have been chiefly the unwise laws and mistaken methods adopted in times past by the national government in Indian administration, the knavery and cupidity of many Indian agents and other white men having relations with the Indians, and the selfish intrigues of spoilsmen and politicians.

In view of the fact that the Indians are increasing in numbers rather than decreasing, Mr. Maynard says:

> Our responsibilities, duties, and obligation in this matter are not likely to be lessened for many years to come, or until, in the process of time and under the operation of wise and enlightened laws, the Indians cease to be "wards," a class apart and distinct from all other people within our borders, and are merged in the great body of our citizenship, where they rightfully belong.

When the German Franks overran Gaul, and after the Gaul and the Frank had united to one common brotherhood, the result was the bright and brilliant French nation. When the German Angles and Saxons invaded Britain, and after they had joined hands with the Britons, they laid the foundation of the present hardy and dauntless English nation. In like manner, when the time shall come, of which Mr. Maynard speaks, and come it will, the time when the Indians cease to be "wards"; when they will be "merged in the great body of our citizenship, where they rightfully belong"; when the sharp, quick, and ready intellect of the Indian shall work together with the talents and the experience of the white man, there shall grow up an "American nation" which will outclass and eclipse everything whatever the world has hitherto done in the line of founding and building up nations. And the better the Indian is instructed and educated now, the greater will be the glory and splendor of the future Real American Nation.

Therefore, do not think it is not worth the time, labor, and expense of helping the Indian, because after a few years his race will have passed. Neither imagine that by contributing toward the Indian schools and missions you are simply helping a dying man to his last meal, or gilding the sunset hours of a parting race. The Indians are with us. They are increasing in numbers and shall certainly play a prominent role in the future destinies of our country.

And now, dear reader, I earnestly and sincerely hope that you, after considering these seven motives (to which I could add a few more, if I were not afraid of tiring you), will not fail to be a friend of our Indian mission schools, and will strive to make Indian-friends among your friends and acquaintances. Remember that whatever you do toward helping our Indian mission schools financially will not be forgotten by Him, who has promised to reward even a drink of water given to the poor and needy in His name.

An Alternative Model: Canadian Indian Policy

We on the Yankee side of the Great Lakes find it, as a rule, quite funny to speak of the "Cannucks" of Canada as a people who are a kind of semicivilized cross between a barbarian and a savage. We speak of them with that air of superiority with which smart city folks usually speak of rural jayhawkers and hayseeds; look upon them as back numbers in this age of progress, still in an embryonic state of development; as stragglers holding on to the tail end of the bandwagon of modern civilization, barely managing to keep pace with the tempo; while we are sitting on the front seat blowing the big horn. I have spent four years in Canada and have had occasion during that time to learn that the people and country there have a few points which, if we would imitate, would raise the standard of our enlightenment and civilization not a little.

Bankruptcy is almost unknown in Canada, because she has a set of the best banking laws in the world. Her criminal laws are as wise as those of any nation and are far better handled than ours. There is no buying the juries and bribing the judges by rich criminals; whoever has violated the law is punished accordingly, be he beggar or millionaire. Religious freedom and liberty are not a dead letter on the Canadian constitution as they are on ours; every Canadian citizen has at least just as much personal liberty as any citizen of the states. Canada has the splendid distinction of being almost the only civilized country in the world that has no divorce court, and in our country the divorce courts are so busy that they are generally referred to as "mills." The separate school system, according to which the taxes of the citizen go to the school visited by his children, is an impossibility here, and according to all indications, it will take us two or three generations to catch up with Canada on this particular point. But the one point to which I wish to draw special attention just now is the treatment of its Indian wards by the Canadian government.

His Majesty's government in Canada has always been very happy in its relations with its Indian wards. Very little or no friction has occurred between the government and the Indian tribes within the Canadian borders. With perhaps the exception of the Riel rebellion the government has never been compelled to use force of arms. Canada will never need a Helen Hunt Jackson to record her "Century of Dishonor," nor will her history ever show up such gory blotches as our unnecessary wars with the Seminoles, Sioux, Cheyennes, Nez Percés, Apaches, and so on, nor will her language ever be disgraced by the phrase, "The only good Indian is a dead Indian." Where differences have existed—and there have been such differences—it has always been possible to secure an amicable adjustment and reconciliation through the channels of diplomacy, common sense, justice, and fair dealing. Wherein, then, lies the secret of the success of the Canadian government in handling the Indian question? Particularly in the following points, largely taken from the *Indian Herald*, vol. 1, no. 3.

1) The Canadian government *has always treated the Indian as a man,* or as a human being who possessed all the qualities and properties of human nature, and it appealed to these qualities and properties and almost always succeeded in bringing out the good sides of the Indian. His vanity was tickled; his love for exterior show and pageant was humored; he has always been placed upon his honor; he was not commanded in the terms and accents of a categorical imperative, backed up by frowning guns and rifles, to live in peace, but was *invited and encouraged to assist the government* in establishing and preserving peace throughout the vast domain over which the Indians are scattered. Almost invariably when treaties were made with the Indians, uniforms, flags, and medals (with the promise that new uniforms would be given every three years) were given to the chiefs and headmen, and these warriors were made *officers of the government* for the preservation of peace and the prevention of crime among the tribes which these warriors dominated.

Such dealing was *bound* to appeal to the best qualities in the Indian. It appealed to his pride, to his self-respect, to his love of dignity, to his sense of honor. It gave him to understand that a trust had been committed to him by the "Big Chief across the broad water." Thus was engendered in the heart of the Indian a deep sense of loyalty to the "Great Father," whom they were told loved his red children, and that loyalty made itself manifest on more than one battlefield in defense of the empire. I have stood on the banks of the Thames River in Ontario, where fell the celebrated Shawnee chief, Tecumseh, in Canada's defense, and the Indian was prominent in the relief expedition sent to Khartoum to rescue Chinese Gordon.

2) The Canadian government has always been *firm and just* in its dealing with the red man. It was firm in the making of its treaties and had the fixed intention of fulfilling them to the letter. It is firm, even today, in the maintenance of their conditions. A treaty once made between the government and the Indians was binding; was "an end to all strife"; it was final; it was to endure "so long as the sun

shines and water flows." Neither party could ignore or recede from its conditions. The Indians have faithfully kept their part of the compacts, and the government has never failed to fulfil its part. *No treaty has ever been broken.* But on two occasions the government, out of its bounty and desire to meet the Indians' wishes, *has gone beyond the claims of the Indian* upon it, and for two tribes increased their perpetual annuity.

3) In getting possession of the Indian lands the government *never summarily appropriated them.* The Indians' rights and claims were always considered, and the lands were bought. In consideration of a certain sum of money paid in hand, a tract of land, some incidentals suited to the needs of the peculiar tribe dealt with, and a solemn pledge that schools would be established and a definite perpetual annuity paid them, the Indians forever ceded their lands to the British Crown. By treating with the Indians in this manner, the Canadian government avoided all possible cause of friction insofar as the question of the rightful possession of the lands was concerned. The Indian sold his land, got his price for it, took the money, and gave up his rights. The transaction was satisfactory to both parties.

Our government either took the Indians' lands peremptorily from them, or employed other means to get possession of them. One of these means Joseph, chief of the Nez Percés, after the Nez Percés' war in 1876, in a speech before General Howard, exemplified in the following words, which show a fine sense of the straight logic and the smooth sarcasm of the red man:

> In the treaty councils the commissioners have claimed that our country had been sold to the government. Suppose a white man should come to me and say, 'Joseph, I like your horses; and I want to buy them.' Then he goes to my neighbor and says to him, 'Joseph has some good horses; I want to buy them, but he refuses to sell.' My neighbor answers, 'Pay me the money and I will sell you Joseph's horses.' The white man returns to me and says, 'Joseph, I have bought your horses, and you must let me have them.' If we sold our lands to the government, this is the way they were bought. On account of the treaty made by the other bands of the Nez Percés the white man claimed my lands.

4) In order that the Indian might have no opportunity to blame government if the lands selected for their reservations were later found to be unsatisfactory, the government decided *to consult the wishes of the Indians.* They certainly knew better than the whites what lands were best suited to their occupation, their needs and wants—according as their inclinations were bent toward agriculture, fishing and hunting, or stock raising. The Indians were, therefore, allowed to select their own lands. But they must be selected within certain specified limits agreed upon at the time the treaty was made, and within the territory ceded by them. Once the Indians had chosen their lands and a government survey of them had been made, it was settled once for always; there was no throwing them open later on for the benefit of hungry, unscrupulous land sharks, neither was there any change of location possible, nor could the lands be disposed of except by and with the permission of the government. The prudence and the wisdom of allowing the Indians to select their own lands are self-evident and have undoubtedly saved Canada many a

crimsoned page of history. [Allowing them to select their own lands] placed the government before the Indians in the light of seeking the best interests of the Indian; of desiring to please and of showing deference to his wishes and preferences as to where he should live. It made the Indian feel that he was a man, a human being, who had a right to some portion of God's earth, and this feeling once engendered in his heart had more influence in making him peaceful and law-abiding than all the powder and bullets in the world.

5) The plan followed by the government in the selection of the Indian reservations was also followed *in the matter of establishing schools.* Schools must be established on the several reservations. There must be a school established on every reservation as soon as there is a sufficient number of children to warrant such a step. And it must be located at *the place which the Indians themselves designate.*

From this brief outline of the Canadian government's policy in its management of its Indian affairs it is easy to see wherein the secret of its success and strength lies. Time has justified the policy of treating the Indian as a man and appealing to the best that is in him; it will show. Time has justified the policy of placing confidence in the Indian; he responds. Time has justified the policy of placing the Indian on his honor; he has endeavored to keep it unsullied insofar, at least, as his relations to the government are concerned. Time has justified the policy of treating the Indian with honesty and justice; his natural sense of these qualities will bind him more securely than chains of iron and steel. Time has justified the policy of keeping the promises and treaties made with the Indians; they will take their cue from the white man. Time has justified the policy of doing to the Indian as one would wish that others would do to himself; the Indian has always reciprocated accordingly. Yes, had we followed up the Indian policy of Spain in our country, as England followed up that of France in Canada, the history of our "Indian question" would be quite different from what it is now.

Notes

1. From FWW 10 (October 1902–May 1903): 152–56, 188–94, 222–27, 260–65, 295–99, 332–34, 369–72, 404–7; 11 (June–August 1903): 10–14, 44–48, 82–86.

2. The usual format for *St. Anthony's Messenger* did not include footnotes or endnotes. The following notes expand and standardize Father Leopold's within-text references.

3. John Gilmary Shea, *History of the Catholic Missions among the Indian Tribes of the United States, 1529–1854* (New York: T. W. Strong, late Edward Dunigan & Brother, Catholic Publishing House, 1854), 39.

4. Charles F. Lummis, *The Spanish Pioneers* (Chicago: A. C. McClurg and Company, 1899), 158, 161, 163–64.

5. Reau Campbell, *Campbell's New Revised Complete Guide and Descriptive Book of Mexico* (City of Mexico: Sonora News Company, 1899), 23.

6. Campbell, *Revised Complete Guide*, 70.

7. Campbell, *Revised Complete Guide*, 142–43.

8. Lummis, *Spanish Pioneers*, 150.

9. Lummis, *Spanish Pioneers*, 168–69.

10. Charles F. Lummis, "Circular letter of W. A. Jones, Commissioner, Office of Indian Affairs, January 1902." This letter, along with a subsequent supplementary order, which, in Charles F. Lummis's words, "practically nullifies the original," is reproduced in Charles F. Lummis, "The Sequoya League," *Out West* 16 (March 1902): 301–2. The portion of the order given here by Father Leopold is from Lummis's quotation of an unofficial portion of the circular letter in the previous issue, *Out West* 16 (February 1902):189. The supplementary order, written in response to "criticisms that have appeared in the newspapers," directs that enforcement of the order be done in a gradual and tactful manner that will not "give the Indians any just cause for revolt," while at the same time asserting that this request for tactful administration in no way represents "a withdrawal or revocation of the circular letter" and its original intent.

11. Charles F. Lummis, "In the Lion's Den," *Out West* 16 (February 1902): 190.

12. Lummis, "In the Lion's Den," 190.

13. "Is Our Indian System a Curse?" *Literary Digest* 25 (November 22, 1902): 667.

14. "Is Our Indian System a Curse?" 667.

15. Lummis, *Spanish Pioneers*, 94.

Part 3

EARLY MINISTRY, 1901–1910

11

Neighbors[1]

Leopold Ostermann, O.F.M.

[As we have already shown, Father Leopold's monthly contributions to *St. Anthony's Messenger* manifested considerable variety in approach and topic. Some were historical essays that combined his reading with personal experience, others were accounts of trips taken, challenges in the mission work, or interesting events and people. Most congenial to present purposes are his reports of daily life as experienced by the working friar, of visits to Navajo families or nearby points of interest, of conversations heard and stories told, stories representing the ongoing oral history of the people. Here he tells of a visit to Hubbell's Trading Post, at Ganado, Arizona, and repeats some stories about the headman in that area, Many Horses, and his father, the renowned Ganado Mucho, "Ganao Muncho" in Father Leopold's terminology. Ganado Mucho's severe treatment of the troublesome medicine man in the story below is not out of character with other incidents in his life. Some time after the people's return to their homeland following their incarceration at Bosque Redondo, he and Manuelito cooperated in a "witch hunt" whereby 40 Navajo men whose resumption of raiding threatened the peace were tried and executed.[2]]

Toward the end of March 1901, Reverend Father Sales, O.F M., Venerable Brother Placidus, O.F.M., and myself paid a visit to our old friend and next western neighbor, Mr. J. L. Hubbell, whose trading post is about 30 or 35 miles west of St. Michael's Mission, at a place called Ganado, in Navajo *Luk'antqel*, or *Luk'akintqel*, that is, "Big House among the Reeds." Ganado is not a village nor a town, but a postal station. Mr. Hubbell's store is the only house there. Following the freighting road over the mountains, we enjoyed one of the loveliest drives imaginable: now we go up hill, then down dale; now over a sage-covered plain, then through a beautiful pine forest; now over a stretch of sand, then jolting over rocky bottom; now through a dry watercourse, then near a deep-gorged canyon. Thus it goes on till finally we drive out into a large, flat valley, where everything is either brown or gray. In this valley, on the banks of a small creek called the Little Colorado Wash, in which there is almost always *some* water, is the trading post of Mr. Hubbell.

Mr. Hubbell is partly of American, partly of Mexican, descent. We were consequently received with genuine Mexican hospitality and frank Yankee cheerfulness. Our host is a man who has a short, striking little story for every and any occasion and entertains his visitors in a manner that makes the visit a pleasant and lasting remembrance. In the past Mr. Hubbell has taken a very active part in the politics of the Territory, is well-read, conversant with all the questions of the day, and perhaps just as well-informed and up-to-date, in out-of-the-way Ganado, as many who live on Broadway, New York. He has a large, well-stocked store and treats the Indians with kindness and justice, for which reason he is much liked by them, and many come 40 or 50 miles, passing other stores on their way, to trade with him. The Indians call him *Nikeesnili*, which is the Navajo word for spectacles, as he wears eyeglasses. He has traded with the Indians about 20 years and speaks Spanish, English, and Navajo fluently. He can relate some very interesting incidents from the times when it was a highly unsafe and risky thing to be in the neighborhood of the Navajo, of which I shall repeat one.

One day Mr. Hubbell and two Mexican gentlemen were sitting at their dinner. The table was placed so that one end touched the wall where there was a window with a pane broken out. They were pleasantly chatting and enjoying their dinner when they suddenly heard a stern voice saying: "Killing a Mexican is like killing a dog!" and looking toward the window, from where the voice came, they saw the athletic form of a Navajo warrior, with bent bow and arrow placed in position to shoot in through the missing pane. The two Mexicans dropped out of sight in "press the button" style and hid under the table. Mr. Hubbell, at whom the arrow was pointed, did not dare to move, knowing well that the least motion would be followed by the twang of the Indian's bowstring and perhaps a fatal arrow wound. He felt that his life was not worth a cent with a hole in it just then; he saw the period which was to be put to his life's course hovering about the tip of that arrow. He made inward acts of contrition, striving to hide his feelings from the Indian, to whom he showed an indifferent front, riveting his eyes on his. Again he heard the ominous words: "Killing a Mexican is like killing a dog!" While the Indian hissed these words through his clenched teeth, he began to pull back his bowstring farther. Slowly the bow bent more and more until the tip of the arrow touched the wood. Then the savage asked him: "Are you not afraid?" Mr. Hubbell, summoning his courage together and preserving his bold front, answered: "If I were, I wouldn't tell you!" Then the Indian, who, it seems, was not in a killing mood just then, slowly relaxed the tension of his bow, thrust the arrow into his quiver, shouldered his bow, turned on his heel, and deliberately walked off, without ever turning back to see if a Winchester were pointed at him. He was suffered to disappear unmolested, but after the two Mexicans had cautiously ventured forth from their hiding place, the appetite for dinner was totally spoiled.

About 10 miles or so beyond Mr. Hubbell's place are the so-called cornfields, flat bottoms where the Indians raise fairly good crops of corn, or maize. Quite a number of Navajo live in this section, but their *qoghans*, or huts, are very far between. There is no such thing as a Navajo village or pueblo. Although very social and company-loving, the Navajo is not at all gregarious. This, no doubt, is the result of the constantly nomadic life of this tribe. The Navajo is pronouncedly a nomad and always was from the time when his forefathers, many centuries ago, left their Alaskan homesteads and began their migrations southward. If he strikes a place that suits him—perhaps a nice valley with good meadows and a spring—and the place is not already occupied, he fells a number of pines, puts up his *qoghan*, covers it with earth, and there is his home, and he will not suffer anyone to locate or build on the land he considers his. Thus the next *qoghan* may be one mile, five, 10, or 15 and more miles away. Sometimes—especially up in the mountains—you may pass within 200 feet from a Navajo's manor that shelters a large family and never suspect it, if your attention is not drawn to it by the bleating of sheep or the barking of coyote-looking dogs. With regard to his home, the Navajo is a seeker of solitude.

This trait of shunning the stranger and seeking seclusion from his presence can be noticed even in their children. Sometimes you will come upon a herd of sheep or goats—these animals are never without a herder, which office generally falls to the lot of the children—look about as you will, you will certainly not detect a shepherd anywhere within your horizon. But after you have passed the herd and are well on your way again, a miniature Navajo—perhaps two or three of them—will crawl out of some arroyo, with a few coyotish dogs, and drive on their woolly charges. If you haven't seen them appear, or rather crawl upon the scene, you will be tempted to believe they have just sprouted up out of the ground.

The Navajo seems to have a special talent for appearing suddenly and unexpectedly. Time and again I have suddenly found myself face-to-face with a redskin—especially in the hills—and could not say from which direction he came. I would then shake hands with him, saying: "*qaláqodsa, si-k'is! qa-dá?*" (Hello, my friend! From whence?). He answers: "*ulu-dá*" (From thence). I continue: "*qagosh dinniya?*"(Whither are you going?) He answers: "*ula-ji*" (Thither). While he says *ula-dá*, and *ula-ji*, he points out the direction of "thence and thither," but not with his index finger, nor with hand or foot, but by turning his face in that particular direction and pouting his lips. This is a general custom of young and old.

Many Horses and Ganao Muncho

The chief or headman among the Navajo living about *Luk'antqel* is Ashki bi-li lani, that is, "The Boy with Many Horses." He is not what his name indicates, a boy, but a man well in the neighborhood of 60, judging from his appearance, which, however, is a very unreliable criterion of an Indian's age. He has visited the mission several times, has shown great interest in the projected school, and has promised to send children there as soon as it be ready to receive them. He is of middle height, with a sad expression lingering about his face, especially about the eyes.

His grandfather was a Moqui Indian who came and stayed with the Navajo of his own accord. The Navajo considered him a slave. He was, like all Pueblos, a hard and diligent worker, industrious and thrifty, and knew how to work himself up. He was an excellent runner and was therefore frequently taken along on hunting trips after deer and antelope, which used to abound between here and Tanner Springs, about 45 miles southwest. His master sent him to herd his horses, which he kept in the just-mentioned country. He would fence the horses up in some canyon and run down deer and antelope on foot. Thus he was always well supplied with meat and acquired a goodly number of valuable hides. After staying at this a year, and having proved himself faithful and trustworthy, his master, feeling himself under obligations to him, treated him as one of his equals, and let him have about 30 horses. From this time he was no longer considered or called a slave. He continued to work hard for himself, acquired a large herd of horses, sold his buckskins, saved what he earned, and bought turquoise—the most valuable gem of the Southwest. In the course of time he was well-to-do and married into the *Tqo-tsoni*, or "Big Water" clan.

His son, the father of Many Horses, achieved renown among the Navajo as an orator. Especially during the time of war he made very eloquent appeals to his fellow tribesmen in the interest of peace, for which reason he was called Bi-tso yeyeitqi, that is, "He Who Speaks with His Tongue." Later on, when he rose to the head of his clan, he was called Tqo-tsoni qastqin, "The Big Water Man." He lived about *Luk'antqel*, in the neighborhood of where Many Horses still lives, and at one time had large herds of horses, cattle, and sheep. The Mexicans, therefore, named him Ganao Muncho [Ganado Mucho], "Many Herds." He was of a peaceful disposition. When, however, there was war he was very much "in it," but was always one of the first to make peace. He was, with Manuelito and Mariano, one of the big chiefs of the Navajo, and he exerted a great influence over the Indians in his neighborhood.

During his time, in the latter part of the 1870s, a certain well-known medicine man of his district began to pose as a kind of prophet and had preached to the Indians certain things which made them quite excited, and which would, if continued, very likely bring on trouble. Ganao Muncho sent word to him to come at once and report to him; he had something to talk over with him, assuring him at the same time that he need fear no harm. The medicine man refused to obey the summons, which was repeated four times. The fourth time Ganao Muncho gave him the same assurance of no harm to him being intended, adding that now he had summoned him four times in a kind and friendly manner, this would be the last invitation. If he disregarded it, he would certainly be killed. The stubborn old medicine man, who by that time had gained a number of followers in whose midst he felt himself quite safe, ignored this last invitation, as he had the others.

Shortly after this, a Hashkawn dance (*dsil k'iji qa'tal*, the greatest dance of the Navajo) took place in the neighborhood. All the medicine men of the vicinity and many from far off would be present. Ganao Muncho here saw his opportunity of administering the threatened punishment to the stubborn old medicine man. He called together his sons and relatives, about 40 in number, armed them, and went to the place of the dance. The medicine man was in a *qoghan* nearby with a number of his followers, also armed. Ganao Muncho went to the door and called him out.

Not being obeyed, he shouted into the hut that all those who wished to keep out of trouble must leave the *qoghan* at once. Those who were within became greatly excited, and all but this particular one left the hut. No one dared go in, as he was armed with a six-shooter. Then they began to throw ropes around the ends of the logs where they met and projected a little, forming the roof of the *qoghan*, so that if the hut caved in he would be buried under its debris.

After the roof was pulled off, the medicine man, seeing how things were going, cried out, addressing Ganao Muncho: "Brother, you are not going to kill me in this way, are you?" But Ganao Muncho answered: "I have been good and kind with you, and have given you plenty of chance. I have called for you four times; you knew you would be killed if you refused to come; you did refuse four times; therefore, you must die." Then, having given his followers a sign, one of them looking in through an opening in the wall caught sight of him, shot in, and killed him. His body was then dragged forth and his brain beaten out with clubs. Now some of the other medicine men came up to Ganao Muncho, remonstrating with him and saying that he should not have killed him in such a manner. But Ganao Muncho turned on them and said to them with flashing eyes and frowning brow, if they did not wish to experience a similar treatment, they had better shut up, and shut up they did.

Many Horses was the constant companion of his father. He says that he stayed with his father from the days of his childhood on until the day of his father's death, and the story of how he treated his sick, aged father is one of filial piety and attachment which may well deserve imitation even among civilized people. Many Horses says that once he was well-to-do and rich (according to Navajo ideas), had nice lands, many flocks of sheep, cattle, horses, and so on, but when his father, being an old man, was taken down by a lingering sickness, lasting five or six years, during which piles and ulcers broke out all over his body, Many Horses sacrificed almost all he had to pay the medicine men for their singing, their dances, and ceremonies. He sent for the best-known medicine men that could be got and had them come and "banish the evil spirits" that were tormenting his father, no matter what they would ask for their services, and medicine men are not backward in asking. He spent in this way the equivalent of about three or four thousand dollars, so that now his property is pretty much dwindled, although he is not exactly poor. He still wears the dagger of his father and finds great satisfaction in showing it and in speaking with respect and reverence of his deceased parent.

Many Horses' father was a so-called *qozhoji*. The *qozhoji* are a certain order of medicine men who differ from other medicine men in a few points. They are seemingly more sincere in their beliefs than others. They make sacrifices of precious things, for example, turquoise and the like, use no idols or fetishes, have songs and prayers, but attribute to them no supernatural effect or power, leaving it to the will of the gods to grant their petitions or not.

When Ganao Muncho noticed that at last the cold hand of death was upon him, he called his son to his deathbed and said to him: "My son, we have always been together, but tonight we must part. I have always loved you very much and did the best for you I could. When I am gone always strive to be an honest, upright, and truthful man. Do not believe in the powers of medicine men, for they have none.

They can never hurt you by any supernatural influence." In this strain he spoke to his son for a long while, and to all appearance "Many Horses" has always followed and lived up to the advice of his dying father.

In December 1890, the whole country was startled by the announcement that the Indians in the Northwest were performing fantastic Ghost Dances. This was universally looked upon as a symptom that serious troubles were brewing among the Indians, and in fact soon the whole Northwest was aflame with wild excitement, and the government was hurrying troops thither. A Messias craze had broken out among them and an Indian millennium was to be inaugurated. The trouble was greatly augmented by the appearance of a fanatic named Johnson, who is supposed to have undertaken the role of the Messias, but who more probably was a Mormon agent. This man told the redskins that when the grass was eight inches above the ground he would appear again, that then the red warriors should have their lands once more, the dead heroes would rise again from their graves, all the cattle would turn into buffalo, and a great wave of mud would arise and sweep the palefaces off the earth. We all know of the furious outbreak which followed this strange craze, and the dear price of human life paid on both sides. The leading spirit in this uprising was Sitting Bull, the celebrated chief of the Dakota Sioux. Being a crafty old medicine man, filled with haughty pride and ambition, and with an implacable hatred of the white man, he fostered by all possible means this superstitious craze. He continually harangued the Indians, inaugurated the Ghost Dances, and sent emissaries to all surrounding tribes to incite them to make trouble and to join in the revolt.

Some of these emissaries, or such who had listened to them, came as far south as the Utes, the northern neighbors of the Navajo, where they spread the news of the coming Messias who would rid the country of the palefaces and restore it to its pristine glory. Bi-hi Lizhini, that is, "He with the Black Horse," a very influential headman of the Navajo in the Carisso Mountains, was among the Utes at that time, and returning home, he brought the news of the impending destruction of the whites and the return of all dead Indians from *ch 'indi 'ta* [and such places] into the Navajo country, where it raised a little stir in some places, especially as in some regions grass for the herds had begun to get scarce. However, it created no disturbances except in the brains of some designing medicine men, notably one near *Luk 'antqel*, or Ganado.

As the story of this medicine man's craze has some connection with Many Horses and will give the reader a still better glimpse of his character, I shall try to relate it according to the facts I could get.

The medicine man, who is still living, and whose name is N-näzi, that is, "The Long, or Tall One," was shrewd enough to see in the prevailing craze an opportunity of gaining prestige and profit. He conceived the idea of organizing a new lodge of medicine men, with new legends and ceremonies, and with such extraordinary supernatural gifts and powers as would awe the people into reverence and induce them to call for him or his associates in their troubles and sicknesses. Thus their herds and possessions would increase and they would rise up high in the estimation of the people. Some distance from his *qoghan*, I was told, he had made a hole in the ground, large enough to accommodate one person comfortably. One night when the snow was falling thickly and N-näzi was sitting in his *qoghan* with his family and some friends around the fire, he, being attired in nothing less and nothing more than a G-string, arose, walked out into the night and snow, and never reentered the hut all that night. The falling snow quickly covered up his tracks. He had simply vanished, but vanished into the hole he had prepared where he lay snugly enough awaiting the morning. At the first faint blush of returning daylight he cautiously came forth from his hiding place and returned to his hut, brushing out his tracks with branches of trees, and the still falling snow soon covered the least traces of them.

He entered with a cold, solemn face, and soon had those present worked up by telling them that he had been on the top of the San Francisco Mountains, a hundred or more miles away. The San Francisco Mountains, *Dok'ooslid*, that is, "It Does Not Thaw," about 12 miles north of Flagstaff, are among the sacred mountains of the Navajo. The country of the Navajo, according to their legends, was bounded by the following sacred mountains: in the east by *Zisnajini*, that is, Black Horizontal Belt, Pelado Peak; in the south by *Tzodzil*, that is, Big Mountain, the San Mateo Mountains; in the west by *Dok'ooslid*, that is, "It Thaws Not," the San Francisco Mountains; in the north by *Debentsa*, that is, Scattered Sheep, the San Juan Mountains. All these mountains and several others figure prominently in Navajo mythology, and consequently also in the songs and ceremonies of the medicine men. They are regarded by the Navajo as something like Mt. Olympus was by the ancient Greeks: the homes of their principal deities.

On the San Francisco Mountain N-näzi said he had an interview with Esdsannadlehi, "The Woman Who Changes." She is the most revered deity of the Navajo, and is supposed never to remain in the same condition. She grows to be an old woman, then becomes a young girl again, and thus continually passes through endless courses of life, ever changing but never dying. Dr. Washington Matthews thinks she is nothing else but the apotheosis of Nature, or of the changing Year. She is the author of all fertility in nature, and therefore her home is in the west, the direction from which the rain and the thaw breezes come. From the top of San Francisco Mountain, N-näzi went on to say, he was transported to mid-ocean, where he met Yołgai Esdsa, "The White Shell Woman." She is the younger sister of Esdsannadlehi, with whom she is associated in the myths. However, the younger sister receives a lesser degree of worship than the elder. Esdsannadlehi, made of an earthly jewel, turquoise, is related to the land, Yolkai esdsan, made of the white shell from the ocean, is related to the waters.

Here he was told that a great many Indians had left their ancestral customs; had forgotten their old traditions, or made fun of them; believed no longer in the gods of their fathers, and so on. Therefore, as a punishment for them, the grass was getting scarce in their land, and their animals, the chief source of their subsistence, were suffering and getting lean. Now, he had been chosen by her to change all this; therefore, she had vested him with great supernatural powers, had commanded him to perform certain ceremonies and to use his powers for the benefit of his people. He then explained some of the ceremonies he was to perform, adding that the Shell

Woman had prescribed for their performance, among other things, four virgins for each cardinal point of the compass, making 16 virgins in all. Although this last request should have stamped him, in the eyes of his hearers, rather a mire-grovelling carnalist than an ocean-floating spiritualist, he nevertheless found faith with some. He had those who were in his hut that night to bear testimony that during that cold snowy night, he was gone all night with nothing but a G-string on, and had not been seen anywhere in the neighborhood. This was to be an absolute proof that he spoke the truth, that he had been transported and had been granted extraordinary supernatural powers. Many listened eagerly to what he had to say and believed his words.

Many Horses, too, had heard of "Longfellow's" nocturnal air journey, his flight out over the ocean deep, and of his doings and sayings. Not believing the least word of it, he made up his mind to go and tell him so. One day he entered the *qoghan* of N-näzi, and being a man who believes in striking straight and square, he opened up on him with

> I heard you are a holy man and have visited the holy people and have many things to tell. You are a . . . liar (the dots stand in place of a qualifying adjective), trash like you are not holy; you are a schemer and are out after the things of others. The holy people would surely not have anything to do with a scrub like you; if you have seen the Shell Woman and spoken with her, prove it to us, she must have given you something by which you can prove that you speak the truth; you lie!

Here old N-näzi began to protest and to complain. His friends, too, began to interfere and to reprove Many Horses for his speech, telling him not to speak so, for the holy man was telling the truth. Upon this Many Horses got his Indian up still more, and turning upon the whole crowd, he repeated with special stress and emphasis, "He is a . . . liar; he is a nice fellow to sacrifice virgins to. He says he has great powers. It isn't so. Let him show his powers: He hasn't any, and can do nothing. I don't believe a word of it. And if the Shell Woman was speaking to such a scrub as he, she, too, is a liar. If she told him that the Indians have grown wicked, and that therefore there was no grass for their herds, she lies. There isn't much grass now because we have larger herds, and because our herds have eaten it," etc.

The plan of N-näzi to gain position and possession failed. He still lives, and does not like to be reminded of his failure.

Notes

1. From Leopold Ostermann, FWW 9 (April, May 1902): 366–71, 402–5.
2. Raymond Friday Locke, *The Book of the Navajo* (Los Angeles: Holloway House, 1986), 30–31. For an alternative view of the "witch purge," which sees it not as a response to raiding behavior that threatened the peace but rather as a traditional response to witchcraft motivated by genuine fear of witches, see Martha Blue, *The Witch Purge of 1878: Oral and Documentary History in the Early Reservation Years* (Tsaile, Arizona: Navajo Community College Press, 1990). For biographical information on Ganado Mucho, see Virginia

Hoffman and Broderick H. Johnson, *Navajo Biographies* (Phoenix: Navajo Curriculum Center Press, 1974).

12

Chin Lee in Retrospect[1]

Leopold Ostermann, O.F.M.

[During Father Leopold's first years as a Navajo missionary he was part of the Franciscan team at St. Michaels, working closely with Father Anselm and Father Berard in helping to master the Navajo language, cultivating rapport with the Navajo people, building St. Michael's School, recruiting students, and striving to create a network of support, financial and political, for the maintenance and expansion of mission activities.

In 1902 he began visiting Chin Lee with an eye to establishing a mission outpost there. In 1904, in a rented building, he began periodic residence in Chin Lee, and in 1906 Father Leopold and Brother Gervase Thuemmel were formally transferred there. He would continue to collaborate with the team at St. Michaels, but from a distance, and he was now burdened with the full responsibility of a mission outpost. He would serve at Chin Lee for 20 years, until failing health necessitated his transfer back to St. Michaels.

The ministry at Chin Lee isolated Father Leopold both geographically and socially. Visits from other Franciscans were few, and while there was plenty of work to do, for a long time there was little evidence of achievement. According to his 1907 report to the Bureau of Catholic Indian Missions, "in four years of mission work he could meagerly report one baptism, and that of an infant in danger of death," and three years later he wrote that "no progress could be made Christianizing the adults who are thorough and intense heathen."[2] A government boarding school was established at Chin Lee in 1910. With it came the opportunity to instruct the resident children, and then, finally, there were the success stories, the observable changes in children's lives, and the baptisms.

Of those long years at Chin Lee, another Navajo missionary, Jerome Hesse, would write:

> What hardships, labors, and trials Father Leopold endured on the missions no one will ever know. He would not tell and none other could. During the many years he spent at the Navajo mission at Chin Lee, Arizona, the only thing that we know for sure is that he divided his time between missionary and ethnological labors, collaborating in the gathering of material for the books on the Navajo

language and customs published by the Franciscan Fathers of St. Michael's. When the altitude forced him to leave the missions, he devoted his time to preparing in simple form a grammar from which others might gain an elementary knowledge of the extremely difficult Navajo language.[3]

We do know that his literary production for general audiences dried up. Father Leopold produced the last of his long series in *St. Anthony Messenger* on "Franciscans in the Wilds and Wastes of the Navajo Country" in 1909. In the next decade he wrote his share of articles for the friars' short-lived annual, *Franciscan Missions of the Southwest*, but they were mostly combinations or extensions of his previous publications, often with minimal editing. What he now had to say to general audiences was what he had already said, and apart from his correspondence, there are no more of the rich, first-person accounts of contemporary events and personalities that made his earlier articles so compelling. Even counting the derivative pieces, his total output of nonspecialist (non-Navajo language) writing for the years 1910–1919 was only a dozen or so articles.

There was even less in his final decade. The brief series in *St. Anthony Messenger* from which most of the segments of the present chapter are gleaned offered, as the series title suggests, merely little stories, vignettes of a page or two in length, and even some of them were repetitions or extractions from Father Leopold's earlier work. The series was entirely retrospective, having begun in February 1927, some time after Father Leopold had come down to St. Michaels for health reasons, and his final contribution appeared in November 1928. The stories pertaining to his first decade of Navajo mission work are combined in the present chapter. Those of later vintage appear in chapter 23.]

In 1902 the writer was sent to Chin Lee from St. Michaels, Arizona, to look the place over as a prospective point for a branch mission of St. Michaels. I had never been there before and knew nothing of the place but that a friend of ours, Mr. S. E. Day, lived there with his family and ran a trading post. I started out with team and wagon west to Ganado, and from Ganado north in the direction in which I was told Chin Lee lay.

Following the road according to directions, I traveled along on a hot summer day, till late in the afternoon I found myself drawing near a beautiful grove of cottonwood trees. (The grove is still there, about one-fourth of a mile northwest of the present mission.) There was no house or hogan, not even a fence post within the expansive horizon. It is in occasions like this, out in limitless wilderness, unknown miles from everywhere, an unobstructed horizon all round, a cloudless sky above, a palpable quietness brooding over everything, and not a living being in sight, that one feels very small, almost, one might say, like an atomized molecule.

However, I thought I saw a hogan, all but hidden from view, under the cottonwoods where, if it be inhabited, I could get some information as to where Chin Lee was, and as to where I was myself. I drove right straight for that point. In making this beeline I drove over a Navajo's field, which had been recently irrigated, came near being mired in, and was glad to get out again safely with my ponies. I was not mistaken; there really was a hogan under the trees, and it was inhabited. I asked the master of the house: "*Qádisha Ch'inli?*" (Where is Chin Lee?) He looked at me as one looks at a greenhorn and, smiling, described a large circle, saying: "*Kwe'e Ch'inli*" (Chin Lee is here.) I then queried further: "*Qádisha Naaltsos Naez baghan?*" (Where is Mr. Day's house?) (Mr. Day was called by the Indians Naaltsos Naez, *naaltsos* meaning paper or book, and *naez* meaning tall. He was a tall slender man and had been for some years chief clerk at the Agency of Fort Defiance. Hence, Naaltsos Naez, the Tall Book Clerk, or Bookkeeper.) He gave me directions as to roads and turns, and after driving about one and one-fourth mile, always according to directions, I arrived at the store and was kindly greeted by Mr. and Mrs. Day and by the three Day boys.

Chin Lee was selected by the late Father Anselm Weber, O.F.M., as a desirable mission station for various reasons: 1) There were at that time already rumors abroad that the government intended to erect a boarding school for Navajo children at that place. A branch mission at Chin Lee, therefore, would bring the fathers in contact not only with the children, but also with their parents and other adult Indians. 2) Chin Lee is situated near the center of the Navajo reservation. Consequently, various parts or regions of the reservation could easily be reached or visited from there. 3) Indians living in the Black Mountain district came to Chin Lee or passed through there on their way to Fort Defiance, St. Michaels, Gallup, and other points. 4) The large peach orchards in Canyon de Chelly brought many Navajo from all parts of the reservation to Chin Lee in the fall, when the peaches were ripe. It was therefore an advantageous or strategic point, where one could easily meet a large number of Navajo, become acquainted with them, make known to them our intentions, and gain their confidence and goodwill. And as such Chin Lee has proved itself to be.

Accordingly, I visited Chin Lee occasionally during two years, staying two or three weeks at a time. Much acknowledgment is due to the Day family, parents and three boys, for the kindness, help, and hospitality shown me on these visits.

The First Mission House at Chin Lee, Arizona

For about two years I had been visiting Chin Lee off and on, two and three weeks at a time, and had become well acquainted with place and people. The time had come when it was considered feasible to establish a permanent mission station there.

Accordingly, in 1904 an old, much dilapidated stone house was rented from a Navajo for this purpose. This old stone house was originally built for a store or trading post but had been abandoned years ago and left to go to ruin. It consisted of three rooms. From one of the rooms the roof was entirely gone, and on the two others, part of the original dirt roof was still on, but doors and windows gone. Wind and weather had left their marks in, out, and around the old house. So it took considerable work and expense to put the old stone house into a fairly habitable condition, and for more than a year it was "though ever so humble" home sweet home to me and to good old Brother Placidus Buerger, O.F.M., who has since gone to his reward.

It was on August 15, the day of Our Lady's Assumption, when Brother Placidus and myself were driving slowly up the Chin Lee valley in a covered wagon, rigged up in the old prairie schooner style, to take possession of our new home. In the wagon was a cook stove, kitchen utensils, two iron bedsteads or cots, bedding, and sundry other articles and things which we would need to start up housekeeping. The wagon was drawn by a sturdy team of horses, of which the one, a big sorrel, was called Dutch, and the other, a large dapple gray, was named Prince. Thus we arrived at the old stone house, unloaded our things, carried them in, arranged them as we saw fit, and settled to stay.

Before our arrival the three Day boys had repaired the house as well as it could be done. More dirt or mud had been put on the roof, windows and doors put in, and the place thoroughly cleaned out. We had two serviceable rooms, one, the smaller one, was rigged out as kitchen, pantry, and dining room; the other, much larger and longer, served as dormitory, parlor, and chapel. At one end of this large room a rude altar was set up; at the other end the beds were placed.

During the warm season, when it began to get dusky in the evening we carried our beds outside and slept under the star spangled canopy of heaven. For want of better material we had stuffed our pillows with hay. One night while sleeping thus in the open, I was awakened by feeling my pillow being pulled from beneath my head. Looking up, I saw old Dutch, who had probably scented the hay, tugging away at the pillow.

The dirt or mud roof was nice enough in good weather. It kept the place cool when the weather was hot, and warm when it was cold, but it was by no means absolutely waterproof, as we were to find out. It was during the rainy season, which sets in any time in July and August, when one afternoon an extraordinarily heavy rain poured down from a heavily clouded sky; it was like a veritable cloudburst; it came down in streaks and sheets. The water found its way through the mud roof in a number of places, and was soon pouring down into the rooms in many miniature cascades. The interior was being flooded; we threw open the doors and with brooms helped out the rushing stream. When I remarked to the brother, "Say, Arizona is some nice place, isn't it?" he replied, "Oh, you bet, the nicest place what gives."

At times I had to lay a two-inch plank before the altar to say Mass and had to gird up the alb sufficiently to keep it from being soiled. One day Charles Day, one of the Day boys, came over to visit us. When we entered the large room, Charley, who was an excellent marksman, suddenly whipped out his revolver and shot a rattlesnake, which had coiled itself snugly for a cool nap right in front of the altar. At another time I went out into the kitchen and ran on to a large bull snake. Again when I lifted up a box I discovered under it a wriggling scorpion. So we were not the only inhabitants of the old stone house. However, in spite of all, it was a dear old place.

The Old Wind Doctor

After taking possession of the old stone house and having made ourselves at home therein, I bought some old boards off an Indian, and the brother and myself made a few rude benches and placed them in the chapel room.

Between 10 and 20 Indians would come to the old stone house on Sundays, accompanied by the Day family, and one of the boys, all of whom spoke Navajo and English equally well, would do the interpreting. At first I told them about creation, the fall of our first parents and its consequences, and the promise of a Redeemer; about the flood and how Noah and his family lived for many years after the flood in the same country. There was but one people then, who spoke the same language, had the same laws, customs, and so on.

By and by the people increased and became too numerous to live together in the same place. So they decided that the different families or clans go out in different directions and look up new homes for themselves and children. But before they separated they had a council and decided to build a very high house or tower, the top of which would reach up to the sky, so that, if another flood came, they could go up and be saved. But God then made them speak different languages, they could not understand each other, had to give up the building of the tower, and the different families and clans went away in all directions to look for new homes.

When the people scattered like that, they came to new countries, met with new things, had to live in different ways, so that their language and their customs became more and more changed. They took their holy history or religion with them, but because they did not have it written down, they by and by forgot much of it, and in trying to remember it, got many things wrong, or fixed it up and added to it to suit themselves. Thus it got mixed up with all kinds of stories and myths. That's why there are in the holy history of the Navajo some points which are somewhat similar to ours.

But our holy history has been written down in a book, in which everything is told how it happened from the beginning, and this book is called *The Bible* or *The Holy Writings*. This book has never been lost and, therefore, the real and true holy history has always been known wherever this book was kept and read. . . . As the holy history of the Navajo has some points which are similar to ours, it shows that there was once a time when they, too, had the right story. . . . Now we have come to them because we wish to tell them the real and true story again of the things that happened from the beginning as they are described in this holy book. . . . There are many more things in this book which they should know, and which I will tell them if they will come every Sunday and listen.

During this narrative, an old Navajo, a *Niłch'i Cateałi*, a Spirit Chanter, whom the whites called Wind Doctor, and who sat on the front bench, would now and then make remarks to his neighbors. After the talk I asked the interpreter what the old man had to say. At one time, during the story of the creation, he remarked to the others, "He's got it pretty correct now," and at another, when the fall of our first parents and its consequences were described, he said, "He's a little off now, but he'll come back again to the right thing."

At another time, when speaking of the Blessed Trinity, one wished to know which of the three divine persons was the first, another, which was the oldest, and another, which was the strongest.

A Threat to Kill

One night, it was about 10:30, I was still sitting up and reading, when I heard a horse gallop up to the house and stop near the door. Presently the door was opened and a tall, burly Navajo entered. He seemed very much agitated and excited; he could hardly speak. He came up to me and, pointing his finger at me, said: "I am going to kill you!" Now, only a short time before this, the agent from Fort Defiance on a visit to Chin Lee had been held up by a number of Navajo, hardly a mile from the house. There was a strong feeling against the whites prevalent among the Indians at that time, some even going so far as to say that all the Americans living on the reservation ought to be killed. Moreover, there was a certain element among the Indians of Chin Lee who had a rather tough and unenviable reputation. [As I remembered] all this, the finger pointing at me began to take on unnatural proportions, and I began to feel rather uncomfortable. However, I told him not to be in a hurry, and to take a smoke, handing him some tobacco and cigarette papers. After taking a few soothing whiffs of the fragrant weed, he became more quiet, and pointing toward the mountains, he said: "I am going to kill you, a Navajo said to me."

It must be remarked here that the Navajo verb has no subjunctive mode; consequently, there is no indirect speech, nor has the Navajo language a word corresponding to the English conjunction, that. The sentence, therefore, "he said (that) he would kill me," must be given in Navajo thus: "I will kill you, he said to me." This man, then, simply wished to tell me that some other Navajo had threatened to kill him, but was at first too excited to finish the sentence.

He then went on to tell his story. He lived up on the mountain with his wife and child. That very same day his wife's father had come to his house and had taken his wife and child away. He had protested against this and made some efforts to hinder it, when his father-in-law made the above-mentioned threat of killing him if he did not leave his daughter alone. He said he loved his wife and loved his child; he wished to get them back again, and asked my advice what to do in the matter. At that time there was an old chief or headman by the name of Qastqin Yazhe living near Chin Lee, who had much influence with the Indians of that region, and whose word carried considerable weight. I told him to go to Qastqin Yazhe, since he was a headman of the Navajo, and explain his case to him; he would certainly look into the matter and fix it up for him. He then told me that his wife was a daughter of old Qastqin Yazhe, and that Qastqin Yazhe was the very man who had threatened to kill him. However, he departed, and I subsequently found out that he mistreated his wife and that old Qastqin Yazhe had good reasons for taking his daughter away from him.

The Spiritual and the Temporal

On August 15, 1905, the site of the present residence, located about a mile west of the old stone house mentioned above, was selected by the Very Reverend William Ketcham, director of the Bureau of Catholic Indian Missions, Washington, D.C., who at the time was visiting at Chin Lee, and by the Reverend Anselm Weber, O.F.M., of St. Michaels, and myself. Ground was broken and work begun the following day. . . . The greater part of the work was done by Indians. About a year later the writer and a brother were sent to Chin Lee to reside there permanently. I made repeated attempts to gather the Indians and induce them to come to "the prayer" on Sundays, telling them I had some very important things to say and to talk over with them. A considerable number would come for a time and then gradually drop off or move away.

Their naive conception of things spiritual, and their way of mixing the spiritual and the temporal, showing that they expected the white man's prayer to supply, in the first place, their corporal needs and wants, were manifested on various occasions. One Sunday after Mass and after I had given them a lengthy talk, one of them, referring to the Mass, asked what was the meaning of that prayer. I explained to them that Jesus Christ, the Son of God, who had come down from heaven, who suffered and died to save us, who rose again from the dead and returned into heaven, had first made this prayer before His death, and told His *ae'ndeishodi* to continue to make it when He would be gone, in order to remember Him; if they would come here regularly every Sunday I would explain it to them further, so they would understand it; I would also tell them many other things which they must know. After this, another one got up and asked when I would give them some clothes and food. I told them that while we would not suffer any one of them to starve or to run about naked, our main object was not to feed and clothe them; for to do that we would require barrelfuls of money, which was not the case. Besides, we thought they were manful enough to do that themselves. Our main object in coming among them was to tell them what they must believe and what they must do and how they must live in order to be happy hereafter. This is what Jesus Christ, the Son of God, told His *ae'ndeishodi* to tell all the people, and that is why we have come. Of course, we would willingly and gladly help them in any other way as much as we were able.

At another time, when I had finished Mass and was taking off the sacred vestments, a Navajo came up to me and put his hand on my shoulder, saying, "My friend, your prayer is *t'aiyisi qozhô*," very happy or good. He then took out his medicine bag, in which he kept his sacred pollen, walked about the room, and sprinkled pollen against the walls, muttering something the while. After this he again said that prayer was very good, and departed. Another one proved the excellency of prayer by the following reasoning: "It is very good for all, Americans and Navajo, to pray. We all must pray; if we pray much, we shall have much rain; if we have much rain, the corn and everything else will grow well; if everything grows well, we shall have plenty to eat." Ergo, prayer is very good.

In January 1907, another father was sent out to Chin Lee, so that the personnel now consisted of Father Leopold Ostermann O.F.M., Father Marcellus Troester, O.F.M., and Brother Gervase Thuemmel, O.F.M. The rumors concerning the erection of a government boarding school for Navajo children at Chin Lee were, by this time, becoming more definite and were gradually taking tangible shape. A site for the new school was selected, plans and specifications drawn up, and by 1909 bids on the buildings were published and solicited. . . . In the fall of 1909 work on the school was begun and the buildings finished the following spring. By April 1, 1910, the school was opened with 49 pupils in attendance. This number increased to 80 pupils the following year. This opened new hopes and brighter prospects for the future of the mission.

The Dying Child

It was early on a Sunday morning, some time between 5:00 and 6:00, when I was awakened by someone rapping at my window. Getting up I opened the window and saw a Navajo man standing outside with a very anxious expression on his face. I asked him:"*Qaat'ila ninisin?*" (What do you want?) He then told me that his little baby was very sick and would not live very long. Would I come along with him, make prayer over the child, and pour water on its head (baptize it).

I asked him where the child was, and, pointing to a clump of cottonwood trees about one-fourth of a mile northwest of the mission, he said it was on the other side of those trees. Judging the distance to be not more than one-half mile, I did not think it necessary to hitch up the ponies, but taking along what was necessary for baptism, I went along with the man. Leaving the mission in a westerly direction, we passed through the above-mentioned cottonwood grove. I expected to be near the hogan (*qoghan*, a Navajo hut) but the man kept walking right on. After walking what I judged to be more than two miles, I asked him if it were still far to the place, and received the answer, "*Doda, t'ayidi*" (No, near by).

We had walked about three miles when I saw a hogan right near the road. My guide said that was the place, turned off the road, and led me in. The mother and several other persons were in the hogan sitting round about, and in the center lay a little baby, apparently only a few months old, bedded on a blanket and some sheep pelts. The child seemed very sick, indeed, and looked as if it might die at any time. After baptizing it, I walked the same way back home. At 9:30 I said Mass and gave instruction to the children. While we were eating dinner at noon, the father came to tell us that the child had died and asked us to bury it, which we did, giving it Christian burial.

A Double Sick Call

One day I was asked to come and visit a sick young Navajo. His home, I learned on inquiry, was 15 to 20 miles north of the mission. I hitched up the ponies and started out. When I got there, I found a young man, Paul Analawudi, lying languidly on a blanket and several sheep pelts in front of a hogan, under a summer shelter. A summer shelter is made by planting four forked posts in the ground, laying poles on top and covering it with limbs, twigs, grass, weeds, or corn stalks. Here the women weave, cook, and so forth, during the hot summer months.

Going up to the young man, I soon found out that he had gone to school, spoke English fairly well, had been baptized, and received his First Holy Communion. Since he seemed to be a pretty sick boy, I heard his confession, anointed him, and gave him the blessing for the sick.

On my way home, when I was about halfway, I saw to my left a Navajo on horseback, galloping across country. He was urging his horse on and seemingly had the intention of overtaking me. 1 stopped my team and waited for him. When he came near, I recognized him as one of our friends called T'la Tso, Americanized into Clatso, Big Lefty. Ordinarily he lived at Mâ'i Tqohe, Coyote Spring, a good distance from here, but just now, he said, he had his sheep over there, pointing to some hills about five miles from the road. He added that his son Lozi (Louis) was with him and had been taken very sick. Would I come over and see him? Of course I would, and turning the heads of my ponies eastward, I followed him over the rough, uneven country, covered with sagebrush, which somewhat hid the hummocks and chuck holes till one struck them. By and by one had the feeling that he was indeed "bumping the bumps." However, I got there safely without breaking bones or buckboard.

I found Lozi to be a very sick boy. He was about 15 or 16 years of age, had gone to school for some years, spoke English fairly well, had never attended any particular religious instructions, and had never been baptized. I stayed with him quite a long while. He expressed his wish to receive baptism, so I gave him the necessary instruction, made an act of contrition with him, and baptized him. I stayed with him a little while longer, and then, giving him the blessing for the sick, I drove and bumped home.

Both of these young men were taken to the hospital at Fort Defiance, and shortly after both of them died.

"Prove It"

Toward the end of May 1907, Father Anselm Weber, having attended a council meeting of Navajo Indians at Fort Defiance, Arizona, was asked to call at the school hospital to see a sick Navajo, who claimed to be a Catholic and wished to see a priest. Arriving at the bedside of the patient, he found a young man of about 20 years in the last stages of consumption. He was known by his school name, Joseph

Lincoln, and had for years attended the government Indian schools at Fort Defiance, Arizona, and at Fort Lewis and Grand Junction, Colorado. He was a very intelligent boy and spoke English quite fluently.

At the last-named place he developed consumption, and when the disease reached a stage that excluded all hope of recovery, he was sent back to Fort Defiance, where his parents could visit him and perhaps take him home. While attending the school at Fort Lewis, he said, he had heard much about the Catholic religion and had received some instruction from Catholic teachers there. He knew he could not live very much longer, and he wished to die a Catholic. Father Anselm, realizing that the hours of his life were numbered, and seeing the goodwill and the wish of the sick young man, and being obliged to go to St. Michaels for the holy oils and the viaticum, promised him that upon his arrival at home, he would at once send Father Fintan Zumbahlen, O.F.M., to see him and give him the last sacraments.

Not knowing where the parents of Joseph Lincoln lived, Father Anselm inquired of another sick boy, who had recently been brought back from Phoenix, Arizona, but could find out nothing more than that his parents lived somewhere about 50 miles from Fort Defiance. However, he succeeded later in locating the parents and notifying them of the whereabouts and the condition of their son.

When Father Fintan, in the afternoon of the same day, came to the hospital, he was very kindly received by the nurse and led to the bedside of the sick young man. Joseph greeted him and asked him who he was. Father Fintan told him that he was a Catholic priest and that Father Anselm had sent him to bring him the holy sacraments. The young man looked at him intently and somewhat surprised him with the words, "Are you a Catholic priest? Prove it!"

Father Fintan proceeded to put on surplice and stole, which satisfied and convinced the sick man. He apologized for his seeming impoliteness, saying that once when he was very sick a Protestant preacher had come to see him, telling him that he was a Catholic priest. So he only wanted to be sure; he had heard so much about the Catholic religion, believed in it, and, as a Catholic, he wished to have a priest about and receive the sacraments before he died.

After giving him some further necessary instruction, Father Fintan asked him if he had ever been baptized. He thought that he had been baptized years ago at Fort Lewis, but he was not absolutely certain. He was then baptized conditionally and also received the other sacraments with earnest and edifying devotion. He now felt satisfied and thought he could die in peace, if only he could see his old home once more.

This, his last wish, was not fulfilled, but he had the satisfaction of seeing his father and mother, who, as soon as they had received the notification, came at once to Fort Defiance to see their sick son and to take him to their distant home, 50 miles beyond the mountains. However, he was already too far spent to stand this long journey, and he died at the foot of the mountains about 25 miles from Fort Defiance.

Notes

1. From Leopold Ostermann, "Little Mission Stories from Our Own Southwest," *St. Anthony Messenger* 34 (May 1927): 634–36; 35 (June 1927): 22–23; 35 (July 1927): 75; "Navaho Indian Mission at Chin Lee, Arizona," FMSW 2 (1914): 27–31.

2. Robert L. Wilken, *Anselm Weber, O.F.M.: Missionary to the Navaho* (Milwaukee, Wisc.: Bruce Publishing Company, 1955), 115.

3. Jerome Hesse, "Obituary: Rev. Leopold Ostermann, O.F.M.," *Indian Sentinel* 10 (Summer 1930): 118.

13

Time in the Saddle, Students, and Sacraments

Anselm Weber, O.F.M.

[The present chapter is divided into five segments, each translated from an article in Anselm Weber's series, "*Die Franziskaner-Mission unter den Navajo-Indianern*" published monthly in *Der Sendbote*. Each part contains, among other things, a progress report on the students at St. Michael's School, either in terms of their initial recruitment, their health and well-being, or their achievements. Often Father Anselm's *Sendbote* articles were like pages from a personal journal, organized chronologically or according to some principle other than the description of a single event or issue. Typically a single article touches on several subjects. The segments below all refer to students and school, but they also treat other interesting topics.

On November 24, 1902, Father Anselm and his interpreter, Frank Walker, began a historic journey from St. Michaels to Red Rock and back, to collect students for the first term of instruction in the new boarding school. Their destination, over 90 miles from the mission, was the home of headman Naakai Dinae'e, who had promised to have several children from his neighborhood ready to go to school. Father Anselm's account of the harrowing trip, over treacherous mountain passes and in dangerously cold weather, was published the following March in *Sendbote*. Two months later *Sendbote* published another product of the trip, Father Anselm's account of the 1892 "episode at Round Rock,"[1] when the Navajo had forcefully resisted an overzealous Indian agent's effort to round up their children. Father Anselm's report was based on reminiscences shared by the assembled Navajo one evening at the home of Naakai Dinae'e. Some of the Navajo there had firsthand knowledge of the event, having been participants in the fracas.

These two pieces first appeared in English in the 1917 issue of *Franciscan Missions of the Southwest*, under the title "Opening of St. Michael's School —Indians' Attack at Round Rock." Actually, the first half of the title is misleading, for only the final paragraph of the article deals with the opening of the school. Instead, the text describes the journey to collect 21 of the school's first 51 pupils, along with the story of the 1892 confrontation as shared by Father Anselm's Navajo hosts.

The 1917 article was recently reprinted as an appendix in Murray Bodo's *Tales of an Endishodi*[2] and is readily available to contemporary readers. Even so, I begin the present chapter with the portion of that article that tells of the journey to Red Rock and back, the part derived from the March 1903 *Sendbote* piece—here entitled "The 'Precious Freight' of the Charisso Mountains"—because the story of bringing in that first "busload" of students for the opening of the school is an essential backdrop to Father Anselm's descriptions of student recruitment in subsequent years. It seemed inappropriate to begin here midstream, as it were, having forced the reader first to consult an appendix of *Tales of an Endishodi*.

Accordingly, I have reprinted the "Opening of St. Michael's School" part of the 1917 English-language article. In preparing that article, Father Anselm edited out several paragraphs from the 1903 *Sendbote* piece. Some few sentences of these, relevant to present purposes, are restored here. That is, what follows is essentially a translation of the 1903 *Sendbote* article, using Father Anselm's translation from 1917 whenever possible, and adding back in relevant portions of the *Sendbote* article, in new translation, where no translation from Father Anselm is available.

The second segment of this chapter, "Challenges of School Year 1903–1904," is a report on the second year of St. Michael's School. It contains both good news and bad news. The bad news is that during the year there was much sickness at the school, and six students died. The high rates of sickness and student mortality created tensions between parents and school administrators, and also a competition between traditional medicine and white medical practice. The incident of the flight of Sister Bridget suggests that the friars and sisters were "running scared" over the possibility that Navajo families might hold them responsible for the deaths of their children.

The good news is that not only did the school survive the episodes of student illness and death with its reputation largely intact, but a majority of the second-year students, the "upper class," requested baptism. There was a "huge celebration," for "these were the first students who had been openly baptized in our chapel."

The need for "time in the saddle" continues, as may be seen in the third segment, "Marriages at Round Rock, 1904," which begins with Father Anselm's report on the opening of the third year at St. Michael's School and of an Indian agent's offer to have his police help Father Anselm round up students. The bulk of the article describes another lengthy trip, this one to perform two marriages, but recruitment of students continues along the way. Also continuing is the need for outside support, especially donations of clothing, for Father Anselm has promised some of the poorer Navajo that he will have clothes for the entire family when they bring their children to school.

Segment four, "Expeditions and Councils, 1906," excerpted from a *Sendbote* article of June 1907, makes explicit the link between Father Anselm's efforts to help Navajo obtain legal title to their lands and the successful recruitment of their children for the 1906–1907 school year at St. Michaels. This segment also has some revealing details about his time in the saddle traversing the "godforsaken" regions east of the reservation.

Segment five, "Problems and Progress, 1908," contains a brief assessment of the 1907–1908 school year, another year marked by student illness and a few deaths and also by more student baptisms. Here Father Anselm offers hard evidence of positive outcomes from student attendance at St. Michael's School: some former students are rejecting traditional marriage in favor of Christian marriage. Once again, he concludes with an appeal for more clothing, for there has been drought and a lean harvest, and the people are even poorer than usual. And once again, it is plain that the necessity for "time in the saddle" continues.]

The Navajo took little stock in the white man's education and were not very favorably inclined toward sending their children to school. Despite the fact that there were but three government schools for the children of 25,000 Navajo, the government, even with the help of its police force, was unable to gather in a sufficiently large number of pupils for these three schools.

I was determined to avoid a similar failure with regard to our mission school at St. Michaels. In 1902, when our school was nearing its completion, and two months before it was ready to receive pupils, I spent most of my time in the saddle, visiting Indians of various regions on and off the reservation, assembling them in the hogans or huts of their headmen, and holding councils with them, listening to their opinions and answering their questions, doubts, and objections, explaining to them the advantages of a religious, moral, and practical education, to thus induce them to send their children to our school and to make them understand why they should do so.

The "Precious Freight" of the Carriso Mountains[3]

I had promised the headman Naakai Dinae'e and the other Indians in the area of the Carriso Mountains to come to them seven days before the opening of our school with our wagon to pick up the children for our school. Eight days before the opening of the school, I, accompanied by our interpreter Frank Walker, started off on our trip to distant Tselchidahaskani (Red Rock). This was on November 24, 1902. Our wagon was rather well loaded with feed for our horses, provisions for ourselves and the children, blankets, and clothing. We traveled all day in a northerly direction and arrived late in the evening at Crystal, where our friend, Mr. J. B. Moore, had a trading post. Mr. Moore received us with his usual openhanded hospitality and kindly offered us supper and lodging for the night, which was gratefully accepted.

The next day we crossed the mountain by way of Cottonwood Pass, which separates the Chuska Range from the Tunicha Range. This pass is the only way by which the mountains could be crossed. After driving about 10 miles in a north-easterly direction through the pass, in which a mountain creek and a growth of aspen offer a pleasing variation to the sight, we arrived at the highest point from where the road first wends and winds itself between large detached rocks, then changes into a steep and perilous descent along the slope of the mountain. Since there was no reason nor necessity for both of us to risk our lives, I left the wagon, took the lead, and, picking out the best road, piloted Frank Walker along. The road was not only steep and rough, but, added to this, there was just enough snow and ice on the ground to cause the horses to slip and the wagon to skid. Several times the wagon was about to capsize and Frank Walker on the point of jumping to a safe spot and letting horses and wagon go rolling down the steep slope. However, we finally reached the foot of the mountain without any damage to speak of done to horses or wagon, but Frank Walker was very emphatic in his opinion that it would be impossible to drive horses and wagon up that same way on the return trip.

I had traversed this same road several times before on horseback, and I shall never forget the sudden surprise with which I checked my horse upon reaching the highest point and letting my glance sweep down the steep incline, over the trees and shrubs covering the wide slope, out over the vast desert—a desert bare and barren, above the level of which nothing appeared but here and there high, fantastically shaped pinnacles of rock, like petrified sentinels of a long forgotten race of giants. Viewed from a distance, all vegetation seems abruptly cut off at the base of the mountains. While it seemed, from this vantage point, but a short distance to the desert, it took several hours to descend the slope and pass over and between the smaller foothills out into the desert proper.

At 4:00 we arrived at Two Gray Hills, so called after two large square rocks that rear their gray crests above the sandy plane of desert. Here we stopped at the trading post of Mr. Wynn Wetherill to bring back warmth and life into our benumbed extremities. Mr. Wetherill very kindly invited us to spend the night in his house, but this I was obliged to decline with thanks, for I intended to spend the night with a certain Navajo, since I expected to get a few children for our school from this region. So after thawing out sufficiently we continued our journey, and after sundown, when it was already getting dark, we reached our destination, only to learn that the Indians whom I wished to see had moved to some other place. There was nothing left for us to do but to unhitch and feed our horses right there, take some of the provisions and a few blankets, and go to the next inhabited hogan, where we found lodging for the night with a friendly and hospitable Navajo.

On the next day we drove 18 miles further through the desolate desert, and as the horses could not travel faster than a walk on account of the deep, loose sand, our progress was correspondingly slow. Passing on our way the sulphur springs at the foot of fantastic Bennett's Peak, toward evening we reached the trading post of our friend, Joseph Wilkins, who was at one time the proprietor of "the ranch" where our mission building now stands. We were received here with a warm welcome. I learned from Mr. Wilkins that the headman, Naakai Dinae'e, had been there on the previous day, expecting to meet me. I had arrived two days behind the appointed time, and this because on the one hand, I could not start out on the day I had intended to, and on the other hand, the drive up here had taken four days instead of three, as I had imagined.

I here met a befriended headman, Naat'ani Ts'osi (Slender Chief) and another Navajo from Bennett's Peak, who promised to send two children to our school and to have them ready for us when we came that way again on our return trip.

From this place we had yet to make a drive of 20 miles to reach the home of headman Naakai Dinae'e, and neither I nor Frank Walker knew aught of the way. I was, therefore, glad to find an Indian who, for the consideration of a half-dollar, was willing to accompany us about 12 miles. He was to ride on ahead of us and pick out for us such places where the deep gullies could be passed by wagon; for although a wagon or two may have passed this way and left a faint rut upon the sand, there was nothing that could be called a road until we met the road that leads from the San Juan River to the mountains, where we finally could dismiss our guide.

Toward evening we reached the home of Naakai Dinae'e, where we were awaited with much impatience. In four days we had covered 90 strenuous and wearisome miles and were now glad to enjoy a day of rest. On the same evening a number of Indians put in their appearance, and we all camped that night in the same large room. On the two following days I said Holy Mass here, partly for the success of our undertaking, and partly to pray for good weather until we should be safe home again with our "precious freight." Although some had promised to send their children to our school and others were inclined to do so, we knew nothing with absolute certainty. Besides, the weather now, especially during the night, was bitterly cold. I had undertaken this trip so late in the season with much concern and uneasiness of mind. In case we were overtaken by a snowstorm on our return trip, with the scantily clad children on our hands, we would be in "a nice fix"; it would then be utterly impossible to cross the mountain, and we would be obliged to take a roundabout way of more than 50 miles.

I later learned that the Reverend Mother Drexel had a "very bad premonition" that we would freeze half to death on the way, whereupon she called all the Sisters in the mother house to Maud, Pennsylvania, and had them pray fervently for the "precious load of little Navajo."

On the next day more Indians came to see us, and by noon I counted 50 heads, all in the same room. Some had come a considerable distance. In order that neither we nor our visitors might feel the pangs of hunger, I had bought two sheep; flour, coffee, and sugar we carried with us. After we all had taken our dinner, squatted in Indian fashion, dispensing with an elaborate array of dishes and the observance of strict etiquette, everybody tried to make himself comfortable. The Indians rolled their cigarettes, and as the blue clouds from the ignited fragrant weed curled up toward the ceiling, conversation became general and animated, and all were in the best of humor. No wonder—the Navajo don't often get the chance to eat their fill.

The talk turned, for the most part, about our mission and school, and about the education of their children. Being the descendants of an independent race, these sons of forest, mountain, and desert will brook no force; they were not going to let themselves be forced to send their children to school. Of course, I told them that their attitude in this regard was perfectly correct; that children belonged, in the first place, to the parents; that the parents had the right to decide to which school their children should go; that nothing brought about by force would be lasting; that there were no means at my command to force them to send their children to our school, and even if there would be, I would not make use of such means. If they themselves could not understand and were not convinced that it was for the best for their children to send them to school, then they should keep them at home. I then addressed a lengthier speech to them in which I explained the purpose of our mission and school and the advantages for time and eternity of a good, moral education.

All of them were much interested and seemed much gratified. Several of them made speeches commenting upon what I had said to them, and promised to bring their children the next morning. Almost everyone said that formerly they were simply told that they *must* send their children to school, and they had persistently refused to comply with this command. Now, however, they understood that it was for their own good as well as best for their children to send them to school. At this juncture a Navajo woman entered, and, shaking me by the hand, said: "*Shichai* (my grandfather), I will send three." "What, three?" I asked in surprise. "Yes, three," she answered. All present laughed and applauded so vigorously that she turned confused upon her heel and disappeared as suddenly as she had come. She was the wife of Mr. Black Horse [one of the principals in the Round Rock episode a decade earlier].

These Indians live in extraordinarily needy circumstances. Thus I was very happy that I had some clothing left over from what Reverend Father Provincial had graciously sent to us from the different order houses. I divided what I had among the most needy of them, and the biggest and best overcoat I gave to "Navajo Killer," a huge, strong Indian who strutted about in it, proud as a Spaniard. When he was about 16 years old, he got in a fight with the biggest ruffian of the whole region, fought him for over half an hour, and at last, in self-defense, killed him—thus his name. And apparently that was not the only victim whose life he had snuffed out.

Unfortunately, I did not have enough clothing to appease all of the needy petitioners. Then I told them that I had "made a paper," written an appeal which would be read by several hundred Americans, asking them to send clothing for the Navajo. When I received this, I said, I would be better able to help them in their need. They received this communication with much joy. In joyous thanksgiving, I can also confirm that I didn't "make" this "paper" for nóthing, that in many instances my appeals in this connection have met with unexpected generosity. Yesterday, a well-filled container with good clothing arrived which our esteemed friend and patron, Mr. Wendelin Holdener from Belleville, Illinois, generously sent to us. We also have received two heavy bundles of good clothing from the parents of our Reverend "Indian" Brother Simeon, Mr. Karl Schwemberger and Mrs. Christina Schwemberger, in part from themselves, and in part collected from their good friends in Cincinnati. It took Brother Simeon a long time to unpack these things, and the Indians who helped him had their mouths watering.

I know that others also responded to our requests and that I will be in a position to report more next time. We express heartfelt thanks, both from ourselves and from the Indians in need and hope that others will follow the good example. Many of the Navajo are in such a poor state that they are beginning to kill their ponies and gather cedar berries to quiet their hunger. . . . But we must return to the desert and to Tselchidahaskani, or Red Rock.

On the morning of our return trip there was much hustle and bustle at the home of Naakai Dinae'e. By and by children began to be brought in. We gave them something to eat, and since they were very scantily dressed, we gave each one a blanket to keep warm on the long trip to St. Michaels. As we were just ready to leave, a Navajo called the American Killer came up to us and begged us to wait yet a while, for he had made up his mind to send his three children to our school also, and they were on the way hither. At last they arrived and we could start. The wagon was well filled with precious freight; we had succeeded in getting 21 children from that region. As there was no place for me in the wagon, I accompanied it on the back of a Navajo pony. However, I was not the only one on horseback. Parents and relatives of the children, most of whom had never seen our mission, came along. The only one on foot, who stood proud and self-confident in front of the group, was "our Fritz," the indispensable assistant of our Brother Simeon, who also hails from this area.

On the first evening, we stopped for the night with Mr. Wilkin, on the second evening with Mr. Wetherill, and in the forenoon of the third day we reached the foot of the mountain. All the children were taken from the wagon, and while the larger ones climbed the steep mountain slope on foot, the smaller ones were taken upon the horses by the accompanying Indians. Frank Walker had a hard and strenuous time in getting up the empty wagon. At the worst place, where a spring of clear freshwater gushes forth from the mountainside, and where the road leads along a precipitous slope, the road was covered by a sheet of glasslike ice. Fortunately, an Indian was there at work with pick and shovel, repairing the road. I took the pick and proceeded to roughen the sleek surface of the ice, while the Indians brought leaves and earth in their blankets and spread it over the place. When, in spite of all this, the horses got stuck, the Indians laid hold of the spokes, and with a ringing war whoop helped the wagon to move up the hill.

Arriving at the summit, we were greeted by an icy penetrating wind. The children were again helped into the wagon and wrapped themselves closely into their blankets. We then mounted our ponies and covered the remaining 10 miles to Mr. Moore's place in an hour. Of course, the wagon arrived much later. On the next day, the last day of our trip, we encountered a blustering snowstorm. However, the cold wave that usually accompanies such snowstorms did not set in till we were almost at St. Michaels. I and a number of Indians rode on ahead, and when the children finally arrived almost half-frozen, a warm room was ready for them.

On the next day, the feast of the great apostle of India, St. Francis Xavier, December 3, 1902, the mission school at St. Michaels, Arizona, was opened with a solemn High Mass, celebrated by the chaplain, Reverend Berard Haile, O.F.M., with 51 pupils in attendance. My companions—I will call them the "Charisso

Indians" in later articles—stayed several more days. And when they were finally ready to depart, sitting on their horses, they were photographed by Father Berard.

Challenges of School Year 1903–1904[4]

Perhaps a whole year has already passed since I last mentioned our Indian school, and many of you probably think that I neglect the school; however, that is not so.

It took more than a little trouble for me to gather the old students again last fall and to recruit the desired number of new students. In spite of all my efforts, I did not succeed in convincing all the parents to send the students of the previous year back to school again. However, the number not returning was negligible. There were more, especially those who had attended a government school before and whose influence on the other students began to have adverse effects, whom I did not accept again, because we only want the best students and no black sheep. This policy had, among other things, the effect that especially the best and most respected Indians sent their children to our school.

How many and what extensive excursions I made to reach the necessary number of children for our school, what occurred during them, what interesting conversations came out of them are all too long and involved to tell, and I have little desire for that, especially since it is all so long ago. I will only mention the happy fact that while I rode south with Frank Walker and headman Ba'jlinni and recruited a good number of children for our school who were nearly totally untouched by [white] culture, Indians from the Lukachukai Mountains brought a number of students to our school without any invitation or demand. The number of boys exceeded the number of girls by far, and because our school is set up for the same number of boys and girls, the boys' section was so overfilled that we had to set up part of Mr. Dan's old house as sleeping quarters for the older boys.

Of the 87 students, 32 were girls, of whom sadly six died during this school year. I hardly need to mention that during the sickness of these and other children, I had no end of trouble with the parents and relatives; nearly all insisted on taking the sick children home to turn them over to the medicine men. One even went to the Indian agent so that he could force us to turn the sick child over to him. When the agent was assured by the doctor that all children in our school enjoyed the very best of care, he let the Indian know that if he took the child out of school against our will, at least one Indian would have cause to regret his actions. When the same Indian still behaved as if he were insane because his daughter was in the same sickroom in which another child had died, and the doctor had assured me that she could be taken home without danger, I baptized the child, loaned her father our lightest carriage, and let her go home with him. Still, she died a few days later.

When the last child died, about a month ago, it happened on the same day that 15 Indians from that region, including four relatives of the dead child, came riding to the school just before noon. They proceeded straight to the kitchen, surrounded the cook, and with stern faces looked her up and down, from head to foot. Most of them had not been here before and had never seen a nun. When the otherwise stalwart Sister Bridget faced these visitors and saw that some were from the region of the dead child, she was seized by panic and fear. She broke through the closed circle of the Indians, hurried up to the second floor to the other Sisters, and told them the horrifying news that the Indians had come to avenge the death of the child. After the other Sisters had calmed her down, she went back downstairs and gave the Indians a good lunch. The intentions of the Indians were actually very peaceful, even though they later spoke with me for over an hour about the sickness and death of the child. They asked me to help them obtain a piece of land that an unscrupulous white man wanted to take from them, which naturally I did willingly. When I told them what a fright they had given the Sister, they had a good laugh.

That such a thing [Indians seeking to avenge the death of a child] could still happen now is shown by an incident which recently took place among the Jicarilla Apaches. Two children died one after another, the last quite suddenly, in the arms of a teacher, Mr. Sales, whom I met here in Fort Defiance. The unreasonable Apaches took him to be the responsible party, and in great agitation, rode up to the school and threatened to do away with Mr. Sales and to destroy the school. Mr. Sales feared for his life and had to be quickly transferred, by telegram. At first there was fear that the military would have to be called in, but the Indians allowed themselves to be appeased before it came to that.

Here it is worth noting that the Navajo are unusually afraid of a corpse and everything that comes in contact with it. If someone dies in a Navajo hut, the hut is not lived in anymore. Because of this, someone who is sick, especially if he is staying in a good hut, is taken into the open air or to a lesser hut before he dies. As more children died in our school, the Navajo thought the whole house was full of ghosts. I tried to appease them, to teach them something better, and told them that no one would be forced to attend the funeral, but that they would do me a great favor if they would overcome their fear and all attend. At the funeral, no one was missing; even the parents and relatives attended. I think that now the ice is broken, so that although I may have some conflict with parents and medicine men who insist that sick children be given to them, we can overcome it.

As mentioned before, religious lessons are given to our students in their mother tongue, because if we were to wait until the students understood English well enough, that would take quite a while, for the Navajo is not a linguist.

At the beginning of June, the older children had been taught far enough that they could be baptized. Many had asked me some time before this about holy baptism. On the first Sunday in June, when I baptized two orphans of about five years of age who were entrusted to our permanent care, many of the older children took offense; they thought they had the first rights to holy baptism.

I had no idea how many of the upper class of 36 students, who were the only ones eligible, would want to be baptized. So that they could speak without embarrassment, I took them out of the somewhat formal classroom into the recreation room, where they could express themselves freely and without pressure. As I wrote down the names of the few students who had already expressed interest, I was more than a little surprised by the large majority of the students who surrounded me and cried: "*Shi do, shi do*" (Me too, me too). Twenty-three asked to be baptized. One of the best school girls, Hilda Adildili, misunderstood me and thought I had refused her because her grandfather is a medicine man. She was inconsolable and cried in a room until I heard of the misunderstanding and assured her that the position of her grandfather would not keep me from fulfilling her true wish.

I spent the second week of June in careful preparation and baptized them on Sunday, June 12. Naturally, this was a huge celebration, not only for those being baptized but also for the whole school, because apart from the sick and a few others who had been baptized as dependents of the mission, these were the first students who had been openly baptized in our chapel.

Marriages at Round Rock, 1904[5]

Last Thursday, October 18, was the designated day for the opening of our school. In spite of only three days passing since then, already over 50 children have arrived. I heard from others that they were on their way. In a few days not only will all the old students have arrived, but their number will be added to by a considerable increase. Such punctuality in school attendance has never existed on this reservation. Just during this vacation I visited a number of parents of our students in different locations and reminded them to be sure to bring their children to school punctually. Moreover, the Indian agent in Fort Defiance, a younger, very capable, and energetic man, assured me of his own free will that if I had any trouble gathering the old students again, and told him about it, he would immediately send his police after them. Such an offer is most certainly rare in the Indian service. Naturally, I would only make use of the offer in an emergency, because we prefer to deal with the Indians "*oozhogo*," or friendly and mildly. However, I secretly let this offer be known to the Indians. It at least shows the Navajo that their agent is very well disposed to our school, and that they have no need to fear discrimination if they send their children to us instead of to a government school. A few days ago I learned that one of our students from last year, under peculiar circumstances, was brought to a government school instead of to us. I informed the agent right away, and he told me an end must be put to this; such a thing could not be allowed, otherwise, all the fickle Indians would want to change each year. He said I should go to Fort Defiance and bring the student back to our school. I must surely treat this very carefully.

Unfortunately, some Indians who bring their children to school are going home disappointed. The charity of some readers of this "emissary" [*Sendbote*] and the enthusiastic activities of some of our fathers to favor our mission made it possible for me to promise some of the poorer of them that, at the opening of our school, I would provide them with such used and worn clothing as was sent by our good friends from the East. Unfortunately, storms and weather, cloudbursts and floods frustrated our plans. Railroad bridges were swept away, and this side of Las Vegas, by Shoemaker Canyon, nine miles of the railroad were washed away by the overflow. The railroad traffic was nearly completely cut off for several weeks. Passengers had to try to come through the Indian territory, through Texas and Arizona, to the western part of New Mexico. As a result, the clothing is somewhere between Kansas and Arizona and hopefully will soon arrive in Gallup, New Mexico. I told the Indians they should come again in a month. By then, hopefully, it will have arrived. I am sure the honorable priests of the different congregations, especially those from our provincial order, would be very willing to forward to us worn or no longer fashionable clothing which the friendly readers of this "emissary" would like to send to us. The address is: Franciscan Fathers, c.o. C. N. Cotton, Gallup, New Mexico. Note that this can be sent cheaply by freight by marking it as "rags." If we get a reputation as Jewish junk traders by doing this, that won't disturb us a bit.

In the hope that the truly sparsely clothed Indians will be richly bestowed upon, I will now expound somewhat about our ride to the distant Round Rock. A while ago, I paid a visit to this far removed area, because the performance of a marriage was waiting on me—a rare occurrence in this area. Not that the people don't marry—sadly, that occurs too often and repeatedly—but rather because for the most part they believe they can do it just fine without their preacher. Father Herculan [Zeug] and I saddled our horses—as well as a third one for our translator, who was with the honorable Father Leopold in the Chin Lee valley at the time—and rode on the same day to Ganado to our friend, Mr. Hubbell. It was very good that we had the third horse, since the horse that Father Herculan rode soon showed unusual fatigue from the hard, extraordinary load; but of course he could change horses. At Ganado I traded his horse for a much larger, stronger mount.

At Ganado I met Mr. Pepper[6] from New York, who was involved in writing an article about Navajo blankets. Later, on his return, Father Berard spent half a night revising and rewriting the lines of the same forthcoming Navajo publication. The above gentleman has it in mind to establish a large hospital for the Navajo Indians with the help of very rich New Yorkers, and he was very curious to learn my opinion about the choice of locality for a hospital. I convinced him that Chin Lee, as the most centrally located point, was the most suitable place for such an establishment. Apart from the fact that the valley referred to, because of its low setting, its mild winters, and other advantages, is more appropriate than any other location for the hospital, for me the thought that we are establishing a mission there, and we would have the opportunity to prepare sick Indians for a Christian death, was the most decisive. The establishment shall be strictly nondenominational. Also, it will assist in breaking the strong influence of the medicine men, the great enemies of civilization and Christianity.

The next day we rode to Chin Lee valley. It was the first ride of Father Herculan through a desert and "badlands." The only water that we found was a dirty spring; it was too bad even for the horses. At noon we rested, sat on petrified wood, and relieved our thirst somewhat with peaches we had brought with us. We stayed at Chin Lee two days. This gave Father Herculan opportunity to see the famous Canyon de Chelly and to see one of the largest Indian dances that takes place in that canyon. Aside from that, it stormed and hailed so much that one could hardly undertake a long ride. One more day's ride through the desert and we reached Round Rock.

My white Protestant and a Navajo were waiting there. The Pope would never unite such a pair! Absolutely not! But the Navajo wanted to receive holy baptism and become Catholic, and the white Protestant had freely promised to make sure that his children received a Catholic upbringing in our Indian school. Because of this, our most honorable bishop had delegated, in this special case, to grant the *Dispense ab impedimento mixtae religionis* [a dispensation for a Roman Catholic to marry a non-Catholic Christian] after I baptized her. The Protestant is proprietor of the trading post at Round Rock.

At the aforementioned post a certain Englishman is cook, bookkeeper, business manager, and baker. Born in India, with a real British taste for travel, he has sailed four times around the world on English ships, walked the world over, and finally ended up in Round Rock. Raised as Protestant, he transferred to the Catholic Church several trips ago. I was very well acquainted with him because he was cook for the entire government personnel at Fort Defiance for a long time, until the "old maid" made his life too bitter and he took to his heels and came to us. Because our Brother Simeon was busy in other areas, I was very happy that he took over our cooking for several months *gratis*. From St. Michaels he went to Round Rock and became engaged to an "Indian princess."

He intended to ride to our mission with her and his protective mother-in-law and to enter into marriage there with the largest possible celebration. For this purpose, he even bought himself an Indian pony and a new saddle with rich, silver fittings and made himself a buckskin suit with silver decorations. I was standing there when he tried to mount his steed for the very first time. The saddle gave way. I hurried to help him, cinched the saddle "man tight," and helped him on, but after just a few feet the Indian horse wouldn't budge. I held his steed as he climbed off again, throwing his right leg over the saddle horn—otherwise, he claimed, he couldn't get off, because the Santa Fe Railroad had broken his leg. I swung myself onto his horse and showed him how one gets an Indian horse to move. After that he mounted his horse again and rode a very small distance away from the house. However, he was now convinced that he couldn't possibly ride his steed the 90 miles to our mission accompanied by his "Dulcinea." Therefore, he, too, decided to let himself be bound by the bonds of marriage at Round Rock.

Unfortunately, neither of the couples had obtained a marriage license from the agent at Fort Defiance. On the same day, the Indian agent from Fort Defiance arrived to visit Round Rock and to confer with an engineer who was measuring to build a dam and irrigation ditches for the Indians. He spent a day and was very pleased to see that one could irrigate much land with relatively little expense, and that many Indians could settle there. Father Herculan accompanied the agent on the trip to Fort Defiance, partly riding, partly traveling with him in a light cart. In two days they reached Fort Defiance, where the agent completed the marriage licenses. With this taken care of, Father Herculan rode home and let Mr. Norbert [Gottbrath] bring the licences to Round Rock. I had, under the circumstances, spent a week teaching both Indian women our holy religion and preparing them for the Holy Baptism. Then, after I baptized them and married both pairs, we rode away. The Englishman gave me a beautiful blanket, the other man gave me a fine Indian buckskin rope.

On our return, we followed the different mountain chains that traverse the reservation and visited the parents of a considerable number of our students who live at the foot of the mountains. Parents and students were pleased with our visits and promised to bring their children to school on time. All kept their word.

Expeditions and Councils, 1906[7]

Last fall, I finally managed to secure 30 new students for our school, so that 116 are now in attendance. The parents of about half of these students live outside of the reservation, between 35 and 50 miles south of our mission. I secured a section of land for 13 Navajo in Sanders, 50 miles from here, from the Santa Fe Railroad Company, and through this I earned their gratitude and the friendship of an influential medicine man named Gischin Biye', who lives in this area. He was the head speaker in the three "councils," or Indian meetings, which I held in Sanders, Houck, and Snake Springs. At the last meeting, about 35 miles southwest of here, I didn't have much time, because I was on my way to the Moqui lands. But Gischin Biye felt compelled by my request in the meeting, and after I had finished my speeches, he promised me to visit with some of the isolated families and to bring their children to the school when, in 10 days, I returned from the Moqui lands. He brought 10 children from this region. Later, I induced the Indian agent, Mr. Harrison, to name Gischin Biye' as chief of this region. I warned him, however, not to misuse his position, gained in this way, to improve his reputation as medicine man, which he sincerely promised me.

I don't want to report any further about my expeditions through the Indian territory, which often lasted over a week. Some of it would hardly be understood, and some would be too monotonous. Several times I rode over 50 miles only to find the Indians whom I had planned to see not at home. I accompanied the Indian agent, Mr. Harrison, on a trip of about 300 miles, traveling east of the reservation into the desert to visit the property of the Indians who live outside of the reservation, and, where possible, to legally secure it for them. Several times we slept on the ground (which was nothing new or unusual for me) and several times rode out of our way, sometimes not knowing exactly where we were. We experienced a real sandstorm in the desert, sometimes traveled over 50 miles in a day, and held two well-attended meetings with the Indians who live in this godforsaken region, one in Seven Lakes, the other at Pueblo Bonito in Chaco Canyon. The result of our efforts is still undetermined, for the government is just like eternity—without end: if I don't come today, I'll come tomorrow. President Roosevelt initiated the so-called Keep Commission some time ago to free the government from the so-called red tape; it has probably entangled itself in red tape and now sleeps the sleep of the righteous. No use in trying to hurry Papa Washington, because you can't do it.

Problems and Progress, 1908[8]

Because we are opening our school again this month, I will share with our esteemed readers that during the past school year, 1907–1908, 127 students were accommodated. Unfortunately, two of these died, one girl here in the school and a boy at home. Sadly, consumption is spreading more and more, not only among the Navajo but among almost all the Indians of the land. And yet they had not known this sickness until they came into contact with the whites. Of course, the government wants to build a hospital for those with consumption, especially for affected students, but as with everything the government does, the process is endlessly drawn out, so we must probably wait years until this plan is realized.

On June 14, 1908, 19 of our students (13 boys and six girls) were baptized, and on the seventh of the same month nine students (six boys and three girls) received their First Holy Communion. Up to now 56 have received their First Holy Communion, and 178 children and adults have been baptized. All whom our school has "absolved" have remained true to their religion and are progressing toward receiving the holy sacrament. Of course, it isn't always easy to offer them this opportunity often. Recently, I traveled 90 miles for this purpose and still didn't reach everyone—one was on the mountain, God knows where.

Some of our students have just married, and it is evident here that we acted correctly when we made not only our students but also their parents aware of the requirements of a Christian marriage. The parents of all of our older students have promised me to see that their children act accordingly. And if an older Indian gives a promise, it is much more dependable than a promise by their young heirs, even when they have attended the school. Polygamy and divorce are common among the Navajo, as with all heathen people, and these practices not only make marriage more difficult but also stand in the way of the conversion of many adults.

One hears the remark here and there that when the Navajo give a daughter in marriage they also sell her. Now this is not correct. How is it then with us civilized people with regard to the so-called dowry? Do the parents give the dowry in order to somehow marry their daughter off that much easier? Hardly! That would be a cynical interpretation. Likewise, it would be cynical to believe that because it is customary with the Navajo that the groom or his family gives the bride or her family a number of horses or sheep or something else for the occasion of the marriage, that therefore he buys his bride.

With the Navajo it is customary that the husband, at least for the first years, moves in with his wife or, more likely, with her parents; and there is then a great deal to be said for the fact that he does not approach them empty-handed. Of course, when an older, wealthier Navajo, who already has perhaps one or two wives, acquires a young girl as wife through a sizable gift, which happens here and there, one could designate that as a purchase, but not in the usual case when two young people marry each other. Also, a respectable Navajo from a "good family" would not sell his daughter for any price to a Navajo of "common" birth, even though he were well off. Naturally, the daughter has little to say about her marriage. Also there is no such thing with them as "acquaintances" [courting]. If a young man were seen very often in the company of a young woman, as is the custom with the whites, both of them would be seen as dishonorable. Such behavior is not befitting of heathens. It happens often enough that the bridegroom and the bride have never spoken a single word to each other before the wedding. Probably this custom is not exactly the best, either.

These singular customs are part of the reason why the "better" Navajo send their daughters to school only reluctantly, especially to a school where the supervision is somewhat lax. They seem to fear that their daughters might fall in love with inferior schoolboys. Of course, such things do happen here and there, but not usually at our school, where the supervision is quite strict. However, also in this case, education paves the way for better relationships.

At the close of school last year a headman and his wife (who at that time lived in the mountains about 100 miles from here and had come here to bring both of their sons home for vacation) told me that they wanted their daughter to be married (last year she did not return to our school). But their daughter did not want to be married in traditional fashion, but instead she wanted us to perform her marriage. "Exactly right!" I answered her parents, for they had promised me a year before that none of their children would enter into polygamy and that they would be married only by a Catholic priest. I intended to come to their region very soon to administer the last sacrament to a sick person and to provide the opportunity for several to receive the holy sacrament; then we could take care of this further. When I came, their daughter told me she knew the boy whom it was intended that she should marry, but nothing more—she did not know whether he was good or bad, whether her marriage with him would make her happy or unhappy. She did not want to let herself be married off by her parents so easily; she had not forgotten what she had learned about marriage at our school. Her parents were understanding enough to value her standpoint and to give in.

Both of their sons were herding sheep 10 miles away in the mountains. The parents sent for them so that they could be at the Holy Mass together the next day. Both arrived as darkness was falling, riding on a donkey. The next morning I held the Holy Mass very early in their house, during which their daughter received the Holy Communion. Her father asked me to be sure not to forget to pray for rain because his fields were drying out.

As I crossed the mountain that afternoon, there was powerful lightning and thunder in that region. Whether a refreshing rain fell there, however, I do not know. I will skip my visits to the other Indians and our students; I will only mention that on this same evening, I tried for about two hours to talk the Indian with whom I was staying out of his belief in witchcraft, at which I was only partly successful. At least he promised me to leave undisturbed those whom he suspected of having hexed his wife.

It was not without reason that the headman asked me to pray for rain, for we have had a very dry year. All spring and summer until the end of July, not only was there not one drop of rain, but in addition there were constant, powerful sandstorms which dried out everything, so that overall the Navajo have bad fields and a poor harvest to count on. As a result of the panic, the prices for wool, skins, and Navajo blankets have sunk to almost half, so that the poor Navajo have already pawned away almost all of their jewelry and their silver work. The coming winter will therefore be very hard for them. Therefore, I ask the honorable readers not to forget them with their generosity, but if they themselves have some worn clothing or can gather some from friends and neighbors, send it to us for the Indians. The best and cheapest way is to sew the clothes inside bags and to send it as "rags" by freight to Franciscan Fathers, in care of C. N. Cotton Company, Gallup, New Mexico. Earlier, many were generous to us in this matter through our preachers. I would like to ask that they do that again this year, and that others follow their good example. Many have also given to our mission very freely, despite the hard times, by sending us clothing and other articles. Many also send us alms money, especially through the editor's office of the *Sendbote*. . . . To all of these, a heartfelt "God bless!". . .

Unfortunately, our superintendent at Fort Defiance, Mr. Harrison, had to resign because his wife was ill. Because I feared we and the Navajo could be burdened with a less-than-desirable superintendent, I lobbied in Washington for Mr. Peter Paquette, who was assistant superintendent here earlier and has now taken the same position with the Arapaho Indians. He is a very capable man and is well disposed to us because he stems from Catholic and French-Indian roots; his grandmother was a full-blooded Indian. It appears his Indian heritage has hindered his promotion so far, but my efforts on his behalf were accompanied by success, and yesterday the news came of his being named as the superintendent at Fort Defiance. It appears that, little by little, Fort Defiance is becoming Indian and Catholic. A Sioux, two Chippewa, two Navajo, and two Pueblo Indians—all Catholic—are now employed there. Aside from that, two shop owners there are Catholic. In this matter things are significantly better than four years ago, and I hope that relations under Mr. Paquette will become even better.

Notes

1. Anselm Weber, FMN 30 (May 1903): 399–405. For an alternate account of the 1892 Round Rock incident, see Frank McNitt, *The Indian Traders* (Norman: University of Oklahoma Press, 1962), 278–81.

2. Murray Bodo, O.F.M., ed., *Tales of an Endishodi: Father Berard Haile and the Navajo, 1900–1961* (Albuquerque: University of New Mexico Press, 1998).

3. From Anselm Weber, "Opening of St. Michael's School—Indians' Attack at Round Rock," FMSW 5 (1917):10–19; and FMN 30 (March 1903): 214–20. Translated by Marie Bradshaw Durrant.

4. From Anselm Weber, FMN 31 (August 1904): 681–84. Translated by Marie Bradshaw Durrant.

5. From Anselm Weber, FMN 31 (December 1904): 1030–34. Translated by Marie Bradshaw Durrant.

6. George H. Pepper published several articles on the Navajo, mostly in popular journals (*Southern Workman*, *Everybody's Magazine*, *Papoose*) over the period 1900–1905.

7. From Anselm Weber, FMN 34 (June 1907): 514–15. Translated by Marie Bradshaw Durrant.

8. From Anselm Weber, FMN 35 (November 1908): 979–82. Translated by Marie Bradshaw Durrant.

14

Law and Order, American Style[1]

Anselm Weber, O.F.M.

[Among the ways that the friars served the Navajo people was to intercede for them or to attempt to serve as their helpers and advocates in those ever more numerous situations where Navajo had to deal with various white institutions, from the federal government down to the local political and educational establishments. Of course, the most obvious of the Franciscans' efforts to help the Navajo deal with white society was the school, where students experienced a kind of "preventive modernization" whereby they learned the ways of the whites and were prepared, to some degree, to participate in the various institutional contexts of the wider society.

For the Navajo, one of the more painful consequences of the intersection of white and Navajo culture was that in many situations Navajo found themselves subject to white legal jurisdiction, white law and law enforcement. In practice, this meant that the Navajo often ran afoul of white law and found themselves enmeshed in law enforcement and judicial proceedings that they only partly understood and in which there seemed to be an institutional bias against them.

The present chapter illustrates the operation of frontier justice in several instances of apparent property crime. Father Anselm, traveling about recruiting students, happens to be in town when an Indian acquaintance is charged with a crime. Observe how, simply as a result of his "being there" when the case comes before the judge, Father Anselm's involvement in the legal proceedings grows from merely lending moral support to serving actively as defense counsel for the accused. His description of the operation of white justice for Indian defendants, in these few personally observed incidents, plainly shows how the system operates to the detriment of the Navajo defendant, and underscores just how critical it is, if an accused Navajo is to receive anything even approaching fair treatment, for the accused to have advocates and allies, preferably white, who understand the system.

In the article reporting these events, Father Anselm did not fully identify the town where the courtroom scenes took place, except as "G—," but his reference to the population of the town, combined with the fact that he was recruiting Navajo students and that there was no other community of any size in or near the reservation whose name began with the letter "G," suggest that he is talking about Gallup, New Mexico.

Note that, as with his efforts to help the Navajo obtain secure title to their lands, his efforts on behalf of particular Indians in court proceedings have direct, beneficial results for his recruiting of students. Eventually, thanks in part to the goodwill his advocacy for Spotted Horse and other Navajo defendants has created, residents of the area promise to send their children to St. Michaels. Father Anselm is motivated by a passion to see justice done, but he is also conscious, with some satisfaction, of having created a rapport and sense of obligation to him, such that children from the area who do attend school are likely to attend the Catholic school at St. Michaels.

The last part of the article summarizes the competition between schools for Navajo students, and it shows Father Anselm's efforts to prevent "his" students, whose parents have signed official papers indicating that they intend for their children to be educated at St. Michaels, from being recruited by or assigned to other schools.]

I had experienced a session of the high court a short time before. But I was more than a little surprised, in light of such extensive experience in a courtroom, when I was given—even forced—to take a "case." Only once in my life had I read something in a law book. But since there was no lawyer in town, and as I had never believed that I was born stupid, I assumed the role of lawyer for the defense.

A wealthy Indian, "Bililikizhi," or "Spotted Horse," had asked me to support him at his court hearing by my presence at the proceeding. Since I had to visit the town at that time anyway, I agreed. On the day of the proceeding, I asked about the court building. I was directed to a wooden hut, 15 by 12, with a door and two half-windows. I am sure that the hut measured only 15 feet in one direction because I measured its shadow as I went by. The 12 feet in the other direction I just estimated in passing. I was a little surprised that a town of some 2,000 residents did not have a better "temple of justice." But as I became better acquainted with the worthy judge, I saw immediately the "eternal right." His Honor came from a land infamous for the mulish stubbornness of its residents. This man would surely have been a good lawyer, because it never seemed to occur to him that the other side might possibly be right.

As I entered, a case between two Indians of different tribes was under way. The accusation was read by the judge in his long-winded dialect. It went as follows: The Indian Petersen (the name sounds Swedish, but it's not) had a calf bound by all four feet in his possession when the owner, a Pueblo Indian, appeared on the scene.

After all had performed the usual oath, the Pueblo Indian gave his testimony, which agreed with the sworn accusation. He had no eyewitnesses to confirm his testimony.

The Indian Petersen gave testimony for himself, saying that he and his companion had been looking for their horses and rode by the Pueblo's cattle herd. They noticed a steer that had wandered away from the herd. They couldn't resist the temptation to catch the steer with their lasso, merely to practice throwing the lasso and to show their skill. After they had removed the lasso, they had ridden on, and soon met two Pueblo Indians. They told them [the Pueblos] that they had caught a steer. "Whose steer was it?" they were asked. "Yours," was the answer. Then all had continued riding. The companion of the Indian Petersen, his only witness, was unfortunately not at the hearing. On cross-examination of the Pueblo Indian [the original charge was amended, in that] the calf suddenly became a yearling. Then it turned out only to be fastened by two feet instead of by all four. The honorable court seemed to have forgotten to send the plaintiff out while his companion testified, and so there was the possibility for the plaintiff later to try to bring his own testimony more into line with that of his witness. Despite some obvious contradictions in the testimonies of the two Pueblos, the judge declared his intention of punishing Petersen as an example. According to his honorable opinion, Petersen had acknowledged his guilt.

"If it please the court," Petersen's lawyer responded, and he went on to make it clear that Mr. Petersen had not pleaded guilty to the crime with which he was charged. He had admitted his guilt to an entirely different crime, if you could call such a thing a crime. To catch a calf by all four legs to slaughter it and to catch a steer with a lasso to keep in practice are surely not the same thing, and a calf is not a steer! The judge didn't seem to agree with this. He claimed Petersen had brought a cow that belonged to another into his possession, and for that he must be punished. The lawyer insisted that if Petersen should be punished for his admitted crime, then he must also be formally charged with this crime. Finally, it was decided to hold a new hearing in four days, to which both parties would be able to bring their respective witnesses.

The lawyer, none other than the Indian agent himself, told the judge he couldn't possibly be at the hearing in four days, because he had to appear before the grand jury of another city on that day—he was required by law. Then the agent asked me whether I would be able to attend the hearing. Of course I could, because I intended to stay several days in this region to find more Indian children for our school. Good! Then I should take his place and take over the defense of Petersen. The judge had nothing to add, and my own objections went unnoticed. So I was advanced *nolens volens* as lawyer.

Since the time to refresh the inner person was approaching, the judge stated that the hearing for the Indian Bililikizhi would take place that afternoon at 1:30. "If it please the court," the lawyer interjected again, "Spotted Horse has reason to believe that he will not receive justice before this court and therefore requests that his case be tried in the neighboring court." The high court saw things quite another way. No justice before him? Laughable! What reason, or much more, what madness could lead "Spotted Horse" to make such a demand?

"If it please the court, according to the law, Spotted Horse is not required to make his reasons known. The simple assurance that, in his opinion, such reasons exist is enough." Now the lawyer must have known this.

When I later inquired where the other court was located, I was told it was in the pawn shop of the German (the Dutchman who beats the limit). Surely an acceptable place for Spotted Horse's hearing on horse theft! When I arrived there that afternoon, the anteroom of the courtroom, that is, the entrance to the room, was crowded with a colorful mix of Indians, Mexicans, and Americans of every type.

Finally, the judge appeared and opened the door to the courtroom right from the entrance. The judge seemed to have a natural aversion to the repetition of the formal oath and wanted all participants and all witnesses to be together right from the first so that they could all take the oath together. He put them all in a row to administer the oath. Only the sheriff, who seemed to be more opposed to a false oath than to a simple lie, raised an objection by saying that he, as sheriff, was always under oath. The lawyer let him know that he was always under oath to fulfill his duty as sheriff, but not, however, always to tell the truth. Another man (called "Senator," because he was a relative of an eastern senator, supposedly his namesake) wanted to know first why he had been summoned to the hearing. He didn't know anything about the whole story. The lawyer responded that Spotted Horse had requested him, and other respected citizens of G—, to serve as character witnesses for him, speaking for the past year. Certainly Spotted Horse wouldn't want the testimonials for him to refer back too far into the past. This observation was met by a burst of laughter, because Spotted Horse had been known in earlier years as one of the biggest thieves and cutthroats in the area, although naturally he had always acted in self-defense.

Charged with other crimes, he had been required to appear before the Indian agent years ago. However, because he possessed large herds of horses, cattle, and sheep, a former military officer and a famous lawyer took his case on, had him take out citizenship papers, and thereby forced the Indian agent to set him free, since, as a respectable citizen of the United States, he was no longer under the jurisdiction of the agent. For this Spotted Horse paid his defenders 801 sheep. The former officer took the herd east, sold them, and squandered the money. The lawyer did not receive one red cent from the episode.

Spotted Horse stood before the court, accused of the crime, during bright day in the open street, of having stopped three Pueblo Indians unharnessing one of their horses and riding away on it. Yet before he had been given time to admit his guilt, a Jewish shopkeeper rose up and said someone should first explain to the Indian what "guilty" and "not guilty" mean before the court. Spotted Horse did not deny the deed but claimed the horse belonged to him; it had his brand. The white court of law wanted to portray his story of ownership as unreliable so that Spotted Horse would admit his guilt. However, this was protested against very energetically, and the Indian was told he should plead "not guilty," which he then did. Order did not reign; each spoke and interrupted the others at will.

Next, they tried to establish who was the owner of the horse. The Pueblo Indian claimed to have acquired the horse from a Mexican for a blanket. Four Pueblo

Indians confirmed this, but the Pueblo Indians couldn't show any receipt, and the horse indisputably carried Spotted Horse's brand. Further, it was established through the testimony of the Pueblo Indians that it is not customary to give mutual receipts and that it is also not customary to destroy the brand when buying an animal. The Jewish shopkeeper argued that according to the law, the horse belonged to Spotted Horse, for it carried his brand and the Pueblo Indians could show no receipt. Naturally, the judge didn't know whether the law really read that way and asked the sheriff to look it up. He took the thick law book and disappeared, but soon returned to say that he couldn't find anything about it in the book.

Now, the informed gentlemen remembered that Spotted Horse had a written contract from the Mexican in question, but who could read it? Asked if I understood Mexican, I pleaded "not guilty." At this moment a hotel owner entered and the judge said, "Now we have one who understands Mexican, because he receives letters from Mexicans." "True," came the answer, "but I have them translated into English by translators." In response I rode to find the Catholic priest of the town. He read the document and translated it into English without any difficulty. According to the contract, Spotted Horse turned over his horse herd to the Mexican for five years; but the Mexican died during that time, and his heirs had given Spotted Horse a further contract which now came into question. Everything went well until the last sentence, where it said that Spotted Horse should receive all the horses back, except those which the Mexican had sold during his lifetime. That was clear. The Mexican had had the right to sell that horse, and the four Pueblo Indians testified that he had done that.

Understanding dawned, winks were exchanged, and we left the courtroom and proceeded to the stall. There it was explained to Spotted Horse how the horse situation had come about. He agreed to give the horse back to the Pueblo Indians and to give them $10 in addition. We proceeded again to the courtroom, where the lawyer let the judge know how the story now stood settled outside of the court. The sheriff protested against this with great vehemence. A criminal case couldn't be settled outside of the court. He insisted that the judge render a decision. The Jewish shopkeeper reminded the sheriff that the story did not involve him one bit. He was only the sheriff, not the judge. The judge tried to mediate by saying that he would have decided the matter the same way: Spotted Horse must give the horse back to the Pueblo Indian. "And the $10 is about sufficient to cover the costs," added another. "Not when the witness costs are counted; if the witnesses don't insist on pay, they don't receive anything." To this the sheriff said he insisted that the costs be paid to the last penny. As you can see, everyone seems to be a judge here.

"If it please the court," spoke up the lawyer, "Spotted Horse did not plead guilty, and you yourselves have granted that he did not act with criminal intent but in good faith, believing that the horse belonged to him when he unharnessed it and took it away from the Pueblo Indian. Therefore, he doesn't need to pay the costs, rather the county should cover them." "I believe the one is as guilty as the other," replied the senator, "and therefore each of them should pay half the costs."

In response, the high tribunal shrouded itself in its ignorance and said it would take the situation under consideration and give its decision the next day. With much dignity, the session was adjourned. The high gentlemen came together again that evening. The sheriff was appeased somewhat—they would pay the witnesses half of what they were actually owed—so the whole story of Spotted Horse cost about $26. Of course the county should have paid the costs—but such a poor county and such a rich Indian! In this case, when the accused is convicted, the court gets a better deal.

Later, Spotted Horse said all seemed to go well until that "Naakai Bich'indi," that cursed Mexican, read the document. He did not know that the "Mexican," who, by the way, was born on the other side of the Rhine, was the local Catholic priest.

As we left the courtroom, an Indian sat on the doorstep who should have been at the first court session that morning. Shortly thereafter, I saw the sheriff come upon him, grab him by the wrist, and take him into his office. I [and some others] followed them. There the sheriff undressed the Indian in a rough manner, searched through his pockets, put handcuffs on him, and dragged him back and forth with them. "I wouldn't treat him like that if he had shown up this morning," said the sheriff. "If that is the reason," said the Indian agent, "the Indian should know that too." With that, the agent asked me to communicate this to the Indian. The Indian, named Shahi, was naturally very upset, and I had to repeat my questions several times. The problem had occurred the previous evening, he said, but he hadn't been able to find the agent, and during the night his horse had come up missing. He had been looking for him since then [until the sheriff took him].

I was filled with indignation over his treatment and had decided, if possible, to free him. So I went with our translator, Frank Walker, to the jail and asked Shahi what he was accused of. He said that an inferior steer who belonged to a Pueblo Indian had persistently attached himself to his cattle herd, and because Shahi couldn't keep the steer away, he had, in order to protect the herd from degenerating, castrated him. I asked him whether someone was witness to his actions. No, no one. He had told the Pueblo Indian himself, and he had appeared to be alright about it. I asked him further whether anyone was present when he told the owner what he had done. Yes, another Pueblo Indian, but the latter was so far removed from them that he could hardly hear their discussion. "Good," I said to him, "then declare yourself 'not guilty' at court. The Pueblos are unwilling to bear witness. They don't have a single thing of importance to say in front of the court."

He followed my advice and was set free. Unfortunately, he had already "sat" in Fort Defiance several weeks for his "offense." What he had done is customary practice for the cowherds of the Southwest. I also explained this to the judge, but he informed me from the law book that such action is unlawful. Perhaps it is, but an Indian doesn't know the written laws and necessarily acts according to custom. What is right for the whites should then be right for the Indian. But the judge didn't see it this way, didn't agree with anything, and if the Pueblo Indian had had witnesses or if Shahi had admitted his act, he would have been punished as an example.

I also saw Petersen in jail and asked him whether he had sent for his witnesses. No, he hadn't had any chance to. I had him give me the names of the witnesses and promised to have them in place on a certain day. To arrange this, I had him tell me his whole story in detail. The next morning, I rode with Frank Walker to see Spotted Horse, the Navajo at the beginning of my report. At lunchtime, the parents and relatives of the Indians Shahi and Petersen appeared and asked me to do anything I could to get them out of jail. In addition, Petersen's companion, his only witness, appeared. He had been away at work for several months and had just now heard how things were with his friend. I had him also tell me how things had happened; his story matched exactly with Petersen's. Also, an American, a shopkeeper in the area and a friend of Petersen, was present and promised to be in attendance at the process. I later wished, by the way, that he would have stayed home.

The next day I visited the Indians in the whole neighborhood and tried to convince them to send their children to our school. Up until then, none of them had sent even a single child. They promised to consider it and to give our school preference, meaning that all of the children of this colony who should be sent to any school, would come to our school. So I could be satisfied with my efforts, and I rode to G— to represent Shahi and Petersen at court.

Shahi was let free, as already mentioned. With Petersen, things didn't go as smoothly. The accusation was again read out loud: Petersen and his companion supposedly had a steer restrained by all four legs in their possession when the owner and two other Pueblo Indians surprised them. This was confirmed by the plaintiff and his two companions. Following this, I had Petersen and then his companion tell the sequence of events. Through different questions I was able to see that their testimony was perfectly consistent. They had ridden by a herd of cattle and seen that one steer had separated himself somewhat from the rest of the herd. Out of mischievousness and to show his skills, Petersen threw his lasso around the horns of the steer. To stop the steer and to get the lasso loose from his horns without danger, his companion also threw his lasso, so that the back legs of the steer were caught. Now it was intended that the steer would be set free again and the two Indians would ride on their way, but they encountered the owner and his companions [who, apparently, were not amused] and in conversation reported what they had done. In the court, I asked several questions and pointed out the fact, confirmed by a half dozen Indians, that Petersen's companion had been away at work for so long that it made a criminal conspiracy relating to the similarity of their testimony before the court impossible. Their complete agreement proved that Petersen's account of things was truthful. Additionally, both had testified, under oath, in answer to my questions that they did not have the faintest idea that one of them had been put in a position to be charged because of this matter and that they had not even spoken anymore about it.

Despite this, the judge aimed his intentions of proper punishment at Petersen—surely not because he believed the Pueblo Indians, but rather because he glimpsed, in what Petersen had done, some horrible crime. To prove that, he read a paragraph of the law to us which had no relation to this case at all. Now the American shopkeeper stood up, praised Petersen above the stars, said that he had committed the same crime many times earlier as a "cowboy," and criticized the judge so severely that the judge threatened to fine him. Infuriated by this attack against his person, his intelligence, and his love of justice, the judge immediately passed sentence: $25 fine and court costs, a total of approximately $60. We would appeal to a higher court: the American and one of his friends put up the required bail of $100 so that Petersen didn't have to return to jail. A few minutes later, however, Petersen told me he had had his fill of this whole business and didn't want to appear in court again. He would sell some of his sheep and pay the $60.

After such an experience, I could only find sympathy with the Indian's mistrust of the rule of law as administered by the American system of justice.

I said that I had visited Spotted Horse and his neighbors to convince them to send their children to our school. When our school had been open for a few weeks and these Indians still had not shown up, I saddled my horse and rode there again—40 miles from here. The Indian with whom I stayed had quite a poor hut, which didn't give us much shelter from the rain and snow during the night. His wife and children slept in an even worse hut—one of the children was covered with many blankets and was literally giving off steam. The rain had actually seeped through the covers onto his warm body. However, he soon got up, bright and cheerful, as if he had slept in the best bed. It is almost incomprehensible that these people aren't all sick after such a night. As I woke up in the morning, the Indian came to me with a large bottle—liquor—and asked me if I didn't want some "medicine." I naturally declined. He, however, was "loaded."

After a short time, a German shopkeeper from the neighborhood arrived. His appearance reminded me very vividly of the verse in "Teutoburger Battle," "He rode in a swamp, lost two boots and a sock and remained miserably stuck," because he was stuck and what one usually wears on the feet, he was carrying in his hands. As he surveyed the hut he said, "It is rather wet here! Ah, you are also wet to the bone! A stream must flow through here somewhere."

Even though he was drunk, the Indian was still not in a nasty mood. We soon rode to the other Indians—some were on the deer hunt, others used work as the excuse why they hadn't brought their children to school. I heard from two Indians here what I had already gathered from rumors earlier, that the translator employed at the government school in Albuquerque, New Mexico, a Navajo and a former student of that school, had been here a few weeks ago to recruit students for that school. He really pushed the Indians to send their children to the government school, and when they told him they had promised their children to me, he told them we were liars and deceivers, just like their own medicine men, that the Americans hated us and he also hated us. The children didn't learn much in our school, he told them; mostly just religion is taught there; and the schools in Fort Defiance and Little Water (government schools) were just about the same as our schools.

The Indians, however, didn't really believe him and said to him that if he were telling the truth, they didn't understand why the most influential headmen were our friends and could send their children to our school. He didn't get one single student from this area. Naturally, I disproved his false statements and told them that even the residing chief of Washington (the president) had praised our work with the Navajo when I had visited there this year.

They promised to bring their children to school right after the first of December. When the trails were very bad and the weather was very bitter—it was 20 below zero at night—I had to go there myself and bring the children in our wagon.

I had heard that the superintendent of that aforementioned Indian school in Albuquerque, Mr. Allen, had convinced two schoolgirls, one from our school and one from Fort Defiance, to come with him to his school in Albuquerque. When I told this to the Indian agent at Fort Defiance, Mr. Reuben Perry, he went with me to his assistant, who thanked me for the information, because up until now he hadn't been able to find out where these schoolgirls were. Our Indian agent wrote immediately to Albuquerque. The superintendent there admitted that he had the two students in his school and asked to be allowed to keep them—actually he needed them. In reference to the student who had attended our school, he wrote he was afraid that if he sent her back she wouldn't go to any school, because her mother seemed to be very angry about our school and wouldn't allow her to attend our school again under any circumstances.

Our Indian agent answered that he could keep his student. He passed his letter on to me and said that whatever I wanted to do in the matter would naturally be his wish. However, he couldn't go there to punish Mr. Allen's behavior. He had heard that his interpreter had spoken to the Indians in very scornful terms about us, unjustly, because we have a very good school. He hoped that he could make his wrong right again.

I answered our agent's question regarding the return of our student in a letter which was actually intended for the superintendent of the Indian school in Albuquerque and was sent to him. I wrote that I really couldn't allow that student to remain in the school in Albuquerque. While we do teach the children the different subjects so that their work in industrial arts and in the different classes could be comparable with any other school, the raison d'etre of our school is, however, religious education (otherwise I would close our school and advise the Navajo to send their children, for example, to the Albuquerque school—there couldn't be a better one if I can believe a certain representative of that school).

After we have spent $150 on the education of that Navajo girl, I would have to be weak in the head to allow her religious education not only to be ended but that on top of that she will be educated as an enemy of that which began her education. I believe I have great cause for this indirect charge. Mr. Allen shouldn't see this as a censure of the government schools in total; if the student, for example, had been brought to the Indian school in Santa Fe, I would not have made any serious objections.

Mr. Allen expressed his fear that the student, if he sent her back, would not attend any school; but the legal guardian of the child, Oastq-Dilaghushi-n-Bitsoi, wished for the child to be sent back and gave me the assurance that she would be sent to our school after her return from Albuquerque, and this with the approval of her blind mother; and if the latter were angry at our school (a somewhat harsh interpretation), I know of no reason for her "anger" other than that I didn't allow her to take her daughter home until I had the permission of her legal guardian.

Without doubt, if Mr. Allen's representative is allowed to continue his statements about us and our school, we shouldn't be surprised if even more people become "angry" about our school.

But even if the blind mother of the girl had been her legal guardian, and even if she actually and with good cause were "angry" with our school, Mr. Allen still had no right to take away the child without my and his (our Indian agent's) permission, because according to my understanding, he (our Indian agent), and not Mr. Allen, has to confirm whether the parents have just cause to complain about our school and have enough reason to transfer their children from our school to another.

I asked the Indian commissioner for an explanation of certain rules and ordinances of the Indian Department. He answered: "The ordinance"—a child who attends an Indian school outside of the reservation and comes home during vacation must be sent back to that school, and they will not allow that child to be sent to another school—"pertains to mission schools as well as to government schools, therefore the same protection will be provided to you in this matter as to a government school."

For these different reasons I have irrevocably decided to insist on the return of the above-mentioned student.

Our Indian agent wanted to soften the seemingly harsh wording of this letter; under the circumstances, this could hardly be avoided.

The letter had its effects. Mr. Allen sent the girl back and told me if his representative made such derogatory remarks about us and our school, he had done it without his knowledge. Thus it was a good lesson, not only for him but also for the Indians. Now they know that they may not send their children from our school into another without notice.

It was not exactly easy to bring the old and new students to the school. A certain inspector, who bragged he stood directly under the president and acted like a pasha with three horse tails, told the Indians they didn't need to send their children to any school if they didn't want. After this person (who understands as much about the local conditions and the Indians as a cow about a pocket watch) spread trouble everywhere, he was quickly transferred.

Many times we had to travel far—40, 60, 90, and 100 miles—with our own wagon to bring the children to school. The worst trip was over the mountains to Tselchidahaskani [Red Rock], approximately 100 miles from here. The Indian who was supposed to bring the children from there to the school had broken his wagon, and so I had Father Berard travel there while I rode to the south. The trip is already hard enough in and of itself, but rain and snowstorms made the return trip nearly impossible.

Fifty-eight miles from here, Father Berard sent an Indian on horseback to us with the request to send him another team of horses to pull the wagon the last 35 miles through the nearly bottomless mire from the rain and snow. After 12 days of absence, Father Berard finally arrived with his coach and four [horses] and his 10 children, just early enough to miss Father Provincial Chrysostom Theobald, who had taught the spiritual lessons for us. I had taken him to Gallup on the day of Father Berard's return. The streets were such that you had to let the horses walk;

as a result of this we arrived at 9:00 in the evening, half frozen, likewise just early enough to miss the likewise late train.

In closing, we would like to express our heartfelt thanks at the year's end to all those who remembered our mission and our Indians in prayers and with loving generosity, and wish them God's blessings!

Notes

1. From Anselm Weber, FMN 32 (December 1905): 1083–88; 33 (January, February 1906): 28–33, 120–26. Translated by Marie Bradshaw Durrant.

15

The Navajo Trouble of 1905[1]

Anselm Weber, O.F.M., and Henry "Chee" Dodge

[The title is Father Anselm's, from his report to Father William Ketcham of the Bureau of Catholic Indian Missions some 15 months after the fact.[2] The commissioner of Indian Affairs was conducting an inquiry into the actions of Navajo Superintendent Reuben Perry during the confrontation, and Weber's report was intended to support the defense of Mr. Perry. In addition to his own retrospective summary and other commentary, and a translation of Chee Dodge's pivotal speech, Father Anselm referred Father Ketcham to his series of *Sendbote* articles on the affair and to the press coverage, including an article by Reverend George J. Juillard, pastor of Gallup, in the *Albuquerque Morning Journal* and two pieces by Father Anselm that had appeared in the *McKinley County Republican*. None of these articles was identified publicly as the work of Catholic fathers. Father Juillard's had run simply as the writings of a "correspondent," and Father Anselm's byline was "one who knows," one who was "on the ground at the time and tells the story of the events exactly as they occurred."[3]

The trouble of 1905 began as an instance of overlapping jurisdictions and the lack of fit between traditional Navajo justice and the U.S. legal system as represented in the authority of the Indian agent and the Department of the Interior. It occurred during a period of growing Navajo resentment against "government officials working among The People and trying to get action and results quickly by personal authority [and who] would resort to orders and sometimes force—with disastrous outcome."[4] For a time it seemed that a minor incident and its aftermath in this volatile atmosphere would precipitate armed conflict between federal troops and the Navajo. After the situation had been defused, the Gallup newspaper credited a speech by "Chief Henry Dodge" to some 2,000 Navajo assembled at a Yeibichai dance as words that "saved an Indian war with its bloodshed and horrors." Another headline proclaimed, "Had it not been for this speech of strong words U.S. troops and Indians would now be at war."[5]

Earlier, the local press had compared the situation to previous uprisings. "History is repeating itself these days" read a front-page piece in the *McKinley County Republican*, "a small incident and a number of Red skins are ready to take the warpath." The article went on to say that federal troops had been sent to Fort Defiance to protect the whites, "to garrison the station and to be on hand in case the Navajo should committee any hostile act toward the white people in the vicinity," and it stereotyped the causes of the confrontation, proclaiming that "the root of all our Indian troubles here is drink."[6] When the crisis had passed, the same paper minimized the action as "the little Indian scare which was made the topic of scare heads in the big dailies all over the country," but even a "little scare" apparently merited a heavy punishment: "What the fate of the prisoners will be is as yet conjecture but it is expected that they will be severely punished as it is the intention of the government to force the Indians to respect the officers and the law."[7]

Father Anselm's biographer casts his role in the trouble of 1905, as in later standoffs between Navajo and U.S. troops in 1907 and 1913, as one of "conciliator and peacemaker between government officials and The People," a service for which "he was admirably equipped by his own peace-loving nature, by his training in patience both as subject and superior in a Franciscan community, and by his intimate understanding of Navajo culture."[8] Without denying these qualifications or Father Anselm's strenuous efforts at mediation (see chapter 26), I believe that to characterize his work primarily as "peacekeeping" is to oversimplify, and possibly misrepresent, his mission. Father Anselm's primary commitment was to not to peace, and certainly not to "peace at any price," but rather to doing the right thing, especially the right thing for the long-term benefit of the Navajo. He was an effective mediator precisely because those who knew him knew that his commitment to moral action, that is, to doing the *right* thing, was more important than his commitment to either party in the contest.

It was in service to justice, and not mercy, to obedience to established law rather than exception to it, that he advised Superintendent Perry against appeasement or even the "retreat" of offering his resignation. Father Anselm warned that unless the government, as represented in Perry, reasserted its authority, the Navajo would be encouraged to even more open defiance. When Father Anselm offered that opinion, it was not at all clear that government efforts to punish the offenders would not escalate the conflict. Indeed, it was because tensions had risen to unacceptable levels that the Navajo headmen also sought Father Anselm's advice, accompanying him to meet with Superintendent Perry and later, at St. Michaels, planning strategy whereby trouble and perhaps bloodshed might be avoided at the coming Yeibichai dance.

The following account of the trouble of 1905 draws mainly on Father Anselm's monthly *Sendbote* reports, supplemented by excerpts from his and Father Juillard's newspaper articles. Note that Father Anselm was involved in the trouble from the very beginning, indeed, from before the beginning. Several days before Mr. Perry's "holdup" at Chin Lee, Father Anselm was warned of a growing hostility among many Navajo toward Superintendent Perry, and also toward white traders. Father Anselm first learned of the potential trouble while visiting Charlie Mitchell at Tsehili, during one of Father Anselm's many journeys to gather up Indian students and transport them to St. Michaels. Thus, Father Anselm's story of the "trouble" begins with his account of that particular trip north. He spent much of his ministry making such trips, and so it is no great digression to follow his lead in this matter and to begin, as he did, the narrative of the trouble of 1905 with that trip over the mountains, with stops both coming and going at the home of Chee Dodge.

The story offers numerous insights on the nature of Father Anselm's ministry. Observe, for example, the inevitable "multitasking." In view of the distances involved, Father Anselm rarely travels anywhere for just one reason. Here, the primary goal is to round up students and bring them back, but the trip is also defined, and its hazards increased, by the need to wait for and deliver important mail to Chee Dodge and then to assist him with his official correspondence. That finished, there is always the need to visit acquaintances along the way to inform, encourage, and in general maintain the network of Navajo support for the Franciscan missionary effort. If, from the standpoint of the impending confrontation, the most important aspect of the trip is the warning from Charlie Mitchell that the natives are restless under the heavy hand of the autocratic Mr. Perry, that information is received too late to prevent the trouble. Yet on the return trip, Father Anselm does communicate the threat to Chee Dodge, who takes it very seriously indeed. It is the combination of an anxious Chee Dodge and a chastened, shaken agent Perry, safely returned from the holdup in Chin Lee, who hurry to St. Michaels for a council with Father Anselm about what can be done.

From this point on, the entire sequence shows just how well connected and influential Father Anselm has become. He advises Superintendent Perry about how the Navajo will interpret various administrative responses. Later, when the military is called in, officers alert Father Anselm and seek his input. Trouble is expected from the thousands of Navajo assembling near St. Michaels for a Yeibichai dance. Prior to the dance, Father Anselm arranges to have powerful Navajo headmen meet with Superintendent Perry at Fort Defiance, where Mr. Perry is urged to minimize criticism by working through the existing structure of headmen rather than being a law unto himself. Later the headmen, anxious to avoid trouble at the dance, meet at St. Michaels to plan strategy, and again Father Anselm plays a central part. At the dance, he is at the heart of the action. Not only are the Franciscans acknowledged as friends of the Navajo in Chee Dodge's memorable speech, but it is Father Anselm who preserves that speech for posterity, translating it from Navajo into German for *Sendbote* readers and into English for the Gallup newspaper. Much later, when those who openly challenged government authority have been apprehended, it is Father Anselm who writes the anonymous insider's account of the disturbance for local readers, and later he is again involved, this time in providing information for the ongoing federal review of Mr. Perry's role in the disturbance. In sum, the scope and variety of Father Anselm's contributions to the successful resolution of the "trouble of 1905," including his efforts to help administrators draw appropriate conclusions from the event, amount to a remarkable case study in what it means to "minister" among the people.]

❖

A few days before Mr. Reuben Perry, superintendent at Fort Defiance, was held up at Chin Lee, Arizona, I was at Tsehili to get some children for our school at St. Michaels. Charlie Mitchell, with whom I was staying, a former scout, policeman, and headman of the Navajo of that locality, told me some of the Navajo were becoming restive under the strict discipline of Mr. Perry. The Indians from the Black Mountains were fostering this restiveness by laughing at the others and calling them cowards; though they were not able to cope with the U.S. government, they could kill the few Americans among them, they said. I intended to warn Mr. Perry of impending trouble, but the occurrence at Chin Lee took place only about four days afterward.

I wish to add that, in 1892 at Round Rock, the Indians made an attack on their agent, Mr. Shipley, bruising him badly, breaking his nose, and so forth. He was rescued by soldiers under Lieutenant Brown and lost his position. Nothing was done to the aggressors; their leader was even made judge shortly afterward. Previous to the occurrence at Chin Lee, the Indians would often speak of the trouble at Round Rock as a precedent, to gain courage to treat Mr. Perry the same way, and that with impunity. All this shows that the occurrence at Chin Lee was the result of a widespread agitation in that locality and the adjoining Black Mountains, which had to be curbed if contagion was to be avoided and serious trouble to be averted. After the occurrence at Chin Lee, I told Mr. Perry, in my opinion, he either had to prosecute the matter or resign. His resignation, however, would constitute a disastrous precedent and would make the position of his successor untenable. I have had no reason to change my mind since then.[9]

A Journey to Tsehili

The Indian chief of Tselchidahaskani, Naakai Dinae'e, who lives about 100 miles from here over the mountains, sent me the news that he could not bring his children and the other students from that region to our school. I should have to come myself and pick them up. I told him he should bring the children by horse the one day's journey over the mountains to Tsehili, where I would wait for him on a certain day with our wagon.

Just as we were getting ready to set off early in the morning two days before the appointed time, I received news from Gallup. A very important letter that would arrive in Fort Defiance on that same day was supposed to be delivered immediately to Henry "Chee" Dodge, with whom we had planned to stay that night. Because of this, I had Frank Walker [Father Anselm's interpreter] go on alone, and several hours later I mounted an old nag that I had been given as a gift a short time before. I rode in a leisurely manner toward Fort Defiance, where I had to wait several more hours for the post.

About 4:20, I got the letter and started on my way to the mountain, 25 miles away, called *So Sella*, "Star," at whose feet was located the house of Chee Dodge. I had decided to reach Red Lake, where the crossing over Black Creek is sometimes dangerous at this time of year, before total darkness set in, and I covered the 15 miles in about two hours. So it was still light enough as I reached Black Creek to make out the crossing. But at full darkness I was still more than 10 miles from my destination and soon noticed that my horse was completely exhausted. If I didn't want to cover those 10 miles alone, I would have to walk my horse, which was, of course, very tedious. There was little danger of losing the road, but five miles from Red Lake I had to strain my eyes to keep from taking the wrong turn. Finally, I saw the dark outline of the mighty peak of *So Sella*. The road passed about a mile north of this "star," and I was supposed to turn left at a small cottage close to the road onto a little-used back road and stop directly at the "star." I hoped to be able to distinguish the cottage itself in the dark.

Long before I arrived there, I saw a blazing fire. At first I thought it must be at the house of Chee Dodge and was meant to serve as a guide for me. As I came nearer to it, I saw that the fire was neither at his house nor on the road, and so I decided it must be the campfire of an Indian herder, and I rode by. Although I nearly stared my eyes off, still I saw nothing of the small cottage near the road. After I had passed a hill on my right, I saw in front of me to the right, a substantial distance away, the outline of a mountain peak, narrowing at the top, named *Tsehitsossi*, or "Slender Mountain," by the Indians, and I knew then that I had ridden too far.

I dismounted, lit a match, and looked at my watch. It was a quarter to ten. I turned around to search for the small cottage again, in vain! Then I remembered that at the foot of the mountain on the north side, a path leads to Chee Dodge's house. If I went from the road directly toward the mountain, I would have to come upon the path. So I rode cross-country.

When I had ridden a good stretch, I dismounted, because from atop the horse it had become impossible to see the path. After I had burned several matches, I finally found the path and followed it. Soon I came upon a deep ditch. By the light of a match I climbed down, but when I reached the bottom I found that the mountain stream had deepened the ditch so much that it would take a real leap to get over it. It was easier for me to make the leap than to get my exhausted horse to jump, but finally he did. I continued to follow the path, which I noticed had not been used for a long time, until I seemed to see a dark area before me. I lit another match and stared in horror—I was at the edge of a dreadful drop-off. Just one step further and I would have fallen into the vast depths.

Now I had to return to the road, following the abyss. After I had used at least a dozen more matches, I found a possible crossing quite a ways further down,. Then I turned diagonally to the previously mentioned path. It was good that I was wearing a suit made out of corduroy à la Charles Lummis, otherwise the under-growth that I had to pass through would have ripped my clothing to pieces. Finally, I saw the white outline of a tent and the muted glow of a light and knew that I had arrived at my destination. I knew that I still had a ditch to cross and was careful to find the right crossing.

Both Henry Dodge and Frank Walker had decided that I had remained at Fort Defiance, since it was already so late. It was 11:00. While I ate a humble dinner, the

Indian entered who had started and maintained the aforementioned fire that was intended to have served as a guide for me. Unfortunately, he had made it too far from the road. Chee Dodge then told me that the path I had been seeking could not be used anymore because the unusually heavy rains of the previous year had made the ditch completely impassable.

The next morning I awoke with a headache. I had Frank Walker start out alone again. I wrote a letter to the trader Mr. J. B. Moore, whose trading post was about seven miles away, asking him for writing materials. After lunch the Indian whom Chee Dodge had sent returned with the writing materials so that I was able to write several letters for him.

At 3:00 in the afternoon I mounted a relative of the horse—called a burro—that Chee Dodge had loaned me. I had had my fill of the nag. I rode the 18 miles to Tsehili, the home of the Indian Charlie Mitchell, where Frank Walker had been waiting for me for three hours. I arrived there just as darkness was falling. Here I was well looked-after. I gave my burro to Frank Walker, entered the roomy stone house of the Navajo headman, and lay down to relax while the women prepared my dinner. Charlie Mitchell was sickly and in a grumpy mood. After dinner, while I tried to relax a little lying on my side, he began to complain about the Indian agent. Our school and my presence served as an invitation for him. He said, among other things, that although I also had my differences with some Navajo, we freely discussed our opinions with each other, expressed ourselves properly to each other, maybe even quarreled a bit, and then everything was right again and forgotten. But the Indian agent, he said, doesn't treat them right. He is too thoughtless, listens too readily to one's accusers, doesn't give an accused person enough opportunity to defend himself, throws too many Navajo in jail for nothing and for nothing again. The Indians were beginning to be disturbed and rebellious. Normally they wouldn't allow themselves to be treated this way. The Indians from the Black Mountains laughed at them and called them cowards. He thought that something was going to happen to the Indian agent. Even if the Navajo weren't in a position to defy the United States, they could still knock off the different traders. If it really came to an uprising, the Indian agent wouldn't be the only one to suffer, but also he himself and others who had always stood on the side of the different Indian agents and the whites as a whole. But he knew not to value what he and others had done for them—he had had enough of the whole affair.

I said very little to his remarks and pointed out to him I could do very little while there. I promised him, however, that if an opportunity presented itself to me in passing, that I would warn the Indian agent, without mentioning Charlie's name, about the feelings among the Indians toward him.

Later, Charlie Mitchell became a bit brighter, and with great enthusiam he told me about his people's conflicts with the Ute Indians and about their first meeting with Americans, the American soldiers under Colonel [James H.] Simpson in 1849. Until then his people had only known Mexicans. His grandfather had observed the American soldiers from behind bushes and told his amazed relatives how the Americans were clothed and armed; how they cooked water and then added something kind of black and then drank the brew; how they cooked and ate white worms (rice) —really! He had seen it with his own eyes! Then they had small, thin sticks of wood which they pushed backward with a striking motion and—*ko adae*—fire appeared! *E-Jei*! Those are people!

Two days later, Charlie Mitchell's son came from the government "farmer" of that region to Tsehili with the order that the Indians in the area were supposed to come to him and work for the wagons and agricultural tools that the agent had given them last year. Charlie said he was sick and couldn't work, and also that the other Indians shouldn't have to work for the tools. They had worked enough for that last year—if they were expected to work any more for the tools they had received, then the Indian agent could come and take his cursed tools back to Fort Defiance again! From all this I gathered that it was about over for the Indian agent, and I resolved to warn him at the next opportunity.

I was supposed to meet the Indian children from the other side of the mountain there at the home of my friend, Charlie Mitchell. When they did not arrive, I had to visit the homes of the Indians in the area, asking that they bring their children the next morning to Charlie Mitchell's house, from which I would then take them to our school. In this way the parents could spare themselves the effort of traveling to the school with their children. Unfortunately, one schoolgirl became sick and wasn't brought to school until a month later. Another student hardly seemed inclined to return to school. When his uncle and I began to urge him, tears came to his eyes; but before I reached the house of Charlie Mitchell, his uncle came riding up with him. His uncle told me that the boy was very sensitive because he had not been able to go to school earlier; when they had come to his region to gather students, his parents had hidden him so carefully in the mountains that even they couldn't find him afterward. Later that same day the boy asked me not to tell his sister that at first he had been unwilling to come.

The patriarch of that region, the father of two of our students and "uncle" of almost all the students of this region (his name is Adilhdilhi), was very sick. I had sent for the doctor for him, but the doctor was too busy to be able to come. I urged Adilhdilhi to come to the hospital in Fort Defiance, but he said he was too weak to withstand the journey.

With 10 students, boys and girls, we traveled in the afternoon of the following day to the home of Chee Dodge, where we stayed overnight. The mother of small Tarcissus had come with us and prepared the evening meal. The next day we arrived at St. Michaels. I rode in the wagon and let the biggest boys ride my nag, which had disappointed me so badly, all the way home, where I promptly gave him away—I had gotten him as a gift myself! I had found myself a fine saddle horse in Tsehilli and promised the owner, Tischinbida, à saddle for it, which would have cost the Indian $35 but which I obtained for $23. He is the best riding horse that I have ever had. I gave him the name "Nlhtschi," or "The Wind," a name he honestly earned.

An Embattled Indian Agent

While we were staying with Henry Dodge, Frank Walker told him of my discussion with Charlie Mitchell about the Indian agent, Mr. Perry, and the animosity of the Indians toward him. The more Chee Dodge thought about it, the more unsettled he became. Three days later he appeared here at St. Michaels to discuss the issue with me. He had understood from Frank Walker that Charlie Mitchell spoke as though representing the Navajo from the Black Mountains as well as his own people. Chee was especially bothered by the remark, "Even if they weren't in a position to defy the United States, they could still knock off the different traders." He thought Charlie Mitchell had spoken his own opinions in this matter, and wanted to share the whole affair with the Indian agent. However, I maintained that Charlie Mitchell had only repeated the statements of the Indians from the Black Mountains, and that his own opinions were very different from this. So it would be contradictory, I said, to create trouble for him because of what he had told me. In any case, I wanted to speak to him again first, and give him the opportunity to clarify himself.

At length Chee Dodge promised me, although with much reluctance, to let the subject rest until I had talked again with Charlie Mitchell. Chee said it would be far better for the both of us if we hadn't heard anything of this sort. Now if something should happen to the agent we would be held responsible, because we hadn't warned him. I responded that he was absolutely correct, but that the situation wasn't as bad as he believed; he was too pessimistic. In addition, I said I would warn the agent at the very next opportunity, but without naming names.

The next morning, Chee Dodge left St. Michaels to return home. When I was called to the door that afternoon, I was more than a little surprised to see Chee Dodge again, accompanied by the Indian agent. Chee laughed at me and asked me now who had been too pessimistic. His fears had partly come to pass, and therefore he had felt it his duty to tell the Indian agent about my conversation with Charlie Mitchell. Then the Indian agent told me about how some Indians had stopped him and violently forced him to guarantee immunity for a certain Indian. It vexed him that he had given in. However, when I freely explained to him the complaints and bitter sentiments against him among many of the Navajo and spoke my conviction that they would have killed him had he not given in, he finally began to understand and appreciate the danger he had faced.

Mr. Perry said he had never broken a promise given to the Indians, and he had to keep his word. However, he had made no promise not to punish the Indians for the violence they had done him and their assault on the government he represented. But he didn't know whether the Indians were shrewd enough to tell the difference. By no means did he want to stand before them as one who had broken his word. Because of this he talked about wanting to resign his office and so forth. I told him that if he let the matter pass, his authority was finished. He wouldn't have to wait long before the Indians stopped him again. And it would not help much for him to give up his position. That would simply place his replacement in a much more difficult position, for Mr. Perry would only have taught the Navajo how to settle matters with their agent.

In response, he explained to me that he didn't know what he should do. He only wanted to tell me that he had telegraphed the Indian inspector, Frank Mead, to meet him in Gallup as soon as possible. When he later learned that the inspector could not be reached, he returned here to St. Michaels with Chee Dodge to consult with me about the advisability of asking the government for military help. Luckily, I was 32 miles away on a sick call, for in such delicate situations I would rather not advise.

One of the biggest Indian dances, the so-called Yeibichai dance, was scheduled to take place very soon, at a place only about a mile distant from our mission. As Mr. Perry was afraid of serious unrest in connection with the dance, he telegraphed for military support.

What were the direct and indirect consequences of all this? Without doubt the Indian agent had made mistakes. When he arrived here a few years ago he was not familiar with the local customs and the character of the Navajo. In some cases he was somewhat hasty. He did not always have the patience to pay careful attention to the very circumstantial defense offered by Navajo accused of offenses. He also did not make distinctions between average Navajo and their headmen; the latter, if thought to be guilty of a crime, were thrown into prison just as fast as anyone else. When he was sent here, they had told him in Washington that his predecessor had been too soft. He was told that he needed to keep a tight rein on things; that was the main reason he had been given this post.

Despite some forgivable mistakes, Mr. Perry was, and is, one of the best agents the Navajo have ever had. He has surely not done wrong on purpose. However, in the last few years we have had an Indian inspector who boasted (falsely) that he stood directly under the president and who behaved himself like a pasha [a Turkish noble]. This honorable man, who, by the way, had to relinquish his office, had explained "human rights" to the Indians and given them to understand that they could do just about anything they wanted. This had its consequences.

Linni's Crime[10]

Chin Lee ("the mouth of the canyon") is a settlement of Navajo Indian farmers, situated, as its name implies, at the mouth of Cañon de Chelly, 75 miles northwest of Gallup. There are also 50 "hogans" scattered in the valley, forming a little village. Chin Lee is a central point from which over 1,000 Navajo get their supplies. In the settlement there is a trading post owned by Mr. Cousins, and a little Catholic mission building where Father Leopold, O.F.M., resides and holds services for the Indians. The U.S. government is represented by a farmer, Mr. Spicher, and a field matron, Miss Spear.

The Indians of Chin Lee have for years had an unenviable, though well-deserved reputation for meanness in the Navajo tribe. It is there that Mr. Reuben

Perry, the Indian agent, saw the first symptoms of rebellion among the heretofore peaceful and submissive Navajo.

In Chin Lee there lives an Indian by the name of Linni. Linni is a man of about 30 years of age. On October 17 Linni, some 20 miles southeast of Cañon de Chelly, was looking for his horse. A rope in his hands, he had for hours looked in vain for his pony. Finally, he passed a herd of sheep, and, approaching the herder, a young girl of 16 years, the daughter of Qastqin Yashe, he asked her whether she had seen his horse. The girl did not answer. He questioned her several times, without eliciting any answer. Angered by her contemptuous silence, he lassoed her. The girl fell down, holding tight to the rope. She cried and shrieked, trying to disentangle herself, protesting that she had not seen Linni's horse. "So now you cry," said he, "now you talk. Why didn't you answer me before? I meant no harm, and even now I do not intend to hurt you; the next time you will be more civil I hope. Now let this rope loose." But the girl was still holding tight to the rope. Linni went to the girl and untied her. He then left and hurried in search of his horse.

The girl soon after left her sheep, went to her hogan, and gave an account of the affair to her father. She told him that Linni had attempted to rape her. Qastqin Yazhe, justly incensed by that report, at once informed a Navajo policeman, asking him to have Linni prosecuted.

A few days later Linni, aware of the impending trouble, came to see Qastqin Yazhe and explained the matter to him. Qastqin Yazhe agreed not to prosecute him if he should give him a white horse. Linni consented to the bargain, and they shook hands. However, another policeman had gone to Fort Defiance and had reported to Mr. R. Perry, the Indian agent, that Linni had raped the daughter of Qastqin Yazhe.

Mr. Perry is a cultured gentleman of uncommon energy. During the two years he has held the position of Indian agent at Fort Defiance, he has been the avowed enemy of the whiskey traffic on the reservation and has fearlessly maintained order. On account of his unrelenting prosecution of evil, wherever encountered, Mr. Perry has caused dissatisfaction among the lower class of Navajo, who are only looking for an opportunity to visit him with their revenge. This class of Navajo even went so far as to state that though they could not hope to overcome the government, still they could kill the different traders and the few white men of the country. Mr. Perry, being told of the outrage at Chin Lee, detailed a policeman to summon Linni to appear before him.[11]

The Holdup at Chin Lee[12]

An Indian police officer named Qastquinsnaes . . . [had] accused Linni of the crime before the Indian agent. So Mr. Perry sent this same Qastquinsnaes to Chin Lee to arrest Linni and bring him to Fort Defiance. Arriving in Chin Lee, he met Linni and Dlad and two other Indians taking a sauna. He demanded that both Linni and Dlad follow him to Fort Defiance. He had hereby actually overstepped his instructions, because he was only supposed to arrest Linni. Dlad replied to him that he did not know of any crime he had committed and refused to follow him. Emboldened by Dlad's example, Linni also refused. He would not go to Fort Defiance. If the Indian agent wanted to see him, he should come to Chin Lee himself. Since Qastquinsnaes was not a match for all four, he went to the government farmer, Mr. Spicher, and told him the situation. Mr. Spicher sent the policeman back to the agent in Fort Defiance with a letter.

The four ended their sauna and then likewise went to Mr. Spicher to explain the event from their perspective. Linni laid special weight upon the fact that his case had been taken care of by a police officer, and as a result of that he was one horse poorer. Mr. Spicher had the police officer, who didn't live very far from there and wasn't supposed to ride to Fort Defiance until the next day, called back to him, tore up the letter that he had given him shortly before, and wrote a complete new letter to the Indian agent. Late the following evening—Chin Lee is 45 miles away from Fort Defiance—Qastquinsnaes reached the agency. The following morning, when he went to turn his letter over to the Indian agent, it turned out that the agent, without suspecting any of these occurrences, had left the agency and was himself on the way to Chin Lee. Qastquinsnaes hurried after him but could not catch him.

When, about noon, Mr. Perry arrived at the mountains and stopped at the trading post of his former interpreter, Nelson Gorman, the trader told him that Linni and Dlad had resisted the arrest, that they had moved with some other Indians back into Cañon de Chelly and had barricaded themselves there, determined to resist. Since the Indians seemed to have limited themselves to the defensive, Mr. Perry, without further concern, continued toward Chin Lee, where he wished to visit the government farmer and field manager, see the new road being constructed, and inspect the fields of the Indians. That evening he reached Chin Lee and went to the house of Mr. Spicher, who explained the situation to him. As overkill, the police officer, Qastquinsnaes, soon came riding up with his letter.

The news that the Indian agent had arrived in Chin Lee spread like wildfire among the Indians. Linni, Dlad, and their gang naturally assumed that the police officer had reported to Mr. Perry in Fort Defiance and that the agent had come for them. They now held a council. At this meeting a certain chief from the Black Mountains, named Doyaltqihi, or "One Who Does Not Speak," took part. In spite of his peculiar name, which hardly seemed to fit him, he incited the Indians to oppose the Indian agent. He himself had had a difference with the agent of the Moqui Indians not too long ago and had forced him to guarantee immunity. He advised them that they should just boldly do the same. . . .

Next morning when the Indian agent was about ready to go to inspect the fields of the Indians and to visit a few headmen, he noticed a large crowd of Indians in front of the house. He went out to them, to be confronted by Linni, Dlad, and their gang. Linni asked Mr. Perry to investigate and decide on his case here and now, without any further ado. Mr. Perry, not wanting to let an accused Indian at the head of a gang of followers give him orders, answered that he had not come to Chin Lee because of Linni. He had other business to attend to here and had no time now for Linni's case. Linni would have to come to Fort Defiance. Linni answered that he did not agree that he should have to make the long journey to Fort Defiance, since both he and the agent were right here. Furthermore, he was not guilty of the crime for which he was accused. Mr. Perry answered that all of that might be true, but Linni had resisted his police officer a few days ago and had refused the officer's demand that Linni accompany him. And now Mr. Perry insisted that Linni come to Fort Defiance where the agent would investigate and decide on his case. With that, Mr. Perry turned around and accompanied Mr. Spicher to the stable to harness his team.

In the meantime, the Indians finalized their plans for the holdup. An Indian by the name of Winslow was to hold the mules, while Dlad was to capture Mr. Perry. In case Mr. Perry should offer armed resistance, they were determined to kill him and to burn down the government building and the store.

By this time the team was hitched up, and Mr. Perry jumped into the buggy, ready to leave. The mules were frisky and impatient. . . . [It seemed that Mr. Perry would barely be able to hold them while the gate was being opened. Then] the Indians surrounded the buggy. Linni and his three friends approached him.

"We wish to be judged now," said Dlad. "No," retorted Mr. Perry, "you must come to the Fort." "Come to the Fort?" said Dlad, "but I have no horse and no time to spare; you are here, you can settle the case at once; I am not guilty of any offense." "It may be so," said Mr. Perry, "but you resisted arrest and must come to the Fort."

The agent would not accede to their wishes. He knew, if he would agree to judge the case there, other Indians would also resist arrest, and it would be impossible for him to perform his duties as an agent in the reservation. Mr. Perry could hardly hold his mules any longer. Suddenly, Linni jumped to the mules' heads, and held them. . . . [It was to have been the Indian, Winslow, who did it, but he] weakened at the last moment. The agent thought that perhaps his motive was to quiet and subdue them, but soon he perceived, by the laugh and the actions of the mob, that they meant to hold him up. He then gave orders to unhitch the mules and jumped out of the buggy. The Indians gave free vent to their anger in approaching him. Seeing his policeman standing near him with his six-shooter in his scabbard, Mr. Perry's first impulse was to jerk it out to defend himself. He made a motion toward it, but realizing that, by doing so, a bloody conflict would become inevitable, he desisted.[13]

At the same moment, the Indian Dlad grabbed his wrists. Mr. Perry tried to free himself by a sudden turn, whereby he discovered that any attempt at escape was useless against the unusual strength of the Indian. His police officer stood inactive next to him, for an Indian named Dolzhi . . . had threatened to kill him if he made any effort to help the agent. Other than that, Mr. Spicher was present, but he was a peace-loving Quaker without weapons. The owner of the trading post, Mr. Cousins, who had once served in the Marines and the Army, also was present, and it was to him that Mr. Perry directed the question of whether it would be possible to overpower the Indians. "Don't even think of it," Mr. Cousins replied. "These guys are all armed."

Mr. Cousins functioned as interpreter for the agent, who now asked the Indian Dlad how long he planned to hold him. "Until you ensure immunity or starve," was the curt answer. "I have seen," he continued, "how you grabbed for the six-shooter of the police officer. It is good that you didn't reach it; otherwise you wouldn't be among the living anymore, and this building would be in flames. I have no parents, no friends, no sheep, no possessions—life is worth little to me. The winter is cold everywhere, and the summer is hot everywhere—it doesn't matter much to me where I am. That is why I do this. You are, by the way, completely in our power." Some Indians maintain that it was not starvation that confronted Mr. Perry, but bloody murder, for they threatened to kill him if he did not pardon them, although the interpreter failed to interpret this to Mr. Perry at the time.

Surrounded by hostile Indians who surely could shoot down any messenger whom he might send for help, and who very likely would kill him should he not give in, Mr. Perry yielded to their demands and promised Linni that he would not be bothered further for the crime blamed on him, nor for the opposition to the police officer. After that Dlad released him, and the Indians scattered. Mr. Perry harnessed his donkeys again and traveled to our holy Father Leopold, in whose company he completed the intended inspections. The next day Mr. Perry returned to Fort Defiance. He was alone, and as he first traveled along the edge of Cañon de Chelly he was overcome by the fear that the Indians were lying in wait for him and would shoot him from their hiding places. However, he arrived at home without any incident.

He realized that he would have to teach these Indians a lesson or give up his office. There was not much he could do about his pair of somewhat unreliable police officers. . . .

Shortly after Mr. Perry requested military support, a certain Mr. Lieutenant [J. H. Lewis], whose name I would rather not make known, was sent on reconnaissance from Fort Wingate, New Mexico, 45 miles from here, to investigate the matter. Since this assignment was made on the evening before a so-called "practice march," he took a wagon of provisions and 13 soldiers with him to Fort Defiance. I happened to be there when they arrived. Their appearance aroused more than a little stir among the whites as well as the Indians. . . . I encountered the lieutenant in the office of Mr. Perry and was introduced to him. He had heard about our missions through the Reverend Father Dumarest[14] and asked about their location. I gave him directions, invited him to come for a visit, and rode home.

The next afternoon, the postal worker told me that soldiers were on their way here. About 11:00 the lieutenant arrived in the company of his Indian scouts. Chee Dodge was present at the time and overheard our conversation. The lieutenant immediately asked me what I knew about the whole situation. When I had finished my explanation, he wanted to know whether I really feared unrest at the forthcoming dance to be held near our mission. I told him that recently at a similar dance about 30 miles from here, a few Indians had gotten drunk in order to cause a riot and to get their courage up so as eventually to resist arrest. I said that I expected a large number of Indians at the dance. If they were successful in obtaining alcohol, then there would probably be some disturbance. However, I did not fear any serious unrest. Chee Dodge confirmed my statements.

In response the lieutenant told us how it was: nothing but rumor and conjecture. He couldn't learn anything for certain anywhere. He only had a handful of soldiers and provisions for only six days. He couldn't go to Chin Lee with that. If he were supposed to arrest the Indians, he would have to have more soldiers and more provisions. If he were to go there, the Indians would all flee, and then he would have to camp on their lands. He had no orders from the War Department to pursue and arrest the Indians. If he were to do it anyway, and if he were captured and his people had to shoot a few Indians in the process, or if one or the other of his soldiers were shot, then he would lose his rank and position.

A few years ago, the Ute Indians had murdered their agent. He and his regiment had been assigned to apprehend the guilty Indians. He followed them for over 80 miles. Every night the Indians snuck up on his camp and fired on them. In pure self-defense his soldiers had to return fire and thereby shot a few Indians. Finally, he went after the Indians personally, accompanied by a few soldiers, and eventually captured them. He was quite impressed with his heroic deed, the miracle he had performed, and confidently awaited praise and reward. Instead the newspapers in the East attacked, scolded, and disparaged him, calling him a monster who unmercifully shot down innocent Indians with their wives and children. And all this because the impossible had been expected of him—to arrest the guilty Indians without bloodshed.

He had learned a good lesson from the experience. Without explicit orders from the War Department he would do nothing. If Mr. Perry wasn't able to arrest the lads with the help of the police, then the Territorial authority was also at his service. If they didn't have any success, then there was always still time to call for military help. In Gallup the Indians also caused a small disturbance here and there. But the Territorial authority had always been able to settle with them without the help of the military. Anyway, he was returning to Fort Wingate with his soldiers. After a few friendly words, he said goodbye.

After the lieutenant left us, Chee Dodge was quiet. It appeared that he was thinking about the situation. Finally, he said it seemed that the lieutenant had not come to carry out orders, but rather to share his preconceived opinions with us. He had only asked a few questions and then, almost without waiting for answers, had carried on the conversation by himself. His report to Washington would surely come out unfavorably. So, he suggested, someone who had no direct interest in the whole affair should send a counterreport to Washington to work against the report from the lieutenant. Naturally, he had me in mind for this and thought that we should stand by the agent. It would work for our good if Mr. Perry's authority were upheld. The agent must demonstrate to the Indians that the government and the army stood behind him and upheld his honor; otherwise the orderly relations on this reservation would be at an end; otherwise everything would be in an uproar. I told Chee Dodge that he was absolutely right, but that I couldn't just agree to write a counterreport, at least not until I had considered it awhile and discussed it with the Indian agent.

That afternoon two headmen arrived, Bilihizhini, that is, Black Horse, who had led the attack on the Indian agent, Shipley, at Round Rock, and Tqayoni, the headman of Ganado, who had just served a sentence for drunkenness at Fort Defiance. They asked if they could stay with us until the dance. We soon learned that both were very bitter against the Indian agent. Chee Dodge came to me late that evening and told me he had set both of them straight and even persuaded them to speak about propriety and order at the coming dance. They were especially incensed that the agent didn't seem to care about the headmen anymore and almost totally ignored them. As they had complained bitterly about that, Chee Dodge had challenged them to go with him to see the agent the next day, to talk with him about the problem. They had immediately agreed to do this, provided that I would accompany them.

The next morning we four, with Frank Walker, rode to Fort Defiance. When we arrived, I was more than a little surprised to learn that the agent was awaiting two companies of soldiers, and I shared with him our discussion with the lieutenant. The agent was thunderstruck. That morning the lieutenant had assured him of exactly the opposite; specifically, he had promised to support the sending of two companies of soldiers, one to Fort Defiance and the other to Chin Lee. He had even talked about sending one company on a forced march directly from Fort Wingate over the mountains to Chin Lee in order to surprise the Indians who had participated in the holdup and, if possible, to capture them. It seemed that the lieutenant must have lied to one of us—but which one? What purpose could he have had to keep me so in the dark? In the end, Mr. Perry thought he had not meant to deceive me but rather Chee Dodge, who had been present and whom, as a half-blood Indian, the lieutenant did not trust. I, however, did not believe that and told Mr. Perry that if that were the case, then the lieutenant must be a master of deception. Mr. Perry decided to telegraph Washington that very evening to get a copy of the report that the lieutenant had, without a doubt, sent to the War Department in Washington. That would clear up the issue. By the way, it turned out that Mr. "Annoying???" [the lieutenant] had not kept me, but rather Mr. Perry, in the dark.

In order to prepare him a bit, I now told the agent why Chee Dodge and the two chiefs had come, and what questions they had hoped to ask him. He immediately had them called in, along with Chief Velo from Round Rock, Chee Dodge, and Frank Walker. Mr. Perry greeted them all in a friendly manner and asked what they desired. The headman Tqayoni told him they had come to hear from his own mouth what he thought about the headmen of the Navajo. Mr. Perry answered that good chiefs who set a good example for the other Indians, who don't drink alcohol, who support the government, and who are friends of the Indian schools are the best that there could be on an Indian reservation. As Mr. Perry mentioned drinking alcohol, Tqayoni closed his mouth in a dark smile and became as red as a crab, because Mr. Perry had, as mentioned, recently slapped him in prison for drunkenness. Mr. Perry noticed his embarrassment and said that he himself was the chief here in Fort Defiance for the whites and the reds. Now, if he were to get drunk and lie drunken in the gutter, what would the consequences be? Soon all would follow his example. Some of his white employees already tended toward such things. This remark was rewarded with resounding laughter. It seemed to do the Indians good to hear from the mouth of their agent that even his white employees were not enemies of the "dark water."

Tqayoni then began to let Mr. Perry see himself as the Navajo saw him, and to give him some good instruction. He said that in earlier years the Indian agent had often called the headmen together and counseled with them about important issues. Formerly, the headmen also had possessed the authority to deal with the smaller issues themselves. Lately people brought all cases to the agent. His precious time, that he could and should better use for the good of all the Navajo, was being taken up with trifles. By doing this the agent also invited all the malice onto himself, because every judgment increased the enmity against him. He hadn't been with the Navajo very long yet, and he didn't know them and wasn't comfortable with their customs and practices, just as he didn't know all the different paths that crossed back and forth on the reservation. If, for example, he followed a specific path, everything went well until another path split off from that one. Then he wouldn't know which path he should follow. On the other hand, they, the headmen, had been born here. They knew all the paths and ways and were ready to show them to him and to support him with counsel and in deed, if he would only give them the opportunity. If any dispute or any misunderstanding arose, if any law were broken, the agent should first speak with the local headman, who was intimately acquainted with the people and their relationships, before making a judgment.

Tqayoni continued in this manner for over an hour, and Mr. Perry listened to him patiently. Among other things, he answered that indeed he had only called the headmen together for a general council one time, but he had often counseled with individual headmen and was always ready to hear their opinions, their suggestions, and their counsel. Mr. Perry told them that he would be pleased to have the headmen judge the smaller issues themselves, so that he wouldn't always be bothered by trifles. However, it was necessary that the bigger crimes must still be brought before him.

The headmen left pacified. It was surely very satisfying for Tqayoni to be able to lecture the agent in this way, and it must have been more than a little difficult for Mr. Perry to listen to him quietly, especially when you remember that he had made Tqayoni "do time" shortly before. By the way, the comments of the headmen contained much truth and many suggestions worthy of Mr. Perry's consideration.

Several days before the Yeibichai dance, groups of Indians were already arriving from every direction. This was somewhat convenient. Normally they would have begun to gather the afternoon or evening before the night of the dance. Their early arrival showed that they had an unusual interest in this dance, that they felt the need to talk about recent events, and that an unusually large number of Indians would come to the dance.

I received inquiries from Gallup as to whether it would be advisable, under these circumstances, for people to attend the dance. My answer was that whatever others might say and fear, I did not believe that there were grounds for any type of worry.

The dance took place during the night of November 15–16, 1905. On November 15, an Indian scout came from Fort Wingate with a letter from the lieutenant. He requested that I inform him if any type of unrest should take place. Shortly thereafter, he called from Gallup by telephone to ask if I had received his letter and whether I feared real unrest. I told him that an amazingly large number of Indians were already present, and that if they were provided with "dark water," then the dance would probably not be completed without some sort of disturbance. However, serious trouble was out of the question.

The same lieutenant carelessly showed his cards on that very day in Gallup. In fact, he had opposed sending troops to the dance because real unrest was exactly what he desired. He expected that the Indians would commit some deadly deeds and that this would give him the opportunity to start an Indian war and earn himself some war decorations. However, Mr. Perry, the Indian agent, wanted to avoid a campaign against the Indians and read the riot act to the lieutenant with so much energy that Troop K of the 5th Calvary, under Captain Willard and Lieutenant Cooly, started on their way to Fort Defiance that very day. They arrived on the following day, the day after the dance.

Even before the dance began, another Indian scout came to me with a letter from the commander himself in Fort Wingate, Colonel George H. Paddock of the 5th Cavalry. The letter stated: "The carrier of this letter, an Indian scout in the service of the United States, has orders to report to you and bring me any type of message that you feel is appropriate to send about the state of things with your mission in relation to the danger of an Indian uprising."

The next morning I sent Colonel Paddock the following somewhat humorous letter by his scout:

> I received your letter, and in response to it I must report that a great number of Indians, over 2,000, were present at the dance; but all of them behaved themselves. Even though alcoholic drinks were available, the consequences of this were not noticeable. Henry Dodge gave a speech, and a number of the most influential Indian chiefs, inspired by Henry Dodge, gave speeches, during which they said Mr. Perry, your agent, was in the right, and they decidedly condemned the Chin Lee incident. With regards to your two Indian scouts, I must say, that they deserve a gold medal as the best dancers in the United States army. Their good dancing was extremely calming because the Indians liked it so much and it quieted the anger of the Navajo war gods.

Instead of inciting unrest, the dance gave Chee Dodge and other well-meaning headmen the opportunity to straighten out the other Indians' heads through their speeches. Chee Dodge, Black Horse, Charlie Mitchell, Tqayoni, Qastqin Yazhe, and other prominent men addressed the peaceful crowd. Chee Dodge had the main address. He is a half-blood Indian; his mother was a Navajo, his father a Mexican who was taken prisoner by the Navajo in one of their raids and was adopted by the tribe. He is the wealthiest and most influential man of the tribe, the best interpreter, and the most eloquent speaker. I cannot help but include his entire speech here to give my esteemed readers an idea of how Indians think and speak, although his marvelous Navajo speech cannot be judged by its English version. It was after midnight when I, along with over 2,000 Indians, listened to this speech.[15]

The Oration of Henry Dodge[16]

It is my intention to say a few words to you tonight. I caught a cold a few days ago, but, as you know, old people always claim that when they are to make a speech.

Black Horse and several of the headmen have made speeches to you tonight, but their speeches were hardly strong enough; for that reason I have a few words to say to you.

One thing I wish you to bear in mind is that the law forbidding you to drink whiskey does not come from the agent nor from any of the headmen; it is a law passed by Congress and approved by the president of the United States. The president does not want you to drink whiskey because it would destroy you. If whiskey drinking were allowed, how many of you would be drunk tonight? You would be lying on the road, in the way of the dancers, drunk, rowing, cursing, and fighting. The president does not want you to do that.

There are some nice and good white people in this camp tonight. They would not be here if you were drunk; neither would any self-respecting Navajo have come to the dance in that case; only drunkards and bums would be here.

You must remember that the president does not mean to keep you from drinking for the purpose of protecting the white people only. No! He means to protect your tribe, every decent Navajo, your own old people and children.

Many of you live off the reservation; the president has given you a long rope so you may graze wherever you please. If a man has a good horse and pickets him out, he gives him a long rope in good grass and lets him graze as far as he can; but if he has a mean horse, he gives him a short rope with his head tied up close to a post so he can get but little feed. The president has given you a long rope. Some of you have a very long rope; you live very far from the reservation. Others who live nearer the reservation have a shorter rope, and those who live on the reservation have a still shorter rope; but the president has a rope on every one of you, and if you do not appreciate the good treatment you are given, if you try to make trouble, he will pull on all the ropes and draw you fellows all together to a tight place. Remember that!

You have many sheep and cattle and horses; the agent does not own them, but you own them, and if you bring trouble on yourselves you will lose your stock, you will be afoot, you will be nothing, you will be wiped out, and the few that will be left will be given a small tract of land, and will be guarded by troops, and everybody will laugh at you and say: "See what a large tribe this was, and this is all that is left of them!"

When the president appoints an agent for you he is going to protect him, and you must not think that you may abuse this agent, take a horsewhip and whip him, or choke him and treat him as mean as you please without the president paying any attention to it. If the president appoints an agent for you, and you disobey that agent's orders, you disobey the president's orders whom he represents. The president is over all the Indians; he is like the sun up in the sky; he watches all the Indians and when they disobey his orders, he sends his troops there to punish them and to make them behave themselves. All the Indian agents appointed for the Indians represent the president; and when you talk mean about the agent and treat him roughly, you should bear in mind that you are treating the president that way. The president of the United States controls a big nation; whenever he sees that his children need punishment, he is going to give it to them; when he makes up his mind that you are troublesome, nobody is going to change his mind. He is the chief of the United States, and when the people do not behave themselves, he is going to treat them as enemies; but when they obey his orders, he will say: "These are my friends and I will look after them and do what I can to assist them."

I understand that Indian traders, some of them on the reservation, and some of them off the reservation, have been saying to you that your present agent is no good. Now I want you to understand that when any white people make such remarks about the agent, they have some personal feeling against him, and they are not thinking of you at all, are not considering at all what is good for you or the tribe. I want you to tell those white people, and I want you to tell them for me, that they are lying to you. The agent is the best friend you have; your protection lies with him, with him and the president of the United States.

Some of you think you may abuse the agent and the president will say: "Oh, well, the agent is no good; I will transfer him and put another man here." The president won't do anything of the kind. When the president knows that he has a good man for you, he is going to stand by him. The president is not going to change any agent to please you. If you get on a drunk, if you commit depredation, or do anything of that kind, and the agent punishes you, the president will certainly not change the agent, but will sustain him against all the troublesome people throughout the United States.

As far as I can see the present agent is the best agent you have ever had: looking after your wants, trying to help you, and to put you in better shape. I do not say this because he has helped me; he has not helped me any; I am not looking for that. I am able to take care of myself; but I know that the agent is trying to help you and to put you in better condition.

These priests here at St. Michaels are also good friends of yours, the same as the agent. They are trying to assist you and to protect you.

I am giving you this advice because I have a warm feeling for you in my heart. I have always had a warm feeling for you and would hate to see you take the wrong view of things, get wrong ideas into your heads, and get into trouble for which I know you would get a good licking. I know that you have been advancing for a good many years. I want you to keep on advancing; I don't want you to fall back; I don't want the old troublesome times to return. If I did not have any warm feeling for you I would keep my mouth shut and let you get into deep trouble; but I think too much of you to keep quiet and not give you any good advice.

(Some of the old people said: "That is good! What Chee tells us is bound to be true.")

Those who are trying to make trouble, and those who support them, will not only get in trouble themselves, but will draw you all into trouble, and you should stop them and help punish them. They are nothing but loafers; they have nothing and look upon you and say: "There is a man who has a nice looking wife; there is a man who has a big band of sheep and cattle; now we are going to start trouble and draw that Indian into it so he will lose everything and we will be the gainers." We don't want any such people among us, and you ought to pitch in and help the government to bring them to justice. I don't care whether these people are going to make trouble for me on account of what I am saying here tonight, or not; I want them to hear it.

The government does not want to have any murder or any rape committed among you, nor that you should become drunkards. I am well pleased to see so many people here tonight, to see no drunkenness among you, and to see you all behaving so nicely. That shows that you have self-respect and some respect for these headmen, and I shall report this to the agent tomorrow morning.

In conclusion, I must tell you something for the first time. When the great chief, Manuelito, was still among the living, he told me he did not want his people to be destroyed and asked me to promise him that I would always advise the tribe the right way, and help them along. He said he knew I was the man who could do it. I gave him my promise. Now this chief has been dead several years, but I always remember the promise I gave him. For that reason I always try to advise you the right way. Though I never mentioned this before, I thought it advisable to mention it tonight so you would know why I am taking so much interest in you.

A Peaceful Resolution

Chee Dodge's noble speech, along with those of the other chiefs, undoubtedly had a good influence on the entire tribe. When the K Troop of the 5th Cavalry Regiment under Captain Willard and Lieutenant Cooly arrived in Fort Defiance on November 16, and Captain Willard and the Indian agent held a council with the headmen where Chee Dodge and Frank Walker functioned as interpreters, they found the headmen inclined to be helpful in the arrest of the Indians.

Three headmen—the silversmith from Crystal, Beshlagai Ilinni Altsossigi; Velo from Round Rock; and Attsidi Yazhe-ni' Biye from Manuelito Springs—were sent to Chin Lee to explain how things stood to the Indians there, and if possible to bring the wrongdoers to Fort Defiance. The silversmith, Beshlagai Ilinni Altsossigi, a very intelligent and cunning Indian, well known for his caustic remarks and his brutal openness, carried out his duty to "explain" the affair with no little distinction. No better calling could have been found for him, since most of the wrongdoers belonged to the tribe of Tqachini, of which this silversmith is the head. Although the Indians encouraged each other to hold out to the end, two of them, Linni and Winslow, got weak in the knees and turned themselves in to Chief Velo, who brought them to Fort Defiance on November 19. Winslow is the Indian who held the mule of the agent; when he lost his courage at the decisive moment, Linni joined him. Linni is the Indian accused of attempted rape—a crime to which he pleaded guilty when he reached Fort Defiance.

The Indian Dlad, who had grabbed the Indian agent and thereby shown his unusual physical strength, disappeared mysteriously with his two brothers, Ts'ossini 'Bihe' and Dinelgai. Different rumors surfaced that they had escaped to the Black Mountains; they had turned themselves in to Mr. Lemmon at Keam's Canyon; or they were camping at Antelope Springs and had gone the direction of the Little Colorado River. In fact, the whole time they were staying in the area of Chin Lee and Cañon de Chelly—an area that is as good as any other to hide out in, especially along the northern edge of the canyon.

Captain Willard then requested the headmen from Chin Lee and the surrounding region to come to Fort Defiance. All came except Qastqin Yazhe, who claimed he couldn't find his horse. On November 28, Captain Willard sent his first sergeant with nine soldiers over the mountains during a heavy snowstorm to "help" the chief find his horse and come to Fort Defiance—an order that they promptly carried out, returning the very next day to Fort Defiance. Along with Qastqin Yazhe, they also brought the Indian Dolzhi, who had threatened to kill the police officer Qastquinsnaes if he should attempt to protect the Indian agent. It was no small deed for the soldiers to ride 90 miles in two days during such weather. When the headman Qastqin Yazhe was brought to Fort Defiance, having been under military watch for several days, he was tired and anxious to demonstrate his friendship to the government.

Captain Willard forcefully reminded him and the other headmen of their treaty with the United States where they promised to obey their agent and to be helpful to him in bringing criminals to justice. In response, the headmen Qastqin Yahze, Qastqin Dilaghushi, Qastqinltsoi, and Nashgalli declared themselves ready to bring the criminals to Fort Defiance in 50 days by signing their names in red ink (they had asked for 40 days, but the captain gave them 50). If they didn't catch criminals in 50 days, they said they were ready to give themselves up to be imprisoned in their stead. The chiefs Beshlagai (the silversmith), Velo, and Attsidi Yazhe-ni'Biye gave their written promise to help the others. The latter of these chiefs—a very intelligent, honest, and influential Indian from Manuelito Springs, stepson of the late famous war chief, Manuelito—was named headman of Chin Lee and the surrounding region seven months later.

A few days later, Captain Willard, Lieutenant Cooly, and the Indian agent, Mr. Reuben Perry, paid us a visit and spent the night here. That same evening, they received the news that the Indians were already on their way to Fort Defiance. As soon as Dlad and his followers heard that all the headmen with a great entourage were after them, they left their hideout and went to the Tunicha Mountains, six miles northwest of Crystal, where they gave themselves up to the silversmith, Beshlagai Ilinni Altsossigi, the head of their tribe. He brought them—Dlad, Ts'ossini 'Biye', and Dinelgai—to Fort Defiance on December 7, 1905.

At the trial that followed, they claimed the mitigating circumstance that a certain chief from the Black Mountains, named Doyaltqihi, or "One Who Doesn't Speak," had incited them to resist the agent. He had had a disagreement with the agent of the Moqui Indians, Mr. Burton, a few years ago and had forced the agent to guarantee that Doyaltqihi would not be prosecuted. He urged that they should just boldly do the same, and so on.

Captain Willard immediately sent several headmen to the Black Mountains to bring in Doyaltqihi. When they brought him to Fort Defiance, at first he denied everything. However, when he was brought before the rest of the Indians, he could not withstand their accusations and admitted his guilt. Without a doubt he really exaggerated things to the Indians in that meeting at Chin Lee. He really had held up Mr. Burton; but as I knew Mr. Burton, I couldn't believe that he had ignored such treatment, and I said so in an article that I was writing at the time for the Gallup newspaper. Soon thereafter, Mr. Burton answered in a letter to this newspaper, in which he forcefully denied that he had been held up by Doyaltqihi or any other Indian. Actually, an Indian who belonged to the tribe of Doyaltqihi had resisted arrest—but Mr. Burton had sent more police after him and apprehended him.

The Indian Department in Washington sentenced the Indians to one to two years in prison in the federal prison on the island of Alcatraz in San Francisco Bay. Lieutenant Lewis accompanied them there. It is strange that the earthquake in San Francisco was hardly noticed on this nearby island. The residents could see the destruction that the earthquake had caused; they could see the fires burning; but they only learned the cause of the destruction that evening when a boat from Alcatraz went over to San Francisco.

A few months ago the Indian Rights Association stuck their noses into the affair, and their representative, the Protestant preacher [William R.] Johnston, also visited me to preach about the guilt or lack of guilt of these Indians. His investigation didn't change anything.

So this episode was brought to a peaceful conclusion. Not only the behavior of the Indian agent and Captain Willard but also that of the Navajo headmen earned recognition for all of them. The situation helped the Navajo, especially the younger generation, to see where insubordination leads. It was a good, almost forgotten lesson that Captain Willard and the Indian agent taught them, perhaps with force but also with much tact.

[In August 1906, because of their "waning health" at Alcatraz, the prisoners were transferred closer to home to Fort Huachuca, Arizona. By June 1907, all had been released.[17]]

Notes

1. Unless noted otherwise, the text is from Anselm Weber, FMN 33 (March, May–September 1906): 222–26, 411–15, 510–14, 596–601, 704–9, and 804–8. Translated by Marie Bradshaw Durrant.

2. Anselm Weber, "The Navajo Indian Trouble of 1905," Anselm Weber to William Ketcham, 15 March 1907. FAC Box DEC.332, Anselm Weber letters.

3. George J. Juillard, "Agent's Coolness Prevented Bloody Indian Outbreak." *Albuquerque Morning Journal*, 21 November 1905, 6; Anselm Weber, "Wise Words Were

These," and "How It All Happened," *McKinley County Republican*, 16 December 1905, 1. None of these articles identify the correspondent, but Father Anselm does so in "The Navajo Indian Trouble of 1905."

4. Robert L. Wilken, *Anselm Weber, O.F.M.: Missionary to the Navaho 1898–1921* (Milwaukee, Wisc.: Bruce, 1955), 173.

5. Weber, "Wise Words."

6. "Navajo Troubles," *McKinley County Republican*, 18 November 1905, 1.

7. "Hostiles Have Surrendered," *McKinley County Republican*, 2 December 1905, 1.

8. Wilken, *Anselm Weber*, 174–75.

9. The above introductory paragraphs are from Father Anselm's memo to Father Ketcham, "The Navajo Trouble of 1905."

10. From Juillard, "Agent's Coolness."

11. The above paragraph is from Juillard, "Agent's Coolness."

12. Here we resume Father Anselm's narrative from *Sendbote*.

13. The preceding four paragraphs are from Juillard, "Agent's Coolness."

14. Father Michael Dumarest, serving under Father Juillard in the Gallup parish.

15. This paragraph combines portions of Father Anselm's introduction to Chee Dodge's speech from the *Sendbote* article with several sentences from Weber, "Wise Words."

16. The text of Chee Dodge's speech, along with Father Anselm's introductory paragraph, are from Weber, "Wise Words." Slight corrections were made by reference to Father Anselm's typescript copy, an enclosure accompanying Weber, "The Navajo Trouble of 1905."

17. For an alternative account of the holdup at Chin Lee and its aftermath, one that blames the entire confrontation provoked by the incident on the egoism of the Navajo agent Reuben Perry, see Daniel Holmes Mitchell, "An Indian Trader's Plea for Justice, 1906," *New Mexico Historical Review* 47 (July 1972): 239–56.

16

The Case of Des Chee Nee[1]

Des Chee Nee, Anselm Weber, O.F.M., and Others

[The present chapter consists of correspondence, mostly one-way, between Des Chee Nee in the New Mexico Territorial Prison and Father Anselm Weber at St. Michaels. The case is an interesting contrast to that of Linni and the holdup at Chin Lee. In that case, Father Anselm's efforts contributed to the maintenance of federal judicial authority on the reservation. The holdup at Chin Lee posed a challenge to that system, and successful intervention consisted of shoring up the legitimacy of the system, and the authority of the agent, while avoiding armed conflict. In the case of Des Chee Nee, Father Anselm's task is to rescue a Navajo man from the inappropriate or erroneous judgment delivered by another branch of government, the territorial judicial system. Father Anselm's efforts to win a pardon for Des Chee Nee do not challenge that system as a whole, but rather suggest a correctable malfunction, a mistake in its otherwise proper operation.

Des Chee Nee's letters offer chilling insight into the vulnerability of tribal people to the imposition of alien systems of social control, systems that they do not understand and with which they cannot cope. Suddenly, they discover that the rules of right and wrong have changed, the stakes are higher, and the old ways of "making things right" no longer work. Coldly, systematically, the alien system chews them up.

The file on Des Chee Nee at Franciscan Archives Cincinnati contains only two examples of Father Anselm's part of the exchange, one his initial request for information to help him decide whether he would "take the case," the other his commentary on the response by the San Juan County prosecutor to his request for a copy of the proceedings of the hearing where Des Chee Nee had supposedly made his guilty plea. What we do have is the story from Des Chee Nee's perspective, as revealed in his appeals for help from within the territorial prison, supplemented by notes and advice to Father Anselm from the anonymous prison helper who writes Des Chee Nee's letters for him, for the prisoner could neither read nor write.

Des Chee Nee's letters, handwritten in pencil by the anonymous prison worker, prompt an exception to the minimal editing rule applied to correspondence quoted or reprinted in this book. Inasmuch as Des Chee Nee's words, expressed in Navajo, were translated, written, and punctuated by that amanuensis—since his words as we have them are expressed in language other than his own, by someone other than himself—it seems no serious distortion of his intent to convey his words in format less distracting to the contemporary reader. Accordingly, I have "smoothed" the text sparingly, and adjusted some of the punctuation, capitalization, and spelling.

To facilitate the flow of the text, we present only the main body of each letter, including salutation and closing, along with an introductory heading that lists the date, addressee, and writer. Des Chee Nee's first cry for help is addressed to the Indian Navajo Red, in care of the trader Charles Day. The next is to Charles Day himself. It is revealing that Charles Day, faced with an apparent miscarriage of justice involving a Navajo, passes the problem on to Father Anselm. By now, with eight years of experience in Navajo country, Father Anselm has acquired the reputation of "fixer." His sympathies with the Navajo are known. He has taken their part in seeking outside resources and has delivered schools, teachers, clothing, and other material benefits. He has helped them secure title to their lands and has supported and advised them in their dealings with white officialdom, even representing them in court. He is respected for his judgment, his political know-how, and his wide personal network. And so the problems find their way to him, in this case, the question of whether Des Chee Nee has been wrongfully imprisoned, and if so, whether the error can be corrected.]

In the District Court, at the October Term, A.D. 1905

The Grand Jurors for the Territory of New Mexico, taken from the body of the good and lawful men of the County of San Juan, aforesaid, duly elected, empaneled, sworn, and charged at the term aforesaid, to inquire in and for the County of San Juan, aforesaid, upon their oaths do present that Des-che-nee whose full first name is to the grand jurors unknown, late of the County of San Juan, Territory of New Mexico, on the 10th day of April, in the year of our Lord one thousand nine hundred and five at the County of San Juan, aforesaid, in and upon one Hos-ton-yaze, a female of the age of sixteen years, unlawfully, violently, and feloniously did make an assault, and her the said Hos-ton-yaze then and there unlawfully, violently, and feloniously, forcibly and against her will did rape, ravish, and carnally know, contrary to the form of the statute in such case made and provided, and against the peace and dignity of the Territory of New Mexico. . . .

And thereafter as follows to-wit at a regular term of the District Court in and for the County of San Juan, being the fourth day, Thursday October 12th, 1905. The following proceedings were had to-wit:

No. 217. Territory of New Mexico vs Des-Che-nee. Now comes the plaintiff by her District Attorney Alexander Read, Esq., and now comes the defendant in his own proper person and the indictment having been read to him in open court for plea thereto says that he is guilty in manner and form as therein charged, where-upon the Court assesses his punishment to imprisonment in the New Mexico Penitentiary for the full term of Ten years from the date of entry and that he pay the costs of this prosecution to be taxed.

It is therefore considered, ordered, adjudged, and decreed by the Court that the said defendant be and he hereby is remanded to the custody of the Sheriff of the County of San Juan to be by said Sheriff safely kept until he can be delivered to the Superintendent of the New Mexico Penitentiary to be so delivered to the said Superintendent, and that he be by said Superintendent safely and securely confined therein for the full term of Ten years from the date of his entry therein, and that he pay the costs of this prosecution to be taxed.

It is further ordered by the Court that a writ of commitment do issue against him. . . .

November 12, 1905: Des Chee Nee to Chee Gema Gay, Red Water Navajo, Care of Charles Day

Shidona,

I am in the New Mexico penitentiary and I want you to see Black Horse and have him see what I am in here for as I do not understand just what the charges were. They took me over to Aztec in the San Juan country and then brought me here for 10 years. If Black Horse will see the agent at Fort Defiance he may secure some information in regard to the case. I want Black Horse to see what he can do to help me. Two Navajo told many lies that I did not understand. Black Horse understands the first part of the case and payment of the five horses and the cow.

Please find out all about it and write and let me know. I am very well. I have plenty to eat and a good place to sleep, and I am very well treated.

Write soon,

December 10, 1905: Des Chee Nee to Charles Day

Dear Friend,

I wrote to Navajo Red in your care one month ago but have not heard from you so I write to you. I have been sent to the penitentiary for 10 years but do not understand what I was sent here for. They accused me of doing wrong to a Navajo woman. The woman they speak of became my wife, according to the laws of the Navajo, and there are a number of witnesses that everything was satisfactory and according to Navajo laws and not against American laws. I would like to have Black Horse see the agent at Fort Defiance and see if he can get an explanation of my case and see if something can be done for me. Peshlaki (silversmith who lives beyond Black Horse's place) knows all about the transaction and there were also five other Navajo present who can give full information in regard to the matter. You will do me a great kindness if you will find out something about it for me and let me know.

I am well treated here, just as well as anyone here, have plenty to eat and a good place to sleep, but there is some mistake about my being sent here which I do not understand. I do not know what I have done that was wrong. I have always been a law-abiding Navajo as far as I know. Will you please do me the favor asked for and let me know?

Your friend,

December 15, 1905: Anselm Weber to Deshchini

Dear Sir,

Your letter to Charles Day was turned over to me, since I am taking up this case for you at the request of Black Horse and Chi Dodge or Henry Dodge. Black Horse has told me all about your case. He related the case to me this way. Your wife was sickly, so you asked her to let you marry her sister. She was satisfied that you should also marry her sister, but her mother did not want you to do so. You then went out with a rope; when you came to the place where the girl was herding sheep, you threw a rope around her and had intercourse with her. When the mother of the girl heard about it, she was mad and did not want you to have the girl for your wife—and the girl also did not want to have you for her husband. Blackhorse then settled the case between you and the mother of the girl, you giving her some horses and a steer.

This is in short the story of Black Horse. Now if his story is true, then that girl did *not* become your wife according to the laws of the Navajo, the way you wrote to Charles Day.

Now I want you to tell me the truth. I will do for you what I can, but you must tell me the truth in answering these questions:

1) Was the girl willing to become your wife before you roped her? If she was willing to become your wife, it seems, you would not have roped her. I hardly think you can explain why you roped her if she was willing to become your wife. I would be glad to know what you have to say about that.

2) Was she willing to marry you after what had occurred?

3) Did she not marry you simply because her mother did not want her to marry you?

4) What were you asked in court during the trial?

5) What did you answer in court during the trial?

6) Who testified against you?

7) Who defended you?

8) Who was your interpreter?

9) Did you explain everything in court during the trial?

10) Did you tell the court that you wanted to marry the girl, and that the girl was willing to marry you?

I am trying to find out everything, and then I will bring the matter before the governor of New Mexico to have you pardoned. But you must answer these questions to me truthfully.

Did the girl not say in court that what occurred after you threw the rope was against her will? And was it not against her will?

Your son is at our school, and I will try to get you out of jail, if possible.

You say you do not understand why you are in jail. The paper of Farmington says that you are in jail because you committed rape, and because you yourself said in court that you committed rape.

And if the girl did not give her consent, if she was not willing you should do what you did, then you *did* commit rape.

Now I am very plain in putting these questions, and I do not like to write such letters, but I am only doing it so I can help you better. Now please write to me and explain matters as good as you can.

Very sincerely yours,

December 19, 1905: Des Chee Nee
to Father Anselm Weber

Dear Sir,

Your kind letter of the 15th at hand and contents noted. I am very thankful that Black Horse and Chee Dodge are taking an interest in my case and that they have prevailed upon you to take up my case and make an investigation. Black Horse has been misinformed as to some of the details. I did visit the girl where she was herding sheep and did have a rope which I was swinging in my hand as I was walking along, but I did not [throw] the rope at or on the girl, nor did I have sexual intercourse with her at that time at all, nor did I have at any subsequent time when she was unwilling. As I understood it the [girl] was willing to become my [wife], as no objection was made to the arrangement on her part. It is true that her parents objected, because they wanted the girl to work at home making blankets [and] herding sheep . . . for she was a good worker and the fruits of her labor brought some little money to her parents.

In answering your questions will reply:

1) Did not rape the girl or have intercourse with her. She was willing to be my wife.
2) Yes.
3) No, she was willing.
4) Was asked in regard to the above transaction.
5) Answered the same as above.
6) The girl's mother testified against me, but the girl contradicted her testimony. The mother told the court that I forced the girl. The girl told the court that I did not.
7) Do not know.
8) A Navajo acted as interpreter. He could not talk much English and I do not think that he interpreted correctly. I think he lied in his interpretation.

9) Yes, as well as I could.

10) Yes, I told the interpreter that, but do not know what he told the court. The girl did not say in court that I raped her, or that anything occurred against her will.

The statement in the Farmington paper was not correct. I did not say in court that I committed rape, nor did the girl say so. Hope you will try to explain this matter properly to the governor and get me out. I think there was a misunderstanding at the court or I would not have been sent here. Please do what you can for me. I am glad my boy is at your school and hope he will do well.

I beg to remain your obedient servant,

Note by writer for Des Chee Nee:

If the alleged transaction occurred on the reservation the territorial court had no jurisdiction and a writ of habeas corpus would release the prisoner at once.

He should have been tried in the U.S. court and was entitled to an attorney, witnesses, and a *good interpreter*.

If it happened off the reservation the court was right but both the court and the governor are fairminded men, and if you find upon investigation that a mistake has been made, I think they will be only too glad to rectify it.

January 9, 1906: Des Chee Nee to Father Anselm Weber

Dear Sir,

Yours of the 4th at hand. In reply to your question I would say that, at the time the alleged transaction occurred, which it is alleged did occur near my residence, I was living west of the Carrizo mountains, a few miles northwest of Black Horse's place. Thanking you for your interest in my behalf.

I am as ever, sincerely yours,

Note by the writer for Des Chee Nee:

I note your remarks in regard to testimony, which are very true, but like you I believe Des Chee Nee is telling the truth. On several occasions I have tried to forcibly impress upon his mind that he must tell the truth in regard to every detail in this matter or I would not render him any assistance, nor could he expect any assistance from you or anyone else.

His manner in stating his case bears the impress of truth, as well as the subject matter of his recital. It is evident that a serious mistake has been made, which has deprived a man of his liberty for a space of ten years.

It is not reasonable to suppose that the prosecuting attorney Mr. Abbott or Judge McFie the trial judge, both residents of Santa Fe, are in any way responsible for this mistake. They were undoubtedly misinformed by misinterpretation as charged by Des Chee Nee.

The governor before issuing a pardon will require the recommendation of both of the above-named gentlemen, and it will be necessary for you to lay the case fully before them, if you find from the facts as adduced you are justified in so doing.

Allow me to suggest that it would be well for you to have a letter of recommendation stating briefly the facts in the case from chief Chee Dodge, whose reputation for veracity and as a businessman is well known. Such a letter would be readily endorsed by both S. E. Aldrich, C. N. Cotton, and others, leaders of the Republican party of McKinley County, N.M., and friends of the Navajo. If you are not personally acquainted with the above-named gentlemen, Father Juillard of Gallup would probably be not only able, but willing, to render you every material assistance. Such a letter so endorsed would undoubtedly aid you in convincing the authorities that your efforts were not alone propagated by missionary zeal and that the facts in the case are alone sufficient as an excuse for any citizen to take up the case in the interest of humanity and justice, regardless of race or nationality. Common courtesy would not allow me to make any suggestions in regard to any other influences which to you, in your wise judgment, might seem fit and proper to bring to bear upon the case. Begging your pardon for the suggestion already made and hoping you will not consider it an undue suggestion.

Believe me to be not only sincerely yours, but as ever a friend to all in distress, "Anon."

January 12, 1906: A. M. Bergere, Clerk, First Judicial District Court, to Father Anselm Weber

Reverend Father,

Replying to your favor of January 4, I beg to state that the Indian De Chee Nee was indicted for rape at the last term of the district court held in San Juan county, he was duly arraigned, and at once entered a plea of guilty, whereupon the court sentenced him to 10 years in the penitentiary. Of course, there being no trial, there was no evidence taken in the case. The evidence taken was all before the grand jury, and of that there is no record, but the district attorney, Mr. Alexander Read of Tierra Amarilla, Rio Arriba County, New Mexico, might be able to give you some information regarding the testimony, if he heard any of it.

I am sorry that I am unable to give you any further information on the subject, but if I can be of any service to you please command me.

Yours very respectfully,

January 17, 1906: Des Chee Nee to Father Anselm Weber

Dear Friend,

I received your kind letter of [January] 13 and will say that I do not remember the form of the questions asked me, that is, as to their exact wording, so that I could properly answer your questions. I thank you and others for the interest you are showing in my behalf. I have not done any wrong that I know of.

Sincerely yours,

Note [from "Anon.," the prison writer]: I am very glad that Mr. [Samuel] Shoemaker has returned. He will undoubtedly aid you and you can depend upon him. I did not know that he had returned or I would have mentioned him to you before.

The new governor may not adopt the same rule that governor Otero has in regard to the prosecuting attorney and trial judge, but it is probable that he will, so you had better be prepared to meet such an emergency.

In regard to the especial idiomatic peculiarity of the Navajo [language] you speak of in regard to affirmative and negative questions, I will say that I am very familiar with their habit of answering a negative question by saying "yes," and Des Chee Nee is particularly afflicted in that manner. Therefore I always put questions to him in the affirmative, and if I should, by chance, address a negative question to him and receive the answer "yes," I immediately change the question to the affirmative and receive the proper answer, "no." This is an occasion where "yes" and "no" mean the same thing. There has not been any mistake of that kind in the interpretation here, as we are very familiar with that fault in interpretation, but—as you suggest—this fault might explain the discrepancy in the present interpretation and the interpretation that was given in court. In fact there is no other explanation unless we assume that there was a willful misinterpretation. Des Chee Nee emphatically declares that there *was* a willful misinterpretation and gives as his reasons that the interpreter was very unfriendly to him and therefore interpreted in such a manner as to convince the jury that Des Chee Nee was admitting his guilt, when the fact was quite the contrary. I am of the opinion, however, that Des Chee Nee is mistaken and that the discrepancy is caused by the court interpreter's unfamiliarity with the Navajo idioms, at least, this is the most charitable view to take of the situation. I am very glad that you have mentioned the subject, as a proper explanation and understanding now might avoid some confusion in the future when the matter is presented to the governor.

In the interest of humanity let me thank you for your interest in this case. Without doubt a very grave mistake has occurred by which a poor unfortunate is deprived of his liberty, and I hope you will succeed and restore him to his family and friends. Allow me to reiterate that a statement from Chee Dodge, endorsed as I mentioned in my previous letter, will be of the utmost importance in the presentation of the case. I have no interest in the case, only as a humanitarian, and therefore hope that you will very speedily succeed. Des Chee Nee was so overcome with his emotions while listening to the reading of your last letter that he was hardly able to converse. I hope and pray that all will be well when presented to the governor.

Believe me to be, sincerely yours, "Anon."

January 26, 1906: Alexander Read, District Attorney, to Father Anselm Weber

Dear Sir,

I have yours of [January] 16, and in reply will say, that I have no copy of the proceedings in the Des Chee Nee case, but will say, from the testimony produced in the case, he no doubt committed the crime of rape, on his sister-in-law, in the county of San Juan in this territory.

As far as the plea of guilty is concerned, I will say that the Navajo interpreter that was there is the official interpreter at the agency at Shiprock, and that no one ever induced the Indian to plead guilty. He was brought into court for the purpose of being tried and when the indictment was read to him, he made a voluntary plea and confessed to the crime.

The mother of the girl was not the accuser. She was brought over simply to prove what the girl told her immediately after the commission of the crime.

The agent at Shiprock was there at the trial and he can inform you who the interpreter was, and all about it. The only thing that can be done now is to apply for a pardon to the governor of the territory, and if a good showing is made that the Indian is suffering on account of a misinterpretation, he will no doubt grant a pardon.

The girl never contradicted her mother. The girl was the only one who testified before the grand jury, the mother being there, as I have said, to testify as to what the girl told her after the crime was committed, as is required in such cases.

I am convinced that if he had been tried, he would have been convicted as charged in the indictment.

I am, sir,

Yours very truly,

January 27, 1906: Father Anselm Weber to the writer of Des Chee Nee's letters

Dear Sir,

Enclosed please find answer from the prosecuting attorney—which looks bad for the Indian. Mr. Shoemaker promised to send me some affidavits from the sheriff and deputy sheriff.

I think the only way of doing anything in the matter will be to see the woman and her mother. I will have an opportunity to send the Silversmith for them in about a week from now.

Without them, I cannot even prove that the alleged crime was committed in Arizona. Nobody would take the word of Des Chee Nee.

Please question him about contents of enclosed letter and then return it to me.

Very sincerely yours,

February 4, 1906: Des Chee Nee
to Father Anselm Weber

Dear Sir,

In reply to yours of [February] 27th, there is nothing more to say, only in reply to Mr. Read's letter. I repeat what I have said from the first, that I never pleaded guilty to the charge, nor did I make confession, as alleged, to anyone, but, on the contrary, told the interpreter most emphatically that I was not guilty as charged. Once again thanking you for your interest in the case,

I am, sincerely yours,

Note by writer:

Allow me to suggest that I do not agree with you in thinking that the statements in Mr. Read's letter look bad for the Indian. On the contrary, I practically gather that every contention that we have made is correct. According to Mr. Read's own statement, Des Chee Nee was dragged at least from the reservation, if not from Arizona, into a court without jurisdiction which does not properly look to the interest of the defendant, as the law distinctly says the court is bound to do. Des Chee Nee stands in this court, without an attorney to advocate his cause, without a friend to advise, with an enemy to give an interpretation. [He is] a stranger among strangers not of his race, accused of a heinous crime of which he has neither knowledge or understanding, without a single witness in his defense or opportunity to procure one. According to Mr. Read's own statement, not a word of evidence was introduced at the trial. But the indictment was read; the interpreter said the Indian was guilty, the prosecuting attorney said he was guilty, the judge said ten years, and away goes the poor Indian with the same railroad speed that has characterized all the proceedings, to the penitentiary, not knowing whither he is going. He arrives there dazed, confused, frightened, and apparently helpless. Finally recovering from his fright and confusion, he begins to wonder what all this tempest in a teapot is about. Mr. Read says in conclusion that he is "convinced that if he had been tried he would have been convicted." He does not give an earthly reason why he is convinced or what convinced him. I venture to assume he does not understand a word of Navajo, has no conception of the idiomatic construction of the Navajo language, does not know whether he had a correct interpretation even before the grand jury or not. Yet he is convinced.

I know that governor Otero would not stand for any such doings as was undoubtedly done in this case and I do not believe the present governor will if the case is presented to him. Do not understand me [to] say that I think the court was willfully guilty of dilatory conduct in this case, but I do think that he placed too much confidence in the prosecuting attorney and allowed him to railroad Des Chee Nee into the penitentiary without a proper investigation. We must also remember that it is the prosecuting attorney's duty to prosecute. He gives his side of the case and he, in some instances, wants a conviction at all hazards. Every conviction, he thinks, builds up his reputation. Having secured a conviction, he wants to maintain his contentions at any price, even if that price be a man's liberty. It is naturally to be supposed that Mr. Read will try to maintain that there has not been a mistake. That is his prerogative, exclusively.

Under all the circumstances, therefore, I cannot see anything alarming in his statement, but rather, if anything, it looks more favorable to Des Chee Nee. I believe you will succeed if you maintain your faith.

According to the tenets of the religion you teach, you must consider yourself an instrument in the hands of God to see that truth and justice prevail in this case.

With many apologies, believe me to be,

Sincerely yours,

July 8, 1906: Des Chee Nee to Henry [Chee] Dodge

Dear Friend,

I wrote you some time ago to know how my family was, and so on, but have not received any reply. I am very anxious to know how all my people are and whether they are well and all right. I also wrote to Black Horse but have not heard from him either. I am also anxious to know what the people at St. Michaels have done with my case, or whether they have given it up entirely. Please write me and give me all the information you can in regard to what I want to know.

Shidona,

n.d. (circa August 1, 1906): Des Chee Nee to Father Anselm Weber

Dear Friend,

Your kind and welcome letter of July 23 was duly received. I was very glad to hear that, so far as you could learn, my family was well and that my son at your school is all right.

I hope you will not fail to attend to the business in your care as regards me personally and that it will not be later than this fall. I am well, as usual, and getting along all right. Tell Black Horse, Chee Dodge Ho, Navajo Killer, Peshlaki, my family, and all inquiring that I am well and send my regards and [hope] they will continue to work in my interest until a good result is brought about. With many thanks for your kindness in the past,

I am, as ever, yours truly,

September 9, 1906: Des Chee Nee
to Father Anselm Weber

Dear Friend,

I received your letter of recent date and was not only glad to hear from you but was glad to hear that my family and friends were also as well as usual. I have been quite ill with stomach and bowel trouble, but I am very much better at the present time. I was placed in the hospital and had the best of care with proper attendance and medicine from the prison physician. All the officers have also treated me very kindly, which I duly appreciate.

The confinement here is beginning to materially affect my health, and I sincerely hope you will use as much expedition as possible on that account in having Peschlaki bring the parties spoken of to your place, so that the proper testimony may be secured in my behalf. I wish that, as you have opportunity, you will convey my regards to Peshlaki, Chee Dodge, Black Horse, and all inquiring friends, as well as my family, and that though I have been quite ill that I am now very much better, and hope to be with them all in the near future.

Also, inform my son who is in attendance at your school that I hope he is progressing well with his studies and that he will be a good boy and continue to do well. I also send an anxious father's love.

Since I cannot write to all my friends (as I am only allowed to write once a month except I have some special business when I can secure a special permit), I am writing to you on this occasion, hoping that you will convey the information herein contained to my family and friends as circumstances will permit. Thanking you for the many favors you have shown "me and mine" in the past, and hoping I shall hear favorably from you soon.

I remain, as ever,

Your obedient Shidona,

November 29, 1906: Des Chee Nee
to Father Anselm Weber

Dear Friend,

I have not heard anything from you for several months and did not expect to hear about my case until about this time.

You wrote me some time ago that you would have my case presented to the governor this fall.

Can you inform me if any move has been made as yet in the matter, and, if so, what has been done?

I am very anxious to have my case considered as my health is very poor and I have been confined to the hospital for some months. If anything can be done for me, I wish it could be done before it is "too late." Will you please make inquiries in regard to my family and let me know how they are getting along? Also give my regards to Black Horse, Peschlaki, Chee Dodge, and all others of my friends. I hope Peschlaki will keep his promise to bring the girl and her mother to you so that you may secure her testimony. Please write and let me know all the news in regard to all of the matters spoken of above.

How is my son getting along with his studies, the one that is with you? I hope he is doing well.

Hoping to hear favorably from you in the near future.

I remain, as ever,

Your obedient servant,

December 9, 1906: Des Chee Nee to Father Anselm Weber

Dear Friend,

I have received your kind and welcome letter of December 3 and am glad to note that I am not forgotten and that you, as well as my other friends, have been active in my behalf. I hope with you that I will be able to accompany you when you return from here, and I believe that I will, if you present all the facts in my case to the governor as they really and truly are, and I have every reason to believe that you will. I hope Mr. Shelton will cooperate with you, as there is no doubt that he can render very material assistance in the case. Let me suggest that it would be well for you to bring all of the correspondence that you have had in the matter, as you might need some of it for reference in the presentation of the case to the governor.

I am very glad to learn that my people are well and that they desire my return. I would surely love to be with them, and hope I may soon. I am very thankful to Black Horse, Peschlaki, and all others who have taken an interest in my behalf. Give my regards to all inquiring friends.

Tell my son to be a good boy and learn all he can. I am glad he is doing well in your school.

I am feeling a little better now than I was, can walk about some with a cane. Hoping to meet you this coming week.

I am, very sincerely yours,

February 10, 1907: Des Chee Nee to Father Anselm Weber

My Dear Friend,

I wrote you a month ago but have not as yet received any answer. I cannot conceive what is delaying matters in my case. Have you heard from Mr. Shelton yet as to what he is willing to recommend in the case, and can you tell me what is the cause of delay, or has the case been abandoned on account of Mr. Shelton failing to give the proper recommendation? It would relieve me of some considerable anxiety to know just how matters stand.

Have you heard anything from my family of late?

My health is very bad. I have not been able of late to eat anything much. Everything distresses my stomach, which is very sore and inflamed. I am still in the hospital under the doctor's care and fear that I will never get out of here alive.

I hope you will answer me this time, and let me know about everything, as I am very anxious to hear. Give my regard to all, Chee, Peshlaki, Charley Tso, and Black Horse, if you should happen to see him, should he be down in that part of the country.

With many thanks for all your kindness to me and mine.

I remain your true friend,

[This is the last communication on Des Chee Nee's case in Father Anselm's penitentiary correspondence folders. Inquiries about the final outcome of the case to the New Mexico State Records Center and Archives in Santa Fe initially were unproductive. After being informed that there was no record of a prisoner named Des Chee Nee, I was told that it might not be possible to document the final disposition of his case because for this historical period the penitentiary records are incomplete. However, additional searching by Ms. Valerie Nye of the Records Center turned up a handwritten ledger page from the Department of Corrections Convict Book, *Record of Convicts, New Mexico Penitentiary*, with the following information about Prisoner no. 1951, Des Chee Nee:

When Received: 28 Oct. 1905	Sentence: 10 years
Term Commences: 12 Oct. 1905	Term Expires: 12 Oct. 1915
Crime: Rape	From What County Received: San Juan
Judicial District: 1st	Name of Judge: John R. McFie
Prosecuting Attorney: E. C. Abbott	Race: Indian
Age: 39	Sex: Male
Weight: 155	Height: 5 ft. 8½ in.
Eyes: Black	Hair: Black
Complexion: Dark	Size of Foot: 7½
Teeth: Good	Beard Worn: Black
Body Marks: None	Where Born: Navajo Reservation
Occupation: Laborer	Married or Single: Married
Children: 1 Girl, 2 Boys	Religion: Catholic
Church of Parents: Catholic	Father Living: No
Mother Living: No	Age of Self Support: 10
Habits/Temperate: Yes	Habits/Intemperate: No
Habits/Use Tobacco: Yes	Education/Can Read: No
Education/Can Write: No	Education/Common School: No
Education/High School: No	Education/College: No

Plea at Trial: [*No entry!!*]   Reasons for Crime: None
Previous Imprisonment: None   Nearest Relative or Friend: [*No entry*]
Remarks: Conditionally pardoned by Gov. Hagerman. Out February 26, 1907.

The ledger entry for Prisoner no. 1951 was unusual because it lacked a "Plea at Trial" entry, while virtually every other prisoner had a recorded plea at trial. Also, for most prisoners there was a name and address entered under "Nearest Relative or Friend." The key entry, however, is the pardon, dated just two weeks after Des Chee Nee's last desperate appeal from the prison hospital that he feared he would "never get out of here alive." Father Anselm's appeal to the governor had been successful. Upon release Des Chee Nee had served 16 and a half months of his 10-year sentence.]

Note

1. Court documents, except as noted, and all letters are from FAC Box DEC.245, fds. Weber, Anselm. N. M. State Penitentiary I (BVI6), II (BVI7).

17

The Last Warrior[1]

Leopold Ostermann, O.F.M.

[The first published report in the Franciscan literature on the death of Dine Tśosi, also known as Slender Man or Slim Navajo, appeared in *Sendbote* of June 1907.[2] Father Anselm's brief tribute included reference to his own service to the old chief and his family. Many times Father Anselm had stayed the night at Dine Tśosi's home, and he had made "near heroic" efforts to help the old chief to obtain clear title to the good lands, complete with rich water resources, that he and his people occupied. The friar had visited the area with Howel Jones, land commissioner for the Santa Fe Railroad, which at that time owned half of the land in question. During that visit Dine Tśosi had told Jones that he and his family had lived on these lands for many years, they were his homeland, he wanted to die here and to leave the lands to his children and grandchildren.

In 1909 Father Leopold Ostermann, for the 101st article of his series on Franciscans in the Navajo country,[3] drew from Father Anselm's German-language article, adding details from his own acquaintance with the famous chief, some of them from a lengthy interview with the old man at St. Michaels, a few months before his passing.

The article reprinted below, from the 1915 issue of *Franciscan Missions of the Southwest*, is a slightly edited and somewhat expanded version of that 1909 piece from *St. Anthony's Messenger*. Part of the expansion is the addition of another full paragraph translated from Father Anselm's 1907 *Sendbote* article. Thus we have here another instance of Father Leopold's' practice of drawing upon earlier writings, his own and Father Anselm's, for the major publications of his second decade as missionary to the Navajo. Although published in 1915, the article derives from the friars' acquaintance with Dine Tśosi in the years 1900–1907 and thus belongs in this section of the book.

On February 22, 1907, there died at his home, in the valley of *Tqelch'int'i*, some 24 miles south of Fort Defiance, Arizona, and about 16 miles south of St. Michael's

Mission, Dine Tśosi, the last of the war chiefs of the Navajo tribe. Dine Tśosi, the Slender Man, had, during his life, taken a prominently active part in many campaigns and raids of the Navajo against their enemies. Apaches, Comanches, Utes, Zunis and other Pueblos, Mexicans, and Americans have seen Dine Tśosi in the front ranks drawing his bow or swinging his lance or firing his rifle, and have heard his war cry ring above the din of the conflict, urging his followers on to the charge. The writer has several times met Dine Tśosi; the last time at St. Michaels, Arizona, several months before his death, when he had a long talk with him about his past life. Dine Tśosi was the grandson of Qastqin Naat'ani, better known to the Mexicans and Americans under the name of Narbona, who is still talked of by the old men of the tribe as one of the ablest and most famous head chiefs the tribe ever had. Narbona was shot accidentally by American soldiers near Two Gray Hills, New Mexico, in 1849. At that time, Dine Tśosi said, he was about 16 or 17 years old, which would make his age about 74 or 75 at the time of his death.

Dine Tśosi was somewhat above the middle height and, despite his age, as straight as a lance. His hair was gray, rather scant, and gathered into a knot at the back of his head, as is customary with the Navajo. A somewhat sad or melancholy expression lingered about his eyes, yet there was that in them which showed that once they could flash and penetrate. His lips were thin, firmly set, and expressive of determination. Time and exposure had marked his face with furrows and wrinkles. He seemed to have little use or taste for American clothes. About his forehead was wrapped the traditional headband of his people. The upper part of his body was covered with a calico shirt of a dark, quiet color, open at the throat, so that a part of his chest was continually exposed. Hands, face, and chest were, therefore, suntanned to a deep, dark brown, almost black, and so weatherbeaten as to give the skin of his chest a leathery appearance. He wore white muslin trousers slashed at the bottom toward the outside, like those of the Mexicans. His footgear consisted of a pair of Navajo leggings, called *yistle*—knit of wool, without toes and heels—and a pair of reddish brown moccasins fastened with silver buttons. Over his right shoulder passed a strap, ornamented with silver buttons, by which hung a leather pouch in which he carried his tobacco, matches, and other small articles. About his neck he wore a triple strand of beads made of small round discs of white shells, with here and there a turquoise. His whole figure was enveloped in the well-known Indian blanket, or robe.

His whole body was a veritable battlefield, covered with the scars of many wounds inflicted by the bullets of Mexicans and Americans, by the lances of the Comanches, and by the arrows of the Apaches and Pueblos. Seven of these scars seemed to have been rather serious wounds, notably one on his chest near the neck. That was the place, he said, where the lance of a Comanche had struck him while he was engaged with them in a fight at Bosque Redondo. After extracting the lance from the wound, he continued fighting with unabated energy, while at every panting breath the blood spurted from the wound as if drawn up with a pump.

The Bosque Redondo, called by the Navajo *T'is nasbas*, Circle of Cotton-woods, was a reservation on the Rio Pecos in southern New Mexico where between 7,000 and 8,000 Navajo had been taken as prisoners of war by Colonel Kit Carson, after his successful campaign against the Navajo in 1863. On this reservation was located Fort Sumner, called by the Navajo *huelti*, a corruption of the Spanish word *fuerte*, fort. Between the Navajo and Mexicans there had always existed a state of feud in which raids and reprisals succeeded each other. Robbing and taking slaves or the recapture of plunder and the punishment of the marauders were the motives which kept this desultory warfare alive. It seems that shortly before Kit Carson's campaign, a company of Mexicans had undertaken one of these periodical retaliatory expeditions into what Dine Tśosi considered his territory. The two hostile parties met at a place called *Tsohotso,* Big Meadow, by the Indians, and *Cienega Amarilla,* Yellow Swamp, by the Mexicans (now St. Michaels), about eight miles south of Fort Defiance. The Mexicans were stationed on a hill some 500 to 600 yards west from where now stands St. Michaels Indian school, while the Navajo were down in the valley, which is between the hill on which the Mexicans were stationed and the quarry from which the stones for St. Michael's School were taken.

As both parties were about evenly matched and a fight would have been very risky for either side, much talk and some negotiations took place which apparently resulted satisfactorily to both parties. However, as soon as the vigilance of the Navajo relaxed and they were about ready to depart, the Mexicans suddenly poured a volley of bullets into their scattered ranks and followed this up with a vigorous charge. A number of the Navajo fell, the rest were stricken with a panic and fled, leaving their leader, Dine Tśosi, and his brother almost alone upon the field. The brother, being shot through both hips, was absolutely helpless. Dine Tśosi, whose warrior spirits were aroused, stood over his wounded brother, raised his rifle, and the foremost of the charging Mexicans fell dead upon his tracks. Then, lifting his brother on his pony and mounting behind him, he with a last shout of defiance galloped off toward the Haystacks, a group of isolated, conical rocks, called by the Indians *Tsetqa*, three miles northeast of the scene of the conflict, and succeeded in making his escape.

When the Navajo were taken to Fort Sumner at Bosque Redondo in 1863, Dine Tśosi found the tame life there irksome and monotonous, and soon had gathered around him a half dozen kindred spirits with whom he left the reservation in quest of "something to do." They encountered a party of nine Comanches, all of whom they killed, took their horses, and returned to the Fort. Had Dine Tśosi in this encounter not received a severe wound in the thigh, this expedition would most likely have been further extended. The commanding officer then forbade him to leave the reservation again without special permission, which brought on a hot argument with the unruly warrior. While this dispute was going on, about 30 Navajo warriors gathered around them holding their rifles concealed under their blankets, but ready for immediate action should the signal be given. To avoid trouble, the officer ordered him to the guardhouse, which orders he promptly refused to obey. Despite the wound in his thigh he began the fight, his followers joined in, and for a time the Fort was a hot and lively place. In the ensuing scuffle Dine Tśosi was knocked down and trampled into unconsciousness, or as he expressed it, he "was killed."

Besides this he took a prominent and leading part in many other fights with the Comanches and Mescalero Apaches during his captivity at the Bosque. It was finally found expedient to send him and a number of other equally turbulent and incorrigible troublemakers to Fort Sill, in Oklahoma. On the way thither, he and his companions succeeded in eluding the vigilance of the soldiers during the night and made their escape. When he was finally brought back to Fort Sumner, he promised to make no more trouble if he were allowed to remain with his people. His request was granted and he faithfully kept his promise. In 1868 General W. T. Sherman came to Fort Sumner and in the name of the U. S. Government concluded a treaty of peace with the Navajo, by which they were allowed to return to their country. Among the chiefs who signed this treaty was Dine Tśosi. With him passed the last surviving signer.

After the Navajo had returned to their country, it was hard for Dine Tśosi to accommodate himself to the altered circumstances. Once more he gathered a band of trusty followers and made a raid upon the old enemies of his people, the Utes. When Colonel Dodd threatened to cast him into prison for his breach of peace, he boldly exposed his chest, covered with scars, saying that prison had no terrors for one who had faced death so often as he. Since then, however, he has lived in peace with the palefaces in the beautiful vale of *Tqelch 'int 'i*, better known as Dine Tśosi's Valley. Here he lived for many years with his family, following the peaceful pursuits of sheep raising and farming and exerting his influence to induce his people to follow his example.

Once more his undaunted courage and consummate leadership were called into action. In 1892 the Indian agent at Fort Defiance put it into his head to bring the blessings of education to the benighted Indian children by the gentle persuasion of main force. He blithely set forth toward the southern part of the reservation into the domains of Dine Tśosi, where he espied just one lonely Indian boy who, blissfully ignorant of his impending doom, was herding his sheep. The agent ordered his policeman to pounce upon the poor urchin and abducted him in triumph to Fort Defiance. When the boy's father appeared the following day at the government school to protest against such high-handed methods he also was forthwith arrested and placed under durance vile.

That, however, was just a trifle too much for Dine Tśosi. No sooner had he been informed of the outrage than he, at the head of 17 well-armed Navajo, rode to Fort Defiance. The agent had not even time to realize what was going on before his office was filled with very determined-looking warriors. The situation looked tense enough, but developed into a piece of high tragicomedy.

Quite coolly, without any threats or open defiance, Dine Tśosi informed the agent that his companions were the most peace-loving souls in the world. Their only request was that the agent also should abstain from any unnecessary provocation. They were not inclined by any means to have their children kidnapped. He insisted that the boy, so unceremoniously taken from his pastoral duties, should be immediately restored to them. The crestfallen agent let his anxious gaze roam through the office. At every door and window it encountered some armed Indian, and before him stood Dine Tśosi ready to emphasize his remarks with a most serviceable revolver. There was but one conclusion to be derived from these premises: he gave orders to return the boy to Dine Tšosi.

While Dine Tšosi was telling me these incidents of his past life I took them down in writing. He was finally curious to know why I was writing all this down on paper. I told him I would put it all nicely together, then it would be printed and many Americans would read it. He could not understand why I should wish that the Americans should read how bad a man he had been. In his past years, he said, he had been a very bad Indian, but now and for many years he was trying hard to be good, to live in peace and harmony with the Americans, and was telling his people on all occasions to do likewise. He wanted all Americans to know and understand this well, and I should not forget to mention it, which wish of the old warrior I am herewith fulfilling.

During his last illness—he had contracted pneumonia—he was frequently visited by the Reverend Anselm Weber, who instructed him in the Christian truths and baptized him some time before his death. He sent the medicine men from his hogan and was very eager to be instructed and baptized. Thus he died on February 22, 1907, and was buried on February 23, from the chapel of the Franciscan Fathers at St. Michaels. With him passed the last war chief and warrior of the Navajo tribe, the last signer of the treaty of Fort Sumner, one of the links which connected the present time with a past epoch.

Notes

1. From Leopold Ostermann, "The Last Warrior of the Navaho Tribe," FMSW 3 (1915): 45–48.

2. Anselm Weber, FMN 34 (June 1907): 513–18.

3. Leopold Ostermann, FWW 17 (September 1909): 118–21.

Part 4

NAVAJO LAND

18

Land Claims: Learning and Using the Law[1]

Emanuel Trockur, O.F.M.

[The process of gaining secure title to the property where St. Michael's Mission and School were to be built took several years. While working through claims and counterclaims to the property, Father Anselm learned things that he would use throughout his life as he helped the Navajo to try to obtain clear title to the lands they occupied. One of the first instances in which he worked against white entrepreneurs to establish legitimate Navajo claim to contested land happened in October 1901, as a direct outgrowth of his efforts to prevent competitive land use on or near mission property. In the selection that follows, published decades later in the *Provincial Chronicle*, Father Emanuel draws upon Father Anselm's reports of the mission land troubles and related events as published from 1901 to 1903 in his monthly articles in *Sendbote*.]

So many factors, costly ones too, were involved in the matter of securing clear and valid land titles in those days, and such great and varied difficulties attended the technical procedure in those instances that the early settlers or squatters made no attempts to comply with legal requirements; instead, each claimant made the best of a policy of taking the matter into his own hands and of settling all disputes in accordance with the accepted western code for the preservation of self and the survival of the strongest. Wherever the enforcing arm of the law had not yet extended its convincing influence there could be found its effective counterpart, not in an officer who stood behind his badge and spoke in the name of law and order, but in an individual who, without a badge, was always prepared to defend his own rights and "enforce the law" with the aid of a deadly six-shooter. This chapter will be devoted to the land status at Cienega and also to a review of some of the obstacles that stood in Mother Katharine's way when she determined to erect an expensive school building for the Navajo, obstacles the kindly friars undertook to remove. In this they succeeded admirably and without recourse to the rough gunplay tactics of the wild and woolly West.

Proceeding with Caution

It should be noted first of all, that at the time of the arrival of the friars, Cienega was not situated within the boundaries of the Navajo reservation, but about seven miles south of the boundary of that tract of land which had been assigned to the Navajo tribe by the U.S. government under the terms of the Treaty of June 1, 1868, and about one mile south of the Executive Order Extension of January 6, 1880.[2]

That this selection of property by Monsignor Stephan in 1895 was designedly made outside the confines of the reservation can scarcely be doubted; with the APA movement [American Protective Association, devoted to resisting the "encroach-ments" of Roman Catholicism] in full swing and with anti-Catholic bigotry bitterly engaged in doing everything in its power to crush the Catholic Indian schools, both he and Mother Katharine had every reason to mistrust the government and to seek indisputable title to federally owned lands, which were subject to the wiles of bigoted public officials, who not infrequently came to their positions via the route of the spoils system. Under these circumstances, the risk of pursuing an easier and less expensive course seemed much too great, and hence Mother Katharine did not hesitate to invest several thousands of dollars in order to secure a legally sound and perfect title to the land upon which she planned to build.[3]

Still, on the other hand, while Cienega was not on the Navajo reservation, it was nonetheless actually within the Navajo country, for when the Navajo, on the conclusion of their treaty, returned from Fort Sumner, New Mexico, practically all who had previously lived outside the newly established boundaries settled upon the sites of their former homes. They had never been *on* the reservation and were not even now.[4] The determining factor of their settling down to live was the proximity of water in the form of a spring or stream, near which they could conveniently herd their small flocks of sheep and goats and plant small fields of melons and corn. The government evidently took no action whatsoever to confine them to the treaty reservation—a silent admission that it realized that the tract would not be sufficient for the entire tribe. A laissez-faire policy was the natural result, and matters were left to adjust themselves aimlessly and automatically. Thus it happened that many of the Navajo, immediately after their captivity, came back unmolested to their old habitats in the vicinity of Cienega to occupy lands which were public domain and open to homesteading and settlement by all comers.

Government Grants to Railroads

Later, with the building of the Atlantic and Pacific Railroad through Gallup and across the southern portion of the Navajo domain to the Pacific Coast in 1882, extensive land grants were made by the government to the railroad company of all unclaimed odd-numbered sections of land on either side of the right-of-way for a distance of 40 miles, that is, at the rate of 20 alternate sections per mile on each side of the tracks; this in accordance with the Enabling Act passed in the year 1866. An additional 10 miles of alternate sections was set aside as a so-called indemnity area, within which the railroad company was permitted to make selections in lieu of lands that might have been acquired within the original 40-mile tracts.[5] These grants extended to and, as Father Anselm Weber was evidently convinced,[6] beyond Cienega, without, however, comprising any of the treaty lands, and made it possible that all or any of the odd-numbered sections within the 1880 extension could be sold or leased by the railroad company to anyone who cared to become a party to such a contract.

To say without reservation that the government totally ignored or failed to take into account any existing rights of Indians that had up to that time occupied these areas would probably be stating the case too bluntly, but the fact remains that these Navajo were constantly at a serious disadvantage. They knew nothing about land laws and their operation, leases, and so forth, and there was no one in the field to advise or protect them, since most superintendents or agents took no particular interest in Indians residing outside the reservation.[7] This made it easy for white settlers who were conversant with preemption and homestead laws to file claims and enter applications for lands being used by Indians and under the law to force them to vacate. The checkerboard ownership of lands further paved the way to a very disagreeable situation, inasmuch as it did not exclude outsiders from the Indian country and allowed white stock raisers to bring their large herds upon the railroad lands, even those that lay within the reservation itself.

Indian Resentment

Prior occupancy gave the Indian an instinctive feeling that he must have, or should be able to acquire, some rights to these lands, but he was helpless to invoke the law in his favor. It should not be surprising, then, that because of its sheltered location[8] and the presence of an abundant water supply, he should in his own way show his reluctance to permit any part of the Cienega valley to fall into the hands of the whites. The first attempt at building a fence here found 50 Navajo looking on from a nearby hill, four of whom daringly came upon the scene to pull up the posts as soon as they had been set and to hinder any further progress in the work. When Mr. Sam E. Day later on began to build a house in the southeastern part of the valley, so many Indians were daily on hand to observe the operations that he and his helpers deemed it advisable to have their Winchesters in constant readiness; and as soon as it was learned that Mr. Day intended to erect a fence, a meeting was held in which the Indians adopted a rather menacing and aggressive policy against the unwanted foreigners. It was resolved that Mr. Day's death should take place at the moment he would attempt to set the first post. Gaining knowledge of the Indians' plans, Mr. Day called on the agent at Fort Defiance, who promptly advised the angry mob that they had no grounds whatsoever for raising objections, that Mr. Day was acting within his rights, and that if they would not withdraw all opposition they would have to suffer the consequences.

The next day about 100 Navajo braves assembled on the hill near Mr. Day's home and invited the "intruder" to a parley. Mr. Day accepted the invitation, though with some fears. Still, lest he should arouse the ire and further suspicions of the Navajo, he wisely decided to leave his Winchester at home. After all, what could he have done against 100 men? And besides, it developed that the matter was not at all as serious as all that; the sole purpose of the meeting was to offer the suggestion that Mr. Day enclose the entire Cienega valley, he furnishing the material and the Indians the labor. Furthermore, a fence should be built through the middle of the valley and, for the sake of peace and friendship, the property equally divided between Mr. Day and the Indians after the custom of the ancient patriarchs. Of course, Mr. Day would never countenance such a proposal, which was quite impossible, since another white man was occupying the unfenced southwestern portion of the valley. Peeved at their ill-success, the Navajo calmly withdrew and resigned themselves to the inevitable.

This incident took place about the year 1885 and was not far removed either in time or place from the tragic and bloodcurdling events that marked the Pleasant Valley War,[9] one of the bitterest and most dramatic feuds of Arizona history. Almost all the principals of this vendetta, no less than 20, died "with their boots on" before peace reigned again in the Tonto Basin below the south rim of the Molgollons. It is true this was a feud of white cattlemen and rustlers, all of whom were quick and accurate with the trigger and who resented any encroachment upon "their" respective ranges; and yet strangers were generally looked upon with suspicion by all occupants in these parts, and it required not only an adventurous spirit but a brave one as well to come here with the intention of making a home and living. It goes without saying, therefore, that those who were looking for trouble were never disappointed.

Experience of George Overton

Again in 1892, when the Negro George Overton built a fence for Mr. Wilkins, enclosing about 80 acres,[10] old threats and menacing tactics became the order of the day. An Indian helper whom he had engaged was so intimidated by his fellow tribesmen that he pretended to be ill and gave up the job. The Negro dared not appear at his work unarmed—not by any means an unnecessary precaution, as a later incident revealed. Returning one day from Gallup, he was informed by an Indian that his cabin had been burned to the ground and that the perpetrators of the deed were lying in wait for him. Sure enough, as he approached the building which in time became the home of the friars, he caught a glimpse of six armed Indians who to all appearances intended to waylay him. With utmost caution he circled around the bushes and hills and gained the house unnoticed. A hurried search for weapons of defense produced just three, one for himself and one for each of his two companions. The Negro tried to hand one of the guns to a Protestant missionary, who at the time was employed here as a ranch hand, but he was forthwith advised to make all possible haste to escape. He harbored no such thought, however, and emphatically so declared as he forcibly thrust a Winchester rifle into the minister's hand with the stern admonition: "If you hesitate to join in this affair, the first bullet will be fired into you." Father Anselm in relating this incident, writes: "This was probably not a courteous way of acting, but, with his life in the balance, regimentation in one form or another must have appeared to the frightened Negro to be his only salvation." The missionary was not to be convinced that this was any of his business, and at the first opportunity he ran to the stable, mounted a horse, and rode away bareback, never to be seen at Cienega again. No battle ensued, and the Negro came through the affair with nothing more than a terrible fright. . . .

Struggle for Clear Title to Cienega

When the friars entered upon the missionary field among the Navajo, the mission property—more correctly, the property purchased by Monsignor Stephan for Mother Katharine—embraced 160 acres, to none of which there existed a full and clear title. To proceed at once with placing costly and permanent improvements on these lands as long as there was the slightest danger of being dispossessed was unthinkable and might well have set the stage for a friar-cowboy feud. . . .

Even before the Wyant deal [May 1901, formally deeding both the land and the trading post on it to Mother Katharine Drexel] had been closed, a Mormon named Robert McJunkin, former cowboy, secret officer, and deputy sheriff, had entered into the picture by purchasing the furnishings of the Wyant trading post. He sought thereby to force Father Anselm to lease the store to him and strengthened his argument with the threat that, if refused, he would open a rival store close by. "Corner lots are very cheap in this country," was his proud and derisive boast. Father Anselm was not in the mood to lease the building, which was the property of Mother Katharine, certainly not to a man who was contriving to wrest lands from the Indians. What McJunkin had in mind was to lease for a short period only, until he could get acquainted with the Indians and guarantee their trade. Then he would build a store of his own nearby and "break" the mission store. But, as Father Anselm was quick to perceive, even though corner lots were so readily available, they must still be valueless without water. There was only one other unoccupied tract of land in the vicinity where water might be found, and Father Anselm had already promised Frank Walker that he would take the necessary steps so that he (Frank) could homestead it. Then Father Anselm decided to rent the trading post to Messrs. Thomas Osborne and George Manning, but refused to close the deal with Wyant unless McJunkin would leave the building and sell the furnishings to the proposed renters. McJunkin finally agreed to this for an extra payment of $50, and the sale was consummated after he gave his promise not to establish himself within a radius of eight miles. . . .

McJunkin did not keep his promise for long. Disappointed and embittered at his defeat, he entered the fray once more with the declaration that if he had enough money, he would erect a new trading post directly west and across the section line from the mission store. To his good fortune it happened that he met two friends in Gallup[11] who gladly furnished the funds for his purpose, and in a short time construction was begun of the building that came to be known as "the store on the hill." The site was a tract of good farming land occupied by a Navajo. Adjoining were 42 acres of arable land which belonged to the railroad company and on which several poor Navajo families raised good crops of corn. Father Anselm immediately put the Indians wise to what was going on and warned them that unless they took proper action, they very likely would lose both their homes and lands; they would have to approach the superintendent at once and urge him to protect them in their rights. They accepted the advice and returned to show the intruders large documents from the agency which indicated that *they* had prior claims to these lands. The agent also notified the squatters that they were taking possession contrary to law, and he tried to restrain them from erecting any buildings on that tract—a warning that was left unheeded.

Father Anselm reported the situation to Mr. Lusk [Charles S. Lusk, secretary to Monsignor J. A. Stephan, head of the Catholic Bureau in Washington, D.C.] and at the same time wrote a letter to Father Victor Aertker, O.F.M., pastor of St. Joseph Church, Los Angeles,[12] requesting him to bring the matter to the attention of officials of the Santa Fe Pacific Railway land department and to urge that they permit no white man to purchase any of these lands and that the Indians be granted prior rights in their purchase.

Most disturbing to the intrusive neighbors was the fact that they had to obtain water from a distance of about one-half mile. Therefore, they started to dig a well in the valley just south of the store, but each morning they found that the Navajo had filled the excavation with ground and large heavy stones. Frustrated in this plan, they had the audacity to ask for permission to dig a well in the field claimed by the mission. Father Anselm replied that since he had rented the field and the store to others, he was not free to give such permission, whereupon the Mormon challenged his right to rent or lease government land and declared that he would file a claim there for no other reason than to be enabled to dig a well. The Indians, he continued, could not claim the land at all, for they were not citizens and, besides, paid no taxes.

The friar did not deny that the land did not belong to him, but he insisted that the fence and other improvements were his—obviously he wished to avoid bringing the Pope into the wrangle—and made it clear that as long as no one else had acquired a right thereto and paid for the improvements he was not disposed to permit the property to be disturbed in any way. The Mormon then came to Mr. Osborne to repeat his threat and to state that since the land belonged to the government, no one had a right to prevent him from filing thereon. But Osborne, widely experienced throughout Indian Territory, Colorado, Arizona, and New Mexico as a hunter, trapper, and chief of Indian police, was not the sort that would so easily be bluffed and he could match his wits with the most brazen in the West. His sharp rejoinder that "you'll bury me here before you dig that well" was enough to silence McJunkin.

Learning the Law

Father Anselm had never heard before that an Indian could claim government land only if he were a citizen. He, therefore, hastened to Fort Defiance to inquire whether this startling news had come to the ears of the agent. The latter, it seems, had no definite information in the matter, and he must have felt that the statement was true. Only after much importuning on the part of Father Anselm did he unearth a recent circular from the Land Office which authorized the allotting of lands to Indians even before a survey had been made; the only requirement was that certain papers had to be drawn up at the county seat.[13] Forthwith, Tsischilli [Father Anselm] offered to accompany his Indian friends to Saint Johns for that particular purpose, since Robert McJunkin had posted a mineral claim on some of the land which they had improved and were now using.[14]

On Tuesday, June 4, 1901, Hosteen Dilaghush-in-Bitsoi (The Howling Grandmother's Grandson), Beshlagai Biye (Silversmith's Son), Frank Walker, and their friar friend set out on horseback for Saint Johns, more than 100 miles away. By 4:00 p.m. they reached the railroad station at Houck's Tank.[15] They had planned to spend the night at the Bennett Trading Post, only a stone's throw from the station, but when they learned that the county seat was still about 70 miles distant, they stopped only long enough to take a light lunch and rode on to the ranch home of the Mormon, Lime Parker.[16]

Frank and Mr. Parker were old acquaintances, and the unannounced visitors were, of course, very cordially received. In a few moments all were happily and interestingly engaged in reminiscing over the cowboy feuds, murders, and the general lawlessness of Apache County.

Father Anselm was here and now convinced that the county in which he lived held first place over all the counties of the Union when it came to bloody memories and disregard for law and order. Recalling that the previous sheriff, only a few days after completing his term of office, had been killed in cold blood by a brother of a man whom he had shot in self-defense, he concluded that to be sheriff of Apache County called for more than ordinary courage; it demanded, too, a very liberal portion of indifference to death, with which that official would be constantly finding himself on intimate terms. The murderer in this instance had not yet been brought to justice, and he was reported to have come from a family of which not one member had up to that time died a natural death.

After supper, which was served at 11:00 p.m., the Indians crawled beneath their blankets and slept under the open sky; the priestly guest enjoyed the comfort of a good bed which had been set up in the kitchen. At 7:00 the next morning they were again on their way, and in two hours they reached Jacob's Well. By 10:00 they had come to the top of an extensive plateau which they crossed about noon. Still another hour's ride down the southern sandy slope of the ridge brought them to Long H Ranch, where they halted for about two hours.

This ranch, erroneously named the Long Edge Ranch by Father Anselm, was the rendezvous of all cowboys and cattle rustlers of the county. The foreman was loud in complaint of the unprofitableness of the cattle business and asserted that the outfit was on the point of selling out; if any of their cattle wandered off to the Apache or Navajo reservations, they could never be recovered; but that was not the worst of it, for the company's greatest losses were attributable to the actions of its own employees who had turned cattle rustlers. There had been a time when these men were so highly organized that they constituted a complete chain all the way from Apache County to the state of Texas. Their method of operation was very simple: at the first favorable opportunity a cowhand would separate a number of steers from the herd in his charge and drive them on to the next link of the chain, and so on until the animals arrived in Texas or wherever they were to be delivered. Father Anselm expressed it as his conviction that this was being done with the fullest cooperation of the wealthy cattlemen of Texas, but he also ventured the conclusion that many cattle found their way from Texas to Apache County by the same route. Other cowhands there were who worked their own independent game by simply driving cattle to the railroad, loading and shipping them, and selling them as their own.

At 3:00 the party resumed their journey, and shortly after sundown Father Anselm and Hosteen Dilaghush-in-Bitsoi rode into Saint Johns far ahead of Frank and the silversmith's son. When the people saw a priest riding into town, their first thought was that he must be the successor to their beloved pastor, Father Badilla, who had died only a month before, but, as Father Anselm records, they were at a loss to explain why he brought the red-skinned grandson of the howling grandmother along with him. The night was spent at the only hotel in town, where Father Anselm met the brother of the deceased pastor, who had come up from Phoenix to look after the priest's affairs.[17]

The following day, Thursday June 6, was the Feast of Corpus Christi, and the Catholics of the town requested the padre of the Navajo to sing a High Mass. He was happy to comply, but when he donned the cassock and alb of the late Padre Badilla, who was a very tall man—six feet, six inches—he smiled at himself as he in his quick and witty humor envisioned the little David of the Old Testament fitting himself out in the accoutrements of the giant Saul.

It was an astounding revelation to the Indians to see their companion step into a strange Mexican church so far away and take hold without further ado. But the Indian mind quickly grasped the significance of the incident and recognized therein a simple and practical demonstration of the unity and universality of the Catholic Church.

After the services, the friar brought his Indian friends to the judge. How fortunate for them that the [Franciscan] missionaries, too, were having land difficulties! For if Father Anselm had not brought this matter to the attention of the Indian Service officials, they might never have become aware of this important provision of the Allotment Act which had been passed 14 years before. All this time Indians were assumed to have no land rights whatsoever off the reservation, and they were constantly being driven off their holdings of many years. Nor was there anyone at Saint Johns who was familiar with this law. Even the judge himself manifested his ignorance of the proper execution of the required documents. Father Anselm then drew up the applications, and the judge merely administered the oaths and witnessed the signatures. It was on this trip that Father Anselm made the acquaintance of a very valuable friend, District Attorney Alfred Ruiz, a staunch Mexican Catholic, who subsequently advised and liberally aided him in his own land troubles at Cienega.

The foursome had intended to start on the homeward journey the next morning, but while they were at supper that evening[18] an Irishman arrived from Holbrook with the report of a fracas which had taken place the night before between Indians and white cowboys at Navajo, a railroad station about 20 miles west of Houck. The cowboys had stolen a large number of Navajo ponies, branded them, and sold an entire carload which they shipped on to Kansas City. In the encounter which resulted it was rumored that two Indians had been killed and one wounded. The relation of the story finished, the conversation shifted to the conjectural lot of the murderers. One speaker incongruously thought that if the Navajo had been the aggressors and the cowboys acted in self-defense, the latter would do well to surrender to the sheriff at Saint Johns. His suggestion brought forth a storm of disapproval from the landlord:

> What? Surrender? Why that would be the greatest folly a cowboy could possibly allow to enter his mind! Surrender without any hope of bail and then be confined in jail until the next district court convenes! Whoever heard such nonsense? If he should own property in these parts, it might be well, but there are numerous other places in this blessed land where a cowboy may find all the things that Apache County has to offer. The sensible thing for him to do under these circumstances would be to shave off his beard, put on a new shirt, get himself a good horse, and make for the wide open spaces. That's what one of them did not so long ago after murdering a wealthy rancher over in New Mexico.

Father Anselm was astonished at this defiant attitude until he learned that the landlord was speaking from personal experience and fully realized what it meant to be locked in the county jail awaiting trial.

Immediately after the meal, Hosteen came to Father Anselm, begging him to start out for Navajo at once; he had some relatives there and feared that perhaps one or the other of them might be among the victims of the tragic shooting. By 8:00 all were on their way through the dark night, and as they neared the Long H Ranch, whose cowhands were reportedly implicated in the affair, the thought came to Father Anselm that if they should be noticed, they might be mistaken for the sheriff and his party in search of the murderers. "That night," he writes, "I would rather have been taken for the toughest criminal in the Southwest than for the sheriff of Apache County."

Arriving at Lime Parker's home the next morning, they were informed that the report of the incident was only partly true and that no one had been wounded, much less, killed. It was therefore decided not to turn off the direct path to go on to Navajo; but they proceeded to Houck, where they remained overnight. Here Father Anselm was consulted by a number of Navajo, among them Debethlizhin Tso (Big Black Sheep), headman of that area, as to what he thought should be done. A large number of Indians, he said, were inclined to take up arms and retake the remaining ponies by force. Father Anselm did not deny that they would be justified in regaining possession of the ponies wherever they might find them, but he was careful to caution them to make every effort to avoid violence or the shedding of blood in so doing. Then he promised to make a report of the affair to the agent at Fort Defiance.

The kindly advice and peace negotiations, however, were not accorded the expected welcome at the agency. The general opinion appeared to be that it would have been the proper thing for the Indians to attack the cowboys en masse and recover their stolen ponies. If in the affray a few of the offenders had lost their lives, it would have been a blessing for the country. The agent believed that the cattle companies could have had no reasonable complaint to offer, for it seemed to him that they purposely were engaging the toughest and roughest rascals they could find to serve as their cowhands. But of course, he explained, as agent it was certainly not within his province to advise the Indians to resort to violence. How, then, could he have expected Father Anselm to do so? While he deplored the slowness and technical flaws of juridical procedure and the fact that before he could get the sheriff to bring the rustlers into safekeeping, their stolen booty could have long ago safely reached Kansas City, he wrote the cowboys a letter in which he demanded that they return the ponies to their rightful owners; otherwise, they would be arrested. The outcome is not recorded by Father Anselm.

Mineral Claims

As soon as Father Anselm returned from Saint Johns he had a visitor at the mission in the person of Mr. Halloway who came to inquire whether he had seen the sheriff. Receiving a negative reply, he stated that since there was gold on the mission property, he contemplated staking a mineral claim there. Suiting his action to his words, he, a short time later, posted a notice to that effect to the rear of the house and, after a few more days, another a little to the west, boldly declaring that now it was time to enter into a compromise, for although gold might not be present in large quantity, his action could give rise to countless complications for the three ensuing years. Elton McJunkin, a brother of Robert and previously engaged for about a month on the mission farm, likewise posted a mineral claim on the mission property.[19] These menacing actions, however, left the friars calm and unaffected, for they realized that these men were not sufficiently supplied with funds to enable them to hold their claims by the expenditure of at least $100 in labor or improvement on each claim per year.

Besides, the matter was also receiving attention in Washington, and Mr. Lusk had called on the commissioner of Indian Affairs, requesting him to instruct the agent to determine the time when the Indian lands should be vacated. An order to this effect was issued by the superintendent and delivered personally: if Robert McJunkin resolved to leave without further trouble by September 10, 1902, he would be permitted to tear down his building and move elsewhere. If he should fail to arrive at a decision by that time, the case would be brought before the district court and the store would become the property of the Indian.

The gold mine claim was abdicated about November 1901, but the "store on the hill" remained.[20] About six months later Halloway sold his interest in the store to Gabriel Weidemeier and started out for himself at Fort Defiance. With the construction of St. Michael's School under way, Weidemeier, as wily and troublesome as his former partner, conceived the plan of moving his "hell-hole" and prospective saloon to a tract of land which Mother Katharine had just purchased from Mr. Day. Being railroad land, this scheme was foiled by Father Anselm's influence with the railroad land commissioner. The latter began to take a great interest in the welfare of the Navajo and worked hard[21] for the enactment of a law by Congress, by which railroad lands occupied and used by Indians might be exchanged for government lands and then legally assigned to them—a measure which was strenuously promoted by Father Anselm, by the Bureau in Washington, and by the local superintendent.

From this it may be seen that the troubles of the missionaries in the Wild West were not chiefly with the redskins, whom they had come to educate and civilize, but with educated and crafty white men who seemed to find their greatest satisfaction and pleasure in scheming and attempting to overreach others. The example of his white neighbors inspired the Negro, George Overton, to come into the conflict. On the strength of labor that he had performed in the improvement of the property for which Mother Katharine had paid $2,000, he now tried his hand at invoking the law in his favor. To quiet him Father Berard Haile crossed the mountain to obtain a statement in writing from Mr. Wilkin, who was conducting a trading post on the east slope of the Chuska Range, more than 70 miles away. Father Anselm drove to the home of Mr. Meadows in the Zuni Mountains for the same purpose. Each declared that the Negro had never before protested against their occupation and use of these respective lands, that he had been fully remunerated for all the work that he had done for them, and that even the log cabin in which he lived was not his own, but had been merely offered to him as a place to stay. The Negro's subsequent correspondence with the land office, in which he represented himself as a martyr to the friars' injustice, was ineffectual. . . .

Building St. Michael's School

Preliminary work on the construction of St. Michael's School was begun on March 1, 1902, with Indians doing most of the common labor, such as excavating, quarrying, hauling rock, and freighting of other material. Specifications called for a very large building, the main part of which measured 136 by 69 feet; the south wing, 77 by 22 feet, and the middle wing, which was to include the chapel on the second floor, 74 by 34 feet. The main structure and part of the middle wing were to be three stories and the rest two stories high, with a nine-foot basement under the front part of the building. Construction was to be entirely of native hard sandstone, available on the acquired land less than half a mile away. . . .

On March 19 the first load of lumber was freighted out from Gallup by the Jesus brothers, half-breed Navajo who lived about 15 miles northeast of Gallup, and on April 16 the first blast was set off in the nearby quarry to procure rock for the foundation. By October the sisters' temporary quarters were fairly ready for occupancy, and on the 19th of that month Mother Katharine arrived with Mother Evangelist, the newly appointed superioress who had formerly presided over St. Catherine School, Sister Agatha, and Sister Angela. Three days later, Miss Josephine W. Drexel came to St. Michaels with Sisters Ambrose and Annunciation. They were followed by four others on October 24: Sisters Inez, Josephine, Mary Theresa, and Gertrude; Sisters Bridget and John of the Cross arrived on December 16 to complete the personnel[22] required to conduct the school.

The hope of finishing the building by November was not realized, and the water system was not installed until the ensuing spring. It was, therefore, under makeshift conditions that the school was opened according to schedule on December 3, 1902,[23] the feast of St. Francis Xavier, with 46 pupils in attendance.[24] On this occasion Father Berard Haile, chaplain of the school, celebrated Mass in the east part of the middle wing, where religious services had to be temporarily conducted. Sisters and children occupied the west part of this wing until about the middle of January 1903, when the entire building was brought to completion.

The first service in the new chapel was a levitical High Mass celebrated by Father Anselm at midnight on Christmas 1902. The sermon was delivered by Father Leopold. . . .

Beginning with September 1, 1902, Cienega became officially known as St. Michaels, Arizona, for it was on that day that a post office was opened in the Wyant store, with John G. Walker, a brother of Frank and a graduate of Hampton, Virginia, as postmaster.[25] This was indeed a most welcome convenience, for hitherto it had been necessary to send and receive mail from Fort Defiance.

The Navajo literally besieged the mission all winter, begging for clothing for themselves and their children, and they lost large numbers of horses, burros, cattle, sheep, and goats as a result of the extreme cold and by starvation. The government made no notable efforts to relieve their sorry plight at the time, but in the spring seeds were distributed to the more needy. The deep snow and abundant rainfall which followed gave fine prospects of good crops for the coming season.

Notes

1. From Emanuel Trockur, "Franciscan Missions among the Navajo Indians: VI," *Provincial Chronicle* 14 (Fall 1941): 37–42, 47–53, and 56–57.

2. The Treaty of 1868 assigned to the Navajo a reservation of 3,328,000 acres in northeastern Arizona and northwestern New Mexico; executive order extensions, so called because they were made by the president himself on October 29, 1878, to the west, and on January 6, 1880, to the east and south, almost doubled the Navajo domain. By executive orders on December 16, 1882, May 17, 1884, April 24, 1886, January 8, 1900, November 14, 1901, May 15, 1905, January 28, 1908, January 16, 1911, December 1, 1913, and January 19, 1918, and by acts of Congress on May 23, 1930, March 1, 1933, and June 14, 1934, further extensions were added, so that today the Navajo reservation comprises about 25,000 square miles or 16 million acres.

3. Cf. Anselm Weber, FMN 43 (November 1916):1027; Zephyrin Engelhardt, *The Franciscans in Arizona* (Harbor Springs, Mich.: Holy Child Indian School, 1899), 208.

4. A misconception of this fact has caused no little criticism on the part of white cattlemen against the government as well as its wards, and has occasioned much embarrassment to the Navajo and deprived him of much of the land which he had occupied from time immemorial. It gave rise to the untruthful and unfair plea of the white man, "Put the Navajo back *on* the reservation where he belongs." As a matter of fact, these Indians had never been anywhere else than off the reservation. The false conclusion that he was trespassing upon these lands gained credence in Washington, where the Indian had no support, since he was not entitled to suffrage, and he was gradually being "squeezed" into the confines of an already overcrowded reservation. It was here that Father Anselm proved himself the great friend of the Navajo by his outstanding activities in urging Congress to extend the reservation and in assisting the Indians to lease railroad lands for grazing purposes.

5. A township is six miles square, subdivided into 36 plots called sections, each one mile square and containing 640 acres. These plots are numbered 1 to 36. The odd-numbered sections within these grants became property of the railroad company; the even-numbered remained public domain, except within the extensions where they became Indian lands. In

effect then, within the 50-mile limit, only one-half of the area was actually reservation for the reason that the government could not give to the Indians what it had already given to the railroad company years before. Some government officials seem to doubt whether there ever were any railroad lands in the extensions that were made prior to the building of the railroad, and even in those that were made after the road construction they have raised the question as to whether certain tracts had been specifically deeded over to the railroad.

6. Accordingly, Father Anselm purchased from the railroad company the 40-acre tract upon which our chapel stands at Fort Defiance and also the "farm" which lies less than two miles northeast of St. Michaels, both in the Executive Order Extension of 1880. These deeds, quitclaims, we have been informed only recently by the land clerk at Window Rock, are not recognized by the Washington Land Office. This, however, should cause no fears to the mission, since a part of the section on which the farm is located was deeded by the railroad company to the United States on September 19, 1915. If the United States accepted this deed from the railroad, it certainly should recognize the railroad company's deed to another party.

7. In the year 1925 the Superior of St. Michael's Mission was advised that the railroad leases, which had previously been attended to by Father Anselm, were in default to the amount of almost $3,000, and that if the money would not be forthcoming within a given time, they would be canceled. Not familiar with the land work, the friar approached the superintendent at Fort Defiance, requesting that something be done lest these lands be lost to the Navajo living along the railroad. "Why, I have nothing to do with them; those Indians are off the reservation," was the answer he received, and the friar's remark that if nothing would be done, they would be forced into the reservation, was received with an indifferent official shrug of the shoulders. During the summer and fall of that year the friar held meetings at various points in Arizona and New Mexico and collected from the Indians and their friends $2,822.80. This sum was sufficient to cover the payments that were overdue, and the railroad was disposed to renew the lease for another year by the promise that efforts would be made to secure future lease monies from the Navajo Tribal Fund.

8. Anselm Weber, FMN 26 (May 1899): 379.

9. Cf. Earle R. Forrest, *Arizona's Dark and Bloody Ground* (Caldwell, Idaho: Caxton Printers, 1936). This book gives a stirring account of the hectic days of 1887 in central Arizona, and its story seems to be reliably authenticated.

10. Weber, FMN 26 (May 1899): 379.

11. Gabriel Weidemeier and Monroe Halloway.

12. This was on the assumption that these lands actually belonged to the railroad company; however, there seems to be some doubt at the Central Agency that this tract had ever been deeded over to them by the government. Cf. Weber, FMN 28 (September 1901): 722 ff.

13. Father Anselm, no doubt, based his contention on Section 4 of the Indian Allotment Act of February 8, 1887, which provided that any Indian not living upon a reservation could settle upon any surveyed or unsurveyed lands of the United States not otherwise appropriated, and have the same allotted to him or her upon application to the Land Office in his district.

14. [Father Emanuel here refers to the "Chronicle of St. Michaels," recorded first by Father Juvenal Schnorbus, with later entries by Father Anselm Weber, Father Frederick Hartung, and, after October 15, 1900, by Father Leopold Ostermann. The typescript version of this document on file at FAC (Box PLA.376 St. Michaels, env. St. Michaels Earliest History 1898–1907), entitled "History of the Ranch, about Seven Miles South of Fort Defiance (Cienega) Arizona, Now St. Michael's Missions," is paginated differently from the copy cited by Father Emanuel. I have added an author entry and changed title and page

references to match the typescript copy in the Cincinnati archives.] Juvenal Schnorbus et al., "History of the Ranch," 22.

15. This was the original name of Houck, Arizona; the station at the time was located at the juncture of Black Creek and the Puerco, a short distance east of the railroad bridge and about one mile west of the present location.

16. Lime Parker lived at Black Springs, about three and a half miles south of present-day Sanders, Arizona. Frank Walker's father had resided here years before, and nearby was the grave of his little daughter, whom he had baptized before she died. This is about one-half mile south of Emigrant Springs. Father Anselm gives the distance from Houck to this point as 15 miles; actually it is less than 10; from Lime Parker's to Saint Johns, he says, was 55 miles. This is about correct. The distance then from Houck to Saint Johns is no more than 65 miles, and not 70, as Father Anselm was informed. When he writes that it was 15 miles from Lime Parker's to Jacob's Well, he again overestimates by about five miles.

17. Father Badilla, a native Costa Rican, died at Saint Johns on May 3, 1901, and his mortal remains lie buried in the church there, which this year is being superseded by a more imposing structure.

18. Weber, FMN 28 (October 1901): 817.

19. Schnorbus et al., "History," 22.

20. Weber, FMN 29 (August 1902): 643.

21. Weber, FMN 28 (October 1901): 821.

22. Schnorbus et al., "History," 24–25; Weber, FMN 29 (December 1902): 997. This was Mother Katharine's fourth visit here. She had been at Cienega for the third time on May 25, 1902, with Sister Agatha, of Santa Fe. Cf. Schnorbus et al., "History," 24. Sister Gertrude, who since August 1941 is stationed at the Tegakwitha Mission School at Houck, supplied the names of all the sisters who first came to St. Michaels. She was in the third contingent, which, she says, numbered four sisters and not three, as the chronicler relates. Of these sisters, all are living at this writing (October 7, 1941), except four: Sisters Josephine, Inez, Bridget, and Evangelist.

23. Weber, FMN 30 (March 1903): 220.

24. Schnorbus et al., "History," 25; FMSW (1917): 19, says 51 pupils, while the *Indian Sentinel* (1908): 23, says there were 57. The latter may have been the actual number enrolled the first year. Writing in March 1903, Father Anselm set the enrollment figure roundly at 50; Weber, FMN 30 (April 1903): 305.

25. Weber, FMN 29 (November 1902): 912; Schnorbus et al., "History," 24, records that the post office supplies had been received on August 22. Both Mr. [Charles S.] Lusk and Mr. [Robert E.] Morrison had used their influence in bringing about the establishment of the post office. [In an earlier note to a section of the article we have not reprinted, Father Emanuel writes that "Mr. Morrison, whom Father Anselm had met in Prescott, was former Attorney General of Arizona and one of the best lawyers in the Southwest. Both these Catholic gentlemen (Morrison and another attorney, Mr. Alfred Ruiz) cooperated in obtaining tax exemption for all mission property at St. Michaels. Cf. Weber, FMN 29 (August 1902): 643."] On August 2, 1902, Mr. Lusk wrote to inform Father Anselm that St. Michaels had been established as a post office and that Mr. Walker had been appointed to take charge. Cf. Letters in St. Michaels archives.

19

White Profits from Navajo Lands[1]

Anselm Weber, O.F.M.

[This early description of a visit to Navajo country by Eastern capitalists and politicians illustrates how the power structure, centered in Washington, D.C., might manipulate events and have its way with the Navajo despite substantial local resistance. In this episode, note the uniform support among white officials, including the local Indian agent, for the "foot in the door" approach to exploiting Navajo resources and "opening the reservation." An 1891 law required that prospecting on the reservation be approved by "a council for the Navajo," and so "an occasional group of Navajo in the affected San Juan or Shiprock area would be summoned to rubber stamp an agreement authorizing such exploration."[2] In the narrative below, Father Anselm shows how such authorizations were obtained. It would become much worse. According to Peter Iverson's *The Navajo Nation*, "by the 1920s prospectors and oil company officials were besieging the Navajo."[3] Whatever the treaties and laws might say, the whites were in charge of the game and could change the rules to suit their purposes. Experiences such as this one must have helped to fire Father Anselm's growing passion to defend Indian lands and resources against encroachment. Another strong point of this chapter is its portrayal of the political acumen and organizational skills of Chee Dodge.]

A few months ago Mr. S. E. Day, our one-time neighbor, remarked to me that it was most strange to him to note how our government in Washington was showing its interest in the welfare of the Indians. What was it that provoked this sarcastic remark? A certain Mr. Huff,[4] capitalist and coal baron of Pennsylvania, arrived in Gallup by private railway car with several other companions about the middle of June. The car was switched to a siding and the party proceeded to Fort Defiance, where they deported themselves in a lordly manner, demanding board and lodging for themselves and feed for their horses as per a letter which they presented from the secretary of the interior. Still another letter, actually a written contract, signed by the same secretary, was produced permitting Mr. Huff and company to explore the reservation for gold, silver, copper, coal, and oil for a period of two years. Wherever minerals would be found within this time, permission was given to conduct mining operations for eight more years. At the expiration of these 10 years they had the option to renew the contract.

The agreement provided that 4 percent of the earnings be entrusted to the secretary of the interior to be appropriated at his discretion for the benefit of the Navajo. For validity this contract required the consent and written approval of the Indians. For this reason the agent was advised by telegraph to call a meeting as soon as possible of the influential headmen of the tribe. The date was set: July 16.

Mr. Huff then returned to the East in his special car, leaving a Mr. Worth as representative of the company. Joined by Mr. Keam, of Keams Canyon, the latter hired an Indian pathfinder and the party set out on their exploratory expedition. Father Berard met them in the Tunicha Mountains; they invited us to attend the meeting. Several headmen now came to us to consult us and to seek our advice. While we were opposed to having the reservation, or only a part thereof, converted into a mining district, since contact with the mine laborers might demoralize our Navajo, we nevertheless were convinced that the reservation would be "opened" if it were found to contain rich mineral deposits, and that even despite Indian objections.

By the evening of July 15 more than 200 had put in their appearance at Fort Defiance, all, for the most part, perplexed and undecided. It was here that Chee Dodge, trader near Round Rock, displayed his intelligence, his great influence over his tribesmen, and his natural leadership talent. After reading the contract he had a complete knowledge of its contents, and several conversations with Mr. Worth had brought the latter to the conviction that he had won Mr. Dodge over to his plan.

On this same evening Mr. Dodge held his own preliminary session in a shed next to the agency stable. He began by stating that the Treaty of 1868 was still in effect and no one could alter it without their consent. It was in their power to retain the reservation or to dispose of it. Neither the secretary of the interior nor the Washington officials nor the agent could take any action in this regard unless the Navajo agreed. And in the event anyone should threaten their rights, they could register their protest and carry their appeal to the people of the nation, because there are always to be found those who will champion the cause of the oppressed. He went on to point out that, if they so wished, they could decide to allow Mr. Worth to prospect for minerals for a period of two years. In case he would discover valuable deposits, then they could come to an agreement as to the value of the findings; another meeting could be held and that particular area of the reservation could be leased for its estimated worth. But to lease the entire reservation without any further ado—such an action, NEVER!

All agreed to this decision, whereupon Mr. Dodge took aside a number of headmen, his personal friends, and instructed them as to what they should say at the meeting the next day. Since he wished to be one of the main speakers at that meeting, it was then unanimously decided that Frank Walker, our interpreter, should do the interpreting.

The meeting began the next morning at about 10:00. I myself, Father Berard, and Father Samuel Gelting, who was staying with us at the time, were present. Soon the spacious hall was filled with about 300 Indians, with the agent, Mr. Worth, Mr. Keam, two stenographers, and the school superintendent seated before them. While the superintendent was ceremoniously calling the meeting to order, Mr. Dodge paid no heed whatsoever, concerned only with assigning his friends to their places and "taking over" as if he were the only one that had anything to say. Frank Walker was unanimously chosen as interpreter, and when the superintendent had read the first words of the long-winded document, construed in technical legal form, he asked Frank to give a literal translation. Frank replied that that was quite impossible. Indeed, the oft-repeated phrases, "the party of the first part and the party of the second part" and "of the afore-said first part and of the afore-said second part" are enough to drive the very best Navajo interpreter to utter despair. Here Mr. Dodge arose to explain that the document simply could not lend itself to a literal translation. Besides, that was not necessary. He stated that he understood the full meaning of the contract and that, if the agent would merely recall its salient points, it would be an easy matter for him to inform the Indians of its contents. With this the procedure went on without further difficulty.

Mr. Keam then took the floor and, in a lengthy, cunningly worded speech, sought to win the Indians over to his plans. Reminding them of his many years of friendly relations with them and how he at all times had promoted their best interests both in word and deed, he went on to say that, were he not convinced that this contract was for their benefit, he not only would remain silent, but he would have remained away from this meeting. He ended by extolling the advantages that would accrue to the Indians: the 4 percent of the profits and, in addition, labor and wages. Furthermore, though they were far away from the railroad, they could now remain in their own homes and find work with the mining company.

An Indian promptly put the question: "How much shall we receive in payment for our labor? Perhaps 50¢ a day? And what kind of work could they do?" Undoubtedly, he thought, it would be only common labor at the surface, while the actual mining operations would be given to white men for a wage of $4 to $5 a day. He was followed by the old stalwart Black Horse, who a few years before had nearly murdered an agent and who, by his vigorous gestures and angry voice, stood out before all the others. With a blast of fiery and furious eloquence he angrily asked when the white man would cease to bother the Indians. Incessantly, gold seekers had been coming into their domain asking permission to prospect for gold. In case none was found, the matter would once and for all be settled, and the Navajo could from then on live undisturbed on their reservation. He alluded to the time when the government had sent General McCook with many soldiers, cavalrymen, and scientists for the purpose of determining whether gold was to be found in the Carriso Mountains. None was found, and the government assured the Indians that this would be the last time they would be annoyed. So now what is this Mr. Worth here for? He must indeed be a very poor, hungry dog thus to be pursuing us. Frank politely refrained from interpreting this last sentence.

Another headman raised the question as to how the reservation could be leased as long as it was not known whether it contained minerals; and even if minerals were to be found, it still was impossible to estimate their value. Why not, therefore, permit a two-year period for prospecting and then define a specified area and estimate its worth? Another meeting could then be called and a lease of that section of the reservation arranged. This was the final decision, which was in accord with the outcome of the deliberations of the previous night.

Protestations on the part of the agent and of Mr. Worth and Mr. Keam had been to no avail. No business organization, they contended, could afford to accept such a proposal. It could not be considered for even one moment, for how could a company be expected to undertake such costly and laborious explorations without the assurance of deriving a profit therefrom? Furthermore, there was a law which decreed that Indians might lease their lands for a term of not less than 10 years; if now they wished to lease for only two years, a special act of Congress would be required. But what do Indians know about laws or Congress or congressional acts? They remained obstinate in their demands, and it became evident that further discussion would be futile.

Asked by Mr. Keam to explain the meaning and significance of an act of Congress, Frank Walker replied that he did not think himself equal to the task. Obviously, then, there was no one who could give an intelligent explanation except Chee Dodge, but he happened to be on the side of the opposition. Finally, Mr. Keam summed up enough courage to ask Mr. Dodge whether he thought he could and whether he would be willing to explain this matter to his tribesmen. With a quick "Why not?" Chee Dodge was on his feet and proceeded to explain that the Navajo had no choice but to grant a lease for ten years. Thereupon Mr. Keam launched out in a lengthy, carefully worded speech in which he gave every possible reason and argument why the Indians should enter into this agreement. Victory for the company appeared in sight when the Indians declared that they were now undecided as to what course they should take. Therefore, they should be permitted to adjourn in order that they might confer among themselves before arriving at a decision. Noontime had arrived and the request was granted.

At the afternoon session it soon became apparent that Henry Dodge had erred completely in believing that Mr. Keam had made a favorable impression by his masterful speech, for the Indians had in the meantime adopted a policy not of mere indecision and postponement, but of open resistance.

Without intending to describe the meeting in all the details of its wearisome procedure, I shall touch upon some of the interesting incidents. On one occasion when Mr. Worth attempted to liven the group with a pleasantry, saying that if the contract would be entered into, the Indians would eventually be riding about in golden carriages, he received the sarcastic rejoinder that this meeting had been called not for the purpose of listening to wisecracks, but rather to deliberate over a very important and solemn matter.

The Indians were not willing to accept a mere 4 percent; they felt that they should receive at least 10 percent. After some hesitation, Mr. Worth did finally make an offer of 5 percent. All were displeased at seeing the agent enthusiastically siding with the company. One of the headmen pointed to him, saying that he ought to take his place next to the Indians and uphold their rights instead of allying himself with the Americans favoring the acceptance of the contract. To this the agent replied that he viewed the matter in quite another light, for in his opinion signing of the contract would be of great benefit to the Navajo, whereas refusal would result in a disastrous prospecting of the reservation by countless irresponsible gold seekers. This remark stirred up a veritable hornet's nest, and the agent was accused of attempting to coerce the Indians by threats to sign the contract. "Are you not our agent sent among us to defend our rights?" they asked, and "Is Washington unable to keep these gold hunters away from our reservation?" and so on.

Toward evening a headman stood up to say that the leasing of the entire reservation was a question of grave importance and one that demanded serious and thorough consideration in advance of any decision. Of course, he added, if it were a mere matter of disposing of a few head of sheep or goats, a unanimous agreement could be reached very easily. He therefore moved that they adjourn so that the matter could be further discussed.

The results of their deliberations that evening were made clear at the very outset the next morning. Headman after headman declared that the tribe was not adequately represented here, because the meeting had been announced on too brief notice. Some of the headmen stated that they were the only Indians present from their areas and that they did not wish to assume responsibility for the approval or rejection of the contract without consulting with other influential members of the tribe. It was the general consensus that a definite decision be deferred and that another meeting be called within perhaps 30 days. The agent was plainly disturbed. Although a Washington telegram had urged that the deal be closed, he would have been blind not to see that further exertion on his part would be useless. He whispered a few words to Mr. Keam and Mr. Worth, whereupon the latter rose to state that he had no thought of compelling them to a decision here and now and that he would grant them as much time as they liked—30, 60, or even 90 days. Besides, he would like to take a number of headmen to Washington or perhaps have Washington officials come here for further discussion of the matter. In view of this concession, he proposed that they now give a token of their goodwill by giving a 10-year lease for a square mile anywhere on the reservation, if need be, of a mere sand hill. After interpreting this to his people, Mr. Dodge concluded by saying that, in his opinion, it would be well for them to make this slight concession. All agreed.

To the question as to the location of his selection of a square mile, Mr. Worth replied that he did not know definitely, but that likely it would be in the Lukachukai or Carriso Mountains. Obviously, the Indians had been taken unawares and it was evident that the selection would be made in the Carriso Mountains, as actually was the case later. Further questioned as to when he would take a delegation of headmen to Washington, he stated that he was leaving that to the government, whether they should go to Washington or whether Washington officials should come to them. In fact, he was leaving the entire matter in the hands of the federal government. Ten headmen were then chosen to sign the contract, which was also witnessed by Frank Walker as interpreter.

Mr. Worth then departed for the East; he soon was back again to start his gold-digging operations with the help of a few whites and Indians within his selected square mile in the Carriso Mountains. With considerable difficulty he managed in 23 days to reach the forbidding mountain country which lies 130 miles from the nearest railroad station. More than once the Indians left him in the lurch. Finding it impossible to cross the Lukachukai Mountains, he had to retrace his course to reach the other side of the Tunicha Mountains by way of Cottonwood Pass and then proceed along the east slope of this chain to the Carrisos.

On November 1 it was decided to call another meeting for November 7. Seven days, however, is much too brief a time to get word to the Navajo living at great distances, and of the six headmen who appeared on the appointed day, only three lived on the reservation. Honoring the meeting by their presence were Messrs. Worth and Keam and also Mr. Huff, who had arrived with Congressman Dazzell of Pennsylvania. These gentlemen presented their case in such a favorable light that the headmen appeared willing to sign the contract. However, they demanded that Henry Dodge be called to the meeting. Late on the evening of November 8 the agent sent a messenger to Mr. Dodge's home only to learn that Mr. Dodge was at his trading post at Round Rock, 75 miles from Fort Defiance. Since Mr. Huff had to leave the next day, he all but insisted upon an immediate acceptance of the contract. All six headmen eventually agreed to sign the document, with the understanding, however, that it would lack validity unless it would later be signed by Mr. Dodge. With this understanding, 13 more Indians affixed their mark to the contract. Frank Walker refused to sign until Mr. Dodge would do so.

Now Mr. Dodge found himself in a predicament: if he would sign the contract he would risk the displeasure of those headmen who had not been informed, and if he refused, he would be on bad terms with the government. On the other hand, the Indians had given their conditional consent, but the document itself did not so state. Soon thereafter, as was to be suspected, it was noised about in responsible quarters that, even though Mr. Dodge would withhold his signature, the secretary of the interior would nevertheless consider the contract valid for the simple reason that the Navajo tribe does not depend upon a single individual. After considerable hesitation and delay, Mr. Dodge and our interpreter *did* sign the contract on November 25, following a telegraphic inquiry by the secretary of the interior as to whether this had been done—a glaring example of how contracts and agreements are entered into with Indians.

I hardly believe that the Huff Company will have reasons to rejoice over their contract. No doubt, there are localities in the Carriso Mountains where gold may be found, but the question remains whether in commercial payable quantity. The Black Mountains in the northwest section of the reservation are reported to contain gold deposits; possibly so. Why, in the vicinity of our mission, prospectors are said to have made a rich find some years ago—one of them, so the story goes, was murdered either by the Navajo or one of his associates, but who cares to rely upon rumors and to seek the location, and find it? Rich copper deposits are rumored to exist in the northwestern part of the reservation; the same is true of other parts of our land, as, for example, Calumet, Michigan, but here rail and water transportation renders production less costly.

As for coal, there is a great quantity in our immediate surroundings, and still more along the San Juan River and beneath the desert sands east of the mountain chains. But why strike out for distant points when abundance is so near at hand, as in Gallup, where an inexhaustible supply is to be found so near the railroad?

Oil? Well, here again we are quite "up-to-date." Gallup and vicinity are witnessing a genuine "oil craze," but I pity the poor victims of the East who become its prey.

Notes

1. From Anselm Weber, FMN 28 (December 1901): 995–99; 29 (January 1902): 24–28. Translated by Emanuel Trockur.

2. Peter Iverson, *The Navajo Nation* (Albuquerque: University of New Mexico Press, 1981), 19.

3. Iverson, *Navajo Nation*, 19.

4. Probably George Franklin Huff, whose financial interests are said to have included banking, coke, coal, railroads, natural gas, and other utilities. Huff served in the U.S. House of Representatives, and was chairman of the Committee on Mines and Mining from 1907 to 1913.

20

The Navajo Indians:
A Statement of Facts[1]

Anselm Weber, O.F.M.

[Father Anselm's pamphlet of 1914, *A Statement of Facts*, was an attempt to educate legislators and other citizens on the true situation of the Navajo and their land. It was intended to counteract misconceptions encouraged by interest groups such as American cattlemen who talked of "opening up" the Navajo reservation to settlement by the non-Navajo and of "excess" land there, or who encouraged the forcible removal of the Navajo living outside the reservation "back" onto the reservation "where they belonged," when, in fact, the traditional home territory of many of the Navajo living outside the reservation had never been within the boundaries of the Navajo reservation as it was then defined.

Between the manuscript and the final printed version of *A Statement of Facts*, Father Anselm made three kinds of changes: 1) stylistic and factual adjustments, as in the inclusion of more accurate official figures from the 1910 census, or altered estimates of that portion of the land within the reservation boundaries that did not really belong to the Navajo; 2) moderations in tone and personal focus, as in the change of the initial first-order heading from "Colonization of the Navajo Reservation" to "The Navajo Indians,"or as when statements addressed to, or made about, Senator Albert B. Fall of New Mexico were softened to refer merely to the Congressional Record or "Congress"; and 3) substantial cuts of introductory and other material, including a quotation from Theodore Roosevelt and several statements revealing how strongly Father Anselm disagreed with the efforts by white politicians to "open up" Navajo lands and displace the Navajo people.

I have added back into the text changes of type 2 and 3, while retaining the corrections, expansions, and factual adjustments Father Anselm made in revising the manuscript for publication. That is, the text below does not reintroduce all deletions from the manuscript, but only those judged to fall into categories 2 and 3. Thus it reintroduces the "straight language" that Father Anselm softened in his final editing, but not the material he judged to be incomplete or inaccurate and therefore altered or expanded.

Father Anselm's biographer states that it was Father William Ketcham, the director of the Bureau of Catholic Indian Missions, who "stripped . . . all direct allusions to personalities" from the original manuscript.[2] Along with the allusions to personalities went much of the passion of the initial draft. Apparently Father Anselm was persuaded that a more measured and diplomatic "statement of facts" was less apt to alienate influential readers. For our purposes, the original version is preferable. It reveals a Father Anselm combative and outraged over the efforts of powerful politicians, and Senator Albert Fall in particular, to displace the Navajo and appropriate their land.

Father Anselm's deletions here reinserted into the text are given in italics. Where the flow of the final text is interrupted by the insertion, as where, instead of simply deleting a section, Father Anselm reworked the surrounding text, thereby introducing an alternative reading, I have bracketed the reinserted material.

In the published version of *A Statement of Facts*, Father Anselm indicated emphasis both by italics and by putting words and phrases entirely in capital letters. Both types of emphasis are retained in the text below, but to distinguish deleted text reintroduced here, shown in italics, from Anselm's use of italics for emphasis, words he italicized in the published version are given in bold rather than italics. Also, I have largely retained Father Anselm's capitalization format as it appears in the published pamphlet.

Father Anselm passed away just as his antagonist was achieving the pinnacle of his power. In 1921, Senator Fall was appointed secretary of the interior in the cabinet of President Warren B. Harding. He would resign in 1923, and soon thereafter came the rumors of corruption associated with the granting of oil leases, then the official investigations that ultimately led to his conviction and imprisonment for taking bribes. Senator Fall would become the first U.S. cabinet officer ever to be imprisoned for felonies committed in the course of his official duties.[3]

Among the ironies of the story of the senator's rise and fall from power is an outcome that Father Anselm would have much appreciated. In 1935, three years after his release from the New Mexico State Penitentiary, Albert Fall accepted baptism into the Catholic Church at the hands of Father Albert Braun, pastor of the Mescalero reservation,[4] one of the reservations that Fall had earlier tried to open to settlement and public use.]

❖

COLONIZATION OF THE NAVAJO RESERVATION

On the 18th of July, 1911, I was speeding from London, England, towards Harwich, on my way to Germany. Four of us were sharing the same coupe, myself, an Englishman on his way to view the Rhine, and two Germans whose physiognomies betrayed their descent from Abraham. Both spoke English fluently, though with a German-Hebrew accent; both had spent 19 years in New York City. Just at that time the tension between France and England on one side and Germany on the other was nearing the breaking point, and this tension soon formed the subject of conversation between the Englishman and the two Germans. After some preliminary skirmishing my Hebrew friend said to the Englishman: "You have colonies everywhere; you have stolen the whole world together while Germany was weak; now when Germany has become strong and wants to steal a little too of what you didn't gobble up yet, then you won't let her." The Englishman objected to the expression "steal," but my Hebrew friend answered him: "Vell, you got it, you got it! How did you get it?"

As long as New Mexico and Arizona were weak, they could do very little by way of opening up and "colonizing" the various Indian reservations, but now, since four Senators and two Congressmen hold forth at the Capitol, conditions have changed. Senator Fall of New Mexico, speaking of the Navajo, expressed it in this way: "New Mexico and Arizona have been wards of the Government for sixty years past. they have had no representatives upon the floor of this body, nor upon the floor of the other House; that is, a representative who had a vote. We have been dealt with simply by the Bureaus of the Government, and it is yet almost impossible, apparently, to convince the different Departments of the Government that New Mexico is now a sovereign state of the Union" (Cong. Record 1913, Page 2317).

And Judge Medler, representing Senator Catron at a hearing in re Pueblo Indians before Mr. F. H. Abbott, Acting Commissioner of Indian Affairs, said: "I have lived under the Territorial Government for years. We were trying for years to get Statehood so the United States would leave us alone. We have got it; now leave us alone; let us manage our own business."

One of the first acts of the NEW MEXICO LEGISLATURE after obtaining statehood was to memorialize Congress to allot to each Navajo 160 acres and then to throw the remaining acres open to public settlement. Before the senatorial election at Santa Fe, the following significant item appeared in the Albuquerque Herald:

Santa Fe, New Mexico. March 18, 1912. An interesting sidelight in the senatorial situation developed yesterday, when a number of influential members in both houses began receiving telegrams from a variety of citizens in the county of San Juan, asking them to ascertain before voting for a senator just where the respective candidates stood on the opening and allotting of the Navajo Indian reservation. . . . It is said here that the San Juan people have not confined themselves to the New Mexico Legislature alone, but that they are sending the same kind of messages to the Legislature in Arizona. The San Juan representatives here, including a delegation of citizens, assert that the senators from Arizona and Utah will join forces with the New Mexicans in an effort to open the reservation.

It would be interesting to know what senators, if any, have pledged themselves before their election to this policy. A few days after his election, on March 27th, 1912, SENATOR T. B. CATRON gave the following statement:

It will be my purpose also to try to enact laws by which Indians who are now in New Mexico shall be made to go upon land which shall be allotted to them, and remain there and adopt civilized and industrious habits. There are reservations now for the Mescalero Apaches, Jicarilla Apaches, and Navajo amounting to many millions of acres and totaling nearly 1,000 acres for each man, woman, and child. The retaining of so much land by these Indians is hampering and keeping back the development of the State and is keeping it from being filled up with settlers and is holding back its progress.

I shall disprove the 1,000-acre assertion later.

Last January (1914) I was told that the delegations of Arizona, New Mexico, Utah, and Colorado were to combine to have the Navajo reservation opened to settlement.

A State Senator of New Mexico lately assured one of the Superintendents of the Indian Service that the present session of Congress would pass a bill making the opening of the Navajo reservation mandatory; that a portion of the Zuni reservation would be opened for the benefit of the Mormon setters of Ramah, etc. (Density of population in McKinley County 2.4 per sq. mile, of the Zuni reservation within said county 5 per sq. mile).

In HEARINGS BEFORE A SUB-COMMITTEE on Indian Affairs of the House of Representatives, 1913, I see on page 12 that $43,000 are asked for the survey of Executive Order Extension of November 9, 1907, and January 28, 1908, embracing 43 townships in Arizona. I shall revert to this item later. Mr. Reeves, of the Indian Office, states: "In Arizona the State Land Commission and the cattlemen and others have insisted on the Office carrying out that provision (Act of May 29, 1908), because they want the surplus lands restored to the Public Domain so they can use them for grazing ground."

I could refer to Congressional Records of June 17, September 18, and December 15, 1913, to show the attitude of Senators Fall and Smith and the Arizona State Land Commission in this regard, but I think the point will be conceded that a strong movement has been started to allot and open up the Navajo reservation.

The Navajo Indians

For several years past there has been agitated the question of allotting lands in Arizona and New Mexico to the Navajo and other Indians and throwing open to settlement and entry under the public land laws the unallotted balance of lands now embraced in Indian reservations. The cry has been loud that these reservations are too large and are not needed by the Indians. Unfortunately, some members of the delegations from these states have appeared to be influenced by exaggerated and untrue statements upon this question, and as the Indians are absolutely dependent upon the federal government for their rights, I have tried hereinafter to show why these reservations should not be reduced in area.

Congress, as a whole, is responsible for the Indian policy and may not conscientiously shift responsibility to delegations from states in which the Indians in question live. Is not the nation, as such, through its representatives, responsible for the wards of the nation? May I not truthfully say some members of Congress represent constituencies or rather some active, aggressive constituents who are enemies of the Indians and their welfare? THEY have responsive representatives in Congress in such cases; but who represents the Indian? Without a vote, placed under federal jurisdiction, he is not a part of the state "constituency"; he is often fought by the constituency and its representatives. The Indian has no representation unless Congress as a whole espouses his cause. Too often, however, Congress as a body relies implicitly upon the delegation from such states for information, guidance, and action, and such delegations are, at times, misinformed by interested constituents. I am stating the case as mildly as possible.

[*A FLAGRANT CASE*] A CASE IN POINT is found in the Congressional Record of June 17, 1913, pages 2317–2321: *I refrain from properly characterizing the remarks of Senator Fall since I could not do so without offending against "Senatorial courtesy"; neither could I place his misleading remarks in the proper light without a long dissertation. I am not now taking issue with Senator Fall on the legislative amendment he advocated; neither do I wish to pass upon the allotments in question in Socorro County. I am only concerned at present with some of his flagrant misstatements of facts to the detriment of the whole Navajo tribe. I shall give Senator Fall's words in quotation marks throughout.* "Within three months the Indian Department has located 137 renegade Navajo in Socorro County, New Mexico, 250 miles from the Navajo reservation, where they have unallotted 12,211,300 acres."

Not 250 miles, *Mr. Fall*, but 54 miles, as the bird flies, from the Navajo reservation.

"Including the Navajo who are off the reserve and the Navajo who are not, there are 1,100 acres to every Navajo, man, woman, and child."

This is a simple question of census, acreage, and arithmetic. According to the Census of 1910 the Navajo tribe numbers 22,455 people. To my own personal knowledge a large number of the Navajo were not enumerated in that census; but let us accept the figure of the last census. Let us also assume 12,000,000 acres as constituting the Navajo Treaty Reservation and the various Executive Order reservations, and a simple example of arithmetic will show that, instead of 1,100 acres, each member of the tribe would have but 534 acres. However, to be more accurate: The Navajo reservation embraces 11,887,793 acres, of which approximately 719,360 acres belong to the Santa Fe Pacific Railroad Company, and approximately 55,400 acres to the state of Arizona, leaving 11,113,033 acres. Consequently, if you take the very conservative figure of 25,000 Navajo and 11,113,033 acres really belonging to them, you would have 444 acres to the person.

"These 137 Indians (of Socorro County) happen to represent the renegades of the tribe, who would not stay home and work, but have been leading a nomadic life for several years in the mountains of New Mexico, existing by fishing and stealing.

Those are the Indians who have been located among the citizens who are compelled to pay the taxes."

It is true, some of these 137 Navajo are renegades, or rather descendants of renegades, but in a peculiar acceptation of the word. The Navajo call them "Dine Ana'i," that is, "Navajo enemies." Years ago, before the Navajo were subdued and taken to Fort Sumner, in 1862, when raids between Mexicans and Navajo were of frequent occurrence and about 1,500 Navajo were held captives by the Mexicans, the Mexicans employed "renegade Navajo," "Dine Ana'i," as their guides in raiding the Navajo. Some of those 137 are descendants of such, and the Navajo would not care to receive them on the reservation.

"For several years in the mountains." Why, many of them have been born right there in Socorro County; at any rate, I have a paper before me, dated June 23, 1894, written by the archbishop of Santa Fe, signed by 43 persons of Socorro County, testifying to the good character and good intentions of these Navajo of Socorro County. Furthermore, the records of the Santa Fe Land Office show that settlement was made by some of these Indians in 1870, and homestead entries in 1883 and 1888. As early as 1886 Judge McComas of Albuqerque tried to dispossess the Navajo, David Torres, claiming the land to be coal land.

"Existing by fishing and stealing." They have small herds of sheep and goats and work as herdsmen for the Mexicans. The records of the District Court for Socorro County for the last 15 years do not show that any Navajo was indicted for any crime during that period. Fishing! I doubt if there is a live fish within 50 miles of their habitat. Besides, fish are tabooed by the Navajo. Organize a fish brigade, armed with fishes tied to switches, and you can drive the Navajo residing off the reservation back to the reservation much easier than with several regiments of soldiers equipped with modern firearms.

I can easily imagine how the United States Senate listened with bated breath to the following IMPASSIONED OUTBURST OF SENATOR FALL:

I want to say to the Senator (Bristow) that possibly he does not understand the conditions as they exist in our country. Possibly he is not aware of the fact that every year, two or three times a year, these Indians are allowed to go from their immensely rich reserves to interfere with white men, American citizens, on the public domain, causing the killing of anywhere from one to a dozen people. This is an unfortunate condition of affairs. I can say to the Senator that we people down in our section of the country can deal with these conditions if we are compelled to; but this sometimes becomes a question of all a man has—of his property rights, of protection to his family and his children. Any white man, any American citizen, will then use such force as is necessary in protecting his family. All that we seek to do is to restrict the further location of these Indians upon the public domain until Congress can act again. The Committee is being appointed, and I presume this matter will be investigated. It has been investigated before, and reports made, and no action taken. But this must cease; it must stop; and I tell the Senator from Kansas that it will stop. (Congressional Record, June 17, 1913, page 2320)

I regret that a senator made this statement. *Is it a matter of no consequence if a senator defames a whole class of people publicly before the representatives of the whole United States? I demand names and dates, Mr. Senator.* I have been among the Navajo for 16 years and I know of not one single instance where a white man was killed on account of the Navajo leaving the reservation, or on account of any grazing or land disputes. If every year the killing of from one to a dozen is occasioned by The Navajo leaving their reserve, how is it that [*Senator Fall is the only resident, or rather non-resident of New Mexico who knows anything about it? His using the present tense precludes the assumption that he had reference to Apache raids of three decades ago.*] no one knows anything about it?

Furthermore, is it true that every year, two or three times a year, these Indians are allowed to go from their immensely rich (?) reserves to interfere with white men? The Navajo living on the very border of the reservation naturally graze their flocks on and off the reservation. (The reservation line is, as a rule, not known to them.) But Indians who live and have their range within the reservation do NOT leave it. When the small Treaty Reservation of 3,225,600 acres was created, in 1868, the Navajo returned from their Babylonian captivity to the homes they had occupied before their abduction to Fort Sumner; they did not leave the reservation; they had never been on the reservation. At a recent council with Indians off the reservation, 193 heads of families attending, each one was asked and each one asserted most emphatically that he had never lived on the reservation and had never ranged his stock thereon.

Why should Senator Fall be so wrathy about Indians off the reservation? Does he himself live on HIS RESERVATION? Is it not true that his RESERVATION at Three Rivers got too small for him, that he resides in Texas, and that his property holdings reach beyond the confines of our common country into old Mexico? If the Navajo reservation constitutes an empire, the land holdings of the two senators from New Mexico constitute a good-sized principality.

One more quotation *of Senator Fall*:

In 1893 . . . a board of army officers, under a resolution of Congress and by direction of the Secretary of the Interior, made a thorough examination of the entire Navajo reserve. They made a voluminous report, which was transmitted to this body and to the other House, in which it was shown that with the expenditure of $65,000 additional to the amount of $20,000 which they then had on hand, a total of $85,000, the Navajo Reservation could be placed in a condition, by the opening of water holes and the development of small streams of water, so that it would amply support every Navajo Indian, man, woman and child, on or off the reserve, and that the 9,000 off the reserve could be taken back to the reserve where they belonged and no longer interfere with the citizens living on the public domain. Congress refused to act; it refused even to appropriate $65,000 for the purpose reported by this board of army engineers. The fault, therefore, lies, to some extent, with Congress. (Congressional Record, June 17, 1913, page 2317)

No, Congress did NOT refuse to act. The following year Congress DID appropriate $60,000 for that purpose. What became of the money? Ask Mr.

Vincent. What became of the subsequent appropriations for development of water? Ask the respective superintendents of irrigation. Very little water has been developed by the government—the suggestions of those army engineers have been carried out to a very, very limited extent. [*Senator Fall has repeatedly referred to this report.*] This report has been repeatedly referred to. I have a copy before me. It shows how conditions were then, 22 years ago. On page 28, the honorable commissioner of Indian Affairs, J. T. Morgan, writes:

> The relations between the Navajo Indians of New Mexico, Arizona and Utah and their white neighbors have been much strained for some time. The Navajo, on account of lack of water and grass on their reservation, located in the Territories named, have been forced to go beyond its boundaries to sustain their flocks and herds. . . . In a letter dated July 16, 1892, Gen. Alex. McD. McCook, U. S. Army, commanding the Department of Arizona, in reference to the condition of affairs on the Navajo Reservation, submitted for my consideration certain recommendations based upon what he deemed an immediate necessity, with a view to settling the differences between the Navajo and the whites upon the borders of their reservation, with a statement that it was reported by the Navajo Agent that 9,000 of these Indians were without the limits of the reservation from necessity; that they had large flocks and herds; that there was no water or grass within the official limits of the reservation to maintain them, and give sufficient water even for limited agricultural purposes to the 18,000 Indians said to constitute the Navajo Nation. . . . The General stated in his said letter that it would, in his judgment, be inhuman to drive the Navajo Indians, with their large flocks and herds, back to the reservation as it now is.

And on page 50, he states:

> Should the appropriation be made and the water developed and irrigation established as proposed, it is believed that the roving, non-reservation Navajo could be returned to the reservation and induced to remain thereon, and that the reservation Indians themselves could be restrained from going beyond the official limits of their reservation for the purpose of securing water and grass for their flocks and herds.

I wish to call attention to the fact that this statement embodies only the opinion of the then Indian commissioner. Nowhere in their report do the army engineers make any similar statement. But let that pass.

The appropriation was made; water was NOT developed, and irrigation, as proposed, was not established to a very appreciable extent. Even if, at present, all the recommendations of said army engineers were carried out, the same conclusion could not be reached now, after 22 years; or is it reasonable to assume (*as Senator Fall seems to do*) that conditions now are the same as 22 years ago? Since that time the Navajo have increased by seven or eight thousand, and their stock has more than doubled. *But enough of Senator Fall.*

Senator Smith of Arizona

During the same discussion in the Senate, Senator Smith of Arizona delivered himself as follows:

> *Mr. President, for thirty years we have been meeting just such statements as the one just read by the Senator from Ohio (Mr. Pomerene). There is not a Papago Indian in Arizona who has not more than enough room on the reservation set aside for the Papagos in Arizona. The Papagos who are not on the reservation are off it because they do not want to stay on it. There is not a Papago on the Public lands of the United States that has not ample room for himself and family free to him within the reservations in the State.*
>
> > *Mr. Pomerene. "I ask, for my own information, is the Senator advised as to how many acres there are in the reservation of the Papagos?"*
>
> > *Mr. Smith of Arizona: "There are several reservations for Pimas and Papagos. I should judge that the Papagos have in Arizona probably a thousand acres apiece—perhaps more—but of the amount I am not certain, but I am sure of one thing and that is, if these Indians were handled with more sense and less sentiment, it would prove a blessing to the tribes and result in a great saving of public money." (Congressional Record, June 17, 1913, page 2318)*

No, Senator, not a thousand acres per capita, but 27 acres per capita of rocky grazing land which cannot be allotted to the 4,775 Papagos living off the reservation since these 27 acres per capita are needed by the Indians on these reservations. Thousand acres was bad, even as a wild guess.

To complete the picture I beg to call to your mind the remark of Senator Catron from New Mexico, quoted above, that the Navajo, Mescalero, and Jicarilla Apaches had reservations totaling nearly one thousand acres for each man, woman, and child.

Will they upon whom the responsibility of a fair and just treatment of the Indians rests, continue to implicitly accept information and guidance in Indian affairs from these senators?

Opening of the Navajo Reservation for Settlement

In discussing this question, the character of the country and its capacity to carry a certain number of stock and to support a certain number of people must be taken into consideration; also the number of stock and the number of people it is actually supporting now.

According to the Census of 1910, our APACHE COUNTY has a population of 9,196 on its 11,379 square miles, that is, 0.8 of a person to the square mile. How does the Indian population compare with the white (American, Mormon, and Mexican) population in this county? While the 5,247 square miles of the Navajo reservation support 5,687 Navajo, that is, one person to the square mile, the rest of the county, 6,132 square miles, supports but 3,510 (whites and Indians), that is, 0.6 of a person to the square mile. Furthermore, in the townships south of the reservation, occupied by whites and Indians, the population averages one person to the square mile, but the portion occupied exclusively by whites averages but 0.5 of a person to the square mile; hence the "Indian country" supports just twice as many people as the "white country" in the same county. Then, why should the Indian country be opened to settlement, since it IS settled already doubly as densely as the white country? Practically every Navajo is a stock raiser, though he may practice, in addition and on a small scale, dry farming and farming by irrigation where it is feasible, but, of the 3,510 whites of Apache County, 1,929, that is, more than half, live in the towns of St. Johns, Concho, Egertown, and Springerville; that leaves 0.3 of a person per square mile. What percent of these town people are stockmen, I do not know. After enumerating the population in four towns, 22 townships and the reservations, the census bulletin states: "Remainder of county 392." Exempting the four townships in which the four towns are situated, that "remainder" comprises 3,288 square miles, that is, 0.1 of a person to the square mile. If the 5,686 Navajo on the reservation in Apache County could be removed as by magic, how many stockmen would that country support? Where over 1,000 Navajo families make a living at present, possibly a few dozen absentee cattle and sheep men would enrich themselves. But the Navajo cannot be brushed aside by a magic wand. To open the door to these cattle and sheep men would ruin an already overcrowded range and ruin the Navajo besides. When the rest of Apache County is as thickly settled as the Navajo reservation, it will be time enough to consider the opening thereof.

NAVAJO COUNTY with its area of 10,300 square miles and its 11,471 people, numbers 1.1 person to the square mile. The Navajo and Moqui reservations, with an area of 4,662 square miles and an Indian population of 4,371, number one person to the square mile; on the Apache reservation 1.3 persons to the square mile, and off these reservations 1.2 persons to the square mile; but if you deduct the population of the railroad town of Winslow, with its 2,381 inhabitants (not to mention Holbrook, numbering 609 inhabitants), you have only 0.7 of a person to the square mile, as compared to one person to the square mile on the reservation.

Within this county is the so-called BUTTE COUNTRY, east of the Leupp, west of the Navajo, and south of the Moqui reservation, a tract of land 24 by 39 miles, which, on May 13, 1908, was withdrawn from sale and settlement for allotting purposes. The 523 allotments, made in 1908 and 1909, are not yet approved. The odd-numbered sections in the west half of this tract belong to the St. Louis and San Francisco Railway Company, while the odd-numbered sections on the east half belong to the Santa Fe Railway Company. The chairman of the Arizona State Land Commission and others demand that this tract be restored for entry and selection. Is this tract unused and unoccupied? Like the balance of Navajo County (deducting the population of Winslow) outside of reservations, it numbers 0.7 of a person to the square mile, though the southwestern portion of the tract is absolutely barren. Within this tract, on 14 townships, carefully canvassed, 335 Indians are allotted, and they have 50,549 sheep, 1,124 cattle, and 1,869 horses; consequently, they have five acres to the sheep, or their equivalent. Deduct the railroad and school lands, and they have but two acres per sheep. Is there room for whites within this tract? The railroad lands of several townships, among them T. 23

N. R. 18 E., have recently been leased to white men. Two of the three springs within this particular township belong to the railroad company, and one to Charles L. Day. Will it be possible for the Indians to remain on this township and retain their allotments—with two acres to the sheep and no watering place?

COCONINO COUNTY with its area of 18,238 square miles and its 8,130 people, numbers 0.4 of a person to the square mile; but the Leupp, Western Navajo, and Moqui reservations in this county, with an area of 5,163 square miles and 2,722 Indians, number 0.5 of a person to the square mile.

Deduct the 2,900 inhabitants of the lumber and commercial towns of Flagstaff and Williams, and Coconino County outside of these reservations numbers but 0.2 of a person to the square mile. In other words, the Indian population on these reservations is more than doubly as dense as the white population in the "white country," that is, there are 3,200 acres to every white person living outside of Flagstaff and Williams, and 1,280 acres to every Indian living on the reservation.

In the LEUPP RESERVATION within this country eight families, 77 people, having 6,400 head of sheep and goats, are living permanently along Canyon Diablo and on the southwest part of the reservation south of the Little Colorado River; eight families are living along the banks of the river, and eight families are living north of the river, more especially around the "Lake" and the "Cornfields."

These Indians, living permanently on the Leupp reservation, have 13,400 head of sheep and goats, 103 head of cattle, and 219 head of horses, while five families, numbering 37 people, and having 2,800 head of sheep, 110 head of cattle, and 75 head of horses, part of the year are living on this reservation.

SAN JUAN COUNTY, with its area of 5,476 square miles and its 8,504 people, numbers 1.6 persons to the square mile. The Navajo reservation (in 1910, when the last census was taken and before the extension in New Mexico was opened), with its area of 2,384 square miles and its 2,693 Indians, numbers 1.1 persons to the square mile, while the population off the reservation numbers 1.8 persons to the square mile.

Deduct the urban population of Farmington and Aztec (1,294 inhabitants) and such as exclusively follow horticultural and agricultural pursuits through irrigation along the San Juan and Animas rivers, utilizing a comparatively small area of land (there are 706 irrigated farms in this county), and the rest of San Juan County will not average 0.7 of a person to the square mile, while the Navajo on the reservation average 1.1.

McKINLEY COUNTY, with its area of 5,506 square miles and its 12,964 people, numbers 2.4 persons to the square mile. The Navajo reservation in McKinley County (in 1910), with its area of 3,060 square miles and its population of 5,527, numbers 1.8 persons to the square mile. The population outside of the Navajo reservation numbers 7,437. Of these, 1,752 are Zuni Indians, occupying 264 square miles in McKinley County, that is, 5.2 persons (Zunis) to the square mile; 4,222 live in the town of Gallup and the surrounding mining towns, which leaves a population of 1,463 people living on 2,181 square miles, that is, about 0.6 of a person to the square mile as to 1.8 on the Navajo reservation.

Summary

In the district covered by Apache, Navajo, Coconino, San Juan, and McKinley counties, taken as a whole, a given area supports through agriculture and stock raising two Indians to one white man; in other words, the strictly rural population living exclusively by farming and stock raising is twice as dense on the reservations as the strictly rural population of the whites living in the same counties in exclusively white districts. Then, why should these reservations be opened up? Because the proportion, two to one, is too small? Must three or four Indians make a living where but one white man could subsist? That an Indian can and does make a living where a white man would starve does not prove that an area which supports one white person can support an indefinite number of Indians. Or, should the reservation be opened to stock their unused area? How does the stocking and grazing and farming on the Navajo reservation compare with the rest of the states of Arizona and New Mexico?

Comparative Stocking and Grazing

According to the last census (1910):

Arizona has	1,226,733 sheep
	246,617 goats
824,929 head of cattle, equal, in their effect upon the range, to	3,299,716 sheep
99,579 head of horses, equal, in their effect upon the range, to	398,316 sheep
3,963 head of mules, equal, in their effect upon the range, to	15,852 sheep
7,104 head of asses and burros, equal, in their effect upon the range, to	14,208 sheep
	Total[5]: 5,201,502 sheep
Acreage of Arizona	72,838,400
Acreage under cultivation 350,173	
Acreage controlled by mining industry 138,963	
	489,136
which leaves for grazing purposes	72,349,264

Dividing this acreage by 5,201,502, the number of sheep, or their equivalent, you have 13.9 acres per head of sheep.

According to the last census (1910):

New Mexico has	3,346,984 sheep
	412,050 goats
1,081,663 head of cattle, equal, in their effect upon the range, to	4,326,650 sheep
179,525 head of horses, equal, in their effect upon the range, to	718,100 sheep

14,937 head of mules, equal, in their effect upon the
range, to . . . . 59,748 sheep
11,852 head of asses and burros, equal in their effect
upon the range, to . . . . 23,704 sheep
Total: 8,887,236 sheep
Acreage of New Mexico 76,467,103
Acreage under cultivation 1,467,191
Acreage controlled by mining industry 467,626
1,934,817
which leaves for grazing purposes 74,532,286
Dividing this acreage by 8,887,236, the number of sheep, or their equivalent,
you have 8.4 acres per head of sheep.
Now, the Navajo have . . . . 1,781,900 head
sheep & goats
43,000 head of cattle, equal, in their effect upon the
range, to . . . . 172,000 sheep
87,000 head of horses, equal, in their effect upon the
range, to . . . . 348,000 sheep
3,795 head of mules, equal, in their effect upon the
range, to . . . . 15,180 sheep
5,440 head of burros, equal in their effect upon the
range, to . . . . 10,880 sheep
Total: 2,327,960 sheep
About one-third of this number, that is, ... 775,986 sheep
are off the reservation, leaving . . . . 1,551,974 head
on the 11,807,793 acres of land on the reservation, that is, 7.6 acres to the head, as
compared to the 8.4 acres to the head in New Mexico as a whole, and as compared
to the 13.9 acres to the head in Arizona, as a whole, or as compared to 11.1 acres
to the head in Arizona and New Mexico combined; in other words, the Navajo
reservation is stocked almost twice as heavily as the rest of Arizona and considerably more than one-third heavier than the rest of the states of Arizona and New
Mexico combined.

In all Arizona there are but 9,227 farms, including cattle and sheep ranches. Of
these, 4,841 are irrigated farms, leaving 4,386 cattle and sheep ranches; 3,206 are
mentioned as Indian farms or ranches, leaving but 1,180 ranches to white men,
showing that the number of Indian families supported through stock raising is
almost three times as large as the number of white families supported by the same
industry.

Range in New Mexico and Arizona Overstocked

It is universally admitted that the range in Arizona and New Mexico is overstocked
and run down and in danger of being ruined, hence the Kent Leasing Bill, H. R.
10,539.

Mr. J. J. Thornber, of the Arizona Agricultural Experiment Station, states: "The present condition of our stock ranges is highly unsatisfactory to everybody. The production of forage, which, at best, is uncertain on account of the climatic conditions . . . has been reduced to such an extent over much of the country by continual overgrazing that the grazing industry is of necessity carried on under most adverse conditions to the stockmen" (Bulletin No. 65, page 354).

But the Navajo reservation is stocked heavier and its range is more overgrazed and run down than the range in other parts of these states.

Mr. E. O. Wooton, of the New Mexico Agricultural Experiment Station, makes the following statement regarding the Navajo reservation and lands occupied by the Navajo in New Mexico:

> That part of the Territory lying northwest of Grant between the Santa Fe Railroad and the Colorado and Arizona borders is a region of rather poor carrying capacity, and has been badly overstocked by sheep for years. It is now able to carry not more than about sixteen head to the section, or an average capacity of about 40 acres per head. (Bulletin No. 66, page 28)

Condition of Range on Navajo Reservation

On February 8, 1911, Mr. Matoon, forest supervisor, wrote to the district forester:

> *Condition of Range.* Due to past overstocking of range during many years, the range is exceedingly overgrazed throughout the portion of the Zuni National Forest included within the Navajo and Zuni reservations. As a result, the soil is eroding badly in many places and the sheep belonging to the Indians make a scanty living. Over considerable areas in the eastern division of the Navajo district very little plant life is left except sagebrush and scrub juniper and pinon. The former heavy stand of grama grass over much of this region is nearly extinct.

In regard to this very tract of land, Mr. Reeves, of the Indian Office, made the statement: "In Arizona the State Land Commission and the cattle men and others have insisted on the office carrying out that provision (Act of May 29, 1908), because they want the surplus lands restored to the public domain so they can use them for grazing grounds."

Where is the "surplus" in this overgrazed district? Allot this tract of land and open it up, and you will ruin the range and the Indians, both. The attitude of white stockmen toward each other is described by Prof. J. J. Thornber as follows:

> Since the country was practically all public domain, each man was free to graze as much stock on it as he was able to possess, without restriction, and without any consideration as to the carrying capacity of the grazing areas. Besides this, there were those from the outside who drove in herds from time to time to graze on the same and adjoining areas, thus sharing further the range with those already using it to its fullest carrying capacity, and, in addition, continually adding to their herds. With this 'free-for-all' scramble for grass into which conditions finally

developed each stockman sought to get all he could while it was yet to be had, for what was left by one lot of stock was sure to be eaten off by another. The nominal possession of a well-managed range was simply an invitation for others to come in and graze it off closely without any regard whatever for the moral rights of the settler or squatter, who might desire to make a home there. No thought was given concerning the maintenance of the range, nor its permanent settlement later, which, above all else, were the things to be most desired. That which was free for all to use came to be regarded as free for all to despoil. The very domain that should have been carefully guarded as a heritage for future generations, was being ruthlessly destroyed by a mere handful of persons in the absence of any laws regulating its proper use. The above state of affairs led not infrequently to recourse to arms, especially between cattlemen and sheep men, of which instances our local histories are unfortunately replete. (Bulletin 65, page 336)

It would be considered very poor business management, indeed, for A, to improve the public grazing lands adjoining his holdings, however much he desired, so long as B, C, and D, his neighbors, could share equally with him all the advantages and none of the expense, and F, and G, tramp sheepmen, could drive in their herds from another section of the country, and appropriate the last mouthful of grass, if necessary, for their own use. The above is but one of a number of conditions which obtains under the empty and deceiving terms, "free grass," "free grazing" and 'free range.' (Bulletin 65, page 341)

If the stockman has water and grass on the public domain for a thousand cattle, no matter how long he has been a resident, another stockman, and perhaps a non-resident, can put down there beside these cattle another thousand head of stock, and the resident stockman can have no recourse. He must share, and share alike, his losses with the intruder, regardless of his improvements and his foresight. (The Practical Application of the Kent Grazing Bill, pages 4 and 5)

In view of this statement, may I venture the question what the attitude of white stockmen will be toward Indians after opening up the reservation? And what the condition of the range will be within a few years?

It is true, there are some portions of the Navajo reservation which are not overstocked, due to lack of water. Development of water in these districts would relieve the overgrazed portions of the reservation. The following statement of Mr. E. O. Wooten, in Bulletin 66, shows that the same conditions obtain among the whites in New Mexico: "The average carrying capacity is still further diminished by the absence in some well-grassed regions of sufficient water to render the forage available. This condition may be changed by developing water."

Open, Unreserved Lands in Arizona and New Mexico

The clamor of these two vast, undeveloped states for opening the overstocked and overgrazed Navajo reservation seems rather ludicrous. According to Bulletin No. 66 of the New Mexico Agricultural Experiment Station, in 1908, only 2.5 million acres were held under patent from the U.S. Government, obtained as homesteads, desert claims, mineral claims, and so forth, that is, about one-thirty-ninth part of the Territory was patented land and 55,000,000 acres of unreserved public lands were subject to entry.

Why should the reservation be opened, since at least 50,000,000 acres ARE open to settlement in New Mexico and are WAITING? In addition, on March 30, 1914, 5,009,412 acres of state land were still unleased and unsold.

In Arizona there are, according to Mr. Carl Hayden (congressman from Arizona), "39,529,195 acres of unappropriated and unreserved public lands."

Hence, if anyone urges the opening of the Navajo reservation, let him advance other reasons than a lack of unappropriated lands in these states.

Amount of Land Needed in New Mexico and Arizona for Support of One Family

Assuming that the lands of the Navajo reservation, as a whole, are neither better nor worse than the rest of New Mexico and Arizona, I proceed to quote competent authorities as to the quantity of land required for the support of a family. Bulletin No. 66 of the New Mexico Agricultural Experiment Station, page 29:

> If forty acres be sufficient to carry one cow, and the rate of increase be 50 per cent, and the yearling be sold at $15, what has the stockman gotten from the forty acres? The gross receipts are $7.40 for the forty acres, but from this must be deducted the interest on the proportional part of all money invested in the cow, fences, pumps, troughs, corrals, buildings, etc., the cost of all service necessary in caring for the cow and yearling, and all other running expenses.

Page 33: "The land is good only for grazing, and its carrying capacity is so small that from 2,500 to 7,500 acres of land (4–12 sections) would be necessary to support a family expending $1,000 a year, assuming cattle worth $15 per head, and that the normal increase of such stock would be 50 per cent (carrying capacity 20–60 acres per head)."

Bulletin 65 of the Arizona Agricultural Experiment Station, pages 346 and 347:

> Under the Texas grazing laws, the advantages are pre-eminently with the permanent settler and the small holder. He may purchase not more than four sections of grazing land at $1 per acre, and lease ten other sections for a period not to exceed five years. . . . The absolute lease district comprises practically all of Western Texas, in which country conditions are quite similar to those in Arizona.

On page 349, the Australian Lease System is quoted in commendation, as follows:

> There are a number of classes of leases to fit the various conditions. Pastoral leases are unlimited as to area, but of 28 years tenure. . . . As an alternative of the pastoral lease is the homestead lease, which is limited to 10,240 acres and to 28 years time. . . . Scrub and inferior land leases apply to their respective types of country, which might otherwise remain unoccupied and unproductive. Their terms

are for 28 years usually, and the maximum area obtainable under either of them is 20,480 acres. One or the other of these may be held in addition to a pastoral or homestead lease.

The author of this bulletin, in his speech before the National Live Stock Association, Denver, Colorado, makes the statement (page 7): "There is little grazing land in the Western and Southwestern States that has a stock-carrying capacity such that even four sections of it would maintain a family in ordinary comfortable circumstances. To make this bill (the Kent Grazing Bill) acceptable, the entries must be much larger."

Mr. A. A. Jones, first assistant secretary of the interior, makes the statement:

A bill introduced in the House of Representatives (H. R. 6637) proposed to provide for a grazing homestead of not less than 640 acres and not exceeding 1,280 acres in area. The bill . . . is not designed to apply to or provide for the entry of lands suitable only for grazing. The maximum area permitted to be entered thereunder, and even the maximum area described in H. R. 6637, would be wholly insufficient for the support of a homesteader and his family upon lands of that character.

Mr. Kent, author of H. R. 10,539, states:

It is obvious that a home supported by the production of live stock is to be gauged not by area, but by the test of the number of head of stock that can be produced. Vast areas, indeed most of our grazing country, would not carry sufficient stock on two sections of land to support a family, so that without some certainty of tenure of adjoining public lands there could be no assurance of a livelihood from that source.

On March 9, 1914, the *Albuquerque Morning Journal* had the following editorial:

Better Land Laws. A bill proposed by Congressman Fergusson for a 640-acre homestead is a distinct improvement over the present law. Better still is the bill which has the hearty support of Mr. Fergusson. The proposition by Mr. Jones is for an expert appraisement of the lands open to homestead. Where the appraisers find a quarter section sufficiently valuable, let that be the size of that homestead; where 320 acres, 480 acres, or 640 acres are enough to afford a living for a homesteader, set that amount aside for entry. Should the land be such that with reasonable economy a man cannot make a living on less than ten or twenty thousand, or even a hundred thousand acres, give him the right to enter such an amount. Such law as proposed by Mr. Jones has in it absolute fairness and unassailable good sense. . . . The *Journal* states without hesitation and with full knowledge of the subject that quarter section homesteads were taken up in South Dakota, for example, during the past quarter century worth more by far than any ten thousand acres now open to entry in New Mexico. We will make it a little stronger and say that more than a thousand homesteads have been taken up in

South Dakota, during the past twenty-five years, any one of which was worth
more than any twenty-five thousand-acre tract now open to entry in this State.

What is true of South Dakota is equally true of the public lands that have
been taken up in North Dakota and Montana during the like period. In making this
statement the underground water, which may be used for irrigation by pumping,
in New Mexico, is given full consideration.

In another issue the same paper made the statement: "But there are other
millions of acres in the arid Southwest which never can be irrigated and where it
would be impossible for a settler to make a comfortable living on less than 50,000
acres." *There are stretches on the Navajo reservation where a thousand acres
would not support a burro and 20,000 acres would not support a family. Even such
as are insistent upon the opening up of the reservation describe portions thereof as
"practically or wholly worthless . . . barren and sterile wastes . . . lava deposits,
rocky peaks and crags; pink, white and blue volcanic clay, pleasing to the eye, but
a stranger to vegetation, and other worthless kinds of lands with which the Navajo
reservation is quite generally marked."*

In the face of all this, what do you think of people who urge the allotment of
160 acres of **such** grazing lands to the person and then the opening of the SUR-
PLUS or balance to settlement? Permit me to quote Mr. Reeves again: "In Arizona
the State Land Commission and the cattle men and others have insisted on the
office carrying out that provision (Act of May 29, 1908), because they want the
surplus lands restored to the public domain so they can use them for grazing
ground."

If it is absolutely necessary for the salvation of New Mexico and Arizona to
open the Navajo reservation, let it be done after adequate homestead and leasing
and grazing laws have been passed and after the allotment laws have been modeled
after these prospective land laws, and after the United States has educated the
Navajo and placed them in a position to cope with their white neighbors.

The Tribe Uneducated

Aside from the children attending the different schools, there are not over 400
members of the whole tribe of over 25,000 who understand and speak the English
language well. Twelve years ago they had but one government boarding school for
the whole tribe; before that time the children were not kept long enough in school
to be benefited. Even now there are no school facilities for 5,000 Navajo children.

The Policy of Allotting Reservations

The policy of allotting reservations to Indians may be a good one where the
reservations are agricultural in character. With the exception of a few favored
places where irrigation is practicable, the Navajo reservation is good for grazing
purposes only; and large tracts of land are not even good for grazing purposes for
lack of water. Allotments for agricultural purposes means, as a rule, allotments for

dry farming; and, in places, bottom lands are so scarce that the allotting agents had been authorized to allot in 10-acre tracts for agricultural purposes, the balance of the 160 acres allowed to be allotted somewhere else for grazing purposes. A large percentage of Americans have abandoned their "dry farms" because they could not make a living on them. Shall we expect an Indian to make a living on a 10-acre or even on an 80-acre tract where an American fails on his homestead of 160 or even of 320 acres? These small tracts of bottom lands will help along; in good years the Indian can raise his corn, squashes, potatoes, and so forth, on them to help support him; but his main support comes, and, in a country like this, must come from his stock. A Navajo Indian cannot, as a rule, make his living from his allotment for agricultural purposes; much less can he make a living from his allotment (160 acres) for grazing purposes. That is obvious to anyone who is familiar with this country. On many a quarter section even a half dozen goats would starve.

Worse than lack of sufficient grazing is the lack of water. Let the Indians who are fortunate enough to have water on their allotments insist upon their right of exclusive control, and self-support will become impossible for the vast majority of the Navajo. These are some of the reasons why the allotting and opening up of reservations in this part of the country are impracticable and fatal to the progress, if not, ultimately, to the very existence of the Navajo.

As to certain parts of the reservation where lack of water has prevented overgrazing, I wish to state that it is absolutely impossible for the Navajo, on account of the very deep snow, to winter their stock on top of mountain ranges and even at the foot of the mountains where the altitude is high. These Indians **must** have a different winter range; and in winter when there is some snow on the ground, which obviates the necessity of watering the sheep, they take their stock into the low lands. Hence, where you find good grass late in summer and fall, you will find it grazed off in spring when the Indians take back their flocks to the mountains. There is hardly any place on the reservation which the Navajo do not use during some season of the year; and their cattle and horses roam over this country all year round.

Now, if water were developed in these places, it would be a help to the Indians, since they could use the range longer and during winters when there is no or hardly any snow. But as to developing water in such a country, in view of placing Indians there to **stay** and graze all year round, that would ruin the range completely. The soil in these desert lands is more loose and sandy, the grass does not form a continuous sod; only scattering bunches and spears of grass; continuous grazing would transform that country into an absolute desert. Lack of water, however, is not the only reason why some places are not grazed even during winter; but lack of protection against storms in large, open tracts of country, and lack of fuel as well.

Even if all the springs and lakes and reservoirs and the best land should be allotted before opening up the reservation, Americans and Mexicans will find a place to build a reservoir and dig a well, and secure it by homesteading, through Desert Act, or by buying or leasing railroad or state lands, and come in with thousands of sheep and cattle and control the country for miles around. Where a number of Indian families made a living, you will have one sheep man and a few herders.

The government is preventing overgrazing in forest reserves by granting permits to stockmen for a certain number of stock, giving the preference to actual occupants and keeping others out. Why not pursue the same policy in regard to Indian reservations in a country like this? Why should Mexicans and Americans be permitted to intrude and overgraze and "eat out" the original occupants?

The aim of the Kent Grazing or Leasing Bill is the same: to protect the range and to protect the original occupants. That aim is obtained by retaining the reservations intact.

Statements of Mr. Roosevelt

Mr. Roosevelt, after traversing through the wildest part of the Navajo reservation in Arizona, from the northwestern extremity to Tuba, through the Black Mountains to Kayenta, to the wilds of the Navajo Mountains, to the Moqui reservation, thence through the better portion of the Navajo reservation to Ganado, St. Michaels, and Gallup, writes in the Outlook *of October 18, 1913:*

> *During the second day of our southward journey the Painted Desert, in gaudy desolation, lay far to our right; and we crossed tongues and patches of the queer formation, with its hard, bright colors. Red and purple, green and blueish, orange and gray and umber brown, the streaked and splashed clays and marls had been carved by wind and weather into a thousand outlandish forms. Funnel shaped sand storms moved across the waste. We climbed gradually upward to the top of the mesa. The yellow sand grew heavier and deeper. There were occasional short streams from springs; but they ran in deep gulleys, with nothing to tell their presence; never a tree nearby and hardly a bush or a tuft of grass, unless planted and tended by man. We passed the stone walls of an abandoned trading post. The desert had claimed its own. The ruins lay close to a low range of cliffs; the white sand, dazzling under the sun, had drifted everywhere; there was not a plant, not a green thing in sight—nothing but the parched and burning lifelessness of rock and sand.*

How many acres of SUCH land, think you, are required for the support of one family?

[*And*] In the *Outlook* of October 18, 1913, Mr. Roosevelt writes:

Among those at the Snake Dance was Father Weber, of the Franciscans, who have done much good work on the Navajo Reservation. Father Weber has attained great influence with the Navajo because of his work for their practical betterment. . . . Father Weber, like every competent judge I met, strongly protested against opening or cutting down the Navajo Reservation. I heartily agree with him. Such an act would be a cruel wrong and would benefit only a few wealthy cattle and sheep men. . . . On my return from this dance (Moqui Snake Dance) I met two of the best Indian Agents in the entire service. The first was Mr. Paquette, a

Wisconsin man, himself part Indian by blood. The other was Mr. Shelton. . . . Messrs. Shelton and Paquette explained to me the cruel wrong that would be done to the Navajo if their reservation was thrown open or cut down. It is a desert country. It cannot be utilized in small tracts, for in many parts the water is so scanty that hundreds, and in places even thousands, of acres must go to the support of any family. The Indians need it all; they are steadily improving as agriculturists and stock growers; few small settlers could come in even if the reservation were thrown open; the movement to open it, and to ruin the Indians, is merely in the interests of a few needy adventurers and of a few wealthy men who wish to increase their already large fortunes, and who have much political influence.

Mr. Francis E. Leupp, former commissioner of Indian Affairs, wrote once upon a time: "The Navajo have learned that thrice blessed is he who has nothing, for from him can nothing be taken away. Denizens of a desert too forbidding to tempt white cupidity, they have escaped pillage because nobody believed the booty would be worth the trouble of robbing them."

But in spite of the fact that thousands of acres of this reservation have not vegetation enough to founder a humming bird, the reservation as a whole is stocked one-third heavier than the rest of Arizona and New Mexico, resulting in overstocking and overgrazing of those portions of the reservation that are blessed with vegetation, yet the reservation is to be allotted "because THEY want the SURPLUS lands restored to the public domain so THEY can use them for grazing grounds."

Opening of Extension in Arizona

In "Hearings Before a Subcommittee on Indian Affairs," I see, on page 12, that the Indian Office has asked for an appropriation of $43,000 to survey the 43 townships in the Navajo Extension made November 9, 1907, preparatory to its allotment. In justification it is stated that the Act of May 29, 1908, requires the president to restore the surplus land to the public domain after the Indians have been allotted. In explanation, I must say that Mr. Andrews, then delegate to Congress from New Mexico, had this act passed regarding the extension in Arizona and New Mexico. The extension in New Mexico has been allotted and opened up—and the consequent conditions are certainly not encouraging. There may have been some reason for the Act of 1908 as far as the extension in New Mexico was concerned, since American cattlemen and Mexican sheep men had been using portions of that tract, but at that time the extension in Arizona was and always had been in the exclusive possession of the Navajo; hence, there was no justification for said act as far as the extension in Arizona was concerned.

On page 20 of said "Hearings," Mr. Reeves states that the Arizona State Land Commission and the cattlemen and others have insisted on the office carrying out that provision (Act of 1908), because they want the surplus land restored to the public domain, so they can use it for grazing ground. Would there be a surplus? The paragraph on Apache County illustrates existing conditions considered by themselves and as compared with the conditions obtaining among the whites in our county.

Description of Extension in Arizona

In describing this tract of land (those 43 townships of the Extension of 1907, in Arizona) I shall include seven adjoining townships to the north—a former extension—just south of the treaty reservation. These two extensions in Arizona contain a large tract of very valuable timberland, about 12 townships having been embraced within the Zuni National Forest. The grazing on this tract is above the average of the Navajo reservation.

It also embraces a number of extensive valleys used by the Indians for agricultural purposes—more especially:

1. Bonito Valley, along Black Creek, extending from Fort Defiance, the agency, 22 miles to the south, and being under the Red Lake irrigation system.

2. The valley along the Pueblo Colorado wash, on which Ganado and the Cornfields Day School is situated, running through seven townships, that is, 42 miles north and south. Part of this valley is to be irrigated by the Ganado Irrigation Project now being constructed at a cost of $60,000.

3. The LeCroix Valley, along Cottonwood wash, extending through five townships, 30 miles to the southwest. These are the principal, though by no means the only valleys within this tract, used and needed more especially for agricultural purposes.

All this land is used and needed by the Navajo. The scarcity of agricultural lands makes it absolutely necessary to retain all the lands in the fertile valleys for them, and as to the grazing lands on this tract, I shall quote again a letter, dated February 8, 1911, from Forest Supervisor Mr. Mattoon to the district forester:

> *Condition of Range.* Due to past overstocking of range during many years, the range is exceedingly overgrazed throughout the portion of the Zuni National Forest included within the Navajo and Zuni reservations. As a result, the soil is eroding badly in many places and the sheep belonging to the Indians make a scanty living. Over considerable areas in the eastern division of the Navajo district very little plant life is left except sagebrush and scrub juniper and pinon. The former heavy stand of grama grass over much of this region is nearly extinct.

For the year 1912 the Forest Department authorized the grazing of only 18,500 head of sheep and goats, and 1,050 head of horses and cattle on the Navajo and Zuni division of the Zuni National Forest Reserve; but the Navajo are grazing, not their proportion of the 18,500 head allowed by the Forest Department, but they are grazing 40,000 head of sheep and goats on the Navajo division of said forest reserve embraced within the tract, that is, on the 12 townships here described. This proves conclusively that the Navajo are in need of every acre of land within this tract.

Railroad and State Lands

But half of this land, that is, 576,000 acres, in actual possession and use by the Navajo *from time immemorial*, belong to the Santa Fe Railway Company, while 55,040 acres belong to the state of Arizona. The Navajo are in possession and cannot get along without these lands if they are to remain self-supporting. The same may be said of the 17 townships in the Extension of 1884 in New Mexico.

I am not urging an exchange of lands, but the purchase of the railroad and state lands from the proceeds of the Navajo timber sales.

In the Interest of the Railroad Company?

Of late I have heard and read so many innuendos, intimations, and open assertions that the recent extensions of the Navajo reservation—Western Navajo, Leupp, and the Extension of 1907 in New Mexico and Arizona—were made at the instigation and in the interest of the Santa Fe Pacific Railway Company, that I am afraid the sentiment thus created might militate also against the purchase of the railroad lands I am advocating; hence a few statements of fact: Major McLaughlin, for years inspector of the Interior Department, a gentleman of sterling qualities, is responsible for the Western Navajo Extension; the Reverend Mr. Johnston is, I am quite certain, responsible for the Leupp Extension. A few months ago the land commissioner for the Santa Fe Railway Company [*knew him so little that he thought him identical with "Pussy-foot" Johnson*] was not acquainted with him .

Besides: Western Navajo was created on June 8, 1900, and Leupp on November 14, 1901, while the law permitting exchanges and lieu selections was passed three and four years later, on April 21, 1904. Where is the connection? Some people owe an apology to these two gentlemen, *and also—if such a thing were conceivable in our day and generation—to the Railroad Company.*

And the extension in Arizona and New Mexico, created on November 9, 1907, and corrected January 28, 1908? For about five years previous the Navajo Indians living off the reservation had been agitating the question of an extension. About two years previous Mr. Brosius, the agent for the Indian Rights Association, made a trip from Farmington, New Mexico, to the south over the country east of the Navajo reservation and recommended, among other things, as may be seen in the report of the Indian Rights Association, that an allotment agent be sent to allot those lands to the Navajo. Mr. Keepers was sent and had been allotting lands to the Navajo on the east side of the reservation. In consequence of Mr. Brosius's trip of investigation the Indian Department sent two of its officials to investigate and report on lands off the reservation occupied by the Navajo. Previous to that, Supervisor Frank Mead, accompanied by Harry Curley, made a trip to the east and south of the reservation in New Mexico to ascertain and report conditions to the Indian Office. The matter was brought to a crisis, however, when the Santa Fe Pacific Railway Company leased to American cattlemen several townships containing lakes and springs improved by the Navajo and used by the Indians. When the Indians found themselves despoiled of their homes and barred from their watering places, they began to raise a fund for traveling expenses to send several of their headmen to Washington to see the president. The money collected was placed with a well-known Indian trader. Things having come to such a pass that serious trouble was feared, their superintendent, Mr. W. H. Harrison, found it necessary to make a trip to that country to council with the Indians, asking me to accompany him. Both Mr. Harrison and myself advised them not to continue to collect money to send a delegation to Washington; we deemed such an expenditure utterly useless, since it was the avowed policy of the department not to extend reservations.

A few weeks after these councils, the commissioner of Indian Affairs, the Honorable Francis E. Leupp, came to Fort Defiance, and the Indians made use of that opportunity to place their grievances and their requests before him. They told him they had been urging this matter more especially for the last five years; one inspector and one agent after the other had made trips over their country and had reported conditions to Washington. While their agents, when writing on small and trifling matters, always received their reply, it seemed that just these important letters had been lost somewhere between Fort Defiance and Washington, since they never received an answer to them. They did not ask the government for any assistance; they did not wish to approach the government, like the worthless Ute Indians, begging for a piece of meat and a loaf of bread; they wanted to be self-supporting; but to be and remain self-supporting they needed the lands they now occupied; all they begged of him was opportunity to make a living, and protection against such as would deprive them of this opportunity by depriving them of their homes and watering places and grazing lands.

Mr. Leupp told them that those important letters had not gone astray; they were in his possession at Washington; but that it was necessary to deliberate a long time over such an important matter; besides, the government was large and moved slowly, like the big freight wagon they saw before them. When he returned to Washington he would tell the president all they had said to him. He did so, and the reservation was extended.

Then a cry went up through all Israel from Dan to Bersabee. A petition to the president to have the extension rescinded circulated in five counties in New Mexico, letters and telegrams of protest were sent to the president, to the governor and to the delegate of Congress, and indignation meetings were held. The opposition was directed against the extension in New Mexico partly because some Americans had leased some of the railroad lands and others had made application to lease several hundred thousand acres, and partly because some Mexicans were wont to graze their herds on this section of the country, especially in winter. None of these Mexicans or Americans were LIVING on this tract; they simply ranged their sheep and cattle on it, while the several thousand Navajo had their homes on it and were depending upon it for a living.

Part of the land was allotted and the extension in New Mexico thrown open.

Unfortunately, the extension did not prevent Americans from leasing railroad lands on the reservation; in consequence, there was more stock owned by Americans on the extension when it was thrown open than there had been when it was created. It is true, the Indians leased a few townships of railroad lands, but not enough to adequately protect themselves. At this time the Indians have five townships of railroad sections leased from the Santa Fe Railroad Company and two from the Frisco, in order to retain control of a portion of the range they need. The Indians could not be made to see the advantage of securing leases of other townships until the white men had secured the leases. *Thereafter, of course, the white men are given the first privilege of renewing their lease every year.* Some of the stockmen are trying to keep the Indians out of the townships they have leased or within the limits of their allotments; this, of course, no Indian can do, as the only value any of the allotments have is the amount of range they can control surrounding their respective allotments. Recently, one man from Chama leased all the Santa Fe lands in San Juan County except half a township, which a Navajo had leased, and he has brought in approximately 30,000 head of sheep. It can easily be seen that these Indians are facing one of the most grave questions that has ever confronted them *on the public domain, that of restricted range for their stock.*

In absolute control of the leased railroad lands, with equal rights on the unallotted public domain, the privilege of renewing their leases and of leasing more railroad lands—the advantages of the large stockman over the numerous Navajo whose small herds do not enable them to lease the railroad lands they need, are apparent, and the outlook is not encouraging.

Off the reservation, in McKinley County, south of the reservation, the Navajo have leased seven full townships and five fractional townships. One of these townships had been leased by a white man, who promptly bombarded the Interior Department with petitions and protests against the "renegade" Navajo whom he wanted moved back on the reservation; he prosecuted them under an old law forbidding anyone to herd his sheep within nine miles of a ranch house, and boasted that he would have these Indians ousted from that township within a year. And he would have succeeded had I not induced the railroad company not to renew its lease to him under the circumstances, but to lease it to the Navajo. In other localities the whites **have** eliminated them from whole townships through the leasing of railroad lands.

Such conditions as described on this and the foregoing pages have been, and are, responsible for the efforts to eliminate the railroad lands from the Navajo country, whether by exchange or purchase.

In the Butte country, as mentioned before, the railroad lands of several townships, among them T. 23 N. R. 18 E., have recently been leased to white men. Two of the three springs within this particular township belong to the railroad company, and one to Charles L. Day. Will it be possible for the Indians to remain on these townships and retain their allotments—with two acres to the sheep and no watering place?

In the southwestern part of the Navajo extension in Arizona, Americans leased a township some years ago, developed water and placed improvements on it costing over $5,000, and applied to buy the railroad lands of this and two more townships. The two townships east and the township south of the one containing these improvements have been leased by the Navajo to prevent further encroachments by the cattlemen. In the last three years, leasing or purchasing applications for five different townships in that part of the extension, and for two townships adjoining the extension, were made by as many cattlemen.

The Navajo are in possession of these railroad lands and use them and need them. They realize if they do not secure the railroad lands, they will, eventually, not only lose half of their holdings to white men, but the other half will be rendered useless through overgrazing—and they will have to "move."

The Indians on and off the reservation pay annually some $2,500 lease money for their protection.

They are unable to raise $8,000 annually to lease all the railroad lands on the reservation, and about again as much to lease the railroad lands occupied and used and needed by them off the reservation. Even leasing all the railroad lands would give them no protection if the railroad company should begin to sell its holdings to white men.

Timber Sale and Purchase of Railroad Land

Realizing all this, the Navajo have signed the following petition: "We, the undersigned Chiefs and Headmen of the Navajo Tribe, respectfully request that an appropriation, reimbursable from our timber sale, be made to buy the railroad lands which are in actual use and occupancy by the Navajo Tribe on and off their reservation."

It is true that Article XIII of the Treaty of 1868 provides, "If any Navajo Indian or Indians shall leave the reservation herein described to settle elsewhere, he or they shall forfeit all the rights, privileges and annuities conferred by the terms of this treaty"; furthermore, that Section 7 of the Act of June 25, 1910 (Stat. L., 855), provides, "That mature living, dead and down timber on unallotted lands of any Indian reservation may be sold under regulations to be prescribed by the Secretary of the Interior, and the proceeds from such sales shall be used for the benefit of the **Indians of the reservation**, in such manner as he may direct." But the Indians are of the opinion that their consent, expressed through their aforementioned petition, supplemented by an act of Congress embodying the words. "To buy the railroad lands which are in actual use and occupancy by the Navajo Tribe **on and off** their reservation," would eliminate these limitations.

Considering the fact that their timber, except four million feet, is on the treaty reservation on which there are no railroad lands, their action might seem ultra altruistic, were it not for the fact that the Navajo on the treaty reservation realize that their brethren will gradually be forced on to their already overcrowded and overgrazed reservation unless the railroad lands are secured for them.

Roughly estimated, the timber on the treaty reservation amounts to about 2.6 billion feet, while the timber on the extended Navajo reservation amounts to about 800 million, half of which belongs to the Santa Fe Railway Company. The Navajo ask that the timber be sold through the Forest Department.

Not Feasible?

I have been told that two things militate against granting this petition:

1.The law of 1904 permitting exchanges of land—rendering a purchase unnecessary;

2. On account of the large area of land held by the Navajo, Congress could not be induced to make such a reimbursable appropriation..

As to the first, if the Department of the Interior wishes to **avail** itself of the law of 1904 in spite of the vigorous opposition of the delegations from Arizona and New Mexico and of Mr. Mulford Winsor, state land commissioner of Arizona, the Indians would not object, I am sure.

If Mr. Mulford Winsor needs all the available good lands in Arizona, also those on the Navajo reservation, as it would seem, to make selections for the state, *When the 12,000,000 acres of the Navajo reservation obscure his vision, Arizona has, apparently not enough good lands from which to make selections; but when his mind is not burdened with the vast empire of the Navajo reservation, he is more optimistic; anyway, I read . . .* the following passages, taken from the *St. Johns Herald* of January 8, 1914, sound rather strange:

> Seven or eight million acres of land in Arizona, outside Forest Reserves and Indian reservations, is reclaimable by irrigation. This is the estimate of the State Land Commission. The Commissioners have now been in office long enough to have visited practically every township within the borders of Arizona. They declare that the public has absolutely no conception of the vast number of reservoir sites, or of areas of land which can be cultivated profitably with pumping water.
>
> There are not hundreds of reservoir sites, but thousands of them. Only a few have been withdrawn under the United States Reclamation Act. Along every stream in the State is at least a small site, the Commissioners say. In some sections of 'dry' Arizona there is more water, if conserved by storage, than there is land. Numerous sites are found along the Little Colorado, Gila and Santa Cruz Rivers. One of the largest in the State is on 'Bill Williams' Fork. There are several on Cataract Canyon, in Coconino County. Several vast valleys in Mohave County can be irrigated from the Colorado or from reservoirs in smaller streams. Cochise County has many sites in the Swisshelm, Whetstone and Dragoon Mountains. Greenlee has more sites than land.

As to the second point, it has been the object of this paper to place facts and figures before the members of Congress and others interested and to make them acquainted with the character of the land, grazing conditions, and so forth, in the Navajo country. I need not repeat.

Reimbursable Appropriation

The reimbursable appropriation ought to be made in the near future. After the railroad lands have been partially leased and partially bought by white men, and the

Indians have lost their homes and watering places and grazing grounds—the means
to make an independent living—it will be too late.

The same holds good regarding state lands. If their timber is sold, [*our friend
Mr. Mulford Winsor*] the state land commissioners will be able to dispose of the
state lands within the Navajo country to the Navajo *at once* much sooner than [*he*]
they could sell to the whites in other parts of the state. *If he is in need of funds, let
him urge a reimbursable appropriation for the purchase of both, state and railroad
lands: The Navajo will thank him for it and pardon his tirades regarding their
reservation.*

Whether the money thus appropriated will be reimbursed in the near future, lies
with the government. The ripe timber is there in abundance awaiting a purchaser.
There are other uses to which the proceeds of the timber sale could be put after the
necessary lands have been purchased: educational and sanitary purposes, the
development of water, upbreeding of their stock, and so on.

If this method is neglected, the Indians and their friends are forced to urge the
only alternative: exchange of lands.

Dead assets are of no use to anyone. It would seem in accord with our business
administration to bring this dead capital to life to help the Indians and to save direct
appropriations out of the pockets of the taxpayers.

Timber Sale for Mescalero Apaches

A similar point in question is the timber on the Mescalero reservation. While their
timber is estimated at several million dollars, the Indians—no, they are not starving,
but there is a condition bordering on starvation when, through lack of food, the
system is so enfeebled that any sickness will carry them off [*into a domain not
controlled by Senator Fall*] to the Happy Hunting Grounds.

The 187 Fort Sill Indians—brought to Mescalero *in spite of the protests of
Senator Fall—hinc illae lacrymae!*—are receiving rations until next October. What
then? The son of Victorio told me they were used to getting enough to eat; they
could not subsist on one full meal every second day—like the Mescaleros! Does
anyone imagine that they can make a living by raising oats in the clouds of White
Tail?

There may not have been a contract; but the Mescaleros received the Fort Sills
to full tribal rights of land, money, and other benefits, and the Fort Sills accepted
this offer, both under the supposition that their timber be sold and the proceeds used
to stock the reservation for both, the Mescaleros and the Fort Sills; but, instead of
that, on January 26, 1914, S.4187 was introduced to convert the Mescalero Apache
reservation into a National Park "for the benefit and enjoyment of the people of the
United States"—without any provision for timber sale (except "for the protection
or improvement of the park") or purchase of the timber by the federal government
to indemnify the Indians, to enable them to buy stock and make a living. The free
grazing granted to the Indians by that bill means nothing to them if they have no
stock to graze.

I hope Congress will not [*disgrace itself by creating*] create "pleasure grounds for the benefit and enjoyment of the people of the United States" amid an Indian population of whom Mr. Meritt, assistant commissioner of Indian Affairs, makes the statement: "While they have great potential resources, they are really SUFFERING much of the time for WANT of sufficient SUBSISTENCE and CLOTHING."

The attempt to relieve this deplorable condition through a direct appropriation was defeated during this session of Congress. The item in the Indian Appropriation Bill providing $200,000 to buy stock and other means of support for them was passed by the Senate, rejected by the House, and lost in Conference.

It is hoped that these facts and figures will command the thoughtful consideration of Congress and other friends of the Indians, so that the justice of the contention of the Navajo and their friends may be properly understood and appreciated: that their reservation should remain intact and that they be enabled to acquire title to the railroad and state lands occupied by them.

(Reverend) Anselm Weber, O.F.M.
St. Michaels, Arizona
July 25, 1914

Notes

1. From Anselm Weber, "The Navajo Indians: A Statement of Facts," FAC Box DEC.241 Weber, Anselm. Writings, Fd. "Weber, Anselm. Original MS—A Statement of Facts, 1914" (AVI2), typescript; and *The Navajo Indians: A Statement of Facts* (St. Michaels, Ariz.: Franciscan Fathers, 1914).

2. Robert L. Wilken, *Anselm Weber, O.F.M.: Missionary to the Navaho* (Milwaukee: Bruce Publishing Company, 1955), 205.

3. David H. Stratton, "The Memoirs of Albert B. Fall," *Southwestern Studies* 4, no. 3 (1966): 4.

4. David H. Stratton, *Tempest over Teapot Dome: The Story of Albert B. Fall* (Norman: University of Oklahoma Press, 1998), 341–42; Wilkin, *Anselm Weber*, 158–59.

5. The published total here is 60 sheep too many for the figures given. Using the correct total of 5,201,442 as the divisor in computing acres per head of sheep does not change the resulting average, 13.9.

21

My Work on Navajo Land Problems[1]

Anselm Weber, O.F.M.

[Perhaps the most poignant aspect of Father Anselm's review and self-assessment of his work on Navajo land problems is his confident statement, in early 1919, that "Thanks to God, my activities in these matters have come to an end." Things did not work out that way, and instead, to the very end, people continued to contact him about land issues, and he continued to be involved personally and politically. In early 1921, in the last months of his life, "he carried on his usual heavy correspondence on Navajo land matters,"[2] and at his death Howel Jones, the land commissioner for the Atchison, Topeka, and Santa Fe Railway Company, with whom Father Anselm had worked so long and successfully, sought desperately to replace him with another friar who might carry on the work. In January 1922 he urged Father Marcellus Troester to "master the facts," to emulate Father Anselm's thoroughness and attention to detail:

> The reason that Father Weber was so successful is that he mastered the facts and his reason for so doing was that the delegation in Congress did not have time to get the details necessary for successfully doing anything in the legislation. Father Weber studied and exhausted the facts and he furnished the details to his friends in Washington and his results were phenomenal. You can do likewise.[3]

Immediate action was needed, for "the situation in Washington is acute and if you want the Indian grazing lands kept intact, you will have to go to Washington and defend their needs."[4] Three weeks later, Jones passed along a statement of frustration from members of a Washington law firm that had previously worked with Father Anselm, "We regret very much that at this time we have not Father Weber with us to explain to the Interior Department the wishes of the Indians."[5]

Father Marcellus was not Father Anselm and could not do the work Father Anselm had done. Neither could Father Fintan Zumbahlen, who worked on Navajo land matters for a time in 1924.[6] With respect to Navajo land, Father Anselm would prove to be irreplaceable, and it is in that light that his self-assessment of efforts and achievements should be read. That, in fact, it is understated may be seen from this description of his workload during one of his trips to Washington, D.C., early in 1917:

> Father Anselm worked an average of eighteen to twenty hours daily during this period while he prepared data at night and accompanied Indian delegations by day through the intricacies of effective lobbying and buttonholing of war-distracted politicians. Largely as a result of this dramatizing of the Indian land problem, the Navajo reservation was increased May 17, 1917, by 94,000 acres in the Coconino County, Arizona, region, and some 60,000 acres were withdrawn from public entry in the Crown Point area of New Mexico for Navajo allotment.[7]

Wilken summarizes Father Anselm's impact on Navajo land in the statement that "it appears that he initiated or promoted every major move made from 1907 until his death in 1921 to procure more land for the Navajo," and compares his commitment in land matters to that of the famed Chief Manuelito, who "begged constantly of every government official for more land: 'Just a little piece more, brother, and when you see the big chief at Washington, let him set aside for us that strip yonder to the east, to the west, or to the south.'"[8]]

For the past 15 years I have from time to time written articles for *Der Sendbote* describing my efforts to aid the Navajo Indians in their land problems. Thanks to God, my activities in these matters have come to an end, and I propose to furnish my readers with a general resume of my labors in this field together with a brief account of the results.

During our first years at St. Michaels we encountered numerous and serious difficulties in gaining title to our mission lands—a fortunate circumstance for me inasmuch as it offered an opportunity to make a study of land laws and to gain some knowledge of a land surveyor's profession. Our neighbor, Mr. S. E. Day, himself a surveyor, proved himself a most willing and competent teacher.

In the year 1904 Indians living off the reservation came to me with the complaint that Mexicans and white men were invading their domain, depriving them of their lands and homes. I could not let their pleas for assistance go unheeded and permit my Indian brothers to be divested of their rights by unscrupulous white men. That, in the first place, was the duty of our government which, however, did nothing.

In years past, it was found, the Indians in their ignorance often moved stone markers of survey monuments, while others had been destroyed or lost in floods or through weather conditions. On the other hand, surveyors often failed in their duties and neglected to set monuments at more important and decisive points. They likely were under the impression that such a God-forsaken region would never be settled, so why waste time there with useless surveys!

To begin with, I had to determine on land maps just where these Indians lived. Then I had to obtain a copy of the "Township" from the Land Office. With this information I would visit the Indians and we would search for the monuments. Having found one and deciphered it, I was enabled to survey each plot and write down a legal description. The Indians were always most willing to assist me, and often large groups were on hand. Provided with the descriptions of their holdings, the Indians then came to the agent at Fort Defiance, who prepared their official applications and sent them on to the Land Office. These Indians lived at a distance of 20 to 60 miles from our mission, and at one time I spent five weeks without interruption among them and surveying their lands, a total of 15,840 acres for 99 Indians.

In the year 1907 I accompanied Supt. [William H.] Harrison on a trip to the eastern part of the reservation, where we attended several meetings with the Indians, one of which was held in the presence of Indian Commissioner Francis E. Leupp. Here the Indians requested that their reservation be farther extended eastward. In reply the commissioner promised that, on his return to Washington, he would relate to President Roosevelt all that they had just spoken. He added that if an extension would be made by the president—executive order—it would hold only for a short time, namely, to offer opportunity for Indians to secure title to the lands they were then occupying. That done, the remaining lands would again be thrown open to sale or settlement.

When the Navajo learned that I was going to Cincinnati later that same year, they urged me to go on to Washington to inquire as to what had become of the commissioner's promise and further to request that this extension be made also southward. On my arrival in Washington I learned that the president had agreed to issue the extension order as soon as the required bill would be presented to him. The commissioner yielded to my urgings and provided for the added extension to the south. I myself defined the boundaries of these extensions, which comprised a total of 2,791,040 acres in New Mexico and Arizona. Of this total, one-half of the land is owned by the Santa Fe Railway Company. The extension southward, comprising 1,221,120 acres, was due totally to my own personal efforts.

Since this extension was made only to enable the Indians to secure title to the lands they were actually occupying at the time, surveyors were engaged on the extension in New Mexico and 216,800 acres were allotted to individual Indians. The extension was now withdrawn in New Mexico and thrown open to settlement, permitting both whites and Mexicans to enter the area with their cattle and sheep herds and to use all lands not allotted, including railroad lands naturally, for their own purposes. This created a precarious situation for the allotted Indians insofar as it was quite impossible for them to make a living on their relatively small holdings alone. I therefore made up my mind to prevent at all costs a similar crisis on the Arizona extension, as soon as Congress, spurred on by Congressman Andrews of New Mexico, enacted a law on May 29, 1908, directing the president to throw open the extensions in both states as soon as the Indians had been individually allotted.

Thus, when the government detailed allotting agent Peterson and surveyor Simington to Arizona for the purpose of making allotments on the Arizona extension, I registered a vigorous protest before the Indian Office which resulted in a suspension of surveying and allotting lands on this area. Instead, it was arranged to have these men do their work off the reservation in Arizona where many Indians were living. In this manner 291 Indians gained title to 46,560 acres off the reservation. Through my further urgings, 121 more Indians living in New Mexico received 19,360 acres.

As was to be expected, this enraged the whites and local politicians, who finally succeeded in having Senator Fall of New Mexico introduce a bill in Congress whereby the government was forbidden to appropriate monies to be used for the purpose of allotting lands to Indians. At my suggestion the Indians now hired Mr. Simington, and out of their own pockets they paid him $1,500; 232 Indians thus acquired a total of 37,120 acres. However, Mr. A. A. Jones, then undersecretary of the Interior and now senator from New Mexico, had since 1913 been doing his utmost to forestall approval of these Simington allotments. Faced with this opposition, I wrote a letter to my good friend General Hugh L. Scott and with his aid finally prevailed upon the secretary of the interior to agree to the eventual allotment of 19,000 acres of railroad lands. In the year 1913 Senator Curtis of Kansas had aided me in the passage of a bill which permitted Indians to acquire title to railroad lands, provided they had occupied these lands for a period of five years.

It was only during my latest visit to Washington that the above-mentioned ban was lifted on April 15, 1918, by Undersecretary of the Interior Vogelsang, so that the remaining Simington surveys and other applications were approved and legally accepted.

Despite the fact that I had foiled attempts to reopen the extension in Arizona in 1910 (our mission is located within this extension), our government, yielding to the demands of cattlemen and others, in 1913 began to contrive ways and means to bring this withdrawal about. Intent upon countering this move and for various other reasons pertaining to Indian land problems, in 1914 I published a 29-page pamphlet titled *The Navajo Indians: A Statement of Facts*. I had a goodly number of copies printed and distributed them to Indian Office officials, the Department of the Interior, the Land Office, and to a number of senators and representatives in Congress as well as to other influential friends of the Indians. Since that time I have heard no more talk with reference to the opening of this reservation. May I add here that the expenses of printing and distribution of my pamphlet were defrayed by a good friend, and our mission treasury was not in the least affected.

By ray of encouragement to build their lines through this region, the government had made land grants of all odd-numbered sections to the railroad company for a distance of 40 miles on both sides of their location of track. As a result, one-half of a great portion of the Navajo reservation was the property of the Santa Fe Railway. In 1904 Congress passed a law by which the railroad company could exchange its reservation lands, with proper approval, for other unoccupied or unclaimed lands of similar nature and worth elsewhere within the state and off the reservation. I have on many occasions written to Senator Curtis and other high officials in Washington, suggesting that they interest the Indian and the Land Office to request the railroad company to relinquish their holdings within the reservation and exchange them for other lands. My contention was that as long as the railroad company owned these lands and could sell or lease to whites, the reservation as such was of little value and protection to the Navajo.

So strong became the opposition to this proposal that I had come to fear that all my efforts had been in vain. However, Mr. Curtis finally called upon President Taft personally and explained conditions as reported in my letters. The president, fully convinced of the urgent need of these exchanges, without hesitation issued his orders to the secretary of the interior. Relinquishment of 327,402 acres by the railroad company to the government followed on February 5, 1913. Later, in 1915, after I had accompanied a delegation of Washington officials on an inspection tour of the respective lands, 303,350 additional acres of some of the best lands on the reservation were exchanged, valued at no less than $1.5 million.

On my visit to Washington in 1916, I was instrumental in bringing about an exchange of 23,040 acres and in April 1918 still another, of 109,880 acres. As he signed the document in my presence, Undersecretary Vogelsang remarked: "I subscribe to this measure even though the heavens should fall!" Now the railroad company owned not even an inch of land within the limits of the Navajo reservation and thus ended one phase of the Indians' many land problems. All lands within their reservation now belonged to them, and it was through my efforts that 1,439,160 acres were secured for them both on and off the reservation. This figure does not include the "tiny reservation" obtained in 1917 when I accompanied nine Indians on our famous trip to Washington. That would have brought the total to 1.5 million acres.

Had I not come to the aid of these Indians, many of them would have lost their little farms, watering places, homes, and grazing lands to the encroaching white and Mexican stockmen. At the same time, my activities greatly increased our prestige among the Indians in religious as well as in other respects.

The only criticism of my labors came from white men who hoped to rob the Indians of their lands and from the Protestant ministers who, in their *The Indians of the Southwest* bewailed the fact that they were time and again reminded by the Navajo themselves of the valuable work that we were doing for them. Hence the complaint that the Indians for that reason inclined more to the Catholic than to the Protestant side.

Of course, much remains to be done in Indian land matters, with many of the plots surveyed by Mr. Simington as also others still waiting to be officially and legally assigned. Almost every day Indians are receiving letters from various land offices requesting sworn statements required before issuance of title. My duties as missionary have made it impossible for me to attend to these affairs, and the agency has been "too busy" to be concerned with them.[9] So, when I was in Washington last spring, I tried to induce the commissioner to send someone to Fort Defiance to handle these and other land matters. This he promised to do, but it was only after

I had written at least a half-dozen letters that he sent Mr. Simington to Fort Defiance for that purpose the early part of February of this year (1919). I delivered a large stack of letters and documents to Mr. Simington, letters which I had left unanswered and unattended to for an entire year, and breathed a happy *adios* to allotment work.[10]

Notes

1.From Anselm Weber, FMN 46 (April 1919): 323–28. Translated by Emanuel Trockur.

2. Robert L. Wilken, *Anselm Weber, O.F.M.: Missionary to the Navaho* (Milwaukee, Wisc.: Bruce Publishing, 1955), 229.

3. Howel Jones to Marcellus Troester, 27 January 1922. FAC Box DEC.235, fd. Troester, Marcellus.

4. Jones to Troester, 27 January 1922.

5. Howel Jones to Marcellus Troester, 16 February 1922. FAC Box DEC.235, fd. Troester, Marcellus.

6. Howel Jones to Fintan Zumbahlen, 11 September 1924. FAC Box DEC.235, fd. Troester, Marcellus.

7. Wilken, *Anselm Weber*, 226.

8. Wilken, *Anselm Weber*, 206.

9. [Translator's note by Father Emanuel.] Actually, Indians living off the reservation were not under the jurisdiction of the agent or superintendent. However, if they could not make a living where they were, they still could return to the reservation, which was already overcrowded and overstocked. Naturally, then, it was to the advantage of the reservation Indians that these off-reservation Navajo remain where they were. Father Anselm's strategy was obviously based on this evident fact, and it must seem clear that the Indian Office agreed with his contention.

10. [Translator's note by Father Emanuel.] These letters were all registered mail addressed to the Indians in question in care of Father Anselm Weber, St. Michaels, Arizona, and I recall how they were still arriving here after I came to the Southwest in August 1917.

Part 5

AMONG THE PEOPLE, 1911–1920

St. Michael's Mission, circa 1900. Courtesy of Franciscan Friars, St. Michael's Mission.

The Navajo gathering for a chicken pull at Chin Lee, circa 1905. Courtesy of the Archives of the Franciscan Province of St. John Baptist of Cincinnati.

At the hogan of the silversmith, Crystal, New Mexico, June 1913. Beshlagai, the silversmith, stands in the doorway; Vincent, son of the sick woman within, is seated second from the right, next to the old medicine man. Courtesy of Franciscan Friars, St. Michael's Mission.

Navajo family at Oak Springs, Arizona, early 1900s. Courtesy of the Archives of the Franciscan Province of St. John Baptist of Cincinnati.

Armed Navajo at Chin Lee trading post of Sam Day, around 1902. Standing at left is Dine Tśosi; seated holding rifle is Naakaii Nez; standing to the left of Nez, holding spear and bow, is Hosteen Kliz-ini. Photographed by Ben Wittick. Courtesy of the Archives of the Franciscan Province of St. John Baptist of Cincinnati.

The home of Tsiischbischi, circa 1908. Courtesy of the Archives of the Franciscan Province of St. John Baptist of Cincinnati.

Navajo "desperadoes" of the Beautiful Mountain disturbance in Gallup to serve their sentences, December 1913. Back row, left to right: Ni'dughullin Biye', Ni'dughullin Benalli, H'asht'al, and the sheriff of Gallup; front row, left to right: Bizhoshi, Attsidi Naez Biye', Hatali Yazhe, and Bizhoshi Biye'. Courtesy of Franciscan Friars, St. Michael's Mission.

Tsiischbischi and students at the Santa Fe school, October 1900. Courtesy of the Archives of the Franciscan Province of St. John Baptist of Cincinnati.

Father Leopold and friends at a summer gathering. Courtesy of Franciscan Friars, St. Michael's Mission.

Father Anselm, Chee Dodge, and medicine man Bizhoshi, of the Beautiful Mountain episode of 1913. Courtesy of Franciscan Friars, St. Michael's Mission.

Father Anselm and first communicants at breakfast, St. Michaels. Courtesy of the Archives of the Franciscan Province of St. John Baptist of Cincinnati.

Students at St. Michael's School, early 1900s. Courtesy of Raynor Memorial Libraries, Special Collections and Archives, Marquette University.

22

The Faith for One and All[1]

Berard Haile, O.F.M.

[Sometime around 1920, when he had accumulated several years of experience as resident priest at St. Isabel's mission at Lukachukai, Father Berard seems to have considered obligating himself to *St. Anthony Messenger*, as Father Leopold had done almost two decades earlier, for an ongoing serial about missionary life among the Navajo. He writes that the editor was interested in the story of the origins of the *Ethnologic Dictionary*, a topic that was less interesting to Father Berard than "a free serial in which Navajo daily life might be described together with the occupation and difficulties of the missionary."[2] Seemingly with that outlet in mind, Father Berard produced a number of manuscripts—potential essays or parts of essays, mostly handwritten—that blended his personal experience in the Lukachukai community with more general commentary on Navajo life and culture. Somehow the projected series never materialized, and most of the drafts and fragments created for it, or aimed at some future opportunity, seem never to have been published.

Chapter 22 combines two of these untitled, undated manuscripts, one handwritten, the other typescript, from Father Berard's Lukachukai period. The first, seemingly intended as an introductory essay, contrasts the dated and distorted public stereotype of the Native American with the reality experienced by the missionary in the field. Beyond that, it makes the case, as the Franciscan missionaries had been doing ever since they arrived in Navajo country, for the humanity of the Indian and the worth of the Indian soul as equivalent to that of any other member of the human family. The second part continues this theme, expanding it to the critique of the ongoing "stepchild" status of the Indian missions, which, because they were located within the boundaries of the Unites States, did not receive financial support comparable to that available to "foreign" missions. If the souls of the Indians were as worthy, and their beliefs as demonstrably pagan or heathen as those of the Hindus or the Chinese, then plainly the shortfall in financial support for the Indian missions was discriminatory and unjustifiable.

Father Berard's essay is an expression of the spirit of the Franciscan ministry over the 1911–1920 period. It is both justification and appeal, and to my mind captures the attitudes of the mature friars—faith, commitment, a willingness to sacrifice self in service, a certain resignation about visible results—that underlay the achievements of that decade. Written at decade's end, it is fitting prologue and context for the selections that follow.]

Letters which reach us from time to time reveal the fact that, after all, work in the Indian missions seems something out of the ordinary. They speak of the "noble work," of its being "wonderful," "difficult," "lonely," or "all alone out there" and wonder "how you can make up with a life like that?" One is almost tempted to reconsider and take a similar view of the situation. Yet there is so much of ordinary prose entering the daily routine that any flashes of an ardent enthusiast are quickly smothered, and we mold our views to suit a matter-of-fact situation such as it is.

Usually, too, an endeavor to repress such views is met by a gentle hint at the "well-known modesty of you missioners." Be that as it may, it is not uncalled for, we think, to present a few sketches of Navajo Indian life, such as our Mission of St. Isabel presents them. The mission will present the background with no pretense at strict chronology. If some of our neighbors be rogues, and others lovable, we have an admixture that is found elsewhere also. . . .

Prosaics of the Ministry

These sketches do not purport to stamp the life and work of the Indian missioner as heroic. It is an old saw that human nature is everywhere alike. So, too, the work in the missions runs parallel with parish work anywhere else. Abstracting from the difference in language and environment, you have the same tasks of calling your parishioners to duties of conscience, administering the sacraments, instructions at schools, regulating marriages, or accepting social calls, at which time you may be quizzed on religious and, more often, on very personal matters. That you have bills to pay and, which is a little worse, to invent methods of your own to meet such bills, is probably a disagreeable side issue. Assuredly, there is nothing exotic in the man that devotes his life to the call of the Church to carry her message to an isolated and strange people whom we have called American Indians. Neither is there anything striking or singular in the devotion of those of the faithful that, for the same reason, are interested in the Indian and his missioner. The Faith is for one and all. It is a gift, yet one that God need not bestow except where and upon whom he so pleases. What is there singular, then, in our prayer that these other sheep, too, may be brought into the fold; that they, too, may receive the light to know the things that are now hidden from their eyes?

Perhaps the Indians present a problem all their own. Theirs is a nation within our nation, and somehow we think of them as something curious that ought to be staged to satisfy this curiosity. The feathered, swarthy warrior with raised tomahawk, such as used to grace or disgrace the stands of our tobacconists, is still in our fancy. History, Wild West stories, shows, and fiction are unattractive unless the Indian acts the part of a gruesome spectre. It cannot be otherwise, so it seems, and the men, therefore, that enter their villages, tepees, houses or homes to evangelize them are by that same token destined to martyrdom and its halo.

Our concept of the Indian is based to a degree upon erroneous notions which picture him as a sulking, stolid, and unapproachable being, lacking in wit and humor or nobler qualities, but responsive to everything that is treacherous, sneaking, and deathly. If we could but remodel our views and din it into our minds that stealth, theft, murder, brutality, and crime are equally as abhorrent to them as they are to ourselves, we might enlarge our interest in them for their spiritual and material betterment. This is not saying that the Indians are angels. Crimes occur among them from motives that differ little from those recorded on the front page of any of our dailies. Yet it should not be overlooked that such acts are deplored by the better class of tribesmen, who realize that the faults of the wayward are wrongly attributed to the tribe as a whole.

It is wholly missing the mark, too, to imagine that the Indian is entirely without a mind of his own, a simple child of nature who eagerly awaits the missioner and his message. As though all that is required were some poetic Blackrobe with cross aloft and baptismal font ever ready, and lo and behold, your Indian bends the knee, falls in line, and beyond cavil will repeat the early fervor of the apostolic times! If it be otherwise and he need instruction like any other mortal, or requires time to convince like you and I and our ancestors did, he is then and there rejected as hopeless, and any effort expended upon him is condemned as of little use. Strange as such reasoning is, we find it nowhere so readily and easily applied as to the Indian mission.

Yet it is well to remember: Christ is not preached to them for their approval any more than we expound the faith for approval to a sincere Protestant seeking the truth. Faith being a gift of God needs no man's approval. The question is whether Christ approves of those to whom this gift is offered. By what right should we except the Indian? The command to go and preach the Gospel to all nations certainly includes our neighbor within our own borders, and we should assuredly make a wreck of charity if we considered our Indian neighbors unworthy of the light of the Gospel.

Granting this right to the Indian, the devoted men that live and sicken and die among them to win their souls are certainly not extraordinary in doing Christ's own bidding. At least the missioners themselves will not think so. They felt the call of the Church to devote themselves even to these benighted races whom she wishes to see within the fold. Yet not all will feel this call as they did. In a sense it is a repetition of the call of Abraham to "go forth out of thy country, and from thy kindred, and out of thy father's house, and come into the land which I shall shew thee" (Gen. 12, 1). It often spells isolation, or at least segregation from congenial companions, and the severance of ties that bind members of the same race. Instead it carries with it life among a strange people of a strange tongue and custom and culture, who are not always responsive to reason, but may be childlike in their simplicity and ignorance, conservative and tenacious in their adherence to traditions and tribal codes. The work of dispelling ignorance and elevating those that sit in darkness to higher standards is a slow one, while progress and results may be scarcely visible. Naturally, the disposition and inclinations of the individual are a deciding factor in the choice of such fields of labor, no matter how much alike priestly labors are everywhere. It goes without saying, therefore, that light in prayer must be sought for such a vocation, and we should earnestly pray the Lord of the Harvest, that he send forth laborers into his vineyard.

The parish limits are, of course, not defined by milestones, and the wandering instincts of the parishioners do not contribute to its stability. And although the church bell rings out its call every Sunday and holiday, its sound cannot reach them in their habitual absence from home. A writer recently set forth that Indian missionaries after years of faithful labor and perseverance have little to show for their efforts, which total probably the goodwill of the people and the affection of the children. If we abstract from such occasional ministrations as those pointed out above we might say that he had the Navajo missions particularly in view. For the missioners must chiefly reach the children in the school, to realize which it is necessary to gain the goodwill of the parents.

This need not necessarily be a revelation unless to those who still consider the Indian in a class of his own. It is true, at least of the Navajo, that this is practically virgin soil for the Church. The days, however, in which the missionary had but to appear with crucifix held on high and the ladle with which to drench the heathen in baptismal waters are not of record with us. Neither does baptism predominate the Navajo convert nor stamp his fervor and enthusiasm as akin to that of primitive Christianity. On the contrary, the Indian is human and intensely so. While readily accepting Christian doctrines after sincere study, the change cannot remove all temptations. And these are many.

The spirit of their new religion has not indeed as strong a hold on them as with the faithful at large who are eager, for example, to have their infants baptized as early as possible after birth. [Among the Navajo] it is either "too soon yet," or "the baby is just born a week or a month ago," or "it isn't sick," or "its mother said to wait," or when wit had difficulty in penetrating his or her cranium, you will be told, "I dunno', I'll see what the mother says." When you persist, and stubbornly at that, it is often possible to have the whole family visit the mission. On such occasions they are guests, horses and all. You baptize the children and have the parents attend Mass and receive the sacraments. The pastor pays the baptismal fees and, if necessary, extends the Easter season just to reach them. Easter, by the way, is "the big Sunday," as the catechism says, and is heralded abroad by wireless communication, that is, the word is passed along from one neighbor to another, as there are no telephones and papers.

There are instances, too, in which every obstacle is disregarded in attending services. An Easter communicant, on one occasion, reached the mission at dawn, saying that he had left home with the rise of the morning star, as he lives some 10 miles distant. When asked if he had partaken of food, he replied, "Oh no! *sizahadot-'at*" (I want it put into my mouth), which is their expression for Holy Communion. On another occasion, at Christmas, the thermometer showed close to 10 below zero. The boys blanketed their horses for the night, as they wished to receive Communion on Christmas morning, which they did, though they were clad in their ordinary daily working clothes. Sunday clothes are unknown, and a blanket often covers a shirt-waist worn for many months!

The Call to the Feast

It is not customary among the Navajo to reveal religious knowledge one to another. Singers who have learned the songs and ceremonies of a particular rite do not feel called upon to become teachers to the inquisitive unless for a substantial consideration. Inquirers into religion or applicants for a singer's candidacy are therefore not very frequent. A similar timidity is felt toward the priest. They see that he undoubtedly performs some rite when Mass is celebrated. He administers the rite of baptism and visits the sick. He is without doubt the possessor of some religion and may, so they surmise, ask a compensation for instruction or introduction into this new religion, much as their singers do. Of course this is different, they argue, because not all believers must necessarily be priests. Married men and women attend the Mass, receive Holy Communion, their children are baptized, they belong to the priest's religion. What about us, then, they ask, who follow our own ways and ceremonies? May we attend Mass? May we learn something of this religion? Do you pray for us, too?

Now I do not doubt a moment that you expect me to say yes immediately to every one of these queries. Yes, I do it gladly. It is an easy problem when you face it as you find it here taken from life. But had I asked you: Is it allowed to permit the Indian, if he is a heathen, to attend at Mass? Would you hesitate a little over the heathen? Of course, there is no objection to being placed in heaven side by side with a Catholic Mexican or Indian. That would settle the question for eternity of whether you and the Negro, Mexican and Indian are good enough, wouldn't it? Yet I have often wondered why we Anglo- and other Saxons draw the color line. Why do we use the subterfuge of special pleading once anyone devoted enough will ask the same privilege of Catholicism for the Indian and "like folk" here below that we are gracious enough to submit to in heaven.

The question may be altered a trifle and worded: Why are there any Indian missions? And in our instance, Why does the Franciscan Indian Mission Aid (F.I.M.A.) devote its men and alms to the mission fields of Arizona and New Mexico when the population is chiefly Mexican and Indian? In an instance like this a reply in dollars and cents is quite out of place. Financial returns can hardly classify with a spiritual harvest. Because these missions are in need and may require our assistance for some years to come does not betoken a meager spiritual harvest by any means. "The poor you will always have with you." If our Mexican and Indian missions are poor, we may as well be spiritual enough to admit that they are worth our attention or financial assistance. It is worthwhile, then, to attend to such missions or to assist them financially.

Our work in these lonely missions strikes me as akin to that of the servants who were sent out with invitations for the marriage feast of the King's son. Suddenly, as it were, a marriage feast is announced. A betrothal does not seem to preceed the marriage. Neither is there any mention made of the bride. The feast is paramount. To have this well-attended seems the King's chief concern. Invitations are sent out, and He sends His servants to call them that were invited. When these refuse, others, from the lanes and byways, are urged to enter. Now that some refuse and others neglect to attend is not the fault of the King nor of His servants. If the wedding feast signifies the sacrifice of the Mass, the sacraments and prayers of the Church—the servants have ought else to do but to call. The King certainly draws no color line; why should His servants do so? The wedding feast, the Mass, is for one and all. The servants may not discriminate, much less is discrimination a privilege of the guests who have already entered. The King reserves the right of discrimination. He silences and punishes only one guest who failed to make use of the wedding garment. Wedding garments are provided for all that respond. Does the garment fit the Mexican or Indian less well than others? Shall we disfranchise them from the wedding feast because they are less cultured, live in the byways and lone places, and are poor?

If we are the servants, our orders read to invite them to the wedding feast. Either we place this feast, the Mass and sacraments of the Church, before them personally as missionaries, or we assist with prayer and alms that this wedding feast may become known through the missionaries. Perhaps, after all, it is not a useless reminder to say that it is yours as much as anybody else's concern to be an invited guest who has donned the wedding garment. If so, you certainly share in the general joy if the room is filled with guests. In other words, do you despise the Indian missions as beneath you, or do you assist them with alms and prayer? Again, did you ever say a prayer for the conversion of an Indian? If not, please join me. No doubt my Indians are much mistaken when they fancy that the Mass and white man's religion are for the whites only just as the native singings are for the Navajo only.

I think there are few of the Faith that would flatly state that the Indian is unfit for the white man's religion. Yet some 20 years in the field have been an occasion to observe that there are not a few who fancy that time, money, and men might be spent with better result elsewhere than in an Indian mission field. They seem to forget that the servants are sent out only to call.

Was that wedding feast suspended because some refused to respond? The F.I.M.A. is ample proof that its desire is to have the missionaries continue their call. They will then report to the King. These reports, it would seem, are perused by higher critics than the King and before the King has a chance. And their verdict, I am sorry to say, is not always in harmony with the opinion of the "Father of all mercy." They seem to prefer that the armies be sent out to settle the question once and for all and be done with this constant, patient waiting and calling. They forget that we must invite only. Let the King mete out the punishment.

The F.I.M.A. is a lead in the right direction. It supports assistance to two classes of poor missions, the Mexican and Indian missions of our Southwest. The Mexican population of New Mexican hamlets and settlements is poor, but traditionally Catholic. It needed priests which the Franciscan Province of St. John the Baptist furnished them. Their spiritual ministrations will not differ from those to which we are accustomed in any well-regulated eastern parish. It is merely a matter of serving up in Spanish instead of German or English. It is hard for many of these good people to meet their priest's support of $1.50 per annum. The F.I.M.A., therefore, wants to provide what is wanting in expenditures which the parish cannot meet, such as school funds, teachers' salaries, buildings, and the like. It wishes to equip the "servants" better for their arduous duty of "calling these poor guests."

The same ultimate end it has in view for the Indian section of the missions. The servants here "call" a strange people of deeply rooted conservatism. Their tribal customs are religion with them, and again their religion is tribal custom. Inherited culture and views, combined with a language that is all-sufficient for the tribe and nothing else, place a very different task upon the servants than we expect in the usual run of parish work. You adjudge and arbitrate family troubles, petty rancors, and animosities; you advise, direct, and instruct, with probably a momentary result. You expect and await, you await and expect, because you are not operating with armies but have been sent out in a byway where a poor and ignorant people awaits the call. This call is not the call of trumpet or cannon. It is not a call that will find immediate response. It is a call nevertheless. Some are gained, others enlightened, still others well disposed, which disposition will in the King's own time bear fruit.

What F.I.M.A. above all needs is the prayers of its patrons. The poor and humble in spirit will give them both for the peoples that F.I.M.A. wishes to reach and benefit, as well as for the ministers who extend the call. Is it too much to ask for the grace of perseverance for our Mexicans or for the grace of conversion for our Indian population?

The poor in spirit, too, will alone contribute their mite to F.I.M.A., which welcomes them for its beneficiaries the Franciscan missions of the Southwest. You needn't be a sentimentalist at all, but I daresay you, too, would appreciate as I have a letter like this. It was a bad scrawl but I could fancy the trembling hand that made a great effort to write:

Dear Father:

I ain't much at rightin. Am bedridden and a widow. But here's 50 cts. for your Mission and excuse rightin. I have the reumatis.

Yours, _____

Thank God the widow's mite is perpetuated not alone in the Gospel. Our Indian missions are obscure. They haven't the appeal that the Chinese and other missions make. Due to false reports and books on the Indians, there are not a few who desire information on the submission of the Indian. "Aren't you afraid to live with those Indians?" is one of the queries that reach me. Not exactly. But I want to say that 20 years ago, F.I.M.A. could not have been launched. That it is like a little lamb or kid frolicking in the sun and has aroused widespread interest is a good omen for a better appreciation of the Indian and other missions of the Southwest. For our mission it spells a central and united effort. This would be a proper place to say a word on so-called United Charities as they apply to Indian missions. However, the editor is growing impatient at the length of this article. Suffice it to say that an Indian mission as a rule has no resources save charity contributions. Parishes here are not [well] established. Pew rents, fairs, euchre parties, church societies, and like sources of revenue seem so natural to our eastern friends that I often receive hints at trying some of these stunts locally. The object is, of course, to help along with trifles and trinkets for such entertainments. I can easily see the finish of a grab bag especially if it were filled with shoes, pants, shirts, stockings, hats, and the like articles which my Indians are sorely in need of. Yet great as this need is, our Indians are far from the perfection which sees charity in grabbing out of a bag for five cents a chance!

The Indian, in other words, is by far not ready to give, but always ready to take. It is not a heathen tenet that it is better to give than to take. This is a Christian and the better view. It is really too early to have the Indian adopt this Christian view.

Notes

1. From Berard Haile, untitled typescript (here "Prosaics"), n.d.; and untitled handwritten manuscript (here "Call"), n.d., BHP Box 1, fd. 12.
2. Berard Haile, "My Navajo Neighbors," 1920?, BHP Box 5, fd. 1.

23

Shortcoats and Longgowns[1]

Leopold Ostermann, O.F.M.

[The Franciscan missionaries to the Navajo had faced sectarian competition, but not at the intensity that came during the second decade of the century. For one thing, there were new government schools on the reservation, with their large captive audiences of Navajo students available for religious instruction. For another, sheer physical access to the Navajo people was easier than it had been. Chin Lee, for example, in the previous decade the epitome of isolation, was now accessible by automobile, and the presence of the government school there meant that a ministry might be accomplished with less punishing travel, less outright pioneering, than had previously been necessary.

The interdenominational competition centered on two issues: getting signatures, that is, getting Indian parents to sign that they wanted their children to be instructed by the Fathers, or by the Protestant ministers; and getting a property base, permission from the Indians and approval from the government, or, in some cases, simply authority from the government, that would allow sectarian missionaries to build living quarters and houses of worship on the reservation.

The reader will observe that the friars rarely have anything good to say about the Protestant preachers, known to the Navajo as "shortcoats." In part, this reflected a perception that the preachers did not "play fair," that they had come to reap where the Franciscan missionaries had sown, that they aimed their ministry at Catholic rather than heathen Indians, that they spread anti-Catholic rumors and fostered anti-Catholic prejudices whenever possible. One of Berard Haile's biographers points to a continuing difference between the politically circumspect Father Anselm and the feisty Father Berard in regard to policy toward Protestants: "To Father Berard, Protestants were a thorn in the flesh, almost as much in need of light as the Navajo, and a good bit more difficult to deal with. Father Berard has left no record of positive encounters with Protestants. Perhaps for that reason he was willing to be much sharper in print about their tactics than Father Anselm thought prudent."[2]

Chin Lee was one of the hot spots of the sectarian struggle. The Franciscans, having already spent almost a decade there, defined the Chin Lee Navajo as "their" Navajo, and while the Franciscan mission there had not distinguished itself in numbers of baptisms or of Navajo attending Mass, it would emerge that most of the Chin Lee Navajo favored the friars, the "longgowns" with their long-term commitment to the area, over the newcomer "shortcoats."

This chapter is a composite of Father Leopold's recollections of his dealings with shortcoats at Chin Lee, as published in the late 1920s as part of his brief series, "Little Mission Stories from Our Own Southwest." With one or two exceptions, notably the concluding "Shipped across the Ocean" story, the events described in these stories happened long before the stories were published. Mostly they date from the years immediately after the government school opened in Chin Lee in 1910. Father Leopold introduces them as "incidents of how preachers, by underhand and questionable methods, succeeded in getting signatures for Navajo children at Chin Lee."

Father Leopold's reference to "underhand and questionable methods" may perhaps be seen as the biased judgment of an old campaigner. The reader may assess Father Leopold's stories on their own merit. However, that his view is not without some support from observers less institutionally committed may be seen in the following excerpt from a letter by a Daniel Holmes Mitchell, a white trader, one who styled himself denominationally neutral, to then president Theodore Roosevelt. The letter, dated December 1, 1906, refers specifically to Protestant missionaries among the Hopi, within the Navajo reservation, but the generalizations about this "class" of people are intended to apply well beyond the strict limits of the Hopi community.

There resides at Hopi, as in all other weak and defenseless communities, a parcel of men too lazy to earn an honest living, who are paid fat salaries by people of misshapen consciences for spreading the gospel according to Saint Baptist, Saint Methodist, or good Saint Presbyter—they never even by accident spread the gospel according to Christ. I know of no class so zealous as these missionaries to stir up strife in a community and turn the moral peccadilloes of their neighbors into current coin. Indeed, upon the success of such endeavors depends their sustenance, for the more evil they can find the field, the more munificent will be their salary. In short, their worth increases with the amount of spiritual carrion they exhume. I speak, your Excellency, of what I have seen, and from a neutral vantage-ground. Being the member of no sect, but merely a man who worships God in His out-of-doors, and tries to do as little harm as may be to his neighbors, I am quite unbiased in my judgment, and I solemnly affirm that among the Indians, where they fore-gather in the greatest numbers, I have never seen a single missionary, excepting the Catholic Fathers—who are, to be sure, educators, and not missionaries—for whom I would dishonor the name of gentleman. At Hopi, these missionaries have been utterly obnoxious. That one of their parishioners, as they are pleased to call these honest, upright people, is a moral man, of honor and integrity, just, kind, courteous, charitable and without spleen, seems as nothing in their eyes. If he is not a professing Christian of the creed which they expound, he is to them worse than his own offal. Could the Hopi forbid them their doors, these missionaries might be bearable, but they are immune from a tithe of the persecution they inflict, for they live under the protection of your Excellency's Government, and some of them are even in your Excellency's employ. They are thus in a position to work incalculable harm. The people, one and all, detest them. Their abuse of hospitality—for they enter a house only to spy upon its inmates—their tale-bearing to the authorities—and they do not scruple to lie to gain their ends—and their double dealings generally, have disgusted all classes oſ society. They welcome any discord among the Hopi, and do all in their power to bring discord about, knowing full well that if they can only bring matters to a crisis, repressionary measures will follow, and they can thus cow this patient people more than ever.[3]

Father Leopold, like the trader, was convinced that the methods of the shortcoat preachers were devious and underhanded, and several of his stories tell of run-ins with them. Here, then, are tales of the struggle for Navajo souls, reported from the battle lines at Chin Lee.]

Some particular, romantic interest seems to cling about foreign missions. The yellow tints of China, her tilted-roofed pagodas, the mysterious ways and customs of her people, and their extraordinary dress and ornaments; the golden sunshine, the trailing wisteria vines, and the cheery cherry blossoms of Japan, and the courteous manners of her people; the mysteries of India with its gorgeous temples, its grotesque, enigmatical Buddhas, its teeming millions of dusky inhabitants, with dreamy eyes and lovable disposition; the aroma of sandalwood wafted from the islands of the Pacific with their peaceful, childlike denizens; even the Arctic regions with their extensive fields of snow, their ice-built igloos, their reindeer and dog sleds, and their hardy, fur-clad people: all this and many other things of an oriental hue and color surround foreign missions with a mystic and romantic veil that appeals strongly not only to the imagination but also to the hearts and the purses of the staid, sober Anglo-Saxon, Teuton, Slav, and Celt of the West.

This is not said to criticize the lively interest in, and the willing help shown, the foreign missions. On the contrary, such interest and help are very commendable and laudable, and worthy of all encouragement. But we must not forget that we have some missions equally interesting and equally worthy of help right here in our own country, at our very doors, as it were. Some of these home mission fields, for instance, our Southwest, seem to be almost as unknown to the majority of our Catholics as if they were situated in Tibet or in Togoland.

What heathen people can, or ought to be, of more interest to us than our own Indians? Are our Indians really an interesting people? Of course they are. Are missions among them worthy of being helped? Of course they are. Although most of the romantic atmosphere that surrounded the Indian, his life, and doings in the old days has now been dispersed; although he no longer hunts the buffalo on the plains and in the valleys, nor, decked out in paint and feathers, sets out singing and dancing upon the gory warpath; although he no longer dresses in fringed buckskin, nor sports beaded moccasins and a plume headdress; although he no longer tortures prisoners at the stake, nor wears their scalps at his belt; although he no longer indulges in marauding expeditions, nor in any other way furnishes material for red pages of history; and although he has forever buried the hatchet and has forever-more smoked the pipe of peace with his pale-faced conquerors; although he has learned the advantages of peaceful pursuits, of agriculture, stock-raising, and industry, and has copied to a considerable extent the ways, habits, customs, and clothing of the white man: yet he is, nevertheless, a very interesting member of the human race.

This is especially true of the Navajo and Apache of the Southwest. A series of little stories or incidents of the country and the missionaries, of the people and their children in our sunny Southwest, will, no doubt, be of interest to the reader.

Signatures

When the government Indian school at Chin Lee, Arizona, opened, and the Navajo began to bring in children, it was required of them, by order of the Indian Office, that they give their signature in writing or per thumb mark to signify their preference as to the religious instruction of their children. Our having been on the ground several years before the school was built and having become acquainted with the Indians and gained their confidence and goodwill, they naturally gave their signature to the Catholic priest.

A few years after the school was in operation, preachers began to nose around at Chin Lee, trying to make an entrance by any and whatever means. After the first preacher, with a trained and primed interpreter, had been there for some time, I was told that they had captured 20 of our people and had induced them to change their signatures in their favor.

It happened that at that time an inspector of the Indian Service visited Chin Lee. He was not a Catholic, but a fair-minded man. When he was told of this, he sent for the Indians, asked them why they had made the change, and explained to them clearly and fully the meaning and effects of the signatures. The Indians told him that the shortcoat (preacher) did not represent it nor explain it to them in that way, neither did they want to do that, so they all recalled the signature given the preacher, or his tricky interpreter, and declared that their first signatures, given to the priest, should alone be considered.

In the few next stories I shall bring a few more incidents of how preachers, by underhand and questionable methods, succeeded in getting signatures for Navajo children at Chin Lee.

Rip Van Winkle, the Father of His Children

At Nazlini, about 20 miles south of Chin Lee, lived a Navajo who was generally known by the name of Rip Van Winkle. He had two children at the Chin Lee school, a boy and a girl, both of whom he had signed over to us and who were regularly receiving instruction with the rest of the children.

At one time I was told that he had changed his signature in favor of the preacher. When I next saw him, I asked him why he had done so and if he knew what the change meant. He told me that an American had come to his house and asked him if he had any children at school. He said, yes, he had two there. The American then asked him further if he were the father of these two children, and Rip again answered, yes. Then the American pulled out a paper and told him, without any further explanation, to put his thumb mark on it. Rip complied, thinking that he was signing to the fact that he was the real father of the children.

When told that the American was a shortcoat, or preacher, and when it had been explained to him clearly what his signature meant, namely, that he was thereby turning over his children to the preacher for Protestant instruction, he was much surprised, declaring that such was not his intention; that he had only been asked if he were the father of those two children and had been requested to sign to the fact. He lost no time in having his second signature annulled.

The two children have since been baptized, were graduated at the Chin Lee school, and transferred to nonreservation schools. The boy is now at the Indian School at Albuquerque, New Mexico, and the girl at Fort Apache, Arizona.

Dine Naez Has a Child at School

One day a Navajo, Dine Naez, that is, Tall Navajo or Tall Man, came to me, of his own accord, and told me that about a month ago he had put his thumb mark on the shortcoat's paper (given him his signature) for his girl, who was a pupil of the Chin Lee school. The shortcoat came to him, he said, and asked if he had a child in school. When he said yes, the shortcoat pulled out a paper and told him to put his thumb mark on it. This he did, under the impression that he was signing to the fact that he had a child at school.

Later on he was told just what this thumbprint meant, and he had now come to tell me about it. He had no intention whatever of turning over his girl to the shortcoat, but wanted me to give her religious instruction and consequently did not want that second signature to count. I told him to take his case to the superintendent and tell him just what he wants. This he promptly did. The girl has been baptized some years ago and was later transferred to Sherman Institute, Riverside, California.

More Shortcoat Ruse

About one-fourth of a mile from the Chin Lee mission is beautiful cottonwood grove. Under the large branching trees is a nice log house and a *qoghan* (Americanized into hogan, a Navajo hut). This log house was at one time inhabited by relatives of our interpreter. These relatives came to me one day and said the shortcoat had been at their place the day before and had given them a long talk, of which they did not understand anything. After the long talk, which was Greek to them, he presented a paper, saying they must all put their thumbprints on it. However, since they had not understood his talk, and did not know for what the thumbprints were to be used, they became suspicious and refused to sign. And so the shortcoat had to pocket his paper and try his methods elsewhere.

I told them they had done right and advised them, as I had advised other Indians before, never to put their thumbprints on any paper, neither for me nor for anybody else, unless they were absolutely sure of what was on the paper.

A Right Bower[4]

Among the Navajo of Chin Lee there was a certain educated woman who while at school had attended Protestant instructions. The shortcoat, or preacher, who had given her instructions during her school days, had certainly done well his work of inoculating her with the germs of bitterest bigotry and hatred of all things Catholic. She, as it were, played the role of right bower to the preachers, who praised her as a good, sincere Christian. In season and out of season her bitter, slanderous tongue was busy.

Among our Catholic children there is a girl, now 19 or 20 years of age, who went through the Chin Lee school and spent a few years at Sherman Institute, Riverside, California. One day while speaking to her, she said to me:

> Father, do you know that when I was first brought to school Mrs. ___ tried very hard to persuade my mother to change me over to the preachers? She told me when my mother comes again to see me, to bring her over to her house. When my mother came, I took her over there and that woman just talked and talked and talked to her about changing my signature for preacher. But I was right there and told my mother, 'No,' and begged her not to do it, and she didn't.

Many Goats and the Horse Herder

About four or five miles south of Chin Lee mission lived an old man by the name of Tłizi Łani, Many Goats. Judging from his name he belonged to the Tłizi Łani clan, the Many Goats people. He was well known at the mission, especially for his pleasant disposition. He always had a joke and a laugh whenever he came around.

One day I was told that he was very sick and wished to see me. So I went to pay him a visit. It was a mild and warm day. When I came near his place, I found him lying out in the sun in front of his hogan. He looked very sick. Instead of the customary smile, his face had a very pinched and painful expression. After some talk with him on baptism and the most necessary points of faith, he declared himself willing to be baptized.

When I visited him a few days later, he was much worse and seemed to be declining rapidly. I anointed him and a few days later gave him Christian burial.

Another sick call took me up the mountain to the home of Łi Neinłkadi, the horse herder. Here I found the woman mentioned in the foregoing story; she of the bitter, slanderous tongue, at the bedside of the sick man. When I entered the hogan and greeted her, she smiled a very friendly smile which, knowing what I did, looked more repulsive than a frown or a scowl would have looked. However, when I approached the sick man, she stayed right there and even condescended to interpret a few things which I wished to say to him. After telling him why I had come to see him, what I wished to do and exhorting him to be sorry for his past wrongdoings, I baptized him. He did not recover, but died after a few days.

Catholic Children in Nonreservation Schools

In 1920, 31 Catholic Navajo children, 19 boys and 12 girls, were transferred from the Chin Lee school to a nonreservation school in southern California. These children used to write to me and let me know how they were getting along and inquire after news from their homes.

One of the girls wrote in one of her letters: "When we first come here, the other girls they ask us: 'To what Church you belong?' We say: 'We belong to Catholic Church.' They say: 'No you don't belong to Catholic Church, you belong to Protestant Church.' I say to them: 'We belong to Catholic Church as long as we live.'"

One of the boys wrote: "Last Sunday some boys ask us to go to church with them. We think we are going to Catholic church. But they take their song books and begin to sing, I know it is not Catholic church, and I get up and walk out. And all the other Chin Lee boys they get up and follow me."

Another girl wrote that she was pestered by other girls asking her to go with them to Protestant services, and added: "I think they want to get me away from my Church, but I bet you they can't do it." The superintendent at this particular school was personally known to me, and I knew him to be a fair-minded man. When I wrote to him about these proselytizing efforts of the pupils, I received the assurance that such things would not be tolerated and would be promptly stopped.

A Sick Call to the Peach Orchard

One day a Navajo dismounted in front of the house, came in, and asked me to go and see his daughter, who was very sick. He said they lived up toward the mountain at a place called the Peach Orchard. Quite a number of peach trees had been planted at that place, hence its name. I knew the place and also knew that there was a long stretch of upgrade, rocky, and bumpy road between the mission and there. I judged the distance to be all of 15 miles.

At that time we had a Dodge car at the mission. I got ready, and taking the Brother along as chauffeur and the Navajo as a guide, we started out. The first part of the way was good until we struck the rough, rocky, uphill stretch. We managed to dodge, rock, and bump up safely and then struck some adobe flats. Adobe is a kind of soil of a dark brownish color which when soaked with water beats Illinois mud or any other kind of mud. It had rained a few days before, and the flats were nice and soft in places. Just as nice as quivering chocolate pudding. At one place, somewhat lower than the surrounding region, the Dodge ran into the mud and came to a dead stop, and neither chains nor low gear or any other kind of gear, nor all the gas feeding, could force it through.

While we were standing there and planning what to do next, a Navajo came driving toward us with a load of wood. He stopped to see what the matter was, and I told him where we wanted to go and why, but our *ch'idi* (Navajo name for automobile) was now stuck in the mud and I did not know how we could get there. We were then yet some five miles from the place. After considerable urging and bickering, he finally consented for the consideration of $5 to unload his wood and take us there. The road was mostly soft and upgrade, and since his horses were about half or more played out already, it took a vast amount of urging, yelling, smacking, whistling, and whipping till we, at last, got to the place.

Upon entering the hogan, which was a rather large one, situated in a woody place, I found a young woman about 20 or 21 years old, apparently very sick. A number of relatives were sitting about. After doing for her what I could and baptizing her, I left again on the lumbering wood wagon. The Navajo driver asked me, "How much you give me if horses give out?" I told him I would consider that later when the horses really gave out; for the present he should just drive on and try to get me back to the *ch'idi*. Arriving at the place where the Dodge had foundered, I saw that in the meantime the Brother, with the help of some Navajo, had succeeded in extricating the car and getting her in condition for the trip home. As I had no money with me, I told the man, while he was reloading his wood, to call at the mission the next day, and I would give him the $5 and an old overcoat. He called promptly the next day and received what had been promised him.

Some Sick Children

About 20 miles south of Chin Lee is a place called by the Indians Nazlini. At this place there lived a full-blood Navajo by the name of Clitso Dedman. In his earlier years he had gone to school, received a fair education, spoke Navajo and English equally well, and for some years ran a trading store at Nazlini. He is a close friend of the mission and has been of help to us on many occasions with the Indians of that region.

March 5, 1923, early in the morning, Clitso called at the mission and asked me to his home and to baptize his little boy. The child was some two or three years old, and was very sick; in fact, was not expected to live very long. He was anxious to have him baptized at once since death seemed so near.

I told him to hurry back home and I would follow just as soon as possible. I instructed him what to do, also how to administer private baptism in case things should take a sudden turn for the worse before I got there. Accompanied by the Brother, I hurried the ponies over the road, which was for a great part rough and stony. Besides, with a rig I could not drive over the trail but had to follow the windings of the road.

We arrived at Clitso's home near Nazlini at 10:00 a.m. Clitso came to meet us and told us that the boy had died about two hours ago. Upon being questioned, he said he had baptized the child when he saw that he was dying, and from his description I could judge that he had done everything that was required for private baptism.

The Brother and myself selected a suitable place for interment on a hill under a tree, dug a grave, and gave the child Christian burial. The father made a neat cross of wood, which was placed at the head of the grave. Returning to Clitso's home, another one of his children, about two months old, was found to be very sick, which I baptized before leaving for home.

Another call to attend a sick child took me some six miles north of the mission. At this place there were several hogans within sight of each other. After baptizing a very sick child, I was told that there were some more very sick children in some of the other hogans. I made the round of all the hogans in the neighborhood, and before leaving for home I baptized four very sick children, all of them little more than infants.

Longgowns and Shortcoats

A few years ago, when the preachers had succeeded, in spite of the protest of an overwhelming majority of Indians, in getting permission from Washington to establish a mission at Chin Lee, near the school, one of the headmen came to me and asked what was the difference between the longgowns and the shortcoats. I told him to bring a crowd of Navajo to the mission on a certain evening and I would explain the difference.

The appointed evening, a number of Navajo having come, I invited them into the chapel. I began by saying:

Some time ago I was asked by some of you what was the difference between Longgowns, the Franciscans, and Shortcoats, the ministers over there on the hill. In order to make it easy for you to understand the difference, I am first going to tell you something which I heard from a very old Navajo man. Perhaps some of you may know about this story.

It was many, very many years ago, when the Navajo were yet living in *Dine'tqa*. One day a number of Navajo, who had become dissatisfied, gathered up their belongings and their families, and left the tribe to look up a different homestead. After they had left the tribe and had found a place that suited them, they settled down and made their homes. Then they began to brag and to say: 'We are the real, true Navajo. Those back there whom we left are a bunch of old scrubs and mixed breeds; they are not real Navajo at all.' And they kept on saying such and similar abusive and untrue things about the old tribe.

Now, a little more than 400 years ago there was only one kind of Christians, only one kind of Jesus-people, who had the same belief, the same prayer, the same holy history. Then some got dissatisfied, and they left the Church and began to deny part of the doctrine, which had always been believed. They began to teach other things, which had never been taught before. When they were told that this was wrong, and were asked to give up their erroneous teachings, they were too proud to do so, separated from the old true Church, and made a belief and a prayer of their own. They began to say that they were the only real, true Christians, the only true believers in Jesus Christ, that they alone had His real doctrine and that those back there, whom they had left, were all wrong, were ignorant, and told all kinds of lies about them. These were the first shortcoats. By and by others who became dissatisfied joined them, and by keeping up their lies and calumnies, they succeeded, in the course of time, in deceiving many to side with them. You will hear some of these lies yourself pretty soon.

Therefore, the real difference between us and the shortcoats is this: We have always believed and held fast to what Jesus Christ and His apostles taught, and to all things that have been taught and believed since the days of Jesus Christ, that is, more than 1,900 years. The shortcoats began only 400 years ago by denying some things and making up others to suit themselves. They behaved just like that bunch of Navajo, who left your tribe in *Dine 'tqa*, in considering themselves the only real, true Christians, and in telling nasty lies about the true believers in Jesus Christ, whom they had left.

The Navajo had listened attentively to all this and when I had finished expressed their satisfaction and their understanding before leaving.

Saved on the Installment Plan

The following incident may give readers an idea of the means employed by the shortcoats in spreading the truth (!?) among the Navajo:

A few months ago a Navajo, who had always been very friendly toward our Fathers, came to me and told me that the shortcoat had been speaking to him about us, our beliefs, customs, and teachings. He cautioned this Navajo to be very careful not to join the Catholics, because the priests are all bad and are after nothing more than money. If, for instance, the Indian's father is dead, the priest will tell him that his father will have to be saved; he is not yet saved but suffering a great deal. He, the priest, can save him by prayers, but to make these prayers, he must have some money.

When the priest meets the Indian the next time, he will tell him that his father is not yet perfectly saved; the head is out alright, but the rest of his body is still suffering intense pains. He will have to be saved completely. This means more prayers, and more prayers mean more money. In this way he will continue to save your father, piece by piece, so long as money is forthcoming. Evidently, he was alluding to the Catholic practice of praying for the dead and of having Masses said for them.

Of course, I explained to the Navajo how utterly absurd and untrue such talk was; that anyone who could say such a thing is either very ignorant or very un-Christian and malicious. I told him that I was born and raised a Catholic, that I am a Catholic priest for many years, but that I never heard anything like that; that it is new to me. This Navajo had gone to school in his younger days and spoke English fairly well. When he was leaving, I said to him: "By and by you will hear some more such funny and silly stories about us, and if you do, let me know." Smiling, he answered: "All right, Fadda."

Shipped across the Ocean

The school year of 1926–1927 I spent in Towaoc, Colorado, helping Father Marcellus Troester, O.F.M., who at that time was kept more than busy at Waterflow and Shiprock, New Mexico. There is a large government school at Towaoc for Ute Indian children. Of the 160 pupils, 61 received Catholic instruction twice a week and attended Holy Mass and sermon on Sundays. Quite a number had already been baptized and received the sacraments every two weeks: one Sunday the boys and the next Sunday the girls.

The rest of the children attended Protestant instructions and services. The preacher who was there at that time was rather narrow-minded and bigoted, maintaining, among other things, that Catholics were not Christians. However, things went on quietly enough until a strange preacher visited Towaoc and gave some talks to the children and adult Indians. This preacher was a full-blood, educated Navajo who had been trained and primed by white preachers in the truth and practices of their gospel, the main point of which is to instill a deep and lasting hatred of the Catholic Church and all things Catholic.

Among other things, he cautioned them against becoming Catholics, because the Catholic priests would take the boys, after they were grown up, and send them across the ocean, where they would have to be soldiers and fight for the Pope, from where they would never be allowed to come home. This silly lie was believed by the Indians and had the desired effect, namely, to work up the Indians and to create strong feeling and hatred against the priest and against everything Catholic. While passing through the grounds I was several times stopped by adult Indians, and some came to the house where I was staying and excitedly told me about what they had heard. I was glad they did come and ask me for information, as that gave me a chance to deny the lie and make an attempt at setting them right.

I also made it a point in my instructions to the children to explain to them what a downright, silly lie had been told them, and how ridiculous it was to say or to believe anything like that. The next day I was somewhat surprised at their senses of humor; when I passed one of the school buildings, before which there was a crowd of children, they lifted up their hands and with much loud laughter asked me: "Say, Fadda, when you going take us across de ocean?"

This same native preacher had, some time before this, told the same vile slander to the Indians and to the children of Fort Defiance, Arizona, and had there, too, stirred up quite a bit of excitement among the Indians.

This same native preacher and his wife were formerly employees at the government Indian school at Shiprock, New Mexico. While there, she warned the Navajo girls not to become Catholic, because Catholics are all going to hell; they should not let the Catholic priest baptize them, because after baptism the priest would take each one into a private room and—the rest is not printable. That's what they call spreading Christian truth. Ye shades of Ananias and Saphira!

Notes

1. From Leopold Ostermann, "Little Mission Stories from Our Own Southwest," *St. Anthony Messenger* 34 (February–April 1927): 466–67, 524–25, 578; 35 (July, November 1927): 75–77, 301; 36 (November 1928): 309–11.

2. Arne Hassing, "Father Berard Haile, O.F.M., and the Navajo," in *Religion in the West*, ed. Ferenc M. Szasz (Manhattan, Kan.: Sunflower University Press, 1984), 94.

3. Daniel Holmes Mitchell, "An Indian Trader's Plea for Justice, 1906," *New Mexico Historical Review* 47 (July 1972): 250–51.

[4. The term "right bower" refers to one of the two highest cards in a card game, namely the jack of trumps.]

24

Tales of Lukachukai

Marcellus Troester, O.F.M.

[At Lukachukai, 35 miles northeast of Chin Lee, there was a trading post and, by Navajo standards, a fairly dense agricultural community. Not that it was a village in the American sense of the word, but rather "a true community of families grouped closely on irrigated farm land and bound by common ties of neighborhood, occupation, and culture."[1] Several former students from St. Michael's School had their homes in the vicinity, and in 1909 the community formally requested that the Franciscans locate there. A chapel was constructed in 1910, and Father Marcellus Troester, stationed at Chin Lee, made monthly visits until 1915 when Father Berard was assigned as resident priest.

This chapter offers three glimpses of Lukachukai, spaced at two-year intervals, the first two from the itinerant Father Marcellus's correspondence with Father Anselm, the last from his formal progress report published in the 1915 issue of the mission's annual, *Franciscan Missions of the Southwest*.

Father Marcellus had been assigned to the Navajo missions after his ordination in 1906. After a time at St. Michaels he was sent to assist Father Leopold at Chin Lee, and working from there, made monthly trips north to visit the Lukachukai community.

Each of the letters describes a difficult journey to Lukachukai, the first in midwinter 1911, the second in summer two years later. A quite remarkable difference in spirit and tone separates the letters from the article. The letters are really lamentations on problems, frustrations, and even apparent failure, while the published report of 1915 conveys a refreshing optimism and sense of accomplishment. Some of that difference is simply a matter of audience: in the correspondence Father Marcellus is often explaining to his Superior why he wasn't able to accomplish what he had been assigned to do, while in the report for public consumption the intent is to put a positive "spin" on things so that readers will be inspired and motivated. More of the difference, I think, is simply a matter of time: by 1915 five years of effort, despite challenges and failures along the way, had produced a substantial amount of real progress. The letters, written in the early stages of the struggle, emphasize the challenges the friars faced: the physical obstacles of great distances to travel, dangerous terrain, and frightful weather, and the interpersonal barriers to be overcome, the suspicions, misunderstandings, and commitment to traditional beliefs that characterized the Navajo of Lukachukai.

Part of the changed outlook at Lukachukai was attributable to the construction of a new government boarding school there, and one of the reasons that boarding school was there was the influence of Father Anselm. In February 1912, writing from St. Michaels, he reported to Provincial Eugene Buttermann that recently he had attended a meeting of the supervisors of federal schools for Indians and that his suggestions to them had been taken seriously:

> As to building a chapel for the Navajo, things are moving rather rapidly here. It was fortunate that I attended the meeting of the supervisors at Fort Defiance last week. I succeeded in having Lukachukai selected for a boarding school for a hundred pupils. If I had not been there they would have suggested only a day school for that place.
>
> Besides that boarding school, two day schools will be built, one about a mile from the railroad at Houck, Arizona, for 40 or 50 children, and one at Wide Ruins for the same number of children, 25 miles from the railroad. Each will be about 30 miles from this place. Both are in a locality where a number of Navajo have their adjoining farms. The Navajo in these two localities belong to our 'sphere of influence' and are sending some of their children to our school. We must attend to those places and a small chapel ought to be built at each of these places. . . .
>
> It was also suggested and urged that the large boarding school at Keam's Canon, now used for the Moquis, should be turned over to the Navajo. There are at present between 3,000 and 4,000 Navajo children of school age without school facilities, and the Government has decided to build schools for them. In new localities worth while where schools are to be built I would like to be the first on the spot, get a piece of ground from the Indians for chapel and a few rooms, obtain their promise to bar 'the others' and thus 'preempt' the place and all the surrounding country. All this will show you that I shall very soon need the money to build chapels where these new schools are to be built. . . . The ten Indian Commissioners (Cardinal Gibbons among them), the Secretary of the Interior and others have at last set the Indian Office in motion to build schools for the Navajo, and we cannot afford to let these new localities slip away from us.[2]

Father Anselm was doing his best to minimize competition from the shortcoats by "preempting" the best locations and working to solidify his already positive rapport with the Navajo people generally. Lukachukai, Houck, and Wide Ruins, all were now targeted for special attention from the Franciscans.]

To Lukachukai, Winter 1911[3]

Reverend Dear Father Anselm:

Was that a trick you played on us, when you said our Boss would be home Wednesday evening, thinking perhaps that I would not go on that trip otherwise, or was he merely mired in again? Well we made the trip anyhow and were gone three days, and a horrible trip we had of it too. We had a fierce blizzard blowing straight in our face all the way until we got to Round Rock. We left here Wednesday morning about 9:00 and took the trail along the canyon, opposite the field matron's. After riding a few miles, we met an Indian and of course held him up. His name is Chetch'oshdilni Biye. He said he has a boy at the Fort [Defiance] school named Ashki Łbai. He put this boy in school himself. He also has two small boys in St. Michael's School, taken there by their uncle Bilaagodi. The mother of the children is dead and he did not know her name (very likely because she is dead, he did not want to speak of her). The names of the two boys at St. Michael's are: Yik'e łał and Wé. The father lives somewhere near Ganado at Kinazini.

We then rode on and met several squaws and asked them about Ts'atqaedot'-lish but it seems nobody knew exactly where it was, even those that lived within a few miles of Qastqin Yazhe, but we found it at last. Qastqin Yazhe signed for his boy Yazhe Bahe at the Fort school. The mother of the boy is Yiłnasba. We also saw Qastqin Bitsiłaba'igi, and he said that is not his son at St. Michael's School, as you say, but the son of his brother Qastqin Naes.

From there we rode on to Lukachukai and of course inquired at once for Dadsiłqeheni Biye. I spoke to him about his son Jessie Davis and asked him to sign for him, but he put me off, saying I should wait till morning, then he would sign. I told him it was very important and in a hurry, but he said he had other things to talk about and we should wait and I had to let it go at that. I was somewhat afraid that he had perhaps signed already to [Reverend] Black, but he said he had signed to no one as yet. We hung around his hogan till dark thinking Black's messenger might drop in any time. Finally, we went to the chapel, where we stayed all night. We had a hard time of it, having one blanket each and the stove is so small that the wood burns out in 10 minutes, and our firewood we had to scratch out from under the snow.

The next morning we took a look at the chapel. The stone cap and step of the front door are both cracked in the middle. The cap is so bad and weak that you can notice it sagging in the center. It is braced with two-inch uprights and cross pieces, but it looks bad. The best thing would be to take the cap out again and put in another, if possible. The plastering looks rather poor, since they did not take the trouble of trying to get it smooth, unless you intend to give it another coat of plaster. The red-stone caps on the terraces of the chapel-front are also wrong. Instead of being bound with the adjoining wall, they only touch it, which causes a weak spot, allowing the rain to wash down along the mortared joints.

We had a hard time getting the doors open and a still harder job to get them shut when we left. We had to pound the front doors shut from the inside and therefore had to take three keys along. They only have one coat of paint and need at least two more. There is a good deal of lumber lying around, outside of the chapel, which ought to be saved, but we did not have the time to stay there long and besides everything was covered with snow.

We soon left and went to Dadsiłqeheni Biye, and had a long talk with him. He signed for his boy Jessie Davis and said he won't sign to Black nor anybody else. He asked me when we are going to move in the Lukachukai chapel, and so on. He said you and the archbishop promised them a school up there and now he is saving his younger children for the new school. He said he saw a lot of flooring left from the chapel and told me to ask you whether he could have it for his house, as he has a dirt floor now. I told him the chapel is not finished yet and very likely you need the lumber to make closets, shelves, and so on, but I would ask you anyhow and you could let him know through some Indian that goes up there.

We inquired, wherever we could, about the other Indians we were to see. We learned that Dine Yazhe, father of Cecilia and Mercedes was at Tsełchidahaskanni, so we could not see him. We heard that Leonard Tqodok'ozhi had been working for [Superintendent William T.] Shelton but had returned, but he lived so far that it would have taken us another day just to see him, and I thought it was not so important as to warrant our staying over in such horrible weather. About Paul Nakai Dine Naes we could learn nothing, except that he lived at Tsełchidahaskanni, [and we] didn't know why he did not go to school.

From Dadsiłqeheni Biye we went to Tqoaqaedlini. He said he is glad to give us his signature and let us instruct his children, because it happened already that Americans, from nonreservation schools, came to the Fort and took children away to other schools without letting the parents know. Tqoaqaedlini said he was on the chapel grounds, when you and [Fort Defiance Navajo School Superintendent Peter] Paquette were there and spoke about starting the chapel, but you did not say anything to him about signing, and so forth. I told him you did not know he was there, because you were anxious to see him. Tqoaqaedlini said he won't sign to anybody else.

At the latter's hogan we met an old man named Tsi Bitsoi, who is very poor and lives all alone. Has nothing to eat and the only clothing, that which he has on. The other Indians said he goes around begging for something to eat. He said he has a boy at St. Michael's School and wanted to write a letter to him. The boy's name is Tqol. He said his boy gets paid for working at the school, which I doubted, but he said he (the father) got several things, food, and so forth, from his boy last summer, and that is the reason he wants to ask his boy to give him food and clothing now, and wants you to speak to his boy about it.

From Tqoaqaedlini's we went to look up Luke, and a miserable time we had to find him. Luke lives on this side of the canyon, that is on the opposite side from Lukachukai, so we had to go around the head of the canyon because we could not cross at Lukachukai, [and] for that reason we could not see Paul nor Charlie Mitchell because they lived in the opposite direction and we were not in a mood for paying friendly visits in such weather. We were half frozen on that trip, looking for Luke, and whenever we spied a hogan, we bolted for it and crawled in to thaw out and dry ourselves, but the hogans were scarce. We could not see half a mile ahead on account of the blizzard, but Chique has a good nose and could smell the smoke and we found him [Luke] at last. You said in your letter to me, that you sent word to Luke about farmwork and so on, but Luke said nobody ever told him a word about it. I asked him whether he wanted the job and tried to encourage him to take it but he hesitated. I finally got him to decide. But he and his uncle who was with him said that the roads are so bad now that his horse could not make the trip. He wanted a month's time, but I told him that would be too late. He then said he would go to St. Michaels in two weeks to take the job, and in case he should back out, he would come to Chin Lee and let me know and I can write to you. From Luke's hogan we could see Charlie Mitchell's place on the other side of the canyon, on the Lukachukai side, but we could not cross. Luke told us it was eight miles from his place to Round Rock but it's fully 16. The way we flew over that trail was a caution. We left Luke's place at 4:00 and reached Round Rock store at 6:00. My, but we were happy.

We had learned on the trip that Maurice Ałts'ihi lives right near the store at Round Rock, so we walked over the next morning. We found his mother and two sisters, but Maurice was not there. They told us that his older brother, who usually takes him to school, came to get him, but Maurice was at Shiprock then, working for Shelton, and had been all summer. He came home about a month ago, but then his brother was gone and they had no horse to take him to school. Then his uncle came and asked Maurice to herd sheep for him, and his mother told him to go and earn a few sheep. Maurice will go back to school next fall and wants to take his brother with him. The mother has eight children, four boys, and four girls. One girl, that was present, is about 10 years old, and was so afraid that I came to take her along. The mother says she thinks it is enough if she sends the boys. But I think you might persuade her to send more children.

On the whole trip we could not learn much about Qastqin Naesk'ai Biye. Some said he lived near the Black Mountain; others said near the sheep dip. Therefore, we went from Round Rock to the sheep dip store and inquired there. They told us that he lives in the neighborhood of Ts'atqaedot'lish and that he often comes to the store. I told the storekeeper to tell him the next time he sees him, that I want to see him and that he should come to Chin Lee, if possible. Now I will wait a while and see if he comes and if not, and if the weather clears up, we will go and hunt him up. There is nobody living at Tqodadastqanni now, no wood nor anything there.

Now I hope you are satisfied with this report and say I'm a good boy. Of the $10 you sent I have $9.60 left, that I don't know what to do with, unless you want me to keep it for future trips. Or in case you ever want to buy me a Christmas present (doesn't matter if it's in February) I might suggest a pocket Breviary, since mine is so clumsy and unhandy to take along on these horseback mission trips. Ha ha.

Sincerely yours,

A Tale of Woe from Lukachukai, Summer 1913[4]

Reverend Dear Father Anselm:
Well I have a tale of woe from Lukachukai for you. I went to see Charlie Mitchell
and found them accidentally, although they had moved. When I entered the hogan
(Big Charlie wasn't there), his wife would not speak to me; she only made signs.
I saw Charlie Jr. lying there, all covered up, and thought he was dead. I went over,
raised the blanket, and saw that he was sleeping. Speaking to the old lady again, she
yelled at me that Big Charlie was up on the mountain. Not wishing to wake the boy,
I waited a while and then uncovered him again. He opened his eyes and recognized
me. Spoke to him, asked him how he felt, whether he could eat anything, and so
forth, and then asked him if he would like to receive the sacraments again. No, no,
he didn't want the sacraments anymore. I asked him why not, what was the matter?
He said, the last time I was there and gave him the sacraments, I made him worse
instead of better.

    Now, when his mother saw what was up, she came over and sat down on the
other side of Charlie and told him he should not listen to me and should not let me
say any prayers over him. And every time I would start to talk to Charlie she would
talk to him, too, so that he would not hear what I said and possibly give in. I tried
to explain to Charlie what the sacraments were for, told him I was no doctor and
that the sacraments were mainly for the soul, and so on. Well, he said he did not
care for his soul. Then I explained about heaven and hell, and so on, but he said he
could not be happy in heaven as long as he is so sick now. Well, I tried everything
I could think of, but all to no avail. And all the time his mother would butt in; as
soon as I would start to talk, she would, too. I hated to give up and started over four
different times, would explain to him, tell him the sacraments would do him good,
and so forth, but no, he did not want them; they make him worse. Thinking that if
I would say the prayers for the sick over him, he might possibly change his mind,
I spoke to him about that, but no, he would not let me pray over him either, his
mother always urging him to refuse me. I simply could do nothing with him. I
finally got him to promise to say a short prayer now and then and told him a few
ejaculations and told him that if he ever changes his mind and would like to see me,
he should just send for me and I would come at once. I left them reluctantly without
even giving him the blessing or anything.

    It was sure a humble *ænishodi* that hit the trail. On my way back, I met Big
Charlie in a buggy. I tried to speak to him about the matter, but he always acted as
if he did not understand what I said. He told me the whole history of Charlie's
sickness and always understood what I said, but as soon as I would mention my last
visit, he did not understand me. I am sure the whole outfit takes me for a witch now
and that my "medicine" only makes people worse. I am pretty sure that it was Big
Charlie and his wife who talked all that rot into their boy. If Charlie feels that way
about our religion, you might guess how he will like it to have us say Mass at his
house, and what damage he could do to our cause by telling other Indians about his
boy's case. I wish you would go for him hammer and tongs next time you see him

and haul him over the coals for his foolish superstitions, though I doubt whether it will do any good, and besides I do not think you will see him for quite a while now. I felt mighty blue about this affair, but I suppose a person needs such a humiliation once in a while.

At the chapel, on Sunday, I had quite a crowd, that is, in comparison to other trips, though I should like to have had a list of all the children around there. As it is, you sent me the names of those whom I know best, but what I need most is the names of those who are in school during the year and whom I seldom get to see, though I think I had all present that lived nearby. Some, of course, were up on the mountain and on the other side and could not come. Had Ralph Kinlichini serving and want to get his brother, too, if you can let me have a surplice. I wrote to Egbert about it. Then I would like to have Benediction and have all the necessary things except remonstrance. Could you manage to get me one or should I write to Provincial for one? As to the list of names, you must have them somewhere, and I wish you would let me have what you have on hand even if they are not arranged yet. I would pick them out and copy them and return your list. . . .

Another thing I wish to mention is the children ought to be taught at school how to baptize in case of necessity. Callista's sister was sick and I told Callista to speak to her about baptism, and so on. I think these children could do a world of good if they were only told how.

Sincerely yours,

Our Mission at Lukachukai, 1915[5]

Nestled at the foot, and adjoining the abrupt cliffs of the Lukachukai Mountains, lies one of the most beautiful and picturesque spots on the whole Navajo reservation. Many might think that the babbling brook, the sweet-scented woods, and the balmy fields of varicolored flowers are unknown quantities in our arid and sunbaked Arizona, and yet we find here such inspiring spectacles of scenic grandeur and beauty as to baffle the most vivid imagination in attempting a description of their existing reality.

It is true that the greater part of the Navajo reservation is absolutely useless for agricultural purposes. Nevertheless, there are some few favored localities where this pursuit may be followed with gratifying results, and it is in such places that the Navajo settle down to wrest from mother earth a livelihood that forms a supplement to the sustenance from their flocks of sheep and goats and their herds of cattle.

Such a naturally favored place is the above-mentioned Lukachukai Valley. Protected on the north and east by the towering Lukachukai Mountains and on the south by the lower foothills is a rich and fertile piece of land, watered by several clear mountain streams and dotted here and there with hogans that look for all the world like overgrown anthills. However, many families possess substantial houses which show traces of the industrial training of some returned pupil. Adjoining each house or hogan are the farms which give evidence of the thrift and progressive spirit of the Navajo and show forth the falseness of the rather common canard that all Indians are an indolent and lazy set and a burden to the community in which they live. Here they raise their staple farm crops, the more abundant of which are corn, alfalfa, wheat, beans, squashes, and melons, and here and there are even seen young orchards budding forth in the more sheltered places of the lowlands.

It affords a refreshing sight, after passing miles and miles of the scraggy sagebrush and sand, to come suddenly upon these velvety plats of rich alfalfa and billowing fields of golden grain, interlaced, as with silken threads, with a network of irrigating ditches that go meandering down the valley from farm to farm. However, one drawback to this El Dorado is the shortness of the season, and it frequently happens that an early frost nips their whole crop in the bud. But necessity is the mother of invention, and the Navajo have hit upon a plan to save and utilize their frozen corn by roasting it in pits, which enables them to preserve it for winter use. In view of the exceedingly rapid progress this little settlement has made within the past few years while being left entirely to its own resources, one can reasonably predict that a great future awaits these Indians when once the government is ready to extend a helping hand by teaching them the principles of agriculture and economy.

It was these existing conditions together with a judicious discernment of the possibilities of the future, but especially the fact that a large number of children from this neighborhood attended our school at St. Michaels, Arizona, that six years ago led the Reverend Anselm Weber, O.F.M., to choose this place for the establishment of a mission. Occasionally, he had visited this place from St. Michaels in order to give the Catholic children an opportunity to attend Mass and receive the sacraments when at home, and had used one of the better Indian houses for this purpose, but it was at once apparent that this was unfit for divine service, and he therefore began to take steps toward acquiring ground for the erection of a suitable chapel. Having learned that the *Yeibichai,* the renowned Navajo dance, was to take place in the Lukachukai Valley on October 9, 1909, and anticipating the presence of a large crowd of Indians, he deemed the time propitious to lay his petition before them and obtain from them a piece of land and their consent to establish a mission there, all of which was most willingly granted. The site selected by the Indians themselves for this mission contains a spring of good, clear water, in fact, the best and most active spring in the whole neighborhood.

A curious coincidence, a case of poetic restitution one might call it, was the bestowal of this site for mission purposes, inasmuch as this very spring has, for centuries past and until lately, been used in their heathenish ceremonies. It was considered sacred by the Navajo, so much so that it was looked upon as a crime and an infallible portent of impending misfortune to use this water for either man or beast. And now this same spring bubbles forth the water used in the regenerating sacrament of baptism, yes, for the sublime sacrifice of the Mass itself.

Qabo'ol'æsi (it is tramped out) is the name by which this spring is known in one of their legends. According to this legend, the Buffalo People, who were considered deities, undertook a journey from west to east in company with the Deer, Antelope, Bighorn, and Mountain Goats, all deities. They left *Dok'ooslid*, the San

Francisco Peak, which is the Sacred Mountain of the West, and headed toward *Tsisnajin*, the Sacred Mountain of the East, near the headwaters of the Rio Grande. Having arrived at the foot of the Lukachukai Mountains, they looked in vain for water wherewith to quench their thirst, whereupon the buffalo began stamping the ground until it became moist, and they continued this procedure until finally there was sufficient water for all to drink. The fact is that the surface water here is so shallow that by digging only two feet one can get all the water necessary for ordinary needs.

Although the land was given willingly and promptly, the funds were, as yet, missing for the immediate erection of the chapel, and it was nearly two years later that the ground was broken and the building commenced. Reverend Anselm Weber had engaged an American to take over the contract. With the help of some Navajo, he put up a substantial stone building consisting of a large chapel with two rooms appended, these latter intended for the use of the visiting missionary. . . .

Fully appreciating the great blessing of having a chapel and not being obliged to use a miserable hogan or Indian hut for the celebration of Mass, still we cannot but entertain the wish that it might be a more fitting dwelling for the Most High, for though the exterior presents a neat and respectable appearance, an atmosphere of extreme poverty permeates the interior. On account of the great distance of the base of supplies—the lumber coming from a distance of 50 miles, the other materials 90 miles—the total cost of the building, as it now stands, was $2,240.82, and since the available funds amounted to $1,940.82, there still remains a debt of $300, and consequently the plastering, painting, and inside furnishings had to be postponed until some later date. As can be expected, wherever the Gospel is carried into new territory, there is absolutely no income for this mission, and it must rely for its support on outside help. Aside from the fact that it would only be detrimental if not entirely fatal to the missionary work, as such, to ask the natives to support a cause, the importance of which they cannot yet fully comprehend, it would also be heartless to expect them to contribute of their meager sustenance when they themselves are often at a loss to know where the morrow's meal will come from. So we put our trust in God, assured that He will take care of His own, and also in the charity of kindhearted Christians with the expectation that they will continue to help along in the future as they have done so generously in the past.

In 1912 the writer was appointed to take charge of this mission, and it is now visited regularly once a month except during winter when most of the Indians move away to find new pastures for their sheep and cattle. The chapel was so far completed that it could be used, and the dedication took place on June 22, 1912. The different schools on the reservation had just closed, and all the children of Lukachukai and surrounding neighborhood were present for the celebration. The neighboring Indians had also been invited, and a large number put in their appearance, eager to see the novel ceremony. The dedication was performed by the Reverend Anselm Weber, after which followed Solemn High Mass and Benediction and an appropriate address in which the ceremonies of the day were explained to the attending Indians.

This mission, as mentioned above, was mainly established for those children who have completed their curriculum at the various schools and returned home to face the vicissitudes of life. True, at school they have been thoroughly imbued with the essentials of religion and have been prepared for the duties of life as far as human patience and self-sacrifice permitted under the circumstances. They have been lifted out of the mire of ignorance and superstition and have received that religious education which alone can elevate the character and make of them true Christian men and women. Still, theirs is but a religion in the growing stage and requires continual care and attention. If such children were left to themselves, never seeing or hearing any more of their faith, it would not take long for the latter to die in the bud, and they would soon relapse into the pagan customs and superstitions of their childhood. Therefore, if their education and religious training, imparted to them with so much patience and under such difficulties at school, should not constitute a mere flyleaf in their book of life, it devolves upon the missionary in the field to supplement this initial acquirement with unceasing watchfulness, by continuing to nourish their famishing souls with the word of God and by weaving, through countless exhortations, the principles of religion into their daily lives.

Unfortunately, on account of the great distance—this mission being situated some 35 miles northeast of Chin Lee—the missionary must be content with supplying them with the benefits of their religion on the installment plan, as it were, by visiting them once a month and whenever an urgent case requires his presence. Sick calls at this distance might seem preposterous and, in the language of the street youngster, might "be going some." Well it is, but with the Indian method of wireless communication news travels like wildfire and nearly every inhabitant within a radius of 20 to 30 miles or more knows of the sick person.

A description of one of these visits might be a revelation to many. The sick or dying person will be found lying on a bed of sheep pelts spread on the ground, occasionally receiving a waft of smoke and a spray of ashes from the open fire nearby, and one of the family will be seen busy shooing the flies away and shaking the ubiquitous ants from the blankets. If the patient be one who had attended school and received Catholic instruction, the missionary has easy sailing in regard to administering the last rites of the Church, for usually a ray of light flits over his countenance at sight of the visitor, and even the pagan parents take the proceedings as a matter of course without the least interference. Nay, more than that, they are highly pleased and flattered to know that the *ænishodi* should come such a distance to pay a friendly visit to the sick and that he should "bring the prayer along with him," as one laconically expressed it. As to accommodations and facilities for administering the last sacraments, there are none, and the priest is fortunate indeed if he can find a crackerbox or something similar on the premises upon which to place the Blessed Sacrament, otherwise he must content himself with spreading a blanket on the ground for the purpose. In most cases it is almost impossible to remain standing in the hogan on account of its low and cone-shaped roof, and should one attempt it where the roof is sufficiently high, he would soon become wise to the fact that smoke rises upward and that the purest air is to be found near the ground.

Should the sick person be a full-fledged heathen, one who had never heard any-thing about God or the future life, the case presents other difficulties besides those mentioned above. Often, the priest on his arrival will find one or more medicine men performing their rites over the sick person and will be greeted variously with a look of fear, suspicion, and resentment. Of course, in such cases it is out of the question to interrupt the ceremony and attempt to gain the attention of the patient, and all one can do is to make the best of the situation by either emulating the patience of the Indians, of which they have an overabundance, or by repeating the visit at some other time. The patients, too, already keyed to the highest pitch of dread by the mysterious doings of the medicine men, and saturated from childhood with their pagan myths and superstitions, must be approached with moccasined feet and with kid gloves, metaphorically speaking, lest the sublime truths of the Christian religion prove to be too much for their apprehensive minds. Still, notwithstanding these difficulties, the results fully justify the attempt at rescuing these souls and are ample compensation for the labors and hardships endured.

Almost as prosaic as these sick calls are also the regular trips to the mission. It is not all spiritual work, by any means, that confronts the missionary upon his arrival. After spending the greater part of the day in the saddle, he is likely to enjoy a huge appetite, but does not find the proverbial ministerial chicken dinner awaiting him. Instead, he must be his own chef, and the first act finds him gathering and chopping firewood. Moreover, his horse needs attention no less than himself, and often considerable time is consumed in securing suitable feed. Such are a few of the minor incidentals of Indian missionary life, but since there is no cloud without its silver lining the missionary, on the other hand, has the satisfaction of knowing that his work is not in vain.

Having satisfied the undeniable rights of nature, he can turn his attention to the spiritual welfare of his flock. Until recently it has been the custom, and somewhat of a necessity, at each visit to go about from house to house and even out to the sheep camps to let them know that the *œnishodi* was there and would hold services the following day. Though it is seldom that all of them are at home or to be found at all, some being at great distances herding sheep, others up in the mountains rounding up horses or cattle, it is nevertheless a gratifying feature to note that the pupils have all remained faithful thus far, and their eagerness to attend Mass and receive the sacraments shows the enduring influence of the training received at school and is an index of their appreciation of their newly adopted religion. . . .

We now have a fair-sized bell with which to call them to church. It has a beautiful, clear tone that reaches out to the remotest parts of this settlement. To think that in these wilds, where but a scant 50 years ago the mountains rang and re-echoed with the bloodcurdling war cry of these savages, we now hear the peaceful voice of a church bell inviting and drawing these same children of the forests and plains to the house of God!

A welcome addition to this settlement in the past year was the erection of a government school building which will be opened for occupation as soon as the necessary furnishings and supplies can be shipped in. With the school right in their midst the Indians will not hesitate to bring their children as when they are obliged to take them 50 or more miles away and are thus separated from them for practically a whole year. Since this school was begun, they are all, parents and children, eagerly looking forward to its formal opening, as they have long ago recognized the great advantages such a training brings to their children.

What is considered one of the chief psychological difficulties to overcome in the education and civilization of the Navajo is the returning of the graduated pupils to their old homes amid the pagan and superstitious environment of their elders to take up once more the Indian life with all its degenerating influences. However, these conditions are unavoidable at present and of a transient nature, nor are they entirely devoid of all good. The young leaven, freshly inoculated with the germ of Christianity, is bound to start fermentation in the lives of the older generation, and even at this early date one can notice a healthy transformation taking place in the minds of the latter. They already realize that the new religion brought home and practiced by their children forms a break in the continuity of their time-honored traditions, and are beginning to look forward with resignation to the inevitable doom of their cherished customs and ceremonies. They perceive the unmistakable superiority of the white man's religion and, like their children, they feel that what the missionary has to offer them seems to fill a certain, undefinable void in their hearts which their own pagan mythology is unable to do.

Hence the signal change exhibited in their attitude toward the missionaries in the last few years. Where formerly these were looked upon with suspicion and somewhat as intruders, they are now welcomed by the Indians, and the one great desire at present, as repeatedly expressed by the natives, is to have the æ'nishodi come and live permanently with them. An occurrence of profound significance is the fact that occasionally on these mission trips a number of older Navajo will call at the house, squat down on the floor along the walls, and then ask to be told more about the white man's God. What seems to appeal to them very strongly is that the Christian religion has something definite to offer them for the next world, whereas their own traditions represent to them some vague and uncertain existence after this life.

In this disposition, then, they are satisfied to have their children baptized and embrace the new faith, but as to themselves, they are as yet undecided and slow in giving up their inborn superstitions and changing their entire mode of life. But if we consider with what difficulty even the civilized races are made to part with their favored superstitions, we can readily understand that it is no easy matter for these untutored pagans to shed their old beliefs of a sudden and accept the religion of the white man. However, they have been aroused from the deadly slumber of paganism, they already stand on the threshold of a new spiritual awakening, and on the horizon of this race appears the dawn of a faith of which we may cherish the confident expectation that it will be of such brilliance and endurance as it is slow and difficult to bring about.

Notes

1. Robert L. Wilken, *Anselm Weber, O.F.M.: Missionary to the Navaho, 1898–1921* (Milwaukee, Wisc.: Bruce), 120.

2. Anselm Weber to Father Provincial Eugene Buttermann, 12 February 1912. FAC Box DEC.247. Weber, Anselm. Let., fd. CIV4. Letters Superiors.

3. Marcellus Troester to Anselm Weber, 19 February 1911, FFP Box 1, fd.4.

4. Marcellus Troester to Anselm Weber, 8 July 1913, FFP Box 1, fd.4.

5. From Marcellus Troester, "Our Mission at Lukachukai, Arizona," FMSW 3 (1915): 30–38.

25

A Sick Call to Crystal[1]

Egbert Fischer, O.F.M.

[The following narrative of Father Egbert's visit to Crystal and his breach of courtesy in dealing with Beshlagai the silversmith is one of the few writings of the early Franciscans among the Navajo where there exists an "internal" critique by another missionary. Reading the piece, the reader may notice a difference in style from the matter-of-fact, sometimes understated accounts of Anselm Weber and Berard Haile. In Fischer's *Sendbote* article, the missionary "I" is more apparent, and he highlights his success in calling upon the powers of heaven as needed in the daily ministry. In correspondence with Father Anselm, Father Berard found fault both with these elements of Egbert's essay and with Egbert's conduct in the incident described, behavior that to Berard smacked of the discourtesy of the Protestant preachers who persisted in preaching to the Navajo and in other obtrusive behavior in situations where their hosts had openly expressed a lack of interest or even rejection of the "shortcoats" and their message.

During the five years he was assigned to the Navajo missions, Father Egbert wrote six articles for Father Anselm's *Sendbote* series, "*Die Franziskaner-Mission unter den Navajo-Indianern*," including three articles in 1912, two in 1913,[2] and his final contribution, the 1915 piece reprinted below.]

It was Sunday morning, June 22, 1913. Just after I had finished the Holy Mass in the school hall at Fort Defiance and was putting away the holy garments, Anna Curley, a newly baptized Navajo Indian woman who was now teaching weaving to the schoolgirls, came to me and asked me to baptize her sick mother in Crystal, New Mexico. This morning she had offered the Holy Communion for her mother. She was sure that a loving God would not withhold the grace of baptism from her.

Crystal, New Mexico, is about 30 miles from Fort Defiance. At breakfast I asked the doctor whether he had been called to Crystal, and when he told me he had not, I asked him to take me with him if he were called there. He gladly promised to do so. On the next Thursday morning, as I was returning to our mission school and getting back to work, nothing seemed to be going right. Without really knowing why, I got myself ready to travel. Behold, at about 9:00 I received news that the doctor had been called to Crystal. The agent was also going along. I could go with them if I reached Fort Defiance in time. Our mission is eight miles from the government school at Fort Defiance. Brother Felix quickly got the Indian boy Theodore from the field and sent him to find the saddle horse "Shanty." Meanwhile, I telephoned Fort Defiance and through the translator asked the agent to wait there for my arrival.

Theodore found the horse quickly, and in a few minutes I was in the saddle. I did not have to spur the horse, it seemed to sense the need to hurry, and so on the way I was able to go over each item that I needed to bring with me. I was planning to conduct the Holy Mass the next morning in Crystal, and nothing could be overlooked. Luckily, I had everything necessary in Fort Defiance, and there would surely be enough room in the agent's car. "What if the agent and the doctor don't stay there overnight?" I suddenly asked myself. "What then? Then dear God will surely find another way."

I was already approaching Fort Defiance when an anxious feeling rose within me that I was likely arriving too late. I met Chee Dodge there and asked him, "Have you seen the agent anywhere?" "He left in a car for Crystal 15 minutes ago," he answered. "The doctor was with him. They seemed to be in a great hurry." So I was too late! Then I must go there by horse, I told myself. The horse was not even one bit wet from the ride, and 30 miles further wouldn't hurt him. So I bought a few pounds of oats and went to the doctor's house to get my saddlebag. There the doctor's wife advised me to use the car of Clitso Dedman, one of the Indians from Naazlin who had befriended us and who had just arrived in Fort Defiance, to catch up with the agent. Clitso gladly agreed, even to drive to Crystal and to stay overnight and bring me back on the following day. So I loaded everything up, and we left around noon.

Clitso had never been to Crystal, but we had the agent's track in front of us, which Clitso never lost sight of, although a white could hardly have differentiated it from a wagon track. One time the agent had made a big detour to avoid some deep sand, but the Indian kept going, undisturbed, and soon we were on the tracks again. Now our water ran out, but Clitso's sharp eye soon spied a cloudy brooklet, and we filled the machine with water using measuring cans. We had been going for two and a half hours without seeing a living soul when we discovered a wide track near Whiskey Creek. "Sheep have come by here," remarked the Indian. "How many?" I asked quickly. "Perhaps 400," was the answer. A short time later we came upon the herd. It actually must have been right around 400 sheep. But now there were no more tracks to follow. "They turned here," Clitso suggested, "whether right or left we'll have to find out." He got out, went to the left, and soon came back. In some thick undergrowth I thought I saw wagon tracks, but the Indian was sure that they were our own tracks. He followed these and suddenly turned to the left. The agent's car was standing there next to a hut and a tent. The doctor got big eyes when he saw us, then he said, laughing, "I am sorry that the agent was in such a hurry. But I knew that you would find some way to come." "Godly providence" was all that I said and I went into the hut.

An emaciated figure lay there groaning on sheepskins in the far corner of the hut. Anna Curley held her mother in her arms, and when she saw me her face brightened up, and she whispered something into her mother's ear. The sick woman opened her eyes, saw me, and said quietly, "*La'a.*" Now the doctor came, took her pulse, and inquired about the symptoms of her illness. I left the hut, and Anna followed me. Outside she grabbed my hand and said she had ridden half the night before to get here and then had not left her mother's side until now. She had prayed constantly that her mother could be baptized before her death. Now her prayer had been heard. Then the doctor came up, and I asked him what he thought about her illness. He hadn't yet determined what her illness was, and he said, "By all appearances she will die, and I am curious to know whom the Indians will blame for her death, me or you. The medicine man is always guiltless." He pointed to the medicine man behind him and then returned to the sick woman. Actually, a ceremony had been well under way when the doctor arrived. The old silversmith, whose wife lay there so sick, had sent for the most famous medicine man for 50 miles around to come, and had promised him, if I am correct, 200 sheep and a few horses as reward.

The silversmith himself now came and welcomed us with his soft voice. He was happy that we were visiting him. "Not you, we're visiting the sick woman," I thought, but I didn't say anything. That was lucky, as I later found out. The doctor now came back, took a few medications from his satchel, and taught Anna how to use them. As the agent made preparations to return with his car, I was glad that I could stay there with Clitso. Anna traveled almost three miles with the agent and the doctor to her house and returned on foot. Meanwhile it was almost 4:00, and the silversmith invited me and Clitso to dinner. Baked mutton was the only thing I could eat. I had watched how the women there had baked the "pancakes," and despite wolflike hunger, I couldn't choke down the pastries. But the meat was very tasty. After the meal, I talked with Wallace, a son of the silversmith who had been in Phoenix, Arizona, at school and had become a Presbyterian there. This conversation made such an impression on him that he later assured Anna that if he hadn't been baptized a Protestant then he would have been baptized a Catholic.

Finally, Anna returned with her brother Vincent. He had been a student at our mission school in St. Michaels years ago, but he had left the school after one year without having been baptized. But now he wanted to be baptized with his mother. When I asked Anna to help me by being an interpreter, she explained to me shortly, "I can't do that." I was puzzled. I turned to all the holy guardian angels of the newly baptized and pressed Anna to try it just one time. "I know it isn't easy," I told her, "but at least give it a try." In vain! I promised the mother of God to baptize the dying one "Maria" if she would intervene here. Then Anna came and said, "Clitso is a wonderful interpreter." So our loving God had sent me not only a car but also a capable interpreter in an almost miraculous way. Clitso was ready and the lesson could begin.

In the middle of the hut a fire was burning, and on the right three female figures cowered. Two women each held a child. Now and then the third stoked the fire. In the far corner lay the very sick woman, Anna at her feet and Vincent sitting at her head. To the left of them was Clitso. I took my place next to him on a sheepskin. Next in the line after Wallace came the brother-in-law of the silversmith, the silversmith himself, the old medicine man, and finally his two assistants. Three or four children were also in the room. A splendid opportunity to explain our holy religion to them—I made extensive use of it. I had a few pictures in my breviary which were very useful in my explanations. At the finish I emphasized the justice of God in punishing sins. When I then stressed the mercy of God in forgiving sins, everyone was visibly touched. When I asked the sick mother outright whether she wanted to be baptized, she declared she was ready. Vincent did the same. Everyone followed the ceremony with expectant interest. After I had performed the baptism for both of them, I went out with my breviary and prayed. I had just enough time to finish before the darkness fell.

Just as I was finishing, Wallace approached and asked shyly, "Will you forbid the singing to begin?" I turned to Anna and tried to discover whether the sick woman had been asked for permission. Anna said succinctly, "My mother doesn't want the medicine man at all. She doesn't believe in it. Every time she falls asleep from weakness, the singer or his assistants shake her awake and order her to sing with them, but she is ashamed. She is not asked for permission." I then turned to Wallace and answered, "My duty here is resolved. I came in peace, I will go in peace. No discord should come because of me. I will not get involved." Then Clitso came and said, "The silversmith is angry that you did not ask him for permission first. You should have waited for another three days. He has been humiliated in front of the medicine men. He is lord of his house." "The house belongs to my mother," said Anna now, "and if she wants the priest and not the medicine man, that is not the silversmith's business" (Anna is not the daughter of the silversmith). "I called the doctor," she continued, "the silversmith didn't want to have him." Clitso continued, "I tried to calm him [the silversmith] down by telling him that is was too late. He should have opened his mouth earlier. The medicine man now fears he will forfeit his reward because the baptism will make the whole medicine ineffective, but out of love for the silversmith the singer will make the medicine even stronger through this night." I did not see the silversmith anymore that day.

Somewhat after 8 p.m. we were given cooked mutton to eat, and soon I gathered several blankets together in the tent. I must have dozed off because as I awoke I noticed that all the blankets were missing. Then one time someone whisked by me. Finally at daybreak, after I had rolled a large sheepskin together and used it as a pillow, I slept for about an hour. I was up before 6:00, sent for Vincent and Anna, and got everything ready to perform the Holy Mass in the tent next to the hut. Then when Clitso also showed up, I asked him to find out from the silversmith whether he would be comfortable if I gave the dying woman the last rites. I feared there would be an unpleasant interruption if a row broke out. The silversmith answered angrily, "Since she is baptized now, I don't care at all what she does." During the Holy Mass which I performed for the dying woman, Vincent and Anna received the Holy Communion for their mother. For Vincent, it was an unusual way to celebrate his First Holy Communion. After the sacrament I turned to the sick woman, and now she received her Savior for the first time, in this case as final rites. For six days this sick woman had not been able to eat anything. The Holy Communion was her first nourishment in that time. After breakfast Anna traveled back with us to Fort Defiance. She couldn't very well stay behind. She needed to stay out of the way of her stepfather for a while.

Within five days, the dying woman was well again and could perform her housework as before. At Christmas while she was in the hospital in Fort Defiance for a few days, she taught another heathen Indian about baptism and the Holy Communion and received the Holy Communion herself by her own accord.

And the silversmith? For four whole months he held a grudge against me, and when the Protestant preacher from Fort Defiance (there are three there) asked the Indians for a building site for a chapel, it appeared that the old silversmith would decide in his favor, provided the preacher employed his son Wallace as interpreter. I had the newly baptized members pray religiously, and what do you know! At the last moment the silversmith changed his mind and spoke emphatically against the Protestant preacher. The Indians withheld their approval for clearing a building site for a Protestant chapel and explained they only wanted one religion for their children—the Roman Catholic. So God governs our missionary work.

A Critique by Father Berard[3]

The December copy of *Sendbote* has an article by E. F. of which a friend writes: "*Was Wunder*! It is to laugh." You make it plain that E. F. is responsible for the article, affectation and "*cordis effusiones*" and all. But, has this policy your approval, or are you giving the author rope to hang and disappear? Is the sequel to be a publication of the correspondence on the first confirmation tour? *Confessio* E. F., or the exposal of E. F., may be a good move, something like the stories of the Arizona Kicker of Give-a-dam-gulch, but Juvenal *resuscitatus* is stamped all over its lines. To me it reads like the triumph of a d'ye-see-what-I-did-Kid, and *let the rest go to Hellas with policy*. It takes some brass to be as frank as the author is; I see the ass follows the brain, but makes a better combination. You were quite right when you maintained, months ago, that the author has no sense. Do you now agree with my friend's "*Was Wunder*"? In one of my letters I wrote that I hoped that the time is far off when I must preach to these Indians and that for courtesy or some other reason they would willy-nilly listen to me. Again I repeat that such a policy is against my grain, and I for one do not see the justice of the preachers in forcing themselves and their doctrines upon these people against their desires, against their protests, and in the face of open opposition. Possibly I would hesitate to publish these views, but I daresay that the action and sentiment described in this article went against my grain just as much, because it publishes that one of us acted like a preacher. To my mind the silversmith did not resent the baptism of his wife so much as the spirit that prompted one of his friends to gain his point stealthily. Courtesy has never hurt the cause of religion, but our religion has been hurt by a lack of courtesy. The silversmith's double [turnabout] and his indifferent dealing toward us is traceable to this incident. I hate the spirit that glories in such a victory. I for one regret that this victory is published, and if ever [readers are referred to this article] . . . I hope it is done in an other than a reference of commendation.

Father Anselm's Response to Father Berard's Critique[4]

I read what you wrote around the "Was Wunder! It is to laugh" with interest and some pleasure. But you are altogether mistaken if you think I had any *intentions* in having him write that story. I had written nothing the month before, and I could not have written anything that month. So I asked him to write up his trip. He had asked me several times to let him write it and publish it in *Der Sendbote*. I corrected it and cut out quite a little what he wrote about Beshlagai. I suppose you know that he died. I did not know of his sickness till after his death. I am sorry for him. He has helped us a good deal till the episode and till I made the blunder of "interfering" in his land trouble with Tsishchilli Ts'ossi. I saw him the last time at Ganado, and he was very friendly to me then. Father Leopold said some in the East made the remark that F. E. F. [Father Egbert Fischer] has a "cinch on Providence." One told me he read it and was surprised at ME, till he read the signature. Well, many people like to read such writings, and it is no fun to write an article every month—for me.

Notes

1. From Egbert Fischer, FMN 42 (December 1915): 1118–23. Translated by Marie Bradshaw Durrant.

2. See, in addition to the present selection, Egbert Fischer, FMN 39 (July, August, December 1912): 595–601, 692–96, 1082–86; 40 (September, October 1913): 782–87, 884–90.

3. Berard Haile to Anselm Weber, 12 December 1915, FAC Box DEC.241. Anselm Weber Writings, fd. Missiology—Anselm and Emanuel, II (AV7).

4. Anselm Weber to Berard Haile, 19 December 1915, FAC Box DEC.241.Anselm Weber, Writings, fd. Missiology—Anselm and Emanuel II (AV7).

26

Navajo on the Warpath?[1]

Anselm Weber, O.F.M.

[One of the more dramatic examples of Franciscan intervention as keepers of the peace was the mediation of Father Anselm in the Beautiful Mountain disturbance of 1913, when General Hugh Scott and U.S. troops were called in to help resolve a Navajo challenge to the authority of Superintendent W. T. Shelton of the Shiprock Agency. Commissioner of Indian Affairs Cato Sells personally requested Father Anselm's assistance in defusing the situation. Over a five-week period in late October and November, Father Anselm's negotiating skills, combined with the persuasive statesmanship of his friend General Scott, helped to resolve the confrontation peacefully, and in a manner fair to the Navajo "renegades" involved.

Summarizing Father Anselm's role in the resolution of the crisis, his biographer observes that although, in the hour of crisis, the U.S. government had urgently requested the friar's assistance, it was reluctant to acknowledge his part in making the peace and never made public the extent of his service.

> For all his strenuous physical effort in crossing and recrossing the Chuskas in deep snow, his tireless and successful efforts to induce the accused Indians to sit at repeated councils at St. Michaels and at Noel's Store, his expenses in feeding his Indian companions, as well as the accused, and providing horse fodder—for his entire effort—not one official word of gratitude or approval was tendered to Father Anselm Weber by the Washington officials.[2]

The extent of that service is apparent in Father Anselm's own story of the episode recorded in a handwritten journal he completed in January 1914, several weeks after the resolution of the affair. In 1919 he published a revision of that journal history as "Navajo on the Warpath?" in *Franciscan Missions of the Southwest*. Most of his changes were cuts, and much of the deleted material is relevant to our objective of seeing the Navajo through the eyes of the Franciscans. Accordingly, for this chapter I have added back into the published version most of the material excised by Father Anselm in the course of his revision, yielding a text closer to that of the manuscript journal than the published article.

Among the conclusions to be drawn from a comparison of the manuscript journal and the published article is that Father Anselm's role in mediating the Beautiful Mountain "uprising" of 1913 and his influence on the outcome, including the light sentences given the "rioters," was even larger than the article suggests. Several of his cuts tended to mask or understate his participation.[3]

Text deleted by Father Anselm and reinserted here is italicized. Where the published article summarized or reworked deleted material, thereby presenting problems of duplication for the present reading, I have bracketed the overlap, which follows immediately upon the fragment reintroduced.]

Many bloodcurdling accounts about the Navajo "uprising" were published in the fall of 1913 in the papers of the country. Fifteen hundred strong—thus ran the reports—armed with the latest high-power guns, well-supplied with food and ammunition for the winter, they were defying the U.S. government in their natural stronghold on top of Beautiful Mountain, New Mexico.

They had threatened to raid the Shiprock Agency, to burn the agency sawmill, and to kill the Indian traders—so the papers stated. They were charged—in the press—with murder, larceny, jail-breaking, polygamy, rioting, assault; women had taken refuge at the agency to protect themselves against the brutality of their husbands, and so on. Here is a fair specimen:

> Farmington, N. M., Nov. 27—To the accompaniment of weird, shrill cries and monotonous chanting, the frenzied braves of Chief Be Sho Shee whirled about one another on a grassy plot of Beautiful Mountain. As their medicine men urged them on in the strange ceremony, the half-clad paint-bedaubed Indians brandished ancient weapons, and sang their war songs in hideous chorus. Sentries stood watching at the signal fires until dawn came and ended the savage spectacle. It was the rarely seen war dance of the Navajo—and there probably will never be another, etc.

The facts are as follows. Considerable enmity and jealousy had existed between Hatali Yazhe and Dine' Ts'ossi Biye'. Failing in repeated attempts to have Hatali Yazhe arrested for killing his wife through witchcraft, Dine' Ts'ossi accused him, in addition, of polygamy, of having three wives, and of having brought whiskey into the reservation. Thereupon, Mr. W. T. Shelton, superintendent of the Shiprock Agency, New Mexico, instructed one of his policemen, Nanl'ghuddy, to arrest Hatali Yazhe and his three wives and to bring them to the agency.

Unfortunately, Hatali Yazhe had left the day before for the Black Mountains; nevertheless, the policeman arrested his three wives and brought them, with their three small children, to the Shiprock Agency.

Returning after an absence of 12 days, Hatali Yazhe found his home deserted. The next day he discussed the matter with his relatives and friends, and the day following they, 11 in number, started for Shiprock Agency to see Mr. Shelton.

Camping that night this side of the San Juan River, they rode into Shiprock early the next morning. Here they learned that Mr. Shelton was not at home. They rode into the police quarters but did not find the women. After repeated inquiries and prolonged search, they at last found the women and asked them to follow them.

In the meantime, the alarm had been given. In consequence, Mr. Jensen, the agency farmer, who was in charge during the absence of Mr. Shelton, two other employes, a Navajo policeman, and a number of large schoolboys blocked the way between an agency building and the garden fence. Old Bizhoshi was in the lead; Mr. Jensen grabbed the bridle reins of his horse on one side; another employee grabbed them on the other side. Bizhoshi begged Mr. Jensen to let them pass, telling him they did not want to take the women home; they only wanted to take them to a store just outside the agency grounds, buy provisions for them, since they had not had any meat since their arrest, and await the return of Mr. Shelton. Mr. Jensen shook his finger at him and told him, no, they could not take those women away. Four times Bizhoshi begged him, and four times he refused, shaking his finger at him. Thereupon, Attsidi Naez Biye' gave the horse of Bizhoshi a fierce whack with his quirt; the horse, rearing and plunging, tore loose from the two employees and opened the way for the rest of the Indians. In the melee the Navajo policeman grabbed the rein of Ni'dughullin Biye's horse. Ni'dughullin Biye' seized the hand of the policeman, placed it on the saddle knob, and held it there. The policeman now released the bridle rein with his one hand and tried to pull the six-shooter out of Ni'dughullin Biye's scabbard—he did not succeed, since the top of the scabbard had been tied so the revolver could not be drawn without untying the string. Then the policeman made an attempt to draw his own six-shooter, seeing which H'asht'al spurred his horse and took the six-shooter away from the policeman. Ni'dughullin Biye' released the hand of the policeman from the saddle knob and rode on. Now the policeman turned on Ni'dughullin Biye's son, but he grabbed him by the nape of the neck, spurred his horse, and then dropped the policeman, who fell flat on the ground. The one "battle" of the "Navajo War" was over—not a shot had been fired. The policeman had been prevented from drawing a six-shooter and using it. Some, not all, of the Indians were armed with six-shooters and rifles, but none made an attempt at using them. Ni'dughullin Biye', for one, certainly had not intended to use his tied-up six-shooter. The Indians rode on to the store, and, after a short stay, during which they ate lunch, they crossed the river and camped there till in the afternoon. They intended to await the return of the superintendent to see him, but when some of the Indians told them the superintendent might make trouble for them, they returned to their homes.

Mr. Shelton, having been informed upon his return of the happenings of this eventful day, intended to ask for troops, but was dissuaded by Mr. Paquette, superintendent of the Fort Defiance Agency, who happened to come to Shiprock the day following the affray and who was of the opinion that Mr. Shelton, through the good offices of some of their friends, could induce the 11 Indians to surrender. Mr. Shelton made indirect attempts to have them come to Shiprock by inviting all the

Indians to his annual fair. Bizhoshi and his followers decided to attend the fair and see Mr. Shelton, when a terrific downpour prevented their coming. After the fair Mr. Shelton went to Santa Fe and swore out warrants against these Indians for "rioting"—thus placing the matter into the hands of the Department of Justice. Then he informed Mr. Paquette of his action, requesting him to ask Chee Dodge, the wealthiest and most influential man of the Navajo tribe, to use his influence toward their surrender to the U.S. Marshal, Mr. Hudspeth, at Shiprock, to stand trial before the federal court at Santa Fe, adding, if they would not surrender, they would get into serious trouble, that is, either a posse or the U.S. troops would take them.

Chee Dodge was at Ganado at the time, 100 miles away from them. Upon his return from Ganado, on October 25 he stopped at our mission at St. Michaels, Arizona. I accompanied him to Fort Defiance, eight miles distant, to see Mr. Paquette, from whom, as I informed him, he was to receive Mr. Shelton's request. In two days the Navajo would have a Yeibichai dance at the foot of the Lukachukai Mountains, 58 miles to the northeast of Fort Defiance, and it was more than probable that some of those Indians would attend the dance. I was going to our mission at Lukachukai anyway, and Chee Dodge had intended to be present at the dance.

We started the next day, staying overnight at Chee Dodge's home at Washington Pass, 25 miles from Fort Defiance. The following evening we reached Lukachukai. At 8:00 in the evening (October 27) I and two of my companions walked the six miles from our mission to the dance, which had just begun and lasted all night. Over a thousand Indians attended. Hatali Yazhe, the man of three wives, was one of the dancers. Three more of the 11 in question were present, but could not be found during the night among such a large crowd. During the "intermission" Chee Dodge kept a splendid speech against polygamy and against such occurrences as had happened at Shiprock. I had seen Hatali Yazhe during the night and had told him Chee Dodge and I wanted to speak to him and his three companions after the dance. At daybreak he and his followers came to me and accompanied me to where Chee Dodge was taking a "nap." In the presence of the chief of police from Shiprock and a number of Indians who had gathered around us, we explained their position to them. At last they agreed to come to St. Michaels the following Saturday and to Fort Defiance on the following Sunday, not to surrender, but to talk matters over with Mr. Paquette and myself. Chee Dodge, Beshlagai, and Charlie Mitchell, influential Navajo chiefs, promised to meet them on that day at our mission at St. Michaels.

They did not come, because Hatali Yazhe became sick and the rest did not get through harvesting their corn in time. Mr. Shelton, superintendent at Shiprock, and Mr. Hudspeth, the U.S. Marshal, had come to Gallup, New Mexico, to be on hand if the Indians should decide to surrender. When they learned that the Indians had not come, they and Mr. Paquette came to St. Michaels Sunday evening. After the discussion, we sent Charlie Mitchell, an influential Navajo, who, together with Chee Dodge, had attended our consultation and had taken part in it, to their camp to find out why they had not come, and to induce them to come the following Saturday.

Charlie Mitchell started the next day, taking Beshlagai with him. It must be remembered that the Beautiful Mountain, their home, is about 80 miles from St. Michaels, across a high mountain range. The following Saturday all came to St. Michaels, accompanied by Chee Dodge, Beshlagai, and Charlie Mitchell.

[Shortly after, Chee Dodge and myself met Hatali Yazhe and three of his followers at a Yeibichai dance attended by nearly 2,000 Indians at Lukachukai, 67 miles to the northwest of St. Michaels. We explained their position to them, and at last they agreed to come to our mission the following Saturday—not to surrender, but to talk matters over with Mr. Paquette and myself. They arrived at our mission a week after the stipulated time, since Hatali had become sick and the rest did not get through harvesting their corn in time.]

When all had taken their supper, Mr. Paquette, superintendent at Fort Defiance, who had arrived in his automobile, opened the discussion with them.

Old Bizhoshi related the arrest of the women, their trip to Shiprock, and how they had taken the women and children away. He said when they started they had not intended to have any fight. They had intended to beg the superintendent four times for the women and children before they would take any steps, but that the superintendent had been away. He acknowledged that some of them were armed, but added that the rifles were and remained in the scabbards strapped to the saddles.

Hatali Yazhe explained his marital troubles. Speaking of his first wife, he said: "When we were living together we had lots of trouble. She left me three times and tore up lots of things." Some time after the third separation he married another woman whom he considered as his real wife. Following the advice of his father, he subsequently was reconciled with his first wife: that made two. He was also living with the sister of his second wife who bore him a child. After the trouble at Shiprock, his first wife took her property and went back to her own people.

I explained to him that he was not to stand trial for polygamy, but for "rioting" only.

After listening to them patiently, Mr. Paquette tried to make them realize that they had been doing wrong in taking those women away from Shiprock, and to impress them with the necessity of surrendering and standing trial at Santa Fe, but Bizhoshi answered: "I do not think we have done anything wrong. They came and stole the women, and we stole them back. You know Mr. Shelton stole those women and children. When we went to San Juan we stole them back. It is just the same. If you had a wife and children, and you were away and somebody took them, when you got back your home would be broken up, and what would you do?" Mr. Paquette answered unhesitatingly; though a bachelor, he had apparently no difficulty in imagining himself placed in such a predicament. But considering the fact of his being part Indian, part French, and in possession of herculean strength, I doubt whether he told the exact truth when he said: "I would go to the man who caused the arrest and straighten the matter out. If you had done that you would not be in this trouble today. You should have waited till Mr. Shelton returned and gone to him and put the case before him."

Bizhoshi answered: "Mr. Shelton is a mean man to us. He is there to be mean to us. He stands out ready to jump on us. We are like little birds hiding among the rocks, to keep him from picking [on] us."

Bizhoshi's son then added: "Mr. Shelton is mean to us. We do not know where to turn over there. For every little thing he puts us into jail. All the Indians over there know this. The women prisoners must weave blankets, and the men prisoners must work. The jail down there is full all the time. All these gardens around the school are worked by them. Some get 12 months, some a little less. For little things he gives them 12 months."

They could not be made to realize that they had done anything seriously wrong. If they had killed someone or seriously harmed someone or committed some great theft, they would gladly surrender and accept punishment, but that they should be dragged away from their home to distant, unknown Santa Fe, and there go to jail, perhaps for years, on account of that little affair at Shiprock, that was beyond their untutored minds, especially since they considered themselves the outraged ones on account of the abduction and detention, for 15 days, of the women and children during the absence of the husband. Neither could they understand the differences and limitations of jurisdiction. That the matter was out of the hands of the Interior Department, that neither Mr. Paquette nor even Mr. Shelton could settle the affair after the warrants had been sworn out against them, was beyond their comprehension. In spite of our explanations, the thought persisted in their minds that Mr. Paquette or I myself could settle the affair then and there at St. Michaels.

We did not urge a decision that night, but told them to consider the matter and talk it over and let us know their intention the next morning.

The next morning they had decided not to surrender. *Hatali Yazhe, the main man, was pretty sick. He was suffering from muscular rheumatism and was running quite a temperature. Bizhoshi, his father, refused the offer of the doctor's treatment at the Fort Defiance hospital, saying he was a medicine man. They wanted to take him home, try their own medicine on him, and then talk about going to Santa Fe.*

Thereupon Mr. Paquette explained to them in plain and unmistakable language the troubles they would bring upon themselves if they persisted in their refusal. I added that there were two things before them—to surrender and stand trial, or to face the soldiers. If they surrendered we would all feel like helping them. I would meet them at Santa Fe and see to it that they would get a good lawyer, a good interpreter, and have a fair trial.

Bizhoshi Biye' then answered: "I promise to go. This is the first trouble I have been in. I have always farmed. This is the first time."

They all promised to surrender, but Bizhoshi begged Mr. Paquette for more time to attend to his sick son, Hatali Yazhe, who was suffering from muscular rheumatism and was running quite a temperature. Mr. Paquette told him that he was powerless to grant this request; that lay with the U.S. Marshal. But Bizhoshi, ignorant of these limitations of jurisdiction, standing upright in the middle of the room, repeated the same request in a quivering voice, called Mr. Paquette his brother and chief, fidgeting in the meantime about his blanket and belt, his fingers coming dangerously near his revolver. Mr. Paquette did not notice this and promised to try to obtain this authority by wire from the U.S. Marshal. That seemed satisfactory to them, and they agreed to surrender in 10 days (on November 12), at Shiprock, if the U.S. Marshal would wait that long. Upon telegraphic inquiry, the U.S. Marshal wired his consent to this arrangement. The Indians left after dinner, Sunday, November 2, for their home, staying the first night just beyond Fort Defiance.

The following Wednesday a Navajo policeman came across the mountains from Tohatchi, about 30 miles east of Fort Defiance, and told the policemen of Fort Defiance that Bizhoshi had been near Tohatchi and had told his friend, Debelchi, in four days he and his followers, 70 in number, would ride into Shiprock, beg Mr. Shelton to pardon them, and, if he refused, they would kill Mr. Shelton.

Mr. Paquette learned of this from one of his policemen in the afternoon of the next day, when the Tohatchi policeman had returned home. There was no time to send for him for further inquiry and investigation, as it was Thursday, the fourth day. To be on the safe side he communicated the story to Mr. Shelton by night letter.

When this night letter reached Shiprock it had changed into a bomb which promptly exploded in the shape of telegrams and telephone calls to the U.S. Marshal for protection, to the Indian Office for troops, to Durango, Colorado, to Farmington, Fruitland, and Aztec, New Mexico, for assistance to protect Shiprock.

Shiprock was placed in a state of defense; the Indian police were keeping a cordon of sentinels thrown out about the agency day and night. The residents agreed upon a signal in the event of the Navajo swooping down upon the place. The bell over the agency office was to be rung. Rifles, six-shooters, ammunition, and the presence of some outside assistance testified to the preparedness of Shiprock.

On November 8 Inspector McLaughlin received a telegram from the Indian Office, calling him from Devil's Lake to Shiprock. Evidently Devil's Lake was all right and Shiprock was not. The same day I received the following telegram from the Reverend W. H. Ketcham, director of the Catholic Indian Bureau, Washington, D.C.:

> Kindly go immediately to Shiprock and do all you can towards peaceably adjusting the troubles that have arisen between Shelton and the Navajo. Situation seems serious; I am authorized to state that Commissioner Sells will greatly appreciate your kindly offices in this matter. From Paquette you can learn details of trouble. As to what move you should make, you are best judge. Bear this in mind in reading this telegram.

That same day Chee Dodge came to Fort Defiance to attend a council of the Navajo. When Mr. Paquette mentioned to him the statement of the Tohatchi policeman, Chee Dodge told him that the story involved a physical impossibility, as Bizhoshi and the rest of them had stayed at his (Chee Dodge's) own home

Monday night; and while the rest of them had left for their home on Tuesday, Bizhoshi and his sick son had stayed with him till Wednesday morning. Bizhoshi could not have been at Washington Pass and near Tohatchi, 50 miles away, at the same time. He had not made the threat of going to Shiprock with 70 followers to kill Mr. Shelton in case of his refusal to pardon them.

Well! Mr. Paquette wired Mr. Shelton that night the *real* state of affairs, and I wired Reverend Father Ketcham that I would leave the next day for the Beautiful Mountain and Shiprock to see the Indians and Mr. Shelton; also that no threats had been made to raid the Shiprock Agency.

The following day, November 9, I started for the Beautiful Mountain, taking our interpreter, Frank Walker, and Gishin Biye', a renowned medicine man, along. I thought one medicine man might have some influence with another medicine man (Bizhoshi).

The next day we were joined by Hastin Nash'a'hi, a friend of those Indians. On this second day we crossed the mountain—a very hard trip—and arrived at Mr. Noel's store, six miles from their camp, after dark. On the way, before reaching the store, we arrived at the government sawmill in the afternoon, where Mr. Ayers, his wife and family, and some white employees had remained at their post in spite of the rumored "Navajo war."

The evening of the second day, after crossing the Chusca Mountain range, we reached Mr. Noel's store, in the valley on the east side of the mountain, where we stayed overnight. Toward evening we had met a bunch of Indians and learned from them that the excitement at Shiprock had become known to the Indians; also that word had been brought to them that *now* it was "all off" with them; that there was "no hope" for them, which had induced them to change their minds about giving themselves up on the 12th, and which made my task so much the more difficult.

The following morning I sent word with the Indians in different directions that I wanted to see them at the store in the afternoon. Bizhoshi and all whom my message reached, with the exception of Hatali Yazhe, who was suffering from rheumatism, came in the afternoon. I gathered them in a nearby Indian house and spoke to them. I explained to them what I could and what I could not do for them. Again they showed their peculiar mentality by expressing their conviction that I could, and their earnest request that I should, settle the matter then and there. I repeated that I had no jurisdiction whatever; that I held no government position, but that I was there to assist them as much as possible. To make them realize their position I explained, at some length, the meaning of a warrant, the purpose of a court, and the court procedure, so they would know what rights and what chances and what means of defense they would have. I urged them to surrender, promising them that I and our interpreter, Frank Walker, would accompany them to Shiprock, or, if they wanted to avoid Shiprock, to Farmington, and thence to Santa Fe. I would stay right with them until after the trial.

They seemed much impressed and well pleased and asked me to come the next day to their camp, or rather, their home on the east slope of the Beautiful Mountain, since Hatali Yazhe, who was sick, could not come down. All would meet there. I readily accepted the invitation. From remarks they made after the meeting I had all reasons to believe that they would surrender. The next day *I, our interpreter, the two Navajo who had accompanied us, a former policeman by the name of "Doctor John," and Dei-ni' Biye', a chief of that part of the country,* [we] started on horseback for their camp. On the first steep trail, a son of Bizhoshi met us and told us, after the meeting of the previous day, Stephen Dale, a brother of one of the accused, a former interpreter and policeman at Shiprock, had told them I could do nothing for them; my interpreter had not interpreted all I said; it was "all off"; if they surrendered, they would "get the worst of it," and so forth. Thereupon they had decided *not* to surrender. *Stephen Dale afterward denied having made all these remarks.*

We proceeded. In winding our way along the steep trails, hugging, in places, the precipitous rim-rock, always exposed and within rifle-shot from the rim-rock, inaccessible from our side, strewn with huge detached boulders and covered with low bushy pinyon trees, I realized that a few well-armed men could, from admirably protected positions, "pick off" a large number of men with almost absolute safety. From their home the Indians have an unobstructed view of the store, the Shiprock road, in fact, of the whole vast expanse to the east. It took us an hour and a half from the store to their camp, a distance of about six miles.

They received us cordially. All were present. A wonderful feat! All the "fifteen hundred Navajo camped in their natural fortress on the slope of Beautiful Mountain, defying the U.S. government," found room in one Navajo hut; *and six of us didn't even belong to those 1,500.*

I myself and my Navajo friends who had accompanied me—we all did our best to persuade them to surrender. They vented their grievances, more especially against some of the Shiprock policemen, against whom they charged intimacy with women prisoners of Shiprock, giving that as an additional reason for taking away those women from the agency. They did not see why they should be punished, and not their accusers and traducers, together with the police force. Neither could they comprehend why the whole world should bother about them, since they had done no wrong and did not intend to do wrong or harm anyone. They were afraid of Santa Fe; they did not know what might await them.

Bizhoshi Biye' added they had no money to defray their expenses at Santa Fe. When I assured them the government would take care of them and their necessary expenses from the time of their surrender, he brought instances where enforced trips to Santa Fe had been rather expensive. As I learned later, the expensiveness consisted in imposed pecuniary fines.

Then again their thoughts would enter another extreme. They would beg me to save them and have the matter dropped. Ni'dughullin Biye' said to his neighbor in an undertone: "Let us take hold of him and entreat him." Gishin Biye' heard only the first part of that sentence and afterward spread the rumor that they wanted to grab me and hold me as a hostage. The sick and suffering Hatali Yazhe got up and, limping over to me and taking me by the hand, said to me: "My friend and brother, you said it was not necessary to entreat you, but in spite of that I beg you very much to have this matter dropped." Their attitude was simply pitiful.

While we were talking, a sheep had been butchered and the women had prepared a good dinner for all of us, which was brought into the hut, and *15 or 16 of us* [we] partook of the repast. After dinner we resumed our discussion. At last I put the direct question to each one. One and all refused to surrender.

Then I said: "You have told me what you are not willing to do; now tell me what you *are* willing to do. Tomorrow I shall go to Shiprock and see the U.S. Marshal and Mr. Shelton. What message shall I bring them?" *Supposing the warrants could be withdrawn, would you be willing to submit to Mr. Shelton, your agent, and receive your punishment at Shiprock?*

They asked me to tell Mr. Shelton that they would gladly go to Shiprock, or would gladly have him come to their camp to see them and be friends. They did not intend to harm anyone. They intended to behave themselves and do the right thing, but they begged him to drop the matter. Then they all shook hands with me and asked me to stop at the store upon my return and let them know Mr. Shelton's answer. They seemed to think Mr. Shelton and the U.S. government might probably grant their petition.

Their answer to my question had not been complete, so I asked big Bizhoshi Biye' whether they would unreservedly submit to Mr. Shelton and accept their punishment at Shiprock. He said, no, they would not submit to any punishment. They wished that the matter be dropped. Shaking hands with me, he said: "You have helped us so far, do not drop us now."

The next day I drove to Shiprock Agency, 28 miles from Mr. Noel's store, where I met Mr. Shelton, Mr. Hudspeth, the U.S. Marshal, and Mr. Galusha, deputy U.S. Marshal. Later in the afternoon, Major McLaughlin, the well-known inspector of the Interior Department, arrived from Devil's Lake, Minnesota [*sic*]. Of course, I delivered my message and gave them all the information at hand.

The next day Major McLaughlin discussed the advisability of his making an attempt at inducing them to surrender. He asked Mr. Shelton's advice. Mr. Shelton advised against it. Since I and Mr. Paquette and influential Navajo chiefs had failed, an absolute stranger to them had no prospects of succeeding. Besides, he added, it might make things worse. Any delay might induce others to join them.

I did not think a short delay would matter; neither did I think any more Navajo would join their ranks. Major McLaughlin thought he and his superiors of the Interior Department would feel more satisfied if he made the attempt, after coming all the way from Devil's Lake and being so near to them. He decided to go if I thought I could induce them to come to Mr. Noel's store to meet him. I had no doubt about that. We had advised against his going to their camp. Since he was a "big man from Washington," the idea might enter their heads to "hold" him and to try and force him to pardon them, which they would not dare attempt at the store.

Mr. Shelton secured an Indian messenger for us. I introduced Major McLaughlin to him and asked him to go to the camp of the Indians to tell them that this inspector from Washington, myself, and Frank Walker would meet them at noon the next day at Mr. Noel's store. No one else would come. Major McLaughlin thought we might promise to help them to get only a short sentence, but Mr. Shelton objected, since the maximum penalty for rioting was rather light.

We spent the afternoon in seeing and admiring the magnificent school plant at Shiprock, the ideal school garden and school farm and stock farm. We also visited the irrigation project in course of construction which will irrigate a large area of land. Shiprock is a monument to the ability and energy of Mr. Shelton, its founder and builder.

[Since Major McLaughlin thought it advisable to make an attempt at inducing them to surrender, I sent a message from Shiprock to them requesting them to meet us at Noel's store the next day at noon.]

Early next morning we started for Noel's store, where we arrived at 11:30 a.m. After dinner all the Indians, even Hatali Yazhe, put in their appearance. The meeting took place in the sitting room of Mr. Noel's dwelling house. I introduced the Major to them, expressing my delight at his coming. The address of Major McLaughlin was a credit to his experience of over 40 years among Indians; none better could have been made. At last old Bizhoshi said: "The same thing over again; urging us to surrender and go to Santa Fe. When we heard an inspector from Washington was coming, we thought he could settle the affair here."

Big, dark Attsidi Naez Biye' said: "Come, let us go!"

But no one stirred. Addressing Major McLaughlin, they said Hatali Yazhe was too sick to go and they had no way of paying their expense at Santa Fe—a more polite way of refusing. They did not heed our assurance that the government would take care of them after the surrender. They pleaded their innocence of wrongdoing and their present peaceful intentions. After explaining their grievances against the Shiprock police force and Mr. Shelton—on which occasion Bizhoshi Biye' made the drastic remark: "Mr. Shelton has been bulldozing us and picking on us; in short, he has been doing everything to us except castrating us, and I think he is going to attempt that next"—they begged Major McLaughlin to report their whole case to the secretary of the interior. He promised to write to the secretary all they had told him. Thereupon all shook hands with us, and old Bizhoshi embraced Major McLaughlin. It seems the poor fellows were in hopes the secretary of the interior would drop the case when he received the Major's report. It was 4:00; the Major returned to Shiprock, and I and Frank Walker returned home, *staying overnight at the government sawmill, 12 miles from the store, and reaching St. Michaels the next day, November 16, after a drive of 61 miles and an auto ride of eight miles that day.*

Bizhoshi is a renowned medicine man, belonging, aside from other lodges, to the Adilniji Hatal medicine lodge, whose votaries practice the art of divination by shaking their hands and arms. They repeatedly tried to fortify themselves by these ceremonies. After one of them old Bizhoshi exclaimed: "Ah; not without reason did I see blood on my hands twice when holding them towards the sun."

During this week I read in the paper conflicting accounts of soldiers sent upon the Navajo reservation, but on November 23 I learned definitely that Brigadier General Hugh L. Scott, the late chief of staff, had arrived at Gallup, New Mexico, with 300 soldiers and sent word to me to come and see him. I had met him five years before, when he spent a day and a night at our mission.

When I learned that he had been sent, I knew a fight would be avoided if possible. Mr. Paquette went to Gallup in his automobile, taking Chee Dodge and myself and Frank Walker, our interpreter, to explain things to General Scott. We arrived late at night, since the auto of Mr. Paquette had gone through a trough bridge and it had taken us three hours to raise it. General Scott was very glad to see us. He had tried to reach us by telephone, but our telephone was, as usual, out of commission. [Mr. Paquette, myself, Chee Dodge, and Frank Walker drove to Gallup to meet him.]

After I had explained the situation to him, he asked *how the Indians could be induced to meet him for a friendly conference. After some discussion he intimated* that Chee Dodge and I should go to the Indians and induce them to meet him at Noel's store the following Wednesday evening. Keeping his soldiers 18 miles from Noel's store, he and his aide-de-camp and our interpreter, Frank Walker, would come alone to the meeting place. After the conference the Indians would be permitted to return to their home if they should choose not to surrender. He suggested Chee Dodge and myself for the task because the Indians knew us, had confidence in us, and would not suspect a "trap" from us. We gladly agreed to this arrangement.

This was Sunday night, November 23. On account of rain and snow and heavy roads we did not arrive at Fort Defiance until 4:00 the next afternoon. The Navajo, Clitso Dedman, volunteered to take us in his auto to Chee Dodge's home, but at dark rain and snow stalled the auto and we camped with an Indian. The auto took us about 10 miles further, when adobe clay interfered with our progress. Fortunately, an Indian team happened along, which we appropriated, and drove to Washington Pass, the home of Chee Dodge. It was too late to go further that day.

The next morning Chee Dodge, myself, Dr. Norbert [Gottbrath], *and several "other Indians" started horseback for a 40-mile ride across the mountain for Noel's store. The snow was rather deep on the mountain. We saw bear tracks at three different places, but no bear. At 2:00 we arrived at the agency sawmill, tired and hungry. The sawmill and houses were locked and boarded up. The sawyer and all the whites had adjourned to Noel's store. I bought a kid from an Indian for ourselves and obtained some hay for our horses. Leaving the work to the others, I lay myself to rest on some sheepskins in the Navajo house until I was called for "dinner." Our stay lasted just one hour during which the kid had been butchered, fried, and eaten. We also had coffee. Two hours more, and we arrived at Noel's store* [Chee Dodge and myself went home the next day, and crossing the mountain horseback, had arrived at Noel's store Wednesday evening] where General Scott, his aide-de-camp, and Frank Walker had arrived a little sooner in an automobile. They had no mountain to pass since the road from Gallup leads along the east side of the mountain, but rain and snow had made part of the road almost impassable. If I remember well it took almost a whole troop of soldiers to get that auto into Tohatchi the first day, while provision wagons were scattered all over the flat, bogged down. Instead of 18, the soldiers were 55 miles away that day—still at Tohatchi *pulling in wagons*.

At Mr. Nelson's store, 15 miles from Mr. Noel's store [On the way to Bennett's store] General Scott had met Mr. Shelton with his whole Navajo police force. When General Scott outlined his plan to him, Mr. Shelton opposed it. The Indians had been talked to too much, he said; a new conference would only make matters worse; he had come with his police force to conduct him to the few trails leading up to Beautiful Mountain. He urged a forced march to prevent their escape. General Scott answered him: "From what you tell me things cannot get any worse. I shall talk to them first, then fight if necessary." He "advised" Mr. Shelton not to come any nearer to Mr. Noel's store with his police force; neither would he permit his soldiers to come any nearer until sent for. Fifteen miles more brought General Scott to Mr. Noel's store, where we met him. During the evening several Navajo came from the mountain to reconnoiter, peering into the general's tent, and into the Indian hut where his aide-de-camp, Frank Walker, and some Indians were. Then one of them rode off in the direction from which the troops were expected.

The next morning we sent two reliable Navajo, whom we had brought with us, John Brown and Tsishchilli Ts'ossi, both belonging to Bizhoshi's clan, to their camp to tell them that General Scott, myself, and Chee Dodge asked them to come to the store for a friendly talk. Neither soldiers nor policemen would be at the store. They would not be arrested. They would be free to return to the mountain if they should choose to do so. Chee Dodge told them to urge more especially old Bizhoshi and his wife to come. Our messengers were hailed on the way, but permitted to go on, upon disclosing their identity. They found five in one hut; all had their cartridge belts and six-shooters on and their Winchesters within easy reach. Attsidi Naez Biye' held his Winchester on his knees. Our men greeted them and shook hands with them and opened the conversation. Attsidi Naez Biye' spoke first and said: "And now they have brought the soldiers against us so that we have to kill and be killed." Our two Indians told them neither was necessary, and delivered their message. John Brown added that I knew their condition; that they had no chance against so many soldiers; that I felt pity for them, and had come again the long distance from St. Michaels to help them. They should not disappoint me.

Bizhoshi was not present. One of the Indians not belonging to the accused guided them to Bizhoshi's home. *On the way they met two mere boys, both armed with Winchesters, looking for horses, they said. John Brown told them where he had seen their horses and induced them to accompany them to Bizhoshi's*. But Bizhoshi was not there. They delivered their message to his wife, a rather young woman, asking her to use her influence with her husband to surrender, and to come with him to the store. Bursting into tears, she promised to do so. *Sending one of the armed boys to find Bizhoshi, they returned.* On their return they met Bizhoshi himself. After a long conversation, during which they expressed the sympathy of their clan and begged him to take pity on his wife and children, he promised to come and bring the rest along with him. John Brown had told him: "It is just as though you would put your wife into one pocket and your children into the other pocket, and then jump from a precipice." In all there were 15 armed men and boys in the camps of Beautiful Mountain. They had *not* selected this mountain as a place of defense; it is their regular winter home. At noon our messengers returned with the good news, and about 2:00 five of them arrived at the store, also Bizhoshi's wife and two daughters. Hatali Yazhe had not been at home; one was absent on a deer hunt, and one had left for Red Rock.

The Indians had all left their fields in the neighborhood of the store and had moved to the foot of Tunicha Mountain, to their winter camps. The evening before and early in the forenoon the store was deserted, no Indians in sight, but the notice of our arrival had begun to spread among them, Indian fashion, and soon they were coming in goodly numbers. At about noon Charlie Mitchell, Kinlichini, a policeman, and four other Navajo, armed with Winchesters, arrived from our side of the mountain. We had sent word to Charlie Mitchell to join us on our way, but he had been near distant Round Rock, hence his delay in arriving.

The following day about 100 Indians had gathered at the store, a number of them well armed, though they made no display of their firearms. They all seemed in good humor, laughing and talking among themselves and with Bizhoshi and his followers. But I knew their temper, and some others did. They had no desire to have the soldiers "campaign" over their reservation, scatter their flocks, and "accidentally" kill innocent people. If Bizhoshi and his followers would not surrender, they would take them—not because they disliked Bizhoshi and his outfit, but because they loved themselves and their property more.

Bizhoshi entered the store and, seeing General Scott behind the counter, walked up and shook hands with him and began to talk. The general, however, told him: "No; not now." They should eat their dinner first, then they would talk. He had meat and provisions brought to them, which Bizhoshi's wife and daughters prepared. Seeing Bizhoshi's little grandson in the store, the general, smiling, held out a silver coin to him. The boy hesitated; I took the little fellow by the hand and led him to the general. He took the coin, his face beaming with smiles. The mother and some others laughed their applause. Some of the others came in to shake hands with the general. When I saw big dark Attsidi Naez Biye', the one who had said, "Now we must kill and be killed," leaning against the counter, I went up to him and shook hands with him. He greeted me by name, but seeing the stern expression of his face, I did not dare to invite him to shake hands with the general; I feared a refusal.

While they were eating dinner, an Indian messenger arrived bringing a letter from Mr. Shelton. Enclosed was a wild, rambling letter from the government clerk at Shiprock Agency addressed to Mr. Shelton. Intelligence had reached the agency that, as soon as the soldiers appeared, Bizhoshi and his followers would swoop down upon Shiprock to raid and kill. All the Indians along the river were scared to death, arming themselves, and so on.

Mr. Shelton's letter to the general begged him to make inquiries from Mr. Noel and others and let him know if he found the situation as stated in the enclosure so that he and his policemen might return to Shiprock for the protection of the agency. General Scott's answer assured him that there was no truth in "that stuff" from Shiprock. Five of the Indians, among them the two most feared—Attsidi Naez Biye' and Ni'dughullin Biye'—were at the store and weakening; they would stay there overnight. Indians had informed him that one of his (Mr. Shelton's) policemen had made an arrest on their way to Noel's store; he hoped no more arrests would be made while this matter was pending; neither were the soldiers or policemen to come any nearer the place of conference till called for.

After their dinner all came into the store—a rather large room with counters on two sides. General Scott took his seat in front of the counter, Chee Dodge, who did the interpreting, to his right, and I to his left. The five Indians sat in front of us to the left; my friend, Attsidi Naez Biye', next to me. Something was bulging in my coat pocket. Attsidi Naez Biye' touched it with his hand and smiled— evidently he thought it a revolver, but it was an innocent Kodak. They themselves had their six-shooters in their holsters—nothing unusual—they belong to the Navajo paraphernalia.

General Scott, in nonchalant posture, speaking in a low, easy tone of voice, but in short, incisive sentences, which were singly rendered into Navajo by Chee Dodge as soon as spoken, opened up by telling them that he had heard they were in trouble. He felt sorry for them, he had come to help them, was glad they had come to see him. The last few nights they had not slept well; they had been troubled and uneasy. He wanted them to feel at home and sleep well at the store. No trap was being set for them; he had come as a friend. He then invited them to tell him frankly what was in their heart.

They selected Bizhoshi Biye' (Bizhoshi's son) as their spokesman. He related the accusations against Hatali Yazhe, the arrest of the women, the occurrences at Shiprock. General Scott again expressed his sorrow and his sympathy with them and then continued substantially as follows: "I have got over 300 soldiers out there. I do not want them to come here. They will not come unless I call them. I don't want to call them; I don't want to fight you. Some of my soldiers have never seen an Indian. They would not know you from my friend Charlie Mitchell here. They might kill innocent people. They would not know a man from a woman; they might kill some of your women and children." Then, pointing at one: "Have you a wife and children?" "Yes." "How many children?" "So many." "Do you love them?" "Yes." "Do you want anything to happen to them?" "No!" "Have you any property?" "Yes." "Any sheep?" "Yes." "Do you want them scattered all over and your property destroyed?" "No." He put these questions to each one, then added: "I don't want to call the soldiers; I don't want to see any harm done to your women and children. I don't want to fight you." Then, turning to one of them and pointing his finger at him, he said abruptly: "Do you want to fight me?" "No." All were asked the same way, and all answered, "No!" He continued: "And I don't want to fight *you*; we don't want to fight. And now it is getting late. I want you to eat your supper and stay here tonight and be at your ease and have a good sleep, and tomorrow we will talk again."

They arose, and each one came to the general, shook hands with him, called him "chief" and "elder brother" and thanked him. It was refreshing to see their relief. After all, it was not necessary "to kill and be killed." After supper the general called old Bizhoshi to the sitting room and asked him all kinds of questions about their captivity at Fort Sumner, about their origin, their history, their former habitat, their religion, and their customs. Bizhoshi, who is 77 years old, and as medicine man well versed in Navajo lore, answered the general's questions so readily and fully that the latter gave him generous praise which flattered the old man immensely. They had become friends. Next morning, we patiently awaited the arrival of Hatali Yazhe. Attsidi Naez Biye' had gone the evening before to find and bring him.

In the meantime I took some photographs of the Indians and the family of Mr. Noel and the school class of Miss Robinson. This photograph shows that Mr. Noel and family and Miss Robinson with all their youngsters had more courage in remaining within six miles of these "renegades" than —. But comparisons are odious. Not all Indian traders preserved their equanimity. One of them wrote he had been staying up for [several] nights till 4:00 in the morning. The soldiers had been on the reservation for six days and had done nothing. He wrote that he believed in fighting first and talking afterward.

While we were standing on a sandy hill near the store, Bizhoshi Biye' approached and asked Chee Dodge to take a walk with him. During that walk, he explained to Chee, Attsidi Naez Biye' did not intend to surrender, and he was afraid he might influence his brother, Hatali Yazhe, to refuse also, *begging him to see them privately as soon as they arrived.* About 11:30 Attsidi Naez Biye' returned, bringing Hatali Yazhe with him; the other two had not yet returned home.

Chee Dodge spoke to Hatali Yazhe first, telling him not to use his sickness as pretense to refuse surrender; he had done that too often. He *had* to surrender, and that was all there was to it He would have the best of care on the way. He agreed. Then he called Attsidi Naez Biye' into the general's tent and opened up on him, *when he was called to dinner. Chee came out of the tent and asked me to arrange so he could take his dinner later; he could not drop Attsidi Naez Biye'. Going back into the tent he continued his conversation.* At first his stubborn friend answered his questions and arguments with a simple "*hola*" (I do not know what I'll do). At last Chee told him if he had no property to lose and did not care for his own life, he ought to consider his wife and children and his companions and the rest of the tribe. At last, after Chee had talked to him and argued with him for three-quarters of an hour, he agreed to surrender.

At about 1:00 they were called into the store. General Scott bade old Bizhoshi sit near him and helped him to his seat. Attsidi Naez Biye' had taken the seat farthest away, and I suspect the general did not trust him; he asked him to come up and sit in front of him, which he did. There the general could watch every movement of his. This time Frank Walker did the interpreting and Chee Dodge took his seat on the counter. *He wanted to be free from interpreting so he could break into the discussion if any opposition should arise.* There were 70 Navajo in the room and about 30 outside.

The general asked Hatali Yazhe, who had not been present the day before, whether he had heard from the other Indians what had been said. He had. Repeating in a few words his remarks of the previous day, he told them that they had had a perfect right to go to Shiprock and see Mr. Shelton about those women prisoners, but that it had been very wrong to take them away as they had done. Mr. Shelton represented the U.S. government; they might like him or they might not like him, but as long as he was their agent, they had to obey him as the representative of the government. Then he explained law and courts to them, the necessity of the law to live in peace and to be protected by it; the absolute necessity of enforcing the law.

"Supposing," he added, "a warrant were sworn out against me and the U.S. Marshal served the warrant on me."

I am in command of over 3,000 soldiers on the Mexican border; don't you think I could whip any U.S. Marshal with them? But in the end I would get the worst of it. Nobody can fight the U.S. government. It is just like fighting that mountain; it is worse, for the mountain won't fight back, but the U.S. government will fight back. I have over 300 soldiers back there. I came to get you, dead or alive. And I will get you. A dead man is no good to anyone. I don't want to fight you. That is the reason I left the soldiers back. Bringing them here would have been like placing a keg of powder near the stove. I don't want to call the soldiers. Now I will give you the same advice I would give my own son over here (Lieutenant Scott, his aide-de-camp). Go with me to Gallup tomorrow, take the train to Santa Fe, and stand trial. I do not know what the judge at Santa Fe will do; I do not know what is in his heart. Three of you have surrendered and their trial is over. The judge gave them a suspended sentence and sent them home. You saw them. He may do the same to you; he may not; I don't know. But you must stand trial.

Thereupon Hatali Yazhe arose, walked up to the general, took hold of his hand, and said: "I am not well, I am sick; but my chief and my brother, I leave everything to you; I shall do what you tell me to do!" The general promised him the best of care; he would ride in an ambulance to Gallup and he would have the services of the Army physician. One after another arose, walked up to the general, and shook his hand. They called him their chief and brother and father, thanked him, and promised to go with him. Then the tension broke among the other Navajo. All wanted to shake hands with the general and express their appreciation. A veritable ovation for General Scott followed. When quiet was restored they begged that Chee

Dodge and myself should accompany them to Santa Fe and that the general should assist them. We promised to do so. But two of them were missing; the one on the deer hunt, and the one who had gone to Red Rock. Besides, they would like to go home first and arrange matters, since they were to be away "indefinitely"; if the general would give them two days leave, they would get the other two and all would meet him again at the store, Sunday evening, ready to accompany him to Gallup Monday morning.

General Scott hesitated just one moment, then granted their request. It was 3:00. Mr. Noel and family had been exceedingly kind to us and urged us to stay till next morning, but we wished to break the long, hard ride over the mountain to Chee Dodge's home. After saddling our horses, a thought struck Chee Dodge. He went back to the store and told Bizhoshi to be sure and keep his promise and see that the others did the same. *Why, of course he would.* Turning to Bizhoshi's wife, he said: "See that he comes." "*La'a!*" was her reassuring answer. Bidding a short goodbye to our host, to the general and his son, we were off *for T'ohaali, 18 miles away, where there is a small Indian school.*

We, that is, Chee Dodge, Doctor Norbert, the four Navajo who had accompanied us, and myself arrived at the school at 6:00. Since there was no horse feed at the school, and accommodation for but two of us, we rode on to the Indian trading store, where Mr. Bloomfield and family, Mormons, gave us a very friendly reception and good accommodations. The next day we crossed the mountain and reached Chee Dodge's home. The next day, Sunday, Dr. Norbert and I drove home to St. Michaels with Chee Dodge's team.

The following Tuesday Chee Dodge and myself met General Scott and his soldiers and prisoners at Gallup. In the evening we accompanied the general to the county jail to bid his friends goodbye. In their presence he handed me a letter he had written in their behalf to the U.S. Attorney. In taking leave of the general, each in turn held his hand and thanked him profusely for saving them. Bizhoshi embraced him. They parted, and General Scott's mission was at an end. Comment on his success is superfluous. The secretaries of the interior and of war knew whom they chose, since the general's record for similar achievements is unsurpassed, and it speaks well for his superiors to have taken him from his important command on the border to save a few Navajo from themselves.

General Scott left the next day for El Paso, or rather Fort Bliss, to rejoin his command. The soldiers, whom he and the prisoners had passed at Nelson's store, followed him to the border, instead of returning to Fort Robinson, Nebraska.

At 2:30 the next morning, Mr. Galusha, Deputy U.S. Marshal, met us at the depot with his prisoners, and soon we were speeding toward Santa Fe, where we arrived at noon.

That same afternoon, Judge Pope, of the federal court, *called me to the bench, and after a short conversation appointed Mr. Wilson, government attorney for the Pueblo Indians, attorney for the indicted Navajo. Court would open again next day.*

[. . . appointed Mr. Wilson as their lawyer. A conference with him and the U.S. Attorney followed.]

About a half hour later, the Navajo were in the spacious library, relating their story to Mr. Wilson, Chee Dodge acting as interpreter. A consultation followed. The regular court session had closed the previous week. To stay in jail till next session of court in April, or give bond, or, if released upon their own recognizance, to return to Santa Fe, did not seem feasible. The best thing to do was to waive a jury trial and plead guilty.

The following morning, the U.S. Attorney arrived at Santa Fe from Albuquerque. I handed him the letter from General Scott. A conference followed. [One of the prisoners] *had been indicted for rioting and stealing the six-shooter from the policeman during the melee at Shiprock. But he had not stolen it. He had taken it away from the policeman to prevent him from using it. He had immediately given it to a Navajo by the name of Adola, who had it returned to the policeman. The U.S. Attorney agreed to have that feature of this case dismissed.*

Ni'dughullin Biye' was indicted for horse stealing and rioting; Tom Dale for horse stealing only. They said they could not plead guilty to horse stealing because they had not stolen the horses. They asserted very emphatically and maintained very vigorously, Mr. Shelton had a certain Navajo in jail for a long time; while he was serving his sentence, his stock scattered and this horse had strayed into their herd. They did not know to whom the horse belonged. When the owner, released from jail, returned to gather his stock, they had turned the horse over to him. No witnesses were there to disprove their assertion.

The U.S. Attorney had refused to issue a warrant against Hatali Yazhe for polygamy. He was of the opinion that the Indians ought to be educated to a certain standard of morality before being prosecuted in the courts for such offenses. Reluctantly, he had issued the warrants for rioting, because Mr. Shelton had insisted that he could not maintain control unless the Indians were punished in the courts. The attorney was of the opinion that such matters ought to be settled on the reservation.

Court opened at 2:00 the following afternoon. The seven Indians pleaded guilty to rioting. Mr. Wilson's narrative and plea followed, supplemented by myself and Chee Dodge at the request of the court. Thereupon the judge lectured the Navajo for about half an hour in a very able, practical way. Chee Dodge interpreted. The judge's address was, in substance: If they (the Indians) obeyed the law, all white people would be their friends and help them; if they disobeyed the law, they would have to be punished. They had been right in some things and wrong in others. They had had a perfect right to go and see Mr. Shelton about the women prisoners. Every man, white, red, or black, has a right to protect his family. But they had been wrong in taking the prisoners away as they had done; they had been wrong in not surrendering until the U.S. soldiers appeared, and so on. He advised them strongly against polygamous practices and other infractions of the law.

He dismissed the case of pistol stealing; released Tom Dale and Ni'dughullin Biye' on the point of horse stealing upon their own recognizance; but if they went home and behaved themselves, they might not be called again to answer that charge.

Hatali Yazhe, on whose account the whole affair had occurred, and Ni'dughullin Binalli, who had quirted the policeman at Shiprock, were sentenced to 30 days in the county jail at Gallup; the other five were sentenced to 10 days in the same jail. He told old Bizhoshi that he would have given him a longer sentence, since his age and experience should have prompted him to advise his sons and followers differently, but he had pity on his old age and would sentence him to only 10 days.

The Indians were pleased with their mild sentences.[3] They said 10 days were as one day. Before leaving the courthouse they called upon the judge in his office room to thank him and bid him goodbye. The evening of the same day we boarded the train for Gallup. The Indians served their sentence, are at their home again on the slope of Beautiful Mountain, and "all is quiet on the Potomac!"

Life is, to a great extent, comic opera.

I shall add an editorial comment which appeared in one of the leading papers of New Mexico [not further identified in the manuscript].

I shall conclude with a few hexameters:

Horace: *Quidquid delerant reges, plectuntur Achivi.*

[Whatever the kings do wrong, the Greeks are beaten.]

Parturiunt montes et nascitur rediculus mus.

[The mountains groan and a ridiculous mouse is born.]

Let me reverse: Nascitur rediculus mus et parturiunt montes to kill it.

[A ridiculous mouse is born and the mountains groan to kill it.]

Risum teneatis, amici? [You smile, my friend?] *Like Hashimuro Togo, I require no answer.*

Notes

1. From Anselm Weber, "Navajo on the Warpath?" FMSW 7 (1919): 1–17; and "Beautiful Mountain Journal, January, 1914," FAC Box DEC.333, Anselm Weber Beautiful Mountain, fd.CI12.

2. Robert L. Wilken, *Anselm Weber, O.F.M.: Missionary to the Navaho* (Milwaukee, Wisconsin: Bruce Publishing Company, 1955), 188.

3. Superintendent Shelton was infuriated by the light sentences. In his report on the situation, "Shelton described, almost in anguish, how several of the Navahos were let off in Santa Fe without any witnesses being called on other charges. . . . Shelton thought that the publicized trial in Santa Fe was no trial at all, and nothing but a farce." Davidson B. McKibbin, "Revolt of the Navaho, 1913," *New Mexico Historical Review* 29 (October 1954): 287.

27

St. Isabel's: The Missing Pages[1]

Berard Haile, O.F.M.

[Father Berard was sent to Lukachukai as the resident priest in August 1915. At year's end Father Anselm asked for a piece on happenings there for the 1916 issue of *Franciscan Missions of the Southwest*. Berard's contribution, entitled "St. Isabel's," ran to about 4,800 words, or about 405 lines of typescript. Father Anselm, in his capacity as editor, found much of the manuscript problematic—in today's parlance it would be labeled politically incorrect—and cut the offending portions, which were many. The sanitized remainder, missing some 230 lines of the original typescript, he published without securing the author's permission for the drastic cuts. Father Berard howled in dismay, and Anselm responded defensively. Even after Father Anselm had curtly demanded a halt to the exchange, Berard persisted. On February 22, 1916, he wrote that "I do not want to deny you the right of the blue pencil the use of which we expect from the editor, but your contributors also have rights which are to be respected," and later in the same letter he reminded Anselm, "On the whole your feelings on the subject are not different than mine. A few years ago some German paper published an article of yours on which you remarked: 'Why, the dam fellows changed it. They must think I don't know German.'" In Berard's view, the cuts were so substantial that "the article in its altered form" was "but a travesty on the original."[2]

The deletions treated two topics: 1) Characteristics of Lukachukai Navajo that Father Berard cast unfavorably, either in terms of their effects upon Navajo solidarity and progress or their impact on the friars themselves, and 2) the efforts, in Berard's eyes, unethical and insensitive, of Protestant missionaries to secure a foothold among Lukachukai Navajo. The previously published, expurgated version of "St. Isabel's," available both in its original provenance and, more recently, in *Tales of an Endishodi*,[3] is not reprinted here. The deleted portions, the missionary's honest perceptions of the problems facing the people he serves and the nature of his opposition, are published here for the first time.

Father Berard's article was a seamless piece, sans headings, but in the present context it seems appropriate to add subtitles to make up for the intervening transitional material not reprinted here. Also, for each segment I have included an

386

italicized sentence or two of overlap with the previously published material so that the interested reader may identify precisely where the offending sections originally appeared in Father Berard's manuscript. Note that this use of italics is opposite from that of other chapters: here it is transitional sentences from the *published* article that are italicized rather than manuscript text missing in a published version.

Given that Father Anselm cut both descriptions of the Lukachukai Navajo and of the activity of the Protestant missionaries, it is noteworthy that Berard's complaints focused almost entirely on the deletions relevant to Protestant activity. In fact, the cuts in Berard's depictions of the local Navajo were just as severe, and for these Father Anselm did not have the "must not offend advertisers" argument to fall back on to justify his editorial decision. Apparently, Berard did not contest the removal of much of his description of the local Navajo because he knew what was wrong, and reluctantly agreed.

For one whose experience was so extensive, whose knowledge of Navajo language and culture already was hardly matched among whites, his depiction of Lukachukai people in the original draft of "St. Isabel's" is surprisingly negative. Perhaps it reflects the contrast between the isolation of Lukachukai and the, by comparison, almost cosmopolitan centrality of St. Michaels; perhaps it merely represents the weariness and frustration of Berard's first months as the area's resident priest. Whatever the cause, in the manuscript submitted for publication Berard highlights the negative—common thievery; lice picking in public; the defects of a clan system that perpetuates inequality and a marriage system that fosters polygamy, family violence, and divorce; the irrelevance of formal education to everyday Navajo life; and the alleged ubiquity of evil spirits and the corresponding perpetual necessity for expensive, time-consuming, protective "sings." In retrospect, he must have agreed with Anselm that such a picture of his charges was hardly likely to generate among readers a sympathy for the Navajo and a willingness to contribute to mission work among them.

There is a certain irony in the fact that one who plainly was already surfeited with Navajo ceremonies—sick and tired of "white, yellow, black, and blue *ch-indi*," and the effects of belief in them upon his parishioners—would in future become even more familiar with the spirit world of the Navajo, attending ceremonials and sitting "through whole nights and days taking notes until I was half mad."[4] He would become the foremost authority of his time on Navajo ceremonialism, a man whom the Navajo identified as one who knew more about them than any other white man. Facing the "How do I detest thee, Lukachukai?—let me count the ways" spirit of perhaps one-quarter of the manuscript, Father Anselm rightly penciled it out, and Father Berard, full of argument about the cutting of his descriptions of Protestant missionaries, hardly peeped.

To contemporary readers, such "slips" of Berard's, coming from one who already was esteemed as a veteran missionary and authority on Navajo life, and revealing the limits of his own tolerance for some of the "bad habits" of his charges, should be reassuring. He, too, continued to struggle over the culture gap. Here, after 16 years in the field, he reveals that he is not resigned to aspects of Navajo life that offend his sense of order, justice, or sin. As is plain in many of his other writings, he also found much that was admirable among the People, and his commitment to them did not waver.]

❖

Effects of the Clan System

As for the Navajo, the Lukachukai district is known for years as a farming district. Yet even now it cannot be said to have overreached its experimental stage. For while it is favored with a rich soil, an abundance of water, and a comparatively close market for its products, it is yet a stagnant community that is held within the grasp and restrictions of its own obnoxious social and clan system.

Matriarchy prevails among the Navajo, that is to say, every child that is born belongs to the clan of its mother, not to that of its father. This implies, according to Navajo marriage law, that the clan of the husband is not related to that of the wife; hence, at any time they may be divorced and remarry into each other's clan, if they so chose. For marriage causes neither affinity nor consanguinity between them. Their children, however, fare somewhat differently. Through their parents they become members of their mother's clan, and relatives of all the clans that are affiliated and related to this clan. On the other hand, they become only related to their father's clan and his related clans, which fact later prohibits, or at least makes marriage into these clans undesirable. Of course, intermarriage with clans related to their mother's clan is entirely prohibited, being equal to that of intermarriage of first cousins among civilized people.

In a small community like Lukachukai the drift is naturally to strengthen related clans to the exclusion of others. In consequence, the women and their children represent one group of related clans into which the husbands have married. As a further consequence one greets the other as brother, sister, uncle, aunt, nephew, niece, or relative of some kind, each belonging to one large family. All of which may seem utopian at first sight, but vanishes before the baneful specter of a foolish clan system that destroys the unity and solidarity of the very family.

Rights exist—at the pleasure of the clan. Property is divided. The husband has property of his own, while the woman manages her own affairs. The family as such has none and is reared by mutual consent, usually at the expense of the father. Divorce, therefore, is frequent, and alimony is never exacted as a penalty.

Thus, late on Christmas eve we were stirred from our first slumber by the voice of a rider, whose silhouette appeared against the moonlight in the window. He called upon us to open the door and then hastily informed us that his mother had well nigh been murdered in a scuffle with her husband. The woman, who shortly entered, was dizzy and covered with blood but managed to explain that the "man" had suddenly attacked her for some reason unknown to her, had beaten her head against the walls of the house, and then landed upon her face with his fist. Just then her son, a lad of twelve, had picked up a forked stick and struck his stepfather a blow in the back of his head, cutting a deep wound. They had then left him unconscious. The woman now refused to live with this man whom she had married only last summer, but after her husband paid her a horse the matter was dropped and settled. The husband had just cleared a fine field for the spring, and thus the solution reached was probably cheap in the long run.

It will be seen, then, that plans for organizing the Navajo and colonizing them in certain districts which some have suggested as feasible are confronted with a gentile system that excludes nonrelated clans as undesirable, and makes a will-o'-the-wisp of marriage and of family ties, that blasts energy and restricts labor to the lowest possible exertion. For, if I lose this woman and family, will any of my future wives consent to live here? Why shall I toil? Why expend my energy when I may be ousted at any moment? This is large enough for present needs! Owing to this suspicious disposition of the clans toward each other, then, only tracts of small area are cleared. Ditches are taken out and repaired by those who participate in their benefits, and then studiously led aside. A private ditch may be cut at any time, and water is permitted to go to waste rather than to allow some "upstart" or stranger to demonstrate that there is enough room for more. A cooperative system in which one farmer assists the other at plowing, harvesting, fencing, and so forth, is never thought of, much less practiced. "The whites do that, we don't." . . .

While some maintain with a slur that the progress which the Navajo have made within the last three decades consists in the possession of wagons, plows, and implements that represent the culls of some large manufacturing plant, it is gratifying to say that the Lukachukai Indians appreciate even these and use them to the limit. In addition, the government maintains many schools, on and off the reservation, for the education of the Navajo. Graduates from these schools are returned to their tribe as a living sample of what education will do for the Indian.

The influence of such graduates is not very marked at Lukachukai and vicinity; in fact, it is often difficult to discover a trace of an earlier education. Some time ago I was called to a dying young man of about 30 years of age. He had graduated at Riverside, California, some 10 years ago, but returned in poor health, suffering with pneumonia. He was known locally as the "Little Singer" from the fact that he followed the calling of his father, who is a singer of some renown. At school he was called Hatral Thompson and this name, with a New Testament and some knowledge of English, was about all that distinguished him as an educated Indian. It was possible, however, to instruct and baptize him before his death.

Another Riverside and Carlisle pupil draws the blessings of two wives upon himself, while his brother, known as the "old pupil" from early school associations, is an undetected cattle thief! Bigamy, you know, is a remnant of Navajo tradition: "Marry the old woman to get the daughter, it saves you the trouble of a mother-in-law," while theft should not be practiced publicly, but whenever you can get there first! . . .

No particular care . . . is bestowed upon the hair, excepting to occasionally bathe it in yucca suds or to inaugurate a vigorous campaign against disagreeable but active heptapeds called lice. No abashment, indeed, is felt in publicly extending this campaign to clothes and body, as there are no official "lisoleums" and the dis-lousing process is left to the energy of the individual.

The Lukachukai Indian is a liberal spender and a good sport. Freight rates are high and often yield from $25 to $30 per load of 3,000 pounds. When times are good, as when the traders stock up for winter, or at the harvest and piñon crops, much freighting is done with the result that the pockets of our freighters bulge with Dago Red and associated brands. Life then looks bright, you share the "fruits" of your trip with anyone that comes along, and after all a night's rest dispels a heavy head and a memory of whatever may have preceded! You provide for the winter—later.

They are superstitiously devoted to their singings. Your mother saw a coyote skeleton, or the carcass of a horse or cow when she carried you in confinement, and now, after many intervening years, that spirit is pursuing you. Witness your fall from a horse, the sickness of your child, the loss of your sheep through storm and starvation, all shows that you should call upon a singer to remove this spell. You do that. Your neighbor has a similar case. After that the district 30 and 40 miles distant announces a mountain chant, a *yeibichai*, or a war dance, which you must not miss by any means. Is it surprising, then, when you learn that the son of so and so is a singer of this chant, another for that, fellows that never were heard of before, yet come into prominence with a rattle, charcoal, and a crow feather?

Still there are many *ch-indi*, large and small, dwarfish and giant *ch-indi*, not to recount the numerous white, yellow, black, and blue *ch-indi*, some striped and speckled, flat, straight, swift, and stealthy *ch-indi*. What with *ch-indi* to the front, to the rear, and to the sides, those above and below, the number of singers should necessarily correspond! Besides a *ch-indi* is crafty, invisible, and stubborn (corresponding to our evil spirit or phantom).

The district is notorious also for its witches, its star readers, its people "that shoot" into you beans, turquoise, bones, hair, pebbles, and other causes of sickness. Tracing and avoiding this caliber of evildoers and removing the causes require ingenuity and sagacity which keep the people constantly alive to the seriousness of such dangers. Indians of other districts that are farther advanced and have largely discarded such hallucinations ridicule them and keep aloof from the vicinity. In consequence [social] intercourse is none too lively, and transient strangers have no reasons for tarrying any longer than necessary, possibly, too, for fear of contamination. In addition, Lukachukai lies somewhat beside the public thoroughfares that connect distant localities with centers of traffic, travel, and interest. . . .

Protestant Missionaries in the Lukachukai District

The Lukachukai district contributed some of the first pupils to the Mission School at St. Michaels. . . . This and the fact that more than five years have elapsed since the erection of the chapel made the appeals of the Indians for a resident [Catholic] missionary stronger than ever. The more so as the inroads of Presbyterianism crossed the expressed desire of the local community and vicinity. Their relations with Protestant ministers have been none too friendly; in fact, the district refused them permission point-blank to extend beyond their territory already established. On the other hand, as said before, we were urged earnestly to make use of our permission to extend our activity by establishing residence at Lukachukai. . . . *As for the Indians, inquiry has been stimulated, curiosity is aroused, and a means is provided to begin religious instruction with something that is tangible and visible, especially so later when the school shall have been opened.*

In the interest of truth it must be said that the designation *æ'nishodi bi æ aḥs 'isigi* does not stand for "short-tail ministers" as some opine. The Navajo cannot vouch for tails that may or may not exist. But it refers to the "ministers with short coats" as opposed to the likes of us, plain, unqualified *æ'nishodi*, "dragging gown."

Last September it so happened that several members of the Presbyterian persuasion had decided to assemble in council near a point called Round Rock for the purpose of obtaining a tract of land from the Indians. The chief of the Western Presbyterian district with Brothers Mitchell, Green, Platt, and other colors, and an interpreter, called on our friend Charlie Mitchell in company of the trader at Round Rock. Their mission was peaceful, but its results remind one of a hornet's nest that is peace itself until it is molested.

At any rate, a number of Indians were gathered in haste, and after his namesake had introduced himself to Charlie as another Mitchell and had received a "devil-I-care" reply, our half-brother Crum introduced the other gentlemen and the purpose of the council by explaining that "these people" desired to build a hospital at Round Rock, and desired the consent of the Indians through Charlie for a small tract of land there. This, Charlie immediately refused, saying they did not need a hospital; with sufficient doctors in the country, that "preacher-and-physician-in-one" brought them no benefit, that, should they require an additional force of physicians Washington would grant them, that doctors wearing short coats and preaching were not wanted; therefore, they would not grant the petition. "Haven't we *ændeishodi*? They talk to us if we want it. We want them only, not 'these people.' We have decided long ago, that from St. Michaels to the railroad, back to Fort Defiance, from there to Crystal, the Wheatfields, Tsehili down to Lukachukai and Big Oak, from Chin Lee to the Black Mountains shall belong to the real *ændeishodi*. No, let 'these people' stay where they came from."

"But," said Mr. Crum, "have you not all along clamored for more doctors, and you now refuse when these men want to build a hospital, where your people will have attention and free medicine?" "'To be sure, I want doctors," Charlie replied, "we want them and hospitals, but let Washington send them to us. We know Washington, but do not know these men. Let me tell you something, young man. Years ago, when your father-in-law built that store at Round Rock, we Indians gave him that piece of land to build a store. The buildings, the shelves, the cans, the dry goods and merchandise, that's yours, the land is still ours. Comes an Indian with a pelt, a blanket, wool, or cash, and wants sugar, and coffee, and calico, and what not, you are there to take that pelt, and to take his cash, and to give him a can of pears, or a piece of calico, or what he may want. There is your place, behind the counter, not here. Take my advice and stay there, and attend to your business, and do not meddle in affairs that do not concern you in the least. You are not a preacher, but if you were, you would not get that land. That settles it."

"Well," said Charlie in explanation, "I thought they might do here as they did at Red Round Rock (*tsełchi dahaskani*) where they also talked hospital, but gave them a 'short-coat.' If I can so do it, they shall never get that land. *Ch'indi, ch'indi, œ'nishodi bi œ ałts'isigi* (double d the preachers)!"

Notwithstanding this send-off, one of them shortly after made his headquarters at the government buildings, and from there visited the neighboring Indian camps. Here he "talked religion" to them nilly-willy, so that he was soon dubbed "*bahani łani* (much talk)." Some, as the Catholic families, refused to listen, while others that listened in curiosity responded with that inimitable Indian grunt which leaves you as wise as you were before. The fates would have it that Charlie Mitchell stumbled on to him at one of the camps, and making the best of a disagreeable situation had to occupy a seat near the minister. This mouthpiece immediately struck up its tune with that air of "Listen to my story too?" so disagreeable to any person, even one as ordinary as Charlie Mitchell. He therefore politely refused to listen, remarking that when the time had come he would listen to the *œ'nishodi* at St Isabel's. "And when the fellow insisted," Charlie afterward related, "I was much tempted to floor him. Why, he even had the nerve to ask me to supper at Shinn's, which I also refused, because it angered me still more. As though he might give me bacon and beans and coffee, and then tell that we want him here. What kind of people are they anyway? You tell them as often as you like that they are not wanted, and yet they return. Much like a dog that you kick off, and then comes back at you wagging his tail." And when the builder with his brother entered the room Charlie related the incident to them also, concluding his remarks with the advice: "Tell him to stay away, children, tell him to get out!"

His thoughts reverted to the same subject that evening. "'Tis strange," he said, "I seem to be alone in this fight. Recently, for instance, I had a long talk with *hastqin yazhe* (Hesús) on the subject, but noticed that he was indifferent. Frank and Chee and the silversmith seem to lay back and do not express themselves freely. The other day I met the Shirley boys at St. Michaels and asked them what they were doing there. "I see you here quite often," I said to them. "Is it merely to get some hay that you come, or a square meal? Perhaps you are here on business, or you seek advice in money matters? Does it ever occur to you to put in a good word for the priests with the people?" "Oh," said they, "we never talk about such things, in fact, never thought of that before." "You see," Charlie continued, "I am practically alone. The situation to me is much like this. When three coyotes attack one dog, there isn't much hope. I am in that position now. And when two coyotes meet two dogs, each side is afraid to attack the other. They eye each other and then gradually withdraw, as neither side has a show. Perhaps I have another friend that is helping me, but I do not know of any, do you? But when three dogs attack one coyote, the coyote has no show at all and runs and runs until he outruns the dogs. That's what it ought to be. All the Indians should get together and chase this coyote out of the country. Then we should be at peace. As it is now here is Charlie like one dog against three coyotes, not knowing whether he should attack or not. *Daani*, it's so. Some of these scrubs will say yes in council, but when some white stranger comes along and shakes hands with them, and gives them a meal of beans and pork and coffee, they will say yes to anything and everything, and you do not know where you are at with them. Therefore, you should call that council which we have planned together, and have all of them thumbmark that protest against these short coats and send it to Washington. That will settle the matter once and for all."

That council is still pending for reasons which would take too much space to explain here. As it is, I fear the editor reluctantly grants me this space for St. Isabel's. I should have written on St. Leonard's at Tselchi dahaskani also, but of that some other time.

Notes

1. From Berard Haile, "St. Isabel's," BHP Box 1, fd. 13.

2. Berard Haile to Anselm Weber, 22 February 1916, BHP Box 3, fd. 1.

3. Berard Haile, "St. Isabel's," FMSW 4 (1916): 21–26; Berard Haile, "St. Isabel's," in *Tales of an Endishodi: Father Berard Haile and the Navajo, 1900–1961*, ed. Murray Bodo (Albuquerque: University of New Mexico Press, 1998), 154–59.

4. Ralph Looney, "'Father Shorty' and the Navajo," *Ave Maria National Catholic Weekly* 59 (5 May 1962): 22.

28

"You Ministers Seem to Make Trouble for Us Wherever You Are"[1]

Berard Haile, O.F.M.

[The council that Father Berard and Charlie Mitchell hoped would settle things and drive out the Protestant missionaries (chapter 27) was held the following March. There the Lukachukai Navajo voted to refuse to make land available to any religious denomination other than the Roman Catholic and affirmed their desire to have the Catholic fathers provide religious instruction for their children. As things turned out, with the establishment of a government day school in the area, the dominant pro-Catholic majority would not be able to keep the area closed to non-Catholic missionaries, but for the moment it was a victory for local community control and the Franciscans.

The present chapter combines the two articles Father Berard wrote for *St. Anthony Messenger* on the Lukachukai councils of spring 1916. They include an exemplary demonstration of the leadership and oratorical skills of the powerful Navajo headman, Charlie Mitchell. His rationale against allowing the Protestant preachers access to the region is a fair reflection of Father Berard's position.]

On March 29, 1916, a council of the Lukachukai Indians was held at St. Isabel's to decide "whether we shall have two ways of thinking, or only one," in other words, "Shall we permit the shortcoat ministers to establish themselves at Lukachukai in addition to St. Isabel Mission?" (The mission was established some five years ago for the purpose of keeping in touch with the graduates of St. Michael's Indian School, which had largely drawn on this vicinity for its pupils. Since August 1915, St. Isabel's has been the residence of one father and a laybrother, with St. Leonard's at Red Round Rock and other points as stations and territory.)

Despite the establishment of St. Isabel's, the Presbyterian missioner residing at Fort Defiance, Arizona, has been in the habit of making visits to the various Indian settlements at Wheatfields, Tsehili, Lukachukai, Round Rock, and Chinli, a circuit of some 90 miles. Accompanied by an interpreter, this worthy evangelist makes it a point to stop at any Indian camp within this circuit, preaching to all and one, young and old, to the willing as well as to the indifferent, in season and mostly out of it. The immediate result of such evangelizing is *nil*, for which the Navajo has a better expression in his *qola*, meaning "I don't know," an expression that is comprehensive as well as unoffensive, but leaves you quite unwise as to the result of a three-hour sermon. A lasting result of this method, however, is that the Indian, like most of us, feels that it is not very opportune, having every mark of coercion. In consequence, repeated protests against this intrusion reached the superintendent, with the result that in reply a plea was made for a "free for all" reservation. On a treaty reservation like this, however, where it seems to be an established fact that the tribe and not the individual Indian disposes of land and rent rights, unanimous consent or refusal seemed to be their only redress. When, therefore, the rumor gained in persistence that the traveling evangelist (or "much talk" as the Indians dubbed him) had succeeded in renting a house at Lukachukai in which to hold occasional services and in securing a tract of land for mission purposes, the time had come to definitely dispose of the matter. It so happened, providentially perhaps, that on the date set for the council the said minister repeated his visit, accompanied by a fairly good interpreter. As our interpreter, like Jacob's son of old, "did not appear" in time for the council, we considered it a fair move to press the minister's interpreter into our service, as curiosity had led him to learn the reasons for the gathering of Indians at our chapel.

As is usual at a council the subject matters were discussed in private confer-ence with the elders or leaders of the local tribesmen. It developed that there was some truth in the current reports and that efforts had actually been made for the rent of a house belonging to one Mr. Redhouse. Also that some converse had been held on securing a tract of land belonging to one Walter Harvey, a graduate of Carlisle, I believe, who is also a nominal adherent of some Protestant persuasion. These disclosures showed a divided camp, which was happily adjusted by the quick action of the leaders. Mr. Redhouse, who was called upon, emphatically denied any intention of ceding his rights, pointing out that he should be without a home if he rented his house to this American, whom he had neither seen nor spoken to. Mr. Blue Eyes, who had originated the report, denied any sinister intention, saying that he had merely hinted at a possibility of renting said house from Mr. Redhouse, but that the matter was now settled by the owner's refusal. Indeed, Blue Eyes proposed to cite the minister before the council in order that he fully understand that he is not wanted in the vicinity. This, however, did not appeal to the other leaders, who preferred that their decision be submitted by the agent and that they ignore the minister. After each and every leader had expressed himself on the subject it was decided to draw up a document which they and the council *in pleno* would endorse. Therein was stated that the Lukachukai Indians refuse "to set aside a tract of land for any church of another than the Catholic denomination, and to rent any land or any of their houses to such other denomination, and to permit any other than the Catholic priests to give religious instructions to their children."

This document was explained by the interpreter, and through Charlie Mitchell to the assembled Indians. One and all, the elders and their people, men and women, signed, that is, thumb marked this document. In like manner, the married people who propose to send their children to the local day school all affixed their signatures which grant special permission to the Catholic priests only to instruct their children in Holy Religion. That closed the first council at St. Isabel's, after which one of the headmen remarked, "Now everything is straight, and there is just one way of thinking now, and that's your way."

Within a month after the council at St. Isabel's, the superintendent of the Navajo Agency at Fort Defiance summoned the Lukachukai Indians to another council. The government had determined to erect a day school in the valley in place of the usual boarding school, and Mr. Paquette was charged with the unpleasant duty of presenting this new plan to the Indians and to use all arguments within his power to induce them to be reconciled with it and to send their children to the new school.

Two or three days passed before all the Indians could be gathered, and the council opened April 30, after the Sunday morning services, at which an unusually large number of Indians were present.

Mr. Paquette ably presented his case. He told them that the school would open for a nine-month term, from April until December, and that classes would be held daily excepting Saturdays and Sundays. The children would return to their homes in the evening and sleep there. Clothing would be given to them and lunch served to them at the noon hour. In the morning the parents would return them to the school at 9:00, washed and cleaned.

The Indian is accustomed to the boarding school which provides the children with clothing, meals, and lodging. This method, Mr. Paquette admitted, was the most practical and the most desirable one for them but, owing to the fact that the appropriations in money to the Indian Office had been curtailed, could not be carried out for the present. He said he confidently hoped that under the circumstances they would abide by this ruling of the Indian Office and that he would be able to report a large enrollment.

In a city with waterworks, timepieces, well-regulated homes, and fixed habits it may seem unnecessary to point out such requisites as cleanliness in appearance and promptness in coming to school. Indeed, some reluctance toward a boarding school might be felt in a community of whites that is accustomed to have its children at home after school hours. Not so among the Navajo. The Lukachukai Valley proper, for instance, is some 15 miles long by eight miles wide, in which the homes of the Navajo adjoin their small farms, while the school is located at the upper end of the valley. Water is found in several of the creeks and is led to their farms in irrigation ditches, which at the same time supply the demands of the home. The ditch is their washstand and basin, and the sun their towel, both of which they dispense with on cloudy days; and soap will last longer if it is not used regularly! Then, too, the idea of having schoolchildren sleep at home! Not that they are particularly sensitive as to where they lie down, as long as they have some sort of a roof, a sheep pelt, and blanket. What's a school without beds? Other schools have beds for the children—what sort of school is this that gives them clean clothes in school and the dirty floor at home? At other schools the children remain all the time; they are fed, clothed, washed, looked after for ten months in the year. That's the kind of a school we want—not this one-day, one-meal affair, which makes you rouse the children in the morning, feed them, chase them off to school, trail them in the sagebrush to see that they actually arrive at the school, and meet them halfway in the evening lest they be lost. That leaves you no time for your own work! Besides, who knows the time? Clocks we have none. The sun is our guide, true enough, but this thing of 9:00, as the Americans count, we cannot do it. A school is a good thing and we want our children there; but keep them there—keep them there; get a frame building with beds if you like, only save us this worry over the children every day! Such and similar were the thoughts and opinions expressed at the council.

The agent, however, could make no definite promises, save to strongly urge and recommend a boarding school with a capacity of 125. And in view of the long distances which the children would be forced to travel, a compromise was reached by which only such children as lived within a radius of two miles from the school should attend. That the Indians agreed to do, but again begged the agent to urge a boarding school with the Indian Office, so that a larger number of children might be enabled to attend.

The agent now called upon the Indians to bring up whatever matters they might have for discussion. After disposing of matters of local and personal interest, such as the preservation of ditches, economical use of water, distribution of implements, wagons, plows, and the like, one Mr. Singer arose to broach a subject which had, indeed, been discussed in a previous council but still seemed unsettled. "I refer," he said, "to the matter of religious instruction of our children in this school, and now that the two gentlemen" (pointing to the writer and Mr. Green, the minister) "are present, it seems a good time to settle this question here in presence of the agent." To which the agent replied that he was quite ready to hear their views, since some insinuations had been made to him that they had been driven to give their signatures to one side, and complaints had been made that their policeman, Charlie Mitchell, in his capacity as policeman, had strongly agitated against the ministers. It was now time to express their views on these charges.

That brought the council Indians to their feet. "Do that for Charlie's sake? Are these Charlie's children? What has he to do with our children? We, we settled that ourselves in council at the 'little priest's' place last month. What has Charlie to do with that? I put this thumb mark on that paper, not Charlie's thumb mark! And I, and I, and I! Charlie tell us what to do? Oh, no! Years ago we, the Lukachukai Indians, decided that we want the priests to locate here, and every one of us gave the little priest our signature when he asked for it. That's settled! There is no use of talking about the matter at all!" Expressions like these and that happy play of a grin with which an Indian dismisses a mooted question left no doubt as to the mind of the council.

There was one dissenting voice, however. Walter Harvey stated that he did not think as the rest of the council. Indeed, as there are several religions among the

Americans, it seemed to him that this minister, too, should be allowed to come among them, so that they might hear the different stories, and leave the children to choose their own religion. He had not signed that paper at the council, he said, because he had been absent. But when questioned about his own children, he admitted that he had none, which fact robbed him of the privilege of speaking in behalf of the children of others. The Indians, too, pointed out to the agent that he might have expressed his views at their council which he had not attended, though he had been repeatedly invited to do so. Mr. Harvey took his seat and kept it.

It seemed that our side of the dispute was ably enough defended by the Indians themselves, a view that the agent apparently shared, since he now called upon the minister to speak in his own behalf.

Mr. Green opened by stating that "this isn't my council, and I haven't anything to do with it. But I will say that last fall Charlie Mitchell himself told me that he did not want me here, and that he was working against me." He then enlarged upon his mission to preach the Gospel, which alone he was trying to do, and not to fight with the people. He had heard, he continued, that a council had been held "down there" (at our chapel); but also that matters had not been explained to the Indians, who had signed something that they did not understand.

As we had pressed Mr. Green's own interpreter into our service at the previous council, and the Indians had sufficiently forestalled such brazen charges of misunderstanding the agreement, it seemed best to follow their own policy of ignoring the charges altogether and leaving the matter to Charlie, who surely would take up the challenge. Though 70 years of age, Charlie is still vigorous and hardy, morally clean and true, as fine a physical specimen of the Navajo as may be found anywhere, a lovable character, always in sympathy for the suffering, the needy, and the distressed, always willing to help with advice and friendship. Naturally, then, he is the spokesman for others who cannot present their cases with ease; the lawyer, the judge, at times even the sheriff who brings the culprit to punishment. All matters of common interest are therefore left to him for settlement or adjustment. His appointment as chief of the local police did not change this tribal position, for there is no other to replace *Chala tso*, Big Charlie.

When, therefore, Charlie opened up in reply, the council faced Mr. Green in that confident attitude which plainly trusted Charlie to voice the sentiments of all. "I *did* see you last fall," Charlie said with some emphasis.

> And I *did* say to you that I and the Indians did not want you here. That's true, and I say it again, my brother, or whatever I may call you. You object to my talking to the Indians that way, why should you? If I am policeman, do I talk to them as a policeman? Or did I just begin to talk that way to them since I wear policeman's clothes? Or will I stop talking for my people because I am policeman? Indeed not! Look at my hair! They are gray, and they got gray in riding around for my people, in working for them, in talking for them before you were born or heard of!

This was duly interpreted.

"You would know why we do not want you and the rest of the ministers?" he continued.

> Well, in my younger days the older folks among us, men that were intelligent and straightforward, used to tell us to be honest, not to lie, not to steal and cheat—in a word, what we ought and ought not to do. They are gone, and the few headmen that are left to represent the people have thought that possibly you and your kind might replace these old folks and tell the younger people such things. Yet you ministers seem to make trouble for us wherever you are. You report the Indian for the smallest of offenses, some of you have even tried to take away or help take away lands that belong to the Indians; in fact, the districts in which you have located report dissension and a world of trouble. On the other hand, we know the priests. They do not meddle with every little trouble that arises; they don't gossip like you do; they do not oppose our singings as you do; they help us along in our lands and other ways and we know them for years to be the same good people they were when they first came to us. Therefore, they are the ones that should talk to us like the old folks used to talk. Let them teach our children, not you. They erected that chapel with our consent years before you ever came here. Had you come first you might have succeeded. But now that we have the school and the priest among us, we think that's enough, and want no more.
>
> And as for your preaching, I do not know how you preach. But from hearsay, I have it that you have a funny way of talking that the people do not like. I am told that you stop at any hogan and pop your questions on things these people know nothing about. It seems much like an American ready with pencil and paper to take down what the people may answer to his questions, 'Do you want to go up to heaven?' or 'down to hell?' What! Are these people dying that you place them before this alternative? You don't talk to people about death when they are hale and hearty! Besides, they say you talk about the earth burning up and somebody coming on clouds. It seems to me that only frightens the people unnecessarily. Therefore we do not care to listen to you, and ask you again to leave us alone.

No reply was made to Charlie's remarks, and the agent closed the council with a final appeal to the Indians to send their children promptly. On May 2, 10 children were enrolled, which number has increased to 14, and will be augmented as soon as the lady teachers arrive to care for the girl pupils. The boys, of course, are very earnest, and even on Sundays readily appear for Holy Mass. Let us hope that we may succeed in instilling true Christianity into their souls, and pray that Christ's message of peace and joy may soon supplant the superstition and fear that until now have held sway among the Navajo Indians.

Note

1. From Berard Haile, "A Council at St. Isabel Mission," *St. Anthony's Messenger* 23 (May 1916): 553–54, and "The Sequel," *St. Anthony's Messenger* 24 (July 1916): 67–72.

29

Life at Chin Lee Mission, 1917–1918: Contrasting Views

Fidelis Koper, O.F.M., and Leopold Ostermann, O.F.M.

[The typical Franciscan mission staff included one or more friars, ordained priests authorized to teach and administer the sacraments, and one or more Brothers, nonordained members of the order who served in many capacities. In the Navajo missions of the early 1900s, the Brothers were assigned many of the duties associated with the physical upkeep of the missions.

Brother Fidelis Koper, author of the letter that begins this chapter, entered the Franciscans as a teaching Brother, but after 20 years as a teacher in the Midwest was sent to Jemez, New Mexico, as a handyman and then, in 1915, was assigned to serve with Father Leopold in Chin Lee.

When he came to the Navajo missions Brother Fidel was no anxious young volunteer, but a middle-aged veteran already set in his ways. Three years older than Father Leopold, he had his own opinions about how things ought to be organized, what his proper place was in the mission outpost's division of labor, and how the Indians should be treated.

By the time Brother Fidel joined him, Father Leopold had already been isolated at Chin Lee for a decade and, perhaps reflecting both his own temperament and the influence of Navajo ways, ran a fairly "loose" ship. There was much in his management style, both internally and in his treatment of the Navajo, that offended Brother Fidel's standards and sensibilities. After two years, he could remain silent no longer and wrote a long letter to Provincial Rudolph Bonner detailing improprieties and unnecessary deprivations at Chin Lee mission, most of them, he suggested, due to the administrative incompetence of the "lovable" Father Leopold.

The provincial's investigation of the problems at Chin Lee included communicating the charges to Father Leopold, and of course also to mission Superior Father Anselm. As may be seen in the second section of this chapter, Father Leopold's moderate response to his provincial's queries about the issues Brother Fidel had raised reveals much about his own priorities and attitudes. Father Anselm's response to the situation, communicated some months later as part of a longer report to the provincial, was both less moderate and more protective of Father Leopold: "I suggest that Brother Fidel be removed."

Brother Fidel was moved out of the Navajo missions, and in his place Father Leopold received the younger, more compatible Brother Julian Elpers, who served with him at Chin Lee until 1924, when Father Leopold's deteriorating health necessitated his transfer to St. Michaels.

Brother Fidel's list of complaints is a useful window to the daily life of the missionaries in an isolated reservation outpost. The current reader comes away from the exchange with an appreciation of the sacrifices involved in life among the Navajo at this time. It is noteworthy that most of Father Leopold's response is not to deny the conditions described, but rather to suggest that, given the nature of things, Franciscan missionaries to the Navajo should expect no better.]

"Father Leopold Is Not a Man to Enforce Rules and Regulations"[1]

Very Reverend and Dear Father Provincial:

Herewith I make an attempt to present to you a pen picture of Chin Lee, not of the "Burg" and surrounding country, but of the conditions, of which, in my humble opinion, you ought to have knowledge.

I assure you, I am not doing this in a rage or revengeful spirit, but calmly and deliberately, and therefore I hope, you will not take it amiss.

In your two visitations I told you, I was perfectly satisfied at Chin Lee. I still am, generally speaking. There isn't a place in the Province I would rather be because Father Leopold is such a lovable character to get along with, and I find the various kinds of work very much to my liking.

To work, to build, make, fix and improve is a sort of a passion with me, and therefore I have been hard at it from morn till night, even working late by lamplight.

Please, Father Provincial, don't take this as a boast.

By this time, perhaps, your curiosity is aroused and are wondering what all this is about.

Had I not taken sick and been compelled to lay off (this is the third week) I'd probably overlooked and forgot as I so far have been doing in spite of the trying part of it.

But now, since I took sick in consequence of it, I feel justified , even compelled, to make this report.

Surely, when a person's health is endangered through mismanagement it is high time to say something before greater harm is done.

And while I am telling you one thing I might as well say more.

What I want to call your attention to mainly are the meals, the food as it has been served right along.

We have 160 acres of land of which about 50 are cultivable. We have three horses, two hired men, and a complex set of farm implements and yet all year round we practically live out of *tin cans*.

Neither this nor the summer before was there anything worth mentioning raised except perhaps three ton of hay.

And why not?

I am not complaining about canned vegetables; have never been particular about food. Anything is good enough providing it is wholesome. Dear Father Provincial, you know as well as anyone that sameness in food, almost day after day, the same stuff the same way is not good for health and that stale, spoiled food plays havoc with the best of health.

This is my fifth year out West. In all this time I have enjoyed excellent health, till of late; never felt better in my life.

At the time I took sick, Father Leopold admitted as did also Mr. Ayze, our interpreter, that they were feeling bad in the stomach region the last few days. This is not in the least surprising.

Times and again have I seen dishes of stale food covered with mold standing on the pantry shelves.

Of late we have been getting mixed dishes which I took for remnants of previous meals, the Lord knows how old, thrown together.

Fred, the young Indian you met at Chin Lee, is hired to do the cooking, baking, washing, and work around the place.

He is a mere boy, and like the average Navajo, light-minded and foxy. He takes no interest in his work, it seems.

Father Leopold, God bless his good soul! leaves everything to the cook *what* and *how* to prepare—and when to serve meals.

Often have I gone to the kitchen for my breakfast and found stove still cold at 7:30, even 8:00.

There is *no* set time for meals; it is entirely left to the cook.

For no apparent reason whatever, we will have dinner one day at 11 a.m., the next 11:30, at 12:00—at 1:00 p.m. and later.

With supper it is much the same. This irregularity is not the exception but the rule.

Of this irregularity I do not complain; I merely mention it to give you an idea of how the kitchen end of the place is being run.

As a rule, the cooking *solely* consists in *warming up already cooked* vegetables. Even then when there is plenty [of] nice beef soup meat on hand *canned soup* is dished up.

Or he will take a can of *corn*, add a handful of *crackers* and lots of *hot water* and dish that up for soup.

Potatoes we very seldom get; it's too much work to prepare them.

Times and again it has happened that friends sent us perishable vegetables that required a little work to prepare. They were left in the pantry till they *rotted* and had to be thrown away.

Rice, macaroni, noodles, hot cakes, pancakes, or any of the many different so-called Muflfynifans [?] are not made. Not even bread is baked.

On the whole, meals consist, from one week's end to the other, of canned goods, simply because it takes less time and work.

Father Leopold does not seem to know or care what effect this has on the contentment and health of his people, nor the expensiveness of such housekeeping.

I have gone to the kitchen for my breakfast but had to content myself with a bowl of coffee. There was not a slice of bread, not even crackers in the house.

I am quite sure the cook would do the right thing if he were only told what is expected of him, and occasionally reminded.

He knows what a fine, easy position he has, and would not care to lose it. But, since Father Leopold doesn't seem to notice, and never says anything, he takes advantage of Father's goodness, or weakness.

We have many, many meatless days during the year. We need not have any, but that's not the cook's fault. Meat he will always prepare if on hand. Indians, at least the Navajo are very, very fond of meat.

Fred the cook is supposed to wash. Tubs, boiler, wash machine, and wringer are there. In all this time I have been at Chin Lee he has not washed *one-half dozen* times. No one is called in to do it, and it is not sent out to be done. Fathers Sixtus, Lawrence, and Ludger did their own while Fred idled. I did some of mine, some I sent to the Sisters at St. Michaels.

What Father Leopold does about his is a mystery to me. Twice I called his, Father's, attention to the fact, that washing was being entirely neglected.

He admitted that Fred was supposed to do it and that he was somewhat negligent. This was six or more months ago. He has not washed since.

Fred is not entirely to be blamed so much. Being a mere boy, light-minded and foxy, he looks for the easy side of life.

He seems willing when Father tells him to do anything. The trouble is, Father does not seem to see nor care, and does not tell Fred what to do. Fred prefers not to see what to do and must be told everything—every time—specially. And that is what Father Leopold neglects entirely.

Knowing Father's goodness, or weakness, Fred takes advantage of it to the very limit. Lately he was sent to St. Michaels on horseback to fetch something. He stayed away eight days. Father Marcellus picked him up in Gallup.

Some time before, sent to St. Michaels on a similar mission, he stayed away 10 days. Had gone to Gallup.

As far as I know, nothing was said to him, and he drew his pay in full.

He draws $20 a month; has free board, free fuel, free oil, and occupies two rooms in the stone building next to the church. He was married last summer.

This building was expressly erected, like the one at St. Michaels, *for the Indians* that stop over to lodge in for the night.

All summer Indians have been lodging in our kitchen.

As the nights became cooler their number increased; one-half dozen, whole families at a time sleep there, and wash there.

At breakfast time I have found the kitchen crowded with Indians, five or six standing around the stove, some squatted on the floor, others washing themselves.

Some may ask, others take it for granted and walk right in anytime, since doors are never locked.

The Navajo are known to be very lousy. They have both head and body lice. Father Leopold has 10–12 woolen blankets and comforters to loan to Indians to sleep in if they happen to be without one.

These blankets in which these filthy, lousy Indians have slept are kept in the pantry with our laundry and foodstuffs.

The consequence is that we ourselves are as lousy as the Indians are.

These body lice are awfully nasty little beasts and hard to get rid of.

Father Leopold knows, has experienced it time and again, that the Indians steal almost anything they can get away with, and yet he leaves them sleep in the kitchen.

Some lazy chaps, mostly young fellows, the cook's friends, hang around for days at a time, getting their meals as if our place were a hotel.

It's to these Indians lots of our meat goes, and we must do without.

How, where look for the cause? The man in charge, of course.

Really, dear Father Provincial, I hate to say a word against Father Leopold; he is such an amiable character; everybody loves him.

But, oh my! If he only had a little ambition, a little push and insight in things.

No wonder Father Sixtus used to get hot, Father Lawrence explode, and Father Ludger got awfully disgusted the first few days already.

Father Leopold truly is what our people out here call him, a fatalist. He does not seem to notice anything, lets everything go as it pleases—and most unconcernedly awaits the result.

You surely must have formed that opinion when you were here.

How primitive and unattended to everything looked in the house, in church, and around the place.

I have tried hard to accomplish something, fix up the place, but it's very difficult since I spend almost half of my time repairing wagons, farm implements, and all kinds of things for the Indians. Father wants me to do it to gain their goodwill. I must have repaired between 25 and 30 wagons this summer.

Except on Sundays and when his assistant who tends to the mail three times a week is away, Father Leopold *never* gets up in the morning till 9:00, almost 10:00. Has been doing so, I'm told, for years.

Often people come and ask for him. Surely, I can't tell the people that he is still in bed at such late hour.

He has no curtains on his windows, and I have seen people, schoolgirls, *peep in on him.*

Before going to Chin Lee I was accustomed to daily Mass and Holy Communion. Now I can hear Mass and go to Communion on Sundays only. In the beginning I use to wait till 8:00, but soon found out, it was useless.

I have no idea when he says Mass. I positively on principle do not watch his habits and doings.

As stated above, we have about 50 acres of cultivable land, three horses, two hired men, and all necessary farm implements.

Our whole harvest this year amounted to about three ton of hay; no corn, no oats, no vegetables, not even a mess of potatoes. A small field of corn had been planted, but the horses were not looked after, horses and cattle got in and feasted. Now hay is bought at $30 a ton; corn $3 per. cwt. shelled. You might be told there is no water, or that things won't grow. There seems to be any amount of water on our place, 20–30 ft. below the surface, surely more than enough for a few acres of vegetables. It's not true things will not grow. The Indians raise lots of corn and lots of potatoes. It's all in the management.

Brother L. will probably tell anyone, potatoes can't be raised in St. Michaels. When here he planted *1,000 pounds* of seed potatoes and got but *700 pounds*, 300 pounds less than he planted.

Through Father Celestine's wise and businesslike management of the farm they got 1,834 sacks of potatoes from only 2,000 pounds of seed potatoes. Each sack weighed 100 pounds. Total, 18,340 pounds.

Besides, they got lots of oats, hay, and vegetables.

Mr. Hubble of Gallup, who has a branch store in Chin Lee, made Father Leopold the offer to put a portion of our land (it looks good to him) in alfalfa hay on half share, but he declined the offer.

Should no effort be made to raise more crops in the future, then, to my notion, we need not keep any horses at all.

They are not used for freighting from Gallup. Outsiders have been doing that at $1 per cwt. while our horses ran around idle and our hired lad did the same.

Not needed for making trips to St. Michaels or Gallup. The stage is always at our disposal, free of charge. Besides there are frequently auto chances.

Perhaps to make mission trips? If you knew how many.

As a rule, every Indian family has its own team and wagon.

Oh yes, our horses are used quite often, but by outsiders.

In all the time I've been in Chin Lee, I can't recall *one-half dozen times* that we really needed our team. Not exactly needed, but used them for hauling.

Surely, Father Provincial, by proper, businesslike management hundreds of dollars could be saved annually without depriving ourselves of anything we are entitled to. We would at least have decent, wholesome meals.

How can a man with a healthy appetite work and keep his health when he sits down to a meal at which there is *no meat*, no eggs, no cheese, no butter, no Muflfynifans[?]—nothing, but perhaps three dishes of warmed-up canned goods, bread or crackers, and coffee. In the last six months I've had but *two* eggs; cheese none at all.

The above is the usual bill of fare. When meat is on hand, and it's not a day of abstinence, that is added.

Then the irregularity. You never know when dinner will be served.

It may be 11:00—it may be 12:00—it may be 1:00, even later, and for no apparent reason, than the cook's convenience.

There is absolutely no excuse for having such poor meals as we have been generally having. Even here at St. Michaels the meals are as good and as regular as they are in the East.

When I took sick three weeks ago I had such pain in the stomach, a hot, burning sensation in the bowels as if they had been scalded. Father Leopold and our interpreter had much the same experience. I took good care of myself in my room for four to five days, hoping it would pass over, but it did not. I am still suffering with more or less intensity. It comes and goes.

There being no doctor at Chin Lee, I managed to come to St. Michaels to be treated by the doctor at Fort Defiance. He gave me different medicines and told me to stay here at least a week. He told me, frankly, my trouble came from the meals. When Father Marcellus asked the doctor what ails me, he replied: "Too much canned food." I dread to think of returning, because I am sure a relapse is certain, unless more wholesome meals are served.

This reform is out of the question as long as Fred has charge of the kitchen.

Father Leopold is not a man to enforce rules and regulations as you can infer from what I stated above. I can't understand why the cook should still be retained at such financial expense to the mission and inconvenience to us since Mr. Ayze is the official interpreter. He is well educated, sincere, and full of fervor, willing to help wherever he can. He is a widower, about 30 years of age. Was engaged as cook before coming to Chin Lee. He told me, he would do the cooking without increase of salary (he gets $25 a month) but, for some reason, Father Leopold is not in favor of this. I have never been in charge of a kitchen, but I venture to say, I can do lots better than Fred has been doing.

Father Leopold is an excellent cook, and he could teach me if I were appointed, although I'd rather do any kind of manual labor.

Dear Father Provincial, I have surely made this report long enough to serve its purpose, to give you a fair idea of the conditions, thinking you ought to have knowledge of same. I am fully aware of the fact that it is a bold undertaking for a Brother to criticize his Superior and report to the Provincial, but I feel justified, even compelled to do so, since my health is at stake. You no doubt will agree with me, that things at Chin Lee on the whole, and in regard to meals in particular, are not as they should be.

Naturally the question arises: What can or should be done?

God forbid that I have the nerve to offer you suggestions. I am withholding information that would throw a lot of light and afford, I think, the key to the situation, but I dare not to forward same unless you request me.

As unbelievable this all may seem to you, it is nevertheless true, as all the Fathers that have been at Chin Lee can testify. Father Lawrence, who complained times and again, told me he had said nothing to you in visitation because he was sure to be transferred and did no longer care. I said nothing because I had been away a few months and had just returned.

In conclusion I assure you again that I like Chin Lee very much for reasons given above, and am perfectly willing to put up with all else, if it can only be brought about that decent meals be served.

If this does not seem possible, then, dear Father Provincial, please send me elsewhere, because I am sure under present conditions my health will be seriously impaired.

Very respectfully and sincerely yours,

"If St. Francis Would Come to Chin Lee, He Would Feel Quite at Home"[2]

Very Reverend and Dear Father Provincial:

I received your letter with enclosed check for $75, for which I thank you very much and very sincerely.

I take notice of the contents of your letter and I like it. I assure you that I take not the least offense at it, so far as you are concerned. Indeed, I am glad you told me all that, since it gives me the reason of the dislike, which some seem to entertain against Chin Lee, and to what ought to be remedied. I do not intend to let this knowledge influence my sentiments or my conduct toward anyone. However, since everything has its two sides, I may be allowed to say a few words.

If I compare my present condition and its circumstances with that of the few first years I spent in Chin Lee, when good old Brother Placidus and myself were camping or bunking in an old stone house with a leaky mud roof and a ground floor, with rattlesnakes and scorpions as occasional visitors, it seems to me that I am now living like a prince. Yet, Brother Placidus used to say: "Shandelier is the best place what gives."

If Father Marcellus and Brother Gervase had been left here another year or two, the house would look different. But even as it is, while it is by no means a palace, it is, also by no means, a hole, being situated on the top of a knoll. Now, supposing I get the money and the material to put the house into better shape, I don't know who would do the work. Brother Fidel has his hands full of all kinds of jobs, indefinitely, which are equally necessary, if not more so. While Brother Fidel is very handy and practical; is really a genius in fixing almost any thing; does good, neat, and substantial work; while he seems at present satisfied here and very interested in putting things in tip-top shape. And while I have no reason to complain or kick about him, but am very satisfied with him, and do not wish to criticize his ways or his work: yet I must say, that Brother Gervase would do three times or more the work in the same time. I see and know that that is his way, and therefore, I let him have his way and try to show myself interested and satisfied with his work, which, as I have said, is good, neat, practical, and substantial. However, I will follow your suggestion and talk house with him. Perhaps some of the other jobs can be put off.

As to meals. When Brother Gervase was taken away from here, no one was put in his place. The boy, who is here, Fred Price, was originally engaged as interpreter, farmhand, and to help the Brother in outside work. He knew as much of cooking as I do of running an automobile. (Yet I have cooked many a meal since then, although before coming out here, I never touched pot or pan in such a capacity). Fred was told to take charge of the kitchen and cook. Good old Father Engelbert would have said: "*Do hesh en Dreck*." Of course, the meals were not à la Delmonico's, and Fred naturally made use of as much canned goods as he possibly could, but the meals never injured me any, nor did they seem to me: "*eines vernuenftigen Menschen unwuerdiges Essen*." Fred went on with his cooking as best he could. I didn't kick, because I didn't know I had to. However, since Brother Fidel is supervising cook and kitchen, very little canned goods come on the table.

As to uncleanliness. I had to be assistant cook, housekeeper, and general factotum. Naturally, things were not as spic and span as in a ladies' millinery shop. No one moved foot nor raised finger to help, and Father Berard one day asked me: "How do you manage to get along, anyway?"

As to fleas and bugs. I never saw any fleas, nor even A flea, in the house, and I do not think anybody else did. So I must charitably ascribe that to an exaggerated flight of imagination. Bugs? Bugs were discovered in the house only the last two or three years, and I suspect they were brought in with secondhanded clothes from the East. We kept these old clothes in the attic, and after the presence of bugs became apparent, their tracks and traces were found to lead downward from above. There are no more old clothes in the attic, and the bug pest is well under control.

Of the rooms in the house, the assistant always had the best one: roomy enough, plastered walls, a spring bed, a table desk, a chair, a place to hang in clothes, a stove, and Navajo rugs on the floor. But there are neither hot and cold water faucets in the room, nor is it connected with a bath and toilet, and when the humble son of St. Francis, who occupies it, lies down and raises his eyes, he sees the joists of the upper floor instead of a rose-tinted ceiling.

Of the two last assistants I had, who, I think, are responsible for this uncharitable Chin Lee rot, one looked upon Chin Lee as his prison or penitentiary, or as he put it: "It was a knock for me, that I was sent to Chin Lee. I was too outspoken; I told the Provincial the truth, and now I am in Chin Lee for it. I don't care to take up the study of Navaho or anything else, until I am assured that my being sent to Chin Lee was not intended as a knock for me." The other one was here hardly two or three days, when he sorrowfully and dolefully declared that it did not look like home to him. He mentioned several modern conveniences, which they have in other houses, even at St. Michaels, and why could we not have them here? It seems that when he came out to Chin Lee (between 80 and 90 miles from the railroad, out in the wilderness), he expected to walk into a palace, take the elevator to the nth floor, enter his boudoir, press an electric button, turn on the hot and cold water, take a bath, use the toilet so as not to expose his precious posterior to a draught, and ring up the bellboy for further orders.

If a person once has his mind set against a place, it is the easiest thing in the world to drum up an array of reasons and embellish them with yellow fringes. Chin Lee is a mission station, out of the way; a pioneer post out in the wilderness, and not a metropolitan palace, equipped with all the modern conveniences conceivable.

Of course, I well know that the house is not perfect by any means, and that quite a few things need change and mending badly, which will be done as soon as possible, and as soon as we can get at it.

Dear Father Provincial, you will have to pardon some of the expressions in this letter, but I think I may indulge a little bit in exaggerating, since such exaggerated reports on the abominable conditions at Chin Lee have gone east from here and found implicit faith there. These things remind me of the graceful compliment which good Father Edward Bleke paid Chin Lee, when he was visitator for our province: "I think if St. Francis would come to Chin Lee, he would feel quite at home." Of course such friars, who seem to have some special privilege or dispensation for wearing the habit only when they say Mass, even on Sundays, will not look at it that way. Why, do you know that we were accused of not even having toothpicks on the table, with a tone and inflection, which showed that that was certainly THE limit.

In one of my former letters to you, I expressed my hope that the next chapter would send me a volunteer. However, before he comes out here, tell him what he is running up against. When he comes to Chin Lee it is like arriving on another planet. There are no electric cars passing the door; no hot and cold water in every room; no toilet room in the house; no heating system nor electric buttons to push; some of the walls are not finished; the upper floor forms the ceiling for the lower, so that the joists and the flooring are visible; things are in a primitive or semi-primitive condition, or, as Zigliara says "*in fieri*," but in the course of time, with a little goodwill and a generous dose of patience, many of these inconveniences will be remedied. If he still balks and wants to back out, then let him go way back and sit down.

There is no use out here for sissies, mama-pets, and softshellers, who act as if they ought to be accompanied by a wet nurse, but a straight-out, unstarched, rough and ready young man, who wishes to do good, and who would take some pride and interest in becoming a pioneer of Christianity, will be a splendid success.

Last Sunday our chapel was filled to overflowing with children, so that I had to pack quite a number of them up into the organ loft. When I looked over this crowd of children from the altar, my heart went out to them and I thought to myself: "Dear children, you are certainly worth the few hardships and inconveniences, which this place and the conditions here entail, and for your sake I would willingly and gladly undergo whole lots more, even to going back to the old stone house with its leaky mud roof and its dirt floor." In the afternoon a large crowd of the little tots came over here to see me, and although I wished very much to be alone and write a few letters for next day's mail, I spent several hours with them, playing with them, amusing them, making music for them, and was glad to see them enjoy it and hear them laugh. There are now about 170 children at the school, of whom four boys go to the preacher's services, and I have the promise of a Navaho father of returning two of these to us. Between 20 and 30 are being prepared for Baptism and First Holy Communion.

It was under these impressions that the thoughts and ideas, expressed in this letter, came to me. I wish, therefore, to repeat that I take no offense at anything you wrote, as far as you are concerned, that I am glad and thankful to you for telling me.

But, at the same time, I cannot help but to tell you what I think of such, who run down a place, because they seemingly prefer their own bodily ease and animal comforts and conveniences to the good that is and can be done. In fact, the latter seems never to enter their mind. Some seraphic modernism!

Once more I most sincerely thank you for your kind and generous contribution toward the instruction of my dear children, but I would like to know if I should carry this into my accounts as a donation from the province, or as a simple donation. I also thank you very much for your kind offer to help us in fixing up the house, and shall gratefully avail myself of it, if necessary.

With kindest regards and best wishes, I am,

Very sincerely and obediently yours,

"I Suggest That Brother Fidel Be Removed"[3]

Very Reverend Dear Father Provincial:

. . . After Father Leopold wrote that letter, Fred was here [at St. Michaels]; he had brought his wife to the hospital at Fort Defiance, where she is expecting a young Price. Fred Price is Fred's name. He told me he had quit Chin Lee. He will be the official interpreter at the Chin Lee school. He promised me to help us as much as possible in that position; and I am sure he will. He said he liked Father Leopold very well, but the Brother had it in for him and for the Indians in general. When the Brother would tell him to tell the Indians to "get out," he would not interpret it that way, but would say that the Brother was busy, and so on; he would also tell the Indians not to mind what the Brother did or said, that Father Leopold was the "boss." Fathers Marcellus and Celestine, who had accompanied the visitator to Chin Lee, told me that the Brother ranted and scolded fiercely about Fred. He expects Fred to cook, attend to the stock, the farm, the house, and the chapel. He wanted him dismissed. When Father Marcellus asked him who would do the cooking in that case, he said: "Father Leopold, of course; he doesn't do anything, anyway."

Do you remember, when you and I and Father Marcellus arrived at Chin Lee at 8:00, Father Leopold had to build the fire and prepare the supper for us, while Brother Fidel was entertaining you? He will not attend to anything at all, except "tinkering." The scaffold is still in the chapel. He is now trying to change around and embellish the residence. Fred plowed three acres of land for planting—three acres among 160—but nothing will be planted, or course; who should do it but Fred? And he has quit.

I suggest that Brother Fidel be removed. Whatever you do, please do not inflict him on one of your friends—and I consider myself among them. I hope you will find it possible to send a Brother to Chin Lee who can do the cooking, and a few other things. The farm at Chin Lee, which can be irrigated, could support the mission, if someone would "run" it who understands something about farming. A "decent' Brother would go a long ways in making Chin Lee more satisfactory to Father

Leopold, who is suffering from the blues, and to his prospective assistant. I am sure if you would send Father Ubald to him, he would not be in danger of being interned.

Notes

1. Fidelis Koper to Provincial Rudolph Bonner, 7 December 1917. FAC Box PLA.376. St. Michaels AZ/St. Michael's Mission, fd. St. Michael's Letters 1912–1923.

2. Leopold Ostermann to Provincial Rudolph Bonner, 23 February 1918. FAC Box PLA.071, env. Chinle AZ. Letters 1910–1918.

3. Anselm Weber to Provincial Rudolph Bonner, 26 May 1918. FAC Box DEC.247. Weber, Anselm. Letters, fd. Provincial Business 1898–1912 (CIV2).

30

The Struggle for Chin Lee

Anselm Weber, O.F.M., Leopold Ostermann, O.F.M., and Others

[Chin Lee was a pivotal battle, perhaps *the* pivotal battle, in the struggle between the Franciscans and the Protestant "preachers" for the souls of the Navajo. If there was one place, one site where the Catholic missionaries could assert they had a *right* to be, and to be left undisturbed, that place was Chin Lee. It was "theirs" by right of priority and pioneering investment, of popular demand for their form of Christianity, of overwhelming community rejection of the competition, of treaty right whereby the Navajo tribe was assured authority over its own land to decide whom might be allowed to live among them and whom they could reject, and by right of demonstrable benefits afforded the tribe as opposed to a history of agitation and trouble.

On all these counts, the Franciscans seemed to have the advantage. For much of the struggle it appeared that, ultimately, they would triumph, and in isolated Chin Lee, at least, they would be able to teach their holy religion and create a Catholic Navajo community without having constantly to confront anti-Catholic propaganda and overt, abrasive competition for students and their families from within the community itself.

Despite these apparent advantages, the Franciscans would lose the battle. In the end, the "opening" of Chin Lee to the Protestants was a lesson in administrative power. Neither treaty rights nor the will of the local majority (in state and national context, a nonvoting, noncitizen majority) could trump executive fiat. If, under any of a variety of guises, the secretary of the interior "granted" a religious denomination right of access and, it necessarily followed, accompanying acreage on the reservation, it turned out there was little the tribe, or the Franciscans, could do about it. Perhaps in today's political climate, treaty rights would count for more, but in the 1920s, Secretary Albert B. Fall's decision was final, and that decision reflected the political realities of the time. Father William Ketcham's Bureau of Catholic Indian Missions might serve as a clearinghouse for information, a lobby for Indian causes, a tool for attempting to "finesse" legislative and administrative decisions and magnify political leverage, but its efforts at behind-the-scenes influence and focused lobbying were necessary precisely because of the minority status of both the Catholics and the Indians.

The struggle for Chin Lee was lengthy and complicated. Here I can only offer a series of more-or-less representative glimpses, brief narratives that, within the range of evidence available, seem to stand out as well expressed or especially significant reports by the friars on what seemed to be happening.

There are four sets of players, incumbents within distinct institutional planes or "plates" which intersect in the Chin Lee affair. They are: 1) the U.S. government, as represented by the superintendent of the Indian agency, other government employees on and off the reservation, and all officials and agencies above them, in a pyramid that extends to the president of the United States; 2) the Navajo, considered as individuals, community members, and members of the less-than-sovereign Navajo nation; 3) the friars, both as members of their mendicant order and representatives of international, historic Roman Catholicism; and 4) the "preachers" or "ministers," agents of their particular, typically American, self-governing denominations and of international, historic Protestantism.

In the present story of the struggle, only one of those institutional planes, that of the friars, is well represented, although to some degree that of the Navajo is reflected in the reports of the councils held, of petitions signed by the Navajo present at those councils, and in reports from Chee Dodge, some of them including representations from other Navajo that he passes "up the line." An account of the struggle anchored in one of the other institutional planes, say that of the Protestant ministers as reported by the Presbyterians, is a very different story. For example, the ministers protested the presence of "competition" in their access to the captive audience of young Navajo in public boarding schools, lamented the "unfair advantage" of the Catholics generally, and in 1920 reported that in Chin Lee "The Work of Grace among the heathen Indians still goes on at this Station and in spite of the opposition of Rome which keeps us from using our building appropriation the little church continues to grow." Moreover, the "intense rivalry" for students which seemed to make the Christian faith "an instrument of disintegration, debate, and pettiness" was, in the Presbyterian view, absolutely justified, especially "when the apparent alternative was Catholicism, an unmitigated evil which precluded any possibility of comity."[1]

This chapter is entirely comprised of excerpts from the friars' correspondence. It is divided into 10 parts, the concluding part being further subdivided. With the possible exception of one letter from Father Leopold to Chee Dodge, which may be seen as having "supporting document" status, the first nine parts all are letters, or extracts from letters, reporting "up the line," to mission Superior Father Anselm, to Provincial Rudolph Bonner, to the director of the Bureau of Catholic Indian Missions William H. Ketcham, or to that organization's secretary, Charles S. Lusk. With the single exception of a 1918 field report from Father Celestine Matz to Father Anselm, these "status reports" all are authored either by Father Leopold or Father Anselm.

In the final part of the chapter, the scene of action moves from Chin Lee to Washington, D.C., and here the progress reports are typically "down the line," from

Washington to St. Michaels. Here the correspondents are the lobbyists on the scene, generally Director Ketcham or Secretary Lusk. At the end, with Father Anselm gone from the scene, the final decision, and an accompanying Franciscan mission policy of acquiescence in the matter, are communicated to Father Leopold at Chin Lee by Father Marcellus Troester, the new Superior at St. Michaels.]

❖

1915: "I Am Afraid the Same May Happen at Chin Lee"[2]

At Chin Lee, there [formerly] was nothing there but a store and our old temporary mission house. Now there is a government school there with a capacity for 200 pupils, our mission house and chapel, and three Indian trading stores. When we selected the place for a mission, there were no prospects for a government school at Chin Lee. I built the mission house so as to have room for a day school on our land on an elevation near the mission house. When the government built the school, we, of course, gave up the idea of having a mission school there.

When the government school was a certainty, the missionaries assembled at Ganado wanted to establish a mission at Chin Lee in addition to ours. All were in favor of it, except a Reverend Mr. Gass, of Albuquerque. At his insistence the idea was given up at that time. . . .

Until recently a certain Dr. Yeagle was government physician at the Tohatchi school. He belongs to the Christian Reformed Church. When a sick call came, he would have all kinds of excuses for not going, so the Indians would ask the Christian Reformed medical missionary, Dr. [Lee Sjoerds] Huizenga . . . to visit them. Dr. Huizenga then made use of his opportunity to induce the Indians to give him their signatures [agreement to have their children attend Protestant religious instruction]. He and Dr. Yeagle were in collusion. But that is neither here nor there.

Dr. Yeagle was transferred to Chin Lee. Not long after his transfer I learned that the Christian Reformed Church intended to establish themselves at Chin Lee. The wife of one of the Indian traders at Chin Lee (both educated Navajo) belongs to the Christian Reformed Church; one of her children got sick, Dr. Yeagle attended to the child, and they, it would seem, inaugurated the movement of having the Christian Reformed Church established there. The Indians of Chin Lee had told me repeatedly that they did not want any other church at Chin Lee in addition to ours. Even the children of the above-mentioned trader went to our instruction, and they and the parents would, at times, come to our chapel on Sundays. All was well until Dr. Yeagle arrived. I went to Chin Lee, called a number of Indians together, and told them about the intentions of the Reformed Church. They were very emphatic in their unanimous assertion that they did not want any other church for themselves and their children than the Catholic Church; they would not give their signatures to them for their children and would not give them any piece of land to establish themselves.

Some weeks later I learned that the Christian Reformed would go to Chin Lee to establish themselves there during the present month of December. Thereupon I composed the enclosed protest and the Indians eagerly signed it. . . .

Last summer the ministers from Fort Defiance began to go among the Indians along the foot of the mountain, and to Lukachukai. Lately the minister made his home with the government farmer for 10 days, going about and forcing his presence upon Indians unwilling to listen to him. He also went to our former pupils, who told him they knew their religion and did not care to listen to him. Some told him they did not want them, they only wanted our Church and no other. They [the ministers] urged the Indians to give them a piece of land to build a hospital at Round Rock, 15 miles west of Chin Lee. The Indian trader urged the Indians on, but the Indians told them they wanted no hospital from them. The government having built a school, a day school, at Lukachukai, the teachers, man and wife, have arrived about a month ago. They are good Protestants. The government farmer is a "genius" and a former minister. Under these conditions the ministers at Fort Defiance thought they might succeed in getting there and establishing themselves there in spite of the opposition of the Indians. Lately, one of the ministers said to Mr. Paquette they intended to get the signatures for the day school at Lukachukai before the school would open. Of course, he added, they were not telling this [to] everybody. Our interpreter, Frank Walker, was present. Evidently, the minister did not notice him or did not recognize him.

The Indians there are just as averse to having them at Lukachukai as the Indians at Chin Lee are. . . .

Across the mountain from Lukachukai, 15 miles distant, is Red Rock, a rather large settlement of Navajo. When our school opened in 1902 the Indians of this locality sent 21 children to our school, though Red Rock is at least 90 miles from St. Michaels. I said Mass there in the house of the headman the first time in 1902, and ever since I would make trips there, say Mass, have our former pupils go to the sacraments, and so on. I left the vestments in the house of the chief, and use his rock house as a chapel. When I went there in 1913 to say Mass and give the pupils, some of them married with families, a chance to make their Easter duty, baptize their children, and so forth, the Indians told me that the Protestants had been there and had told the Indian trader they would establish a mission there. They had not asked them, the Indians, about it. The chief told the trader that they did not want any other church than ours in that locality; that they had sent their children to our school, that I came there to say Mass and to pray, that I always had been a father to them, and they did not want any other denomination among them. All this happened before I knew anything of it and before I came to Red Rock. During my presence there, information came that the ministers had several loads of lumber on the way to build a mission house. The Indians came to me and asked me whether they could do that without their consent; the land belonged to them, and they did not want them. I told them they were on the treaty reservation and from all I knew they could not build without their consent. They were determined not to let them build. They did not need any urging on; they had made up their mind before I arrived there.

When the lumber arrived and they began building, 58 Navajo went there and protested against their building and told the workingmen to stop. They did not heed the Indians and completed their building. I asked Mr. Lusk to inquire whether they had the permission of the department. They had not even asked the permission of the department. *Possibly* Mr. Shelton of Shiprock had given them permission. Possibly they knew they could not get the consent of the Indians and thought by going ahead and building without permission of the Indians and the government, they would have the "fait accompli" in their favor.

Thus matters were standing when I came to Washington. I reminded the commissioner of the letter I had written to Mr. Lusk and of their building without the consent of the government and against the protest of the Indians. [Commissioner of Indian Affairs] Cato Sells told me he was utterly opposed to have anyone try to keep any denomination out of any particular part of the reservation. That it was bad policy and would work both ways. He went on in that strain, and intimated very strongly his opinion that I had put up the Indians to refuse, and that the Indians would not have refused if I had not put them up to it. I told him that the Indians themselves had protested against their establishing themselves there and that I had not put them up to it. "You didn't? Not this time? You wouldn't do anything like that!" he yelled at me. . . . I simply said: "Well, I didn't." . . .

The next time I saw Cato Sells, I referred to the incident again, telling him I thought it due to myself to explain. I told him about the attitude of the ministers at Fort Defiance, bringing the *Menace* [anti-Catholic magazine] into it, having it sent to Catholics and Protestants, having it where the children could get a hold of it, and so on. I also showed him a clipping from the *Menace* which read: "Ft. Defiance, Ariz.—I am a Presbyterian missionary among the Navajo Indians and am fighting Rome and its priests who are determined to get this tribe under its power."

Cato Sells said: "That is bad." I told them of all the charges they had brought against me, and so forth. Well, he said the rules and regulations ought to be followed, proselytizing should be avoided, and there would be no trouble. . . . Very well. But the ministers built that house at Red Rock and no one ever bothered about it, whether the Indians wanted it or not.

I am afraid that the same may happen at Chin Lee and at Lukachukai. They may go to either place, get the written request of one or two or three Indians, send that to the Indian Office, and obtain the permission to establish themselves. Or they may do as they did at Red Rock: Build against the protest of the Indians and without the permission of the Indian Office, and be upheld by the Indian Office after the thing is done. At Chin Lee, for instance, that trader, whose wife is a Christian Reformed, may tell them: You may build on the land I am using, near my store, and the Indian Office will not object.

I have explained matters now, and I am leaving it to you to make use of the protest or not. Since Cato Sells is utterly opposed to having anyone try to keep out any denomination from any particular part of the reservation, the use of the protest might have the opposite effect of the one desired. All I would like to have is this:

That the Protestants be treated as we are treated: No establishment of a mission without the request of at least the majority of the Indians living in the locality in question. I never attempted the establishment of any mission or mission station without having first the signature of *all* the Indians living in such locality.

1916: "I Am Not 'Giving Up the Ship'"[3]

I mentioned in my last letter that I and Chee Dodge would make a trip to Chin Lee and that I would write you the result. We found that Mr. J. A. Garber, principal at the Chin Lee school, has abused his position to establish the Presbyterian mission at that place. When Indians brought new pupils to that school, he asked why they all gave their signatures to us, why they did not give them to the Reverend Mr. [Frank A.] Green, telling them they ought to give them to the Presbyterian minister. In one instance the parents had given their signatures to Father Leopold, then took the children, six of them, to the school. Not succeeding in his endeavor to have them change their signatures, he entered their names accordingly. The mothers of the children left the school and came to our mission. The interpreter of the minister, Hosteen Yazza, temporarily employed as industrial teacher at the Chin Lee school, and his brother, George Yazza, followed them to the mission, telling them they had done wrong in giving us their signature, that Mr. Garber had said if they would change their signatures, he would give the children other names and would fix it up. Hosteen Yazza has been especially active in that line. He is a Presbyterian, educated at the Albuquerque school; when he was a pupil at that school he tried, by letters written to them, to induce his three Catholic sisters, pupils at the Fort Defiance school, to become Presbyterians. Mr. [Reuben] Perry put a stop to his activities in that line. Upon his return from the Albuquerque school, the Presbyterian ministers at Ganado employed him and used him to induce his father to give the ministers "second signatures" for his three Catholic sisters at the Fort Defiance school. Now Mr. Garber employed him temporarily as industrial teacher at the Chin Lee school. In view of his and Mr. Garber's "activity" it is not difficult to guess at whose instigation and for what purpose he left the employ of the ministers to assume his double role at the Chin Lee school. He has succeeded in inducing his father to give his "second signature" to the Ministers for his three Catholic brothers, attending the Chin Lee school. There is a movement on foot to have his father appointed policeman for the Chin Lee district.

On one Sunday Mr. Garber kept all pupils not yet baptized, for whom we have the signatures, from coming to our chapel, sending them to Mr. Green's services; on another Sunday, when, on account of bad weather, the smaller children could not be sent to our chapel, he sent the smaller boys to Mr. Green's services. He has sent other pupils for whom we have the signatures and a former pupil of St. Michael's School, where he had been baptized, to Mr. Green's services.

Some representations and misrepresentations of Reverend Mr. Green to obtain signatures and second signatures for pupils and for the mission site at Chin Lee:

That Catholics are bad; that no Catholic can ever become president of the United States; that he has been sent by "Washington" to obtain signatures; that the Catholics pray to the devil first before praying to God; that Mr. Paquette is one of us (which is not true), and that they, the Presbyterians, can get rid of him at any time, and so on. The Presbyterian minister at Kayenta told the headman of Chin Lee, Attsidi Yazhin Biye, that Mr. Paquette is the "naaltqe," the "slave," of the Catholic priests. I have it on pretty good authority that Mr. Garber intends to supplant Mr. Paquette at Fort Defiance (through the help of his Presbyterian friends, I presume).

I do not know how many, or how few, Indians have signed the petition for the mission site at Chin Lee. Several have revoked their request. Mr. Garber and Mr. Green have been saying that the site has been granted. Hosteen Yazza, the industrial teacher, told Smarty Brown they did not need his signature for the mission site; his own signature (Hosteen Yazza's) alone would be sufficient to obtain it from Washington.

From all this and my former letters the conclusion is inevitable that the Presbyterians, as represented by the poor specimens they chose to send among the Indians, are endeavoring—not to build up their own church out of converted heathen Indians—but to destroy our constructive work of years of patient labor at Chin Lee, and to destroy it by misrepresentations and vilifications and through the active assistance of government officials; and if Mr. Garber is permitted to remain at Chin Lee and thus perpetuate the impression created among the Chin Lee Indians that the government wants them to turn Presbyterian, and if the mission site is granted them through a petition obtained from a few and obtained under such influences, the Indian Office becomes a party to what I can only characterize as their "pernicious activity"; but I expect better things from the fairness and impartiality of the Indian Office. Father Egbert has left Fort Defiance in disgust and Father Leopold is losing courage, but I am not "giving up the ship," and I know you will assist me in holding it.

1917: Council at Chin Lee[4]

On March 28, 1917, the Indian Office wrote to you regarding the investigation of the Chin Lee affair as follows: "Regarding the advisability of granting a mission site for which Reverend Mr. Green is asking, the inspector recommends that it be granted only on condition that a representative number of Indians who will patronize the school, make written requests therefor. This recommendation will be carefully considered before any determination of such request is made."

I must write you further developments. When I arrived at Gallup, New Mexico, from my long sojourn at Rome City, Father Lawrence [Rossmann], who had come from Chin Lee the day before, told me Mr. Paquette had called a council at Chin Lee for the following Saturday to ascertain the wishes of the Indians of that district in regard to granting a mission site to the Presbyterian Church. I felt a little chagrined thinking that the ministers had urged this council and that Mr. Paquette had called it, taking advantage of my absence, not knowing that I would return that soon. I went to Chin Lee, arriving there two days before the council convened. Chee Dodge urged me very much to be present at the council to correct misrepresentations and refute accusations and charges continually brought against us and our religion by the ministers; he (Chee Dodge) would have the Indians ask questions to give me a chance to vindicate ourselves. Though I might have followed the example of the Christian Reformed minister who attended the Zuni council last year, put his arm around the interpreter before the council, and shook hands with the governor after the council, congratulating him on the stand he had taken against us, I preferred to stay away not to embarrass anyone by my presence.

As I learned from the Indians after the council 11 headmen or representative men of different localities of the Chin Lee district voiced their opposition to granting a mission site to them. No one spoke in favor of it. Eighty-eight signed against granting the site, and 11 signed for granting it. Since I was not present at the council, I cannot give a detailed description. I shall mention but a few things. The headman of Chin Lee said the government gave their children a good education at the Chin Lee school, and Father Leopold instructed them in religion; they were perfectly satisfied with that arrangement; but that was enough; too many religions were bad and only apt to confuse their mind; the religion of Father Leopold was the only one they wished for. After voicing his opposition to granting the mission site, he added, if the government would grant the permission in spite of their protest, he would be on hand when they would start the building to kick over the building rocks. The other speakers emphasized, among other things, the troubles caused by their [the ministers'] coming to Chin Lee and opposed the granting of the mission site.

Mr. Paquette reminded several of the fact that they had given their signatures to the minister for the Protestant instruction of their children, intimating that they, to be consistent, should give their signatures for the granting of the mission site. One of them answered him, he had given his signature to us first; then the ministers had come time and again and bothered the life out of him till he gave them his signature just to get rid of them; since that time one of his children had become Catholic and the others would follow her example. Another Navajo said his case was the same, and he asked Mr. Paquette to put his children on the Catholic list again.

Those who signed for granting the mission site were: Mr. and Mrs. Nelson Gorman, Mr. and Mrs. John Gorman, Sam Gorman—all belonging to the Christian Reformed, not the Presbyterian Church—and William Gorman, a heathen, and his wife—seven. The other four belong to the Fort Defiance district and should not have been permitted to give their signature, namely: Mr. and Mrs. Watchman, who live on the mountain and send their children to the Fort Defiance school, and who gave me their signature last year, for the Catholic instruction of the children they would send to school from that time on, though one or two of their older children are Protestant; they happened to be at Chin Lee and Mrs. Nelson Gorman induced them, at the last moment, to give their signature for the Chin Lee mission site, which they did reluctantly; Matthew and Fred Peshlakai, brothers of Mrs. Nelson Gorman, who live at Whiskey Creek in the Fort Defiance district and simply happened to be working for Nelson Gorman when the council took place. William Gorman's daughter is a good Catholic, but it seems he had to herd with the rest of the Gormans.

Of these 11, Nelson Gorman is the only one who has any children—one boy—at the Chin Lee school. There are, it is true, three Peshlakais, Francis, Luke, and Maimie Peshlakai, at the Chin Lee school, over whom Mrs. Nelson Gorman seems to claim guardianship, and whom she sends to the Presbyterian instruction. If the father of Francis (also the father of Mrs. Nelson Gorman) were still alive, he would have him attend our instruction like the rest of his children attending school since 1910. He is the same Peshlakai or silversmith of whom Attsidi Yazhin Biye speaks in the enclosed letter of Father Leopold—but he is dead now and has nothing to say, even about the religion of his son Francis, or his grandchildren, Luke and Maimie. Though the mother of Luke and Maimie is dead, their father is still alive, married again, and living in the Fort Defiance district.

Here I wish to refer again to the sentence quoted from the letter of the Indian Office in the beginning of this letter.

None of the ministers were present at this council. I do not know why they stayed away. I presume, however, that they did not want a council which would make known the real attitude of the Indians; that they wished to obtain the mission site in consequence of the few signatures obtained last year through the grossest misrepresentations and through the unwarranted assistance of Mr. Garber and Hosteen Yazza, then industrial teacher at Chin Lee. I have written you and the Indian Office very fully about that last fall, and I am sure my protest against granting the site upon the few requests obtained through such means and under such circumstances will remain effective. Some of those requests have been withdrawn; some withdrawals I filed with the Indian Office last fall. I enclose another retraction, because it shows their methods. Signatures for the Presbyterian instruction of pupils have also been withdrawn since that time.

The reasons for my opposition to such a grant I stated fully in my letter to you and to the Indian Office last fall. The conclusion of my last letter read something like this: "All this and my former letters make the conclusion inevitable that the Presbyterians make the attempt not to build up their own denomination out of converted heathens—but to destroy the results of our patient, constructive activity of many years at Chin Lee through misrepresentations, slanders, and vilifications and through the active assistance of government employees. . . .

The land belongs to the Indians, at least on the treaty reservation, and Chin Lee, Lukachukai, and Red Rock, or Tselchidahaskanni, are on the treaty reservation. Article II of the treaty reads as follows: "and the United States agrees that no person except those herein so authorized to do, and except such officers, soldiers, agents, and employees of the Government, or of the Indians, as may be authorized to enter upon Indian Reservations in discharge of duties imposed by law, or the orders of the President, shall ever be permitted to pass over, settle upon, or reside in, the territory described in this article."

Would they be justified, in consequence, in putting Mr. Green on a wagon and bringing him beyond the confines of the treaty reservation? Some of the Indians were contemplating such an act last fall.

Another reason for my opposition consists in this that the Presbyterian ministers at Fort Defiance and Chin Lee consider the destruction of our work and the "conversion" of Catholics, not of the heathens, their main object. Their continuous efforts at proselyting, to have parents change their signatures in their favor, their vilification of our religion, the literature they distribute among the Indians, and so on, are ample proof of this. I enclose a leaf out from "My Life in the Convent," found in possession of an educated Navajo at Fort Defiance, together with "Roman Catholicism Investigated and Exposed," and "Who Started This War?" Of course, the *ignorant, educated* Navajo know no better and believe such stuff, and I am ashamed to be seen in company of the Sisters or to look any woman, who has read such books, in the face. I confess I feel like murdering the whole outfit. Some of the Navajo, who resent their aspersions against us, feel the same way. . . . I beg you to bring these matters to the attention of the Indian Office, together with my vigorous protest against granting a mission site to the Presbyterians at Chin Lee.

1918: Death at Dinner[5]

The father of the preacher's interpreter lives up in the Canyon [de Chelly], and he has been having some trouble with other Navajo regarding some lands or fields. The interpreter (and I think the preacher too) were up there the beginning of the week, and invited the people concerned to be at their place in two days to talk over the matter and get it settled probably before Mr. Clark, the principal. Last Thursday the people were down, and with them the two headmen Qastquin Bisadi and Daghanaezi. These two headman, together with another Navajo Dinenaez, were received into the preacher's tent, where dinner was given them. Right after dinner *all three of them* were taken violently ill at the stomach with great pains and vomiting spells. The two headmen managed to get as far as Stagg's store. Mr. Staggs put them in that old stone house just behind the store, in which Brother Placidus and myself used to live. Both of them began to swell up abnormally, and by morning Daghanaezi was dead. Qastqin Snaez was over here and told me that not only his stomach, but his legs, arms, face, and head were swollen up out of all shape, and when they tried to wash him the skin began to peel off. We helped bury him on our place Friday afternoon. Qastqin Bisadi was also horribly bloated, but he is slowly recovering, although still very sick. Of course, there is quite a bit of excitement among the Indians over this, and I heard they want to keep a meeting (at the school, I think) in three or four days to talk this matter over.

Qastqin Snaez also mentioned that Indians had been getting meals at our place hundreds of times and never anything had happened to them; that these men were poisoned, and that they wished to chase them (Mr. Peck and his interpreter) out of this place. I should write to Mr. Paquette to come out as soon as possible, and so on.[6]

I know that the Indians who became sick of poisoning had intended to come over here for dinner, but the preacher invited them to his tent and insisted that they be his guests for dinner. Also, after dinner when they began to feel bad, they wanted to come over here, but got no farther than Stagg's store. The government physician at the school here pronounced it a case of poisoning. I heard yesterday that the other side is trying to explain the case by saying that the men were drunk. Queer that the preacher should have taken three drunken Navajo into his tentorial sanctum; queer, too, that the men should be taken ill right after dinner before they had a chance to swig. And even *if* they had drunk some whiskey (which I do not believe), would [that] cause them to be taken violently ill, swell up abnormally, and even cause death to one of them, and what kind of whiskey was it that would turn victuals into poison?[7]

Mr. Paquette went to Chin Lee as soon as he heard of it and held a meeting with the Indians. When one of the Gormans maintained that the Indian died of whiskey, Mr. Paquette called the government physician, who pronounced it a case of poisoning. It was a stormy meeting and only the presence of Mr. Paquette prevented open violence. They maintained that the minister or his interpreter had poisoned them. They promised Mr. Paquette to abstain from violence. Mr. Paquette advised the minister, Mr. Peck, and his interpreter to leave that part of the country for a while until the excitement had died down. They did not do so but are going around among the Indians as though nothing had happened.[8]

About 10 days after that Mr. Paquette met Reverend Mr. Mitchell at Chin Lee and pointed out to him the mission site they wanted. Some Indians who found out the reason of their meeting asked Mr. Paquette to call another meeting, but Mr. Paquette is not going to call another meeting.

I suspect that the ministers *have* made application for the mission site at Chin Lee through Mr. Paquette, and that is the raison d'etre of this letter and the enclosures.

And I beg you to acquaint Mr. Sells with the attitude of the Indians toward the ministers and toward the granting of the mission site. If the site is granted in spite of the opposition of the Indians, there may be serious trouble. Even now the Indians are talking about taking Mr. Peck forcibly off the reservation.

I heard that the ministers said at Chin Lee that they did not need the consent of the Indians, since Chin Lee was off the treaty reservation. It is true that on some maps Chin Lee is marked about six miles off the treaty reservation, but anyone who has been at Chin Lee, and knows the location of Chin Lee in reference to Canon de Chelly and the Naazlinni Creeks, knows that those maps are wrong, and that the treaty reservation line is about two and three-quarters of a mile west of our mission, and three miles west of Chin Lee. Even the maps that are wrong in regard to the location of Chin Lee are correct in regard to location of the above-mentioned creeks.

I am utterly opposed to the granting of a mission site to the Presbyterians. The enclosures show clearly enough that their only object is to destroy our own work among the Indians through *Menace* tactics.

I don't know what Mr. Paquette may have written in regard to their application, but I am afraid Mr. Paquette is too much afraid of the ministers to oppose them and to uphold the Indians in their opposition to granting the mission site. For the last eight years they have been accusing Mr. Paquette of favoring us, untruthfully, I assure you, but their constant accusations against him have intimidated him, I am afraid. Other superintendents would fight back, but Mr. Paquette is not built that way. Very few men would stand as much from them as Mr. Paquette has stood.

The Navajo cannot understand why all their protests should be of no avail. Three years ago they sent in a protest, signed by 139 Indians of that district, last year one signed by 88; after [that] they protested to Mr. Paquette against the activity of the ministers at Chin Lee, but without avail. Abusing and slandering us and our religion before the Indians only arouses the Indians so much the more against the ministers.[9]

Council at Fort Defiance, July 29, 1918[10]

On the 29th ultimo [last month] was a big council at Fort Defiance, called by Mr. Paquette for the purpose of appointing new headmen, defining their duties, and so on. The council had been called last February, but on account of a heavy snowfall, so few Indians appeared that it was postponed. About 300 Indians attended. After the marriage relations of the Navajo, the improvement and sale of their stock, dipping of their sheep had been discussed, one of the Indians from Chin Lee broached the Chin Lee matter. In a short time pandemonium reigned in the assembly hall. Very little was interpreted to Mr. Paquette, since several attempted to speak at the same time, and speakers followed each other without order in rapid succession. They represented the various districts of the reservation. When John Curly, the interpreter of Reverend Mr. [Howard A.] Clark, of Fort Defiance, a mission helper who has studied in one of their schools or seminaries, the same one who had told the Chin Lee Indians about that foundling asylum in Texas and the girls visiting priests in confession, and so on, when he and Tsehe Notah, a graduate of the Santa Fe school, arose to defend the ministers, their attempts only aroused the opposition of the council so much the more. Their pointing to the picture of Abraham Lincoln and telling the council to follow his teachings did not impress the audience; neither did the assertion that their religion came over to this country with the Pilgrim Fathers, and had been growing stronger ever since the time of their landing. All speakers with the exception of these two (and one who stated that he belonged to the Episcopal Church and that he did not oppose any one) were very emphatic in demanding that the ministers should leave the reservation or that they should be "run off" the reservation. Some of the sentences uttered were:

Why should we wish to have those among us who poison people?

The ministers have done nothing for us; Mr. Paquette, Chee Dodge, and the priests are the only ones who are helping us.

We don't want the religion of the ministers; we only want the religion of the priests, and no other!

The priests are at St. Michaels, Fort Defiance, Chin Lee, Lukachukai, and Tohatchi; and there is where we want to send our children to school.

The ministers are talking against Mr. Paquette, our agent, against the priests, the headmen, and the policemen and all of us; we ought to run them off! They only make trouble for us!

The rest of the assembly gave their assent to the sentiments expressed in a loud and demonstrative way.

When comparative quiet had been restored, Chee Dodge, who with Mr. Paquette and William Ayza, the interpreter, had his seat on the stage, and had been interpreting at times, addressed the assembly and Mr. Paquette in Navajo. His speech was interpreted by William Ayza, the official interpreter.

He began by recounting certain provisions of their treaty with the government: 1) the building of schools, 2) the punishment of whites who commit any wrong upon the person or property of the Navajo, and 3) that no one except government officials and employees of the government shall ever be permitted to pass over, settle upon, or reside on the treaty reservation. Having described the protests of the Indians against the ministers as expressed in protesting petitions, in councils and meetings at Chin Lee, and now here at this council, where practically all had demanded that the ministers be put off the reservation, he voiced his surprise that no attention is being paid to all this, that the provisions of the treaty are not executed, and that Mr. Paquette is taking no action and no steps to comply with their demands in this respect. He then asked Mr. Paquette whether he was going to wait a few years longer, to see perhaps whether the other side would not obtain the upperhand in the meantime. Turning to the audience he asked whether he had not voiced their sentiments. The assembly yelled its assent and its approval.

All eyes were now turned to Mr. Paquette, expecting his answer.

Mr. Paquette told them, during all the years he had spent in the Indian Service he had tried to do the right thing; while a subordinate, he had kept aloof from religious questions; as superintendent he had always tried to be fair and just. He assured them the power to comply with their wishes and move the ministers off the reservation had not been granted him by the department; he had to obey the rules and regulations and the orders of the Indian Office. He reminded them that at least 100 Navajo had given their signatures to the ministers, requesting that they give religious instructions to their children; "they at least," he added, "do not wish that the ministers be moved off the reservation." Here a Navajo jumped up and interrupted him, saying: "Yes, but how did they get these signatures?" "They go from hogan to hogan and ask the Indians: What is your name? They write down the name and get his mark and then, after they have his signature, tell him: Very well; we will give religious instruction to your children." Mr Paquette ignored this remark and detailed to them his calling the council at Chin Lee last July a year ago, the attitude of the council, the absence of the ministers, their subsequent request for a mission site at Chin Lee, and so on. As near as I can remember, he concluded his address by saying: "Since the land they asked for was not needed for school purposes, I sent their request to the Indian Office, informing the office that the land in question is on the treaty reservation, and that 88 Indians had given me their signature against granting the mission site and 11 for granting the site. All this I sent to the Indian Office and am now awaiting a decision and instructions from Washington."

The council then asked Mr. Paquette to report all that was said by this council in this matter to the Indian Office. Mr. Paquette answered them, he would await the answer of the office to his report regarding the mission site at Chin Lee *first*, before he would do so.

Now, my dear Mr. Lusk, you will readily see that the communication of the vigorous protests and emphatic demands of this large council, made after the decision has been given in the Chin Lee matter, would be belated and nugatory. You will also see that Mr. Paquette refuses to make the sentiments and wishes of the Indians in this matter known to the Indian Office. On that account Chee Dodge and the other leading headmen have requested me to inform the Indian Office of these proceedings. I have but one explanation of Mr. Paquette's refusal: that he is afraid of the influence of the ministers with the Indian Office. In the fall of 1916 one of the ministers said they had the *assurance* that Mr. Paquette would be removed. Now one of the former interpreters of the ministers, Wallace Peshlakai, is telling some of the Indians that Mr. Paquette "is going to go." Mr. Paquette knows this, knows that the ministers have been trying for years to have him ousted, knows of the actions and sayings of one of the late supervisors, and is, evidently, afraid to represent the wishes of the Indians to the department.

I do not admire the shrewdness of the ministers. Their talks against me and us and our religion and their talks against Mr. Paquette infuriate the Indians. The ministers have sown the wind, and are now reaping the whirlwind. On a par with this is their insistent obtrusion at Chin Lee. This year the fourth Minister is holding forth at that place: Mr. Green, who left Chin Lee last spring, is now running a restaurant at Gallup; Mr. Baldwin did not last long; Mr. [H. Dudley] Peck, accused of poisoning the two Chin Lee Indians, has now been replaced by a Reverend Mr. [David K.] Ward, from Tuba, Arizona.[11]

If they should be successful with the Indian Office, obtain a mission site at Chin Lee, and oust Mr. Paquette, the whirlwind might change into a hurricane.

It would be of a piece of their tactics if they would accuse me before the Indian Office of having instigated and engineering that uproar during the council at Fort Defiance. I assure you the thing was altogether spontaneous; I had absolutely nothing to do with it, neither directly nor indirectly; I knew nothing of it. I had seen but one man from Chin Lee before the council, and he told me they would bring up the poisoning case at council, since Mr. Paquette had not done anything in the matter. And that is as far as my knowledge went.

One reason why I think they might do so is that their interpreter and mission helper, Mr. John Curly, came to me during the council and after the council, and asked me in great excitement whether I was in favor of running all the ministers off the reservation; whether I thought that Reverend Mr. Peck had poisoned the Indians, and a number of other questions. I did not give him much satisfaction, though I assured him I had nothing to do with that uproar. I asked him, however, whether he thought I should be quiet and say nothing while they were distributing the *Menace* among the Indians and books like "My Life in the Convent," "Who Started This War?" "Roman Catholicism Exposed"; while they were telling the Indians such stories like the one about the foundling asylum in Texas and girls visiting the priests during confession; while they were trying to destroy our work by such methods and by trying their best to have Catholic pupils became Protestant, and to have parents change their signatures in their favor, and so on.

In answer to his accusation that I was impeding the spread of Christianity by opposing them, I told him different people had different views as to what Christianity really is, but Christianity most certainly did not consist in slandering, misrepresenting, and vilifying those who differ from us.

I beg you to communicate these occurrences to the Indian commissioner as an additional protest against granting a mission site to the Presbyterians at Chin Lee.

"We Surely Don't Want Such People among Us"[12]

I am writing you this letter at the request of several Navajo of Chin Lee. Not long ago two inspectors were here to look at and to report on the site which the preachers want for their mission. These inspectors, especially one, seemed very favorably inclined toward the preachers. Since these inspectors left here, the preacher here received a load of lumber. Whether he wants this lumber to put up a temporary shack for the winter, or whether it is only an advance load for more to come, or not, nobody knows. It has made some of the Navajo about here excited, especially since John Gorman told Jake Tom, the headman, that the inspectors had given the preacher permission to build.

Attsidi Yazhin Biye, Hashtl'ishni Naez, and Jake Tom protested very emphatically, saying they absolutely don't want the preachers here. Wherever they come, they said, they act as if they owned everything, and once they have a house here they will act as if the whole reservation belongs to them. This is a part of the treaty reservation; it does not belong to the Americans; it was given to the Navajo by special treaty. What right, therefore, has anyone to build a house on it against the wish and will of the Indians, and in spite of their repeated protests? We don't want them to build.

Years ago we gave our consent to the building of a Catholic mission, and we think one mission is enough for us here. We don't want any more missions. The priests have done the Navajo lots of good, not only by teaching and advising, not only by giving them food and lodging, but also in many other ways. The preachers have never done them any good, but wherever they came they stirred up trouble and quarrels. That's what they have done here and will do much more once they have a house here. Therefore we don't want them. If they once start to build and the headmen go there and throw over their stones, there will be trouble; if we let them build their house and then go and tear it down, there will be more serious trouble. Therefore we don't want them to start building. Three cases are known where the preachers caused the death of the Navajo and we surely don't want such people among us. John Brown, Hastin Dilawushi, Bidagha Naezi, Hastin Snaez, and others think and speak the same as we do.

These and other things were said and they asked me to let you know. They also asked if you could let them know if Washington had given the preachers permission to build, and advise them what to do. They seemed very anxious that you should know this, and very anxious to know what you will say to them, and would be glad to hear from you soon.

"They Will Simply Tell Him That He Must Go"[13]

Dan Kinlichini arrived here from Chin Lee yesterday evening before supper, and after supper he asked me to write to you, and to tell you that the headmen, Attsidi Yazhin Biye, Doyał'ihi (Cannot Talk), Bidagha Naezi, and others, want to know the exact lines of the treaty reservation, because the preachers claim that Chin Lee is not on the treaty reservation and that therefore they do not need the consent of the Indians to build there.

Furthermore, he said that Hastin Snaez, Attsidi Yazhin Biye, and others intend to go to the preacher at Chin Lee in a friendly way and kindly ask him to move away from Chin Lee, since they don't want him there. If he refuses to go, or if he begins to quarrel with them, or if he uses any harsh words they will simply tell him that he must go, that they will force him to go, and that if he threatens them in any way, either with a gun, an ax, or any other instrument, they too will use violence and do him bodily harm and if necessary kill him. Dan said that Hastin Snaez is still very much worked up over the death of his two brothers, and that he attributes the death of Bisadi to the poisoning affair of several months ago, and that some of the other Indians say that in consequence Hastin Snaez is liable to do almost anything in an unguarded moment and do harm to the preacher, and that even some of the younger Indians may go to his assistance.

Dan wants me to tell you that he is doing all in his power to help our cause by telling the Indians of his own experience with the preachers at Shiprock for seven and a half years, by telling them that the preacher there used to tell him and others that they must not hate anybody, that they must not tell lies, and so on, and that this very same preacher hated Mr. Shelton, made accusations against him at Washington, practically caused his resignation, and the like, and thus acted contrary to his own teachings to the Indian children, and that he has found out from his own experience what the preachers are. He mentioned some other points that are contained in Leopold's letter to Chee, and therefore it will not be necessary to repeat them.

Mr. Paquette was here on Wednesday and told me that he had a talk with preacher Clark on Tuesday. He said that Clark told him that Mr. Ward, the preacher at Chin Lee, had written to him (Clark) that Leopold had called a council of Chin Lee Indians and that at this council a delegation was elected to call upon the preacher and ask him to leave Chin Lee, but that said delegation had not yet come to him (Ward). Dan said that this is not true, but that Indians had called upon Leopold, as stated above, and had told of their intent at various levels of going to the preacher and telling him in a friendly way (as brothers) to leave Chin Lee, since they did not want him there.

Clark told Paquette further that they (Presbyterians) were going to fight the Chin Lee affair to a finish or to the bitter end. He also told Paquette that the Presbyterians do not want him (Paquette) to be removed from Fort Defiance; that he (P.) was as good a friend as they could ever expect, but that he might just as well go now since he had served the Catholics' purpose. He did not mention in what this "Catholic purpose" consisted, neither did Mr. P. ask him in what it consisted, but Paquette told him that he thought they had no reason for complaint, since he always tried his best to be fair to both sides. . . .

"Even Now They Are Combing the Black Mountains"[14]

I shall try my best to get Mr. Paquette to write a good letter to the Indian Office. I shall compose it, if he lets me, which I think he will. Mr. Linnen [E. B. Linnen, a federal investigator in the inquiry into the conduct of Superintendent Peter Paquette] thinks that the site should not be granted, since it is on the treaty reservation, and since the vast majority of the Indians vigorously object to it. He told me if he were called back to Washington now, he would speak against this grant and explain matters.

I realize the "delicacy" of the position of Catholics advising the secretary in this matter. But would Presbyterians feel the same delicacy in the opposite case? Not upon your life!

You are right in saying you did not know how our Catholics are going to buck up against this proposition, namely: the argument of Mr. Sells that the minority must have right of representation and right of religious instruction—if that alone were the question, and if the Chin Lee case was an ordinary one. But, first of all, the Presbyterians do not want to establish themselves there mainly to give religious instruction to *their* children, which number two or three, but to give religious instruction to children that were Catholic, or for whom *we* had obtained the signatures. Even now they are combing the Black Mountains and making a fierce drive to induce the Indians to change their signatures, and they have succeeded with some; with how many I do not know. One Indian that was here a few days ago said they had obtained second signatures for 90. I am sure that is an exaggeration, but it shows that they claim a large number of our children right now. A few years ago they had obtained through misrepresentations and fraud some 18 or 20 second signatures. Last spring they claimed about 20 of our children. But since Mr. Paquette's ruling stood, and they had to appear before him to ask for the change, none of them did so. When the ministers had left them, they were sorry they had given in to their persistent urging, and were glad the second signatures did not count without going before Mr. Paquette. I have written you before about the slanders they are persistently spreading against us and our Church and its Priesthood. I hear now (though I had no chance to verify this) that their interpreter is intimidating the parents by telling them if they did not change their signatures, they would be arrested. I have no doubt they are telling the Indians that Mr. Paquette, whom they have called our slave, was going to be dismissed, that they have the permission to build at Chin Lee, and that it is much better for them to change their signatures in their favor.

Then the "poisoning episode" has aroused the Indians so much that it would be inadvisable to grant the site to them, if the Indian Office wishes to avoid trouble. I am afraid that the Indian commissioner and possibly Mr. Lane [secretary of the interior] is of the opinion that the Indians at Chin Lee would not be opposed to the grant of the mission site, if I had not been in the back of it. The Navajo have refused a mission site years ago at Red Lake, before I was in the country, and Lieutenant Plummer made the ministers stop building. At Red Rock they refused without [my] having anything to do with it, in fact without my knowledge. The same is true at the Wheatfield under Commissioner [Francis E.] Leupp. It is true, I have upheld the Chin Lee Indians in their opposition on account of the *Menace* tactics and on account of the proselyting of the ministers, but I did not originate their opposition, nor am I responsible for the intensified opposition on account of the poisoning episode.

If I were the secretary of the interior, I would call in Mr. [Thomas C.] Moffett[15] and I would tell him that until his ministers desisted from bringing such outrageous charges: our ravishing girls, having an asylum in Texas filled with children of priests, our leading the whole tribe straight to hell, and God knows how many other variations: until they desisted from fighting tooth and nail to get the parents of our children to change signatures in their favor; until they desisted in bedeviling the superintendents if they do not assist them in their pernicious activities, neither the Chin Lee mission site nor any other mission site would be granted to them.

"I Shall Continue to Oppose Such Skunks"[16]

I must write you some more developments in the Chin Lee affair. On the 23rd ultimo Major McLaughlin stopped off here on his way to Fort Defiance, where Captain Throwbridge was waiting for him. He did not know what they were to investigate. Their instructions awaited him at Ford Defiance. I sent an Indian up to find out. He brought the following letter from Mr. Paquette: Major McLaughlin and Captain Throwbridge will leave for Chin Lee tomorrow morning. The rest you can guess. We are not wanted there." [In Chin Lee, Chee Dodge served the inspectors as interpreter, having borrowed Father Anselm's car to get there] . . .

I awaited his return at his home. The inspectors only called the headmen of Chin Lee to inquire about their attitude toward the granting [of] the mission site to the Presbyterians. The Indians told them they did not want the Presbyterians there, and if they started to build, they would tear down the building. They told them the place was on the treaty reservation, and they had a right to refuse They told them about where the treaty reservation line is.

Once the Indians had had a meeting at Father Leopold's place and there decided to run the preacher off. The inspectors inquired from the Indians why the meeting had been held at our place. Whether they had been called, and whether I had been present. The Indians answered them: they kept all their meetings at Father Leopold's mission; that we had nothing to do with it, however, and that they had not been called: they had gone there of their own accord; and that I had not been at Chin Lee at the time. One said he had told the Indians at that meeting that it would never do to start out from Father Leopold's place, since that would be misconstrued; that they decided to go to the minister from their own homes and tell him to leave. They added that someone from the Gorman crowd had been listening during the meeting, that he informed the preacher of their intention, and when they went to tell the preacher, he had left already.

He returned, however, and later began to put up a temporary shack. Thereupon, they told the inspectors [that] Hastin Snaez, the brother of the two they claimed were poisoned by the preacher, went to the preacher and told him to leave; that Hastin Snaez had done this of his own accord, without their knowledge.

The ministers had the signatures for the mission site from 63 people. The inspectors inquired very minutely about these signatures and found that the names of a number of little children, one only four years old, were on the list. If I am not mistaken, they had not only the names of women and small children, but also the names of such as do not belong to the Chin Lee district.

The inspectors went to see the Gormans, practically the only ones who favor granting the mission site. Chee Dodge does not know what was said by them, since several of them speak English very well, and the inspectors did not need Chee Dodge as interpreter and did not take him along.

The Inspectors told Mrs. Nelson Gorman that, even with the 63 signatures, those who wanted the mission site granted, represented only three percent of the Indians belonging to the Chin Lee district.

I have written to you what the ministers and others said about the end of the world being near at hand. The inspectors inquired of Mrs. Nelson Gorman what had been said in the respect. She told them and tried to prove to them from the Bible that the end was near. They told her they did not wish to discuss the question, but were only inquiring what had been said.

I saw both inspectors after their return from Chin Lee, but they said *noddings* about the investigation: they only inquired of me about the location of the western boundary line of the treaty reservation. I told them I had a tracing of the plat made by the surveyors, obtained from Santa Fe Land Office, which showed conclusively that Chin Lee is on the treaty reservation. On their way to Gallup they stopped at our place to look at that tracing. Aside from the question of the boundary line nothing at all was said about the investigation by the inspectors. All the information I have, I have from Chee Dodge. From what he told me, I am inclined to think that they will make an adverse report.

You know I never made any secret of it that I encouraged the Indians to oppose the granting of the mission site. But we had nothing to do with that meeting in which they decided to run off the preacher. We never encouraged them to run them off, or to tear down their building; neither did we coincide with their assertion that the minister had poisoned those Indians.

All we did was to tell them Chin Lee was on the treaty reservation and that they had a perfect right to refuse a mission site to them, and that, if they refused, it could not be granted; that we did not want them there, giving our reasons for not wanting them.

One of the Indians told the inspectors that at one time, when they had a meeting at Chin Lee in the presence of the archbishop (Pitaval), they had agreed that ours should be the only mission at Chin Lee; that they wanted to keep their agreement; but even aside from that agreement, they did not want them.

The preachers have sown the wind and are reaping the whirlwind. And some more whirlwind is coming.

Only last week the Reverend Mr. Clark, minister at Fort Defiance, told three young married Navajo women, one a graduate of our school, the other two graduates of the Fort Defiance school, all three Catholic, that *all Catholic priests* had children, and were calling them, their children, "Jesus." Then he went on to talk against confession and the Mass, and so on. He told them this in Mr. G. U. Manning's store at Fort Defiance.

Of course, I shall continue to oppose such skunks. They ought to be lynched if there is no other way to stop them.

The End of the Chin Lee Affair

[During Father Anselm's final illness the struggle for Chin Lee was much on his mind. In one of his last letters, written from a convalescent home a little over a week before his final relapse, he wrote Father Leopold: "The final hearing in Chin Lee case took place before Secretary Payne on 12th instant [this month]. Preachers, Indian Rights crowd, women, and one of the *Gormans* from Chin Lee and Reverend Mr. [Frederick G.] Mitchell were present. Mitchell interpreted for Gorman. What Gorman was it, I am wondering. Father Ketcham thinks the decision will be in our favor; he will let me know as soon as the decision is made known."[17] The next day he wrote Father Ketcham that "I am sorry I could not be present at that hearing before Secretary Payne. It would have been so very interesting for me." He went on to reminisce about the Navajo family that had "sponsored" the Protestants in Chin Lee: "Before the preachers 'worked on them' and turned them, the Gormans were friendly to us. One of their daughters—possibly the daughter of that 'missionary'—was Catholic, but turned Protestant and is now at Riverside. Even Nelson Gorman and his wife, the former trader, their mainstay, used to come to our chapel and have their children come to our chapel at times."[18]

Father Ketcham helpfully responded with the following description of the hearing before Secretary of the Interior John Barton Payne, but there is some question whether Father Anselm ever read the letter. Written in Washington, D.C., on February 22, it would have arrived in Rochester, Minnesota, about the time Father Weber's relapse necessitated emergency surgery (he received Last Sacraments on February 26, the emergency surgery on February 28, and passed away March 8, 1921).]

Hearing on Chin Lee before the Secretary of the Interior, 1921[19]

You say that you would be glad to know what was said at the hearing by Gorman and Mitchell. So far as I can remember, Gorman made a speech telling how he used to be a pagan and used to pluck out his beard and throw it to the bears, and how he worshiped snakes and other animals; he said that he had been a liar—an awful liar; he also said: "I don't mind telling you that I had stolen." But he explained how he had listened to the teaching of the "shortcoats" and had become a Christian man. He begged the secretary of the interior to let him have a prayer house at Chin Lee where the Navajo could learn of the true God.

Mitchell interpreted for him. Nothing of a bitter nature was said by Mitchell or Gorman, their contention being that non-Catholic Indians—Gorman and his family, and others—should have the privilege of worshiping God according to the dictates of their own conscience.

The secretary asked Gorman if he had ever attended a Catholic church. I think he said he lived about a mile and a half distant from it, and that he had never attended it, but that his daughter had and that she reported to him that they followed quite a different system in the Catholic Church from what they did in the "shortcoat" chapel. Gorman also said that he was very glad he had made the trip to Washington, that he had stopped off at Kansas City, that he had found many, many friends, and that he now knows what he never knew before—that there are a great many "shortcoats" in the United States, whereas he had been told that there were hardly any. He will now be able to enlighten his people on all these points, so that they will not be deceived hereafter by reports that there are not any "shortcoats" in the country.

The secretary of the interior asked Gorman why it would not be all right for them to build their chapel just off the treaty reservation. He replied that that might be a solution to the question. Mitchell, also, when questioned, said that might be a solution, and that he would take it under advisement; after a few minutes he came back with the statement that off the reservation the chapel would be located in the red hills where there would be no water.

Mitchell made much ado of his knowing the Navajo language, and gave out some enlightenment regarding the Navajo verb. When the secretary asked him how he learned the language he replied that he had "lived and slept and scratched with the Indians." Several times in his remarks he referred to "our Catholic friends." He made the statement that because the Catholic missionaries were first among the Navajo, the expression for missionary in Navajo is "longcoat," and hence, to designate the Presbyterian missionary they had to call him the "shortcoated longcoat."

[As it happened, it was not Secretary Payne, before whom the hearing had transpired, but the new secretary of the interior, Albert B. Fall, whose decision finally would end the struggle over whether the Protestants could have a mission site in Chin Lee over the protestations of the great majority of the Navajo residents.]

Progress Reports from Father Ketcham in Washington, D.C.

April 5, 1921: As for Chin Lee, the matter has not yet been decided. We had two hearings before the secretary of the interior, Mr. Payne, and after the last hearing the Presbyterians seemed to become alarmed and in some way or other the matter was sent to the attorney general. The attorney general then referred it down to the Interior Department for an opinion from the solicitor. Of course, we do not know what that opinion was, but we find now that it is before the present attorney general—the unpleasantness having been passed on from our former "brave" administration to this one. There is absolutely nothing to be done. The matter will now be decided and we will get the notification, I suppose, in due time. Appearances seem to be in favor of the contention of the Indians of Chin Lee, but, of course, we are never sure of anything in this world. The matter should have been settled by the last administration. It is a pity that such an embarrassing legacy should have been handed over to a new administration just coming in.[20]

June 29, 1921: Things have not been going well in the controversy about Chin Lee. The other administration left this question as a legacy to the new secretary of the interior and commissioner of Indian Affairs. Recently the Presbyterians have been extremely busy and they have so engineered things that they have gotten up to the secretary himself a letter, for his signature, approving the authority for the Presbyterians to locate at Chin Lee. At this moment, the Catholic side of the question has been brought to the attention of Secretary Fall, and he is holding up the matter for consideration and some further investigation.[21]

July 16, 1921: On speaking to various parties in the Indian Office concerning the Chin Lee case, we consequently meet with the statement that the case is closed, and that the permission was granted the Presbyterians. They do not seem to realize that the case was reopened and that the permit of the Presbyterians was suspended, pending an investigation concerning the contention as to whether or not Chin Lee is in the treaty reserve.[22]

October 6, 1921: Has anything transpired in the matter of the contention of the Presbyterians to locate a resident missionary at Chin Lee? . . . As for me, I have heard nothing and the secretary is away from Washington just now. . . . Please let me know just how far the site that was set apart for the Presbyterian mission at Chin Lee would be from the school itself and also how far the Presbyterian site would be from your church site.[23]

The Response from Chin Lee

October 28, 1921: [S]ince the last two months or so, there is a resident Presbyterian missionary here at Chin Lee. He resides in a building, which was formerly owned by Nelson Gorman, a Navaho, and used by him as a trading store. I was told he has dropped remarks of intending to build a church and a residence.

Some time ago there were rumors floating about out here, that the Presbyterians had received permission from Washington to put up mission buildings out here. When the Indians heard this, they, of their own accord, and on their own initiative, held several councils on this matter and protested emphatically against granting land and giving permission to erect buildings thereon contrary to the wishes and protests of an overwhelming majority of the Indians, especially since Chin Lee is on the old treaty reservation, and they had in no way been consulted and asked for their consent. They had, moreover, protested several times already to inspectors.

These councils were held, at some distance from Chin Lee, either in the latter part of July or the fore part of August, so far as I can remember. After holding these councils, the Indians came to me and asked me to write a letter for them to Washington with their protest and their signatures, asking the government to help them in their rights and to uphold the stipulations of the treaty. Since none of them was able to write, and believing them to be in their rights, I did so, addressing the letter with about 230 signatures to Mr. Dockweiler. I sent the letters to Father Marcellus, at St. Michaels, and he has probably by this time forwarded it to you.[24]

January 22, 1922: I am enclosing copies of letters, recently sent me. Please look them over and let me know if this thing is true, after all the protests of a vast and overwhelming majority of Indians of this region, repeatedly sent in to Washington?

Chin Lee is three miles within the lines of the Navajo treaty reservation, and this fact is one of the main objections of the Indians to anyone taking up land and putting up buildings against their will and consent. The Indians look upon the treaty with the government somewhat like we look upon our Constitution, that is, they consider it a document, a pact, or a contract, which ought to be honored, respected, and held sacred by both contracting parties, and which ought to be upheld religiously according to stipulations and agreements contained therein. Consequently, they cannot understand how Washington, or the government, can break its given word and its solemn promises against the repeatedly expressed protests of an overwhelming majority of Indians, and then expect them to honor and respect the laws of the country, or to uphold their end of the treaty.

They are under the impression, which according to their treaty is correct, that nobody has a right to take up any of their treaty land and build upon it, except with their will and consent. Therefore, it looks to them as if their treaty rights have been grossly disregarded and violated, or, to use a phrase, frequently used in the few last years as if their treaty were a mere "scrap of paper."

If the above is really true, it seems as if another chapter is to be added to "A Century of Dishonor." . . .

P.S.— I was contemplating sending something like the above letter to several newspapers, and making this latest injustice against Indians public, but I will await your answer and advice.[25]

"There Is Nothing More To Be Done"

[Had the Presbyterians lost at the level of the Department of the Interior, it was rumored they would appeal to the president. Instead, the Catholics lost, and there was no further appeal. To judge from occasional combative statements by the late Father Anselm, had he still been present there might have been further fight. Perhaps even, as Father Leopold suggested, an appeal to public opinion. But Father Anselm was gone, and so, by year's end, was Father Ketcham. Father Marcellus Troester, the new Superior of St. Michael's Mission, was cautious, and so was Mr. Charles Lusk, the longtime secretary of the Bureau of Catholic Indian Missions. Father Marcellus even thought he spied a silver lining in the final resolution of the controversy. He stated, with some finality, the conservative policy the Navajo missions would follow.]

Your letter received, also enclosure to Mr. Lusk which I am sending on to him. There is nothing more to be done in the case, as far as I can see, with a view of having the permission rescinded, since the attorney general gave the decision in favor of the Protestants. Neither would I consider it good policy, at the present time, to publish this affair in the papers, first, because our opinion in regard to the treaty has been [judged to be] erroneous, and second, because this very decision of the Attorney General will most likely be our own advantage in the near future. [The Franciscans were trying to gain a foothold at Zuni Pueblo, where the Protestant minister was circulating a petition seeking to have the Catholic Fathers prevented from establishing a mission, and a majority of the Zuni were opposed to allowing in the Franciscan missionaries.] . . .

As to Chin Lee, I would not lose courage and consider everything lost, but rather take things as they are and make the best of them. After all, we could not expect to keep the Protestants out for ever anyhow. What if the reservation were thrown open? As it is, the vast majority of Indians adhere to us and we should make every effort to hold them. Give them to understand that it is in their power to freeze out the ministers. Let the Protestants spend their thousands in putting up buildings, and if the Indians steer clear of them, keep all children away from them, and don't let them interfere in their home life, they will soon be sorry for having forced themselves in and the Indians can still have only one religion for their children.[26]

[Father Marcellus's advice to Father Leopold to accept the defeat and move on was strongly seconded by Secretary Lusk of the Bureau of Catholic Indian Missions.]

Father Marcellus Troester has forwarded to me your letter of January 22, in regard to the decision of the secretary of the interior in setting aside the site at Chin Lee for the Presbyterians. While, of course, we do not think the secretary was warranted in making the decision in question, it has been made, and is based upon an opinion of the attorney general. *The matter is therefore closed*, and it would be useless to attempt to bring about a reversal of the secretary's action. Going into the press and indulging in criticism of the secretary would, I venture to suggest, do no good, and might do us a great deal of harm. His answer to any criticism that might be made would be that his decision was based upon the advice of the attorney general, who is the legal adviser of the president, and this would be a complete answer. Newspaper criticism of the secretary would necessarily offend him greatly and might have a tendency to prejudice him in regard to other matters which we may have occasion in the future to submit for his consideration and action. We cannot afford to take any chance in this regard. I therefore trust you will accept the situation as philosophically as possible and regard it as a closed incident.[27]

Notes

1. Bruce Lee Taylor, "Presbyterians and 'The People': A History of Presbyterian Missions and Ministries to the Navajo" (Ph.D. diss., Union Theological Seminary, Richmond, Virginia, 1988), 945–46, 964, 971.

2. Anselm Weber to William H. Ketcham, 8 December 1915. BCIM Series 1, Box 93, fd. 1.

3. Weber to Charles S. Lusk, 14 October 1916. BCIM Series 1, Box 98, fd. 21.

4. Weber to Lusk, 1 October 1917. BCIM Series 1, Box 109, fd. 1.

5. Under this heading are excerpts from three letters, each identified by the citation at the end of that excerpt.

6. Leopold Ostermann to Weber, 2 June 1918. FAC Box DEC.248. Weber, Anselm Let., fd. Weber, Anselm. Ketcham & Lusk. 1915–1924. DI14.

7. Ostermann to Weber, 18 June 1918. BCIM Series 1, Box 109, fd. 1.

8. Apparently, nothing ever did happen with regard to "solving" the case of the poisoned Navajo. About a year later Father Anselm, writing in defense of the beleaguered Fort Defiance Agency Superintendent Peter Paquette, who at the instigation of the Protestant ministers was being investigated on charges ranging from favoritism to incompetence, described Paquette's initial inquiries about the poisoning and his obtaining a commitment from the Chin Lee Navajo that they would abstain from violence. Father Anselm concluded, "No further investigation was ever made of this case. If I had been in the place of Reverend Mr. Peck, I would have demanded an investigation to clear myself in the eyes of the Indians. I am quite certain Mr. Paquette never reported this episode to the Indian Office." Weber to E. B. Linnen, 7 June 1919. BCIM Series 1, Box 113, fd. 27.

9. Weber to Ketcham, 4 July 1918. BCIM Series 1, Box 109, fd. 1.

10. Weber to Lusk, 8 August 1918. FAC Box PLA.071 Chinle AZ, fd. Chinle AZ Letters 1910–1918.

11. For further information on Presbyterian ministers involved in the Chin Lee struggle, see Taylor, for example, 968–71, 1018, 1036–38, 1054–55.

12. Ostermann to Henry C. (Chee) Dodge, 18 December 1918. FFP Box 1, fd. 6.

13. Celestine Matz to Weber, 10 January 1919. FFP Box 1, fd. 6.

14. Weber to Ketcham, 18 June 1919. BCIM Series 1, Box 113, fd. 17.

15. Thomas C. Moffett was head of the Presbyterian Mission Board, later president of the Indian Committee of the Federal Council of Churches, and a powerful lobbyist for the Presbyterians.

16. Weber to Ketcham, 6 October 1919. BCIM Series 1, Box 113, fd. 28.

17. Weber to Ostermann, 15 February 1921. FFP Box 1, fd. 3.

18. Weber to Ketcham, 16 February 1921. BCIM Series 1, Box 124, fd. 14.

19. Ketcham to Weber, 22 February 1921. BCIM Series 1, Box 124, fd. 14.

20. Ketcham to Ludger Oldegeering, 5 April 1921, BCIM Series 1, Box 124, fd. 14.

21. Ketcham to Marcellus Troester, 29 June 1921. BCIM Series 1, Box 124, fd. 14.

22. Ketcham to Isidore B. Dockweiler, 16 July 1921. BCIM Series 1, Box 124, fd. 14.

23. Ketcham to Ostermann, 6 October 1921. BCIM Series 1, Box 124, fd. 14.

24. Ostermann to Ketcham, 28 October 1921. BCIM Series 1, Box 124, fd. 14.

25. Ostermann to Lusk, 22 January 1922. BCIM Series 1, Box 124, fd. 14.

26. Troester to Ostermann, 25 January 1922. BCIM Series 1, Box 130, fd. 10.

27. Lusk to Ostermann, 8 February 1922. BCIM Series 1, Box 124, fd. 14.

31

Influenza Epidemic

Berard Haile, O.F.M., and Anselm Weber, O.F.M.

[The influenza epidemic of fall and winter 1918–1919, and its less devastating reprise the following winter, were the worst calamity to befall the Navajo tribe since their incarceration at Fort Sumner in 1864. The 1918 epidemic was a national and international disaster as well, killing over a half-million Americans and, worldwide, perhaps as many as 21 million souls.[1] The effects of the epidemics were notably severe among American Indians, and the Navajo proved especially vulnerable. Survival seems to have been contingent upon the victims of the disease receiving appropriate care, and most Navajo not only lacked access to such care but followed cultural practices that heightened mortality, such as exposing the very ill to the elements rather than allowing them to die in the family dwelling, seeking the ministrations of itinerant "singers" who carried the infection about with them, and assembling family members and neighbors in ceremonial "sings."[2]

The Navajo who lived through it remember the time as "when that flu came and killed all the People."[3] Some sense of the immediate impact of the disease is conveyed in a pair of eyewitness accounts. Franc Newcomb, wife of white trader Arthur J. Newcomb, wrote:

> The first persons to die were buried in the accustomed manner, but soon death struck too fast and the living members of the family were too sick and too weak to attend to the burials. Throughout the valley there were many deserted hogans containing two or three corpses, wrapped in their blankets and covered with a little brush, loose earth, or ashes. The fleeing relatives did their best to block the doors and the smoke holes with logs and brush to prevent entry by coyotes and wild dogs. Small children and old people were the first victims, but the flu played no favorites and soon the death rate was just as high among the strong men and women. The whole atmosphere was filled with dread and nervous tension that no one could escape.[4]

Rose Mitchell, who experienced the epidemic in the Chin Lee area, remembers:

> That sickness hit us in the fall; it started spreading across the reservation almost overnight and lots and lots of people died from it. People would feel fine during

438

the day, get sick in the night, and by morning, they'd have all passed away. It was like that. It killed whole families overnight; up to about twenty people in a family would die in one night. It seemed to really hit the young children; little children all over the area were dying day and night, night after night. People died right and left. No one knew what it was. . . . Because no one knew what it was, no one knew what to do about it; even the people trained to find out the causes of illnesses . . . even they couldn't determine what was happening or what should be done about it.[5]

The ravages of the epidemic were a major demographic shock to the Navajo people. Estimates of overall mortality run in the range of 10 to 15 percent.[6] There were also attending psychological costs to the survivors, long-term emotional reactions to suffering and loss that several commentators have identified[7] but no one has analyzed well, perhaps because the data are so sparse, and this, too, because of a Navajo cultural trait. In the words of Rose Mitchell, "I don't remember who else we lost at that time; when people die, we don't talk about them ever again. We don't speak about those things, mention their names, or think about it. Those are our rules about that; we just try to stop thinking about it after they've been lost like that."[8]

Where medical facilities were available, as at Fort Defiance, near St. Michaels, the Franciscan missionaries helped to nurse the sick who filled the hospitals to overflowing. Father Anselm, responsible for the well being of the Navajo students at St. Michaels, imposed a strict quarantine on the school that, miraculously, minimized the impact of the epidemic there (a visiting sister, infected while traveling, died of the flu isolated at St. Michaels, but the careful quarantine kept the disease from spreading to the children). About a month into the epidemic, after the worst of it seemed to have passed, Father Anselm sent a status report to Provincial Rudolph Bonner. A few weeks later he commented briefly on the epidemic in letters to Secretary Charles S. Lusk of the Bureau of Catholic Indian Missions. His most detailed record of the epidemic appeared early in 1919 as part of his *Der Sendbote* series. We begin chapter 31 with these reports by Father Anselm on the influenza epidemic as experienced at St. Michaels and Fort Defiance.

In more remote reaches of the reservation such as Lukachukai, where there was no access to modern medical assistance, little could be done but to try to make the victims comfortable, administer last rites, bury the dead, and wait for the plague to run its course. Thus did Father Berard watch, serve, and wait out the affliction. Early in December 1918 he reported to the provincial:

Of course we are snowed in for the winter but this is a month earlier than usual. West of us the Flu is still raging and decimating the Navaho. Here I have lost some of the Catholic parishioners, so far four or six. It's so hard to get a line on them as they were hidden in the piñons and then fled almost anywhere. Some were not even buried as whole families took sick and had nobody to look after the rest. We buried some but could not do justice to all. The brother took a severe cold so I put a stop to the sexton's job. It kept us busy for a while but now the situation seems normal again, at least in our valley.[9]

The chapter concludes with Father Berard's extensive notes on the epidemic at Lukachukai. Apparently these were intended as the initial installments in a series of articles on Navajo life and culture. His manuscript includes some lengthy digressions on his Navajo friends, stories that have no direct or necessary connection to the influenza epidemic. However, because they are relevant to our general interest in the Navajo as seen by the Franciscans, and because, for Berard, the path to these narratives begins with the epidemic, or perhaps wanders through it, they are presented here as he set them down.]

❖

Fort Defiance and St. Michaels, Fall 1918

Report to Father Provincial Rudolph Bonner, November 2[10]

Monday evening [October 21] I got a message from Chin Lee that Father Leopold was very sick and had asked for one of us to come to Chin Lee. Father Marcellus was at Tohatchi, and heavy rains had made it impossible for him to make the trip at night, so I sent an Indian to Sammie Day, 30 miles away, to come with his auto at once and take me to Chin Lee. We started about 10:00 and got to Chin Lee about 3:00. Father Leopold was up again. Sunday night he had an acute attack of indigestion, I think; all day Monday diarrhea; but Tuesday when I arrived he was well again. I had passed through Fort Defiance, and Father Emanuel told me he was well. But that same evening I got a message from the Fort that Father Emanuel was very sick. After visiting some sick around Chin Lee and baptizing a few I returned the next day to Fort Defiance. Thirteen children were sick in the Chin Lee school with the influenza; the other children had been dismissed from school and sent home before they got sick.

Father Leopold and myself visited those sick children Wednesday morning. Father Emanuel was sick in the government hospital with influenza, and Father Marcellus had arrived there the evening before and has stayed there ever since. I stayed at the Fort from Wednesday till Thursday afternoon, when I went home again. Father Marcellus was not exactly well, but he preferred to stay at the Fort where he would have medical attention; besides, he said, if he and I got the influenza the same time, things would be worse; I should let him get it first and then come up and take his place. He is well and Father Emanuel is up again; he did not get pneumonia, though he caught cold and was in danger of getting it. Dr. [Albert M.] Wigglesworth and his wife and three children are down with the influenza at Fort Defiance, but are getting well again. Dr. Hailmann is at Fort Defiance to look after the sick.

On the sixth I attended to Fort Defiance, and five children were sick, which sickness the doctor from Gallup, now dead also, pronounced a simple cold. On the ninth 250 were down with the influenza.

On the 12th I went to Gallup to see Father Elig and returned on the 14th. On the same day I went to Fort Defiance, where 300 were in bed.

Father Emanuel returned from Carlsbad on the 16th, so I went home on the 17th, after I and he had given the sacraments to those who were seriously ill. Thirty-six have died at the Fort so far, and one or two are not expected to live.

To keep our school from getting the influenza I have "quarantined" it, and am enforcing the quarantine as well as I can. I sent Father Celestine down there to stay at the school, so no one from here would infect it. They fixed a room for him in the rear of the south wing. Of course, they had to get the permission of Mother Katharine to do so. I had to be pretty harsh with the Mother and others to make them observe the quarantine. If I had gone away to Roswell, I am afraid the school would have been infected. The influenza is among the Indians in different camps now, but they seem to get over it, very few dying.

I was sorry to learn of the death of Father Theodore. I am going to Gallup this afternoon to attend the funeral tomorrow and to help out Sunday, returning here Monday.

Since Father Marcellus is building, I suppose I shall go to Fort Defiance Tuesday and relieve him, so that he can return to Tohatchi.

I am surprised that Father Marcellus and myself did not get the influenza, since we spent so many days and so much time each day among them.

Mother Katharine was here for a long time, and her companion, Mother Philip, died here at the school on the second ultimo [October 2].

I am not going to write for *Der Sendbote* this time. . . .

I have not begun to work on the magazine [the annual, *Franciscan Missions of the Southwest*] yet on account of the influenza. I hope to start soon now.

Father Elig was pretty sick, and it took him a long time to get over it. I was afraid Father Rembert would get it also, since he worked like a trooper day and night busy with sick calls especially the first week the influenza was prevalent in Gallup. I only put in three very hard days at Fort Defiance, when I first went up there.

Reports to Charles S. Lusk, December 1918 and February 1919

I do not remember how much or how little I have written you about the investigation of Fort Defiance, ourselves, and Chin Lee by Inspector Coleman and the newly appointed Inspector Endicott. I cannot say that I like them very much. They talk too much, especially Mr. Coleman; and they listen too much to people who are disloyal, liars, and no good in general. Several times they have made disparaging remarks about the way the influenza was handled, comparing our school, where I kept it away, and Fort Defiance, and the many deaths at Fort Defiance, and so on. Explanations do not seem to affect their attitude in the least.

They, at Fort Defiance, were taken by surprise. A few cases of sickness pronounced as ordinary colds by the doctor called from Gallup, and a few days after that the whole school—300—down with influenza. Dr. Wigglesworth arrived three days after the school was down. Dr. Hailmann a week or 10 days later. I was at Fort Defiance from the time the first deaths occurred for nearly a week, and after that, at intervals, to relieve other Fathers.

I know Mr. Paquette, the nurses, and employees called in immediately from Tohatchi and Chin Lee, did all they could, some working day and night. All, with very few exceptions, deserve the praise. Mr. Paquette did all that possibly could be done to relieve the situation. After such heroic work and sacrifices it must have sounded strange to the employees to be told in a meeting called by Inspector Coleman that every employee who did not do his or her duty was going to be fired, and so forth.[11]

They have also investigated the number of Navajo that died in the camps of the influenza! Mr. Paquette did all he could for the camp Indians, visiting them with the doctor, bringing them to the hospital in his auto, and so on. Of course, he could do nothing for those living very far from the agency. There is a limit to everything. Or did the Indian Office have spare doctors and nurses that would have been sent to those distant camps if Mr. Paquette had asked for such? What about our military camps? Why not investigate and suspend and decapitate everyone in authority whose "subjects" died in large numbers for want of attention?[12]

Report in *Der Sendbote,* March 1919[13]

On October 6 I conducted the worship service in Fort Defiance because Father Emanuel had traveled to Carlsbad for spiritual exercises. After the service I visited the hospital, and the hospital orderly informed me that five students were sick. If they were not suffering from the Spanish influenza, he said, then they couldn't explain their high fevers. In my ensuing conversation with Mr. Paquette [Peter Paquette, superintendent, Fort Defiance Agency] about the manner in which we can protect our schools against this disease, I brought up the question whether it wouldn't be wise to send all the children home before the outbreak of the disease, where they would be better protected from infection in their homes which are spread widely apart from each other. However, Mr. Paquette thought he would rather wait to make the decision until the doctor, called from Gallup, arrived and evaluated the sick children. He had learned that a few cases of this influenza had appeared on the reservation; to send the children home would hardly protect them from infection and would deprive them of medical and other help for their illness. The next day the doctor arrived at Fort Defiance and explained that the five students suffered from a very common cold. Three days later about 250 students there were in bed with true influenza. Mr. Paquette informed me that so far no one was seriously ill and promised to let me know immediately if the sickness should take a turn for the worse.

At that time we had 250 students in our school at St. Michaels. I conducted a strict quarantine there and ordered that no one leave the school grounds, and that no one, neither red nor white, could visit the school. Because we missionaries were daily placed in danger of infection, a few days later I had the music room of our school set up as living quarters and "banished" Father Celestine Matz, O.F.M., the chaplain of our school, there. We can thank these precautions and the prayers of the Sisters that our school has so far been completely protected from the influenza. Actually, not completely, because we had a death in our school. Around the end of September the honorable Mother Katharine Drexel, in the company of Mother Philip from the mother house at Cornwells Heights, Pennsylvania, arrived on their visitation trip to St. Michaels. Unfortunately, Mother Philip had picked up this sickness somewhere on their trip and arrived at St. Michaels with it, without knowing it. Despite the best care and medical help she passed away on October 2. Her sickness was short and her death, in keeping with her holy life, highly uplifting. On October 4, at the celebration of our Holy Father Francis, she was buried at our church. When our school was founded she had a great desire to be transferred here and to dedicate her life to the Navajo. Her wish was not fulfilled, and now her earthly remains await a glorious resurrection surrounded by her beloved Indians. Only Mother Katharine Drexel, Mother Loyola, and the hospital orderly, Sister Eduard, had cared for her and stayed with her day and night, thereby protecting the other Sisters and the school from the danger of infection. When the mother house learned of the illness of Mother Philip, there was great fear for Mother Katharine, and a telegram was sent to me to make sure that she was kept far from the sick. As if such a thing were in my power! She had been closing the eyes of the dead for days before, and our Lord in his goodness had protected her from infection. Because of this epidemic she had to stay at St. Michaels for about a month.

The influenza made a fearful sweep through Gallup. The coffins were soon all used up, and in order to prepare the needed number of graves, the railroad workers had to be called in. Luckily for Gallup, the new, spacious hospital run by the Sisters had been completed one year before. Our fathers could hardly manage the needs of the sick, and on October 10 the disease struck the preacher of the congregation, Father Eligius Kunkel, O.F.M., who had been weakened and exhausted by the constant work. After I visited him in the hospital and had returned home, Grant Baloo from Fort Defiance rode up with the news that many Catholic students were also close to death.

I went immediately to Fort Defiance, where I found both hospitals, all bedrooms and other rooms, filled with the sick—300 in number. Just after my arrival in the late afternoon I administered the last sacrament to many, of whom one died during the night. After supper I accompanied the doctor to visit many of the rooms filled with the sick. The doctor, Dr. Wigglesworth, praised many times in my letters, was exceptionally, successfully employed at Fort Defiance for 12 years. He had been appointed to the Indian Bureau in Washington and installed as the head of medical services for Indians. But he didn't especially enjoy that work, and he arrived at Fort Defiance with his family during the raging epidemic. During the evening we also visited the orderly assigned to the tuberculosis hospital, Ms. O'Connell, who had also contracted the influenza. She directed my attention to an old, heathen Indian in the hospital named Hastin Zo, and made the observation that she would not allow him to die without holy baptism. Ms. O'Connell has Catholic and Indian, French, and Irish blood. Since she took over the above-mentioned position, she has always informed us when anyone seriously ill is brought to the hospital, and if no priest can come in time, she has often herself performed the holy baptism for the dying. A few days later, when the influenza was followed by pneumonia, she received the final sacrament herself, but our Lord kept her alive so that she could continue her healing work with the sick. Our next visit was to the old Hastin Zo, but the doctor told me he wouldn't die for a long time. However, when I was administering the extreme unction to Loholo the next morning in a neighboring room, the doctor came to me and said the old Hastin Zo was near death. I went straight to him, found him still fully coherent and happy to be able to receive the holy baptism. He died that same day.

The seriously ill were not separated that far from the rest, and it wasn't easy to decide where my help was needed first. A Catholic employee had called me to Hanzesbah, who lay dying. I had just arrived there when Ms. Tobin, who had come from Chin Lee to help care for the sick, informed me that a young student who had attended the Chin Lee school shortly before, Casey Jones, lay in the hospital dying and was not yet baptized. When I arrived at the hospital Casey Jones had just died. But luckily he had recently been baptized at Fort Defiance. So I returned to Hanzesbah and gave her the final sacrament. Despite the fact that this elderly student was very sick, later suffered from pneumonia, and was not out of danger for about a month, she did again regain her health. Many times she asked for the Holy Communion and asked Father Emanuel for a prayer book. I believe she prayed herself well. Of the 10 sick people to whom I administered the last sacrament on that day, six died.

On the following day Father Emanuel returned from Carlsbad and came directly to Fort Defiance. He knew his sheep, and I didn't need to search through our church books and our lists to find which students were Catholic, which had been baptized, and which had received their First Communion. The doctor and his assistants had now separated the seriously ill from the rest. I stayed two more days at Fort Defiance, and during this time we baptized the new students who were sick and looked after the very ill. Then I returned to St. Michaels.

When I had arrived at Fort Defiance, a government employee, a Russian Jew whom I will only call the "Bolshevik," was making fun of us and told a Catholic Navajo Indian he saw that I had come there and was visiting the sick. He said that if a sick person died without his priest present, he would have to stay a long time in purgatory. The Indian answered him, "If you talk like that you will never get out of purgatory." A good answer even though it may not be theologically correct!

A few days later I received the news that Father Leopold was sick in Chin Lee. Since the influenza had also broken out among the Indians at Chin Lee, I decided to go there immediately. I received the news in the evening. Father Marcellus was at Tohatchi with our automobile where he had taken charge of the building of a new chapel. On the telephone he told me that a constant rain had made the way there nearly impassable and that the trip by night would be impossible. He said he would try to come to St. Michaels the next morning and take me to Chin Lee. So his arrival on the next day was not exactly guaranteed. I sent for a neighboring Indian, gave him our good riding horse and a letter for Mr. Samuel Day, the son of our neighbor who, along with his good car, was in the area of Wide Ruins, about 31 miles from St. Michaels. The Indian arrived there before sunrise, and at 9:30 Mr. Day stopped in front of our mission with his car. By about 3:00 in the afternoon we had reached Chin Lee, 55 miles away. Luckily, Father Leopold was not sick with the influenza. His violent bout with sickness had only lasted a short while, and he was already in a state to get out of bed. On the same evening the bad news came over the telephone that Father Emanuel at Fort Defiance was very sick with the influenza. After supper I visited the sick Indians of the neighborhood and performed several baptisms. On the next day Father Leopold and I visited 15 sick students of the Chin Lee school—the rest of the students had been sent home before the outbreak of the sickness—and in the afternoon I traveled with Mr. Day again back to Fort Defiance. The high fever of Father Emanuel had remitted somewhat, and Father Marcellus had returned from Tohatchi the evening before. They had given Father Emanuel his own room in the hospital in Fort Defiance, and with medical help and good care he had soon overcome the influenza. Father Marcellus gave me the good advice to go home. If we both stayed there we could both be hit at the same time by the influenza. It was now his turn. When he became sick, I could relieve him. Despite this, I stayed until the next afternoon.

The sickness also raged with the Indians on the reservation, and Father Marcellus visited many of them from Fort Defiance on out, and I from St. Michaels on out, to perform the Catholic final sacrament and to baptize the heathens. Wherever possible, the sick were brought to the hospital in Fort Defiance, where many lives were saved through medical help and good care. On one day I accompanied Mr. Paquette and the doctor to a hut where six were down with the influenza. Mr. Paquette brought all six in his car to the hospital and all survived.

To let you know what efforts were made for the Indians, one case should be mentioned. A young Indian was brought to the hospital from the reservation. He had the influenza but appeared to be improving. One beautiful morning as I was in the same room making preparations to administer the extreme unction to one of our earlier students, a sudden change occurred. The orderlies gathered around his bed, the doctor was quickly brought in, and the sick boy appeared to be drawing near to the end. His hasty speech, his quick breaths, blood gushing from his nose and mouth, his hands and feet becoming colder—everything seemed to be pointing to his approaching demise. The doctor couldn't explain the sudden turn until the Indian told how he had left his bed shortly before, walked by the window, fallen out, and then dragged himself back into the bed. The doctor said, "Adios, he will not live much longer." But in spite of that he and the three orderlies, one white and two Indians, went to "work," as if it were to save the life of a king. After two hours of effort he was out of danger and is now healthy again. As soon as the doctor had given his orders, I asked the Indian, whom I did not know, if he wanted to be baptized. Apparently I was not unknown to him because he looked at me and said I was his friend and he wanted to do anything I advised him to do. After I had quickly instructed him and said a few prayers with him, I baptized him.

A 17-year-old student had been baptized and received the First Holy Communion when his mother committed him to the preachers. At first he refused to attend the Protestant service, but finally he seemed to want to give in to the pressure from his mother, the preachers, and his interpreter. But during his long illness the preacher didn't even visit him one time. His Catholic sister had me called in, and he was happy to be able to go to confession. I could hear his confession without making it known to the others, but I didn't dare do more for fear of getting into a disagreement with the preacher and the government. In spite of our fears he got well again. Now he is 18 years old and with this age he has the right to self-determination and may therefore remain Catholic.

The doctor mentioned previously, Dr. Hailman, was sent to Fort Defiance from the Indian Office to support Dr. Wigglesworth. Years ago he had married an Irish woman at Colley's ranch in the Apache region. He was raised Lutheran and is descended from a Hohenzollern. Despite this he was very successful and kept all his patients alive; in this he differed from the head of that family, the late Kaiser Wilhelm. Luckily, the Indian Office sent him here because shortly after his arrival Dr. Wigglesworth, his wife, and his three children became sick with influenza. All of them soon recovered from the illness, but Dr. Wigglesworth had a setback and hovered between life and death a whole week long. He was Protestant, but during his stay in Washington he had decided to become Catholic and had come every Sunday to services with his family. On November 8, at midnight, I took him, to the great joy of his family and his Catholic friends, into our church and administered the last sacrament to him. To the great joy of us and the Indians, he survived the illness.

Lukachukai, 1918[14]

Some time ago the editor of *St. Anthony Messenger* suggested a story of the making of the *Ethnologic Dictionary* as a serial of interest to readers. The appeal struck little response in one who has spent his best years in reserve and desert. It seemed anomalous suddenly to make a run on the typefonts for capital I's. However, a free serial in which Navajo daily life might be described together with the occupation and difficulties of the missionary among the Navajo seemed suggestive of a variety of topics. The flu epidemic of 1918 offered timely material. Some of the notes were left as they were written then at the height of the epidemic. Others have been enlarged upon without striving to retain a strict narration. The notes strive to picture the Navajo as they are, not what we might expect of them or what in our estimate they ought to be. For Christian ideals and standards are difficult to imbue when contact with them is only spasmodic as we find with these nomadic Indians.

The condition of alarm, anxiety, and high tension during the recent epidemic was noticeable also in our Navajo camps. American railroad towns and settlements were stricken during the greater part of the month of October. Visiting and laboring Navajo at these points immediately left their labor once they took sick, and in this manner carried the infection back to their camps where it spread with amazing rapidity. This was a surprise to some degree in view of the scattered condition of their camps, as well as their fresh-air life in the piñon districts where the season for gathering these nuts was on. That, it was hoped, might offer an efficient check to the spread of the disease.

Nevertheless, the St. Leonard's district, north of us in the Carriso Mountains, reported 20 deaths within less than a week, due to the fact that Indians who had sought employment at Cortez, Colorado, returned home carrying the germs of the disease with them. The most natural thing for the sick Navajo to do was to call upon a singer to cure him. Any disease is religious in origin and is dispelled by religious ceremony only. Hence, too, as the character of the disease was yet unknown, no harm was suspected in attending such singings in a body as usual. In consequence these unsuspecting visitors, too, became easily infected, in view of the utter lack of preventive precautions with regard to coughing, sneezing, and expectoration. Indeed, subsequent indisposition was still looked upon as nothing more than indisposition and a cold that would wear off in due course of time. Visitors returning from such singings would stop with friends on their way home, just long enough to leave the germs of disease. In this manner quite often an entire family was stricken.

On the whole, the inital stages of the epidemic were not viewed with alarm at all, and the usual preparations for war dances, *Yeibichais*, and the like, were carried on without the least concern. As the war dance is celebrated on three successive days, and is carried to points distant from one another, and huge gatherings from every direction are a feature of this dance, infection *en masse* was particularly to be feared, the more so as apparently there was no suspicion of the malicious character of this disease.

Agents and physicians advised, therefore, that these dances must be postponed and that parents must not visit their children at the agency and other schools. These were wise measures in themselves as they helped to restrict the disease to the schools, most of which suffered heavily. To an outsider that may seem indicative of solicitude for the welfare of the Navajo at large. So it is, for those who are residents in the immediate vicinity of a physician. But the Navajo territory is a vast expanse. Schools with resident physicians are distant and far between, and physicians had their fill with the schools. There they did their work admirably and fearlessly. When we leave the school grounds, however, and penetrate vast stretches of valley and mountain for the Navajo camps, drugs, nurses, and physicians are unknown and unseen!

During the entire epidemic nothing was done in the way of relief, but when it had well disappeared, statistics of the deaths were taken. The injunction on public dances was indeed a preventive measure. It was one way of checking the spread of the disease. But it was also the only measure taken. There is no physician here at Lukachukai. One is stationed at the Chin Lee school, while 75 miles west and 60 miles east of us there is neither physician nor drugstore. North up to the San Juan River, another distance of some 55 miles, God's providence is your only physician. Hence when a Navajo takes sick he seeks a native cure and that is always some *hatal* or singing. And that was precisely what they did when the flu swept over them. The singers were called, and because of attendance as usual at such ceremonies, contagion spread. What with numerous cases on hand and daily new ones, nobody felt much of a desire to hold or attend a public dance.

On the other hand, it was futile to argue with an ignorant people that their chants, instead of remedying the disease, might unnecessarily be a means of its rapid spread. "The American has his own medicine and religion. How can they compare with our singings that we hold to cure every disease?" Yet this attitude by no means makes the Navajo spurn our drugs. They use them if available, as they are cheaper in the end than native singings.

When deaths occurred without regard to routine and the usual singings it was forced upon all willy-nilly, that visits to districts where so many deaths occurred were quite unsafe. Hence chants and public dances ceased of their own accord. Much damage, however, could not be undone. Fortunately, some were able to withstand a serious attack and get by with a slight cold and fever. Others, and not a few, fell victims to the epidemic. Thus one, the head of a family, occupied a tent where he was left to die, while his wife, not many paces away, died that same night with nothing to protect her but a brush windbreak!

There is a hush on the Lukachukai valley as well, much like the lazy, leaden clouds of mist that drag along the foot of its mountains on a rainy day. When will they be lifted? When will this dread disease end? Young men and women, faces that were cheerful once and familiar only a short time ago, are no more, and the end is not in sight.

The other day an aged fellow stepped into the office ordering me to take pad and pencil, that I might figure for him the cost of a door and frame for his new house. He carried a cord which was of the proper length and was knotted down the line to show the desired width. The Navajo are ignorant of measurements and know no equivalents for the denominations of our yardstick. In consequence a cord which indicates the distances by knots placed at proper intervals is used in taking measurements for blankets, windows, doors, or logs and lumber. I figured that the lowest possible cost for frame and door would be $3.58, and advised him so. "Rub out those figures you made," says he after a moment's reflection. "I'll go around to the hogans and try to pick up some old boards, nails, and you might lend me a saw to make that door myself. It'll be cheaper that way, my brother!" This is a very pleasant way of indicating that your services are now no longer required.

At that the fellow was not altogether unappreciative, at least after a fashion, for after dismissing the subject of a door, he reminded me of a promise I had made him in summer that he might have a supply of vegetables as soon as they matured. Ordinarily, truck gardens are not a fashion with the Navajo, who limit the growing of vegetables to corn, potatoes, beans, and squashes. Lettuce, radishes, turnips, beets, and onions are not trifled with, though many are familiar with onions and cabbage and their preparation. Perhaps it is because vegetables are usually classified with grasses which animals eat. Still, numerous species of native flora are classed as edible in the shape of medicine, tea, or greens, so that modern vegetables naturally go as (white, red, etc.) "edible grass." Initial attempts, too, have been made to raise them in this valley with some success, though not for home use, but simply "to see if they'll grow" or "because the seed was given to us."

Our vegetable harvest had been quite plentiful, and so the remnants were gladly placed at his disposal. Cabbage, beets, turnips, and carrots he tied into various bundles which were strapped to his saddle, or lost in the folds of his robe. He mounted his horse, his son back of him, and rode off contented. I have not met the poor fellow again, nor was he able to frame that door, because the flu took him three days after his visit. Nor was his case the only surprise in store.

As it was piñon season when all hands are needed to gather this valuable fruit, the valley was practically deserted for a time, only to be quickly peopled by the returning sick and dead! A neighbor of ours left his crop of piñons in charge of the store and then barely was able to drag himself home. Dizzy and weak, he was helpless and died before his family realized what had happened. That was the signal for alarm. The flu exacted a heavy toll of 13 from the four neighboring families. Others were equally stricken, some families losing five, six, and seven members. One family scarcely knew the condition of its neighbor as all hands were busied in caring for their own sick and dead, while it frequently happened that the convalescent members were too exhausted to give any attention to their surroundings.

Presently I am informed that Lucy Belaganayiyisxini is dead after only three days of illness. She was a Catholic girl who for a time attended Mass regularly, and thereafter at least in intervals. As I had not seen her for some weeks I had surmised that she, too, had gone to the piñons. I was therefore particularly grieved at not having been summoned to her bedside and expressed myself so to my informant. "La'," he replied in the most sonorous drawl and pitch you can bestow on that sententious monosyllable, which means "that's true!" "Well," he explained, "she never had much sense anyway." Isn't there a saying of reporting only good things of the dead? His comment upon his sister's judgment did not strike me as particularly appropriate. Perhaps it was good diplomacy. At any rate, when he had finished his report on those that were left of the family and were too weak to walk, with only himself to do the chores, he asked for assistance to the tune of $3 with which to purchase flour for the living. "Four dollars will be better, though," he added, which is also true in a manner.

Off and on within the last two years I have endeavored to instruct the wife of one of my Catholic parishioners preparatory to baptism. She argued that, as her husband is baptized and her children, too, receive baptism, it is not quite proper for her to remain unbaptized, especially since her husband has made a cursory review of Christian doctrine with her. They have a farm about a mile from the mission but divide their time between it and a small herd of sheep and goats whose range is about 18 miles west of here. While she was at the farm for a day or two her husband would look after the herd, or vice versa. I suggested that she make use of the intervals which would find her at the farm to receive a more thorough instruction in religion. This she promised but unfortunately one or other circumstance intervened which allowed her just two instructions. Then the flu came with a mild attack upon herself and her children. In that crisis she sent word through her husband that I should be ready for her whenever the sickness might take a serious turn, that I might come and baptize her. She recovered, however, but insisted more than ever that she be baptized with her child. This I did in the hope of continuing instructions with her next spring.

To the Christian, death undoubtedly has its sting, but doubly so to the heathen. Supernatural motives avail them not such a divine Providence nor the hope of a future resurrection and union with those they loved. They know no prayers for the dead; in fact, all that reminds them thereof is painful if not injurious. What with the memory of days gone by when any of their children cheered them and made them swell with pride, their loss is all keen and poignant. Charlie Mitchell's is a case in point. His boy, Charles Jr., was the pet of his father, a boy whom he fondled and endeared, who loved his father and had no secrets from him. Death snatched him when he was scarcely 20. George, his youngest, was unlike his brother Charles, not as tenderly attached as Charles was, yet he was also their boy and of considerable help to his aging parents. He took sick, it was claimed, owing to a hurt taken in trying to adjust a wagon to the road when the horses failed. A few days of sickness spent him. Some so-called stargazers who divine from the position and color of the stars, advised Charlie that natural causes had nothing to do with his boy's death, which was due to violence from a Navajo. Upon hearing this Charlie and his wife questioned their son. Did he remember the Navajo that killed him? And when he answered negatively and assured them that he had no such recollection, they left him in peace.

That afternoon George realized that there was little hope for him and bade his parents carry him outside to die, so that in the event of his death the house might be spared. He expired about dusk. Upon investigation the next morning they found that the wrap which covered him was bloodstained. That set them to revert to the verdict of the stargazer, so that again they held a consultation of the constellations. These seemed to confirm the statement of the first visionary, so that they were forced to the conclusion that the statement of their son as to the innocence of an outsider had been made in delirium, and also that the report of a strain from lifting a wagon could not be invoked as true. Moreover, the spot where the wagon had slipped the road was examined and found insufficient to have done the harm.

When, therefore, the result of the star readings was known, it was learned that a young boy who had been herding in the neighborhood had visited a singing with George shortly before. As boys will be boys, the two had wrestled and in the fray the small boy had picked George from the ground bodily, thrown him down flat and then sat upon him. The boy was described as mean and always "out for a round." Warnings by elders he left unheeded and was independent to the extent that he became unmanageable. Putting all these reports together rendered a decision which spelled anything but blessing for the victorious wrestler. The family jury found that George's death was not due to natural causes but to violence. This violence was the result of a wrestling bout in which George, a lad of 18 years, had succumbed to the superior skill of his aggressor, a mere boy though he be. The aggressor is therefore guilty of murder pure and simple. For we cannot speak of an accident when a wrestling bout ends with the death of the defeated. The bloodstains which were found after George's death should be evidence enough that deliberate murder was intended. Consequently, the wagon theory is of small import and must be discarded as irrelevant. The wrestler is the murderer.

The news thereof spread among the opposing clan members. It was evident that it was now not a private family affair, but one of the Toaxaedlini (waters meet clan) against the Totsoni (big water clan), to which latter the lightweight wrestler belonged.

Inasmuch as I had been instrumental to some extent in having the government physician of the Chin Lee school visit George in his sickness it appears that I became an interested party, not so much because of this fact as because that physician had accepted the wagon theory, but erroneously held that George, owing to his youth, ought easily to outgrow his injury. In addition, Charlie had upheld this same theory when asking my assistance in securing the doctor's visit. Accordingly, then, Charlie explained that the theory could not be upheld, as he had every evidence now that his boy did not die a natural death.

To corroborate that and to show the impossibility of the wagon theory he called upon a star witness, a young man who had helped George in loading and hauling wood and had accompanied and helped him with the obstreperous wagon. This youth described how they had helped one another in loading each log, that George had even suggested a final, very heavy log, although to the youth the load had seemed sufficient. They managed to load this last log also without mishap. Their good fortune continued until they reached this small grade in the road. As the horses were tired, they were obliged to unload some of the logs and take turns at the wheels to get the wagon up. That evening George ate very little, so that his parents concluded he might have been injured by an overstrain. They had retained this opinion throughout his illness until, after the Chin Lee physician had left them, the singers informed them that a Navajo had "killed" George. This they now knew to be a fact. Some women who had been at the particular singing had witnessed the wrestle, others had seen the two in the struggle, still another had testified to having heard the thump of the fall. These witnesses had noticed that the small boy had been picking on George, that George had brushed him off, then had left the hogan, followed by his tormentor until, in self-defense, he had grappled with him, only to be worsted. "That," continued Charlie, "shows plainly that my boy was killed, and killed by this Totsoni!"

To me it seemed an accident pure and simple due to rough and tumble work between the boys. Neither of them could be blamed for deliberate malice in measuring their strength with one another. The fact that George had not spoken of the matter, had gone after wood, and had worked without noticing the effects of the wrestling bout, and when questioned directly had, by his replies, not attached any importance to this friendly bout, this evidence would certainly clear the boy of malice if brought to the agent's notice. I for one should not accuse this boy of murder. "Is that what you call sympathy?" Charlie asked of me. "Here I have lost my boy and you tell me that he was not killed?"

"My sympathies," I told Charlie, "were never more with you than now where you have sustained the loss of this second boy. You haven't forgotten your first boy, for he was attached to you more than the other two ever were. You are not as strong now as you were then. Their mother, too, is aging so that what help you have had from George you will miss more than ever. As for Mark, who never was healthy, what hope can I give you for him? His is only a question of time, which will leave you and their mother alone. Why, then, should I not sympathize with you? Just now, however, grief has taken possession of you and blinded you against fairness, which should tell you that this boy had no evil purpose in wrestling with George. If the latter's death is due to the wrestling match, it can hardly be stamped anything but an accident. Wait awhile at least before you take action. You may do something which you are not justified in doing."

Charlie appreciated my expressions of sympathy but as to the murder he would see the family! This meant that prominent leaders of his clan were to hold a council in order to decide what ransom was to be paid by the Totsoni clan.

Some years ago an innocent agent was asked what should be done with a witch whom the Navajo had caught. He promptly replied to hang him, not knowing that a gang of clansmen of the witch's victim were awaiting some such reply. And the case of an enterprising evangelist who had invited two traveling Navajo to a cup of coffee and was accused of poisoning one of them with coffee is still within vivid memory. All of which is evidence that little distinction is made between accidental and willful murder, and that clan vengeance knows no mercy. The custom in its earlier stages may have placed an effective barrier upon murder just as the clan system was to some extent a safeguard for the life and property of the wife. Yet it opens the way to friction and mob violence without fairness to the innocent, while the matriarchate opens a channel of clannishness which makes a family such as we understand it an utter impossibility or at best a notable exception.

It is with pleasure that we record Charlie's family as one of these pleasing exceptions. If loyal to his friends, he was above all loyal to his wife, which made her justly proud of him as an exception among the Navajo. In consequence, too, their property was undivided excepting that when she wanted to make debts he reminded her that she had to pay it, while she was equally ready to assist in paying his debts which Charlie is easy in incurring. Maybe this is his one failing, which is easily pardonable if you study the natural grace with which the debts are made. Their love of their children was intense, so that the loss of Charles Jr., of whom mention was made previously, left a vacancy which never was filled again. Months and years after, we found that big man crying and sobbing over this son as though his death had been only very recent.

Councils and conferences which Charlie held privately induced some of the leaders of the opposition to admit that their clan had killed his boy. Some of his friends, however, tried to induce Charlie to drop the case. They pointed out that the wrestling theory should not be invoked because of his son's own testimony and that star readers should not find evidence in the face of the probability of the strain caused by adjusting the wagon. In addition, if it were made known that George was known as a tormentor and had sought opportunities with boys above and under his size, and that Charlie himself had met with little obedience from this boy whenever he had yelled at him to do certain things, these and like instances would certainly cast suspicion on George's peaceable character. To all of which Charlie had but one stubborn reply: "I shall always remember it!" and pressed the case during the entire summer.

After the leaders of the opposing clan, however, had made the admission, it was clear that some such admission would be extracted from the boy, or that he must be banished from the country. The Totsoni seemed to favor or at least to be reconciled to the latter course by way of placing the boy at some nonreservation school. That closed the case so far as they were concerned. But when Charlie's horses went astray, he accused a Totsoni of absconding with them, demanded search and pay for the stray horses, and continued to press his case against the reputed murderers of his boy George. It was evident that Charlie was as relentless as ever. As one Navajo put it, "Charlie has been very angry since that boy died."

The headmen whom he consulted, his friends, and the agent could give him no encouragement. Their views confirmed the original impression that if anything an accident was responsible for the death, with a possibility of combining the two theories, the wagon and the wrestling theory. The fact that the star readers had concurred in the opinion of a malevolent death found little credence for a time, because this opinion was voiced after the wagon theory had been established.

At first Charlie refused to carry the case before the agent, but wanted a native trial before judges selected by himself. These were prominent clan members of his wife's and his own clan. Such action presumed the guilt of the Totsoni clan to which the wrestler belonged. This clan, moreover, must abide by the decision and, as Charlie stated, if that ever turned unfavorable to himself, he should take the matter into his own hands. What this meant we understood when Charlie visited the wrestler's hogan armed with a rifle. There, the report told, he found the boy's brother whom he might have dispatched if the error had not been pointed out to him. In consequence the Totsoni were advised to abscond the boy until the day set for the trial.

Fortunately, Charlie visited elsewhere about this time, saw some of his friends at the agency, and was thereby induced to have the case tried in the regular manner before the agent. These trials occurred on set days with the result that the boy repeated a story which he had given originally. This was in effect that not he but another young man had actually wrestled with George, that George, however, had started the fray but could not hold his own. As a reaction he had a habit of picking on smaller boys, like the accused himself, and George had actually thrown him so that his head hurt him considerably from the fall.

The young man whom the wrestler had accused neatly denied the accusation, so that it was necessary to call in him and others as witnesses. In the meantime the accused boy was kept in custody at Fort Defiance School. Possibly he was prevailed upon to make the admittance. At any rate, some time in September he confessed that all that had been said about the wrestling was true and that he was therefore guilty of murder. Charlie had won out by sheer perseverance. It is more than probable that the boy was prevailed upon to make what confession he did and to admit all charges made, that is, the killing of Charlie's son in a wrestling bout. Charlie, therefore, carried his point without convincing his friends.

It occurred to the agent that this confession took the case out of his hands, transferring it to the higher jurisdiction of the county and federal courts. Preparatory correspondence had been inaugurated when the Spanish flu stepped in and claimed the wrestler in a final bout. And now, said one of the Totsoni, "I suppose Charlie is satisfied!"

To understand all this it must be remembered that the Navajo group themselves into clans or gentes which, according to tradition are not interrelated. The clans or phratries are legendary in origin, yet are sanctioned by tradition. . . . Navajo law also exacted "eye for eye, tooth for tooth," one man's life for that of another. If the deceased had risen to prominence and leadership through wealth or merit the opposite clan might ransom the murderer's life providing, however, both parties could agree on the price. This ransom was an equivalent in slaves, cattle, horses, robes, and buckskins which frequently pauperized the clan, and gave no guarantee of pardon. Today, too, the same rigorous justice is meted out to offenders once it has been established that death occurred through violence of another. Death by accident is not allowed, as such a claim might be invoked in any instance. Thus, when at a war dance, the gun of a young man unloaded accidentally, the bullet striking a friend of his, from which in the end he did not recover, the claim of accident was not allowed. Instead, a heavy fine was imposed upon the boy's clan. Similarly, 25 head of cattle, 70 sheep, and some horses could not induce the clan to silence the case of a murderer who deliberately aimed a gun at an old man and killed him instantly. Sudden death was at first suggested, as the man had been deaf and blind and ailing. Yet the empty cartridge found near the spot gave a clue for the murderer, who was tracked and confessed the deed, whereupon his clan offered the ransom.

What are called bean shooters or wizards, too, are summarily dealt with once traces and proofs of crookedness are established. Indeed, it is not so long since charges preferred against innocent men and women for the practice of witchcraft brought them to speedy grief without a possibility of defense. That offenders of this kind have been tried in the courts and sentenced to a few years in the penitentiary and then returned to their own apparently does not satisfy clan justice. Their old camping grounds become unsafe for a quiet and peaceful life.

Animosity, however, must subside in the wake of the grim reaper, as both clans in the George Mitchell case have been hit hard. His death seemed to have broken his mother's heart. She wept continuously, and even travels to distant districts could not efface his memory. Small wonder, then, that a slight attack of fever found her spent and broken and ready to lie low. She died after an illness of scarcely three days.

The duties of a sexton are not inviting and agreeable to most of us. To the Navajo the duties of the undertaker are unknown excepting that it is customary to bathe and dress the corpse. Its disposition is expedited with no loss of time and with all lack of ceremony. One Saturday my friend Charlie Mitchell asked as a special favor that we deposit his wife and boy on the mission grounds. Both were sick at the time and there was no telling what might happen. I promised to take care of them—as an exception and special favor—with the proviso that it was impossible to attend to every case in this manner.

The following Monday we were called to get the corpse of Charlie's wife. Fortunately, we had reconstructed an old Ford car so that it was suitable for draying stone and heavy material. This car, therefore, served us as a hearse in which we hauled the corpse some eight or 10 miles. As it is unusual here to carry a corpse any distance at all, and equally unusual to use a car for this purpose, we had to give the death signal to travelers that met the cortege. This consisted in waving your hand vigorously in token of arresting the attention to something very unusual. When in hailing distance the chauffeur must not speak, but by giving the road strict attention and staring rigidly ahead the intent of the death signal was obtained. At least from the way the riders and drivers turned aside and urged their horses with their whips it was evident that the car might have the road all to itself.

Fortunately, we were not asked to attend to the ablutions and dressing of the corpse. Mrs. Mitchell belonged to the heavyweights and represented the 200-pound class nicely. But by shoving and bracing and pulling we managed to load her. The attendants, like her daughter and husband who directed our actions, had inserted twiglets of sagebrush in their nostrils, possibly to avoid death's breaths, more likely to prevent her spirit or spirits from taking that entrance. For death knows no friendship and attachments, and the spirit of the dead is inimical like the rest of injurious influences. These considerations did not occur to us; therefore, we saw no reason for decorating our nostrils with sagebrush twiglets. As there was neither box nor coffin, an old comforter was used as a wrap to load her into the car, with instructions to burn that comforter as too old and worn to be placed in the grave. With many pleadings to bury her securely so that her grave might remain untouched we left Charlie a broken man.

Upon our return we placed her in a box of rough lumber, selected a soft spot for digging, and buried her without ceremony. A cloud of smoke in the direction from which we had come showed that the hogan in which she had died had been destroyed. It is customary also to destroy shovels and hoes or any tool used in burial. We ignored this custom, as we needed the tools for other purposes. There was no following at the burial as such action is absolutely tabooed. The sole attendants were the two grave diggers, or as the Navajo call them, "the depositors." That was November 11.

I was just about ready to begin Mass on the following morning when Adits'ai, the interpreter, so called because in the days of Fort Sumner captivity he spoke and interpreted in Spanish, asked to see me. His story informed me that two of his sons—one of whom, Neumann, who was a Catholic in his St. Michael's School days and had been attending Mass and the sacraments occasionally—had just expired. What with only a temporary camp about a mile below the mission, there were only women therein to assist Alphonsus, his brother, in burying the two boys. Since Adits'ai reported them dead, however, I asked him to return a little later in the day, which he did. Upon condition that he furnish Alphonsus with a shovel I agreed to help the boy bury his two brothers, as he begged insistently and the man had my full sympathy.

Accordingly, equipped with a shovel I walked to the camp which he pointed out to me, but to my surprise I found Neumann in agony, about to breathe his last. Evidently, then, as he was beyond hope of recovery, they had considered him dead and reported him as such. Indeed, he lay under a sagebrush in the open, a pair of new pants, a new shirt, and such other things as were to dress his corpse or were to be deposited with him being placed in readiness. Only's Neumann's sister and wife sat near him at a smoldering fire. They had painted their own faces while Neumann's face was covered with his blanket, though the heavy heaving of his chest showed that there was still ample life in his body. As sickness had somewhat changed his features I made sure that the young man Neumann lay before me, and though his people urged that their brother be buried and that by that time Neumann, too, should be ready, there was no time to lose with him if I should be able to prepare him for near death.

Such indifference and stoicism bespeaks anything but genuine affection between sister and brother, wife and husband, father and son. Is this relationship nature's bidding, or is it an irresistible correlary of our constant training and surrounding only, that rouses our ire and indignation at such heartless behavior? There was little time, however, for reflections of this kind, or preachment either. The priest is quick to forget the failings of the living when there is question of life and succor to a departing soul. Let the chamber of death be a cozy, well-ventilated room with the sick call outfit spread and sympathetic friends and relatives ready to assist in prayer, or let it be the shadow of a brush with merely a sheep pelt offering scant comfort to a tired, dying body; the priest's *"proficiscere,"* "Go forth Christian soul," is equally welcome in either place. Just as he meets that soul first in its career in life with baptism, so, too, is the priest its last parting friend on the threshold of eternity! Evidently, death was upon Neumann, since his feet and right side were cold, his eyes glassy, and his face showed the yellowish dark hue of the plague. Quick action was called for.

Accordingly, I threw down my shovel and told his people that I should attend to Neumann first. They did not seem to grasp this, yet consented indifferently. After saying a few prayers and speaking an act of contrition into his ear, I gave him absolution, then rushed back home to get the holy oils. While I was getting ready the brother [Gervase Thuemmel] brought in my horse, which had to cover that mile in breakneck speed. I was happy to find the lad still breathing, whereupon I administered extreme unction and had time to recite the prayers for the dead over him. I am hopeful that God gave him the grace to repeat the prayer with me and consciousness enough for a good preparation for death, though speech and recognition had already left him. His own angel must have prompted me to accept of his father's pleading, for I had scarcely finished the prayers and removed my cassock when he breathed his last. Evidently, the heathen considers a human dead when his sickness is beyond recovery. The Church, however, closes the course of a human career only when, beyond the peradventure of a doubt, death is master. That struck me forcibly when I closed Neumann's eyes in the shade of that sagebrush. What a poor, uncomfortable chamber of death! But even such considerations are brushed aside so long as the priest can reach his own.

The reply when I announced that Neumann had breathed his last was characteristic and savors of a dispassionate fatalism: "He has been dead long ago." Now that he was dead in reality, Alphonsus and myself agreed to bury the two brothers together in a single grave which we set about digging while the women were bathing and dressing Neumann's body. His dead brother lay ready in an opposite direction. We embedded them upon a layer of sagebrush, jammed a saddle, bridle, and blankets which belonged to his brother with the brush between them, and covered them generously with a mound of earth, while the rest of the family were getting ready to leave that vicinity!

The dread of the dead was upon them, as well as of everything the dead had possessed and frequented. To us it may seem like wanton extravagance to deposit Pendleton robes that retail at $12 and $16 apiece, bridles and saddles which average $40 and $50, silverware worth more than its weight in currency, especially in these days of strict economy. Yet the family deposits them without as much as a remonstrance, as something that belonged to the dead, and that settles it. "That's our way of putting them away," is the stubborn reply you get.

As a corpse is an unwieldy object to handle without a stretcher or box, they brought us Neumann's rope with which to fasten the comforter about him. There was no objection to my claiming the shovel which Alphonsus had used and this rope. These are now my possessions.

Mark Mitchell, the eldest son of Charlie Mitchell, had had all symptoms of a consumptive for the last few years. He was therefore an object of concern to his father, who for this reason anticipated his demise as inevitable. On the morning of his mother's death Mark had sent word to his father that he was feeling somewhat better and that his blood-spitting had ceased. Nevertheless, like so many of his tribesmen, he evidently lacked sufficient stamina to withstand and passed away on Wednesday, two days after his mother. The messenger brought a pair of new pants and a string of turquoise, both of which were to adorn the corpse. He asked that I carry these to the family, as he had to return to Charlie, his father-in-law, after showing me the road. By using low gear on the Ford I managed to make what he called a road. Upon my arrival at the hogan, which was situated upon the top of a hilly mesa, I was asked to bathe and dress the corpse. After all, it needed little persuasion to induce them to render this last service. His wife excused herself with having a baby to take care of. A friend of the family pointed out that he could ill afford to go into mourning for four days, as he would be obliged to do. Mark's wife's brother, therefore, had to strip, bathe, and dress the corpse. This we lifted into a large box into which we also placed a good saddle, blankets, and a buckskin rope, and then nailed the lid. We deposited Mark beside his mother. A cloud of smoke down the valley showed that the family had moved and left that neighborhood. Apparently, too, it must be unsafe for the herds of the diseased to pass the "death line," that is to say, the route the corpse is to take. For when the car was about ready to move on the driver was asked to wait until the herd could be driven to the right side ahead of the car.

Whatever may happen to the so-called "depositors" is apparently a matter of little concern. In the days of slavery the burial of the master of his family was forced upon the slaves, who were then shot and left unburied there. Now that the days of slavery have been outlived it devolves upon the family to take care of the dead, which they do with utmost reluctance and as hastily and superficially as circumstances allow. The rule, therefore, is to limit the entire proceeding to absolute necessity in order to prevent disturbance from animals and men. A crevice in the rocks which, after disposition, requires only filling in with stones or logs is a very favorable method. Some waterless ditches away from the roadside or routes of travel are also chosen. An occasional glance at the grave convinces the family that it is undisturbed. At times, however, the contrary is established, and it is learned that men, making a practice of ravaging graves for their treasures, will stalk as coyotes and approach the graves in such a garb. And although such stalkers usually come to grief, grave robbing is at times practiced. The practice, however, is hardly widespread enough to justify [more than] superficial work in burying their dead. On the other hand, resident whites have been induced to extend a helping hand, and it is surprising how many friends they have as soon as death visits a Navajo family. Baptism, which was never thought of in health, is readily accepted for the patient by the family once it is known that the missionaries will bury the dead of those baptized. I have known singers who, after realizing the inevitable, will suggest that the patient be baptized in order to secure burial by whites. However, as in the Mitchell family, friendships might secure the same service, and baptism is not necessary for burial.

It is not good taste to speak of burial excepting in very general terms, so long as there is hope of recovery. It is a fact that some day we must die, but you must not say that someone will die. Making matters personal in such manner may cause suspicion of maliciously wishing or causing their death and that brings to grief. But if it has been established that one is beyond hope and nothing can be done to prolong his life, then it is quite likely that not a single Navajo would refuse baptism at that juncture. Possibly the sincerity of such conversions might be questioned with some justice, yet none of us would refuse the benefit of a doubt to a patient when there is a question of life and death. Our efforts, however, are for conversions among the living, which require patient and continuous instruction, and, undoubtedly, a strong foundation upon the belief that there is a better life awaiting us hereafter must replace the prejudices against death which are prevalent among the present generation.

As mentioned, the flu year saw a very abundant piñon crop, and it was thought that open camp life might spare many pickers. Yet death's toll was heaviest among the pickers and to crown the climax of the ensuing panic the stricken were more than eager to leave the district and thus carried the disease down the valley. Navajo Dick and family joined the piñon harvesters only to find that they were as easy a prey to the disease as those whom Dick had tried to cure of it. Indeed, Dick had boasted that he and family were immune, as he had the cure for the disease! Yet one day it took his daughter who, they told me after her death, wanted me to visit her. Upon my questioning her husband about her baptism, he said he was quite positive that she had been baptized, because at school she had been baptized and then afterward again by a priest.

Tom and Joe Dick, too, took sick, while Robert, their mother's present husband, also succumbed to the disease. Little hope seemed to be left for Tom when Dick removed him to the small timber and Tom felt that he had to pass his checks. While quite conscious, therefore, Tom begged his father to leave him what he had and bury him at least in his silver belt. Dick promised to do so. Yet no sooner had Tom lost consciousness and death seemed inevitable than Dick kindly removed the silver belt. This he carried to the store and pawned for $20. To those who were present he remarked that he should hardly be able to ever redeem the belt, stating, too, that his son had asked him to leave it. It proved more profitable as pawn than as a burial ornament. At that a small brush enclosure marked the spot of Tom's demise until some charitable American dug his grave. Rank cynicism is it? Be it! Quite recently the agent visited here saying: "I want that fellow who was up for rape. We can't let such things go. Where is he?" "Quite safe," I replied, "he is dead and buried."

Tom thus was disposed and it is said that Navajo Dick cursed those of the East, of the South, the West and North, the Earth and the Sun, when all his singings and prayers were fruitless. Joe, however, and a small daughter were left, although reports had it that Joe was on the way to recovery. So I was not much surprised when a hollow-eyed, high cheek-boned emaciated fellow entered my office. His skin showed the usual blackish yellow pallor of our flu types which often reminded me more of descriptions of eastern cholera than of flu cases. Joe Dick was a veritable skeleton, thinly clad in a rag of a shirt and wrapped in a thin blanket. He was convalescent, he said, but at that seemed to have lost every ambition for life, and when I remonstrated with him for venturing out before entirely recuperating, he said he thought he would be better off dead than alive. After clothing him in a better shirt my endeavors were to persuade him to take better care of himself. He recovered finally, but has ever since been in trouble and a source of annoyance to neighbors as well as whites.

Returning from a trip one day, two visitors were awaiting me. The one asked for a board with which to make a baby's cradle and a nipple to nurse the child. It happens frequently that such requests are made, and the trading stores usually keep a supply of nipples on hand. Diluted canned milk and a soda pop bottle with a nipple furnish available substitutes for nursing bottles. This isn't exactly in my line so that I had to refer him to the stores. The other visitor informed me that his father asked me to visit his (the boy's) wife, who like himself was a graduate of St. Michael's School. His wife, he said, had given birth to a child and had been doing well ever since, but had refused to eat the evening previously and was now unconscious and about to die. Therefore, his father asked him to notify me.

When I arrived at the camp I found the girl had been carried outside. Snow which had fallen in the night had been cleared in a depression which was protected to some extent by a heavy growth of sagebrush that formed a natural windbreak. There the patient lay on pelts covered with a robe and comforter. A sagebrush fire was kept up which spread warmth only in close touch with it and was apparently not kept up for the patient. Mr. Bitter Water explained that the girl was from a good family, had been to school at St. Michaels, that he and I were old acquaintances, and that as local headman and elder I surely was glad to assist the girl and his family in putting her away. "For," he said, "She has about till evening." That was evident as well as the invitation to attend to her burial. Her husband, after delivering his message, had received no further orders from his father and consequently felt no necessity of being present at the last rites. Death severs all connection and the closest ties. While administering the rites, as absolution and extreme unction, it occurred to me how easily this young mother might have been saved in a local dispensary. Such an establishment should, undoubtedly, have saved a number of patients that were carried out prematurely because the fear of death was upon the living, whereas some opportune attention would have saved their lives as it has elsewhere. In these distant districts death is appalling, the more so as we are destitute of all medical aid.

Mr. Bitter Water is, like numerous others in the valley, a singer whose services are much in demand at present. He watched my ministrations in silence and when afterward we reviewed the toll of death he remarked that it is not surprising that so many deaths occurred. In his immediate family he counted six. Whereas we the singers who pray and have their rites, "like you and me, did you notice we have recovered? That's because of the power of our prayer. The singers and the *ednishodis* (priests) don't die, the rest do!" This is blissful ignorance and presumption. Yet these men cannot but seize every opportunity to advertise their prowess and at that it is successful advertising, for the very simple reason that no knowledge of the rest of the country is available to the Navajo. They cannot read reports and probably never realized the full malice of the epidemic. As to ourselves I doubt not but that my confreres in the priesthood and such whose duties called them constantly to grapple with death have added special fervor to their daily petition, "Thy will be done." I am not ashamed to admit that in my instance it was the sole antiseptic at my disposal. The priest is not given to boasting, yet as a class, I daresay, none have faced death with more courage than they. This I took occasion to point out to my friend and instanced that Daǧatso (Big Beard, as Father Theodore was called) had recently succumbed [Father Theodore Stephan, stationed at Jemez, New Mexico, died October 30, 1918] and that throughout the country the priests had been victims like the rest of mortals. None of us can defy death, and he had better be modest in his claims! The following morning, Sunday though it was, I assisted at digging the grave, which was blessed before interment.

Notes

1. Rose Mitchell, *Tall Woman: The Life Story of Rose Mitchell, a Navajo Woman, c. 1874–1977*. Charlotte J. Frisbie, ed. (Albuquerque: University of New Mexico Press), 426–27.

2. Robert McPherson, "The Flu Epidemic of 1918: A Cultural Response," *Blue Mountain Shadows* 1 (Spring 1988), 67–72.

3. Mitchell, 25.

4. Franc Johnson Newcomb, *Hosteen Klah: Navaho Medicine Man and Sand Painter* (Norman: University of Oklahoma Press, 1964, 144–46. Newcomb states that the scenes she describes occurred in the winter of 1919–1920, when the "dreaded flu" first arrived "on our side of the Reservation," but her summary statement that "it has been estimated that one-tenth of the entire Navajo population died that winter, and I believe that estimate is far too low" would seem to apply to the 1918–1919 outbreak.

5. Mitchell, 128.

6. For estimated mortality rates by region or school, illustrating the range and wide variation in mortality from the influenza epidemic, see Scott C. Russell, "The Navajo and the 1918 Influenza Pendemic," in *Health and Disease in the Prehistoric Southwest*, Anthropological Research Papers No. 34, ed. Charles F. Merbs and Robert J. Miller (Tempe: Arizona State University, 1985), 380–90; Garrick Bailey and Roberta Glenn Bailey, *A History of the Navajo: The Reservation Years* (Santa Fe, N.Mex.: School of American Research Press, 1986), 119–20; and McPherson, 71–72.

7. Works including reference to the emotional consequences of the epidemic include Mitchell, McPherson, Russell, and Garrick Bailey and Robert Glenn Bailey, *Historic Navajo Occupation of the Northern Chaco Plateau* (Tulsa, Okla.: Faculty of Anthropology, University of Tulsa, 1982).

8. Mitchell, 129.

9. Berard Haile to Father Provincial Rudolph Bonner, 2 December 1918. FAC Box PLA.323. Lukachukai, AZ: St. Isabel, fd. Lukachukai, AZ: B. Haile, A. Weber Letters 1918–1925.

10. Anselm Weber to Father Provincial Rudolph Bonner, 2 November 1918. FAC Box DEC.245. Anselm Weber Beautiful Mountain, fd. Egbert, O.F.M. Fort Defiance Church (CI10).

11. Weber to Charles S. Lusk, 16 December 1918. BCIM Series 1, Box 109, fd. 1.

12. Weber to Lusk, 1 February 1919. BCIM Series 1, Box 113, fd. 27.

13. Anselm Weber, FMN 46 (March 1919): 223–28. Translated by Marie Bradshaw Durrant.

14. From Berard Haile, "Random Notes," typescript, 1918, and a combination of selections from four handwritten drafts and sets of notes, undated, apparently penned 1918–1919, all versions of Father Berard's experience of the flu epidemic. BHP Box 5, fd. 1.

32

Priorities

Anselm Weber, O.F.M., Egbert Fischer, O.F.M., and Others

[Along with the external challenges—a people steeped in traditional tribal religion and in thrall to the medicine men, a federal bureaucracy in the process of withdrawing support from denominational schools, a growing presence of Protestant preachers on the reservation, and powerful local interests devoted to "opening" Navajo lands—the missionaries faced challenges from within. There were confreres and superiors with differing ideas about how to conduct mission work among the Navajo; there were the conflicts of personality and priority that arise even among saints, differences sometimes magnified by the isolation and deprivation of mission life; and there was always the poverty, the lack of reliable, continuing funding for a growing mission establishment. This chapter, based in letters and fragments of letters, offers glimpses of Father Anselm's guiding priorities in the last decade of his life, as they surfaced in his responses to external challenges and to questions from other Franciscans about his leadership.

In portraying Father Anselm's work, and his statements about what he was doing and why, I have skipped back and forth across the decade to some extent, presenting some of his letters in their entirety, in other instances linking statements from different letters, and sometimes drawing two or more segments, perhaps reflecting different principles or themes, from the same letter.

Most action represents a compromise among several, often competing priorities. In choosing among the more obvious priorities apparent in an incident or a communication, one highlights some things at the expense of others. The present chapter is organized around several competing objectives of action, combined according to my interpretation of Father Anselm's personal priorities and commitments. It is illustrative, not definitive, and most of the selections cited might reasonably have been used to illustrate other priorities as well. Each first-order heading involves at least two competing objectives, ordered as they seemed to be in Anselm Weber's hierarchy of values. Thus, "service over comfort" means that, in Anselm's rating of things, it was expected that service to the Navajo would

require deprivation and sacrifice by the missionaries, and that such sacrifice was
seen as an appropriate and necessary cost of providing the service.]

Secular Works over Preachments, and
Long-Term over Short-Term Benefits

[Not everyone, even among the Franciscans, agreed with Father Anselm's policy
of serving the Navajo's present needs and, where possible, their long-term interests,
in the faith that present good works would open the door to future receptivity to the
spiritual message of the Church. Sometimes the notion of exchange—we help them
now, they help us later—was a direct, explicit part of the friars' strategy, but more
often the guiding principle was less obviously quid pro quo than simply to
demonstrate goodwill and a willingness to help in the faith that good things would
follow. Perhaps by creating a reservoir of friendship and trust, or by making Navajo
reliance on the friars habitual, the reasoning went, in future times of spiritual need
the people would turn to those whom they knew and trusted. Added to that, of
course, was the idea that if the friars educated Navajo children to Catholic belief,
eventually there would be adult Navajo who were practicing Catholics.

Critics complained that the friars' activities ought to be more specifically
religious, or at least that the mix of spiritual and secular service under Father
Anselm's direction was too heavily secular. Father Anselm seems to have expected
that, in time, the scales would balance, that secular good works now would in the
future produce the desired spiritual fruit, but he was less concerned about the
magnitude of future returns from present investments than in doing what seemed
to be necessary here and now, and leaving to heaven the balancing of accounts.
When he sought Navajo support for some decision or action, Father Anselm was
not above reminding them of his efforts in their behalf, but his service, and
especially his work to protect their lands, went far beyond the point necessary to
secure their cooperation and to assure that some of them would be willing to learn
about the white man's religion.

Father Anselm was driven by a passion to see justice done to the Navajo
because that was the right thing to do, and whether his actions supported the
immediate objectives of the Franciscan missionaries was less important than that
they serve the long-term interests of the Navajo. Occasionally, to trusted associates,
he admitted as much, as in the following excerpt from a letter to Father Berard,
written from New York City on May 17, 1911:

> Since the train passes through Washington anyway, I spent all day yesterday there
> and did some fine work. I saw Senator Curtis, Vice President Sherman, the Indian
> commissioner, and Mr. Hauke, the second assistant Indian commissioner. . . .

Now, I think I have worked for the Navajo like a Trojan, and I hope Chee and Frank and the silversmith and Charlie Mitchell and others will work for us also, especially that council in June, and I hope the Navajo in general will appreciate my work done and will not place us on an equal footing with Mr. [Alexander] Black, who never does anything, and the others who do mischief.

Of course I would do these things whether the Navajo favored me or not. I did not do them in order to get their support in a religious way; they ought to know that by this time; but if the younger generation is to leave their Navajo religion and become Christian, they might as well chose the *right* Christian religion and become Catholics, as to choose a renegade and wrong so-called Christian religion.[1]

If one of Father Anselm's guiding priorities was to do what ought to be done—to act now, in faith, to do one's best in the light of present contingencies—another was a pragmatism about how things might be accomplished. If by pointing to past successes he could increase the probability of a present achievement, he was quite willing to do so. But the motivation for the original action was neither to bind a recipient of his services to future recompense, nor to generate praise for himself. "Happily Father Anselm Weber had not entered the Navaho mission field with any design on recognition or status to be achieved; neither would his efforts toward maintaining peace on the reservation alter in the least because of any man's thanks, or the lack of it."[2]

Among the Franciscans who questioned Father Anselm's priorities was Father Egbert Fischer, who thought that Father Anselm's "hobby" of working to secure land for the Navajo distracted him from weightier matters, that having the U.S. Post Office located at the mission was another distraction, that too little time went into religious exercises for the friars, and that resources were wasted on the Navajo, especially on the interpreter Frank Walker, whom Egbert said he would have fired immediately. Moreover, Father Anselm's leadership style bothered Father Egbert. He wanted a leader who would show interest in his work, give him assignments, and then follow up and evaluate, rather than the freedom that came with working under the overcommitted Anselm to make his own decisions and suffer from his own mistakes. Father Egbert laid out his grievances in a long letter to Provincial Rudolph Bonner early in 1916.]

"Things Are Far from Ideal Out Here"[3]

Dear Father Provincial:

Your kind letter to me will ever be a source of great encouragement and ever since I received it, I have been debating how I should write to you again. As you, no doubt, remember, things are far from ideal out here, and until you would be stronger physically, I thought it best not to write. On the other hand I fear I would be lacking in truthfulness if I wrote that all is well, or would let you believe all is as it should be. Perhaps I have no business to write at all, and yet, with so much out of joint, I think it well if you are posted in a general way, and can find a way out of the difficulties.

At the present writing, Father Superior [Anselm Weber] is in Gallup. He has been sick for weeks now, one day in bed, then up again. Doctor Wigglesworth says frankly he should have a milder climate and recuperate entirely, but that he will not get well staying at home. I honestly believe he is not happy at St. Michaels, no doubt, the younger element there get on his nerves for various reasons. The sorest spot is Frank Walker, our drunken interpreter. Father Celestine, Father Marcellus, and myself are of one opinion: Frank Walker *must* go. He is a positive curse unmitigated, for our mission. But Father Superior would rather give an eye than see him go.

The next thing is the utter independence of Brother Felix [Bruening]. But there are two mitigating circumstances, absence of religious exercises and his age.

Another thing is the Printing Press. Father Celestine is determined to print at St. Michaels, only Father Marcellus must do the printing. To be sure there's a printer hired but that adds to the complications, I fear.

Father Celestine's limbs are badly swollen and Doctor insists he must remain quiet, wherefore Father Marcellus must attend to St. Michael's School, the post office, and the printing, and as he has Tohatchi to attend to, that government school (Tohatchi) is neglected first.

Now I have no suggestions to offer, and ask you, dear Father, to take no action, as possibly some things might right themselves, although I hardly can see such a thing possible.

To my mind Tohatchi could be attended to more easily from Gallup, instead from St. Michaels, but I do *not* mean that the Fathers at Gallup now should add that mission to their numerous ones at present. Another thing I am in favor of is to have our printing done elsewhere and keep every outsider from boarding at our mission.

Personally I would rather not have the post office, and think it a handicap to missionary activity. The hobby of Father Superior to secure land for the Navajo is so all-absorbing that there's precious little left for missionary activity. Our mission, to be true to its reason for existing, should be mainly (rather exclusively) for soul conquest, and since we are religious, religious exercises should be daily pabulum (not only in retreat). I need not tell you that dissatisfaction is rife. Take away religious exercises, and let everyone do as he pleases, and you have hell in a convent. As to myself, my heart is wrenched beyond expression. I am staying at the new chapel mostly. Brother Fidelis [Koper] is still here (as Father Leopold is satisfied) and he assures me he was never happier. As soon as he finishes the little work remaining to be done he will leave for Chin Lee. He sleeps at the chapel, receives Holy Communion *every* morning, attends my Mass at 6:00, and takes his meals at the employee's mess. I eat and must sleep at the Doctor's. I do not know just what to do. If I go back and forth to St. Michaels I must either have a team and there's no provision to feed them here, or if I stay here all the time, I am practically alone. When I ask Father Superior he says: "Yes; sure; alright," to any question.

Temporizing takes you nowhere. The work here is more than enough for one man, as there are now two hospitals, instruction is every Tuesday and Thursday evening from 7:00–8:00 p.m. and Mass on Sundays at 10:00 a.m. The preachers are doing their meanest, the agent connives at it, and Father Superior is supinely indifferent. At times I feel almost desperate. I am looking for advice, for a leader, and find empty phrases and promises. When I report the doings here to Father Superior I hear: "Paquette has no right to do that," or "I'll settle that," and the matter is dropped—forever. I am at my wits' ends.

Now please don't do anything in this matter until you are called upon by Father Superior, in writing, or can come out to see for yourself.

Possibly Father Celestine will write for a temporary change, although he is now almost indispensable, as he is trying to watch the unnecessary waste of money for which no account is given (Frank Walker and other Indian favorites are a big item); possibly Father Superior will ask for another man, at least if two Fathers leave St. Michaels for their health.

Father Marcellus is uncomplaining, but he is *not* satisfied, and his health not so good.

Dear Father Provincial, I do not want this letter to weigh upon you, nor do I ask you to take my word for anything, but hope you will try to get to the bottom of things as they are, and have been for these four years that I am connected with our mission.

I do not know a remedy. Perhaps the Lord will enlighten your reverence. As I am away from the trouble I can write better than if I were just now coming from an argument.

In fact I have no arguments, as I mortally offend Father Superior whenever I disagree with him, Father Celestine uses me (very willingly on my part) as a relief valve, and I try to encourage him and Father Marcellus wherever I can, but see no relief anywhere. Let me ask you: "Would Brothers Simeon and Ewald still be with us, if they had never been to St. Michaels?" and "Would Father Norbert still be a Franciscan had he never studied medicine?" I don't want an answer, but please, Father, think and pray it over.

Gratefully yours

Trust over Control

[Father Anselm was no micromanager. He was criticized for not spending more time overseeing the daily activities of the friars under his direction, and for being too lenient with Navajo employees. Yet when attention to detail was absolutely critical to success, as in his own research on Navajo lands and the appropriate administrative and political maneuverings, his performance was remarkable, successful, and widely respected.

The "faults" noted by Father Egbert seem to be matters of conscious choice on Anselm's part. Certainly the constant demands on his time would favor his laissez-faire style of leadership. In a subsequent letter to the provincial, Father Egbert commented that "I have been under such unbearable strain for the past six months, that I wonder, my reason is not unbalanced," and then pointed again to the lack of detailed direction from his Superior:

[A]ll I wish to have is a good understanding with my Superiors, but in the past there was only misunderstandings without end. Once I have some Superior, who will tell me just what to do, when I am confronted by the thousand and one problems here, and will back me when I do as he says, not leave me in the hole at the critical moment, there is not anything I would not do in the line of missionary work. . . . I ask that my Superior show enough interest in my work, that I know how far I should go in everything, and that he will back me if I do as he says. Should I ask him: 'How about lantern slides?' and he will answer: 'Sure! Father Leopold has them too,' and I ask for a curtain, or material, and then he will either not say anything, or 'I have no money,' it tries me almost beyond endurance.[4]

Father Anselm made his leadership policy of minimal administrative constraint explicit in correspondence with Provincial Rudolph Bonner over problems Father Fridolin Schuster was having with his superior, Father Eligius Kunkel, then pastor at Gallup. Father Anselm blamed much of the difficulty on Father Eligius's overcontrol:

Now, about Father Fridolin. He is thoroughly disgruntled with his work and everything else, it seems. . . . The meals, especially during vacation, when he cannot take his meals with the absent employees, but must live on Indian fare, do not agree with his stomach. Neither can he 'stomach' his Superior. I think, however, Father Elig is at fault. He ought to have more confidence in him and should let him do his work according to his own fancy. If his work brings him to Santa Fe and Albuquerque, I see no reason why he should object. I think Father Fridolin would not object to staying if he had a free hand.[5]

Father Fridolin, who was working at Laguna, apparently had helped some of his people on land issues, and thereby provoked criticism from his Superior of both his own and Father Anselm's involvement in the politics of Indian land. Father Anselm retorted that

Whether I and Father Fridolin spend some time in looking after the lands of the Indians, well, I do not see why that should make Father Elig sick. The children are not going to the devil, on that account, as Father Elig said. Anyway, his responsibility does not extend to the Navajo. If Father Elig were a little less sensitive and impulsive, it would be better for his own health and the health of others. Of course, if Father Celestine represents me at Gallup (and possibly at other places) as a good-natured old fool, people begin to believe it; but that does not affect my health.[6]

Father Anselm dismissed Father Egbert's criticism without bothering to repudiate each particular. More serious, because it might indeed affect someone else's spiritual health, was Father Egbert's transfer to another mission site. Advising Provincial Rudolph Bonner, Father Anselm wrote,

As to my opinion, it is this, that Father Egbert is crazy. If he goes to Shiprock and starts out the way he did at Fort Defiance, he may get the children baptized and make their First Holy Communion. He *may*, if he starts in enthusiastically. But there his work stops. He cannot HOLD the children and cannot hold the goodwill of the government officials any length of time. In my mind it is a pity that he was not taken somewhere else to make another one free to go to Shiprock. . . . I am not speaking metaphorically when I say he is crazy. He is, and you will agree with me in due course of time.[7]

Also taken seriously, and prompting the detailed response, were subsequent criticisms of Father Leopold Ostermann's leadership at Chin Lee by Brother Fidelis Koper (see chapter 29). In Father Anselm's view, Brother Fidelis's attitude, and especially his inadequate performance in supporting Father Leopold by shouldering, in good spirit, his share of the work at Chin Lee, constituted a real threat to Leopold's mental health. Further, Brother Fidelis's attitude toward the Navajo threatened the positive rapport with the Chin Lee community that Father Leopold had cultivated so carefully over the years. Father Anselm acted with authority and dispatch in recommending to Provincial Rudolph Bonner the Brother's removal and the assignment of a more "decent" Brother to Chin Lee. And so it happened; Brother Fidelis was transferred out of the Navajo missions, replaced by Brother Julian Elpers.]

Generosity over Petty Frugality, Sharing over Stinting

[The complaint that the mission under Father Anselm was too generous to the Navajo, or at least to certain Navajo, appears fairly often in the writings of those who questioned Anselm's priorities. We have already seen Father Egbert's charge that Father Anselm overlooked Frank Walker's failings. Father Celestine Matz was described above by Father Egbert as one for whom he served as "relief valve"and as an "almost indispensable" critic of "the unnecessary waste of money for which no account is given." Much less charitable than his Superior about Navajo needs and appropriate Franciscan generosity, Father Celestine saw Anselm's open-handedness as a weakness. Writing to Father Berard about the possibilities of collecting money owed to Berard, Celestine reported:

> If I would know these scamps personally, that is the ones who owe the money, it would be a great help to me in going after these fellows. Chances are that some of these fellows come here and that I do not know them and that the Boss [Father Anselm] does not ask them for the money for fear of offending them. He surely is afraid of offending the Indian and if he can get out of asking them for anything he surely does it. Only a few weeks ago he donated five gallons of gasoline and one gallon of oil to Edward's father who came here with a hard-luck story and that he had no money to buy gasoline, etc., but when he came back two days later and asked for more gasoline for nothing I put up a howl and told the Boss that if he was going to establish a precedent and give away gasoline in the

same manner as he is doing with hay that I was going to write to the provincial and ask for a change, because I thought it was simply overdoing things. Well, as a result of my kick he made Edward's father pay for the gasoline which he got that day and he has been paying ever since, and if I can help he will pay for every drop he gets here. Don't you think I have taken the right stand in this matter?[8]

Father Anselm's working principle seemed to be, whether with regard to mission resources or his own time and energy, that when in doubt, and when giving was possible, one should give. His biographer writes, "He and his tireless labors for the good of The People were more or less taken for granted, as if such service for the Indians were the expected function of a missionary. Perhaps the finest expression of their appreciation for the friars' work in their behalf was to be found in the Navaho's increasing demand for the priest's time and help in solving their personal and tribal problems."[9]

Works over Words, Deeds over Declarations

To give, to travel, to help, simply to exist meant the consumption of resources, and Father Anselm was much troubled by the lack of sufficient economic support for the Navajo missions. He and his associates might view themselves as heaven's messengers, but they needed earthly financing to do the job.

In 1910 things reached a point that Father Anselm decided to take a direct role in fund-raising, and to make a creative appeal to subscribers to *Der Sendbote*, whether the powers that be liked it or not. His plan was to recruit "promoters" who would raise funds for the mission, and who would be repaid with premiums of Navajo artwork. He announced his plan in a letter to Father William H. Ketcham, director of the Bureau of Catholic Indian Missions. The letter, reprinted below, manifests Anselm's remarkable personal commitment to the mission's creditors. He even threatens to resign from the mission and do private fund-raising if he is blocked in this attempt to raise money within the system. His threat may be the venting of frustration at continuing financial insecurity, but the pragmatic "I'll do it myself" attitude is characteristic of the man. It shows up later in his personal efforts to cajole donations from well-to-do Eastern churches and in many other contexts throughout his life.

Father Anselm's defiant stance bore fruit. The next year, with the cooperation of the appropriate administrators, he was in New York City speaking and collecting donations, appealing to funding agencies such as the Marquette League. In the second excerpt below, he reports his successes to Father Berard.]

"I Cannot Continue to Live on Credit"[10]

Very Reverend Dear Father Ketcham:

I have never been able to ascertain just upon whom devolves the support of our missions. No one is willing to "plead guilty," no matter whom I may address.

The $1,000 which our province had sent me annually is now transferred to Chin Lee. Mother Katharine gives us three a salary of $1,000. No matter what the cost of living may be and how conditions may change, the salary remains stationary.

The archbishops permitted me to introduce the Preservation Society in the parishes of our province for the support of our missions, but the 600 and some odd dollars realized are inadequate. We are living on credit and borrowed money; but that cannot go on indefinitely.

Under existing conditions I am determined to write an article, at the end of this month, for the German *Sacred Heart Messenger* [*Sendbote*], urging the readers to volunteer as promoters for this society, and offering small premiums in Navajo industrial work, amounting to about ten cents to every dollar sent in (two and a half cents to every 25 cents).

I have written regularly for the last 10 years for this *Messenger* and am confident I have aroused enough interest in our work to induce a number of readers to offer themselves as promoters.

I shall also write a letter to the promoters in our parishes offering them the same premium and asking them to extend their efforts beyond the limits of our parishes, and, if they can induce others in neighboring parishes to accept appointments as promoters, to do so.

In this way, I am confident, I can reach a number of people whom you have not reached and whom, very probably, you would never reach.

I should certainly prefer to receive adequate support without any special effort on my part from the proper authorities, whoever they may be; but if they, as is the case, do not give that support, and should, besides, effectively block my way to raise such support, I shall then make a tour East, collect the necessary money to pay my debts, and resign. If the Church as such, as an organization, does not feel obliged to support missionary endeavor, individual responsibility ceases to exist.

Since you are the president of the society I beg you to write to me, either approving of my intended course, or, if you think you cannot do so, registering your sentiments, lack of disapproval, or whatever they may be. Nothing but your categorical prohibition will deter me from going ahead. I hope you will not deem it necessary to place the matter before the archbishops, first because I have no time to wait, and, second, because their approval or disapproval would not faze me very much since they fail to make provision for the support of the missions, which they could if they really wanted to.

In trying to introduce the society I shall not hedge behind your authority; I shall not mention your name so no one can "blame" you for my ungodliness.

Since we have so many Indians to attend to, chapels to build, and so on, and since I can reach people whom you very probably could not reach, I hope I will have your good wishes. Unless otherwise directed, my article leaves here for the editor's desk on the last of this month.

Very Sincerely Yours,

PS. My intended course has the good wishes of Mother Katharine who urged me to write to you.

PS. Should anyone, bishop or archbishop, wish to disapprove and to hold you responsible, you have this letter to prove my "defiance." That is one of the reasons why I wrote it and why I wrote it the way I did. I meant no disrespect to you in the least; but I cannot continue to live on credit, and I know the "authorities" do not bother, least of all our dear bishop who is serenely indifferent.

"I Preached Six Times and Was "All In" after That"[11]

Today I paid a visit to the Marquette League, and I hope to get either $500 or more from it for our chapels. I only saw the secretary and promptly fell in love with her. My reasons for expecting that much from the league? I placed a letter with it in reference to our two chapels, endorsed by the archbishop; then and here is a nice story: when you returned the $1,000 to Bishop Granjon, he wrote to the Marquette League that he had turned over the money to Father Mathias or Matthew, O.F.M., who would build four chapels with it for the Papagoes. But the donor had stipulated that *one* chapel should be built with that money and that it should have the name of *Annunciation*. At last the president decided to ask the bishop to return $500 of the money and they would make up the other $500 and build the Annunciation chapel somewhere else.

I told her: all right; give us the money and we shall gladly call either the chapel at Chin Lee or at Lukachukai "Annunciation" and consider the donor as the founder. She will place the matter before Mr. Philbin, the president of the society, or rather the league, and will let me know the outcome.

Tomorrow I shall write to the Ludwigs Missions Verein in Munich and to the Leopoldinenstift of Vienna for a contribution and for *perpetual* assistance. I am certain I will get something from Munich.

Through the assistance of the archbishop and the provincial here I got some good, rich churches to collect in.

I enclose $252, last Sunday's collection. I preached six times and was "all in" after that. Next Sunday I have a better church still at Yonkers, and hope to send you between $300 and $400 dollars next week. . . .

Conciliation over Confrontation

[Another aspect of Father Anselm's pragmatism, perhaps an outgrowth of his experience trying to influence politicians, was a willingness to negotiate, to "go along to get along," to put aside personal feelings in the interest of a practical outcome. His preference for positive, practical outcomes over the personal satisfaction that might be taken in public embarrassment of his opponents is manifest in his sharp difference with Father Berard over public denunciation of the misbehavior of the Protestant preachers on the reservation, of activities the friars thought unethical or foolish. Many advertisers in the Franciscan Fathers' annual journal, *Franciscan Missions of the Southwest*, were Protestant, and given the choice, Father Anselm preferred the good that could be accomplished with the income from those advertisements over the satisfaction that might be taken in publishing the Franciscan assessment of the practices and character of the Protestant missionaries.

The following excerpts from two of Father Anselm's letters to Father Berard explain his stance on the matter. The first informs Berard that Anselm has edited out parts of Berard's manuscript that he thought unnecessarily provocative; the second answers Berard's caustic comment that Anselm was being too easy on his "Protestant friends." In this second letter, Father Anselm warns that Berard has overstepped his bounds; the freedom Anselm allowed his associates to do things their own way did not extend to expressions of personal disrespect for their Superior.]

"Almost All the Advertisers Are Protestant"[12]

Now about your article, I cannot publish all of it. Almost all the advertisers are Protestant, and it would not do to let them read about short-tail ministers. The part is good, especially the remarks of Charlie about the affair, but not for the magazine largely read by Protestants. I will make use of it for *Der Sendbote*.

Neither will I use all what you say about the Lukachukaini. I would not like to have people think the Lukachukainis a set of sifted son-of-a-guns. Many people would misinterpret that and would think our work useless, and useless to send us money and men. . . .

Mother Loyola told me about your letter, what the Indians said, and how they acted when they saw the statues put up at Lukachukai. . . . If you would write that to me, also something about the services at Lukachukai and something about the former schoolchildren: not that they let the children die without baptism, however, I would gladly put that in. I think something about services and the children ought to go in. . . .

"I Shall Not Stand Another Letter of That Kind"[13]

In your last letter you wrote me: "And in anticipation of your views on the subject of the Navaho, as well as your timidity to offend your Protestant friends by references such as the article contains I sent the article unfolded, and desire that you return it to me unfolded also." Very well, then you should have written me that you wanted the article published unaltered and in full or not at all. In that case I would have returned the article, of course. Your letter contained no more than the assumption that it would be published as written, and that was contained in it only by implication. In the absence of any definite instruction on your part, I assumed that it was sent to me like any other article from anyone else.

As it is, when your letter arrived, the article was not only set, but all the copies were printed already, hence I could not comply with your request. I did not make use of any of your letters, or parts of letters: nothing but what was in the article was used. I return the article by this same mail.

If you had stopped to think you would not have made that invidious comparison with Father Egbert's article. Our magazine is not the *Sendbote*, nor have they the same readers. Last year I cut out many things from his article on Fort Defiance which had appeared in the *Sendbote*. When I asked him this year to write, I told him to omit his troubles with the ministers and the employees. I have not discriminated and am not discriminating.

I thank you for the "timidity to offend Protestant friends." We received over $1,000 this year from Protestant advertisers, and to slap their ministers is hardly a good way to induce them to renew their advertisements.

I do not remember [trader C. N.] Cotton's qualification of [Stewart] Culin's politeness,[14] neither do I recall what I had written in the fore-part of my letter to justify your remark that it bore the stamp of "*dona ferentes*." At any rate, it was not necessary to give me that slap in the face for fear that, otherwise, I would not realize your offensiveness in full. I shall not stand another letter of that kind.

[Father Anselm's preference for negotiation over confrontation, and for the resolution of differences in private rather than before the world, was not an absolute priority. There were limits to his willingness to compromise, and he was pragmatic enough to know that there are times when confrontation is unavoidable. He saw the the threat of "going public" as a useful weapon, to be used sparingly. In 1908, reacting to a U.S. military plan to frighten the grumbling Black Mountain Navajo into submission by moving large concentrations of troops through their homeland, Father Anselm threatened to use the media to magnify the Navajo "howl" over such treatment. Writing to Father William Ketcham, he exclaimed,

> Submit to whom and to what? I know some of the Black Mountain Indians and I assure you that such a course would be preposterous, not to say criminal. If such a course is pursued, I shall join the Black Mountain Indians and 'howl' with them so that the whole United States will hear us. . . . All those Indians need is a good competent, reasonable superintendent. . . . The Navajo are men who resent mere coercion.[15]

In 1919 Father Anselm again threatened to appeal to the general public. He was frustrated over years of official inaction, negative responses, and discriminatory administration by Cato Sells, Commissioner of Indian Affairs. In particular, Father Anselm was dismayed by the apparent success of Protestant ministers in discrediting Indian agent Peter Paquette of Fort Defiance, and the Indian commissioner's apparent acquiescence, if not connivance, in Paquette's transfer. So Father Anselm appealed to the Knights of Columbus, a powerful Catholic organization, to lodge an official protest with Commissioner Sells, and urged that if the protest was unsuccessful, then evidence of Mr. Sells's discriminatory behavior should be published "in some large eastern paper." The letter, dated April 21, 1919, was addressed to Mr. E. P. Davies of Santa Fe, New Mexico.]

"Not to Convert the Pagans, but to Pervert Our Catholic Indians"[16]

Since my efforts and those of my friends at Washington seem to prove futile, I must appeal, through you, to the Knights of Columbus for assistance against the actions and proposed actions of Mr. Cato Sells, commissioner of Indian Affairs at Washington, D.C.

Mr. Peter Paquette, superintendent of the Navajo Agency at Fort Defiance, Arizona, has tried to be fair to us and to favor neither us nor the Presbyterian ministers, but since he could not and would not accede to their bigoted demands, they have been calling him our "slave" and have reported him a number of times to the Indian Office, and have tried ever since 1911 to have him removed. I am firmly convinced that his present investigation and suspension are the result of their agitation and the aggressive demands of the Reverend Thomas C. Moffett, who is at the head of the Presbyterian Mission Board in New York.

Mr. Paquette is to be sacrificed to their bigotry.

I am enclosing a copy of my letter to Senator Ashurst, also a member of the Knights of Columbus, to show you the outrageous way in which his investigation was conducted.

I am convinced that Inspectors Endicott and Coleman have been sent to accomplish a twofold end: to oust Mr. Paquette and to secure a mission site for the Presbyterian ministers at Chin Lee, Arizona, where we have a mission since 1904. Not to convert the pagans, but to pervert our Catholic Indians and our pupils at the Chin Lee government school, do they wish to establish a mission at that point. I enclose copy of my letters to Mr. Lusk, describing two Indian councils, to show how utterly opposed the Indians are to the establishment of this Presbyterian mission.

In spite of all their protests and mine, and the absolute right of the Indians, according to their treaty of 1868, to refuse such mission sites, Mr. Sells seems determined to grant this site to the Presbyterians. Inspectors Coleman and Endicott went to Chin Lee to investigate and report, but they only saw the Gormans, the one outfit who is favorable to the granting of that site, but they did not speak to one of the headmen, not one of all the numerous Indians opposed to the granting of the mission site, except John Brown, the Navajo policeman—not to investigate, but to upbraid him for not helping the Presbyterians as much as the Catholics. Certainly a thorough and impartial investigation! Of course they recommended the granting of the mission site to the Presbyterians. I am sure Mr. Sells will grant it, and grant it in the near future, if the Knights of Columbus do not come to our assistance and to the assistance of the Indians with a prompt and vigorous protest. And I beg you very much to do all you can to have this protest lodged with Mr. Sells or Franklin K. Lane, the secretary of the interior, for our protection against the destructive efforts of the ministers of the *Menace* [an anti-Catholic periodical] type, and the protection of the Indians in asserting the rights granted them through the treaty of 1868. Prompt action is necessary; otherwise, it will be too late.

In further substantiation of the attitude of Mr. Cato Sells toward Catholics, I mention the transfer of Mr. McQuick, superintendent of San Xavier, Arizona, involving a demotion, and the shameful treatment accorded to Major Ernest Stecher, superintendent at San Carlos, Arizona. He joined the army and was lauded to the skies by Secretary Lane for doing so; but he returned to find his place filled permanently by a Texan. Thus were he and his son, also in the army, rewarded for their services to the country. Mr. Sells offered him, instead, the superintendency at Moqui—an impossible position for him on account of the lack of educational facilities for his young son and on account of the ill-health of his wife. The offer was equal to a dismissal from the service. This only to show his attitude; but I beg your assistance especially in the Chin Lee case and the case of Mr. Paquette. I am sure a protest to Cato Sells or Secretary Lane against the granting of Chin Lee mission site to the Presbyterians, and against the removal of Mr. Paquette from Fort Defiance, lodged by the head of your powerful organization would force them to do justice to us and to the Indians.

Should his efforts not have the desired result, I would beg you to have the Knights of Columbus pass a resolution, denouncing the actions of Mr. Sells, and publish his attitude in some large eastern paper. Publicity alone may induce Mr. Sells to refrain from discriminating against us and from yielding to the bigoted demands of Protestants of the *Menace* type. By the way, I begged Mr. Sells, some years ago, when the *Menace* was mailed to some employees and even to some of the pupils of the Fort Defiance government school, to exclude this paper from the school grounds, but he would not accede to my wishes.

Mission Productivity over Missionary Preference

[Father Anselm's pragmatics include a personal tolerance for idiosyncrasy and diversity, along with an awareness that the wishes of less-tolerant others must be taken into account. In one of his reports to Provincial Eugene Buttermann, speaking of problems some of his colleagues have had in getting along with a certain very difficult missionary, he insists that he himself has learned to live peaceably with almost anyone.

> Your sentence: *"Er wuerde auf diese Weise den anderen doch kaum im Wege sein,"* seems to indicate your impression that the main objection against him is his attitude toward us and our attitude toward him. It is true that Father Berard and Father Fintan were utterly opposed to live with him and would have insisted to be removed if he had stayed; but that was not the case with me; I *am* living and *have* been living with so many different kinds of people that I am getting rather indifferent; my main objection against him was and is his utter unfitness for this work which makes his presence not only useless but harmful to our work.[17]

It was that characteristic, the man's potential detriment to the work, that to the pragmatist Anselm was the ultimate disqualification. He continued, "Alone at

Lukachukai he *might* land in an asylum; he *would* ruin that part of our mission." Father Anselm concluded his argument against the friar's transfer to the Navajo missions with a forceful statement of the daunting challenge that Navajo, by their very nature, presented to the would-be missionary. Success elsewhere was not an indication of fitness for the more demanding Navajo missions: "I have no doubt in the world that he does exceedingly well at Padua; but Padua is not the Navajo reservation, and the good religious people there, vowed to obedience or preparing themselves for such vows, are not the stubborn, independent, sensitive, semi-barbarous Navajo; neither is the equanimity, incident to Noviciate routine, to be found at Lukachukai."[18]]

Action over Image, Work over Retirement

[We have already seen, in Father Anselm's report of April 1919 about his work on Navajo land problems (chapter 21), that he had arrived at a convenient and defensible stopping point in his 15-year struggle to secure and augment the Navajo land base. He had even publicly affirmed that he was through, telling his *Sendbote* audience that "my activities in these matters have come to an end." He was 58 years old and in poor health. Late in 1917 he had had a kidney removed, and from that time until his death on March 7, 1921, he was in and out of the Mayo Clinic for continued treatment of cancer.[19] After his thousands of miles of horseback ministry, the intrepid horseman was no longer in saddle. In a letter of May 1918 to Provincial Rudolph Bonner he apologized for a tardy response, on the grounds that "yesterday . . . I took my first horseback ride—10 miles—after a year and a half, and I felt a little broken up."[20]

Father Anselm's personal experience in trying to influence legislators and government administrators had taught him how "things got done" in Washington, and he had become adept at behind-the-scenes political maneuvering, both in his work on Navajo land and in his efforts to influence federal appointments. His very success became a source of criticism; people jealous of his influence suggested that government workers, and not a Catholic priest, ought to be representing the Navajo.

He might be "cut up," and "broken up," but he could continue the influential correspondence and, to some extent, the essential visits. A less committed missionary might have been content to bask in the memory of solid accomplishment and pass the torch to others, but Father Anselm continued the struggle, defending the rights of the Navajo to decide who might occupy land on the treaty reservation, defending a beleaguered agent, Peter Paquette, who had been targeted for removal by the Protestant ministers, insisting on fairness in the treatment of the Franciscans and the Catholic Navajo by government employees who favored the Protestants, working behind the scenes to try to prevent the appointment of a new commissioner of Indian Affairs known to be anti-Catholic, and warning of the dire consequences to follow if, as was rumored, Senator Albert B. Fall were to be appointed secretary of the interior. He also continued to lobby for Indian ownership of lands they occupied, but lacked title to, in New Mexico, and there was hardly a pause in his cooperation with Howel Jones of the Santa Fe Railroad. I cannot find that he ever used the phrase, "enduring to the end," to refer to himself, but he was one for whom image or reputation of past accomplishment was never enough to justify a halt. For Father Anselm "enduring to the end" meant continuing to fight the good fight until he could fight no more.

So in his final years the battle went on. The variety and intensity of his late work may be seen in the following four selections. The first, excerpted from a February 1919 letter to Charles S. Lusk, secretary of the Bureau of Catholic Indian Missions, is a defense of agent Peter Paquette, but it informs us on a variety of other topics, including the Navajo' feelings about Father Anselm. The second letter, written two weeks later to Indian Service Inspector S. A. M. Young, argues for the continuation of a policy designed to prevent the acceptance of "second signatures" from Indian parents who have been tricked or browbeaten into changing the formal religious affiliation of their children in government schools. The third, to Howel Jones, land commissioner for the Santa Fe Railroad, asks for assistance in lobbying against a potential candidate for commissioner of Indian Affairs. The last, to his old friend General Hugh Scott, written just weeks before Anselm's passing, pleads that the well-connected general use his influence in Washington to support the appointment as Indian commissioner of a courageous assistant commissioner of Indian Affairs who has worked to protect Indian lands from illegal incursions by white cattlemen, or failing that, to seek that the same man be continued in his present office. This is also the letter in which Father Anselm laments the baneful consequences that will follow the appointment of Senator Albert B. Fall as secretary of the interior.]

"They Say That I Am Getting Old"[21]

Dear Mr. Lusk:

Yesterday I received the first letter from Father Leopold on the investigation of Messrs. Coleman and Endicott at Chin Lee. I enclose copy. That investigation was certainly a marvel of impartiality, seeing only a few Protestant Indians and calling but one of the Indians on our side, John Brown, not for purposes of investigation, but of abuse and intimidation. . . .

If I made known the character and mode of procedure of these inspectors to the Indian committees, I do not think Congress would be willing to make appropriations for inspectors of the type of Messrs. Coleman, Endicott, and Wilson.

Father Leopold's statement that eight out of the 10 pupils the ministers now have, had been Catholic, and the efforts of Mr. Gorman and the preacher's interpreter to secure Catholic children for their class, again prove my contention that they wish to establish themselves at Chin Lee not to convert heathens, but to pervert Catholics.

John Gorman, mentioned in Father Leopold's letter, and Louis Watchman, from near Fort Defiance, a former interpreter for the ministers, are the only Indians

I know of who wish Mr. Paquette removed. The latter told some Protestant employees at Fort Defiance that, unfortunately, hardly any Protestants wanted Mr. Paquette removed; if he were transferred and they got a Protestant superintendent, they would be treated better. These same Protestant employees told me of this remark and resented it very much, telling me, at the same time, that Mr. Paquette had always treated them fairly.

Bunches of Indians are coming to our mission and beg me to do all in my power to keep Mr. Paquette at Fort Defiance. They say that I am getting old and am "cut up" so much that I cannot go around and visit them and help them as much as I could formerly, and that there will be no one to look after their affairs if Mr. Paquette is removed; that he has been the best superintendent they had since their return from Fort Sumner in 1868; that he has done more than any other superintendent in improving their stock, in showing them how to farm and to improve their farms and raise more crops and make a better living; that they never had any trouble since he is here; that he goes among them and visits them and gives them good advice and settles their troubles fairly and justly like no other superintendent had ever done before.

One of the transferred pupils to the Albuquerque schools, George Peshlakai, wrote to his sister, Nellie Peshlakai, at our school as follows: "I hear that the supervisor is trying to let Mr. Paquette go from being superintendent of the Navajo. I believe it is going to be a great loss for the Navajo to lose such a good man as Mr. Paquette. I felt sorry about that because you know Mr. Paquette has adopted me as his son. I believe no one else besides Mr. Paquette knows how to handle the Navajo because some people do not know the character of the Navajo. Mr. Paquette and Father Weber are the only men that are great friends of the Navajo Indians."

Some have threatened to take their children, not Catholic, but Protestant children, out of the Fort Defiance school to send them to some other school if Mr. Paquette is sent away, and pupils at the Fort Defiance school are threatening to run away if Mr. Paquette leaves. This gives you an idea of what a hold Mr. Paquette has upon the Indians, children, and adults, and of how much they like him and appreciate his work for them. . . .

To Father Leopold's remarks on their assertion that the Protestants were not notified to attend the council at Chin Lee in 1917 . . . I wish to add that . . . it seems to me that the whole affair was prearranged and "staged.". . . This frame-up, probably engineered by the ministers, and the assertion that they knew nothing of the council could have had no other object than to *discredit* the council. . . .

That Mr. Paquette had no idea of favoring us in the matter of that council [when the Navajo denied a Protestant application for a mission site] is clearly shown by his calling the council during my sojourn in the sanitarium at Rome City, Indiana; by the fact that Father Leopold had to find out about it from the Indians; that Mr. Paquette notified the ministers and sent out the policeman and headman of Chin Lee to make it known to the Indians (and the large number of Indians present at this council from all parts of the Chin Lee district proves that these men did their duty); that, during the council, when they were signing their names, Mr. Paquette reminded several Indians of the fact that they had given their signatures to the ministers for the Protestant instruction of their children, and expressed his anticipation that they, at least, would give their signatures for the granting of the mission site. One of them answered him [that] he had given his signature to us first; then the ministers had come time and again and bothered the life out of him till he gave them the signature just to get rid of them; since that time one of his children had become Catholic and the others would follow her example. Another Navajo said his case was the same, and he asked Mr. Paquette to put his children on the Catholic list again: which Mr. Paquette did not do until the Indian had come to Fort Defiance, 47 miles, and signed the paper before him to that effect.

You would oblige me very much by bringing this letter and the enclosed letter of Father Leopold to the attention of the Indian Office.

"I Cannot Counter with Similar Weapons"[22]

Dear Mr. Young:

On February 24, 1919, Mr. Sells wrote to Mr. Lusk as follows:"Referring to the letter of Father Anselm Weber, addressed to you on January 11, concerning certain rules of practice formulated for the use of Superintendent Paquette on the subject of religious instruction of schoolchildren, you are advised that these rules were returned disapproved, with instructions to revise them in accordance with the regulations, and submit to the office for further consideration."

Before these rules of practice revised and submitted to the office for further consideration, I wish to submit the following observations:

When the Indian Office formulated the "General Regulations for Religious Worship and Instruction of Pupils in Government Indian Schools," it was, in my judgment, the intent of the office to simply and exclusively formulate rules, expressed in No. 2,(a) and (c), by which the church affiliation of the pupils should be determined, without intending that said No. 2, (a) and (c), should cover any change of church membership. "Change of Church membership," when pupils themselves desire such a change, is provided for in No. 4 of said General Regulations.

But no paragraph of said regulations touches "change of church membership" when desired by the parents or guardians of the pupils. Hence I do not think that Mr. Paquette acted contrary to the regulations when, on March 14, 1911, he sent notice to me (which I enclose) and to the ministers that no second signatures would be honored unless the parents or guardians would come to him personally, of their own free will, and request a change in church membership.

In January 1912, when this matter was brought informally to the attention of the Indian Office, Mr. Paquette's "position in regard to second signatures was upheld as the proper one." I do not care to enumerate and explain the conditions and considerations which made this ruling of Mr. Paquette advisable—they were of such a nature as to induce the Indian Office to sanction his ruling.

I did not suggest this to Mr. Paquette, but after the ruling was made, we adhered to it scrupulously and I have always been in favor of it, since *we* did not establish our missions among the Navajo to make converts from Protestantism, but from paganism. If not asked, or urged or cajoled by anyone, very few, in fact hardly any, would even think of having the church membership of their children changed. With ignorant pagan Indians, who know nothing of Christianity and do not know the difference between Christian denominations, it is comparatively easy to induce them to change the church membership of their children, especially if the one who solicits the change pits his American resourcefulness, persistence, resolute will, and firm determination against the ignorance, helplessness, and wavering mobility of the Indian. Under the circumstances he may give way, really against his will, and put his thumb mark on a piece of paper then and there. But if, when his solicitor has left him and the spell is broken, he must appear before his agent to make that paper valid, he will do so if he is in earnest and really wants the change. In that case distance is no consideration to him; it gives him a chance to make a trip; and he visits the agency at times, anyway. Instances are not wanting where they appeared before the agent and told him that they had signed second signatures, but they had been *made* to do it, and did *not* want their children to change their religious affiliation. In my judgment Mr. Paquette's ruling should stand; that these *ignorant pagan parents* should *not* be requested (much less urged and cajoled) by anyone, to change the *Christian* church membership of their children, and that if they have been so *induced* to make the change, the change should not be recognized or executed. And even where the *pagan* parents make the request unsolicited and of their own free will, I do not think that the children that have reached the age of discretion should be forced by their parents or anyone else to change their church membership against their own will. Religion and religious convictions and sentiments cannot and ought not be changed—put on and put off—like a garment. Their parents have no conception of the Christian religion and do not realize that their children, when instructed in a certain form of Christianity, have their religious ideas and convictions and sentiments; if they did, they would not be so apt to force them to change their church affiliation and thereby do violence to their conscience and their religious sentiments. Besides, these changes must, of necessity, destroy all religion in these children, since one day they are told to believe and revere what they are told the next day to disbelieve and despise. The whole thing seems ridiculous and preposterous, and I would not like to enter the arena in such a combat.

After writing thus far and thereby concluding my general observations on this matter, I received a letter from Father Leopold this evening, containing such unusual and unbelievable news that I decided to add a few remarks on the practical phase of this question and its present status, and to quote part of Father Leopold's letter.

Since Inspector Colman has been at Chin Lee, and, in all probability has told the people there that Mr. Paquette's ruling had been revoked, the "turning over" of Catholic pupils and detaining them from attending our instructions has begun. The Reverend Mr. Ward of Chin Lee has secured a complete list of all the pupils at the school—all were on the Catholic list, except two, when Mr. Coleman arrived—present and past, that is, not only the children who go to school now, but all who have gone to school from the opening up of the Chin Lee school; also such as have left school, or have been transferred to other schools, and this together with the names of their parents or guardians.

Of course, that is only a preliminary preparation for trying to convert the Catholic pupils to Presbyterianism through securing the mandate from their heathen parents. Since ordinary means would not lead to success, it seems the ministers at Chin Lee and Ganado have agreed to work in the Chin Lee school district on the superstitious fears of the Indians and to create something similar to the "Messiah craze." The Indians, having lost many members of the tribe through the dreadful "flu" epidemic, and having lost quite a portion of their flocks through the unprecedented deep snow of this winter, seem well disposed for such an onslaught.

In a previous letter Father Leopold had written to me that Mr. [David K.] Ward was telling the Indians that the end of the world is due next summer; in the letter received this evening he [Father Leopold] writes: "A few days ago, an Indian, Tsinnajini, from Ch'al Sedahi, near Nazlini, was here, and today Qashtl'izhni Naez, from Tqodok'ozk, or Salina Springs, stopped here and they had some queer stories to tell. It seems the preacher of Ganado has that whole region: Nazlini, Tselandi (Tqodok'ozk/Salina Springs), on to the Black Mountains in excitement and is baptizing the Navajo right and left. One Indian said that he is telling them there will soon be a big flood, but a nice place, nice fields, sheep, flocks, and so on, are being prepared for them in heaven. They must be baptized now, and then when the flood comes he will come and take them into heaven with him. Others said he is going to every hogan and baptizing whole camps from babies to *qastqui*. He is being much helped by an Indian called Two Teeth.

Just now Naat'ani Jumbo, (a former Fort Defiance pupil) told me the preacher had been out to his place with Two Teeth. He wanted to baptize Naat'ani's sister, who said she had been baptized long ago and didn't want to be baptized again. Two Teeth told him that the preacher had some good strong stories to tell him, and the preacher told the Indians if they believe what he says to them they would soon have large flocks and be rich.

The same thing is done around here. Last Sunday Zonnie Van Winkel (a former pupil of Fort Defiance, Catholic, 22 years old) told me [that] Mrs. Nelson Gorman had told her that the world is soon coming to an end. Then all good people would be taken up into the clouds for seven years. In the meanwhile the bad people would remain here on earth and die off. Then the earth would be renewed and the good people would come down again out of the clouds, take possession of the new world, and be happy.

Well I cannot counter with similar weapons.

"Our Work ... Is Constantly Exposed to the Attacks of Bigots"[23]

Dear Mr. Jones:

I must ask your assistance in a very important matter and I am going to be very frank and open. . . . I have reliable information from a gentleman in the Southwest that a movement is on foot of making H. B. Peairs of Haskell Institute commissioner of Indian Affairs. . . . Peairs would have the solid backing of the Indian Rights Association, the Mohonk Conference, the Boston Indian League, the Y.M.C.A., and of the Missionary Board of New York with Mr. Moffett at its head. The predominant membership of these organizations is and has been for years hostile to our work among the Indians.

I am sure you have no idea to what extent bigotry is still embodied in these organizations. They will go to almost any lengths to secure the appointment of a commissioner of their own type. We would not get fair treatment under Mr. Peairs as commissioner. . . .

At best our work among the Indians is constantly exposed to the attacks of bigots and bigoted organizations to an incredible extent, and we need a just and fair-minded commissioner; one who is hand in glove with them would cripple our work among the Indians not only in a religious, but in every other way. It may seem strange to you but it is a fact that vigorous protests have been made by ministers against my assisting the Navajo in their land matters, under the plea that that was none of my business, but the business of the government.

I was in hopes the incoming administration would appoint a superior man in every respect as commissioner of Indian Affairs; I hope we are not coming from the frying pan into the fire. We need an able, broad-minded, efficient man of affairs as Indian commissioner—not a Y.M.C.A. worker or religious fanatic who would deem the abolishing of Sunday baseball and kindred amusements, card playing, dancing, and so on, and casting the gloom of our estimable Pilgrim Fathers over the schools and reservations as the apex of his achievements. . . .

"We Cannot Expect Even Fair and Just Treatment"[24]

My Dear General:

Since you have shown yourself such a good friend of the Indians, and of the Navajo in particular, I must write to you in regard to the appointment of the new Indian commissioner. Since you belong to the Board of Indian Commissioners, I am sure you are taking an even greater interest—if that is possible—in our affairs and have a right to be heard and can exert your influence within that board of distinguished men.

I enclose copy of letter I have just written to Senator Cameron of Arizona, elected last November on the Republican ticket, in behalf of Mr. Meritt, which shows you our wishes in regard to that appointment and the grounds upon which they are based. I have written a similar letter to Senator Ashurst of Arizona. But there are other weighty reasons which I could not mention to these senators, but which I am writing to you, knowing that you and the Board of Indian Commissioners will appreciate their vital importance.

It is well known that the senators and representatives of New Mexico, Arizona, Colorado, and Utah, but more especially the senators of New Mexico, are in favor of opening up the reservations for the benefit of white stockmen and of forcing the Indians with their stock from the public domain back on the reservation. We cannot expect even fair and just treatment from them, much less any favors. I see that Senator Fall has been prominently mentioned for secretary of the interior. If he secures that position and the appointment of an Indian commissioner according to his own heart, we might as well give up and move into old Mexico; but I am afraid Senator Fall's sinister influence would follow us even across the border. It would be a calamity for us if anyone from these states, especially from New Mexico, should be appointed secretary of the interior or Indian commissioner.

You remember our trip to Washington in 1917. With the exception of a few townships set aside at the juncture of the Little and big Colorado rivers in Arizona, nothing was achieved. It is true, in consequence of our trip and at the urgent request of the Board of Indian Commissioners, the secretary of the interior was ready to make a reservation of the Crown Point District, in McKinley County, New Mexico, when Congress took away the power from the president to create or extend reservations. Since that time things have been going from bad to worse. In the Crown Point District American cattlemen have fenced illegally 12 whole townships, and part of three townships, fencing in the public domain and 281 Indian allotments. In a number of cases the Indian homes and improvements were destroyed and the Indians driven off; in other cases adverse conditions created by these cattlemen forced them off. The Indians of this district are certainly in bad shape and on the road to pauperism.

Now Mr. Meritt, the assistant commissioner of Indian Affairs, had this matter thoroughly investigated and has taken steps to have these cattlemen prosecuted and forced to take down their illegal fences. That will be a big fight, and when it becomes known that Mr. Meritt has taken such action, he will have to face the strong opposition of these cattlemen and their supporters, Senators A. A. Jones and A. B. Fall. On other occasions as well Mr. Meritt has shown his intrepid courage as well as his appreciation of our position and his sympathy for us. He has proven that he has our welfare at heart.

For these various reasons, we, I and the Indians at whose request I am writing this letter, beg you to do all you can to have Mr. Meritt appointed commissioner of Indian Affairs. Should that prove impossible, we hope at the very least that he will be retained as assistant commissioner so we can feel that we have in him a strong friend in the Indian Office.

Believe me, my dear general,

Your good friend,

Notes

1. Anselm Weber to Berard Haile, 17 May 1911. FAC Box DEC.245. Weber, Anselm. Beautiful Mountain, Let., fd. Haile, B. Letters 1904, 1908, 1909, 1911 (CI5).

2. Robert L. Wilken, *Anselm Weber, O.F.M.: Missionary to the Navaho* (Milwaukee, Wisc.: Bruce, 1955), 189.

3. Egbert Fischer to Provincial Rudolph Bonner, 11 January 1916(?). FAC Box DEC. 062. Fennen–Fischer, fd. Fischer, Egbert. Letters 1915–1917. Letter apparently undated; penciled date added by a previous researcher.

4. Fischer to Bonner, 30 June 1916. FAC Box DEC.062. Fennen–Fischer, fd. Fischer, Egbert. Letters 1915–1917.

5. Weber to Bonner, 26 May 1918. FAC Box DEC.247. Weber, Anselm. Let., fd. Provincial Business 1898–1912 (CIV2).

6. Weber to Bonner, 26 May 1918.

7. Weber to Bonner, 2 August 1916. FAC Box DEC.062. Fennen–Fischer, fd. Fischer, Egbert. Letters 1915–1917.

8. Celestine Matz to Haile, 2 April 1918. FAC Box DEC.077. Haile, Berard, fd. Weber, Anselm–Berard Haile Letters (II6).

9. Wilken, 189.

10. Weber to William H. Ketcham, 14 November 1910. FAC Box DEC.250. Weber, Anselm. Let, fd. Weber, A. Letters, Misc. (DIV1)

11. Weber to Haile, 16 October 1911. FAC Box DEC.245. Weber, Anselm. Beautiful Mountain, Let., fd. Haile, B. Letters 1904, 1908, 1909, 1911 (CI5).

12. Weber to Haile, 23 January 1916, FAC Box DEC.241. Anselm Weber, Writings, fd. Missiology—Anselm and Emanuel II (AV7).

13. Weber to Haile, 13 February 1916. FAC Box DEC.241. Anselm Weber, Writings, fd. Missiology—Anselm and Emanuel II (AV7).

14. The reference is to an exchange between Gallup trader C. N. Cotton and ethnologist Stewart Culin, at one time director of the Brooklyn Museum of Art and Science. Culin accompanied the friars on a 1903 trip from St. Michaels to the San Juan River Basin.

15. Wilken, 180.

16. Weber to E. P. Davies, 21 April 1919. FAC Box DEC.250. Weber, Anselm. Let., fd. Weber, Anselm. Letters (DIV3).

17. Weber to Provincial Eugene Buttermann, 29 May 1912. FAC Box DEC.246. Weber, Anselm. Let, fd. Scott, Gen. Juvenal Schnorbus (CII3).

18. Weber to Buttermann, 29 May 1912.

19. Wilken, 228–30.

20. Weber to Bonner, 26 May 1918. FAC Box DEC.247. Weber, Anselm. Let, fd. Provincial Business 1898–1912 (CIV2).

21. Weber to Lusk, 28 February 1919. FAC Box PLA.071. Chinle AZ, env. Chinle AZ. Letters 1919–1942.

22. Weber to S. A. M. Young, 13 March 1919. FAC Box PLA.071. Chinle, AZ, env. Chinle, AZ. Letters 1919–1944.

23. Weber to Howel Jones, 16 November 1920. FAC Box DEC.242. Weber, Anselm. Let, fd. Weber, Anselm. Letters. 1920 Land (BI9).

24. Weber to Hugh L. Scott, 13 January 1921. FAC Box DEC.242. Weber, Anselm. Let, fd. Weber, A. Schools, Land (BI4).

Part 6

NAVAJO CUSTOMS AND CHARACTER

33

Navajo Land and People[1]

Leopold Ostermann, O.F.M.

[In 1905 Father George J. Juillard, pastor of the Gallup parish, sponsored a new monthly magazine, *The Catholic Pioneer: A Monthly Literary, Political and Religious Review*. Perhaps intending to broaden its potential readership, before a year had passed the word "Catholic" had disappeared from the title, which now read *The Pioneer: A Magazine of Southwestern Life*. In addition to the Anglo settlers in the surrounding country and residents of Gallup, Father Juillard's far-flung parish included Pueblos, Navajo, and Hispanics. Judging from the available issues of the journal, Father Juillard intended the magazine to emphasize and capitalize upon that diversity. He had already been associated with the missionaries at St. Michaels in several cooperative ventures, and now he asked that they contribute to his magazine. Father Leopold accepted the assignment, and the series that bears his byline seems to have lasted as long as the magazine did, that is, for one year.

There have been approximately 1,500 English-language serials containing the word "pioneer" in their title. Scores of these are, or were, simply named "The Pioneer." A perusal of these titles yields only two entries identifiable as Father Juillard's short-lived magazine, one each for the initial and the altered title. It appears that only two libraries have any issues of the journal, the only nearly complete run held by the Arizona State Library, Archives and Public Records, in Phoenix. The *Catholic Pioneer* seems to have lasted through only a dozen issues, never moving beyond volume 1. It is by far the most obscure journal to publish Father Leopold's writings.

Obscure perhaps, but not deservedly so. The articles by Father Leopold, representing an interweaving of his wide reading on the Navajo with a half-decade of personal experience among them, are informative and energetic. Years later he would dust off some of them and adapt them for republication, without mentioning their prior appearance, in the mission's annual, *Franciscan Missions of the Southwest*. For example, his fine article, "The Navajo Indian Blanket" (1918), first appeared more than a decade earlier in the *Catholic Pioneer*. Father Juillard's transitory journal also published some gems by other authors, including a rare piece on Navajo character by trader J. B. Moore (see chapter 34).

I take pleasure in reclaiming from obscurity, combined in the present chapter, nine of Father Leopold's contributions to *The Catholic Pioneer*.]

Partly in the northwest corner of New Mexico and partly in the northeastern corner of Arizona is a vast tract of land known as the Navajo reservation. It is a territory comprising more than 4 million acres of land, set aside by the government of the United States for the Navajo Indians. The American people in general know very little about this country; many probably know nothing of its existence, and few, perhaps, know that it is marked off and named on the maps of their geographies.

Having spent several years on the Navajo reservation, during which I visited different parts of it and came in frequent contact with the Navajo Indians, I shall try in the course of these "Notes and Sketches" to tell the readers some things about the Navajo and their country which, I hope, may be of interest to them. The Navajo reservation is a part of America's "Wonderland." A bird's eye description of this country is about as easy as describing a peep into a kaleidoscope; for just as the next slightest turn of the tube of a kaleidoscope will completely change the figure, so, too, a description of any one place of the Navajo country will not be recognized at the next turn of the valley, or on the next hilltop, or on the next plain, or in the next forest, or at another season. Even the same place which you have passed several times, and which you think you know well, will often appear strange when approached from a different direction. It is a country which almost baffles description scription, for the contrasts are so frequent and so abrupt, the scenery so diversified, the seasons so peculiar, the climate so un-eastern, the distances so deceptive, the altitude so high, the atmospheric effects so magic, the weather so freakish that a description which fits for one place seems untrue and absurd a few miles further on or at another time of the year.

Charles F. Lummis says of New Mexico:

> But every landscape is characteristic, and even beautiful—with a weird, unearthly beauty, treacherous as the flowers of its cacti. . . . Its very rocks are unique—only Arizona shares these astounding freaks of form and color carved by the scant rains and more liberal winds of immemorial centuries, and towering across the bare land like the milestones of forgotten giants. . . . The Navajo Reservation—which lies part in this Territory and part in Arizona—is remarkably picturesque throughout, with its broad plains hemmed by giant mesas split with cañons.[2]

Such is, indeed, the Navajo country. It is a land of sandy deserts and wastes, where for miles and miles no tree can be seen—nothing but sand and sage-brush—and the eye tires of the surrounding monotony; where the sweeping breeze picks up clouds of sand, whirls it about in wild fury, carries it along for miles, and dashes its tiny grainlets with stinging force against the face of the traveler, who can see hardly yards before him for sand and dust. Again it is a land of woods and forests where the spreading piñon, with its tasteful nuts, grows beside the graceful spruce and fir, the fragrant cedar and juniper, the noble pine and the white-gleaming cottonwood, the quaking asp and the aromatic sumach, the mountain mahogany and the box elder, clusters of willows and patches of scrubby mountain oak; a land of meadows covered with bright grass; a land of flowers where not only the forest but also the hilltops and slopes are starred and studded from spring till fall with wild flowers of every kind, color, and description; a land of fields where yellow dwarfish cornstalks bow their tasseled ears and wave their plumed tips in the breeze.

Now it is a land of heat, where the atmosphere frequently trembles and quivers in excessive heat 25 and 30 feet above the soil; where the vault of heaven sometimes seems to be an immense dome of heated steel, the sun a disk of polished brass in white heat, and the breeze a breath from some fiery furnace, yet where the shaded places are always comfortable, where sunstrokes are unknown; then a land of cold, where snow blizzards and hailstorms rage, where the hoary frost casts his silvery net over the landscape, covered with the "beautiful white"; where the icy breath of Boreas pierces even into the marrow, and mercury hovers about below zero.

At one season it is a land of drought, where the soil is frequently cracked and cloven, yawning, as it were, after the refreshing drops from the clouds above; where once the parched tongues of Uncle Sam's soldiers, on their march against the Navajo, protruded from between their dried and shriveled lips; at another season it is a land of clear, limpid springs, oozing ice-cold from the rocky mountainsides or bubbling up playfully in the valleys; a land of freshets and cloudbursts which send the gushing streams rushing down the mountain slopes and thundering down the rock-bound canyons out into the lowlands, covering them many feet deep with their surging and tossing flood, tearing deep arroyos with steep abrupt banks into the adobe soil.

It is a land of sunshine, where the bright glorious orb of day enters upon his course through the rose-colored portals of the East, climbs radiantly up into the sky, runs his fiery chariot overhead, bathing and flooding everything with ambient light, and penetrating everything with his dazzling heat, and then sinks to rest behind the gold, amber, and orange-tinted curtains of the West; a land of starlight, where after the glowing twilight has gone out, the yellow stars, with a smiling twinkle, bud forth on heaven's canopy and shine like beads of burnished gold; where the silent planets of the night set out blazing upon their invisible courses and run their airy circuits, while from behind the thickets or from behind the ridge of some distant mountain range, the moon rises slowly and solemnly, throwing, like a huge magic lantern, ghostly and ghastly traceries of silvery light and sable shadows across the lovely landscape.

It is a land of "magnificent distances," where the clear, light, pure air acts like the lenses of a telescope, bringing distant objects seemingly almost within reach; where one can ride or drive toward a nearby peak or grove for hours until the intervening distance is perceptibly lessened; where 25 or 30 miles is deemed close neighborhood.

It is a land of fascinating wilds and fastnesses, of dreary wastes and deserts, of gaunt monoliths and fantastic peaks, of grotesque crags and bold cliffs, of yawning gulches and unearthly canyons, of frowning mountains and weird valleys. It is the land of the cactus and the yucca, of the burro and the bronco, of the sheep and the goat, of the sagebrush and the greasewood, of the bear and the wildcat, of the puma and the prairie dog and the coyote, of the centipede and the rattlesnake.

Such is the land where the Navajo lives. It affords him all the change and variety he can wish for. This land he loves with the fervor and enthusiasm—or call it patriotism—of a Tyrolese for his matchless Alpine hills and valleys. For this land its dusky denizens have fought and bled; here they love to roam in all the liberty and freedom of their forefathers, to build their hogans wherever they choose, to raise their crops of corn, beans, and squashes in its valleys, and herd their sheep and ponies in the shelter of its mountains. They are glad if the land-hungry, encroaching paleface does not cross its boundaries, but welcome with liberal hospitality the visits of their friends.

For yet another reason this country is intensely interesting; it is a land where romantic cliff dwellings and ruins of walls and foundations, scattered potsherds and flint chips and lonely desolated cemeteries tell of a dense population which has passed over its surface prior to the coming of the Navajo, even as the children of Assur have passed over the face of Assyria and left the vestiges of their occupied buildings and houses. Many a time, when wandering about amid such ruins and trying to picture the scenes that once took place there, I thought of the following lines, which I once clipped from the *Ranch and Range*, published in Denver, Colorado:

In the gay Southwest in that mystical sunland,
Far from the toil and turmoil of gain,
Strange are the heights and the vales of this our land,
Beloved of the sky, but bereft of the rain.
In this wild weird land where the south winds are sighing
And breathing their requiems o'er ruins grown gray,
'Mid heights that are dizzy or vales where the gloom
Is strange to the light of the day.

After having given a description of the Navajo country, it would now be in order to begin at once to speak of the people who inhabit this strange and interesting country. But before saying anything about the Navajo as a people, or about their customs, arts, mode of living, and so on, the readers will not, I think, find it superfluous or out of place to know something definite concerning the pronunciation, orthography, and signification of the word *Navajo*.

The Name *Navajo*

I have heard the word *Navajo* pronounced in diverse ways, have seen it written in several variations, and have been asked repeatedly what it means. A short discussion of these points, therefore, will, I trust, be of interest.

According to *Webster's Dictionary* this word ought to be pronounced thus: Navaho, that is, *a* having the sound of *a* in arm; according to general usage in the Southwest it is pronounced Navaho, that is, *a* having the sound of *a* in have. In both cases the accent is on the first syllable and the *h* is strongly aspirated. Navajo is undoubtedly of Spanish origin, and the old Spaniards who first used it may possibly have accented the last or the second syllable. At any rate, the Mexicans of New Mexico and Arizona lay a special stress upon the last syllable. The *Columbian Cyclopedia* places the accent on the second syllable, but does not give any reason or authority for doing so.

It will, therefore, in general, be safe to follow the second method, which has become common among Americans. The Navajo very seldom apply this name to themselves, and when they do it is only when speaking of their people to white men. They then pronounce it Nah-veh-ho.

In late years the word *Navajo* has frequently been written and printed Navaho, with *h* instead of *j*. Why this should be done, even by editors and scholars, is not apparent. This arbitrary and unwarranted exchange of letters has been tried to be justified by declaring it to be more in conformity with English orthography. Now, if English orthography is such an exact and such a sure guide as to writing and spelling of words, why then should we write corps and pronounce it core? Why should we write Worcester and say Wooster? Why should the plural of index be indices; of radius, radii; of memorandum, memoranda; of stigma, stigmata, and so on? If these and a great many others are English words why not give them plurals according to the rules of English grammar and orthography? The syllable "ough" must be an orthographical outlaw; compare, for instance, the words cough, *hiccough, dough, lough, plough, rough, through.*

If, therefore, such orthographical sticklers would direct their attention towards ridding our "already overweighted language" of some of its real burdens and orthographical freaks, instead of shying at an old, time-honored, historical proper name, their efforts would, no doubt, be better employed, and more instrumental toward laying the foundation of some future real English orthography.

Again, it has been advanced that the name *Navajo* is only found within our borders, and if we change the spelling here it will not conflict with the spelling elsewhere. This remark is not quite as ingenious as it seems to be. The name *Sioux*, for instance, is also found only within our borders. If we made the spelling of this name more in conformity with English orthography by changing it into Soo, Su, or Sew, or if we dropped the *s* in Illinois, or the *c* in Connecticut, or changed the *ch* in Michigan into *sh*, would that conflict with the spelling elsewhere? And yet, anyone who would attempt this would be held up to the ridicule of every intelligent American, and be branded as a hopeless ignoramus.

These remarks, I think, are very timely. During the last few years the number of visitors from the East to the Southwest has become greater each year, and it will continue to increase as the interesting places and peoples of our Southwest become more and better known. If we do not insist upon preserving our old historical names as they have been written for centuries, we shall soon be blessed with such orthographical gems as Burnaleeyo, Albookerkay, Serreeyos, Loss Krooses, and so on.

Dr. Washington Matthews, M.D., of the U.S. Army, who spent many years among the Navajo studying their customs, religions, ceremonies, arts, and language, and who is a recognized authority on Navajo mythology, folklore, and sociology, says in his notes to his *Navaho Legends*, note 1:

> How and when the name Navajo . . . originated has not been discovered. It is only known that this name was given by the Spaniards while they still claimed the Navaho land. The name is generally supposed to be derived from *navaja*, which means a clasp-knife, or razor, and to have been applied because the Navaho warriors carried great stone knives in former days. It has been suggested that the name comes from *navájo*, a pool or small lake. The Navahoes call themselves *Diné* 'or *Diné*, which means simply, men, people.[3]

Let us follow up the trail pointed out by Dr. Matthews. It is certain that the Navajo received their name from the Spaniards. Therefore, if it has any specific meaning whatever, it must or ought to be found in some of the old Spanish records or reports, for the first Spanish explorers and missionaries were diligent students, close observers, and busy writers as their numerous *documentos*, *collecciones*, *procesos*, *geografias*, *diarios*, *cartas etnograficas*, *discursos*, *descripciones*, *noticias*, and so on, testify.

Now, in a memorial to the king of Spain, written by Fra Alonso de Benavides, O.F.M., in 1630, the writer, after describing the Gila-Apaches, says that more than 50 leagues north of them, "one encounters the Province of the Apaches of Navajó."

> Although they are of the same Apache nation as the foregoing, they are subject and subordinate to another Chief Captain, and have a distinct mode of living. For those of back [yonder] did not use to plant, but sustained themselves by the chase; and today we have broken land for them and taught them to plant. But these of Navajó are very great farmers [*labradores*], for that [is what] Navajó signifies—'great planted fields.'[4]

Fra Alonso de Benavides was one of the first missionaries of the Southwest, and himself a born Spaniard. He wrote his memorial about 275 years before our time, that is, he was 275 years nearer to the origin of the name *Navajo* than we are. From his expression "the Apaches of Navajo," it is evident that the word *Navajo* was originally not given to the people, but was the name of their province or territory, or in other words the Indians themselves were called Apaches and their country was called Navajo, until later the name Apaches was dropped and the name of the territory applied to its inhabitants. This was frequently done by the Spaniards. Thus, for instance, the Acomas, Lagunas, Santo Domingos, Cochitenos, and a few others, although they all belonged to the same Queres nation, are named after their territory or their pueblo. The English themselves have often named people after their land or country. Compare, for instance, the names of the Chinese, Australians,

Japanese, Greenlanders, Africans, New Zealanders, Canadians, Icelanders, Mexicans, and so on, with the names of their countries.

Navajo, therefore, being originally the name of a province or territory, what is its signification? Fra Benavides says: great planted fields, or large planting fields. It is certain that the Navajo, despite their roving and roaming mode of life, have always done some planting and tilling of the soil, although they may have learned this from the more thrifty Pueblos, being very practical, intelligent, and imitative. It is also certain that they claimed and inhabited vast tracts of territory as their country, so that "large planting fields" would fit their country and their occupation quite well. Dr. Brinton says that "when the Spaniards first met them (the Navajo) in 1541 they were tillers of the soil, erected large granaries for their crops, irrigated their fields by artificial water courses or *acequias*, and lived in substantial dwellings, partly underground."[5] "The Navajo," says Bandelier "cultivated by irrigation, and lived in log cabins."

Now, the Spanish dictionary has the word *nava*, signifying a flat, even piece of land, a plain or field. This word *nava*, like the English word *field*, is sometimes used as a part of a local name. Compare, for instance, the famous Navas de Tolosa, the Plains of Tolosa. where the combined Spanish forces broke the Arab power in Spain by a decisive victory on June 16, 1212. From *nava* the word *Navajo* may be derived just as *lagunajo* is from *laguna*, *yerbajo* from *yerba*, *latinajo* from *latin*, and so forth, and this would explain the signification given it by Benavides. The old Spanish suffix *ajo*, like the modern Spanish suffix *acho*, seems to give to a word, not only an augmentative, but also a depreciative signification; thus *laguna* means a pond lake, and *lagunajo*, a pool or puddle; *yerba*, an herb, and *yerbajo* a weed: *latin* means Latin, and *latinajo* bad, ungrammatical Latin. According to this, *nava* would be a field, and *navajo* a large field which is not of much account. Whoever has been over the Navajo country will not deny that a great part of their fields richly deserves this name. This adds, undoubtedly, to the interpretation of Benavides. His expression, "the Apaches of Navajo," therefore, means "the Apaches who live on the large, more or less worthless fields."

Navajo Origins

It has already been mentioned that the Navajo call themselves *Diné*, which is their word for men or people. Before going any further it may be of interest to inquire into the stock or family to which the Navajo belong, and into their origin. By "stock or family" is meant a group of Indian tribes whose languages are found by comparative study to be but variations or dialects of a common ancestral tongue. Take, for instance, the Algonquin stock or family. To this stock belong the Abnakis, Algonquins, Arapahos, Cheyennes, Crees, Delawares, Foxes, Illinois, Kickapoos, Mohicans, Massachusetts, Menominees, Miamis, Micmacs, Narragansets, Otchipwes, Ottawas, Pequods, Pottawotomis, Sacs, Shawnees, and others, the languages of all of whom resemble each other sufficiently to justify the conclusion that at one time they had been but one people with one language.

The similarity or resemblance of speech spoken by different tribes, or by a group of tribes, is determined by a comparison of words, especially root words. If these are similar or identical, the tribes are said to belong to the same stock or family, just as the Germans, Scandinavians, Dutch, and Anglo-Saxons belong to the same stock because their languages have the same root words and many other linguistic peculiarities in common, thus showing them to be descendants of one common parent stock.

Now, in the *Columbian Cyclopedia* I read that the Navajo are "the most northerly band of the great Shoshone and Apache family of Indians," but in the first place neither the Navajo nor the Apache belong to the Shoshonian stock, and second, there are Shoshonian or Snake tribes up in Oregon, Idaho, and Wyoming, which is far way north from the Navajo.

There is, however, a faint strain of Shoshone blood in the Navajo tribe, which has been derived from their northern neighbors, the Utes, who are said to belong to the Shoshonian stock. But lately even this opinion has received a shock by the discovery that the Ute language greatly resembles the language of the Quiche Indians in Central America, who are of the Mayan stock or family.

In former years the Navajo were almost continually on the warpath with the Utes, and the prisoners taken on their raids were kept and either made slaves or adopted into the tribe. Thus in the course of time a Ute clan developed within the Navajo tribe, the Noda' Diné, or Mescal People. (Noda' is the name by which the Utes are known to the Navajo.)

It may be of interest to give here the legends of the Navajo concerning the Ute clan in their tribe, as told by Dr. Washington Matthews in his *Navajo Legends*. A long time ago, back in the gray dim past,

> a number of Utes visited the Navahoes. They came when the corn-ears were small, and remained till the corn was harvested. They worked for the Navahoes, and when their stomachs were filled all left except one family, which consisted of an old couple, two girls, and a boy. These at first intended to stay but a short time after their friends had gone; but they tarried longer and longer, and postponed their going from time to time, till they ended by staying with the Navahoes till they died. . . . One of the girls, whose name was Tsá'yiskid (Sage-Brush Hill), lived to be an old woman and the mother of many children. From her is descended the gens of Tsa'yiskídni (Sage Brush Hill People).

Some time after this,

> some Utes came into the neighborhood of the Navahoes, camping at a place called Tsé'di'yikáni (a ridge or promontory projecting into the river). . . . They had good arms of all kinds, and two varieties of shields—one round and one with a crescentic cut in the top. They lived for a while by themselves, and were at first unruly and impertinent; but in the course of time they merged into the Navahoes, forming the gens of Nota' or Nota' Diné', Ute People.

About the time they were incorporated by the Navahoes, or soon after, a war party of Utes made a raid on a Mexican settlement, somewhere near where Socorro now is, and captured a Spanish woman. She was their slave; but her descendants became free among the Navahoes and formed the Nakaídine' (White Stranger People), or Mexican gens.[6]

Time and again individuals, men as well as women, have been pointed out to me as having originally been Utes, who had been taken prisoners by the Navajo, had been held as slaves, and finally adopted into the tribe, or who were descendants of such prisoners. Besides from the Utes, the Navajo tribe has received recruits from other tribes and pueblos, as we shall see later.

Others associate the Navajo with the Toltecs of Mexico, the alleged predecessors of the Aztecs, and J. D. Baldwin, in his *Ancient America,* sees in them changed communities of Pueblos. Speaking of the Mandans he says: "They may have been, like the Navajo, a changed community of Pueblos," and again: "The Navajo began their present (roaming) condition by fleeing to the mountains from the Spaniards."[7] These two opinions are wild guesses, and need not be considered at all. They are equivalent to jumbling together Norwegians, Turks, and Poles as Anglo-Saxons.

Other writers make the Navajo descendants of the Aztecs. Thus Gregg in "Commerce of the Prairies" says:

They (the Navajo) reside in the main range of the Cordilleros, one hundred and fifty to two hundred miles west of Santa Fe, on the waters of the Rio Colorado of California, not far from the region, according to historians, from whence the Aztecs emigrated to Mexico; and there are many reasons to suppose them direct descendants from the remnant, which remained in the north, of this celebrated nation of antiquity. Although they live in rude *jacales,* somewhat resembling the wigwams of the Pawnees, yet, from time immemorial, they have excelled all others in their original manufactures.[8]

Lieutenant Simpson, in his *Report on the Navajo Country, 1850,* after quoting Gregg, remarks:

As regards the hypothesis which Gregg advances in the above, that the Navahos are the direct descendants of the Aztecs, it is possible they may be. But if, as is likely, and as Gregg also supposes, this ancient people once inhabited the pueblos, now in ruins, on the Chaco, how is it that they have retrograded in civilization in respect to their habitations when they have preserved it in their manufactures?

I know but two ways to account for it. Either the Navajo are descended from a cognate stock, *prior* to that which built the Chaco pueblos, which stock lived as the Navahos do now in lodges . . . or, in process of time, the cultivable and pastoral portion of the country becoming more and more reduced in area, and scattered in locality, the people of necessity became correspondingly scattered and locomotive, and thus gradually adopted the habitation most suitable for such a state of things—the lodge they now inhabit.[9]

Now as a matter of fact the Navajo, with the Apache—who, as Bandelier remarks, were originally nothing else but outlying bands of Navajo—are neither Shoshones nor Toltecs nor Pueblos nor Aztecs but they are the most southern branch of the great Diné, or Déné nation of Indians, very inaccurately and inappropriately called the Athabascan stock or nation by modern ethnologists. All the tribes belonging to this stock or family call themselves by a name meaning men or people, which is more or less similar in all dialects. Thus we have Dane, Déné, Diné, Dinje, Dune, Nde, Tinneh, Teni, and so on. It would, therefore, seem to have been more appropriate and more accurate to call them by one of these names, for instance, Diné, the name by which the Navajo, who are by far the most numerous of all the tribes belonging to this stock, call themselves. Reverend A. G. Morice, O.M.I., who is an ethnologist and philologist of note, has suggested Déné, because it is the name by which the most centrally located, and one of the most populous tribes (the Carriers of British Columbia), calls itself.

Athabasca is the name of a region or district in western British America or Canada, inhabited by a number of tribes of the Déné nation. To call all the tribes belonging to this nation, collectively Athabascans, is, therefore, about equivalent to calling all the inhabitants of the United States Kentuckians or Californians, because a part of them live in a district called California. What would the Missourians say to that? However, the name Athabascans, like many other blunders—even like the name Indian itself—it seems, will stick and stay to designate this Indian family for all future times.

Yet the name Athabascan is not altogether objectionable, as on the one hand the district of Athabasca comprises a very considerable area of country inhabited by Déné tribes, and on the other hand it seems to be a genuine Déné word. I shall now try to interpret its meaning.

The Athabascans

J. W. Powell in his "Indian Linguistic Families of America," quoting Lacombe, gives the signification of the word *Athabascan* as a "place of hay and reeds."[10] None of the Athabascan dialects justifies this interpretation, as hay is called either *t'lo* or *t'lu*, and reed *luk'a* or some other word which has not the shadow of any semblance to the word Athabasca. If instead of "a place of hay and reeds,"it were called "a place of lakes and ponds," it would be more accurate, as we shall presently see.

The western and northwestern part of British America is dotted with almost innumerable lakes. There are a few large lakes, as the Great Bear Lake, the Great Slave Lake, Lake Athabasca, and so on, and any number of small lakes, which either have no connection whatever with the larger ones or are connected with them by rivers. In the words of Horatio Hale, this country east of the Rocky Mountains is "a dreary region of rocks and marshes, of shallow lakes and treacherous rivers," and west of the Rockies, says Father Morice, O.M.I. [Oblates of Mary Immaculate], "the country inhabited by them [Northern Dénés] is rugged and heavily timbered, dotted with numerous deep lakes, and intersected by swift, torrential rivers."[11] These remarks and descriptions are necessary to understand the following.

In the Navajo language we have the word *tqaba*, signifying shore (water edge), and *saka*, used of liquids contained in a shallow vessel or receptacle. By uniting these two words, the Navajo forms the compound word *tqabagisaka*, and by it he designates a small pond or lake situated near the shore of a larger lake, with which it has no connection, at least not a perceptible one.

In pronouncing the word *tqabagisaka*, the syllable *gi* (in, ab) is almost totally inaudible, as also the *a* in the second last syllable—*sa*. With regard to the initial *a*, this, in Navajo, as in other Athabascan dialects, is in a great many words of no importance whatever. It may be placed or omitted without changing the significa-tion, frequently serving simply as an intonation. *Tq* and *th* are equivalent and in-terchangeable, and represent in the Athabascan languages a strong guttural *h* (a German *ch*, or a Spanish *j*) preceded by a *t*, with which it is pronounced almost simultaneously.

After all this, the word *Athabasca* means in Navajo "small shallow lakes situated near the shore of larger lakes," which exactly describes the lay and condition of almost the whole western and northwestern part of Canada.

Of the extent of territory over which the Athabascan stock is spread, Father A. G. Morice, O.M.I., says: "No other aboriginal stock in North America, perhaps not even excepting the Algonquian, covers so great an extent of territory as the Déné. The British Isles, France and Spain, Italy and any two or three of the minor European commonwealths taken together would hardly represent the area of the re-gion occupied by that large family."[12]

The historian Hubert Howe Bancroft, in his *Native Races of the Pacific States*, tells us that the Tinneh are:

> a people whose diffusion is only equaled by that of the Aryan or Semitic nations of the old world. The dialects of the Tinneh language are by no means confined within the limits of the Hyperborean division. Stretching from the northern interior of Alaska down into Sonora and Chihuahua, we have here a linguistic line of more than four thousand miles in length extending diagonally over forty-two degrees of latitude; like a great tree whose trunk is the Rocky Mountain range, whose roots compass the deserts of Arizona and New Mexico, and whose branches touch the borders of Hudson Bay and of the Arctic and Pacific Oceans.[13]

Of the northern Athabascan or Déné tribes in Canada and Alaska, Father Morice says:

> West of the Rocky Mountains, they are to be found . . . to the borders of the Eskimo tribes, while on the east side of the same range they people the immense plains and forests which extend from the Northern Saskatchewan down almost to the delta of the Mackenzie River. From west to east they roam, undisputed masters of the soil, over the almost entire breadth of the American continent, though a nar-row strip of sea shore country separates their ancestral domain from the waters of

the Pacific and those of the Atlantic. With that unimportant restriction, they might be said to occupy the immense stretch of land intervening between the two oceans![14]

South of the Canadian boundary, Déné tribes or remnants of them are found in Oregon, northern California, Arizona, New Mexico, and down in Old Mexico; the Navajo (Déné), Apache (Nde), and the Lipanes (Ipa-nde) being the most southern. The Navajo and Apache, therefore, seem to have been the vanguard, as it were, of some great national migration, started from some cause or causes on the steppes of Asia, over Behring's Straits southward. For there can be no reasonable doubt whatever that the Déné tribes came to this continent from Asia by way of Behring's Strait. The dialects of their language can, without any difficulty, be traced from the banks of the Rio Grande up to the very shores of the Strait.

By the way, the Asiatic origin of all North American wild Indians, that is, Indians of a nomadic or roaming disposition, is at present almost universally accepted. J. D. Baldwin, quoting from Kennan's *Tent Life in Siberia*, says:

> The wild Indians of North America were profoundly different from the ancient people of Central America and Peru. The Pueblo or Village Indians of New Mexico have scarcely anything in common with the Apaches, Comanches, and Sioux. Even the uncivilized Indians of South America are different from those in the United States. Our wild Indians have more resemblance to the nomadic Koraks and Chookchees found in Eastern Siberia, throughout the region that extends to Behring's Strait, than to any people on this continent. Those who have seen these Siberians, traveled with them, and lived in their tents, have found the resemblance very striking.[15]

Further studies of the northern Indians induce Mr. Baldwin to say: "I find myself more and more inclined to the opinion . . . that the wild Indians of the North came originally from Asia, where the race to which they belong seems still represented by the Koraks and Chookchees found in that part of Asia which extends to Behring's Strait."[16]

What is said here about our wild Indians in general is particularly noticeable in the tribes belonging to the Athabascan stock. They are decidedly nomads. Even now, after having a definite reservation for many years, at least one-third or more of the Navajo still roam and rove beyond its boundaries, and the Apache, until late years, were preeminently *the rovers* among the Indian tribes of North America.

How and when the Navajo entered their present country is a subject of speculation rather than of positive or even probable knowledge. According to some authorities they came in the 13th century, while others place their advent in the 14th, or in the 15th century. At any rate, the first Spanish explorers and missionaries found them—Los Apaches de Navajoa—in full possession of their territory, and judging from their own sayings and traditions they must have occupied their present habitat and adjacent lands for at least 500 years. The home of the Athabascans was far to the north—the whole interior of Alaska being still peopled by tribes of that stock. It is, therefore, likely that the Navajo, being the foremost of these roaming, migratory tribes, traveled by slow movements and pushed on southward by easy stages along the eastern ranges of the Rocky Mountain region, until they met the sedentary Pueblos of New Mexico and Arizona in their fixed homesteads and permanent villages, where their progress was arrested.

Characteristics and Domestic Life

The Navajo are the most numerous of all the tribes belonging to the Athabascan stock. They are said by some to number about 20,000 souls, exclusive of the Apache. The Navajo are far from being a pure, unmixed tribe. From traditions, and from the names of some of their clans, it is evident that they, from time to time, received recruits from the Zuñis, Jemez, Moquis, and other pueblos, from the Utes, Mexicans, Yumas, and others. But despite these frequent and numerous additions of strangers to the tribe, the stalwart figure, and the bold, independent bearing of the primitive Navajo or Diné, has not been totally destroyed, neither have his intellectual faculties deteriorated thereby, nor his language been affected to any great extent.

There is, therefore, nothing like a pronounced or prevailing Navajo type. Every variety of form, figure, face, and features can be found among them. There are tall, athletic men with bronze skin, aquiline noses, clear-cut features, piercing eyes, and bold carriage, such as we read of; and small men with subdued, rounded features, light brown or light yellow skin, and noses almost approaching the pug. Between these two extremes there is every intermediate variety of color and contour. Some faces remind one very strongly of the Tartars or the Japanese.

The facial expression of the Navajo is, as a rule, intelligent. In the words of Dr. Matthews:

> Some are stern and angry, some pleasant and smiling, others calm and thoughtful; but seldom are any seen that are dull and stupid. These characteristics are to be noted among the women as well as among the men. The social position of the Navaho women is one of great independence; much of the wealth of the nation belongs to them; they are the managers of their own property, the owners of their own children, and their freedom lends character to their physiognomies.[17]

The Navajo women, as a rule, are strongly built and well developed, but rather short of stature and waddling in gait. This last may be accounted for by their custom of squatting on the ground when sitting.

The domestic life of the Navajo, while it is very simple, is peculiar to themselves. The husband owns perhaps a few blankets, his saddle and horse trappings, his weapons, ornaments, clothing, and probably some other small articles wrapped up and stowed away separately. Everything else belongs to the wife. She owns her own sheep and horses, and marriage gives the husband no claim whatever upon them. Her position is a very independent one. If her husband mistreats her or does not behave to suit her, she may pack up her things, drive her flocks elsewhere, and leave him. This, however, is not always done, as the following incident will show.

Some time ago at Chin Lee, near the center of the Navajo reservation, a squaw thought her husband was showing too much attention to another woman. She did not leave him but waited her chance, pounced upon her suspected fellow-tribeswoman, pulled her raven locks with much vim and vigor, threw her to the ground, throttled her till her eyes began to bulge and her tongue to protrude, and would probably have killed her but for the timely intervention of a government field matron.

On the other hand, if the husband has any cause for dissatisfaction, he may leave or chase away his wife, and take up with another. In very rare cases acts of violence are resorted to, as such acts may bring the woman's family, and probably her whole clan, on the trail of the pugnacious husband, who would make things extremely uncomfortable for him. Or the beaten wife may lodge complaint against the beating husband with the agent, who may summon him to appear at the agency and give an account of his actions, and give his passion time to cool down in the guardhouse or at manual labor. And the guardhouse or manual labor without wages go strongly against the grain of the average Navajo.

Polygamy is practiced among the Navajo to some extent. Although the greater number have but one wife, there are some who have two or three. There is no law or custom as to the number of wives one may have, nor need a Navajo consider how many wives he can support, but how many he can manage, and in most cases the line is drawn on one. A Navajo with two or three well-to-do wives has a comparatively easy life, and this seems to be the chief motive for polygamy, for the squaws, as a rule, spend the greater part of the time between the cooking of meals in spinning and in weaving blankets, which is a source of revenue for the family. However, as we shall see later, the men are neither too lazy nor too proud to perform manual labor if the same is remunerative.

The popular conception of the Indian squaw dragging and drudging out her life in miserable thraldom as the silent, patient slave of her haughty liege lord, with no will of her own, does not apply to the Navajo woman at all. She has full control and management of the family affairs. The husband must plant the cornfield and the melon patch, at which the wife may assist him if she chooses. The children belong entirely to her. The father has nothing, or very little, to say with regard to his children, even by way of correction or discipline, and that only with the consent or acquiescence of his wife. Navajo parents have a deep and tender affection for their children, and children display a strong attachment to their parents, so that corporal punishment need never, or but very seldom, be resorted to. Children separated from their parents are easily and strongly affected by homesickness. Cases are known in which boys who had been sent to distant schools ran away and came back home afoot hundreds of miles.

Both men and women are addicted to gambling, and like white gamblers, frequently trust to luck until they have nothing but the scanty clothing upon their backs; but unlike white gamblers, they do not curse ill luck and fate, but take their loss very stoically, even joining in and laughing at the jokes and jests made at their expense. I once watched a party of Navajo gambling near a place called Bis Dot'lisi Des'ahi. In the circle of players sat a young man, who, after losing his money, beads and ornaments, and saddle, pawned his horse to another Navajo for $2; then he returned to the game, lost the $2, and with the most unconcerned air, as if nothing in the world had happened to him, started out for home afoot, seemingly as light in heart as in purse, and he lived a far distance away.

They also like the taste of the white man's fire water, and will imbibe as long as they can stand straight, whenever an occasion is at hand, paying $5 and more for a bottle of the vilest "stuff," such as is commonly termed "tarantula juice" in these parts. However, there are not a few who denounce gambling and drunkenness as "*d'ayisi doyashonda*," "very bad," and will touch neither a card nor a drop of the "dark water." Some time ago an old Navajo brought a young man to me, saying that he was his son, and asked if I had any work for him. As recommendation for the young man he said: "*Dodakada*," "He does not play cards." Playing cards and gambling are synonyms with the Navajo. In the last few years, too, the laws against selling intoxicating drinks to Indians have been more vigorously and strenuously enforced on and about the Navajo reservation, and several unprincipled liquor sellers along the railroad have been brought to justice. Except near the railroads, one very seldom sees a drunken Navajo, and he generally lands in the jail at Fort Defiance, where he is given time to get sober in meditative solitude, after which he is, perhaps, treated to a wholesome turn at public labor by way of a fine, as a preventive of future overindulgence.

Both men and women smoke, but the pipe, so intimately associated with Indian life and customs in white man's ideas, is not in use among them, and, it seems, never was. They smoke cigarettes, using corn husks for wrappers, although they now mostly get regular cigarette papers and the modern brands of smoking tobacco at the trading posts. They inhale the smoke, seem very contented, and get quite talkative when the smoke ascends in curling columns and gathers in miniature clouds of transparent blue above their heads. Of the calumet, or pipe of peace, they know about as much as they do of the parallax of the stars.

Dress

The ancient national costume of the Navajo, especially that of the men, has about all but disappeared since the advent of the white trader among them. When Lieutenant J. H. Simpson met the Navajo in 1849, he found them "gorgeously decked in red, blue and white," the men wearing "helmet-shaped caps, which were in some instances heightened in picturesque effect by being set off with a bunch of eagles' feathers." The women "wore blankets, leggins, and moccasins—the blankets being confined about the waist by a girdle."[18] Scant remnants of their old typical costume may still be found, for instance, the moccasins, which are worn by the greater part of both men and women, although the American shoe is gradually gaining more and more favor with a great many. Besides some squaws still wear the old girdle or sash, and leggins of buskin wrapped about the nether limbs, and some of the men still carry the old headband and wristguard as reminders of bygone times.

However, as the typical old costume of the Navajo has practically disappeared, the dress and the exterior makeup of the Navajo must be described as it is found at the present time. Let us begin at the head, and take the men first.

With a small whisk broom made of a bunch of dry stems of a particular species of grass, the hair is all brushed smoothly to the back of the head. Here it is gathered into a solid knot, and tied with a white woolen cord in such a manner as to give it the approximate shape of a small dumbbell. But there are not a few who wear their hair cropped off in a straight line, about one-half inch below the ear lobes.

A sash of red or other color, sometimes variegated, often a large handkerchief of the bandana variety, is worn turban-fashion about the forehead, probably to keep the stray locks out of the eyes and face. This turban or headband is sometimes decorated with turquoise or silver ornaments. It has already been, to a great extent, displaced by the broad-brimmed western hat, usually of a whitish color.

They all have the lobes of their ears pierced, and from them are dangling ear pendants consisting either of a flat piece of polished turquoise, a small string of turquoise beads, or of good-sized silver rings. These rings are sometimes quite heavy. I have seen Navajo turn them up over their ears when riding, as the jolting of the horse's gait caused them to jerk uncomfortably at the ear lobes. About their necks they wear strands of beads, either of coral or turquoise, and thin small disks of white shell, or heavy necklaces of silver beads and other silver ornaments.

The upper part of the body is covered by a short shirt of bright-colored calico or velveteen, sometimes fitting very loosely and sometimes quite snugly. With this are worn loose breeches of calico or white cotton, slashed at the bottom like those of the Mexicans. However, coats, vests, and pants of American style, especially corduroys, are not infrequent.

About the waist is buckled a belt, either a leather cartridge belt or one of large oval disks of silver strung upon a strap. On their feet are low moccasins of buckskin, dyed either a dull reddish brown or black, and soled with rawhide. The lower part of the legs are often encased in leggins of dyed deerskin, tied below the knee with red garters woven in fanciful designs.

To all this is added a heavy woolen blanket or robe. There is little or no difference between their summer and winter dress. Instead of deerskin leggins many wear woolen stockings without toes and heels, and in winter they make a kind of overshoes of sheepskin with the wool inside.

Firearms have displaced the bow, arrow, lance, and shield, although in former times these were an essential part of the everyday costume of a Navajo man. An interesting relic of the habitual use of the bow survives in their still wearing upon their left wrist the leather silver-mounted wrist guard as an ornament.

The women dress their hair the same as the men, but never wear a headband. Their ears, too, are pierced, but very few wear ear pendants. Besides their bead necklaces, which also are like those of the men, they wear a number of silver bracelets, rings, and so on.

The typical dress of the Navajo woman was a heavy woolen tunic of dark blue with red ornamental borders. In fact, it consisted of two small closely woven blankets, sewed together from the bottom to the waist, and the upper corners tied together at the shoulders. It reached just below the knee and was held tight about the waist by a red woven girdle. The old-time dress is now very seldom seen, as also the buskin wrappings for the legs. Instead the women now wear dresses of bright flashing calicos, made in the simplest style, a loose jacket, and petticoats reaching to the ankles. Their blankets or robes and their moccasins are the same as those of the men.

The children are dressed about the same as the adults, only that their clothing is smaller in size, and often very scant.

Clans

The Navajo tribe is divided into a number of clans, or *gentes*, a division or an institution found among all nations—except our own, which is composed of all the nations of the world. Thus we find the gentes among the Romans, the clans among the old Celts, and the *sippschaften* among the ancient Germans, and so on. And the more primitive the people, the more defined and compact is the organization of their tribal clans or gentes.

There are about 52 clans in the Navajo tribe. Of these some have taken or received their names from the locality where they originally lived, or where they were found. "There is little doubt," says Dr. Washington Matthews, "that in the majority of cases if not in all, the names of Navaho gentes, which are not the names of tribes, are simply designations of localities."[19] And A. M. Stephen says: "In an earlier time, when the organization of the gentes or clans was more compact, a scope of country was roughly parceled out and held as a clan ground, and many of the clans take their names from these localities."[20] For instance, the *Tqoyedlini*, Meeting of the Waters People, are so called because they originally lived at a place where two rivers joined. The *Tset'lani*, Rock Bottom People, derive their name from the fact they were found, so their legend says, encamped in the bottom of a canyon, and were adopted into the tribe.

Others take their name from the places from which they came, that is, their original homes from which they migrated. After meeting with the Navajo in their own country, they were received into the tribe, and retained the names of their old homes, for example, *Hashk'angatso Diné*, Big Yucca Place People, so-called because they came from a place called *Hashk'angatso*, Big Yucca Place, or Yucca Country; *Tqabaha Diné*, Shore People, so-called after their original country *Tqabaha qalgai*, Prairie on the Shores.

Again, other clans have names of alien tribes of Indians. They are the descendants of people from other [places], either captives or refugees, who have been received and adopted into the tribe by the Navajo in the early days, for example, *Maideshgishni*, Coyote Pass People, or the Jemez Clan; *Noda' Diné,*

Mescal People, or the Ute Clan; *Flogi*, Hairy People, from an ancient pueblo near Jemez, probably Cia, or Silla; *Nanasht'eshi*, Black (or Charcoal) Streaked Stranger People, or the Zuni Clan.

Finally, other clans owe their name to some peculiar circumstance or accident which happened before the clan had a definite name, for example, the *Tqodichini*, Bitter Water People, are said to take their name from the fact that the woman with whom the clan originated tasted first of a spring which the people had found in their wandering, and pronounced it *bitter*. In the same manner the *Tqodok'ozhi*, Saline Water People, are said to have received their names.

Although this, and whatever else is said and known concerning the origin and formation of clans among the Navajo, is now legendary, that is, embodied in their legends and myths, it nevertheless seems to have some historical foundation in actual facts which happened in the early days of the tribe, and which in later times have become more or less distorted, embellished, and enlarged upon, as was natural with a people who had no written language but transmitted their history from mouth to mouth.

Members of a clan consider themselves almost as closely related to each other as members of the same family. This may sound well and philadelphic [brotherly loving] enough to white people, but perhaps it does not sound so well to a thrifty young Navajo, who marries into a numerous clan: all his fellow clansmen have a claim upon him, and upon what is his. If he is industrious and earns some money, his dear relatives will not be long to know of it, and will be at hand on payday to help him reap the benefits of his labor and industry, which, as a rule, are willingly shared with them. The Navajo is far more clannish than either Scot or Teuton: to share his earnings with his clansmen seems to him quite in order. When two strangers meet, one of the first questions asked is: *Qaat'ish bashin ntchin?* meaning: To which clan do you belong? and at once both set to work and try, for their mutual benefit, to work up some degree of relationship.

The ties of kindred or relationship are recognized and observed by the Navajo, even to those remote collateral branches which among civilized nations have long been lost sight of. Indeed, they go still further and often cling to some imaginary degree of clan relationship as fondly as white people do to blood relations of the first and second degree. I have had about a half dozen or more old squaws, in different parts of the reservation, introduce themselves to me as the mother of a certain rich Navajo, with whom I was well acquainted. Somewhat surprised that this particular Navajo had a mother in every nook and corner of the reservation, I inquired about it and found that they merely belonged to the same clan: the *Maideshgishni*, or Coyote Pass Clan. Other Navajo of the *Tqabaha* Clan, which is affiliated to that of the Coyote Pass, claimed the same person for their elder brother.

Not only are members of the *same* clan considered related to each other, but, as may be gathered from the foregoing paragraph, relationship exists, or is supposed to exist, between different clans, so that the 52 or more clans of the tribe are bunched into 10 or 12 interrelated or affiliated groups or phratries.

In the Navajo tribe descent is in the female line, so that a Navajo always belongs to the clan of his mother. When asked to which clan he belongs, he will invariably give that of his mother, totally ignoring his father's clan. Clanship constitutes an impediment of matrimony with the Navajo. No man is allowed to marry a girl of his own clan, and this forbidden degree of kindred is extended to his whole phratry or other clans affiliated to his, and even to his father's clan, although, as Dr. Matthews remarks, exceptions may be made with regard to phratral clans when the phratral relationship is obscure or not well defined.

The clans of the Dené tribes of the far north, at least most of them, if not all, are totemic, i.e., the clan is usually named after some animal, and even when not it has some animal which—or rather the spirit of which—is considered by the members as the tutelary genius, or what civilized superstition would call the mascot of the clan. This animal is called a totem, and its form is sometimes rudely carved out of wood and affixed to the houses, or erected on large carved poles in front of the house. The totem poles of Alaska are well known.

Whether totemism ever was in vogue among the Navajo, that is, whether their clans are of totemic origin, and they ever used clan totems, is now impossible to determine, as they, at the present time, certainly do not use any. Yet Dr. Matthews says there are some passages in their legends which seem to indicate that at least a few of the Navajo clans were once totemic. Thus the goddess Asdsan Nadlehi is said to have given certain pets to some wanderers from the West, to guide and to protect them on their journey. Before setting out, and while taking leave from her, she is represented saying to them: "It is a long and dangerous journey to where you are going. It is well that you should be cared for and protected on the way. I shall give you five of my pets—a bear, a great snake, a deer, a porcupine, and a puma—to watch over you. They will not desert you."[21] These pets accompanied the people on their journey, keeping watch over their camps at night, especially the bear, until subsequently they were set free at different places. The awe of reverence in which the Navajo still hold some animals, for instance, the snake, bear, eagle, coyote, and the like, may possibly, at least partly, be a vestige of the totemism which once may have prevailed among the clans.

The clans of the Navajo tribe are not linked together by any bonds of law or authority into a political or civic organization governed by a set of officers under a central head, like the Pueblos. Neither has each clan a specified territory or certain defined limits which separate it from the other clans. In a pueblo, each clan has its specific quarter, or, as we may call it, its ward, inhabited by members of a particular clan; the whole pueblo is governed by a governor and a number of subordinate officers, all of whom are elected, and whose duty it is to see that the tribal laws and the customs and traditions of the ancients are well kept and observed, and whose words are law for all the people.

Livestock

New Mexico and Arizona came into the possession of the United States in 1848, by the treaty of Guadalupe Hidalgo. Prior to that time the Navajo supported themselves chiefly by war and plunder. They were the highway robbers of the plains, the terror of the country, and like the Ismaelites of old, their hands were raised against all, and the hands of all against them. The chief contributors toward their temporal welfare and their gratuitous livelihood were the Pueblo Indians and the Mexican settlers. To this day, old weather-beaten Mexicans tell of the dangerous times when, at any moment, a band of Navajo raiders might suddenly dash into sight and destroy or carry off their flocks or the fruit of their hard labor.

When the Israelites, in the days of Nehemias, were rebuilding the walls of Jerusalem, their enemies, the Samaritans, Arabians, Ammonites, and Azotians became exceedingly angry and began to attack and harass the Jews. Then it was arranged that "of them that built on the wall, and that carried burdens, and that laded with one of his hands he did the work, and with the other he held a sword." At certain intervals watchmen were posted with trumpets, to sound the alarm when the enemy came into sight, and whenever the flare of the trumpet was heard, the workmen dropped their tools and stood together for mutual protection. The history of the foundation of the Mexican villages and towns in New Mexico and Arizona is very similar to the history of the refoundation of Jerusalem. With one hand the early Mexican pioneers guided their plough or wielded their hoe, with the other they held their sword or their gun. At different advantageous points, sentinels were posted to give the danger signals, when the implements were dropped and the workmen turned into soldiers, and hastily gathered together to repel the attack by force of arms. But despite their utmost vigilance, they were often taken by surprise and suffered heavily. Quick, alert, and experienced, the Navajo frequently appeared in numbers as suddenly as a flashlight, took what they wanted, killed those who resisted or took them along as slaves, and as suddenly disappeared again.

The thousands of sheep, goats, cattle, and horses which were captured and driven off in these raids upon the Mexicans and Pueblos were to a great extent the beginning of the large flocks and herds which constitute the main wealth of the Navajo today. Nowadays, when the glorious old fighting days of the Navajo are a thing of the past, when war and plunder are dangerous occupations, when Uncle Sam's sheriffs and soldiers are set upon the trail of raiders and robbers, when the already acquired herds, and those given by the government later, have increased and multiplied, the shrewd and cunning Navajo has changed from a warrior and hunter into a harmless, peaceful shepherd. Such a step, from warrior to shepherd, is neither a long one nor a hard one to take for a people who possess so adaptable and imitative a nature as the Navajo.

A change of circumstances always necessitates a change of life and customs, and under the stress of changed circumstances, the once wild and warlike Navajo have become a peaceful pastoral tribe, living by, with, and of their flocks and herds. And as time rolls on and circumstances continue to change, this new pastoral tribe is slowly developing into an agricultural tribe. In many places favored by nature with a supply of water, corn, beans, wheat, melons, potatoes, alfalfa, hay, and so on, are raised with considerable success, although in a limited and primitive way; for example, corn is planted by making a hole into the ground with a stick or with a mattock, dropping about a half dozen grains into the hole, and covering it up with the foot.

The Navajo country is perhaps better adapted to the raising of sheep than to anything else. The quick eye and the practical sense of the Navajo were not slow in recognizing this. Therefore, almost every family has a flock of sheep and goats numbering anywhere from 100 to 2,000–3,000. These constitute their staple supply of food and clothing. One never sees a flock of sheep without a number of goats intermingled with them. The casual traveler or passerby may perhaps find nothing extraordinary in this, or may probably think it a queer combination; but the Navajo knows that a goat will always take a very determined stand against a coyote, and that he, consequently, is a greater protection for his sheep than a half dozen of his dogs. The Navajo dogs are a set of cowardly mongrel curs of unknown breed, or rather an undeterminable mixture of breeds, some resembling dogs proper, others having the appearance of coyotes. However, they do excellent service in keeping a flock together or in driving it from place to place.

Some few have small herds of cattle, originally gathered in and picked up on the borders, and appropriated without asking the consent of their erstwhile owners, the Mexicans and Pueblos. Besides this, most of them have a band of stocky, sturdy little ponies. These ponies are said to be the descendants of the Arabian steeds brought over by the first Spanish discoverers. Whether this is true or not, one thing is sure: they are tough and enduring. Nothing can be more deceptive than the appearance of a Navajo pony. Sometimes one sees a Navajo pony that seems to be the "scrubbiest of the scrubby"; he looks as if a slight shove would make him roll over. But saddle him up beside a well-groomed, grain-fed American horse, and when the latter falls down exhausted, the pony will go 10 miles further and then recuperate on sagebrush and dry weeds of last season. Moreover, the pony does not only serve as a means of transportation but is also a much prized addition to the Navajo's larder; for the Navajo relishes horsemeat just about as much as an American does his turkey on Thanksgiving day.

Besides their ponies, many Navajo have a number of shaggy little burros, originally acquired in the above-named cheap but strenuous business manner. I cannot help but devote a few words to the burro, as many people seem to think that he was created for no other purpose but to be the clown or the idiot among the animals. Nothing can be further from the truth than such an illusion. The burro is the most imperturbable philosopher of the animal kingdom; the ideal of the Stoics. The greatest avalanche that ever thundered down the rocky sides of the Alps; an eruption of Mt. Pelee; a Baltimore fire; a Galveston flood; a Louisville tornado; a Caracas earthquake: any one of these disasters, or even all of them taken together, would hardly have any other effect upon him than to cause him to prick up his ears inquiringly, and perhaps to sing a little song of his own composition.

He is personified equanimity and contentment: he will eat what a mule will not touch, and will thrive where a horse will starve. Work? I have seen loads moving along, which after careful inspection revealed two long waving ears in front and a little wagging tail in the rear; the motion seemed to be effected by four neat little hoofs, about as large as ordinary ink bottles. His corporal equilibrium is equal to that of his temperament. He will amble along with his load, safely and without hesitation, on trails which a horse will refuse to tread, and which will make a mule nervous and uneasy. His head is free from vertigo, his feet as sure as a fly's, his nerves seem to be of steel wire, his blood as cool as quicksilver in zero weather, his life as tough as that of the proverbial cat.

His song is the fortissimo of the cry of the peacock and the grating of the guinea fowl combined, alternating with the toot of a Mississippi steamer, and although it is not very melodious, it is certainly very stirring, especially when heard in the dead of the night. His gait, as a rule, is such that if he does not arrive at his destination today, he may arrive there by the end of next week. He is the genius of the Southwest, where nothing and nobody is in a hurry, except the Yankee; where there is always plenty of time *mañana* (tomorrow), and where it is thought foolish to worry.

But more than all this, the burro is one of the pioneers and carriers of civilization in the Southwest. Patiently and without murmur or complaint, he has carried the pack and the burdens of the early settlers, discoverers, explorers, prospectors, surveyors, and the like; with his aid and endurance it became possible to build long railroad lines across the plains and deserts of New Mexico and Arizona, and the railroads, in the laying of which he was so instrumental, brought people into the country, and with the people came development and progress, peace and enlightenment. Therefore, let no one despise the burro, nor make him the target of ill-timed jokes or jests. He has done more for the spread of civilization than many a senator in the halls of the capital, yea, even than many an LL.D. on the chair of a university.

Navajo Pastoralism

On account of the scarcity of grass in the greater part of the Navajo country, and the difficulty of procuring a sufficient supply of water for the stock, it is necessary that the Navajo almost constantly keep their flocks on a move and drive them from place to place.

These facts explain the roaming condition of the Navajo tribe; also the absence of Navajo villages, their scattered mode of living, and their having more than one home. The Navajo country is the largest of all the Indian reservations in the United States; yet at least one-third of the tribe lives scattered about outside of its limits. However, despite all this, and despite the fact of their driving their flocks to and fro, they are not, properly speaking, nomads, as the stock range of each individual family is comparatively small. Neither can they be said to be a sedentary tribe, as they have nothing which could in any sense of the word be called a village. Places where two or more hogans or huts are within speaking distance or even within sight of each other are rare and far between. The nearest approach to a village, in the writer's knowledge, is at Chin Lee, near the center of the reservation, where in a beautiful cottonwood grove there are about a half dozen hogans or huts within hailing distance of each other. As a rule, the next hogan or hut may be one mile, perhaps two, five, or 10 miles away.

Every family, or almost every family, has two, three, or more hogans or residences, which they occupy according to the season of the year, or the number of their flocks, or the condition of the grass and the supply of water. For on the one hand, if a flock be kept too long on the same pasture, there is danger of the grass being cropped too closely, or even of being pulled out by the roots, so that the place will either be spoiled totally, or at least rendered worthless for several years, and on the other hand, many of the springs are fed by surface water and dry up sometimes early in the summer. These conditions must never be lost sight of by the Navajo shepherd. Thus each family keeps moving back and forth between its several residences, over an area which is frequently very small. For this reason it is, as a rule, difficult to say just where any particular Navajo who has sheep is at any particular time.

As a result, the Navajo shepherds drive their flocks during the summer into the mountains, or up on the high table lands, near a spring or a pond or a running creek. In the winter when the snow comes, they take them down again among the lower foothills, or out into the valleys. During the winter while the ground is covered with snow, flock and shepherd depend on the snow for their water supply, and if the snow is very deep, so as to cover even the sagebrush, the Navajo often chops down a piñon tree or two for his sheep to graze on. When the snow melts in the valleys and begins to disappear, the flocks are driven by slow stages back again into the mountains.

For the welfare of his flocks as well as for the success of his crops, the Navajo depends greatly upon a good heavy snowfall during the winter. A heavy snowfall in winter and a slow thaw in spring means a great absorption of moisture by the ground and consequently plenty of corn, melons, and grass in the summer and fall; whereas an open winter, with fair weather and no snow, means a drought during the summer, a failure of crops in the fall, and the loss of much stock, except in some few especially favored localities.

Excepting the San Juan River in the northeastern corner of the reservation, and the Little Colorado on the western boundary, there are no continually running streams or rivers in the Navajo country. There are watercourses, canyons, and arroyos, but they run only in the spring, when the snow melts on the mountains, or after a rain, and serve rather to drain the land than to irrigate it. There are also a few live creeks, which run the greater part of the year, but which often run dry just during the season when water is most wanted. In some localities there are good perennial springs, but such localities are not overly numerous.

Many of the Navajo who have fields or cultivable land practice irrigation to some extent by throwing out rude ditches which carry the floodwaters upon their fields, and a few who possess good continual springs have gone to the trouble of constructing small reservoirs, by the means of which they are able to flood their fields whenever water is badly needed. Of course, in such regions as along the San Juan River, irrigation is carried on more systematically and on a larger scale than in the interior of the reservation. In the future more may be expected of the Navajo in this direction, as their present agents are very anxious and have taken steps to induce the government to lend them a helping hand.

In the latter part of July, during the month of August, and sometimes in the forepart of September, the so-called rainy season sets in. During this period of time short heavy showers, often accompanied by terrific thunderstorms, are frequent. These showers are at times so torrential that in a few minutes the hillside is one sheet of rushing water. During a thunderstorm it is unsafe for a person to be out on one of the large flats or plain, as there is nothing within sight to attract the lightning but the human form; almost every year from three to six Navajo are reported killed by lightning.

During the rainy season the dry sandy soil absorbs enough moisture to allow the plants to grow and thrive for some time, but most of the water rushes off hurriedly through the deep-channeled canyons and arroyos toward the San Juan and Little Colorado rivers. Pools and small lakes are formed in many places which last for some weeks, and sometimes several months and even years. About 15 miles south of Chin Lee, and about six miles south of Fort Defiance, both places on the reservation, are good-sized lakes formed in this manner, where four years ago there was not a drop of water.

At times when water gathers in this manner in pools and lakes, the Navajo shepherd takes advantage of this and keeps his flock in the vicinity. When they dry out, other pastures are looked for, always with an eye to water. As a rule, all waters are regarded by the Navajo as common property of the people. Hence a Navajo will water his stock wherever he finds water, and the Navajo on whose land the water is located will raise no objection to his so doing.

In speaking of the flocks and herds of the Navajo, we must not forget to say a word or two concerning the person of the Navajo shepherd. In the Navajo family, descent is in the female line; the children belong to the mother and become members of her clan; all the property, except horses, cattle, and personal apparel, belong to her. Sheep and goats are hers exclusively; the head of the family has no right whatever over them. He cannot even sell a sheep or goat to a passing traveler without first obtaining the consent and approval of his wife. Therefore, when the flocks are on the move from one pasture to another, they are usually in charge of the women, very seldom of men or grown-up young men, while when the family has settled anyplace and has established its home, the duty of herding the sheep falls almost entirely upon the lot of the children, oftentimes mere tots.

The sheep are not only the staple food supply of the Navajo, but are also a source of revenue for them. The meat and pelts are either kept for family use or sold. The wool, too, is either sold to the traders or is spun into a coarse, loose yarn, from which the celebrated Navajo blanket is woven.

Notes

1. From Leopold Ostermann, "Places and Peoples of Our Southwest: The Navajo," *Catholic Pioneer* 1 (July 1905): 8-9; (August 1905): 7-9; (September 1905): 3-5; (October 1905): 14-16; (November 1905): 12-14; (December 1905): 10-11; (January 1906): 12-14; (February 1906): 10-12; (April 1906): 10–12.

2. Charles F. Lummis, *The Land of Poco Tiempo* (New York: C. Scribner's Sons, 1893), 6–7.

[3. Washington Matthews, *Navaho Legends* (Boston: Houghton, Mifflin, 1897), 213.]

[4. Alonso de Benavides, "Benavides's Memorial, 1630," translated by Mrs. Edward E. Ayer, *Land of Sunshine* 13 (December 1900): 441.]

[5. Daniel G. Brinton, *The American Race: A Linguistic Classification and Ethnographic Description of the Native Tribes of North and South America* (Philadelphia: David McKay, 1901), 72.]

6. Matthews, 144, 146.

7. John D. Baldwin, *Ancient America, in Notes on American Archaeology* (New York: Harper & Brothers, 1872), 68, 74.

[8. Josiah Gregg, *Commerce of the Prairies, or the Journal of a Santa Fé Trader, 1831–1839*, vol. 1 (New York: J. & H. G. Langley, 1845), 285–86.]

[9. Frank McNitt, ed., *Navaho Expedition: Journal of a Military Reconnaissance from Santa Fe, New Mexico, to the Navaho Country Made in 1849 by Lieutenant James H. Simpson* (Norman: University of Oklahoma Press, 1964 [1852]), 96–97.]

[10. J. W. Powell, "Indian Linguistic Families of America North of Mexico," *Seventh Annual Report, Bureau of American Ethnology* (Washington, D.C.: Government Printing Office, 1891), 52.]

11. A. G. Morice, *Notes Archaeological, Industrial and Sociological, on the Western Dénés, with an Ethnographical Sketch of the Same*, Transactions of the Canadian Institute 14 (Ottawa: Canadian Institute, 1893), 11.

12. Morice, 10.

[13. Hubert Howe Bancroft, *The Works of Hubert Howe Bancroft. The Native Races, Vol. III. Myths and Languages* (San Francisco: A. L. Bancroft & Company, 1883), 583–84.]

14. Morice, 11.

15. Baldwin, 65–66.

16. Baldwin, 185.

17. Matthews, 11.

[18. McNitt, 62–63, 67.]

19. Matthews, 31.

20. Alexander M. Stephen, "The Navajo," *American Anthropologist* 6 (October 1893): 349.

21. Matthews, 149 ff.

34

The Character of the Navajo[1]

J. B. Moore

[J. B. Moore, a former Texas ranger, purchased the trading post at Washington Pass in 1896, renamed it Crystal, and over the next 15 years worked to improve the quality and marketability of Navajo products, especially their weaving. Among his innovations were sending Navajo wool East to be cleaned, dyed, and returned. He would then issue it to his better weavers. He also sponsored new, more intricate designs. In 1903 he began doing mail-order business, and his illustrated catalogs set the standard for Navajo rugs for the time. He was the first trader to credit weavers by name in rug advertisements.[2]

Mr. Moore was a great friend of the Franciscans. The Crystal post was a familiar stop on the way from St. Michaels to the San Juan area, its proprietor "always friendly with us and insisted we stop there every time we passed by and stay overnight with him." Father Berard writes that Moore "butchered up the Navajo language almost better than anybody I ever heard, but the Indians got used to his peculiar Navajo speech, and they readily understood him after a while."[3] Father Berard's reminiscences in *Tales of an Endishodi* include a chapter on trader Moore, "The Crystal Trader and the Navajo Witch."

The trader's experience with the Navajo, shared with the friars, expanded their own perspectives. His wise and sensitive article on Navajo character, published a century ago in the ephemeral *Catholic Pioneer*, continues to be relevant and deserves a current audience.]

I know a little of Indians, Navajo Indians in particular. Not much, but a little. And I have learned it from many years of living among and constantly associating with them.

I have learned that one having the necessary mental caliber and receptivity may learn about as much from, as about, the Navajo. Perhaps a little more; for he has the trait in common with the white man of being more willing to impart than to receive instruction. And I believe that efforts for his betterment would prove a great deal more resultful if his white teachers could be brought to take the role of pupil in some matters as well as that of teacher in others.

The Navajo is neither all saint nor all devil. He has good traits, and many of them; but he has others that are not good. He is simply a lump of the great leaven of humanity in its totality, but a lump of such a different consistency that he makes a wretched misfit in the preconceived theories of his zealous but misguided "tenderfoot" friends, who arrogate to themselves the duty of redeeming him and directing his destiny.

By his own efforts and of himself, he has reached a by no means inconsiderable stage of development, but has settled back into a conservatism that clings tenaciously to that which he has tried and found good, and is far less plastic than other tribes not so well advanced. This conservatism makes him perhaps the most difficult proposition of any tribe of the American Indians, and it would seem the part of wisdom to learn of the good he really has and build on that, leading onward by degrees, rather than attempt to uproot his whole system of life and beliefs and substitute one we imagine fits his case better.

There can be no doubt but he has the foundation in him on which to build. Not a day but one may learn lessons in patience, persistence, and tolerance from him. He is patient in his dealings with you, usually accommodating himself to your convenience and inclinations. Patient, too, in what he regards as an unwarrantable interference on your part with affairs he considers peculiarly his own; not to say meddlesome injustice. He is persistent in all his own ideas, and clings tenaciously to his purpose until it is accomplished, if accomplishment seems possible to him. He is tolerant of your different views and different ways of life, and concedes them as fitting and proper to yourself, but cannot comprehend why you should not be willing that he should hold and act on his own, which experience has taught him to believe proper for himself.

He is respectful and considerate of the aged, and kind and indulgent to children, not only to his own, but to all children. And his children are dutiful and obedient too, and considerate of one another. One never sees a larger boy bullying a small one as is so common among white children, and in all the years lived among them, I have [yet] my first time to see a Navajo child receive a blow from either parent, or brother, or sister. Allowance being made for his circumstances, his treatment of his children is so far ahead of that of white parents as to put 99 out of 100 to shame.

He has an innate love for the beautiful, as is shown by the various things he makes, but finds its best expression in the Navajo blanket. This to them is more than a commodity, though necessity demands they make it such. There is a deep sentiment of love and admiration for its meaning underlying its making, as is shown by the interest one of them excites even after it has passed into the trader's possession. If a fine Navajo blanket is spread on the counter, it would be a safe wager that 49 of the first 50 Navajo coming into the store would walk over to it, finger it, and study and comment on that blanket before they noticed another thing in the store.

Patience, persistence, tolerance, respect for old age, love for children, love for the beautiful, make a pretty good foundation on which to build a character, and the Navajo has them. How many whites have all of them? But along with these the Navajo has other traits that are a mixture of the good and bad, and yet others with the good as we understand it all left out, but these may have had a reason for being in some long past phase of life that we know nothing of.

He can, and will lie himself, but expects and demands that you speak the truth. And this raises the question, was he not in his primal state a truth-speaking and truth-loving being? And has he not become a liar because contact with other peoples seems to point out the expedience of lying upon occasion? Certain it is that they do not regard lying with favor, though they practice it so generally. I once heard one of their ablest and most influential men deliver his opinion thus: "He speaks up, and he speaks down; he speaks to the right, and he speaks to the left; but he will not speak straight out as a man should."

The Navajo is a petty thief, and yet may be trusted with sums of money that seem wealth to him, and thousands of dollars worth of property, and will safely deliver either according to his instructions. He sees no wrong in stealing that for which another is responsible, but if a thing be given into his custody he will be strictly honest.

No people on earth like better to trade on credit, and none hate more to pay their debts. Yet, if the debt is due him, he is the most persistent and resourceful of collectors.

Nothing affords one of them keener pleasure than to best a white man in a trade, by short change or in any conceivable way. The little "tots" practice this from the time they can reach their hands to the top of the store counter, and have all become adept in the art when they arrive at adult age. They plan, study, and connive with each other to beat the whites and count it something to be proud of if they succeed.

So in casting up his general character, we find our Navajo a very human sort of being: With good in him, but not all good; with evil in him too, but not all evil either. Allowing for his viewpoint, I am sometimes tempted to think he averages up on the whole better than we do. Certain it is, the good in him deserves as well, as it would if we placed it there, and that if much is to be done for his advancement, this good must be studied, recognized, and built upon, instead of being rooted out of his life along with his faults.

Theories are beautiful things, and good intentions are very laudable, and that the many good people who are theorizing about and planning the betterment of the Indians are actuated by the best of intentions, I have not the least doubt. But we go about the proposition wrong end to. It would be wiser, more humane, and a great deal more effective, if we learn from and of the Indian, and then fit our theories about him as he is, instead of elaborating the theories first, and then setting about tearing his system of life all to pieces, and working him over to fit the theories. Possibly the last course may be made successful, but I fear we will run out of Indian material before the reconstruction process can be made complete.

Notes

1. From J. B. Moore, "Characteristics of the Navajo," *Catholic Pioneer* 1 (May 1906):12–15.

2. Willow Roberts Powers, *Navajo Trading: The End of an Era* (Albuquerque: University of New Mexico Press, 2001), 69; John Bradford (J. B.) Moore, *The Catalogues of Fine Navajo Blankets, Rugs, Ceremonial Baskets, Silverwork, Jewelry & Curios: Originally Published between 1903 and 1911* (Albuquerque, N.Mex.: Avanya, 1987).

3. Murray Bodo, ed., *Tales of an Endishodi: Father Berard Haile and the Navajo, 1900–1961* (Albuquerque: University of New Mexico Press, 1998), 89.

35

Navajo Names

Leopold Ostermann, O.F.M., Anselm Weber, O.F.M., and Berard Haile, O.F.M.

[Here is offered another composite selection, this one arranged chronologically. It combines three statements on Navajo names and naming practices written over almost two decades, beginning in 1904 with Father Anselm's musings on creative and potentially profitable name selection. There follows Father Leopold's 1918 article on the origins and multiplicity of Navajo names, the most serious and straightforward of the three pieces. Here again, Father Leopold enlivens his account with the meaningful encounter, this time a glimpse of the stubborn pride of old Palm of the Hand at the trading post, and the tale of how he got his name. Father Berard's contribution, a fragment from a longer unpublished, undated manuscript, dates from about 1921, when he was writing for possible publication in a series for *St. Anthony Messenger*. It is excerpted from the handwritten manuscript transcribed as "Family Love and Family Work" (see chapter 36).

As time went on, the complexity and multiplicity of Navajo names proved increasingly problematic as Navajo were drafted into military service and incorporated into the bureaucratic organization of the military, veterans' programs, Social Security, corporate pension rolls, and the formal roster of the Navajo tribe itself. Father Emanuel later wrote about the efforts of the Franciscans to help the tribe and the external bureaucracies deal with the "tangled names" of the Navajo.[1]

❖

In Search of Suitable Names: A Modest Proposal[2]

In connection with the baptism of our students, we found out that the Indian Department in Washington wants the name of the fathers of the students to be given as the family name whenever possible. We also do this as long as the Indian names are suitable. But when, for example, the father's name is the Grandchild of the Screaming Grandmother, or the Son of the Dead Liar, or the Son of the Ugly Wife, or the Cousin of the Great Burro, or Shaggy Burro, it is probably not appropriate to burden the children with such a family name. The famous names Grover Cleveland, Bryan McKinley, Russell Sage, and other similar names are already overused for the Navajo students in the different government schools. It also sounds strange to hear or read that Russell Sage is suffering from poverty, Grover Cleveland spent a week in jail, or Thomas Morgan put his sheep out to pasture. How Bryan McKinley can live peacefully together in one person is also a mystery.

It is really not so easy to give suitable names as it would seem at first glance. Therefore I came up with the idea to give them the names of residents of a certain settlement somewhere in *Mitchi Sawgyegan* (Indian name). Earlier, this settlement was called South Bush by some, although that isn't its actual name. I had already been told that part of the settlement was called Hell's Gate, but this is also not quite right, at least in a literal sense, although something like "doors " or "gate" is common in some known place names. I began with the name Anselm Endres, not exactly unattractive, and wrote my intentions to the reverend preacher of that region, with whom I am quite well acquainted. He thought it was a "great idea" to immortalize the local names among the native Indians.

However, he reminded me that I had not set my sights on the financial possibilities of this plan. I should charge the original owners of these names at least $5 to $10, according to the pleasing sound of the name, for the privilege of adopting Indians into their families for our mission. His own name should be worth at least $5. I should give his name to a good, talented Indian boy, and if this boy wanted to become a priest later, he could count on him for his maintenance during his studies. That is certainly very generous, and I will not forget his offer. There are several among the Navajo students who are surely talented enough to be trained for the priesthood, should God grant them the grace of this calling. This preacher also suggested that I extend the plan across the settlement in "South Bush" to richer people who could give more. Wonderful! Whoever wants to adopt Indian children into their family under the above-mentioned conditions, please let us know before we get new "nameless" students, with the stipulation that the name doesn't sound as bad as Shaggy Burro.

An Understandable Reticence[3]

The Navajo has, in his own language, only a personal or individual name, by which he is known to and called by others. Family appellations are not used. However, the individual is never addressed, when spoken to, by the name under which he is known. This would, in the first place, be contrary to Navajo decorum, and second, in many cases, as we shall see, the name would be anything but flattering to the bearer. The general name or title by which a Navajo is addressed, when spoken to, is *Qastqin*, Mister, corresponding exactly with the *Senor* of the Spaniards. Besides this they use such titles as *sik'is*, my friend; *shinai*, my elder brother; *sitsili*, my younger brother; *shichai*, my grandfather, or some word expressing a greater or lesser degree of relationship.

The Navajo is very backward and bashful about telling his name. Upon the question: *Da inlye*? How are you called, or what is your name? he invariably answers: *Qolla*! an expression used in Navajo like *quien sabe* in Spanish, for I don't know, or he will say: *attin*, I have none, or there isn't any. If you inquire further: How do the other Navajo, your father and mother, and the like, call you? the same answer is given. At first one thinks they do this out of some kind of religious fear or superstitious dread, but after hearing a number of Navajo names, one finds bashfulness and reticence on this point quite in order.

The Navajo, as in fact almost all Indians, do not call each other by such highly poetical names as we sometimes read in novels and romances. There are no Fleet Antelopes, Prancing Horses, Soaring Eagles, Towering Pines, and so on, but we do meet with such prosy names as the Liar's Son, the Man Killer, Frozen Feet, Mister Mud, the Stutterer, Little Yellow Man, Little Horsethief, Shaggy Burro, or any other name referring to some natural defect or abnormal deformity in the exterior appearance of the individual. Of course, no one, not even a white man, when asked his name would be very eager to say, for instance, my name is Shaggy Burro, or Squint Eye, or Club Foot, or perhaps even Chan Nt'lisi, which would not sound well at all in plain Anglo-Saxon.

A great many of the Navajo are, therefore, not at all anxious to be known under an individual name in their own language, and try in different ways to avoid or to get rid of an undesirable and noisome nominal appendage.

For this reason some have two names, one by which they are known to their fellow tribesmen and one which they use when it becomes necessary or advantageous to tell their name. Having had occasion of employing some Navajo to work, I, of course, took down their names, telling them by way of encouragement that I could pay wages only to such as had names; it was impossible for me to keep track of nameless people. One, who gave his name as Qastqin Naez, the Tall Man, I heard later on called Janaez Lani Biye, the Son of Many Mules, by his co-laborers (Janaez Lani, He Who Has, or Owns Many Mules, was the name of his father). Another, whose name was Qastqin Lizhini, the Black Man, gave his name as Tqachini, which was the name of the clan to which he belonged. Still another who said his name was Qastqin Diloi Biye', the Son of Diloi (or Mr. Diloison), was known as Daghalba'e, Graybeard. Yet another, whom the other Navajo called Qastqin Bizadi, the Stuttering Man, had me put down his name as Harry.

In late years many Navajo have adopted American names, received either at school or otherwise. These are, of course, not at all backward in telling their names. There is therefore no trouble to get Bryan McKinley, Grover Cleveland, Russell Sage, Hoke Smith, Harry Jones, Chester Arthur, Sammie McClure, and so on, to speak when asking for their names. Neither will Smarty, Slinky, Pinky, Shorty, and so on, nor Loco and Tonto (Crazy), refuse to give their names willingly, so long as the English or the Spanish, and not the Navajo name, is wanted. For all these have also a Navajo name, besides their Caucasian name, some even two or three. Thus Harry Jones is called by other Navajo, Mister Mud, or the Little Sorcerer, having been dreaded very much a few years ago on account of his supposed proficiency in witchcraft, or Scar Eye, from a scar below one of his eyes.

Others take the name of a relative, adding to it a word expressing the degree of relationship, as Woda Bizhe'e, Woda's Father; Atsidi Biye', the Smith's Son; Dilaghushin Bitsoi, the Late Howler's Grandchild; Qatqali Naez Binali, the Tall Chanter's Nephew; Atsidi Dloi'n Bida', the Late Smiling Smith's Uncle, and so on.

Many use the name of their clan instead of an individual name, for instance, Tqachini, Tqodichini, Tqabaha, Tsi'najini, Naakai Dine'e, Tli'si Lani, and the like. These neither refuse to tell their names, nor do they object to being called by them. But they, as also those mentioned in the foregoing paragraph, have, as a rule, still another, more or less complimentary name, used by their fellow tribesmen when speaking of them.

As has already been said, they have no family appellatives, excepting such as have assumed American names. The nearest approach to a family name is the clan name, which is often used, accompanied by some distinguishing adjectives, for the members of a whole family. If, for instance, in the family of the Tqodichini (Bitter Water Clan) there are several sons, one may be taller than the others. He will be called Tqodichini Naez. Another may be fleshier than his brothers; his name is Tqodichini Dil. A third may be of a large, massive frame; he is Tqodichini Tso. A fourth is of slender build; he is called Tqodichini Tsosi, and so forth. To the headman of a clan is sometimes given the clan name, with the word Qastqin, that is, Mister, or Senor, added; for instance, Tqotsoni Qastqin, the Senor of the Big Water Clan, something like the Scotch *The* McGregor, *The* McIntosh, and so on.

Some are known by names occasioned by some event or accident which happened to them in bygone times. Thus Dine Yiyisqini, the Man Killer, has his name from the fact that, being one day violently attacked by another Navajo, he fought with him for more than one-half hour, when he got the advantage of him and was obliged in self-defense to kill him.

On the 25th of last September I met an old Navajo at the trading post, who goes under the name of Palm of the Hand. He was an old-timer. He wore a straw hat with a high-peaked Mexican crown, which was kept from flying off by a string tied under his chin. The hat was tilted a little to the southeast, toward the rear of his right ear, which gave the old man quite an air of buoyant chic. Besides the hat, he wore a pair of muslin trousers slashed at the bottom in Mexican style, a shirt of botanical calico, and a silver belt of round disks about two inches in diameter. His face was a collection of wrinkles, which seemed to indicate he had seen many winters, but he was still alive and his muscles full of energy. In his hands he held a blanket of an old pattern, white with blue horizontal stripes. The blanket was filled with wool, and the ends were pinned together with small sticks about three inches long. The wool was full of cockleburs, so the storekeeper told him he did not like to spoil the good wool he had by getting it full of burs, and kindly asked him to pick out the burs, then he would gladly buy his wool. But old Palm of the Hand pinned up his bundle again and the wrinkles of his face moved and twitched like a cinematograph when he said he would take the wool back home and see it rot first rather than pick out the cockleburs.

This man came to his name in the following manner: Back in the times when the Navajo were at war with the Apache he was out one day with a scouting party when they suddenly happened upon a number of the Apache encamped. The Apache, surprised and not prepared for a fight, fled, and the Navajo charged after them in hot pursuit. One of the Apache stumbled and fell, and this Navajo galloped up to him, whipped an arrow out of his quiver, and was about to pierce his fallen enemy to death when the Apache begged for mercy and for his life. "All right," said the Navajo, "I will not kill you, but I must put my mark on you. Hold up your hand and I will shoot you through the palm of your hand." The Apache held up his hand and the Navajo's arrow pierced his palm. From that time on he was known as Palm of the Hand.

It may be remarked here that Navajo names are very incorrectly given, as a rule, when translated into English. For instance, Black Horse is not the translation of the Navajo Bili Lizhini, which literally means: He whose horse is black, or he who has, owns, or rides a black horse. The same may be said of Roan Horse, Sorrel Horse, and other names.

Naming Customs[4]

We find it quite natural that a boy or girl should be named. Equally natural, too, that our parents addressed us John, Joe, Anne, or Kate. It is a custom so old as Adam, who called his sons Cain and Abel and Seth. This custom is not in vogue with the Navajo. He addresses his boys "*siye,*" my son, throughout life, and his daughter "*sitsi,*" my daughter, as long as she lives. The children, too, address their parents "my father," "my mother." Any other address is quite foreign.

Such names as are given them later are of two kinds. Their secret name is some appellation referring to war as tribal custom has it for names of boys and girls. Such names are The running warrior, At war, Warring chief, The speaker, or for girls, She was born when they returned from war, Went to war, or Were preparing for war, and the like, names which are selected by parents in the child's youth and remain theirs for life. Such names are used only in ceremonial address, as at a war dance. At present they are also mentioned in the records of the school. As a public address and one to be a general mode of calling the title holder's attention, such names seem objectionable or at least not quite in harmony with tribal etiquette or tradition.

Some other name is therefore sought and easily acquired, as the Son of so and so. Some peculiarity which the boy or girl may develop with advancing years will suggest a name. Therefore, we find such names as the silversmith, the hunter, the slim, tall, short, chunky, heavyset man or Navajo or clansman, the tall, small, yellow, white, or clanswoman, and so on. Some people are cheerful and laugh, others have a bodily defect by which they are easily recognized and such peculiarities contribute to tribal nomenclature, hence a laughing man or woman, singer or Navajo, or their sons and daughters. In this manner one may possess two, three, and more names. One of my neighbors is a walking list of names and answers the call of The little witch or beanshooter, Mark below his eye, The one who has a brand, Harry McKinley, Mister Dirt, and The crow-eater (because it is claimed he relishes crow meat). Epithets of this caliber are not often applied directly, but with discretion at times. One of my neighbors overheard himself referred to as *aiki naasts'osi*, Mouse boy, and quite angrily repudiated such a label, saying that he was known all over as Todic'ini Bitter water (his clan). Later his friends claimed that his mouth was that of a mouse and it is quite natural for him to steal like a mouse does and to draw his lips with a squealing noise in mouse fashion. "Why," they said, "should he get angry over his own name?"

At that, one's names are frequently not of your own choice, they say! It may explain to some extent that when you inquire for a Navajo's name he will tell you he doesn't know and thus refer you to others for identification. The implication is, of course, that his name is quite an impersonal affair which, although it cannot be shaken off, is not one's own property like your or my name, but is imposed and forced upon by others. "They know, why ask me, they did it, let them tell you." Hence it is customary to ask a man's companion for the name, not the bearer himself, or to get the information in the bearer's absence. It doesn't seem polite to ask a man's name from himself, nor to expect him to speak his own name either privately or in presence of others, especially strangers. It is done, to be sure, if they are pressed, but not without reluctance.

Notes

1. Emanuel Trockur, "Tangled Names," *Indian Sentinel* 24 (February 1944): 25–27.
2. From Anselm Weber, FMN 31 (September 1904): 765–66. Translated by Marie Bradshaw Durrant.
3. From Leopold Ostermann, "Navajo Names," FMSW 6 (1918): 11–15.
4. From Berard Haile, untitled handwritten manuscript beginning "The Navajo is, of course, a heathen tribe," n.d. (circa 1921). FFP Box 5, fd. 1.

36

Family Love and Family Work[1]

Berard Haile, O.F.M.

[The undated, untitled, handwritten manuscript from which this chapter is taken was penned some time around mid- or late 1921, and thus barely qualifies for inclusion in the present volume. There was a typhus outbreak and quarantine on the reservation in spring 1921, to which Father Berard refers in the final pages of the manuscript (not included in the present chapter): "Quite recently we did not hesitate to make our mission police headquarters. That was on the occasion of a quarantine for typhus fever."

In addition to deleting a few paragraphs that are tangential to the manuscript's main theme of family economics, like the reference to the typhus outbreak, I have folded in all but the last few lines of a charming two-paragraph note on "Mother Love of the Navajo" that Father Berard published in the *Indian Sentinel* in 1924. It seems to belong here.]

❖

The Navajo is, of course, a heathen tribe, and while his actions are largely based upon heathen and tribal standards, he possesses many good and enviable traits of character. With all his superstitions, tenacity, and innate stubbornness for tribal customs and traditions, there is much good, natural goodness which makes him attractive and lovable. By comparison with the Asiatic peoples, for instance, much is in favor of the Navajo. Reports tell us that the Chinese expose their own offspring, which are gathered into orphanages and asylums by missionaries to those countries. We find no such custom here.

Love Does the Rest

On the contrary, both parents and relatives are much interested in and attached to their children. A *sitsui*, or grandchild, is coveted by grandparents, and it is general custom to allow them to raise such a child. Nieces and nephews are as brothers and sisters and equal to their own children in the estimate of an uncle or aunt. A widow is not despised, and a widow with children is a desideratum in marriage. Indeed, the child is the center of the family, the father's heart, a mother's "little one." "I am its father, there's its mother, it is our child," describes the genuine unity of this trinity. Affection is equally extended to all. If there are many, who is the proud father? And what greater distinction is there than if the mother can recount on her fingers that, "I gave birth to these, so many sons and so many daughters, albeit some have died!"

What a fortunate tribe where race suicide is unknown, motherhood is appreciated and respected, family life is clean and sound. Felicitations are heaped upon the father and mother of twins, and the event is heralded by neighbors as well as relatives. Every precaution and care is taken and showered upon them and their mother. And if boy twins, they are a special blessing of the Twin Gods, *Haye-uerg'ani* the Enemy Slayer and *Tobajiscini* the Water Child, after whom they are named and spoken of.

Naturally, then, the labors of parturition are not shunned by the Navajo as they are in modern society. Indeed, some lessons might be derived to advantage from this primitive people. Their women are not jacketed in ribbed or unribbed corsets and other tortures of fashion, but dress for convenience and to meet the requirements of propriety. A loose waist or shirt jacket and suitable dress which is girthed about the loins with a soft native belt allow all freedom of action and sufficient fresh air. Natural healthy development therefore is assured, and it is not at all surprising that deaths in childbirth are very rare.

The biblical injunction that "in sorrow shall thou bring forth children" holds true, of course. Yet there are no maternity hospitals; the hogan is quite sufficient. There are no midwives and physicians. Neighbors and experienced women render such support and assistance as the mother requires. There is no special chamber or apartment in the hogan set aside for the event; any suitable spot therein suffices. By means of a constant cord secured to a hogan pole the laboring woman is held in a sitting or slightly upright position, and such assistance as seems required is rendered by attending women. The couch is the ordinary sheep pelt which custom finds quite comfortable.

There are, of course, deaths of mother and child. The percentage, however, is insignificant when we consider the complete absence of modern equipment and conveniences. It is apparent, too, that the expense item is not unduly large; in fact, a few swaddling cloths, as Our Lady had them for the Holy Infant, cover the bill. A mother's love does the rest.

Tender and sweet is the mother love of the Navajo. Poor clothes and soft bark in a native cradle may be the best she has for baby's comfort. When he graduates from the cradle the only clothing she may have for him is a pair of overalls. But she cares for her baby devotedly and as best she knows how. She has no buggy in which to wheel him and no roads or walks on which wheels could go. But nature has given her a strong back to carry him. She wraps a blanket around the child and herself so as to make a safe pack for him and a warm covering for both. In the Navajo country water is scarce, although air is plentiful. Changes of clothes must be few when the infant brave carries his entire wardrobe on his person.

The child is early trained in herding sheep. A blanket is given him for protection against storms that sweep over the open country, but exposure does not always promote hardiness. The Navajo herder travels light. His Sunday clothes are like his smile, the same for every day and all weather. But he does not relish the idea of having his children rough it as he has had to do. The Navajo desires to have his children better cared for, even at the sacrifice of separating from them by sending them to school. He trusts the priests and sisters absolutely. But he sees that for the Navajo children the day school is only a makeshift at best. It cannot attract the children from their scattered and distant camp homes and train them as the Catholic boarding school can.[2] . . .

Bodily defects, too, rather increase the affection and care of the parent for its child. A limping, cross-eyed, stammering, or otherwise deformed child is not at a disadvantage at home. On the contrary, sympathy extends them larger privileges. Modern school life has to an extent changed matters. "When the first schools were opened and the first attempts made to get children for the schools," said an old Navajo the other day, "I remember the old folks used to turn away their heads and refuse. How can we put our hearts, as it were, in those places where you say our children will be? No, we couldn't stand that. It is different now. They know better and understand the schools a little."

"Still," he continued, "when we are sleepless at night, we think of our children."

I, for instance, am getting old, my hairs are quite gray. The 'one that I lived with' (my wife) is buried, a good sensible woman, that talked matters over with me, accompanied me on trips, made suggestions, bought and sold with me, prepared food, and saw to it that the floor was clean and our goods kept in order and clean. Our children grew up with us. Two went to school and it was always as if we were with them all the time.

One died in my arms embracing me. The other two were good but not like him. They too grew larger and were promising lads, both of them, when they died. For a time after they and their mother were laid away it seemed as if I couldn't think of anything else. I used to see them as we were at home. How could I talk for others, do the thinking for others? It's better now as time goes on. But even now, I often lay wide awake and those early days come back to me with visions of what those boys might be now if alive.

Perhaps you don't feel that way because you never had and never will have wife and children. If you had you would know. I didn't get much sleep in those days, shortly after you filled them up [buried them] out there. I don't know what I should have done if I hadn't had tobacco to smoke and water to take an occasional drink. But it's a fact. A cigarette makes you quiet and forgetful. The same with good water! But that shows how we feel for our children!

Family Economics

The Navajo are classed as a tribe that is self-supporting. This term, however, is a fictitious distinction and implies only that as a tribe they are not classified with a number of others, such as the Southern Ute, to whom rations are regularly issued every month. The Navajo do not receive monthly rations which, in government parlance, is the equivalent of self-support. When you come down to brass tacks, as the saw goes, and consider them at close range the situation takes on a different hue and what is called self-support does not imply a regular income, but simply that they eke out a livelihood one way or another.

We speak here particularly of the district within radius of the [St. Isabel] mission, which we believe is fairly representative of the tribe. This radius covers the Lukachukai, the Tsehili, the Wheatfields, Round Rock and Red Round Rock districts, a radius of some 20–30 miles in every direction.

The residents are made up of farmers, not exactly settlers, but families that till a plot of ground in these sections which are therefore known as farming districts. Some of these families own all the way from 400 to 2,000 head of sheep apiece. Others count as few as 30 goats, while still others are imbued with an ambition someday to possess a herd of sheep and goats. These sheep owners also add cattle to their possessions, some having five and some as many as 60 head. Horses, too, are desirable, and at least one or two are found at every home. Burros are negligible but a desirable addition in moving with the herds.

While the aggregate of these various herds is considerable for the area, the distribution favors only a select few who may be said to be in fair circumstances due to their herds and cattle. Even the largest sheep owners, however, do not abandon their farms, so that there is scarcely one family in the entire district that does not possess at least a small farm. While discussing their herds and farms we take it for granted that poverty does not exclude thrift. Indeed, the Navajo are by no means of the lazy kind. Poor as they are, both men and women are industrious.

Sheep and goats are hybridal and unimproved. They are better travelers than feeders. In fact, the sheep must hold their own with the goats of the herd. Goats and sheep are not separated, and both are usually lean and hardy except in the later summer and fall when they are expected to take on enough flesh to carry them over the winter.

The grazing is not the best. In fact, the country offers little grass. Instead, it is covered generously with sagebrush, which with cedar and juniper offers a meager winter forage, while in spring and summer it hides tufts and blades of tender grass. Even the goats and sheep, then, must work hard to make a living, the more as scarcity of water does not allow a wide range and necessitates constant use and overgrazing of a limited range.

Only when the snows are very deep do a few owners give an occasional feed of hay or provide this for lambing ewes and lambs. Otherwise, regular feeding at the troughs is not thought of. Should cattle or sheep starve for want of pasture, that is a misfortune. An effort to save them with hay and grain cannot be thought of, as a rule, because such commodities are expensive and total considerably where the herd is of some proportion. In consequence, the spring of the year finds many so-called stragglers, sheep that are too weak and poor to follow the movements of the herds. Cattle, on the other hand, are so gaunt and stalky that their owners do not judge them fit for slaughter, and horses show such plain signs of starvation that even a saddle is too much of a weight. Travel is therefore made afoot or by very slow stages to allow the horse a breathing spell.

Small boys and girls usually shepherd the herd, and very few of the larger sheep owners can afford the hire of a herder at $15 a month or the equivalent. The usual method is to herd and raise sheep exclusive of every expense, using all profits for the support of the family. The profits accrue this way. The sheep or goat as such is an article of exchange and may be used to barter for articles of the household such as comforters, coffee, sugar, a horse, beads, or even to pay for the services of the singer. The cuisine will require some, because the craving for meat must be satisfied even in the humblest home. On hoof the sheep normally is worth $2 to $3, war prices having trebled these figures. Meat sold to us at six cents per pound in the earlier years soared at 12 cents in wartime. Cost is now reduced to about nine cents. For range stock this is considered fair, and they sell for even less among the natives. There is small satisfaction in being the victim of meats with the flavor of bucks and rams, corrals and sagebrush!

The wool is lowest grade, short and bristly, unclean with cockleburs and sheep refuse. Its price varies from 46 cents wartime to six to eight cents per pound peacetime price. Hides and pelts are graded according to quality and usually yield a small figure. Wool, meat, and pelts are used as revenue to cover household expenses for flour, coffee, and sugar, or to redeem pawns which were placed to obtain the necessities of life. The sheep owner, therefore, cannot expect to go to heavy expenses for the upkeep of the herds. It is useless to speak of wealth where the risk of loss is greater than the value of the possession. In fact, the loss of the herd is considerable owing to poor range in the winter. Only the rainy seasons of summer present anything like range at all, and even then the herds have hard work of it.

The women usually are owners of the sheep, while the men hold title to the cattle and horses. All stock is branded by the owner's brand, and sheep in addition are earmarked, which is to say, that an ear of the sheep is slitted in one way or another that will differentiate it. It is not usual that sheep of one herd will seek association in another herd unless that be done forcibly by thieves.

Working with the Wool

While wool is sold when a fair price prevails and especially when the winter's pawn has been heavy, a very profitable use is made of it otherwise. It is spun and woven into exquisite blankets which then become an added source of revenue. As there is scarcely one family in all of our districts that can thrive without pawning such articles of luxury as silver belts, rings, bracelets, and the like, the general practice is to sell the bulk of both spring and fall clippings. Only a small portion is reserved for weaving purposes. In winter, the weaving season proper, wool is repurchased for weaving purposes, or small dabs are clipped from the hardier sheep before the shearing season proper is on.

This wool is thoroughly scoured to remove dirt and excessive greases, then spread out over brush or pole to dry. Empty coal oil or gasoline cans are much desired for scouring purposes. Card boards with wire bristles are then used freely to straighten out the strands and make them fluffy for the dyes. Some women dye the wool before spinning, which seems to give better satisfaction and uniformity than dyeing spun wool. The native clay pot appeals to them best for boiling and the preparation of dyes, though modern aniline dyes are rapidly dissolved in water and the wool dipped into this solution.

In spinning, the woman squats down conveniently and makes use of a slender long stick provided with a wooden disk. By twirling the wool strands with this contrivance she is able to shape it into a rough yarn which can be retwirled to any desirable consistency and thickness. These yarns are wound into balls of white, black, red, gray, or any color they may desire. When a sufficient supply of these balls of yarn is had, the loom is erected by the husband. You have two uprights planted firmly in the ground anywhere, outside in the shade or sun, or inside in some corner of the hogan. These two uprights support the loom proper, which is strung on two healdsticks. These again are suspended from a crossbeam which is tied to the uprights, the healdsticks being fastened with a cord wound around them and crossbeam. A similar crossbeam is found at the bottom of the frame with healdstick and tie rope. Naturally, these two tie ropes allow the loom to be raised and lowered to a convenient position for operation.

Warp strands of wool yarn in better blankets, and of cotton binding twine in cheaper ones, run up and down and across the healdsticks, which allows an opening between the warp strands. Between these the yarn is passed by means of a wood shuttle, then pressed in place with a batten comb and rammed taut with the batten stick. To obtain the effect of darning in inserting the yarns a provision is made to draw the rear warp strands forward. A stick the width of the loom shows loop strands in which the rear warp strand is caught. By drawing on this, these are drawn forward and cross the front strands as only the alternate strands are looped. This in outline is the usual method of weaving, which shows that, though primitive, it is all well adapted to environment. All tools may be obtained from local hardwoods, while the framework is such as to require little time in dismantling and mounting elsewhere.

The designs, too, are not woven according to pattern but are left to the fancy of the individual weaver. Round and curved and even diagonal sections are not woven into the design, as square corners offer less difficulty in the use of long tools like the batten stick. It is very poetic, or course, to imagine that the weaver always thinks of romance or some religious symbol in selecting a given design. As a matter of fact, neither enters the concept. The design is usually some rude copy of a pattern noticed elsewhere, for example, in prints of calico or the borders of some newspaper advertisement. As a rule, however, colors are well harmonized, although our

American-made dyes are not as fast and brilliant as English and other European fabric. Less skill and time, too, are required nowadays to produce the usual commercial article. So long as these bring the price, little effort is made to produce the really admirable product of the earlier Navajo weavers. However, it will be seen that here, too, the sheep is put to good advantage. The condition of the wool which in an Eastern market would classify it with shoddy articles is here intensely worked to a product that is appealing in strength, texture, and harmonious appearance.

The wool, as well as the time and labor entailed, count as little in the expense side, as the expense item of a blanket is practically covered by the dyes. It is evident, too, that the chief reason for having the herds is the possibility of weaving. There is no woman owner of sheep who is not also a weaver of blankets, no matter how poor the grade of the sheep may be. It is expected of the Navajo woman that she weave, and the woman that does not weave is an encumbrance and a suspect. While one objection to school graduates is their ignorance of sheep culture and weaving (although the latter is now a "branch" in some schools), the camp girl familiar with both requisites of a Navajo wife is still the ideal of the home. "She hath sought wool and flax, and hath wrought by the counsel of her hands" (Prov. 31, 13).

Farming and Other Work

While, therefore, the care and ownership of the herds belong to the mother of the home, the heavier work such as shearing, lambing, dipping of the sheep, and building of corrals is reserved for the men. As a rule this labor does not interfere with the attention the farm may need. Plowing, harrowing, and planting are done after the frosts have disappeared and the indications of approaching spring are good. With that the lands must be irrigated, as rainfall cannot be expected until the early summer months, say in July. Where alfalfa is grown, as in our district, the hay cutting and harvesting require attention. The fields are usually pastured in the early spring to get the horses in shape for other farmwork. The crop is usually sold at the stores and only a very small supply of the last cutting, say enough to carry the best horses through the winter, is preserved and housed. When the winter is open and mild no thought is given to regular feed, as the horses are turned loose to range on the open country.

Corn, beans, and squashes, with tracts of spring wheat, are also raised. Wheat and corn are sold in part as are beans, while squashes and melons, if there are any, are kept for the household. Wheat and corn, however, go far toward furnishing a winter supply of breadstuffs and are therefore cultivated wherever moisture will warrant a crop. Wheat is not cut by machine like hay, but is harvested by reapers who use a hand sickle. Like the fields of the Gospel which showed cocklebur among the wheat, Navajo wheatfields, too, show an abundance of weeds among the wheat, which, to retain moisture better, is planted in bunches.

No attempt is made to clean the wheat lest they eradicate the wheat with the weeds. The reapers simply ignore the weeds, but cut the wheat stalks and gather them in bundles. These bundles are brought into the threshing floor which is a small corral. Here five or six horses are driven and enclosed, while drivers outside the corral force them to tramp out the wheat by racing them in the corral. After that the corral is dismantled, the chaff is removed, and both men and women winnow the wheat. Some construct a sieve with screen wire bottom and work the wheat through the meshes of sandscreen. The more common way is to fill their native baskets and toss the wheat in the air so that the wind will carry the chaff but allow the kernels to land in the basket again. Threshing machines, binders, and reapers, no, we have not progressed so rapidly.

Corn shellers, too, are exceptions. A good method is to fill your blanket, tie the ends, and let two men club this sack. Even corn cannot resist this beating. This is called clubbing the corn, because it is clubbed to separate the kernels from the ears. It ought to be good and ripe and hard to ensure quick results. As the corn cannot always fully mature in the available short season, it is customary to spread out the ears in the sun and air, say on the roof of the house or the floor of a corral. In due time the air absorbs the moisture and the corn can get its beating. One understands, then, the occupation of men when they say that they are picking, husking, clubbing corn or laying and drying it in the sun.

Naturally, too, there are no flour mills. To obviate the difficulty in grinding corn and wheat for flour or grinding coffee, these are rubbed between two millstones. The lower one is a flat-surfaced stone of convenient shape, placed at a slight angle, the other an oblong round-edged stone much smaller in size. Between these the kernels are crushed and powdered for home use. Though a bit gritty, new wheat bread is very substantial and handy to take along in travel, as it is usually shaped after the upper millstone. Grinding flour is the work of the womenfolk.

With the close of the harvest all profitable labor ceases for the men excepting occasional freighting with teams for the various stores. When piñon nuts are plentiful the family will move to these woods and gather nuts which are sold at the stores. Piñon nuts do not appear annually but intermittently or in certain districts only.[3] . . .

Freighting lasts until the winter snows obstruct the roads. The farms, too, are then abandoned and the herds moved to the valleys or wooded countries for the winter. Small sheep owners and such as have no sheep frequently travel to American settlements in search of work, although many are not so fortunate as to find work for the winter. The number of willing workers that would gladly face the inclemencies of a hard winter for a remunerative occupation is by no means small, and it is regrettable indeed that arrangements seem impossible in this regard. Neither their sheep nor the products of their farms are sufficient for the winter.

The men are, therefore, practically forced to indolence over a period of three to four months because of unemployment in the winter. The women come to the rescue of the family by weaving. Yet that requires much time. It is general custom, therefore, to store supplies of corn and wheat in their farmhouses or, too, in underground dugouts or pits made near the farms. In this manner starvation at least can be prevented.

Loans and Pawn

Not many of our neighbors are adept at the silversmith's craft. Some are quite proficient basket weavers. Where these arts are known they are pursued in winter. Otherwise, it is common usage to resort to another means of a livelihood, that of pawning. Such valuables as a saddle, moccasins, a silver bridle, ring, or belt are easily dispensed with, as they are more or less articles of luxury. Of course, there is the desire of retaining their ownership. But when necessity compels to obtain the necessities of life which may be had at a trading store, common usage suggests such valuables as pawn. The pawn is then simply a security to the trader on credits advanced.

The practice, too, is much in vogue among themselves, and their vocabulary is quite rich in reference to pawn transactions, such as placing or redeeming pawn, or maturity and extensions. If a friend of yours has some money or an article you need, you will give him a horse or saddle and agree upon a certain day to redeem it, or you will ask, say, $6 for a month and promise $1 extra at the end of that month as a token of good faith.

For inducement or security you leave a necklace that is worth twice that amount among the natives. However, among themselves there is no appeal from maturity. Neither can you offer a plausible excuse unless you have agreed again with your creditor on an extension. Otherwise, failure to meet a debt automatically spells forfeit of the security, no matter how much in excess the value of the latter may be. Such a security can then be sold immediately.

While this is tribal practice, the American traders are not so fortunate, but are governed by a regulation which prohibits the sale of pawn before 12 months of tenure. It makes little difference if an agreement for a lesser period has been entered with the Indian. As the 12 months elapse, however, the trader is at liberty to sell pawns.

There are times, of course, when it becomes impossible to redeem a pawn, such as in recent years when the price of wool and sheep were low, and no sheep and cattle could be sold. The usual practice, however, is to redeem pawns with wool and sheep money, as such a method presents better chances for the coming winter. Silverware and beads and similar luxuries like buckskins are really letters of credit, which in turn is extended in view of the value of the article itself as well as the ability of the lessee to redeem that article. Those in possession of sheep or a hay field and cattle or a wagon are considered good security which can cover the pawn.

If, then, pawning must be resorted to by weavers and sheep owners, farmers and teamsters, to meet the expenses of the household, little can be said of the wealth of the tribe. Most of this wealth finds its way over the counters of the merchants. In turn, these merchants secure the markets for Navajo rugs, sheep, wool, pelts, and hay and are entitled, therefore, to reasonable returns. Some succeed; others go bankrupt through excessive crediting.

Our Catholic parishioners cannot fare better in this regard than their heathen neighbors. Excepting for usurious interests and securities which are regularly charged for loans by native lenders, there is little that is objectionable in the practice of pawning. It amounts to about the same as a mortgage or loan at a pawnbroker's. The difference is that nobody here will think of mortgaging his lands or house. These have no value, as they are not held by patent or title, while it is not generally possible to secure loans on sheep and cattle at a bank, as reservation property is protected by government dominion and writs of court do not apply there. Usually, then, the natives make such loans for small sums, albeit the security and interest are out of all proportion.

During the building of our residence, for instance, one of the laborers was approached one day by a rider who evidently was hard up for cash. He needed $12 and figured that the hire most certainly yielded some money to the laborer. There was some objection and parley, as is usual, until an agreement was reached which landed the $12. The conditions, however, were an interest of $1 after 10 days and the horse as security. When the 10 days had elapsed the capital and interest had not been paid. Consequently, the security was forfeited, and the horse exchanged owners. Such transactions are considered fair to both parties, as more leniency would inevitably spell a loss to the lender. Moreover, a legal rate of interest is not in vogue and any interest is binding that has been agreed upon.

It will be seen, then, that our parishioners have about enough to vegetate and live. Sheep, farm products, blankets, and such luxuries as silverware all go toward obtaining a livelihood. Such a thing as the support of a pastor or a school and teachers is out of all question. Misled by eastern notions of a parish, some friends have suggested a fair or party to which an entrance fee might be charged. A grab bag, fishing pool, and the usual features of a church fair were suggested with a view to kindly furnish small gifts for these departments. That cannot be thought of.

My parishioners haven't even a change of Sunday clothes or an extra pair of newer shoes, and are usually indebted heavily at the stores for their pawns which, as said, go toward maintaining them in the hard season of winter. The bulk, however, that live within the parish are not affiliated as church members and are heathens. A fair or barbecue, like any gathering, invariably implies that gifts of food, hay, and eatables generally are distributed free of charge. These are always an expense item.

Notes

1. From Berard Haile, untitled handwritten manuscript beginning, "The Navajo is, of course, a heathen tribe," n.d. (circa 1921). BHP Box 5, fd. 1.

2. The above two paragraphs are from Berard Haile, "Mother Love of the Navajo," *Indian Sentinel* 4 (July 1924): 117.

3. Text from several following pages of Father Berard's manuscript, not included here, was published as part of his "The Navajo Country," FMSW 10 (1922): 28–37, and recently reprinted in Murray Bodo, ed., *Tales of an Endishodi: Father Berard Haile and the Navajo, 1900–1961* (Albuquerque: University of New Mexico Press, 1998), 162–71.

37

The Navajo Woman and Her Home

Gertrude Honaghani

[The author was a pupil at St. Michael's Indian School, St. Michaels, Arizona.]

The Navajo woman takes good care of her home and her children, and all her other property, such as sheep, horses, and cows.

She helps the men to plant seed in spring and also works on the farm all summer. During the harvest they are all very busy with the crops. They get them ready to store away for winter supplies.

We raise corn, potatoes, beans, melons, and pumpkins. Our most important foods are coffee, mutton, cornbread, cornmeal, boiled pumpkins, and corn.

They are especially busy in spring between planting corn and tending to the sheep and little lambs. The goats and kids are very troublesome, but the goats are kept to feed the young lambs who have no mother. Sometimes one goat has to feed two lambs.

They tend to the sheep and goats first and leave the farmwork until some time late in May. On real cold days in spring, some lambs just freeze to death if they are left outside.

Even children three or four years of age are kept busy looking after the lambs and feeding them with hot milk and carrying them into warm places. They have to know the lambs that belong to each sheep, and when there are about 40 or 50 lambs, spotless white, you can hardly tell which two go with each other, and besides, the sheep don't know their own.

Sometimes the sheep try to get out of it, but they cannot because they are tied together with the lambs as soon as possible and remain tied for three or four days, when the lamb is able to run about.

A small boy is appointed to take these sheep and small lambs out a half mile away and let them feed there until they get enough, and then bring them home again, and this child is to see that not one is lost.

When the lamb gets tired following its mother around it will lie down someplace under a bush and go to sleep and cannot find its way home.

Sometimes the coyote will eat them up. So when the sheep are home they are inspected to see if all are there. If any are missing they go out looking for them right away.

Sometimes lambing season lasts six weeks, and the lambs have to be cared for until they are three months old. Then it is shearing time, and they all must be sheared, and the wool is sold, but not all of it. Some of the wool is saved for weaving blankets. There are many designs in weaving, and they all have names.

The men and boys mind the horses and the cows. They see that every horse and cow is branded. They break in the horses and make them work. Some horses are trained to be race horses.

In harvest time everybody is busy on the farm. They dig up the potatoes and put them into sacks, and also the beans are put into sacks and are stored away in an empty house. The pumpkins are buried in the ground and covered over until needed. The corn is husked and dried in the sun and then taken off the cob and sewed up in bags. All winter they eat this corn done up any way they want it. It is hard work to grind a bushel of corn between two stones, and kneeling there all the time. You grind it four or five times; then it is mixed with milk and made into small cakes and baked.

When many men and boys get together, they try their horses at a space of three miles to see which one is the best runner. They bet against each other. It is good to watch them on horseback.

The Indians get up very early, before sunrise, and the children are obliged to run a race as soon as they are awake. They are good runners. They are not forced to obey. They mind sheep when they feel like it or stay at home. But they don't allow their children to get too lazy. They are permitted to do any kind of work they want to. The wood is brought in once a week by the boys, and the water is hauled in twice a week in barrels on the wagon.

When a girl is six years old she learns to cook and keep house and mind the baby for her mother. Before a girl is ten years old she learns to comb and spin wool and weave blankets.

Note

1. From Gertrude Honaghani, "The Navajo Woman and Her Home," FMSW 9 (1921): 35–36.

38

Mealtimes with the Navajo[1]

Leopold Ostermann, O.F.M.

[This early essay is one of Father Leopold's finest. Other friars would later, necessarily, treat the same topic, often as part of instructing new missionaries, but I do not believe anyone ever surpassed Father Leopold's humorous, yet sympathetic and respectful, approach. For comparison, here is a brief statement by Father Berard on Navajo "cooking."

> Cards need not be printed for this menu, as the Navajo's fare is simple and not much varied. Canned goods, if they can be afforded, meat, coffee or tea, and native breads baked in a Dutch oven, or on a hot stone or iron griddle, are the usual meagre fare. Even dishes, such as plates, saucers, knives, and forks are dispensed with. You might use your pocketknife, or the usual Arbuckle meat knife for carving and, if that is inconvenient, your fingers will do to pick up or break off morsels of meat and bread. When cups cannot go the rounds, do not hesitate to share your cup with another, because you can replenish your supply from the common pot! So, too, if you desire your bread in the skillet with broth or gravy, like the rest. The camp knows little of table etiquette. Do not expect a napkin and finger bowl after your meal, but use, well, the back of your hand will do, and rubbing your hands after the meal has about the same purpose as using glycerine in winter for chapped hands! Toothbrushes are not in demand, their teeth being close and excellent. Smacking and drawing the teeth is general custom and is not considered indecorous.
>
> The point of emphasis here, however, is that, if physical ills have their origin in the displeasure of the deities, this indifference to everything that is conducive to health and preventive of sickness is not at all out of order in their system.[2]]

The Navajo, being of a rather lighthearted and social disposition, are always glad and pleased to have the *a'neishodi* to come and visit them in their homes. They deem such a visit an honor for which they show their appreciation by extending to the priest the broadest hospitality. Although it frequently is not much which they can offer, yet it is the best they have, and the longgown is welcome to it, even if the host must go hungry. It affords them special pleasure and enjoyment if the priest has the knack of accommodating himself in some degree to their ways and customs, for example, if he, at mealtimes, takes his place in the circle, squats down with the rest around the fire, and eats heartily of the viands, prepared à la Navajo, helping himself with his fingers, as they do, and with his pocketknife, if he has one.

This is not always an easy thing to do and like every other art requires predisposition and practice, and in some cases a fast-anchored stomach which is proof against sea sickness, all inordinate desires after New York, and against other similar high-strung or unstrung sentimentalities.

By the way, it is an indisputable fact that these same occasions of practicing mortification and self-denial are met with not only among the Navajo and other barbarians of color, but even among civilized folks who have a real white skin. And this, too, not only among what are generally called the lower classes, but even among the upper tens and elevens, who find a delicious flavor in moldy cheese, certain kinds of which are most palatable when in a condition to walk away; and do they not eat birds' nests, the digestions of snipe, pickled and jellied rain worms, and oysters with exteriors and interiors, in all styles? Do they not let meat get just to the turning point to give it the real *haut gout*?

To eat heartily with Navajo the two following rules ought to be observed: first, don't be too dainty or particular. When dinner or any other meal is called, and the viands have been set out in the middle of the floor, on the ground, pull your blanket or sheepskin nearer, same as the rest do, and form with them a circle around the sooty, but steaming pots and pans. The best position is to sit Turk fashion. You need not bother your imagination with pictures of the men lying on their blankets or sheep pelts, smoking while they are waiting for the meal, and spitting about on the floor in their efforts of trying to hit the fire, but when your neighbor reaches into a pan or pot, fishes out a piece of mutton or goat, and hands it to you with a kind and friendly smile, take it and eat it. Do not investigate his hands, with which he may have been cleaning his moccasins, or rubbing down his pony, just before dinner, and remember that water is a very precious thing in this country, and must not be wasted without a sufficient reason. Do not be so impolite as to look into the kettle, nor be suspicious of the meat. It is fresh, perhaps the blood was warm in it yet when it was brought in to be cooked. The Navajo are no Huns or Kirghis, who used to put their meat under their saddles and ride around on it a few days to make it tender. They have either very fresh meat or jerked meat, that is, meat cut into thin strips, then dried in the sun, and finally hung up in the hogan where it takes the place of our old-fashioned flypaper until it is used.

Do not let the newfangled theories about germs, miasmas, and microbes bother you. Mathusalem did not know a thing about these modern medical theories, which would have a man live under a glass globe, and notwithstanding this to the contrary, he lived to see his 969th year. Besides, if any germs have been on the jerked meat, they have all found a sizzling death in the frying pan, are just as dead as that muttonized emblem of patience and meekness of which you are holding a piece in your hand. So do not be too particular. Take it and eat, and if you are hungry tell them it is *d'aiyisi lakan*, very sweet, and they may help you to some more, for the Navajo is not stingy, whatever else he may be.

If they hand you something in a plate or skillet that looks dark and dubious enough to be Spartan broth, don't you believe it. Appearances are deceptive; it is gravy; a hotel menu would call it bouillon. Dip your bread or meat into it, same as the rest. The little round white disks that gather around the rim as it cools off are mutton tallow, which will greatly aid the other more substantial victuals on their southward journey. You may tell them it is *d'aiyisi yaat'ä*, very good; they will give you some more, and you will find the second dip like the second oyster, the first one generally being taken with eyes closed.

As an especially choice tidbit they may perchance have roasted prairie dog for dinner. This roast is prepared in the following manner: The prairie dog having been shot and brought in, the cook rips it open with a knife, takes out the intestines, relieves them of their contents by stripping them through the fingers, replaces them with some salt, scrapes together a pile of hot ashes and live coals, buries the prairie dog therein and leaves him to roast in his own hide. The taste and flavor are excellent. Civilized persons whose stomachs would rebel against this should remember three things: 1) the Navajo way of preparing prairie dog—which by the way is as clean in its habits and as particular in its food as a squirrel, and about which there is nothing doglike except in its name—stands no chance when compared to the manner in which many a civilized dish is prepared, for example, snipe; 2) they know just exactly what they are eating, which is very frequently not the case with civilized food; the Navajo practice no adulteration of food; 3) whites who have eaten prairie dog prepared by the Navajo, and the same dish prepared by whites, invariably give the Navajo way the preference.

Therefore, the second rule is: do not be too inquisitive as to their way, mode, and manner of preparing meals. Remember that the Navajo squaw has never had the opportunity of taking a course in cooking or housekeeping, as taught in some of our eastern schools and institutes, founded for that especial purpose. Her cooking would by no means bring about the gout, but I am not so sure that it would not sometimes cause dyspepsia. Therefore, do not make it your business to see whether or not the squaw sets a high value on the scarcity of water. If she has been on the hunt after overzealous pedicular natives on her own or on her daughter's head; if she has been busy with her baby, attending to some natural events to which our mortal coil is heir by reason of its gear and construction; or if she has handled some other similar *et cetera,* and then has gone to cooking without washing her hands with soft water and perfumed toilet soap, it is none of your business, or ought not to be.

The manner and mode of eating with the Navajo do not apply to every Navajo home. Many of them, especially such as have Americanized stone or log houses, have besides other pieces of American furniture, stoves, tables, chairs, knives, forks, and spoons, even tablecloths and china dishes. While they themselves prefer to take their meals in Navajo style as did their fathers and grandfathers before them, they insist that the priest, or the American visitors, take theirs in the style of their own people, using table, chairs, and so on.

By the way, I may here remark that every white man not a Mexican or a Spaniard is an American, a *Belagána*,[3] with the Navajo, come he from Westphalia, Shropshire, Tipperary, or Missouri, just as everything beyond Albuquerque is Washingdón. The president is called: *Naat'ani Washingdón di setqini*, the Chief who resides at Washington. In fact, Washingdón means either the whole government of the United States or any branch of it or anything pertaining to it. Very distant places, such as Chicago or New York, are said to be places beyond Washingdón (while Europe is the land on the other side of the Broad Water).

The Mexicans are called *Naakai*, White Enemies or Strangers, and the Spaniards, especially with reference to the first Spanish explorers, *Naakai Diyini*, the Holy (or Supernatural) White Strangers. *Ana'e* is a Navajo term used very much like the Greek *hoi babaroi*, to designate strangers, foreigners, enemies, or persons not Navajo. The initial *a* in this word, as also in other Navajo words, is frequently dropped, thus *Na Lani*, Many Enemies, the Navajo name for the Comanche Indians; *Naakai*, Mexican, and so forth. *Aná* means war, and *nashba,* I go on the war path.

But to return to the Navajo eating question, which, as we have seen, ceases to be a question if one is not too particular or too inquisitive. This reminds me that all, or at least the greater part of the sensitiveness of the digestive organs with regard to certain foods, or with regard to their preparation and their preparers, is the work of a quick, vivid imagination.

I remember that, about three years ago, while traveling on the railroad, and having become hungry, I went to the "dining car in the rear" and ordered beefsteak with bread and coffee. The beefsteak had a peculiar, pleasant, appetizing flavor, which made me think it was the best beefsteak I had ever eaten. After dinner, wishing to return to my car, and no waiter being in sight, I went back to the kitchen to pay my bill. Here the stove or range was boxed up in a small tin-lined apartment, about four feet square. In that apartment was a colored cook bending over the hot stove, frying beefsteak for some other customers. He was perspiring like a fishnet: large, round, heavy drops stood on his shining forehead, and in two seconds my imagination had the mystery of the peculiar, pleasant, appetizing flavor of the beefsteak solved. It was caused by the sweat from the brow of the African cook rolling into the frying pan.

I could see the steaming drops of toil coursing down the sable incline, then halt a few moments when they reached the tip of his nose, just as one halts who is about to take a desperate leap and looks for the best place on which to land. I fancied how the rays of the sun, coming in through a small bull's-eye window, struck the crystal pearls of labor and were reflected by them in a twinkling glitter on the tin lining of the apartment, and how they then made their final leap, landing in the hot frying pan with a mirthful sizzle and splurt. From that very instant the steak, then in process of digestion, seemed to turn into lead. I paid my bill in a hurry, and when I got back to my seat, my forehead was covered by a cold dampness which was accompanied by a sensation that would have been a nightmare had it come on during sleep.

All this was, of course, only imagination. However, there are things which one sees in Navajo camps, or hogans, that are not always imagination, but real things. About two years ago, while on a visiting tour northward on the reservation, I stopped for a few days with a prominent Navajo friend. Knowing that I would get mutton for breakfast, dinner, and supper, I took a few pounds of bacon with me to bring some variation into the muttonous monotony. Arriving at the house, I turned over the bacon to the *qastqin,* who took it into the kitchen.

By the way, the house was a fairly good log house of three rooms. The center room, which had the entrance, was what might be called a combination room: at meal hours it was the dining room. Outside of meal hours it was a lounging room, that is, the family spent their leisure hours there when it was too fresh or cold to be outdoors. Among civilized people it would be a drawing room; at night it was a dormitory. To the right was a spare room which was turned over to me during my stay. In it there was an old-fashioned wooden bedstead, which took up about one-fourth of the room; besides there was a small table (on which I said Mass), several trunks, and the walls were decorated with baskets, belts, beads, guns, revolvers, clothes, and the like. To the left of the drawing room was the kitchen. What was in there I do not know. However, through the partly open door I could get occasional glimpses of a few squaws, and from a hissing and sizzling sound I could infer the presence of a stove.

One of these peeps into the atelier of the culinary artists showed me the chief cook sitting on the floor preparing something (perhaps a conundrum), and just behind her was my nice piece of bacon lying on the ground; in fact, she was almost sitting on it. A coyote-like cur was quietly and cautiously sneaking up toward the bacon and smelling and nosing about at it.

I felt my stomach begin to sink at the prospects of having some of the bacon for dinner. I said to myself, "If the old coyote would only snatch up the whole piece, and hike off with it, I would think him a pretty decent kind of a dog." The wish was followed by the act; he presently took the bacon between his teeth and carefully made his way for the door. My best wishes and compliments were with him: "Nice doggy," I said inaudibly, "make yourself superlatively scarce now, and remember the 11th commandment; finish up the piece of pork bosom before anyone detects its absence and starts out to trail it up." It seems this wish, too, was fulfilled, for there was no bacon served up during the whole stay of four days.

If you, dear reader, find yourself at any time among Navajo at mealtime, and see the *qastqin* wash a table knife by spitting on it, and then wiping it on the seat of his trousers, remember that your hide-clad forefathers did not do any better; or if you see an old squaw take the washbasin, in which she and perhaps others too have washed themselves, throw out the water, and then use the basin for serving up the mutton, remember that she could have done worse; or if you see another throw a stick at a dog who was licking out a bowl, then take the bowl and arrange it with the other dishes for coffee, remember that the dog may have done you a favor by emptying the bowl; or if the squaw who does the cooking has taken a heavy cold the night before, and must, in consequence, blow and clean her nose about twice every minute, and you see that she does this with her fingers, which she occasionally wipes on her skirt with the same motion with which a bird wipes his bill on a stick, and continues to knead the dough, cut the meat, and so on, remember some of the incidents with which Napoleon's troops met on the snow-covered steppes of Russia on their retreat from burning Moscow, such as eating the intestines of sheep without going to the trouble of relieving them of their contents; or if you see another dive with her arm into an Arbuckle coffee box, in which old clothes, tools, and the like, are kept, and fish up from the bottom several strips of jerked mutton, which she without any further washing cuts up into small bits and puts into the frying pan for your supper; be glad that you are not obliged to go to bed hungry; or if you see another using a table knife to scrape off his moccasins, then wipe it with his handkerchief, which he had shortly before put to its proper use, take it; he is robbing himself of the use of the knife and showing deference to you.

If you see such and similar things, remember four little points: 1) remember the story of the creation of man, that is, of what the first man was made; 2) remember that you neither know the ingredients of those French soups, English sauces, and the like, which you relish so much, nor do you know the condition of the eggs used in that light, fluffy omelette, which seems to you a perfect poem; if you did, it might perhaps be an awfully prosy thing; 3) remember that you are not running so great a risk as did our soldiers in the Philippines with their highly civilized canned beef; 4) remember that you will not see these things in all Navajo houses; many squaws are as neat and as clean in their work as their Caucasian sisters.

Notes

1. From Leopold Ostermann, FWW 12 (December 1904, January 1905): 225–27, 258–61.

2. From Berard Haile, "Cleanliness, Hygiene?" typescript, 1922. BHP Box 9, fd. 10, pp. 4–5.

3. A corruption of the Spanish word *Americano*. The initial *a* is easily and frequently dropped by the Navajo, even in words of their own language. *M* and *b*, *c* and *g* are closely related, consequently easily convertible. The Navajo language having no *r*, that letter is generally rendered by *l* in foreign words. Finally *a* is far more frequently used as a terminal vowel than *o*. Hence, Americano becomes *Belagána*.

39

Pawn, Games, Gambling[1]

Berard Haile, O.F.M.

[Long before he wrote the present chapter, Father Berard published an authoritative, though fragmented, statement on Navajo games (excerpts from his correspondence were scattered throughout a 1907 Bureau of American Ethnology report).[2] His treatment of games in the present manuscript seemed to duplicate some of that earlier material, and therefore I have deleted the description of games covered in more detail in that report.

Although pawn and loans were already treated briefly in the "family economics" section of chapter 36, Father Berard's more exhaustive discussion here adds enough additional information that the separate chapter seemed warranted. It is one of the earlier essays on the topic and so has some historical interest. Besides, pawn and gambling are the topical connections by which Father Berard leads the reader to the fascinating Navajo family anecdote that concludes the chapter.

More extensive and recent descriptions of the pawn system on the Navajo reservation and how it has changed over the years are available in the now sizable literature on Navajo trading. See, for example, Frank McNitt's *The Indian Traders* and the recent work of Willow Roberts Powers.[3]]

[Among the Navajo] every loan is made with a full knowledge of the hard conditions imposed. Where a time limit has not been set, as when the lessee gives security for a certain loan to be repaid at some time or other, the interest accruing is not increased or compounded, as the creditor is supposed to take only the interest agreed upon and wait until the lessee redeems the security. This practice is not agreeable among members of the tribe, possibly because it is too well known that such securities will be allowed to age and it is felt that the creditor is bound not to dispose of such security for the simple reason that, as no time has been agreed upon, it is property of the borrower in custody of the creditor.

A Navajo does not like the idea of holding such trusts; hence their preference for short-term loans with quick returns either in big-interest money or valuable securities like cattle, horses, beads, or silverware which become property, as said, of the creditor on default. Americans who are not quite familiar with Navajo banking methods or who lend a merciful ear to pleadings of men and women in feigned or real distress are preyed upon for large or small loans according to their disposition, which a Navajo is quick to divine.

Pawns are taken extensively at the trading posts especially in the winter and spring seasons. Almost anything is pawned so that the trader is easily a pawnbroker who lends money on a coat, a pair of moccasins, a saddle, silver headstall, coral and silver beads, belts, baskets, and rings. It is redeemable at shearing or cattle-buying season, but may be redeemed before such maturity, though short terms of 30 and 60 days, too, are stated. Within this period the article must not be sold, lost, or stolen, lest the trader be held responsible for its full value. It is generally understood that these articles have not been disposed of as secondhand goods, but merely placed as security for a given period after which the owner will redeem them, or relinquish them by default. Once, however, this time is expired the trader may consider the pawn his own and exhibit it for sale to anyone paying the debt thereon or extend the time upon payment of a small interest or advance money.

Much pawn is valueless to an American, excepting for the few that collect curios. For we cannot imagine the freak that would bedeck himself with Navajo silver trinkets or should wear moccasins, women's sashes, or belts for the satisfaction of having advanced a given amount of money thereon and lost it. As a security much of the pawn is valuable locally only as it may be disposed of to patrons whenever they have money.

It appears, then, that pawns of this kind are much in favor. The Navajo certainly prefers this method to making loans from tribesmen who will pocket the security as sure as the sun goes down. The trader may be pleaded with and few there are who are as inexorable as the sun. As compared to loans from tribesmen the Navajo is quick to see the advantages of the pawn system. The American, as a rule, is open to argument and has no such conception of the iron sunset rule as his tribesmen. Extensions are readily granted to such as show some willingness by paying part of the pawn debt.

It will be seen that such transactions represent no mean investment when it is remembered that some stores capture between 15,000 and 100,000 pounds of wool in one season, much of which represents redemption of the winter's pawn. Wool averaged between 35 and 45 cents per pound, so that even small owners reaped a nice sum of money. This will ordinarily redeem their pawns and last them through the summer. If not, the same article will return to the pawn section for another credit.

In the fall when the herds are culled for withers, lambs, steers, and calves, another source of revenue is at hand to redeem a pawn, for sheep realized as high as $5.50 and $8 in the last two seasons, while cattle sold at $30 and up or not at all. Add to these such extraordinary resources as piñons, which yield 6 and 8 cents a pound, and hay at $30 per ton, with blankets and silverware as reserves, and you have approximately the sources of Navajo revenue. At that the Navajo is a good spender and disposes of currency often as quickly as he can count it. Thus his pawn is a credit reserve and as a rule will be redeemed or is at best salable.

In addition, much of pawn trinkets are valued as heirlooms. The family will therefore as a rule ask credit on them with the expressed purpose of redeeming them at first opportunity. In the dull seasons of winter, spring, and midsummer the pawn system represents an easy and satisfactory method of extending credits, though as a matter of course good pawn is such as is redeemable for reasons mentioned or will have an easy sale if not redeemed.

True, there are traders who are adamantine and charge as much as 50 cents on the dollar for short-term pawn loans, possibly because of past sad experiences where clemency was abused. Moreover, there are laws protecting the Indian but which apparently consider the trader a natural shark bent on the exploitation of the government wards. Thus the government insists that it will not collect in court the Indian's debts, that they cannot be forced to pay them, which leaves the expressed alternative of having the trader see as best he can how debts may be collected. The trader is thus at the mercy of the Indian.

Should it happen that an Indian has delivered a beef and the agency is forced to await the appropriation therefor in the regular routine of office work, the Indian will frequently present his credit memorandum at the store. This voucher is good, no doubt. Yet if presented by the trader on payday he cannot claim the check of the Indian in payment for any advances made in merchandise. The Indian must receive the check personally. This is done for better identification, as undoubtedly in the pioneer days many frauds were committed through false signatures and thumb marks.

There should be no objection to this system excepting that no effort is made to have the Indian meet his honest debts. It is customary in an instance like that just mentioned that the Indian will accept the check, cash it elsewhere than at the post which aided him when in need, and allow the trader to look for reimbursement elsewhere or forget it entirely. Indeed, it has been observed that the store which allows credits is not patronized during the period in which a debt or pawn is held. Many traders, therefore, refuse credits and limit their pawns to short terms and valuable articles. The advantage of a government protection, then, is evidently too one-sided to be practical and acts in disparagement of those more deserving and honest.

It is evident, too, that the missionaries are frequently singled out as easy marks by a people who seek credits on the lightest pretext. They are more or less of a charity institution and frequently make small loans to gain the popular goodwill. These loans are not always necessarily advances in money, but frequently take the shape of orders for goods from catalog houses with the promise of reimbursement at some more opportune season. Unfortunately for the missionaries it is found that the phrases "later, at some opportune time, or when I have money" are easily vague enough to be forgotten. Since, too, the missionaries do not press their claims and are easily satisfied by promises of paying in life, or, as one put it, when he dies of old age, it would appear that such practices are not lucrative, charitable though they be. The principle that business is business, and that, therefore, no other consideration should enter such transactions has little if any attraction for the missionaries who usually prefer to share and even lose what little they can command.

Instinct or human nature, I do not know, but the fact is that gambling debts must be paid and credits are never allowed. Whatever is staked goes, and frequently the only regrets are that nothing more is available for stakes. Gambling is inseparable from games of chance. Such are card games like Coon Can and Monte, which are probably of Spanish introduction. The old Navajo knew no cards (dáka) but had a so-called seven-card game at which small wooden disks, seven in number, were used which would approach our dice more than cards. These disks were painted dark on one side, leaving the other the natural color of cottonwood. The seventh was painted black on one side like the rest but red on the other, which accounted for the name, the red one. It scored points with either black or white in falling. The method was to toss the disks up and catch them in a basket. In falling the color must show all black or white (with one red) to score. The number of points was arbitrary and agreed upon beforehand, for the game as well as the scores. The stakes or wagers might consist in a dime to a dollar, or in an excitement one might wager the last stitch of clothes on his body.

In the fall and snowless winters much time was spent in the hoop and pole game, which was a game for the day. . . . Another popular game which . . . is still in vogue is the moccasin game. . . . It is a pastime of the night and for results and passion is equal to cards. Indeed, where cards are wanting the moccasin game is a fitting substitute. When speaking of gambling, therefore, both cards and the moccasin game are implied. . . . The laughing or, better, the no-laugh game (dojodloi), is a wager between two parties on which of the two will not laugh at the sight of a grimace, distorted features, ridiculous gait or dress, a joke, action, or anything which may excite laughter. While humorous, the aim of the game is the winning of a wager. . . .

There are, of course, other games such as horse racing, foot racing, shinney, bouncing stick, and others. Yet all these represent one or better means of gambling, and it may be said that none are played for the mere sport of the thing, but for the stake that is wagered. Games are played with a vengeance, that is to say, time is no limit or barrier. If one day is not sufficient another day is at your command, and you do not allow the night or sleep to interrupt your sport so long as there is an acceptable stake. Whoever has best control of sleepiness wins out in the end with keener wits. You cheat if you can without being detected; you may bribe a jockey, edge in on a racing horse, anything is fair in a horse race, but if you lose you must pay the bet or stake. That's just as fair as a race.

It would appear that the rules of life and games are few and very simple: eat when you have something to eat; eat little when there is little, much and your heart's fill when there is plenty, especially at another's expense. If you have food for your horse give it to him, it will make him fat and strong; if there is none let him go without food because you have none. Work when there is work to be done; in winter there is no work; therefore, we do none. If you are sick, invite the singer; if you are not sick, what reason is there for religion? If you have something to stake, gamble; if all is lost, what use is there for games, gambling, or sports? Simplicity itself!

Gambling and whiskey are nationally prohibited, but prohibition of these amenities of life always existed so far as the Indian is concerned. His mental caliber does not stamp the Indian as sufficiently firm in controlling his desires, and it was a wise policy, no doubt, that strove to remove temptations which tend toward pauperizing and making of him a curse to society. That these salutary laws are sidestepped and disregarded is no fault of the legislators and custodians of the law. Indeed, it is well known that despite an enormous host of Secret Service men and detectives, many familiar containers and flasks are seen in the possession of Indians or disappear in the folds of that most serviceable of Indian apparel, the robe. As for gambling, the native games are indulged in without objection, while horse and foot racing are quite usual and publicly instituted, although it is well-known that every race features much betting. Cards, as a rule, are not sold at the posts, yet they make their appearances from time to time and visit districts much as an epidemic. The best are infected, as it seems quite reasonable that one may be as easily a winner as others of whom there are reports. That there must be losers is not thought of until the victims are counted.

The so-called Black Mountain district which affords the best of range for sheep and cattle and is therefore the home of large sheep owners was known as a zealous gambling district. It was therefore singled out for sharps who made raids, as it were, among those residents with the result that much of the wealth was transferred to less fortunate districts. Spasmodic efforts were indeed made to eradicate this condition, though the results limited the evil to that district only. When the flu raged with undisturbed vehemence it was thought best to introduce the pastime wherever players might be found. It so happened that the gamblers convened regularly in the neighborhood. In one instance, after a game of three days and nights the players were so drowsy and subconscious that one of them could easily bury the deck in the hot embers and then go to sleep. Just whether he was conscious of his act is not stated but the cards were burned the next morning.

On another occasion the missionary made the rounds of the hogans and interrupted two men gambling at cards. He had taken them by surprise because it is known that the mission has quite a collection of decks of cards that were taken from gamblers. Naturally, this deck, too, was added to the collection. The missionary simply stated with a smile that just that one deck was missing in his collection![4]

In another instance, the wife of one of the gamblers quietly searched his pockets, which seems a privilege of the wife. She found the deck and could now explain the prolonged absence of her husband. She quietly threw the cards into the stove and claimed the fire had burned them.

A credit memorandum which one of the stores had issued for cash practically made the rounds at one of these tournaments. It called for $7 and was handed in exchange to a singer who had charged $5 for a singing. The singer owed his patient $2. At a game he placed this paper in the pot at its full value and lost. The next night the trick was repeated and fortune smiled upon the singer, who, however, lost it again to a third party. This party cashed in on the paper for part of its value, placing the rest in the pot in the next game. In the meantime, the patient demanded his $2 and, as the paper had not been cashed, was repaid in hay. When the paper was finally redeemed it had to be divided among three parties, two of whom had claim upon it in some game. The transaction thus caused some comment and a desire to check gambling.

It became evident that much of what a good bishop once called the "idiotic pastime" was traceable to an outsider, a young lad who was visiting since fall and apparently had no desire to leave the country. The reason for this developed to be a school order for $40 worth of wood to be delivered at the Chin Lee school. This, as a rule, represents an equivalent for the same amount of money—if the wood is delivered. The store at that place, accordingly, accepted and honored the order for its face value, only to learn that the original owner had failed in his part of the contract.

Naturally, it seemed healthier to this lad, who by the way is an educated Indian, to disappear from the stage. In addition, he received an advance of $5 from a kind government employee, who in all patience is now awaiting his return, and incidentally of the $5 also. It would appear, then, that our friend's money has been liquidized and flows readily. At that he is quite willing to seek work. Witness his being engaged in herding a bunch of sheep to market and thereafter being employed at various chores about a trading post. Excepting for a deck of cards which the trader had used in solitaire, the loss was not very heavy so far as was traceable. But the deck disappeared and our friend knew it not.

Mysterious gatherings, however, which consumed the better part of a few days in succession with continuation at various other hogans, gave rise to various surmises. And when one of the party left the fray $30 to the bad, and our friend with his father were mentioned in this and other gains, the assumption seemed warranted that the cards originated there. Investigation identified the deck as belonging to the trader. Our friend had probably borrowed them and cut the corners to identify them properly! To divide ownership, the deck was exchanged for an older one and was then found in the pockets of the husband's coat and burned.

The young man's mother is a Mescalero whom his father had left years ago and is now married to another woman. It would seem necessary, then, to speak of the father and of the mother as distinct parents. At any rate, his father is married to a woman who is the mother of three young local lads, two of whom are fairly well educated. The elder of these three died last December a straggling victim of the flu, while the other two at present are at large seeking work. Mrs. N.N. no. 1 paid her old husband a friendly visit on which her two boys accompanied her and have since remained with their father.

Father Abraham's family was disrupted of old when he faced the mothers of his two sons. You may imagine Mr. N.N.'s predicament when the interests of his two families were presented to him from each side of the hogan fire. After all, Mr. N.N. did not want to abandon the boys of his first marriage. Neither did the boys of his present wife, their mother, wish to see their aging and industrious mother taunted by boys out of a strange wedlock. In the interests of peace the best solution would seem to be to return the first wife and their two boys to their Chin Lee home. Their father dislikes to do this, although he is aware that they are accused of mischief, like purloining horses and abusing their stepmother.

The ramifications, however, of the now Mrs. N.N. are intricate and extended sufficiently to bring the matter to a crisis. And in this manner gambling was incidentally suppressed because those interested had promised to abandon the practice, upon condition that the Mescalero woman with her boys return to her former Chin Lee residence.

Mr. N.N. had long ago divorced himself from the Mescalero woman and married his present wife, who is called the deaf woman because of ear trouble. Both are well in the years of middle age, and excepting for a nocturnal bout in which the deaf woman escaped the ring with a black eye that cost her husband a horse, they have lived in little suspense for the last four years until the return arrival of the Ismaelites, that is, the Mescalero woman and her two boys. As was intimated the affections of Mr. N.N. were divided between his boys of the first wife and those of his present wife.

The situation would not be clear if I omitted to mention that his present wife, the deaf women, has a marriageable daughter by a former husband. As it is, custom taboos the sight of a mother-in-law. To obviate the inconveniences of this custom, which forbids the husband to see the face of his mother-in-law, many have recourse to a nominal marriage with the mother of a marriageable girl who later becomes the wife. Plural marriage is not tribally forbidden. It was natural, then, that the deaf woman should accuse her husband of such intentions, which, because they were unfounded, induced her daughter to abandon her home.

She attempted marriage with the elder of the Mescalero boys who, however, already held a marriage paper. This showed him married to a schoolgirl in the legal way. His wife, in turn, was dissatisfied, left him, and married another to her liking. For this reason the lad, too, considered himself free to select the deaf woman's daughter. This arrangement, however, suited neither the deaf woman nor the Mescalero woman. The deaf woman objected to the boy on family grounds; the Mescalero woman, because of fear of the law which would hold her boy to the marriage certificate.

In addition to this mixup, it appears that the deaf woman took charge of the wagon, harness, horses, and tools of her new home. She is known as an industrious woman who is at a disadvantage only because of her defect in hearing. Naturally, much conversation escapes her, and in her desire to keep the property under control, friction with the Mescalero boys who come to borrow such property is unavoidable. The more so as her husband, their father, is not averse to extending courtesies to his own boys.

The family connections on the female side, as the sisters of the deaf woman and the widow of her eldest son, sided with the deaf woman in the effort to stop the gambling and to remove the Mescalero boys and their mother.

In the meeting which culminated out of these conditions it developed that the deaf woman had charged her daughter with the sale of a blanket she had woven, instructing her at the same time what to buy. Practice has taught them the approximate values of blankets, so that, if one store will not pay the price, another store is tried for better results. When the daughter returned with a smaller price than the mother's mind had fixed, the deaf woman withdrew the blanket, stating that she would try the other store.

Returning, they met the Mescalero boy with whom the deaf woman remonstrated for estranging her daughter. That brought one word upon another, which was renewed at home in the presence of the Mescalero woman. Owing to the present wife's deafness, the scuffle was carried on in what seemed to be a spirited fashion so that the boy, having stepped outside for wood, imagined that his mother was being attacked. He rushed inside, therefore, only to find that his affianced and his mother had grasped the deaf woman and were warding off her blows.

She was a sight. Her shirtwaist was torn off, baring her arms, her hair was disheveled, while with head bent low she was making efforts with her free hand to reach her aggressors. It was an easy matter for the boy to assist his women in conducting her outside and barring the entrance. Not to be outdone, the deaf woman tried to work the door with a stout pole, and when that failed her, she armed herself with pebbles, climbed the log on up to the smoke hole, and assailed the inmates with a shower of stones from above. That brought them out, she said with a chuckle, but the combined efforts of the three brought her down from her perch and sent her off along the road to her sister.

It was decided at the meeting [with the missionary] that to restore peace the Mescalero woman must be dismissed with the boys, the elder of whom must return to his wife. The disreputable condition of the daughter is matter for reflection, as a school should not profit by the atmosphere created by such an acquisition.

Notes

1. From Berard Haile, "Pawn, Games, Homelife," handwritten manuscript, n.d. BHP Box 5, fd. 1.

2. Berard Haile, "Correspondence on Navajo Games," in *Games of the North American Indians*, 24th Annual Report of the Bureau of American Ethnology, 1902–1903, edited by Stewart Culin (Washington, D.C.: Government Printing Office, 1907), 92–93, 96–97, 385–86, 457–59, 624, 668, 766–67, 781, 789–90.

3. Frank McNitt, *The Indian Traders* (Norman: University of Oklahoma Press, 1962); Willow Roberts, *Stokes Carson: Twentieth-Century Trading on the Navajo Reservation* (Albuquerque: University of New Mexico Press, 1987); Willow Roberts Powers, *Navajo Trading: The End of an Era* (Albuquerque: University of New Mexico Press, 2001).

4. This paragraph is excerpted from a different handwritten draft in the same folder, Father Berard's untitled manuscript beginning, "The Navajo is, of course, a heathen tribe," n.d. (circa 1921). BHP Box 5, fd. 1.

40

Navajo Ethics[1]

Berard Haile, O.F.M.

[Initially, I had thought to combine this undated, apparently unpublished fragment with Father Berard's "Navajo Religious Concepts" in a "religion and ethics" chapter, but the tone is too different from that scholarly summary of the philosophical and theological underpinnings of Navajo ceremonialism. Here, Father Berard offers practical conclusions drawn from years of living among the people, with homey examples ranging from the stolen pocketknife to the raided pantry, and generalizations about the moral principles, or lack thereof, applicable to everything from kleptomania to murder and adultery. A problem with the present selection is that plainly there is much more to be said on the topic, and in fact ethical issues are touched upon in some of Father Berard's unpublished writings on law and crime among the Navajo.[2] Still, partial though it may be, this brief interpretation to Navajo moral standards is worth knowing.]

The Navajo code of ethics is a natural standard of morals sanctioned by custom and tradition. Something is good because everybody so holds it. Likewise an action is not good because "good men and women do not do those things." This rule is usually drilled into children at home in matters of everyday occurrence. Little lies that are harmless or which are told on the spur of the moment or by force of habit are not nice things. They arouse distrust and suspicion. To say the least, one should not tell a lie. Small thefts, too, should not be customary in families of good parentage and standing. Only people of inferior breeding and small means are likely to help themselves to the property of others.

Persuasion of this kind and chiding are not sufficient barriers to evil tendencies, and complaints are frequent that children are notoriously given to lying and stealing. That is true to a large extent also of grown-up people who see no particular malice in lies and thefts that cannot be detected. By a similar standard the ethics of adultery, slander, rape, murder, assault, cheating, and the like are gauged. These are crimes and evils because they are resented by others. And this resentment is shown by the penalties which one must pay if detected and convicted of such misdemeanors. Natural instinct and self-preservation, therefore, dictate that you hide your tracks and plan your deeds so that others cannot detect them. The criminal also considers the favorable and unfavorable side of the penalty.

It is unfavorable if one has property, a family, and children who could suffer by a long absence in jail. But the favorable side shows that adultery may be practiced for a consideration and in secret, while bigamy is often a matter of a few months on the rock pile or some other fine of money, and murder is not always followed by death but gets a sentence of only five or 10 years. Principles of this standard are at times met and are cause for anxiety among better balanced minds. The fact that a sane person goes on a rampage and is unconcerned whether he loses his life or not and commits thefts and assault at any provocation stamps that person as a dangerous member of society. As a rule such a person is given to the government authorities for correction.

Yet the tribe as such had no recognized ethical code of law which stamped a set of deeds as either criminal or as righteous. Neither do the legends anywhere prescribe and proscribe certain acts as ethically right or wrong. This is reflected, too, in the poverty of words with an ethical bearing. The language has no word for law, order, justice, penalty, for right and wrong, for just and unjust, or associated ideas like conscience, conscientious, conscious, guilty, and a host of others. The wrong and injustice done are felt by the perpetrator, but not as a conscious guilt. It is rather something that must be righted in one way or another. A penalty is attached and this penalty must be paid. Sex jealousies are rampant, suspicion is easily aroused, family discords are not infrequent, conjugal fidelity is insecure. On the other hand, many are trusted and tried friends, even of foreigners. They are hospitable to a degree, and you may easily entrust a sum of money to them for transportation, where you could not think of giving the same fellow a chance at your money vault. Anomalies of this character are possible in a system which ignores any appeal to conscience or a moral sense. The unexpected may happen in the best of families.

At times you hear of kleptomaniacs in better families. It came as a surprise to his parents and friends when Blackgoat Harry was imprisoned, because he had wantonly broken a store window, had entered and picked an ordinary cheap saddle and bridle, and then cached it in some out-of-the-way dry creek. They followed the thief's tracks, which he made no particular effort to hide, and found the goods carefully deposited. The tracks then made directly for Harry's home. Yet when the policeman questioned the parents about the matter, they confessed that the boy had no reason to take the things, as he had a better saddle and bridle of his own. Upon his return, however, the boy confessed to the deed, saying that he had no particular use for the goods, but just felt that he might use them sometime. Kleptomaniacs of this caliber who show a diseased craving for theft are met occasionally.

Purloining cattle, horses, and sheep is common when conditions are favorable. Summer houses which in agricultural districts are used for hay and other storage are insecure for the winter unless windows are removed and boarded up and the door well-locked and nailed. Even then the owner must frequently visit the premises for inspection; otherwise, it may happen that his chimney is removed, and hay and grain are carried away through the forced opening in the roof. A thief thus detected is strictly held for damages by the owner and then some. Little mercy is shown.

Where a custodian is hired in the absence of the owner, one's property is comparatively safe. The trick is then to engage the custodian while others of a party help themselves. On one occasion I remember an incident which was more amusing than premeditated. It was necessary to make a trip to the railroad, 90 miles distant, and leave the premises in charge of a custodian. The urchins and other neighbors were particularly alert on such occasions, and we left with a kindly suggestion to this effect. The custodian, however, happened to be a resident of another district, and the urchins soon learned that he was rather kindly and not particularly wise to the ways of the brush. That afternoon, they entertained him with gossip of the vicinity, while two of the boys inspected the pantry and made their getaway with crackers and canned goods. That was easy. So the next day they again repeated their visit, and one of them confided to him how the thing had been done and even offered to show him the brush behind which they had left the remnants. And while this inspection was going on, two other boys made an entrance into a dugout cellar where they found canned milk and such fruits as boys like. They were slow, however, in leaving this feast, so much so that the custodian was upon them in the act of leaving the dugout. He was somewhat crestfallen and expressed his surprise at the skill displayed in decoying him. And yet that very custodian when not engaged in that position was a confirmed kleptomaniac.

On one occasion I missed a pocketknife and fountain pen. The latter I never recovered. But the knife I was asked one day to give to an Indian in the neighborhood. Upon inquiry I traced the knife to the district of the custodian and promptly claimed it without any protest. On another occasion I had to remind the custodian of his forgetfulness in replacing a second pocketknife which he had used to trim his fingernails. On a third occasion a bridle which had been left in our care lacked two silver conchas. After cross-examining several visitors who had camped on the premises in the interval, no suspicion attached to our friend until the owner took him privately aside. After repeated denials the thief finally embraced the owner and told how he had taken the conchas and pawned them at the store for food. Being poor and hungry and having children caused him to do what otherwise he would never think of doing. After [the thief promised] to redeem and return the conchas, the owner let the matter rest there.

It has been said by older Indians that schoolchildren and graduates show greater tendency to thefts than the children of the camps. No allowance is, of course, made for kleptomaniacs, as such a condition was unknown in former years. The thief is always a thief. On the other hand, it is true again that camp children find many tempting things at the schools which are novel and desirable to them. The practice to break into commissaries, pantries, and storerooms is checked and punished as much as possible. Yet unless some better force be substituted than mild persuasion and public opinion, many pupils leave school not much the better for it. The tendency to take the loose property of others tempts them above all. They are true to their tradition which stamped the tribe as raiders and marauders. The saving feature is that petty larceny is practiced in daylight only.

Where there is a will to despise larceny, the force of example is felt in the family. In families of moderate and small means, however, one can hardly claim that the example of others is looked upon as a moral force in the training of youth. The practice of rustling cattle, of driving off sheep, of using and appropriating the property of others without the knowledge of the owner, or of sanding and watering wool for the market, of cheating in games of chance and bargains, and like practices which grown people discuss and plan in detail in the presence of their children have a tendency to develop malpractices and dishonest dealings. The idea is to get away with anything, if you can, and have the laugh on yourself if you can't get there first. Cynically enough, too, the estimate and opinion of others are not much of an incentive, and no deterrent at all.

Notes

1. From Berard Haile, "Navaho Ethics," typescript, n.d. BHP Box 5, fd. 1.
2. See Berard Haile, "Law and Crime," handwritten manuscript, n.d., BHP Box 5, fd. 10, and portions of other handwritten manuscripts in BHP Box 5, fd. 1.

41

Prayer and Sacrifice
in Navajo Perspective[1]

Berard Haile, O.F.M.

[Most of the stack of manuscript that Father Berard seems to have produced there at Lukachukai in the years immediately following the influenza epidemic, apparently written with an eye to that potential series in *St. Anthony Messenger*, did not see print. One of the segments that did is a two-page response to the question, "Do the Navajo Pray?" That brief article probably amounts to less than one-tenth of his writings of the period on prayer and related concepts as they may, or as often, may not, fit into the Navajo scheme of things.

Chapter 41 begins with that published response to the question of whether the Navajo pray. It then proceeds to the related question of the role of sacrifice, which may be defined as the offering of activities or valued goods, in contrast to the verbal plea of prayer, in an effort to influence or propitiate the unseen powers. If the question is framed in terms of whether the Navajo pray and sacrifice as Christians do, the comparison does not favor the Navajo, and the author can suggest that his faithful readers "cherish the privilege of a better prayer." However, Father Berard goes on to suggest that in many ways contemporary American motivations and practices resemble those of the Navajo more than of true Christianity, concluding that "as for dupes and plaster seekers our uncultured Navajo are verily no worse than our high-browed society stars."]

❖

Do the Navajo Pray?

When occasion calls for it, prayer is performed at any season by the Navajo. Some prayers, however, may be said only in the summer months, others exclusively in winter, or with slight variations either in summer or winter. The more elaborate ceremonial prayers occur in the fall, which inaugurates winter with the first frost.

At this season the harvest is on, corn and wheat and eatables are plentiful, hay is abundant, stock and cattle are fat, and work with the herds and farm is not as urgent as in the spring. The fall season, therefore, seems better suited to meet the expenditures of an elaborate ceremony.

In accord with the teaching of our Lord to pray and to pray always, a prayer of the individual as well as community prayer is quite familiar to us. Neither individual nor common prayer, however, is a tenet of the Navajo religion. Indeed, the Navajo prays only when he or she is sick, and it seems passing strange to him that there is a call for prayer outside of sickness or accident. Such acts of praise and thanksgiving as we sing in our beautiful Preface and Gloria of the Mass, or the Te Deum, are not known among them. The Navajo cannot conceive a reason for such acts. Even a private prayer in which the individual pours out his soul to God is unintelligible to him. Their prayer is, indeed, clothed in words and stammerings, if you will. But even these prayers are known to only a few. The ordinary Navajo has no knowledge of them and must rely upon the knowledge of a few singers who, naturally enough, exploit this knowledge at the expense of those less fortunate.

It follows, then, that in order to have a prayer performed, the Navajo must take sick, because prayer is the remedy. This sickness need not be real, but may be imaginary, and is so especially when an elaborate ceremony is desired regardless of the expense.

Every sickness has its origin in religion; which is to say that misfortune like poor crops, the fall from a horse, injury by lightning, or a fall, indisposition, or bodily pains, all trace their origin to some evil influence. It may be that the wind and cloud gods, the lightning, eagle or hawk, coyote or bear, porcupine and ant divinities are at work and must be appeased by their own special sacrificial prayer.

The ordinary Navajo man and woman does not know these prayers. Neither is he able to trace the causes of his malady or misfortune, which, however, always leaves its mark, either in the past or in circumstantial evidence. To ascertain this cause as well as to determine which ceremony or prayer will appease the proper divinity and remove the spell, each case must be diagnosed. This diagnosis is made by so-called readers or seers, who gather the evidence in the case and then consult the stars, the winds, or such divine animals as are noted for their keen sight or hearing, such as the eagle and the turkey. These seers then determine the cause of the disease or injury, and usually, too, suggest which ceremony and singer are to be selected.

Should the guess not hit the mark, neither seer nor singer nor prayer is at fault. For it is then evident that one or the other circumstance in the evidence has been omitted, which fact has blurred the vision of the seer. If the patient recovers he is quite satisfied despite the fact that these various trials relieve him of much property.

In very few instances prayers are recited, or rather, audibly repeated by the patient and the singer. Otherwise, the usual form of prayer is the song which is exclusively performed by the singer. The patient is a passive listener. Their prayers are, therefore, properly called chants or singings, and the conductor thereof is properly "the singer." The melody is introduced in a head voice note or refrain of meaningless syllables like: ho-ho-ho, or eya, eya, e-e-eya-aa, and so on. To these, words descriptive of some legendary event are added, and the tune closed by a repetition of the refrain. Time is kept or not kept to the beat of a basket drum, and usually the melody is accompanied by the shake of a gourd, or other rattle.

The Navajo prayers are a repetition of fixed formulas rather than a spontaneous outpouring of the heart. A certain amount of individual variation is permissible in dedicatory offerings to the hogan poles which are accompanied by a short prayer, or similar offerings of corn meal to masks and ceremonial paraphernalia. But even here these short prayers are a repetition of some phrase borrowed from stereotyped ritual prayers rather than a spontaneous outpouring of the heart. The individual as a rule has no need of prayer excepting when sickness and continued misfortune dictate it.

In this event the general form of the prayer and its phraseology are expressive of a compulsive request rather than of a petition implying a possible refusal. The general belief is that the formula alone, fixed by tradition, is all that is required. The singer should be familiar with some or all prayers that have been handed down for the chant of which he is a representative. If the patient feels that his prayer formula may assist in removing occult influences of disease, he may decide to go to the expense of having certain liberation prayers said. In other words, prayer is not essential. But when the patient requests a certain prayer, it seems essential that he repeat it verbatim with the singer. If recited faultlessly no prayer can be ineffectual, for the reason already mentioned that, as a properly initiated person, the singer has the power to confer the sanctity or immunity which the patient desires. And if we interpret Navajo songs as prayers in native rhythm, which the facts warrant us to do, the same may apply to the numerous sets of songs in possession of the various chants.

The singing man is, therefore, never referred to as a medicine man, because he is chiefly singer, not a man of medicine. What we, and the Navajo as well, consider taking medicine is true only after a fashion. The whole ceremony is medicine, so that no medicine as a remedy is applied without ceremony or singing. If disease is religious in origin the remedy must be similar in character. Accordingly, such medicinal herbs, for instance, in the case of rheumatism, as are applied in the course of a singing, have no medicinal qualities for curing rheumatism, except insofar as they are part of the ceremony. They are medicinal because the ritual requires them. That becomes clear from the manner in which they are applied. Quite frequently the ritual requires that no local application be made, but the herb be sputtered over the patient when an application is prescribed. Similarly, those present may apply liniments, lotions, and potions to themselves if they so desire. Herbs and similar adjuncts are, therefore, merely integral parts. The singing is essential to the cure.

Similarly, too, a singing must be of one, three, five, or nine nights duration, which again is decided by the seer. These notions and practices, as here outlined, offer little that is inspiring. They impress us, undoubtedly, as childish and as the product of a people intellectually not far advanced above the age of a child. At that, they seem about as blissful as a child in their ignorance of higher matters. When we reflect, however, that large numbers of our own countrymen prefer the less onerous ignorance in religious matters to a change that might impose burdens of a personal nature, the notions and practices of the Navajo seem human after all. We who cherish the privilege of a better prayer than theirs will do well to ask its extension to this benighted race.

Prayer and Sacrifice

The subject of Navajo sacrifices is not without interest. Whereas many primitive people offered sacrifices and destroyed their victims, even human lives, in sacrifice, we have apparently no such concept of a propitiation among the Navajo. The destruction of the victim or offering as essential to a sacrifice does not seem to be practiced. In fact, one is at a loss to find anything like even the surrender of the means of life, say, victuals, either of meat or breadstuffs. Slaughtering of sheep, beeves, or horses is quite customary at a ceremonial but never enters as part of it excepting to furnish the meals of the singer and attendants. So, too, the gifts to the singer are no part of the ceremony.

When a sacrifice proper is made, this is frequently done in the shape of a smoke which is expressed in words about like these: "I have made your sacrifice, I have prepared your smoke (cigarette)." This would imply, for instance, a number of prayersticks (*K'et'an* cut wands) which have been cut according to ritual, colored as required with or without facet, and dressed with plumes and stones which are precious, such as turquoise shell and the like. Ground herbs or meal furnish the tobacco, which is inserted in the hollow of the prayerstick or strewn beside it. If the stick be solid it is sprinkled with pollen. The ceremony over, such sticks are deposited in the shelves of rocks or the branches of trees, or when the figures of dogs, ducks, dolls, turtles, and the like are to be made of wood, or a porridge of cornmeal. Some burrow or lonely spot far from traffic is selected for deposit.

Such practices may be symbolic of destruction, but destruction is not intended. The deposits are invariably made in the belief that the respective deity will find and carry them off with them and thus be satisfied. Should they not find them, the fault is not man's who has indubitably posited what was required of him for his physical restoration. The idea is obviously that Navajo reason has dictated the measure, not that it seems to be the due of the deity. Hence the object of a true sacrifice to restore the true relationship of creature and Creator is apparently secondary. The worship is mechanical and involves no change of heart.

One hesitates to speak of a sacrifice with regard to such offerings. The Navajo tenets on the soul seem to exclude anything like a consciousness of obligation to the deities excepting for the duration of the sickness. But where there is no consciousness of guilt it seems useless to speak of a substitute for man's life in the shape of a sacrifice, bloody or unbloody. Man is not conscious of having forfeited life by an offense. Why, then, should he redeem his life through sacrifice? The idea seems foreign to all appearance. Here a sacrifice implies ought else than positing symbolic goods which will propitiate the irate deity.

In fact, once posited, there is no alternative for the deity but to withdraw. Prayer and sacrifice are given begrudgingly and under duress, simply because they happen to be a last or necessary resort to regain one's health. If such acts be propitiatory, they are not far from a mere formality. Navajo prayer and sacrifice require no interior disposition which might be symbolized in the exterior acts. If his prayer supplicates, begs, and entreats, it is so because prescribed by tradition. It *commands*, as any set of mechanical formulas usually do.

Therefore, the individual does not pray, even if we understand by prayer nothing else than a formula of supplication. The singer posits that for him. He is hired to do so. This is a religious act, to be sure, and is the expression of some sort of worship. But it is hardly more than a mechanical recital to some being which is manlike but just a little superior to man and now exacts this tribute.

Religion itself is not a sense of the dependence of man on the deities as much as a sense of fear and awe of these superhuman powers. Love of them is pretty much excluded, while fear dictates obedience and a forced service. For we could hardly say that the worship is rendered because honor and thanksgiving are *due* these overruling powers. Of course, the Navajo recognizes many dominions of this order. The winds, the sun, dawn, twilight, the animals, and a host of other shadows may press him in sickness. Perhaps because of their multitude the character of the sacrifice, too, was changed, making it possible to satisfy these multitudinous deities in the least cumbersome manner.

A Navajo, therefore, does not speak of praying with devotion or of honoring God by a prayer and sacrifice of thanksgiving. All he is concerned with is: Does the singer whom I engage know a given set of prayers? Did he miss anything in the recital of them? All else is immaterial, and you may just as well as not ridicule the singer for his slim voice or praise his round and loud voice. Neither is irreverent.

For the period of the ceremony, then, hospitality is extended on an unusual scale. The singer's fee, too, is a settled feature, be this a sum of money, a horse, cow, sheep, or calico, or whatever else is required, like the native baskets—which must be furnished for lotions—and the cloths or calicos on which to place the patient and the paraphernalia, all are included in their fee. Such payments are anticipated and accepted stoically. So, too, the idea of making a sacrificial payment in settlement is probably the easiest way of defining a sacrifice. This would place the weight and essence of a sacrifice not on the act as one of worship so much as upon its character as a payment. For a sickness is the unmistakable sign of displeasure, or of a spell that some unseen power is inflicting. This power demands something. Unless this something is paid, it may cause final death. Therefore, if life is worth anything, the demand ought to be satisfied.

If some similarity with a sacrifice be found in the performances just described, the measure of worship is no doubt very meager. The ceremonies preceding and accompanying such acts are elaborate enough, but certainly do not involve a better service of the deity or a change of heart for what is better. In reality, then, it would seem that their tenets of animism postulate only the minimum of religion. If sickness is caused by exterior forces only, and these forces are powers which are manlike but overrule man and are thus superhuman, they indubitably postulate some worship. This worship pacifies them and restores the harmony between man and these powers which for some offense was temporarily disturbed. The prayer song restores this harmony and incidentally removes sickness, which is a token of the displeasure of these powers.

By paying this tribute to that unseen power, the matter is settled. The unseen withdraws, and consequently this tribute (in Navajo the price) really gives you life (that which will let you live). . . . [We should not equate] the idea of payment to the worshipful act of a sacrifice itself. [For in the Navajo view] the weight and essence of the sacrifice would be placed not in the act of worship so much as upon the ransom, the small gift which is offered as pay. Navajo fashion would formulate it thus: They, that is, the powers, get their pay (bi'daina' nahalin) for the life stuff (be'ina' duleli) that by which one will live.

Indeed, these are minor considerations, because after all is said the evident thing to do is to inquire which unseen power is irritated and what the price is that is demanded by way of a sacrifice. This information obtained, the result is never a matter of conjecture, once you have selected the appropriate sacrifice, because these unseen powers themselves have prescribed this tribute. It were folly to withhold it, when settlement is so easy and assured. No further obligation is involved, and the unseen are of no further concern, because experience will have taught that it is better to let them alone and not irritate them. . . .

It is of little concern if you lose the last sheep of your herd in the attempt to meet this sacrificial payment, because this spells life or death. At least there is that possibility, and debts or loss of property that you may sustain are a matter for future ponderation. This outlay, however, as well as the fee which must be tendered the singer, are in reality a minor consideration. Friends and neighbors will assist to an extent in defraying these expenses. The chief concern is to pay the score which is due. The so-called sacrifice is the tribute or price which must be paid some time or other. As an act of worship the sacrifice is a secondary matter. Its essential weight rests rather upon its character as a sacrificial payment or indemnity. The penalty of some kind of offense is always sickness. This is unmistakable. Something, therefore, must be paid to indemnify the offended powers.

Whether the statement that the legends and ritual prescriptions furnish a precedent or pattern on which to govern the tribal code of actions be true or not is of small moment. In matter of fact strong parallels are furnished by the clan code which settles its disputes by ransom rather than punishment. With practically no tribal government as a head, the tribe is divided into peoples or clans that in one way or other have been added to the tribe known as Navajo. Of these clans there are 50 or more, some of which are related by blood and do not intermarry. Others have no relationship at all and are just as likely to be friend as foe.

These are clan groups, therefore, with a matriarchal regime, because the children without exception adopt the mother's clan. No contention is likely to arise between related clans that cannot be settled amicably as between brothers and sisters. Injury, crime, or disputes occur, therefore, only between nonrelated clans. Immediately, both sides muster relatives and you have two groups opposing each other. They are governed by the clan code in such instances, that is to say, the tribe as such keeps aloof from any disputes among two clan groups. Thus the old clan code exacted life for a life. One clan demanded the life of a murderer, making the "murdering clan" instead of the individual accountable to the "murdered clan." The offense was now against the clan, a member of which had been killed. The clan, therefore, had a case against the offending party and clan. If the offender was a prominent clansman, the chances for his delivery to the offended clan were small, as his friends would rally to his support. The case, therefore, was settled otherwise.

A bargain was entered by which the offender's clan had to pay a tender in buckskins, robes, beads, and livestock in amounts which would satisfy the offended clan. Such payment always settled the case and usually pauperized the offending clan. Quite recently, a gambler resisted arrest but was finally subdued and turned over to the American authorities for attacking the police. Realizing his predicament, the fellow offered the policeman $20 to drop the matter. This is quite Navajoesque, and the policeman would have considered the offer but for the handicap of the Americans.

There is no objection, then, to settling such matters as crimes, inheritances, or injuries in "Navajo fashion," by pitting one clan against the other. In fact, once you appeal the matter to the clan, your opponent accepts the bluff and the consequence is some sort of ransom or other.

If, then, the tribute, ransom, or pay is invoked in settlement of disputes or wrongs in the social order, a like process might obtain in the religious realm. And we find that a sacrificial payment corrects any disturbance or disarrangement there. If this be the pattern for the social order, the marked difference in the tribute asked is quite apparent. Among themselves men are exacting, but they are grouchy and hesitating to the divinity.

With some show of reason, it may be maintained that the gift surrendered is in no proportion to man's capability, so as when the [offering of] scratchings of [from] a bead necklace or one small disk of turquoise pendant, and the like, leave him the possession of such treasures, practically intact. Even if we plead for manifold sacrifices which might be required at a future date, yet it seems permissible to accept a symbolism in the entire series of sacrifices. The fact that true turquoise or bead shell is offered does not alter this conception, because the portion allotted is quite minimal and between men would hardly be considered as a gift.

Moreover, the sacrificial gift is surrounded with an elaborate ceremony, the whole of which is considered part and parcel of this gift. Of these a prominent feature are the sand drawings which in Navajo are called "spreads" from the fact that originally the drawing was made on spreads of cloth or buckskin. At present the figures are drawn in sand which is spread out on the floor of the hogan. This base layer of clean sand or soil supports the figures of more renowned deities or events of their legendary lives, which are represented with lines of varicolored sand. On this account some speak of Navajo sand mosaics.

It would seem permissible to consider many of their sand drawings as sacrificial. These are "spread out," to paraphrase the Navajo word, in the hogan and the patient is made to enter this spread and sit upon it while the dedication or offering act is made. That done and the ceremony over, the whole spread, or mosaic of sand as some call it, is gathered into blankets and carried outside to a ritual depositing place. In connection with the prayer wands, this performance shows some symbolism of destruction. In fact the patient himself is the offering if the sand drawing be considered his [image or personification] . . . and the destruction of the sand drawing and deposit of the prayer stick could symbolize the completion of the sacrifice. This is mere conjecture, however, which is based on the fact that the prayer wands and drawing are part of one and the same ceremony.

The postulates for a sacrifice to the true God are happily better defined. If so, the fact that our Navajo have only a very hazy notion of a true sacrifice again demonstrates that man becomes a slave of caprice in the measure that he turns away from God. The burden of their ritual is quite heavy, because as heathens they have used their reason, and so on, to destroy their true dependence on one God. Instead, they worship the created things. Perhaps that only increases the impression that their notion of a sacrifice is a distortion and a travesty.

It will be seen, then, that among the Navajo sacrificial worship is limited to a minimum. It is done because there is no alternative and sickness alone forces the Navajo to become religious, and so on. It is quite unintelligible to them that prayer and worship should be the routine as it were of a well-ordered life, especially when health and fortune are one's possessions. "Why should I pray? I am not sick," was the remark of a postgraduate who had been reminded to live up to his new faith.

Yet that expresses the Navajo mind pretty well. One of the most puzzling things to them is to witness that the missionaries devote time to prayer every day. Puzzling because the individual Navajo is not accustomed to such communion with God. "Why do you pray? And do you pray every day?" are frequent questions. That we do this is well known, and the Sunday services announced by the church bell are regular, with not the slightest proof that anyone is sick at the mission. The example is even inspiring enough so that permission is sought and given to attend Holy Mass. Yes, no hesitancy is felt in asking the missionary to pray for them when they attend Mass. Their request is granted, to be sure, yet in a way that may set them to thinking.

The expression, "please pray for me," sounds familiar enough to all of us and we usually seek an intercessory act in our behalf, implying that you combine your prayers with mine. In Navajo the term "pray for me" conveys the traditional concept of praying in my stead because I am ignorant of the required prayers. You get the trend pretty well when it is explained: "I'll be. there, you'll do the praying for me! I can't. But if you do it, I'll be or walk happily; my children and family will be so; my property is safe, every evil and misfortune will be distant." The Mass and prayers take on the shape of something that is evidently similar to the native rites. It can do no harm, seeing that it is practiced so regularly, and "These people are surely good." Thank you! The Mass is far from a nostrum. We call attention to this and to the duty of individual prayer. While, then, we do not refuse admittance and prayer, our fervent petition is that God may soon "enlighten them that sit in darkness and the shadow of death."

Intercessory prayer, so familiar to us, is unknown to them. They hire others to do the praying, much as the old Romans absolved themselves from prayer by hiring and paying their priests to do so. With the Navajo, healing and praying go hand in hand. Prayer must heal. It must cure a disease, it must effect rain, it will prevent anything you ask for.

You do not ask, you posit a prayer, and the thing is done. Otherwise you are a liar and a fakir. To accept an invitation to pray for rain always means that you can make rain. If rain was not forthcoming, you have not prayed, or your prayer is mighty poor.

Baptism, for instance, is a form of prayer, and did you ever know it was a healing prayer? Well, the other day in speaking of baptism a visitor related how years ago he had allowed one of the Fathers to baptize his boy. "He wasn't well at the time and we thought that he might do better if we got that water on his head. By the way what kind of water is that? Where does it come from?" When I explained that any water that is pure will do, he said: "Perhaps it will!" which implied that he knew better. At any rate, he continued, that boy hasn't been sick since and he is so big now. It surely did him some good, this "water put on his head!" "It's a good medicine for the head. There are not a few that say so!"

A Navajo woman brought her married daughter one day to the mission, saying that she didn't have much to say but would like to have me sit down and listen. I did so. "This daughter of mine isn't quite right in her head," she said.

> Last year she suffered such a spell and we had to hold and tie her down lest she jump in the fire or hurt herself. It seems this comes on occasionally only, because she is quite normal at times. Here of late, however, we have noticed the thing coming on again, because she swoons, holds her head, and stares ahead of her just as she did the other time. Her husband, my daughter, and myself therefore have studied the matter, and he said that this 'water on the head' of yours is just the thing. Therefore, we said that she ought to be baptized.

"And what about her?" I asked. "Oh, she wants it, too, because she knows that she isn't right at those times. Therefore, she said she would be baptized." "Is she sick?" I asked again. "No, she's not sick, only this thing."

There was no objection to taking instructions if it had to be, and we arranged to have an interpreter explain to their satisfaction. It was fully explained to them that baptism is not a healing medicine, and all ceremonies had to be relinquished and a life according to the faith they would learn had to be led. Yet I doubt if they were convinced, excepting to be more firm in their conviction that, like some big singer, I didn't care to let them have the benefit of this water. The spells continue and with them the desire to get the water on their heads. But they never applied for further instruction.

Quite recently, I learned that vaseline or petroleum, which is for sale at the stores, is a fine curative because it is made of the fats of snakes. And snakes are mysterious and holy. However that may be, it is not unusual that free medicines are sought at the mission. A singer one day applied for some curative for his child who had refused food for three days. Anything in the line of liniment would do, he said. I had none at the time, and the school supply, too, was accidentally short. Through his son I suggested that if the child was very sick we might at least baptize her. "Will that cure her?" he asked. "No," I said, "We do not administer baptism as a medicine." "Then," said he, "it is useless to apply it. If it doesn't cure her I don't want it." . . .

A prominent weekly in a recent article headed, "The Hunt after Happiness," remarked:

> It seems but natural that people should want to be healthy and happy. Most of them would hardly be able to define their notion of what happiness, for themselves, would mean. But they feel aches and lacks and dissatisfactions and confusions, and since they have never been taught that wisdom, which is hard to come by, may help them out, they run after nostrums. It is extraordinarily interesting to watch the religious notices in the Sunday press. There is Christian Science, popular, powerful, and almost conservative now. Thus there is also a 'divine science' that competes in the art of healing. . . . all these are nothing in their pretensions to what one might call the freelances of the new Healing and the new Thought. There is a lady who calls herself a 'curative psychologist and personality builder,' declaring she has helped many to 'health, happiness, and success.' There is a gentleman who proposes to establish the 'volitional empire,' a lady who promises to heal you of your habits, a lady and gentleman who teach 'healing in the voluntary way.' There is still another lady who preaches on 'How to Get the Things You Want,' and there are various other 'healing services,' and 'houses of prayer and healing,' and lectures on 'Stock-Taking for Success.' The lady responsible for the latter performance adds with almost sweet simplicity: 'These lectures are helping people in business. They will help you.' The Theosophists top off this whole display with their discourses on 'psychism, occultism and magic,' and their promise to teach you the 'secret doctrine.' And next someone of whom you had thought better drops in to bore you about Love.

These quacks have nothing on our Navajo singers (pardon the parallel). As for dupes and plaster seekers, our uncultured Navajo are verily no worse than our high-browed society stars. Let a Navajo singer hang out his shingle in any large city, the enterprise might be very lucrative. He, too, might learn that such methods "help people in that business."

It isn't so strange after all, then, that like these people of our civilized society, the Navajo, too, desire a plaster more than a cure. "They do not want to change their social habits or views," the article continues, "or to think hard, or to seek for the causes of things." They seem to prefer living in their own traditional fashion and then by some formula or charm or bit of magic be cured of ills which their traditions have traced or caused.

Note

1. From Berard Haile, "Do the Navahos Pray?" *St. Anthony Messenger* 29 (January 1922): 353–54; the handwritten manuscript for that article, BHP Box 5, fd. 1; and untitled manuscript, n.d., beginning, "The subject of Navajo sacrifices," BHP Box 5, fd. 16.

42

The Natural and the Supernatural[1]

Anselm Weber, O.F.M., and Leopold Ostermann, O.F.M.

[This chapter illustrates the pragmatic practice by the Franciscan missionaries of using the same basic piece, or portions of it, in a variety of publication outlets. It also manifests the nonchalance about claiming or crediting authorship that characterized much of the missionaries' work, to the frustration of later scholars. In the relationship between Father Anselm and Father Leopold, sometimes authorship seems to denote translation of another's piece as much as origination of the piece.

In 1900, in the *Sendbote*'s monthly series "Die Indianer-Mission unter den Navajo," Father Anselm published an essay on the beliefs and superstitions of the Navajo. In 1902, a segment of Father Leopold's monthly article on "Franciscans in the Wilds and Wastes of the Navajo Country" treated "Red and White superstition." It included a first-person account of the narrator's (presumably Father Leopold's) recent journey with a Navajo companion in which he personally witnessed the intensity of Navajo belief in their dreams. In 1916, much of Father Leopold's piece, including that same first-person account, appeared in Father Anselm's article "On Navajo Myths and Superstitions." The time reference had been altered from "a few months ago" to "some years ago," but the personal pronoun was unchanged. The reader wonders whether the "me" in the incident refers to Father Leopold, Father Anselm, or both.[2] Two years later, Father Anselm included several paragraphs from this 1916 piece in his article for the *Indian Sentinel,* "Origin, Religion, and Superstitions of the Navajo."[3]

The chapter below combines most of Father Anselm's 1900 *Sendbote* essay[4] with his 1916 *Franciscan Missions of the Southwest* article. Leopold Ostermann is listed as coauthor on the basis of the paragraphs from his 1902 *St. Anthony's Messenger* article that made their way into Anselm's 1916 article, and also because I have added in the concluding page of Father Leopold's article, which Father Anselm did not use. Despite the joint authorship, where personal pronouns were singular in the source documents, they remain so here. Editing in the spirit of the

Franciscans, I have freely shifted paragraphs about in an effort to smooth the transitions and stitch together the various pieces into a single essay.

Much of the attraction of this selection is in the personal anecdotes that illustrate the friars' generalizations about Navajo myths, taboos, and medicine men. Here are some priceless stories: the Navajo who sold the hindquarters of his burro as venison, but couldn't pass off the hide to the same white wholesaler; a Navajo's shocked reaction to a white trader's application of the coyote taboo to protect his pawn from thieves; the frenzied flight from fish water of a Navajo kitchen worker; the people's reaction to an eclipse of the moon, and the basic astronomy lesson it provoked; a friar's attempt at a wedding to defuse the traditional mother-in-law taboo, and then his second thoughts about doing so. Explicitly, too, there is the Franciscan version of cultural relativism, in which Navajo superstitions are set against the superstitious practices of civilized white Americans, and both are seen as misguided efforts to appease the unknown, each foolish and ineffectual as compared to the way of faith.]

Lest it appear that the writer considers the Navajo Indians the only superstitious people in the world, let it be said at the outset that the highly educated white man who becomes uneasy when he finds himself at table with 12 others, or who breaks the shells of eggs lest they become the vehicles by which the fairies might sail away with his good fortune, is after all not so far behind the Navajo.

According to their myths the Navajo have emerged from 11 different underworlds into this, the 12th one. A small lake in the San Juan Mountains in southwestern Colorado is given by them as the place whence they came into this world. This small lake, the Indians say, is surrounded by precipitous cliffs and has a small island near its center, from the top of which rises something that looks like the top of a ladder. Beyond the bounding cliffs there are four mountain peaks which are frequently referred to in the songs and myths of the Navajo. They fear to visit the shore of this lake, but they climb the surrounding mountains and view its waters from a distance.

Though they do not believe in one supreme being, their pantheon is filled with many gods and superior beings: Esdsa Nadlehe, the Changing Woman; her sister, Yołgai Esdsa, the Shell Woman, married to the water; war gods, giants, alien and inimical gods, good and evil spirits. Besides, the first man and first woman never died, they are potent still, immortal and divine. Also, all the animals have their divine ancestral prototype, and some of their mortal descendants, for instance, the bear, the coyote, and the snake, are the subjects of some kind of a superstitious dread. The Navajo may kill a bear in self-defense, but if they do, they must get a medicine man to perform some kind of an expiatory ceremony over them.

Coping with Nature

To the Navajo the roll of the thunder, the flash of the lightning, the sweep of the wind, rain, hail, and snow, the roar of the water, the flight of the clouds, the resound of the echo, the bubbling springs, and so on: all these things are the bearers of mysterious, supernatural forces and influences that may harm or benefit him. The eating of fish, the killing of a rattlesnake, the shooting of a bear or a coyote, and so forth, are foolhardy deeds, sure to be followed by disastrous and direful consequences. In the dark he is ever expecting to see ghosts and goblins loom up and take after him. He will never knowingly enter a house in which someone has died; he will never kindle his campfires with wood from a tree that has been struck by lightning. Thus his whole life—we may almost say his every step—is haunted, and most of his efforts and frequently all his property are spent in trying to dodge or to ward off the evil influences of the *ch'indi*.

His surroundings, his education, the practices and traditions of past centuries, all lead him to the conviction that there are supernatural powers and wonders which can be enlisted in his behalf, or can be inimical to him if scorned or disregarded. In his native wilds and desert wastes, in the deep valleys and upon the mountain summits, in the somber forests and in the deep-shadowed canyons, he is constantly brought into close contact with nature, and has always believed that unseen powers were near him and in active operation. It is not difficult, then, to understand his faith and his confidence in his medicine men, whom he believes to be in actual communication with the spirit world, and possessed of extraordinary supernatural powers.

Natural phenomena are very simply accounted for by the Navajo. When the wind blows—and in these parts it does stir rather violently once in a while—it is the wind god Nilthchi puffing his cheeks. When the thunder rolls, the thunderbird is flapping his wings. The lightning flash is nothing else than the divided tongue of the snake god, which is shown when goblins or ogres above are practicing marksmanship. Proof of this is to be found in the fact that when a firearm is discharged in the dark, a light is seen first which is immediately followed by a loud report. Thus it is that we see the lightning before we hear the thunder; ergo—at least that is the argument of our friend Blind Luke—thunder and lightning are derived from some form of shooting.

Furthermore, a Navajo will never use for firewood any part of a tree that has been struck by lightning, and if some paleface should be so irreverent as to do that, a Navajo will keep his distance from the fire so that he will neither feel its heat nor smell its smoke. He would rather go to bed without a fire and even without his evening meal than to warm himself or to eat of food that has been prepared by such a means. It is the Navajo belief that when he in any way comes into contact with a fire of that nature, he takes unto himself something of the nature of lightning. This will draw lightning, and therefore he becomes vulnerable to be struck by it.

There was a time when the Navajo, like the orthodox Jews, would eat no pork. When they were brought to Fort Sumner in 1864, where they remained for four years, pork was on their daily menu. The old-time Navajo attributed the increase of their mortality rate at that time to this circumstance alone.

Mutton and goat flesh are both good, but horse meat is a delicacy, claim the Navajo, who cannot comprehend the white man's aversion to the latter. They claim that the flesh of a young horse is much more palatable than that of an old cow. It is not true that the Navajo eat the flesh of dogs and mules; they go so far as to say that whoever does eat the flesh of a mule is barred after death from the spirit world. However, they will usually be found willing to try to sell a white man the flesh of a mule and deceive him into believing that it is venison or beef. Only a short time ago a Navajo sold two hind quarters of this beef to a wholesaler in Gallup. Ten days later the Indian presented the hide of a burro for sale. The dealer remonstrated with his customer and told him he should be ashamed to offer such "junk" for sale. The Indian replied: "Ten days ago I sold you the meat and you told me it was very good; I don't see why you can find any fault with the wrapper."

It is true, however, that the Navajo eat prairie dogs, but these are not dogs and have no relationship to the genus *canis*. They are small, short-legged animals having some resemblance to the squirrel, and they live in underground burrows. They multiply almost as fast as rabbits and are very numerous on the Navajo reservation. There is a little village of them right near the mission and often as many as 40 or 50 may be seen at one time. As soon as a human approaches too near, a "watchman" prairie dog sounds the alarm and all scurry to their mound entrances. Since they feed on herbs and plants they are naturally a nuisance for the white farmers who rid their lands of them by poisoning. The Navajo shoot them or trap them or drown them out of their burrows. The latter procedure is very common during the rains when water is led from the hillsides into the burrows, which soon brings the drowning little animals to the surface.

Their preparation for the table is a primitive process: without being skinned or drawn they are roasted over a fire of hot coals, and no one would suspect that what was placed before him was anything else than *Hasenpfeffer*. This was the ruse that Brother Placidus played on the Fathers at St. Michaels during the first year of our stay in the Navajo missions. When one's bill of fare varies year in and year out from mutton to goat meat and from goat meat to mutton, prairie dog *Hasenpfeffer* tastes mighty good for a change. Brother Placidus seems to have made up the story that during the following night in my dreams I imitated the barking of a dog. Of course I would not deny this story, but neither can I vouch for its exact truth.

A Navajo will not kill a bear, except in self-defense, but if he should do so, he cannot be persuaded even to touch the carcass. If there are white people nearby, he may come to them and offer to show them where a dead bear may be found provided he receives a few dollars for his service.

A similar attitude is held by the Navajo with regard to the prairie wolf or coyote, which they will not kill at any price, even though the coyotes inflict great losses to the Navajo flocks when they are left unattended. No wonder these preying animals are so numerous, so that we hear their howls almost every night. When a Navajo wishes to express his highest contempt for anyone, he calls him *mai*, coyote, or *mai bakagi*, coyote pelt. Some time ago a Navajo gave his silver armband to a white man for safekeeping. The white man placed the armband in a small chest which he covered with a coyote pelt. Of course, this was a very efficient way of keeping other Navajo from stealing the treasure. When the owner later returned and learned that his armband had come into contact with a disreputable coyote skin, he became enraged. His friends were likewise indignant over the matter, and it was only with considerable effort that serious trouble was averted. Until late into the night the Indian was seen scouring his precious armband with sand and water as he avowedly sought to erase the profanation. Thereupon, he took the band to a medicine man, who finally removed the evil influence entirely.

The Navajo's repugnance to snakes is even greater than that of the white man. He will kill a snake only in self-defense. Should he encounter one on the way he will either walk around it or with a stick remove it from his path. A snake chant which the Navajo sing to bring luck at gambling goes as follows: "I threw it away, I threw it away; I wonder where it is, I wonder where it is." Recently, a white man accompanied by several Navajo came upon a number of rattlesnakes. He forthwith killed them all and was surprised that his friends had made no offer to assist him. When he had dispatched the last reptile, one of the old Navajo called him aside and earnestly warned him to go to a medicine man to have the snake spirits driven out of him. If he should fail to do this, these spirits which had entered his body would kill him within the year.

This singing ceremony, by the way, is quite an expensive affair. It costs four or five head of sheep or a young horse. It consists in making a small wooden snake into which the spirits are driven from the patient by the singing, praying, and incantations of the medicine man. The wooden image is then destroyed. The Navajo attribute great wisdom to snakes; they believe them to understand human languages, to be good listeners, and to be able to turn to evil account what they have heard. For this reason, Navajo sacred legends may be related and their most sacred ceremonies performed only in wintertime, when the terrestrial snakes are hibernating and the celestial snakes (lightning) do not make their appearance.

Still another characteristic of the Navajo is that they will never eat fish, although they are fully aware of the fact that there are other Indian tribes who subsist almost exclusively upon fish. The Navajo will not even touch fish. It is related that the owner of a small hotel had hired a young Navajo to assist her in the kitchen. He was willing to do anything, but he drew the line at preparing fish for meals. He would eat anything, but under no circumstances would he touch fish. One day the lady jokingly poured upon him some water in which she had just washed some fish. The Navajo screamed in fear and ran away tearing off his clothes. He took a bath and "made much medicine" to free himself from his uncleanness.

The Apache Indians share with the Navajo this superstition with regard to fish, although they do not shrink from eating the flesh of horses or cattle that may have died several days previously. Many explanations are given for this aversion. A pupil of the San Carlos school gave the following reason: Long before his "first grandfather" was born, the Apache did not have enough to eat; deer and antelope were rarely to be found, because there were too many hunters. Then the wise men said: "We must begin a great war and kill many people, so that those who remain may live." At a large council meeting between the Indians from the mountains and those along the river, all took a solemn oath: the former swore never to eat fish, the latter never to partake of venison. With this agreement war was avoided and all had plenty to eat. True it is to this day that the Mojave and Yuma Indians of the Colorado River Valley live only on fish and vegetables and never eat venison. Since the Apache seem to keep this promise only when they find it to their advantage, it is very likely that today they do not consider themselves bound by the oath of their forefathers.

The Navajo has his explanation, too: Since he inhabits a desert land where water is extremely scarce, water is considered something sacred, and since the fish live in it, they themselves become holy. Some Indians believe that the fishes can pray to bring water from the rocks. Others claim that when the god, Najanesgani, had killed all the giants that inhabited the earth, he was nauseated and vomited into the river, creating the fishes, frogs, turtles, and the like, and for that reason the Navajo have a horror and disgust for all aquatic animals that eat and chew and breathe water.

One day a Navajo chief of high standing and influence took dinner with us on a fast day. When fish was put on the table, he eyed it very suspiciously and began to move with his chair toward the lower end of the table. The same Indian would eat no chicken, because a ceremony was once performed over him in which the form of a chicken was used. Another one would eat no peaches because a medicine man had forbidden him to eat anything that grew on trees.

Some time ago a small whirlwind, such as may frequently be seen in this country in the summer or fall sweeping along over the land, struck the house of Tsinnajini, an Indian living about a mile north of us, and played a little havoc with things that were not nailed fast. Great consternation in the family; nothing but a *ch'indi* could have done that. Therefore, the first thing to be done was to get the medicine man, who sang and ceremonied in the house a whole night long and banished the evil spirit.

Some years ago an Indian from the neighborhood, Wodda bi-zhe'e', accompanied me on a trip of about 80 miles north to see a Navajo friend of ours who had been reported very sick. We stayed overnight at an Indian's house about halfway. That night Wodda bi-zhe'e' dreamed his wife was sick. Next morning no power on earth could induce him to go along any further. He was absolutely convinced that his wife was really sick or that some misfortune had befallen her. There was no use talking; it was his duty to go home and see that the *ch'indi* was ousted.

When an eclipse occurs they imagine that the sun or moon is dying and must be prayed back to life again. One evening, I had a pretty large "congregation" of Navajo herders assembled around the fire in the middle of their spacious hut, or hogan, at the foot of the Tunicha Mountains. They had listened to me with interest and even eagerness for over an hour when one of them, looking through the large opening at the apex of the hogan, which, in their huts, serves as chimney and window, put the question, "*Da'ci k'os it'ae?*" "Is that a cloud?" (before the moon). He was joined by several others, and the amazing answer came: "*Dooda, olje daasts'a.*" "No, but the moon is dead." All were much alarmed, indeed. Taking a potato and an onion to represent the earth and the moon, the fire in the middle of the hogan representing the sun, I explained the eclipse of the moon to them. They felt very much relieved to learn that the moon was not in the throes of death and did not need their assistance. Our friend, Chee Dodge, happened to be on a visit that same night at Tse'illi with the Indian headman Charlie Tso [Mitchell], who requested him very urgently to join them in their prayers for the moon, but Chee went to bed, telling them the moon would undoubtedly recover without his assistance.

Medicine Men

There are among the Navajo an extraordinary large number of medicine men, called by them *qatqaɫi*, singers or chanters. Some of these form special societies or lodges, each of whom has a set of myths and legends, of songs and prayers, of sacrifices and ceremonials, of medicines and dances. They pretend to possess certain supernatural powers given them for the good and the benefit of the people, especially in cases of sickness. Their ceremonials may vie in allegory, symbolism, and intricacy of ritual with the ceremonies of any people, ancient or modern. They possess lengthy myths and traditions so numerous that one can never hope to collect them all, a pantheon as well stocked with gods and heroes as that of the ancient Greeks, and prayers which for length and repetition might put a Pharisee to the blush. They have a knowledge of hundreds of significant songs or poems, as they may be called, which have been handed down for centuries. They have songs of travel, of farming, of building, songs for hunting, for war, for gambling, in short, for every occasion in life from birth to death, not to speak of prenatal and postmortem songs. And these songs are composed according to established rules and abound in poetic figures of speech.

Based upon their myths and legends and in conformity to them, a multitude of rites and ceremonies are practiced by their medicine men, in which occur songs, prayers, sacrifices, making of sandpaintings, and representations of their deities. Sometimes pertaining to a single rite there are 200 songs or more, which may not be sung at any other rite.

Some of these ceremonies are nine-day affairs, for instance the *Yeibichai* and the *Dziɫk'iji Qatqaɫ*, or Mountain Chant, during which men appear, painted and masked, representing gods and heroes and other mythical characters. They never speak, but utter a peculiar cry. Dances at the end of these ceremonies, though accompanied by religious symbolism and performed often by men wearing sacred costumes, are intended largely to entertain the spectators. Especially on the last night of the Mountain Chant, also called Hashkan Dance, Corral Dance, or Fire Dance, the dances are picturesque and varied, rhythmical and well timed: figures are often introduced similar to those of our quadrilles. The most weird dance is the Fire Dance, when a number of Navajo, covered only with a breechclout, their otherwise naked bodies coated with a thin layer of white clay, pursue each other and lash each other with flaming torches made of bark.

Sandpaintings or sand altars, made during these and many other ceremonies, are figures representing mostly their deities and mythical characters. The groundwork consists of sand spread over the floor of the medicine lodge to the depth of about three inches and smoothed over with the broad oaken battens used in weaving blankets. Various colors are used to make the figures on top of this groundwork. The ingredients are sometimes mixed with sand or dirt to allow them to flow more readily in drawing the lines. White is obtained with a kind of gypsum, which is pulverized; yellow, with yellow ochre; and red, with pulverized red sandstone. Black consists of charcoal, obtained from burned scrub oak, or for the Night Chant, from dry cedar charcoal, which is mixed with dirt. Blue is obtained with a mixture of pulverized charcoal and gypsum added to the dirt. Varicolored pebbles, however, are not used for the sandpaintings.

These preparations are put on bark trays, from which a pinch is taken between the index finger and thumb and allowed to drop on the layer of moist sand, or the "altar" forming the foundation of the drawings. The singer usually superintends the work, directing and correcting his assistants, of whom as many as five and more are at work on the larger drawings. These drawings vary in size and number for the individual chants, of which few, if any, are entirely without them. The patient is seated on the finished drawing. Moistening his palm, the medicine man takes the colored dust from various parts of the "sacred" figure and applies it to similar parts of the patient's body. Thus, if he suffers from headache, the singer takes the dust from the head of the figure and applies it to the head of the patient. After various invocations and rites the drawing is erased and the dirt and sand removed from the medicine lodge or hogan.

While they have ceremonies for planting, harvesting. building, war, nubility, marriage, travel, and many other occasions in life, most of them, including the *Yeibichai* and Mountain Chant mentioned above, and the *Nda*, or War or Squaw Dance, are employed to cure the sick. Sickness with the Navajo, as in fact with all Indians, is not an organic disorder but an independent entity which has its own individual existence outside of man. It is a supernatural evil influence, floating about, as it were, and injected into the system either by witchcraft or by evil spirits. The only thing which can banish it or scare it out of the system again are the songs, dances, prayers, charms, incantations, and so on, of the medicine man, who, by the way, must be paid well in advance for his services. Hence, also, their abject fear of the dead, especially such as have died of some sickness. The sickness is still with the dead body or is hovering about in the neighborhood, waiting for a chance to enter or to be witched into anyone coming too near.

In cases of sickness the diagnosis is often made by men who read the stars and speak to the spirits; then the medicine man of the corresponding rite is called to remove the magic influence by his specific chant. The offended holy person must be appeased by a propitiatory sacrifice, or the power of a higher divinity must be invoked to remove the witchery and malevolent influence of an inferior one. Should the sickness continue after a given ceremony, such a fact cannot be attributed to the impotence of that ceremony, but clearly shows that the offense has not been properly traced and must be sought elsewhere. In consequence there is often no end of singing in one form or other until death ensues or relief is obtained. When the approach of death is certain, every ceremony subsides and the officiating singer withdraws before the inevitable issue.

The knowledge and specialty of a singer are gauged, not so much by his familiarity with the sanative qualities of herbs, the application of which is of minor and secondary importance throughout, as by his greater or lesser knowledge and dexterity in performing a given rite. In fact, when it is known that his medicine pouch is possessed of paraphernalia of some antiquity and difficult to acquire at present, or when others have been cured of a similar disease through his services, the demand for a given rite and the singer becomes greater regardless of the disease.

There are among medicine men some charlatans who pretend to suck disease out of the patient and then draw from their own mouths pebbles, pieces of charcoal, or other small particles, claiming that these, shot into patients through some witchery, are the causes of their sickness. One of these medicine men, called by the Indians Ch'idi Adildonni Yazhe, the little devil shooter, stayed at our mission for a while and communicated to us the secrets of his lodge. The other Indians were afraid to sleep with him in the same room; had he left us at that time they would have killed him, as they had killed his partner. A few years ago he reverted to star reading and talking to the spirits to confirm the suspicions of some that a certain member of their tribe was guilty of witchcraft and responsible for the death of several of their relatives. They, four of them, forthwith killed the alleged wizard and are now serving a 10-year sentence in the federal prison at Atlanta, Georgia, while our star reader spent several months in jail awaiting his trial. Star reading and killing witches are getting to be rather unhealthy occupations among the Navajo. Their belief in witches who can cast spells upon animals, fields, and people and cause them to wither and waste away is pretty general. These witch powers are not only attributed to human beings but also to animals. Some witches are said to appear in the form of bears or wolves. The belief in charms and dreams is also rather strong.

The Navajo—at least a great many of them—waste no love upon their medicine men. I have heard them scold about them, run them down until nothing but shreds were left of them, deny their power and influence, call them cheats, thieves, who "need killing." And these very scoffers and scolders, when taken sick, will send for them, and have them to sing, dance, and hocus-pocus over them.

A Navajo may not look upon his mother-in-law, nor vice versa, without incurring the risk of going blind. Mothers-in-law and sons-in-law, therefore, carefully avoid each other, and when they accidently meet, they abruptly turn from each other, and speedily get out of each other's sight. Their word for mother-in-law, therefore, is *Doyish'inni*, that is, Whom I May Not See. I know a mother-in-law who was creating trouble incessantly and had almost succeeded in inducing her daughter to leave her husband, when the latter, augmenting his courage by a copious draught of firewater, jumped upon his horse and, yelling like the savage he was, rode into the open brush summer hut where his mother-in-law was staying, and where she could not escape, facing her with a superhuman courage and giving her [the dickens]. She left them in peace ever after.

Some time ago I married one of our former pupils, the daughter of a widow, to a youngster who was to make his home at the house of his mother-in-law. I thought it exceptionally inconvenient for the two to continually dodge each other and urged the prospective mother-in-law to discard this preposterous custom. She remained present during the marriage ceremony, then arose, walked up to her son-in-law, looking at him steadily, shook his hand, and called him *shaye*, my son-in-law. Afterward I felt a slight scruple whether I was doing the right thing in trying to break up this beneficent (?) custom. What do the mothers- and sons- and daughters-in-law think of it?

Many may smile a very pitying smile at all this, but before casting stones by the carload at the untutored children of nature, let "white civilization" be careful lest it be living in a glass house. Yes, the Navajo are superstitious; but I believe St. Paul called the highly civilized and cultured Greeks "*superstitiosiores*." They have their superstitions as we have ours.[5] For if we place the white man, who has drunk deeply from the fountain of our boasted *modern civilization*, but not from the fountain of *faith*, side by side with the red man, it is very difficult to decide which of the two is the more superstitious.

Let us compare. How many of the former type will undertake a journey, or any other transaction they consider important, on a Friday, for fear of a fatal accident or mishap? How many, when traveling, will occupy "Room No. 13" in the hotel, or sit down to their meal with 13 at the table, because then one of them must infallibly die? How many will not pick up a pin, if the point is toward them, for fear of ill luck? How many have horseshoes nailed over their doors to ward off evil? How many will turn deathly pale when in the dusk of evening, they hear the innocent screech of a night owl? How many carry a buckeye, or a rabbit's foot, in their pocket for luck, and wouldn't be without it? How many believe in dreams, charms, and amulets, in ghosts and hobgoblins, in haunted houses and witcheries, in omens and fortune telling, in spiritualistic mediums, clairvoyants, and Christian science, in mascots, hoodoos, taboos, and in several scores of other superstitious practices too abjectly silly and too supinely nonsensical to mention? By the way, isn't it just this class that delights in speaking of Romish superstition? Several years ago one of the officials at Fort Defiance, whose faith was limited to the existence of a Supreme Being of some kind, when asked why Catholic missionaries and Catholic schools are more successful with the Indian than other missionaries and schools, answered because the Catholic religion contains more superstition than the others, and that attracts the Indian.

Some time ago I heard of a navy officer, who was described as a man of high culture, who openly avowed that every night before retiring he consulted his planchette. I read of a young lady who committed suicide because she fancied herself "hoodooed" by No. 13. Another one in Philadelphia went violently insane because a fortune-telling quack had predicted ill luck for her, and so on. It is an old truth, as old and as unerring as twice two is four, that the less faith a person has, the more he takes to superstition. The lack of faith, therefore, in our times is the reason why we find among a large portion of our so-called highly civilized and enlightened people about just as much superstition as among the savages, with this difference, that civilized superstition is by far more silly, more trivial, more nonsensical, and more prosy than that of the savage, who knows no better.

However, let us hope and pray that the good God may give to *both* the light and grace of faith, and that *both* may have intelligence and goodwill enough to follow that light which leads to the freedom of the children of God.

It is an encouraging fact that, of late years, the superstitions of the Navajo are vanishing and that the influence of their medicine men is diminishing. This is due to a number of causes, among them education, Christianization, the opposition of the government, hospitals, and the service for the last 12 years of an exceptionally good physician at the head of the medical work of the Fort Defiance superintendency, who has gained their complete confidence through his ability, his tact, and unvarying friendliness, and, last but not least, through his acquisition of their exceedingly difficult language. Even medicine men themselves go to him or send for him for treatment and medicines instead of trusting to the efficacy of their own remedies, songs, dances, and so on.

At a council held at Fort Defiance seven or eight years ago they were urged to discard their ceremonies and dances, but while the medicine men objected very vigorously against such a proposition, they promised at the same time not to teach their songs and myths and ceremonies to the young people of the tribe, so that their religion would die with the medicine men. Even at present, some rites and ceremonies cannot be performed, because there is no one anymore among the living who knows them.

An old Navajo expressed his thoughts regarding these changes to one of our Fathers in the following words: "When we were young everything was much different from what it is now. Our children know nothing of how it used to be. . . . They forget more and more the Navajo ways, and by and by will be like the Americans. We see all these changes, and we cannot stop them. They are bound to go on. . . . But we old folks are too old to change."

Even the medicine men share this attitude. Some of our best Catholics are the sons and daughters of medicine men. . . . Possibly, our attitude toward them is responsible for this attitude on their part. Direct, aggressive, tactless, unsympathetic opposition would arouse their unyielding antagonism and would only retard the death of their heathen religion with all its attending superstitious practices. May it soon rest in peace!

Notes

1. From Anselm Weber, "On Navajo Myths and Superstitions," FMSW 4 (1916): 38–45; FMN 27 (April 1900): 284–89, translated by Emanuel Trockur; and Leopold Ostermann, FWW 9 (May 1902): 405–7.

2. This recounting of the same personal experience by the two different narrators appears in Leopold Ostermann, FWW 9 (May 1902): 406; and Anselm Weber, "On Navajo Myths and Superstitions," FMSW 4 (1916): 42–43.

3. Anselm Weber, "Origin, Religion, and Superstitions of the Navajo," *Indian Sentinel* 1 (April 1918): 4–7.

4. The translation by Father Emanuel Trockur appears under the title "Superstitions, etc."in FFP Box 50, fd. 12; cf. Box 51, fd. 3.

5. The preceding two sentences are from Weber, "Origin, Religion, and Superstitions of the Navajo," 5.

43

The Navajo and Christianity[1]

Leopold Ostermann, O.F.M.

[The following essay has three parts: 1) an historical introduction that summarizes the first efforts by Franciscan missionaries, in 1746–1750, to teach the Gospel to the Navajo; 2) a list of 10 traits of Navajo adults, traits that have changed but little over the 150 years since the failure of those early missionaries, that continue to make Christian missionary work among the Navajo very difficult; and 3) identification of two "bright spots," characteristics of contemporary Navajo that may make them receptive to the message of the missionaries and which thereby justify a certain hope for the future success of the work. The enumeration of traits, reasons, arguments, or qualifications is typical of Ostermann's writing. Recall chapter 10, his writing on "what are we doing for the Indians?" where he systematically worked through seven motives that should prompt Catholic readers to maintain Catholic schools for Indian children, and offered five characteristics of Canadian Indian policy to which he attributed its success, in contrast to the policies of the United States. There is no date on the typescript manuscript from which the pages below are drawn, but judging from its report that "several hundred Navajo children have been instructed in the sacred truths of salvation at St. Michaels, Fort Defiance, and Chin Lee," it may date from about 1915 or a little later. The government school at Chin Lee opened in 1910, and by 1914 some 76 Navajo children at Chin Lee were receiving regular instructions from the padres, with another 50 from Chin Lee and its environs attending school at Fort Defiance and receiving instructions there.[2]

Reference to Father Leopold's "silver lining" is a good way to conclude this initial volume of glimpses of the Navajo through the eyes and pens of the Franciscans. The definition of things summarized here is not incongruent with Father Anselm's long-term view. Anselm's passing in 1921, and the pending "retirement" of Father Leopold from Chin Lee in 1924, mark the conclusion of the incredible first quarter-century of Franciscan work among the Navajo. In retrospect, it truly had been a time of "giants in the land,"and their passing left a gigantic emptiness. The death of Father Anselm, who had directed the work for almost that entire period, left sandals no one could fill. The Navajo missions were literally unbalanced by his loss, and there would be years of stressful searching, of reassessment of policies and personnel, before a workable restabilization could be achieved.]

❖

The first attempts at Christianizing the Navajo were made by the Franciscans in 1744, when in the month of March Fray Carlos Delgado and Fray Irigoyen set out from Jemez for the Navajo country, with the intention of bringing the tidings of the Gospel to the Navajo. They had "interviews" (meetings or councils) with a large number of Indians, their own estimate being about 4,000. The Indians were very friendly, listened willingly to the words and proposals of the padres, and seemed well disposed toward Christianity. When the padres reported on this in June, the governor advised the sending of several new missionaries to the Navajo, but a number of adverse and vexatious delays occurring, nothing was done until 1746, when the viceroy authorized the erection of four missions among the Navajo.

Fray Juan Miguel Menchero then took up the enterprise with much zeal and fervor. He visited the Indians in person and induced some 500 or 600 of the roaming and nomadic Navajo to settle temporarily near Cebolleta, New Mexico. Prospects seemed promising until a year or two later a bitter war broke out between the Navajo and the Utes and Chaguaguas, which frustrated the work that had been done. In 1749 the reestablishment of the missions among the Navajo was authorized. However, they were not to be located in the far north or Navajo country proper, but in the Laguna district. Accordingly, two missions were established, one at Cebolleta, the other at Encinal.

Means of support and soldiers for protection were granted to the missionaries by order of the viceroy, as well as church vestments and agricultural implements. These missions were giving well-founded hopes for success when fresh troubles broke out, and the Navajo, on June 24, 1750, left the missions and returned to the hills and haunts of their country. As their reasons for so doing they said that they had not received as much material help from the missionaries as they expected; that pueblo or village life did not agree with them; they were born free as the deer, and had to roam; that Christianity was good for the padres, and their own religion good for themselves; they were too old to learn new ways. However, they added that they would always be the friends of the padres; they would always be glad to see them, and welcome them in their homes if they came to visit them; that they had no objections whatever if they baptized and instructed their children, and if their children, when they were grown up, wished to become Christians, they would not hinder them in doing so.

Thus the first attempt at Christianizing the Navajo ended in total failure. And owing to the circumstances of place, time, and people, the Navajo country was an absolutely unknown territory. In those times vast unexplored distances had to be traversed frequently on foot; the Navajo were not a sedentary, but a nomadic people; the missionaries were few. Owing to these and similar circumstances, the work begun with the adult Navajo could not be continued with the children. When in 1898 Franciscans again entered the Navajo country to renew the attempts made by their confreres 150 years ago, they found that the adult Navajo of today has changed but very little in the last century and a half; that he is still as friendly and affable, as free and independent, as expectant and yielding, as superstitious and roaming as were his forebears 15 decades ago. These very qualities constitute the stumbling blocks on the way toward a sincere acceptance of Christianity. To make clearer what I mean, I shall enumerate in particular some of their traits which make missionary work among the present adult generation of the Navajo very difficult.

1) Their intense attachment to their old superstitious rites, ceremonies, and practices. There are a multitude of rites and ceremonies practiced by the Navajo, some of which are of nine nights duration. In these ceremonies occur songs, prayers, sacrifices, and representations of their deities, in conformity with the myths and legends upon which they are based. These myths and legends are kept alive and told by old medicine men with all the earnestness and solemn candor of one who is convinced of what he says, and are believed with all the sincerity with which a Christian believes the narratives of the Gospel. To deny or ridicule them would so touch their sensibilities as to make all further missionary efforts among them superfluous. The same may be said concerning their songs and dances. They all have a certain religious signification, the meaning and interpretation of which have for many centuries sunk deeply into their hearts and minds. And since the Navajo are a very independent people, and quickly resent any affront, since their vocabulary does not contain the verb "must," it requires much slow, patient, and perseverant work for many years until one may expect to see the beginning of any result.

2) Their religious indifference, or rather their set idea, that each religion is equally good for the respective people who profess, believe, or practice it. One may tell a crowd of the Navajo the entire story of the Christian revelation, from Creation to the Last Judgment, and after it is finished, they will tell you how they enjoyed it, how interesting, how nice and beautiful it is; how good and appropriate it is for the Americans or white people. Then they will go on to say that they also have their holy history, which is also very nice and equally good for the Navajo, and since they have patiently and respectfully listened to you, you will now listen to them with equal patience and respect. As to having made any impression upon them, such as would induce them to forsake their pagan myths and beliefs and accept the truths of Christianity, you have probably made a little more than did the British cannon balls on Jackson's cotton bales at New Orleans.

3) The influence of the medicine men. There is among the Navajo an extraordinarily large number of medicine men, called by them *qatqaḣ*, singers or chanters. Some of these form special societies or lodges, each of whom has a set or string of myths and legends, of songs and prayers, of sacrifices and ceremonies, of medicines and dances. They pretend to possess certain supernatural powers given them for the good and the benefit of the people, especially in cases of sickness. This is impressed by them upon the timorous and superstitious minds of the people, and this once achieved, their influence is almost absolute. All reasoning to the contrary is like making ropes of sand. So long as this influence continues, the hopes of seeing large numbers of the present adult generation becoming good, sincere, and fervent Christians are very faint. In this the Navajo are not much different from our

own forefathers in the forests of Germany and in the groves of Britain and Gaul. After the superstitious influence of the [early pagan religions] and druids was broken, they soon became Christians.

4) Their idea of sickness. Sickness with the Navajo, as in fact with all Indians, is not an organic disorder but an independent entity which has its own individual existence outside of man; a supernatural evil influence, floating about, as it were, and injected into the system either by witchcraft or by evil spirits. The only thing which can banish it, or scare it out of the system again, are the songs, dances, prayers, charms, incantations, and so on, of the medicine man, who, by the way, must be paid well in advance for his services. Hence also their abject fear of the dead, especially such as have died of some sickness. The sickness is still with the dead body, or is hovering about in the neighborhood, waiting for a chance to enter or to be witched into anyone coming too near. This idea of sickness and its cure is so deeply rooted that it is like talking up against a stone wall to try to tell them anything different. However, in late years many of them, even medicine men themselves, when anything serious occurs to them, are prompt and quick enough to go to the missionary or the American doctor for medicine, instead of trusting in the efficacy of their own remedies, songs, rattles, dances, and the like.

5) Their implicit belief in dreams, signs, charms, spells, omens, and witchcraft. A combination of all these really seems to make up their religion. Their belief in witches, who can cast spells upon animals, fields, and people, and cause them to wither and waste away, is incredible. These witch powers are not only attributed to human beings, but also to animals; some witches are said to appear in the form of bears or wolves. Their belief in charms and dreams is equally dense and intense. You may reason with them on this point till your vocal cords cleave together, it will have about as much influence as if you spoke into a galvanized tube running from ear to ear, the words escaping on one end as fast as they enter the other.

6) Sectarian influence. Since the missionary in the Southwest need no longer look forward to a martyr's death as a reward for his efforts, sects and societies of every dye and stamp seem to feel a special calling of Christianizing the Indian, each one with its own special brand of Christianity. Although the Indian is said to be intellectually a big overgrown child, yet he is very observant, and knows enough to put two and two together. After hearing a half dozen or more different conflicting versions of Christianity, and after seeing that the various teachers do not agree among themselves, some even vilifying others, what wonder is it that the Indian despises the white man's religion, laughs about it, perhaps even finds it ridiculous, or becomes thoroughly indifferent toward it, and prefers to remain what he is?

7) The materialistic trend of the Indian's mind. All his ceremonies, songs, and prayers have some material gain or benefit in view, be it the cure of a sickness and restoration to bodily health, the banishment of some evil influence from his fields and herds, or rain so that his corn and fruit may grow and he have plenty to eat. The same, or even greater temporal benefits, he expects from the white man's prayer. He is not given to looking beyond the horizon of his present life on earth. Although in a way he may be said to be very spiritual-minded, seeing the influences and powers of supernatural agencies in almost everything, yet he is looking in first place

for the gratification of his present animal comforts. If, therefore, the missionary can supply him with wearing apparel, and give him a substantial free lunch as often as he comes to services, he will probably come pretty regularly so long as this is kept up. There is, therefore, some truth in the saying that the way to the Indian's heart goes through his stomach. This is a point which the missionary must take into consideration; it is one of the secrets of the success of the old padres, who gathered the Indians into communities where one worked for all, and all for each other; where they were taught, beside Christian doctrine, how to increase the yield of their fields and the numbers of their herds.

8) The example of the white man. While it is true that many of the whites who lived with or among the Indians were good Christians and exerted a good influence upon the Indians of their immediate surroundings, it is likewise true that the greater part of the white men with whom the Indian first came in contact, especially along the railroads, on the outskirts of the reservations, and in the camps and railroad towns, were as a rule such, by whose exemplary Christian life he was not very apt to be much edified. Often, the first words of the English language which the Indian learns are oaths and curses; often the first steps in the white man's ways are drunkenness, theft, and worse things. Therefore, a large portion of them will be thoroughly prejudiced against the white man's prayer or religion, and the words of the missionary without effect.

9) Their mode of life. The Navajo are essentially nomads, always on the move. There is nothing like a Navajo village or settlement; some have two, three, or more homes, between which they are constantly moving, so that one can never say for sure where a certain Navajo is at present, although one may well know where his home or homes are. A Navajo who is at a given place today may be 25, or 50, or 80 or more miles away tomorrow. You may see a certain Navajo today, and the chances are that you will not see him again for five, six, or seven months, perhaps not for a year, perhaps never again. So there are many with whom very little effective work can be done.

10) Their set ways and ideas. While the Navajo in his childhood, youth, and middle age is plastic and pliable enough, he seems in his old age like a block of cement that has become thoroughly set and can never be molded into anything else but what it now is. One day while out among the Navajo of Tsehili I was speaking with an old man. In the course of his talk, he alluded to the changes of things since he was a boy. "When we were young," he said,

> everything was much different from what it is now. Our children know nothing of how it used to be. They wear American clothes; we send them to the white man's schools; they are taught the same things as white children; you priests teach them the white man's religion; they forget more and more the Navajo ways, and by and by will be like the Americans. We see all these changes, and we cannot stop them; they are bound to go on. We are not opposed to these changes so far as our children are concerned; they are for their good. We are satisfied that they go to school and learn something; we are satisfied that they pray the same as you do, but we old folks are too old to change; we have our ways and ideas, and we cannot change them; we must remain just what we are.

To try to make them understand that one is never too old to learn or to change for the better would be like trying to argue with a confirmed fatalist.

These are some of the points which make missionary work among the adult generation of the Navajo very trying, and tax the patience, perseverance, and optimism of the missionary to a decided degree. However, since according to an old saying, every cloud has a silver lining, there are also some bright spots in the makeup of the Navajo which encourage the missionary and give him well-founded hopes for the future. Of these bright spots I will here mention but two:

1) The Navajo shows no antagonism toward the missionary. He does not oppose or try to frustrate his work but, on the contrary, willingly helps him whenever and wherever he can. Although as a rule he expects some pecuniary or other remuneration for his help, yet he goes into it earnestly, treats the priest with kindness, deference, and respect, and feels himself honored to harbor the priest in his home or to accompany him on a trip. He will go to a great deal of trouble to call together a council at the wish of the priest and will exert his eloquence in placing his views and intentions before his assembled fellow tribesmen. Although individually he makes no effort of accepting the teachings of the missionary, of forsaking the beliefs of paganism and conforming his life sincerely to the truths of Christianity, he nevertheless thinks the work of the missionary good and beneficial and speaks well of it on all occasions. Yet it might be more auspicious for the success of Christianity if he were not quite so yielding; if he had more antagonism; if he opposed the missionaries, and seized one or two of them and put them to the stake, as the Iroquois and Mohawk did. For the blood of martyrs has always been the seed of Christians, whether shed at an Indian stake or in a Roman arena. This way the Navajo at least leaves open the door of hope, through which he may sooner or later enter by following the call of grace.

2) He is very willing to have his children instructed in the white man's prayer or religion. Most of his own ceremonies and rites are accompanied by songs and prayers. Therefore, prayer and the invocation of supernatural powers are with him a matter of course. And since his children are studying the white man's knowledge and learning the white man's ways, they should also practice the white man's prayer or religion. Very little or no difficulty has therefore been found, whenever the intentions of the missionaries have been clearly explained to them, in obtaining their written consent for the Christian instruction of their children. In consequence, several hundred Navajo children have been instructed in the sacred truths of salvation at St. Michaels, Fort Defiance, and Chin Lee, many of whom are now baptized, have made their First Holy Communion, and been confirmed. So it looks as if among the grandchildren of the present adult generation of Navajo there will yet be a rich harvest of good, sincere, and practical Christians.

Notes

1. Leopold Ostermann, "The Navahos and Christianity," typescript, n.d., FFP Box 45, fd. 6.

2. Leopold Ostermann, "Navaho Indian Mission at Chin Lee, Arizona," FMSW 2 (1914): 31–32.

Appendix

Franciscan Friars of the Province of St. John Baptist Serving the Navajo Missions, 1898–1921

1898–1899	**St. Michaels:** Schnorbus, Weber, *Buerger*
1900	**St. Michaels:** Weber, Ostermann, Haile, *Buerger*
1901–1902	**St. Michaels:** Weber, Ostermann, Haile, *Schwemberger*
1903	**St. Michaels:** Weber, Ostermann, Haile, *Holtmann, Schwemberger*
1904	**St. Michaels:** Weber, Ostermann, Haile, Zeug, *Holtmann, Schwemberger, Thuemmel*
1905	**St. Michaels:** Weber, Ostermann, Haile, Zumbahlen, *Buerger, Schwemberger*
1906	**St. Michaels:** Weber, Schnorbus, Ostermann, Haile, Zumbahlen, Troester, *Schwemberger, Thuemmel*
1907–1908	**St. Michaels:** Weber, Haile, Zumbahlen, *Schwemberger* **Chin Lee:** Ostermann, Troester, *Thuemmel*
1909	**St. Michaels:** Weber, Haile, Zumbahlen, *Drees* **Chin Lee:** Ostermann, Troester, *Thuemmel*
1910	**St. Michaels:** Weber, Haile, Leary, *Drees* **Chin Lee:** Ostermann, Zumbahlen, *Thuemmel*
1911	**St. Michaels:** Weber, Haile, Helmig, Fischer, Leary, Bruening, Boehler **Chin Lee:** Ostermann, Troester, *Thuemmel*
1912	**St. Michaels:** Weber, Stephan, Haile, Helmig, Fischer, Leary, *Bruening* **Chin Lee:** Ostermann, Troester, *Thuemmel*
1913	**St. Michaels:** Weber, Haile, Fischer, Gottbrath, Auweiler, Springob, Bruening **Chin Lee:** Ostermann, Troester, *Thuemmel*
1914	**St. Michaels:** Weber, Haile, Matz, Fischer, *Springob, Bruening* **Chin Lee:** Ostermann, Troester, *Thuemmel*
1915	**St. Michaels:** Weber, Matz, Fischer, Troester, *Bruening* **Chin Lee:** Ostermann, Kopp, *Koper* **Lukachukai:** Haile, *Thuemmel*
1916	**St. Michaels:** Weber, Matz, Klinger, Troester, *Bruening* **Chin Lee:** Ostermann, Rossmann, Koper **Lukachukai:** Haile, *Thuemmel*

Franciscan Friars of the Province of St. John Baptist Serving the Navajo Missions, 1898–1921 (continued)

1917	**St. Michaels:** Weber, Matz, Troester, Trockur, Bruening
	Chin Lee: Ostermann, Oldegeering, Koper
	Lukachukai: Haile, *Thuemmel*
1918	**St. Michaels:** Weber, Matz, Troester, Oldegeering, Trockur, Bruening
	Chin Lee: Ostermann, Koper
	Lukachukai: Haile, *Thuemmel*
1919	**St. Michaels:** Weber, Troester, Oldegeering, Trockur, *Bruening*
	Chin Lee: Ostermann, *Elpers*
	Lukachukai: Haile, *Thuemmel*
1920	**St. Michaels:** Weber, Oldegeering, Trockur, *Bruening*
	Chin Lee: Ostermann, *Elpers*
	Lukachukai: Haile, *Thuemmel*
1921	**St. Michaels:** Troester, Oldegeering, Trockur, *Bruening*
	Chin Lee: Ostermann, Elpers
	Lukachukai: Haile, *Thuemmel*

Sources: Annual *Tabula Definitionis ad S. Joannem Baptistam* (locations and assignments of friars and brothers belonging to the Franciscan Province of St. John Baptist, Cincinnati, Ohio), 1898–1921. The standard for inclusion in the table is that a friar was listed as formally assigned to one of the Navajo mission locations. Temporary appointments, such as transfers during the year for health reasons or other short-term service, are not included, and therefore some friars who served in the Navajo missions only briefly, or whose service at particular stations was short-term, are not shown here. Full names and birth and death dates are from George Hellmann, O.F.M., et al., *A Necrology of Friars, 2001 Edition*, Franciscan Archives Cincinnati, Province of St. John Baptist, Cincinnati, Ohio, 2001.

Notes: There is a distinction in the Franciscan friars between the "Father," who is an ordained priest, and the lay "Brother." Both have made vows but only the ordained priests have ecclesiastical authority and the power of orders, that is, the authority to celebrate the sacraments of the Roman Catholic Church. Most of the written materials produced by the Navajo missions were written by the Fathers, not the Brothers. In the table above, the names of Fathers are in regular type, those of Brothers are italicized.

Places denoted by abbreviations are, respectively, St. Michaels, Lukachukai, Fort Defiance, Fort Wingate, and Keam's Canyon. Many locations not listed specifically above were served by the friars. For example, Chin Lee was originally served from St. Michaels, and later Lukachukai from Chin Lee.

The published list of the friars' assignments reflects only their location at the time of the year the records were submitted, and there is considerable movement that is not reflected in this annual "snapshot" of assignments and locations. Thus the table above should be considered only a rough guide, and for a particular friar or location other sources should also be consulted.

The friars' surnames appear in the table above. Typically they were known by their Franciscan name, for example, Father Berard or Brother Gervase. For their full names, Franciscan and Christian, see the list below. Friars who left the Franciscan Order are designated "disc." (discontinued). As above, ordained priests are in regular type, lay brothers in italics.

Auweiler, Edwin Joseph (1881–1970)
Boehler, Ewald William (1881–disc. 1912)
Bruening, Felix Joseph (1862–1931)
Buerger, Placidus Joseph (1852–1906)
Drees, Germain John (1860–1942)
Elpers, Julian Thomas (1875–1946)
Fischer, Egbert Aloysius (1879–1953)
Gottbrath, Norbert Joseph (1879–disc. 1916)
Haile, Berard James (1874–1961)
Hartung, Frederic Edward (1871–1942)
Helmig, Romuald Francis (1879–1913)
Holtmann, Arnold Bernard (1847–1936)
Klinger, Boniface John (1881–disc. 1922)
Koper, Fidelis John (1860–1945)
Kopp, Sixtus Peter (1883–1959)
Leary, Edward Jeremy (1884–1965)
Matz, Celestine Edward (1880–1936)
Oldegeering, Ludger Aloysius (1889–1948)
Ostermann, Leopold John (1863–1930)
Rossmann, Lawrence Joseph (1883–1951)
Schnorbus, Juvenal Francis (1862–1912)
Schwemberger, Simeon George (1867–disc. c. 1907)
Springob, Liborius Joseph (1866–1934)
Stephan Theodore Anthony (1862–1918)
Thuemmel, Gervase Peter (1879–1949)
Trockur, Emanuel John (1890–1977)
Troester, Marcellus Joseph (1878–1936)
Weber, Anselm Anthony (1862–1921)
Zeug, Herculan Joseph (1875–1917)
Zumbahlen, Fintan Frederic (1879–1947)

Bibliography

Bahr, Howard M. *Diné Bibliography to the 1990s: A Companion to the Navajo Bibliography of 1969*. Lanham, Md.: Scarecrow Press, 1999.

Bailey, Garrick, and Robert Glenn Bailey. *Historic Navajo Occupation of the Northern Chaco Plateau*. Tulsa, Okla.: Faculty of Anthropology, University of Tulsa, 1982.

——. *A History of the Navajos: The Reservation Years*. Santa Fe, N.Mex.: School of American Research Press, 1986.

Baldwin, John D. *Ancient America, in Notes on American Archaeology*. New York: Harper & Brothers, 1872.

Bancroft, Hubert Howe. *The Works of Hubert Howe Bancroft. The Native Races, Vol. 3. Myths and Languages*. San Francisco: A. L. Bancroft & Company, 1883.

Benavides, Alonso de. "Benavides's Memorial, 1630," translated by Mrs. Edward E. Ayer. *Land of Sunshine* 13 (December 1900): 441.

Blau, Peter M., and W. Richard Scott. *Formal Organizations: A Comparative Approach*. San Francisco: Chandler, 1962.

Blue, Martha. *The Witch Purge of 1878: Oral and Documentary History in the Early Reservation Years*. Tsaile, Ariz.: Navajo Community College Press, 1990.

Bodo, Murray. *Tales of an Endishodi: Father Berard Haile and the Navajos, 1900–1961*. Albuquerque: University of New Mexico Press.

Bretell, Caroline B., ed. *When They Read What We Write: The Politics of Ethnography*. Westport, Conn.: Bergin & Garvey, 1993.

Brinton, Daniel G. *The American Race: A Linguistic Classification and Ethnographic Description of the Native Tribes of North and South America*. Philadelphia: David McKay, 1901.

Campbell, Reau. *Campbell's New Revised Complete Guide and Descriptive Book of Mexico*. City of Mexico: Sonora News Company, 1899.

"Chronicle of the Order: Pena Blanca, New Mèx." *St. Anthony Messenger* 12 (1904–1905): 322.

Engelhardt, Zephyrin. *Franciscans in Arizona*. Harbor Springs, Mich.: Holy Childhood Indian School, 1899.

Fischer, Egbert. "Die Franziskaner-Mission unter den Navajo-Indianern." *Sendbote* 39 (July, August, December 1912): 595–601, 692–96, 1082–86; 40 (September, October 1913): 782–87, 884–90; 42 (December 1915): 1118–23.

Forrest, Earle R. *Arizona's Dark and Bloody Ground.* Caldwell, Idaho: Caxton Printers, 1936.

Franciscans, St. Michaels, Arizona: Papers. University of Arizona Library Special Collections, Tucson.

Gregg, Josiah. *Commerce of the Prairies, or the Journal of a Santa Fé Trader, 1831–1839.* New York: J. & H. G. Langley, 1845.

Haile, Berard. "Correspondence on Navajo Games." Pp. 92–93, 96–97, 385–86, 457–59, 624, 668, 766–67, 781, 789–90 in *Games of the North American Indians*, 24th Annual Report of the Bureau of American Ethnology, 1902–1903, edited by Stewart Culin. Washington, D.C.: Government Printing Office, 1907.

———. "A Council at St. Isabel Mission." *St. Anthony Messenger* 23 (May 1916): 553–54.

———. "Do the Navahos Pray?" *St. Anthony Messenger* 29 (January 1922): 353–54.

———. "Mother Love of the Navajo." *Indian Sentinel* 4 (July 1924): 117.

———. "The Navaho Country." *Franciscan Missions of the Southwest* 10 (1922): 28–37.

———. "Navaho or Navajo?" Pp. 145–50 in *Tales of an Endishodi: Father Berard Haile and the Navajos, 1900–1961*, edited by Murray Bodo. Albuquerque: University of New Mexico Press, 1998.

———. Papers. University of Arizona Library Special Collections, Tucson.

———. "The Sequel." *St. Anthony Messenger* 24 (July 1916): 67–72.

———. "St. Isabel's." *Franciscan Missions of the Southwest* 4 (1916): 21–26.

Hassing, Arne. "Father Berard Haile, O.F.M., and the Navajos." Pp. 91–98 in *Religion in the West*, edited by Ferenc M. Szasz. Manhattan, Kans.: Sunflower University Press, 1984.

Hellman, George, et al. *A Necrology of Friars, 2001 Edition.* Cincinnati, Ohio: Franciscan Archives Cincinnati, Province of St. John Baptist, 2001.

Hesse, Jerome. "Glimpses into the History of the Catholic Church in New Mexico." *Franciscan Missions of the Southwest* 6 (1918): 24–31.

———. "Obituary: Rev. Leopold Ostermann, O.F.M." *Indian Sentinel* 10 (Summer 1930): 118.

Hoffman, Virginia, and Broderick H. Johnson. *Navajo Biographies.* Phoenix: Navajo Curriculum Center Press, 1974.

Honaghani, Gertrude. "The Navajo Woman and Her Home." *Franciscan Missions of the Southwest* (1921): 35–36.

Hurdy, John Major. *American Indian Religions.* Los Angeles: Sherbourne Press, 1970.

Hurley, Daniel. "*St. Anthony Messenger*: 100 Years of Good News." *St. Anthony Messenger* 100 (June 1992): 10–17.

"Is Our Indian System a Curse?" *Literary Digest* 25 (November 22, 1902): 667.

Iverson, Peter. *The Navajo Nation.* Albuquerque: University of New Mexico Press, 1981.

Juillard, George J. "Agent's Coolness Prevented Bloody Indian Outbreak." *Albuquerque Morning Journal*, 21 November 1905, 6.

Kaberry, Phyllis. "Malinowski's Contribution to Fieldwork Methods and the Writing of Ethnography." Pp. 71–91 in *Man and Culture: An Evaluation of the Work of Bronislaw Malinowski*, edited by Raymond Firth. London: Routledge & Kegan Paul, 1957.

Kluckhohn, Clyde, and Dorothea Leighton. *The Navaho*, rev. ed. Cambridge, Mass.: Harvard University Press, 1974.

Lanzrath, John. "Emanuel Trockur's Bequest."*Provincial Chronicle*, n.s.1 (Fall 1978): 77–83.

Little, Margaret Olivia. "Seeing and Caring: The Role of Affect in Feminist Moral Epistemology." *Hypatia* 10 (Summer 1995): 117–37.

Locke, Raymond Friday. *The Book of the Navajo*. Los Angeles: Holloway House, 1986.

Looney, Ralph. "'Father Shorty' and the Navajos." *Ave Maria National Catholic Weekly* 59 (5 May 1962): 20–23.

Lummis, Charles F. "In the Lion's Den." *Out West* 16 (February 1902): 190.

———. *The Land of Poco Tiempo*. New York: C. Scribner's Sons, 1893.

———. "The Sequoya League." *Out West* 16 (March 1902): 301–2.

———. *The Spanish Pioneers*. Chicago: A. C. McClurg and Company, 1899.

Malinowski, Bronislaw. *A Diary in the Strict Sense of the Term*. Stanford, Calif.: Stanford University Press, 1989.

Matthews, Washington. *Navaho Legends*. Boston: Houghton, Mifflin, 1897.

McKibbin, Davidson B. "Revolt of the Navaho, 1913." *New Mexico Historical Review* 29 (October 1954): 259–89.

McNitt, Frank. *The Indian Traders*. Norman: University of Oklahoma Press, 1962.

———, ed. *Navaho Expedition: Journal of a Military Reconnaissance from Santa Fe, New Mexico, to the Navaho Country Made in 1849 by Lieutenant James H. Simpson*. Norman: University of Oklahoma Press, 1964 (1852).

McPherson, Robert. "The Flu Epidemic of 1918: A Cultural Response." *Blue Mountain Shadows* 1 (Spring 1988): 67–72.

Meyers, Florentine. "Peña Blanca: The First of the Franciscan Missions in Modern Times in New Mexico." *Franciscan Missions of the Southwest* 8 (1920): 29–32.

Mitchell, Daniel Holmes. "An Indian Trader's Plea for Justice, 1906." *New Mexico Historical Review* 47 (July 1972): 239–56.

Mitchell, Rose. *Tall Woman: The Life Story of Rose Mitchell, a Navajo Woman, c. 1874–1977*, edited by Charlotte J. Frisbie. Albuquerque: University of New Mexico Press, 2001.

Moore, John Bradford (J. B.). *The Catalogues of Fine Navajo Blankets, Rugs, Ceremonial Baskets, Silverwork, Jewelry & Curios: Originally Published between 1903 and 1911*. Albuquerque, N.Mex.: Avanya, 1987.

———. "Characteristics of the Navajo." *Catholic Pioneer* 1 (May 1906): 12–15.

Morice, A. G. *Notes Archaeological, Industrial and Sociological, on the Western Dénés, with an Ethnographical Sketch of the Same*. Transactions of the Canadian Institute, Vol. 14. Ottawa: Canadian Institute, 1893.

"Navajo Troubles." *McKinley County Republican*, 18 November 1905, 1.

Newcomb, Franc Johnson. *Hosteen Klah: Navaho Medicine Man and Sand Painter*. Norman: University of Oklahoma Press, 1964.

"Notices of the Order." *St. Anthony Messenger* 7 (December 1899): 283.

Ostermann, Leopold. "Franciscans in the Wilds and Wastes of the Navajo Country." *St. Anthony's Messenger* 8–17 (February 1901–October 1909).

———. "The Last Warrior of the Navaho Tribe." *Franciscan Missions of the Southwest* 3 (1905): 45–48.

———. "Little Mission Stories from Our Own Southwest." *St. Anthony Messenger* 34 (February–May 1927): 466–67, 524–25, 578, 634–36; 35 (June–November 1927): 22–23, 75–77, 301; 36 (November 1928): 309–11.

———. "Navajo Indian Mission at Chin Lee, Arizona." *Franciscan Missions of the Southwest* 2 (1914): 26–36.

———. "Navajo Names." *Franciscan Missions of the Southwest* 6 (1918): 11–15.

———. "People and Places of Our Southwest: The Navajos." *Catholic Pioneer* 1 (July 1905–February 1906, April 1906): 8–9, 7–9, 3–5, 14–16, 12–14, 10–11, 12–14, 10–12, 10–12.

Palladino, Lawrence Benedict. *Indian and White in the Northwest: A History of Catholicity in Montana, 1831–1891*. Lancaster, Penn.: Wickersham, 1922.

Powell, J. W. "Indian Linguistic Families of America North of Mexico." *Seventh Annual Report, Bureau of American Ethnology*. Washington, D.C.: Government Printing Office, 1891.

Powers, Willow Roberts. *Navajo Trading: The End of an Era*. Albuquerque: University of New Mexico Press, 2001.

Roberts, Willow. *Stokes Carson: Twentieth-Century Trading on the Navajo Reservation*. Albuquerque: University of New Mexico Press, 1987.

Russell, Scott C. "The Navajo and the 1918 Influenza Pendemic." Pp. 380–90 in *Health and Disease in the Prehistoric Southwest*, Anthropological Research Papers No. 34, edited by Charles F. Merbs and Robert J. Miller. Tempe.: Arizona State University, 1985.

San Juan Times. 10 November–17 November 1899.

Schnorbus, Juvenal, Anselm Weber, Frederick Hartung, and Leopold Ostermann. "History of the Ranch, about Seven Miles South of Fort Defiance (Cienega) Arizona, Now St. Michael's Missions." Typescript. Box PLA.376 St. Michael's, env. St. Michael's Earliest History, 1898–1907. Franciscan Archives Cincinnati, Cincinnati, Ohio.

Schuster, Fridolin. "The Mission at Jemes." *Franciscan Missions of the Southwest* 1 (1913): 22–27.

Shea, John Gilmary. *History of the Catholic Missions among the Indian Tribes of the United States, 1529–1854*. New York: T. W. Strong, late Edward Dunigan & Brother, Catholic Publishing House, 1854.

Stephen, Alexander M. "The Navajo." *American Anthropologist* 6 (October 1893): 345–62.

Stratton, David H. "The Memoirs of Albert B. Fall." *Southwestern Studies* 4 (no. 3, 1966).

——. *Tempest over Teapot Dome: The Story of Albert B. Fall*. Norman: University of Oklahoma Press, 1998.

Taylor, Bruce Lee. "Presbyterians and 'The People': A History of Presbyterian Missions and Ministries to the Navajos." Ph.D. diss., Union Theological Seminary, Richmond, Va., 1988.

Trockur, Emanuel. "Background of the Indian Missions." *Provincial Chronicle* 11 (Fall 1938): 3–16.

——. "Fifty Years among the Navajo." *Indian Sentinel* 28 (November 1948): 131–33.

——. "Franciscan Missions among the Navajo Indians: II." *Provincial Chronicle* 12 (Winter 1939–1940): 64–75.

——. "Franciscan Missions among the Navajo Indians: IV." *Provincial Chronicle* 13 (Winter 1940–1941): 73–90.

——. "Franciscan Missions among the Navajo Indians: VI." *Provincial Chronicle* 14 (Fall 1941): 37–57.

——. "Incidents in Navajoland." Typescript. Franciscan Fathers Papers, AZ500 Box 47, fd. 1. University of Arizona Library Special Collections, Tucson, Ariz.

——. "Tangled Names." *Indian Sentinel* 24 (February 1944): 25–27.

Troester, Marcellus. "Our Mission at Lukachukai, Arizona." *Franciscan Missions of the Southwest* 3 (1915): 30–38.

Van Valkenburg, Richard. *A Short History of the Navajo People*. Window Rock, Ariz.: Navajo Service, U.S. Department of Interior, 1938.

Weber, Anselm. "Catholic Missions and Mission Stations among the Navajo." *Indian Sentinel* 1 (April 1918): 18–27.

——. "Die Franziskaner-Mission unter den Navajo-Indianern." *Sendbote* 30–47 (October 1902–December 1920).

——. "Die Indianer-Mission unter den Navajos." *Sendbote* 26–30 (April 1899–September 1902).

——. "The Navajo Indians: A Statement of Facts." Franciscan Archives Cincinnati, Ohio: Box DEC.241, Weber, Anselm. Writings, fd. "Weber, Anselm. Original MS—A Statement of Facts, 1914." (AVI2).

——. *The Navajo Indians: A Statement of Facts*. St. Michaels, Ariz.: Franciscan Fathers, 1914.

——. "The Navajo Indian Trouble of 1905." Memorandum, Anselm Weber to William Ketcham, 15 March 1907. Franciscan Archives Cincinnati, Ohio: Box DEC.332, Anselm Weber letters.

——. "Navajos on the Warpath?" *Franciscan Missions of the Southwest* 7 (1919): 1–17.

——. "On Navajo Myths and Superstitions." *Franciscan Missions of the Southwest* 4 (1916): 38–45.

——. "Opening of St. Michael's School—Indians' Attack at Round Rock." *Franciscan Missions of the Southwest* 5 (1917): 10–19.

——. "Origin, Religion, and Superstitions of the Navajo." *Indian Sentinel* 1 (April 1918): 4–7.

——. "The Sisters of Blessed Sacrament for Indians and Colored People." *St. Anthony's Messenger* 9 (January 1901): 262–68.

——. "St. Michael's Mission and School for the Navajo Indians." *Indian Sentinel* 5 (1908):14–27.

——. "Eine Weihnachtsfeier unter den Navajo-Indianern im fernen Westen." *Sendbote* 26 (March 1899): 199–203.

——. "Wise Words Were These," and "How It All Happened." *McKinley County Republican*, 16 December 1905, 1.

White, Leslie A. "The Ethnography and Ethnology of Franz Boas." *Bulletin of the Texas Memorial Museum* 6 (April 1963): 1–76.

Wilken, Robert L. *Anselm Weber, O.F.M.: Missionary to the Navaho, 1989–1921.* Milwaukee, Wisc.: Bruce, 1955.

Index

About the Contributors

Howard M. Bahr was awarded a Ph.D. in sociology by the University of Texas at Austin in 1965. He has taught sociology at Brigham Young University for over 30 years. His other works include *Diné Bibliography to the 1990s* (Scarecrow Press, 1999), *American Ethnicity* (1979), and *Native Americans Today* (1972).

Henry "Chee" Dodge (1857?–1947), the most influential Navajo of his time, came to prominence as official interpreter for the government agent at Fort Defiance. His courage, charisma, and keen intellect led to an early appointment as chief of Navajo police, and to later success in business and ranching. A skilled orator, negotiator, and mediator, he served two terms as chairman of the Navajo Tribal Council.

Egbert Fischer, O.F.M. (1879–1953), was invested in 1897 and ordained in 1905. He served in Cincinnati as seminary teacher and chaplain until 1911, when he was assigned to the Navajo missions. After five years at St. Michaels and Fort Defiance, he was transferred elsewhere. A variety of assignments followed, including more seminary teaching and chaplaincy of the public hospital in Louisville, Kentucky. He did not return to the Navajo missions.

Berard Haile, O.F.M. (1874–1961), invested in 1891 and ordained in 1898, was sent to the Navajo missions in 1900. Over the following decades he became the foremost non-Navajo authority on the Navajo language. In 1915 he began a ten-year assignment as pastor at Lukachukai. Later he served Tohatchi, Fort Wingate, and Fort Defiance. From 1929–1931 he took graduate classes at Catholic University of America and did fieldwork with University of Chicago anthropologists. He then worked in Gallup, and Acoma, New Mexico, returning to St. Michaels in 1938. His contributions to the study of Navajo language and ceremonial life are unsurpassed.

Gertrude Honaghani was a pupil at St. Michael's Indian School before 1921, probably in the 1915–1920 period.

Fidelis Koper, O.F.M. (1860–1945), was invested as a Teaching Brother in 1881 and in 1889 was professed in the First Order. After 20 years of teaching in Cincinnati and Detroit, he was sent to the Southwest as a handyman. He served 27 years in the New Mexico missions, four of them (1915–1918) at Chin Lee with Father Leopold Ostermann.

J. B. Moore owned and operated the trading post at Crystal, New Mexico, 1896–1911. Among the most influential of traders, he is remembered for working with weavers to improve the quality of their rugs, for beginning the "Crystal rug" design, and for innovative marketing via illustrated mail order catalogs.

Des Chee Nee (1866–?), middle-aged father of one of the early students at St. Michael's School, was accused of rape and brought to judgment in a New Mexico court in 1905. He spoke no English. His plea was erroneously translated as "guilty," and he was summarily sentenced to 10 years in the territorial prison. Father Anselm Weber appealed to the governor on his behalf, and Des Chee Nee was pardoned after serving 16 months.

Leopold Ostermann, O.F.M. (1863–1930), was invested in 1882 and ordained in 1890. His ministry in the following decade included teaching seminary, four years as an assistant pastor in Canada, and a pastorate in Illinois. In 1900, he enthusiastically accepted a call to St. Michaels. He spent the rest of his life as missionary to the Navajo. He was Superior and pastor in Chin Lee from 1907 to 1923, when poor health forced him to return to St. Michaels.

Emanuel Trockur, O.F.M. (1890–1977), was invested in 1903 and ordained in 1916. He joined the friars at St. Michaels the following year, and except for two years in the early thirties as an assistant pastor in Peoria, Illinois, spent the rest of his life among the Navajo. He served at St. Michaels, Chin Lee, Houck, Tohatchi, and Gallup. His reputation as historian of the Navajo missions is based on his many publications, voluminous diary, and efforts to collect and protect the writings and records of his fellow missionaries.

Marcellus Troester, O.F.M. (1878–1936), was invested in 1898 and ordained in 1906. His first assignment, to the Navajo missions, turned out to be a lifetime call. He served in St. Michaels, Lukachukai, Tohatchi, the Shiprock area, and, briefly, among the Colorado Utes north of Shiprock. Following Father Anselm's passing, he was Superior of St. Michael's Mission for several years. Much of his later ministry was devoted to expanding and maintaining the Navajo census created by the friars.

Anselm Weber, O.F.M. (1862–1921), was invested in 1882 and ordained in 1889. In 1898, after almost a decade as a seminary teacher, he volunteered for the new mission to the Navajo. In 1900 he became Superior at St. Michaels and held that post until his death. His gifts to the Navajo include spiritual and secular education, advocacy for land rights and legal justice, and numerous instances of helping to keep the peace. A fitting summation of his ministry was offered by historian Frank McNitt, who said that Father Anselm "gave a lifetime of selfless effort in fighting for any cause that would benefit the common lot of the Navajo tribe."

DATE DUE
